MW01076389

GEORGE CUKOR'S PEOPLE

FILM AND CULTURE

FILM AND CULTURE

A series of Columbia University Press

Edited by John Belton

Death by Laughter: Female Hysteria and Early Cinema, by Maggie Hennefeld

The Rebirth of Suspense: Slowness and Atmosphere in Cinema, by Rick Warner

Hollis Frampton: Navigating the Infinite Cinema, by Michael Zryd

Perplexing Plots: Popular Storytelling and the Poetics of Murder, by David Bordwell

Horror Film and Otherness, by Adam Lowenstein

Hollywood's Embassies: How Movie Theaters Projected American Power Around the World, by Ross Melnick

Music in Cinema, by Michel Chion

Bombay Hustle: Making Movies in a Colonial City, by Debashree Mukherjee

Absence in Cinema: The Art of Showing Nothing, by Justin Remes

Hollywood's Artists: The Directors Guild of America and the Construction of Authorship, by Virginia Wright Wexman

Film Studies, second edition, by Ed Sikov

Anxious Cinephilia: Pleasure and Peril at the Movies, by Sarah Keller

For a complete list of books in the series,
please see the Columbia University Press website.

George Cukor with François Truffaut, the French director who as a young critic admired his work but felt "the trouble is that Cukor isn't the kind of director you write about; he's someone to talk about with friends on the street or sitting in a café." They're chatting at the American Film Institute preview party for Truffaut's *The Story of Adele H.* in Hollywood, 1975. Author Joseph McBride looks on at right.

Source: New World Pictures.

GEORGE CUKOR'S PEOPLE

ACTING FOR A MASTER DIRECTOR

JOSEPH McBRIDE

COLUMBIA UNIVERSITY PRESS / NEW YORK

Columbia University Press
Publishers Since 1893
New York   Chichester, West Sussex

Library of Congress Cataloging-in-Publication Data
Names: McBride, Joseph, 1947– author.
Title: George Cukor's people / Joseph McBride.
Description: New York : Columbia University Press, 2024. |
    Series: Film and culture series | Includes bibliographical references and index.
Identifiers: LCCN 2024021667 (print) | LCCN 2024021668 (ebook) |
    ISBN 9780231210829 (hardback) | ISBN 9780231558617 (ebook)
Subjects: LCSH: Cukor, George, 1899–1983—Criticism and interpretation. |
    Motion picture producers and directors—United States.
Classification: LCC PN1998.3.C8 M33 2024 (print) | LCC PN1998.3.C8 (ebook) |
    DDC 791.430233092—dc23/eng/20240603

Cover and book design: Elliott S. Cairns
Cover image: Katharine Hepburn, George Cukor, and Cary Grant on location
for *Sylvia Scarlett* (1935). George Cukor papers, Margaret Herrick Library,
Academy of Motion Picture Arts and Sciences

To my son and teacher, John McBride

You never had to put a label on the bottle, because it was unmistakable.
All the people in your pictures are as goddamned good as they can possibly be,
and that's your stamp.

—Katharine Hepburn to George Cukor

CONTENTS

Introduction: Is George Cukor an Auteur?
And Why Does That Matter? 1

1. Lew Ayres in *All Quiet on the Western Front* and *Holiday* 43

2. Fredric March and Ina Claire in *The Royal Family of Broadway* 57

3. Kay Francis in *The Virtuous Sin* and with Lilyan Tashman in
   Girls About Town 65

4. Lowell Sherman in *What Price Hollywood?* 73

5. Katharine Hepburn and John Barrymore in *A Bill of Divorcement* 85

6. John Barrymore and Jean Harlow in *Dinner at Eight* 97

7. Katharine Hepburn in *Little Women*; the Ensemble of
   David Copperfield 111

8. Katharine Hepburn and Cary Grant in *Sylvia Scarlett* 127

9. Greta Garbo in *Camille* 143

10. Katharine Hepburn and Cary Grant in *Holiday* 157

11. Vivien Leigh, Olivia de Havilland, Hattie McDaniel,
    and Butterfly McQueen in *Gone with the Wind* 169

12. Norma Shearer, Joan Crawford, Rosalind Russell, and Joan Fontaine
    in *The Women* 183

13. Joan Crawford in *Susan and God* with Rita Quigley and in
    A Woman's Face   195

14. Cary Grant, Katharine Hepburn, and James Stewart in
    The Philadelphia Story   209

15. Ingrid Bergman and Angela Lansbury in *Gaslight*   223

16. Spencer Tracy and Katharine Hepburn in *Adam's Rib* with Judy Holliday
    and in *Pat and Mike*   237

17. Judy Holliday in *Born Yesterday*, *The Marrying Kind* with Aldo Ray,
    and *It Should Happen to You* with Jack Lemmon   257

18. Thelma Ritter and Company in *The Model and the Marriage Broker*   275

19. Spencer Tracy and Jean Simmons in *The Actress*   285

20. Judy Garland and James Mason in *A Star Is Born*   301

21. Ava Gardner in *Bhowani Junction*, Kay Kendall in *Les Girls*,
    and Sophia Loren and Anthony Quinn in *Heller in Pink Tights*   317

22. Marilyn Monroe in *Let's Make Love* and *Something's Got to Give*   331

23. Claire Bloom, Jane Fonda, Glynis Johns, and Shelley Winters in
    The Chapman Report   343

24. Rex Harrison and Audrey Hepburn in *My Fair Lady*   357

25. Anna Karina and Dirk Bogarde in *Justine*   381

26. Maggie Smith, Alec McCowen, Lou Gossett, Robert Stephens,
    and Cindy Williams in *Travels with My Aunt*   393

27. Jacqueline Bisset and Candice Bergen in *Rich and Famous*   411

28. Katharine Hepburn and Laurence Olivier in *Love Among the Ruins*   427

Acknowledgments   439
Filmography   447
Notes on Sources   457
Index   489

GEORGE CUKOR'S PEOPLE

0.1. The actress George Cukor was the closest with was Katharine Hepburn. He directed her ten times, including in her film debut, *A Bill of Divorcement* (1932), and here with Cary Grant in *Holiday* (1938). This social satire/romantic comedy with Hepburn as a disillusioned upper-class woman who falls in love with a self-made man is based on the play by Philip Barry.

Source: Columbia Pictures/From Katharine Hepburn Papers of the Margaret Herrick Library, Academy of Motion Picture Arts and Sciences.

INTRODUCTION

IS GEORGE CUKOR AN AUTEUR?
AND WHY DOES THAT MATTER?

George Cukor is a widely admired but little understood director. Most critics and cinephiles acknowledge his extraordinary talent in directing actors and will admit having several Cukor films among their favorites, from *Camille* and *The Philadelphia Story* to *Adam's Rib* and *A Star Is Born*, but the critical literature about his work is skimpy. That's largely because what he did is difficult to express in the inadequate vocabulary that still hampers the nuanced discussion of acting, directing, and authorship in film studies. Cukor was respected but taken somewhat for granted in the film industry; he won only a single Academy Award, late in his long career, for *My Fair Lady*, which in turn is unfairly disparaged by most critics because of its popularity and derivation from theatrical classics. And unlike such other great directors from classical Hollywood as John Ford, Frank Capra, and Alfred Hitchcock, Cukor has never achieved a degree of public recognition commensurate with his talent.

"Would you tell them who I am?" Cukor rather poignantly asked Sidney Poitier when he walked onstage to accept Katharine Hepburn's Oscar for *Guess Who's Coming to Dinner* in 1968. Both the announcer and then Poitier mispronounced Cukor's name, despite the industry setting (it's "*Cue*-kor," not "*Koo*-cur" or "*Koo*-kor"). Writing about Cukor's films, with their self-effacing, discreet, subtle approach that does not show off or foreground the director's style but works largely through his intimate collaboration with actors, has always seemed a virtually insurmountable challenge for critics even though his film career over more than half a century offers a rich, multifaceted, and deeply personal view of the world.

On Cukor, Gavin Lambert's lively, revealing, yet sometimes tantalizingly oblique interview book (1972, updated in 2000), is the closest thing to an autobiography Cukor ever gave us. The partially closeted gay director flirted with the idea of a formal autobiography in concert with various writers and even tried unsuccessfully to market a book of his correspondence, but his lifelong discretion made those kinds of books too problematical to be published. After he and Lambert began their interview book, "he wanted me to write his biography," the author recalled, "but I declined when he set very definite limits on what he would reveal about his personal life. Was it so important to tell everything? he asked. Not in the tabloid sense, I said, but can you separate an artist's sexuality from his creativity? 'It's so good of you to consider me an artist,' George said with an ambiguous smile, and an edge to his voice that I recognized as his way of closing the subject."

Cukor did give future biographers and other scholars a wealth of material by donating his papers to the Academy of Motion Picture Arts and Sciences' Margaret Herrick Library. I attended the ceremony at which he bestowed those papers upon the library, as well as numerous other public events involving Cukor over the years, including a screening of his 1933 classic *Little Women* (his "secret favorite" film) at the Academy theater. After that screening, in a fine display of indignation, he rebuked some in the audience who had misbehaved by hooting at it. The feisty Cukor could not contain his fury and contempt, telling the audience that they had responded with what he called "a bum's laugh."

Over the past fifty years, I have published several pieces on Cukor in film magazines, including a long interview for *Film Comment* (with Todd McCarthy) in 1981 on Cukor's later work. And that year I spent a day on a soundstage at MGM watching him shoot his last film, *Rich and Famous*. His set, we wrote, was "an unusually civilized and well-organized creative workshop, with the elderly director quietly but firmly in command. He spent much of his time sitting in his chair, continuing his long-standing practice of huddling intimately with his actresses, out of earshot of interlopers." Unlike most directors I watched at work, Cukor couldn't be heard much if at all, since he spoke so quietly and intently to his actresses, Jacqueline Bisset

0.2. The one time in his long career that Cukor received an Academy Award as best director was for *My Fair Lady*. At the Oscar ceremony on April 5, 1965, Cukor characteristically said he was "very lucky—I had wonderful material to work with" and "wonderful artists to work with." Cukor previously had been nominated for directing *Little Women*, *The Philadelphia Story*, *A Double Life*, and *Born Yesterday*.

Source: Academy of Motion Picture Arts and Sciences/ABC-TV; frame enlargement from *American Masters: George Cukor: On Cukor*, PBS.

and Candice Bergen. I understood and appreciated his sense of discretion but found it frustrating for my observational process. About all I could hear him saying was, often, "Come on, let's get on with it," and when the camera rolled, "At a brisk clip, ladies." Those exhortations were characteristic of Cukor's style of pacing and impatience with actors he thought were dawdling.

And one time I did hear him give a more specific and significant direction. Bergen, in the scene of her New Year's Eve party, was supposed to be lost in thought because she was considering slipping away and going to the country to see her old friend, played by Bisset. Bergen was having trouble with the focus of the scene and wanted to know where to look. Cukor said, "Look inside yourself." The result in the penultimate scene of the film is one of her character's most moving moments of introspection, the high point of Bergen's uneven performance.

Having tried, like other film critics and historians, to capture Cukor's work in print with some sense of frustration, I feel an invigorating challenge in hoping to finally do justice to the subject with this book. I wrote in a 1971 *Film Quarterly* review of a critical study of the filmmaker, "Cukor's work is more difficult to evoke or analyze than that of almost any other major director. . . . Plot is to Cukor what tune is to Duke Ellington: merely the departure point for a stream of sensations, intonations, and rhythms. How is a critic to explain the workings of Judy Garland's broken monologue on her broken husband in *A Star Is Born*—sudden unveilings of hysterical agony twisting her childishly painted harlequin face into a tragic mask in the raw glow of dressing-room bulbs? . . . The critic can describe the way Cukor gets from *this* to *this* to *this*, but how can he freeze each frame and tell you what *this* is?"

Discussing his cinematic style, Cukor said, "My work really begins and ends through the actors. And it seems to me, the more successfully you work through the actors, the more your own work disappears." Cukor's virtuosity and artistic range have often been missed or undervalued by critics who lack the vocabulary to analyze directorial storytelling in relation to the guiding of actors' behavior in their embodiment of characters. A master director of actors such as Cukor works through their facial expressions, body language, and verbal intonations and rhythms, as well as the more intangible aspects of actors' personalities. But what film acting is and is not and how to evaluate it still are widely misunderstood today by both the public and film scholars, to the detriment of a great actors' director such as Cukor.

Even less attention has been devoted to Cukor's visual style, his mise-en-scène, another aspect of directing that because it does not easily translate into words, often remains somewhat vaguely grasped. As a result, how Cukor's way of seeing the world surrounds and provides context for his actors' behavior and movements through space and time remains inadequately explored. Those two aspects are intimately interrelated, and both are crucial to understanding who Cukor is as an artist. His mise-en-scène became more sophisticated as his work in the 1930s progressed in such black-and-white films as *Little Women* and *Sylvia Scarlett* and fully flowered in his often lushly textured color work from *A Star Is Born* in 1954 through the end of his career.

Furthermore, Cukor's diverse, seemingly self-effacing body of work, characterized by fidelity to the text and a discreet way of channeling his feelings through his actors, presents important questions about the validity and usefulness of the auteur theory. That is the case even though the French critics who propounded its precursor, *la politique des auteurs*, in the 1950s considered him a major artist. François Truffaut and others who admired Cukor devised the *politique* largely to account for directors who did *not* write their own films, such as Cukor with his penchant for directing theatrical and literary adaptations. Cukor emerged from the glittering New York theater scene of the 1920s, and one of his lifelong credos was respect for the original author. Cukor was known for carrying the script pages of the scenes he was shooting with him all day long, and by the end of the day the pages had gone through such a workout they would be crumpled up in his hand. Late in life he received an unprecedented award, for a director, from our Writers Guild of America, West, for his rare degree of fidelity to the written word.

The *politique des auteurs* was transmuted into the auteur theory by Andrew Sarris for American consumption in 1962. While recognizing that "the notion that a non-literary director can be the author of his films is difficult to grasp in America" and that "the studio system victimized the screenwriter more than the director," Sarris reserved his highest accolades for "Pantheon" directors with "a personal vision of the world." Nevertheless, the understanding that such a vision could coexist with fidelity to texts by literary authors or that a director's use of the camera can be considered a form of "writing"— what the French critic and director Alexandre Astruc in 1948 called the "caméra-stylo," or camera-pen—tended to be lost when Sarris's theory became vulgarized by popularizers in the mass media and, indeed, in the film industry. That has led to the widespread misconception in the United States that only directors who write their films can be true auteurs, which Sarris did not claim. That confusion has been made more pervasive by the somewhat cynical adoption of auteurism as a marketing tool by studios, reviewers, and other arms of the film industry.

The lingering uncertainty about whether Cukor is an auteur or not has long been one of the roadblocks to understanding what he brought to his dazzling list of classic films, including *Little Women, Dinner at Eight, Sylvia Scarlett, Camille, Holiday, The Philadelphia Story, Gaslight, Adam's Rib, The Marrying*

0.3. "My last good picture," Cukor jokingly inscribed this photograph when he signed it for Audrey Hepburn during the making of *My Fair Lady*. With a commanding gesture often seen later on film sets, this is Cukor around the age of three in New York City, where he was born in 1899. He was the son of Helen and Victor, prosperous Hungarian Jewish immigrants.

Source: From the Core Collection, Biography files of the Margaret Herrick Library, Academy of Motion Picture Arts and Sciences.

Kind, *Pat and Mike*, *My Fair Lady*, *Love Among the Ruins*, and his mutilated masterpiece, *A Star Is Born*. What are often shortsightedly viewed as his limitations (fidelity to the text, collaboration with major stars) can more accurately and fruitfully be viewed as among his greatest strengths. But even Cukor fell prey to the popular misconception of directorial authorship. At the beginning of the original edition of Lambert's interview book, Cukor declares: "I'm not an *auteur*, alas. And the whole *auteur* theory disconcerts me. To begin with, damn few directors can write. I have too much respect for good writers to think of taking over that job. Also, to be frank, not all directors can direct." Tellingly, Lambert cut that quote from the later edition. More cogent than Cukor's disclaimer is Lambert's observation in his introduction to the first edition that "in making his films, and in talking about them, Cukor's first instinct is to *defer*—to his actors, his writers, and so on. The 'I' exists but doesn't care to advertise itself."

The reasons for the relative undervaluation of Cukor may seem idle in light of the esteem in which he was held among his peers and by many mainstream film reviewers throughout his long career. But in American academic circles, auteurism is in disrepute at least theoretically, even if not in practical application, because it conflicts with what the influential French literary theorist and semiotician Roland Barthes in 1967 proclaimed as "the death of the author." The prevailing trends of academic film study in subsequent decades—largely Marxist, stressing the sociopolitical and industrial factors involved in cultural products—have continued to militate against the concept of the individual artist as central to the filmmaking process.

Since screenwriters and actors have long tended to be devalued in film criticism as well as in academia, Cukor's reputation has suffered because of his self-effacing nature and deference to the importance of those two crafts in the collaborative art of filmmaking. And what the French film critic and historian André Bazin called "the genius of the system"—his thoughtful tribute to the positive aspects of the classical Hollywood studio system in which Cukor thrived for decades—has been distorted as dogma by theorists and historians who stress the collective nature of filmmaking over the role of individuals working within the system. As a result, in some circles Cukor has been regarded as a minor director, not a studio hack but a director the quality of whose work fluctuates along with that of his assigned scripts and casting.

The locus classicus of such arguments is Pauline Kael's condescending summation of Cukor's work in her 1965 collection, *I Lost It at the Movies*: "I would say, give Cukor a clever script with light, witty dialogue, and he will know what to do with it. But I wouldn't expect more than glossy entertainment. . . . Cukor has a range of subject matter that he can handle and when he gets a good script within his range (like *The Philadelphia Story* or *Pat and Mike*) he does a good job; but he is at an immense *artistic* disadvantage, compared with [Ingmar] Bergman, because he is dependent on the ideas of so many (and often bad) scriptwriters and on material which is often alien to his talents." Kael's view expressed what has long been a conventional way of dismissing Cukor with faint praise, as Ernest Callenbach, the editor of *Film Quarterly*, did in his review of Lambert's *On Cukor*: "The result certainly shows Cukor to be a gentleman of culture, tolerance, and taste. It is less certain whether it embellishes his reputation as an *auteur*, since a dominant theme of the talk is his great modesty (despite some enthusiastic prodding) in confronting the projects that fell to him during his long, successful career: his sense of originality—indeed almost of responsibility—seems confined to the task of realization of works which in essence were already in existence. His sympathetic and sensitive attitude toward performers is very much a part of this, of course."

It was a mark of Cukor's relatively modest critical standing that Sarris put him into "The Far Side of Paradise" section of his seminal 1968 book *The American Cinema*, a category in which he relegated directors "who fall short of the Pantheon either because of a fragmentation of their personal vision or because of disruptive career problems." Ironically, "The Far Side of Paradise" has since yielded some of the most abundant treasure troves in the study of American film. It's striking to recall that, despite his quibbling about where to rank Cukor, Sarris's commentary on the director in that book found nothing to fault him:

> George Cukor's filmography is his most eloquent defense. When a director has provided tasteful entertainments of a high order consistently over a period of more than thirty years, it is clear that said director is much more than a mere entertainer. . . . There is an honorable place in the cinema for both adaptations and the non-writer director; and Cukor, like Lubitsch, is one of the best examples of the non-writer auteur, a creature literary film

critics seem unable to comprehend. The thematic consistency of Cukor's career has been achieved through a judicious mixture of selection and emphasis. . . . He is a genuine artist.

In one of his latter-day upgradings of directors once exiled to the "Far Side," Sarris found more personal resonance in Cukor's "chromatically delirious canvases" from *A Star Is Born* onward, along with his "very imaginative form of sensuality" in other late films, although that influential critic still hedged in 1978 on Cukor's ultimate standing in his auteurist hierarchy. It should also be clarified that Ernst Lubitsch always did work closely with his screenwriters, and Cukor did as well, although Lubitsch's writers considered him an equal collaborator on the scripts of the films he directed, while Cukor was more a shaper, an influencer of scripts along the lines he found congenial. As Cukor told Carlos Clarens, the author of an insightful 1976 critical study of his work for the British Film Institute's Cinema One series, "Now I'm not a writer, but I can contribute ideas, suggestions, dramatic effect." And Cukor said of his frequent collaboration with the screenwriters Ruth Gordon and Garson Kanin, "We worked very closely together, sometimes even through the telephone, when they were in New York, trying out scenes, lines of dialogue."

The auteur theory not only is often distorted to apply just to writer-directors but also is often misconstrued by its opponents as unfairly claiming for journeyman studio directors the same kind of authorship as practiced more obviously by such celebrated writer-directors as Bergman, Orson Welles, Billy Wilder, Yasujiro Ozu, and Woody Allen. But Cukor was far more than simply a loyal functionary of the studio system, although his detractors often use his long and mostly happy work at MGM, RKO, and other studios as proof of their claim that he was more a product of the "genius of the system" than an artist with a personal vision. Cukor transcended the label of journeyman by making the system work in his favor, maintaining high standards in his films, rebounding resiliently from any setbacks, and winning commensurate respect within the industry.

Truffaut and the others at *Cahiers du Cinéma* in the 1950s (several of whom also went on to become directors) were scathing toward French directors who made slavish, unimaginative adaptations of literary works as a "Cinema of Quality," but Cukor was not similarly criticized by those influential tastemakers. What's forgotten is that their *politique* was created largely to account for the recognizable visions of such individualistic Hollywood studio directors as Alfred Hitchcock, Howard Hawks, Raoul Walsh, Nicholas Ray, Otto Preminger, and Cukor, who managed to put their stamp on their work without writing (or taking credit for writing) their own scripts, even if this meant that they relied on other people's material.

Reviewing a film Cukor himself disparaged, the 1950 Lana Turner vehicle *A Life of Her Own*, an uneven blend of largely formulaic romance and corrosive observation of the dehumanizing nature of the New York fashion industry, Truffaut wrote that "this admirable film" displays "the beauty of Cukor's work, that extraordinary man who makes, out of every five films, one masterpiece, three other very good ones, and the fifth still interesting." Although Turner is stolid and emotionally arid, and Ray Milland is bland as her married paramour, two supporting actresses are extraordinary: Margaret Phillips, in an unclichéd portrait of Milland's neglected, crippled wife, and Ann Dvorak, in a searing performance as an aging model who commits suicide. Cukor was disgruntled by MGM's tampering with Isobel Lennart's script, including the studio's refusal to keep the ending he had filmed of Turner also killing herself at the end. Truffaut admitted his critical conundrum about Cukor in his review of a 1954 film he considered a "masterpiece," the Judy Holliday–Jack Lemmon neorealist comedy *It Should Happen to You:* "The trouble is that Cukor isn't the kind of director you write about; he's someone to talk about with friends on the street or sitting in a café." And the British film historian Edward Buscombe wrote in 1973, "The Anglo-American critical tradition is not equipped to deal with a director like Cukor. . . . The almost total lack of serious treatment of Cukor's films in English testifies to it. . . . Cukor has presented a problem to film criticism. He is a great director, but there is, literally, nothing to say about him."

I intend this critical study of Cukor to disprove Buscombe's notion that "there is, literally, nothing to say about him" and Truffaut's claim that "Cukor isn't the kind of director you write about." I am setting out to evolve a vocabulary that fully comprehends Cukor's viewpoint, his relationship to his material, and his approach to style; that puts his films and collaborators into realistic working contexts; and that pinpoints precisely what it is that makes him a great director. And in so doing, I hope to elucidate more clearly what film directing is all about.

THE CUKOR STYLE

Henri Langlois, the archivist and cofounder of the Cinémathèque Française, eloquently but all too briefly summed up some of what makes up the Cukor style: "*knowledge of the world*—elegance of style, distinction of subjects chosen, distinction of actors, refinement of cutting, a world in which everything is in half-tones, suggested and never over-stressed." And the actress Olivia de Havilland, with whom Cukor worked privately on *Gone with the Wind* even after his firing from that intimate 1939 epic, perhaps suggested best what Cukor could bring to a scene: "George Cukor is the Cellini of directors. He has a marvelously intricate imagination which works on a very fine scale. Take a look at the scene where Mammy's lacing up Scarlett—it's crammed with tiny fleeting expressions and motives —and then at the next one, where Scarlett sits on the stairs eating a chicken leg. There's no other scene in the film with so much details, such richness—those were Cukor touches." *Tiny fleeting expressions and motives.* Despite his characteristically modest claim that he was not an auteur, "alas," the intricate expressiveness of Cukor's style is not only distinctive but pervasive in his films. His style is recognizable from small details to richly textured and sweeping visuals and expressively fluid narrative movement. Few directors are as attentive as Cukor is to the subtle nuances and shadings in human behavior. His keen knowledge of psychology and shrewd, diplomatic way of handling actors—gently in most cases, commandingly when needed, and all points between—flowed from his ability to understand their individual personalities, to bring out their strengths and make intelligent use of their limitations.

Cukor views the complexities of human beings in a similar way to the approach followed by another great director, Jean Renoir. In a filmed discussion with the actor Marcel Dalio about the revealing close-up in *The Rules of the Game* in which Dalio's Marquis de la Chesnaye expresses his complex feelings about displaying his prize possession, a musical organ, Renoir said, "I think it's the best shot I've ever done in my life." He told Dalio what he found so eloquent about the shot was the way the actor expressed a mélange of humility and pride, a sense of achievement and doubt, "Rien défini. En marge—en marge de beaucoup de choses" (Nothing definite. On the margin—on the margin of so many things). In much the same way, the nuanced, finely detailed style Cukor favors allows his actors to explore their feelings "on the margin of so many things."

Cukor was a master of subtext. His own "double life," as his biographer Patrick McGilligan has called the partially closeted queer director's lifestyle in Hollywood while he carefully navigated the different strata of society, helped him probe beneath the surface and see behind people's social masks and disguises. That tendency came naturally to a man who was difficult to categorize because he led his unconventional life on the margins of society as a gay man, a Jew, and the son of Hungarian immigrants to New York. His "double life" and family background made him adept at recognizing and bringing out the subterranean levels of meaning in the screenplays he directed and knowing how to help his actors bring out the various layers in the text they were performing in oblique and often subversive ways. Having outsider status compels people to engage in masquerading, literally and figuratively, and to play roles as they navigate the tricky rules of mainstream social games.

Cukor preferred to express himself not in an overtly revealing way, as some directors do, but more covertly, through the text and subtext. He did so while attempting to capture the essence of his source material through careful study and research and involving his screenwriters in every phase of production. His conviction that the text was his guide led him to a belief in adapting classic novels such as *Little Women* and *David Copperfield* even with their structural flaws intact rather than risking disrupting their basic qualities. And he was known for his unusual practice of halting production to ask screenwriters to write new lines rather than indulging in improvisation. That respect for the text is a byproduct of his formative work in the theater and goes hand in hand with his immersion in the art of performance. His films encompass a breathtaking range of behavioral traits and personalities, but he often gravitates to characters who behave "theatrically" or with irony and self-conscious introspection, engaging in all sorts of role-playing. That helps make his films so fascinating to watch and study.

Cukor's films were often based on plays, which he made seem effortlessly cinematic with his fluid, creative, and well-motivated blocking in relation to the camera and often virtuosic yet little-noticed camera movement. One of his peers, King Vidor, recognizing this quality in Cukor's 1933 film version of Somerset Maugham's play *Our Betters*, wrote him, "I would never have tackled a subject with so little locomotion but you have a faculty of keeping it

0.4. Cukor had the unprecedented distinction of winning an award from the Writers Guild of America, West, for the respect he showed for writers. Here he confers on the set of *A Double Life* (1947) with his frequent screenwriting collaborators Ruth Gordon and Garson Kanin and the film's star, Ronald Colman, who won an Oscar for playing an actor obsessed with his role as Shakespeare's Othello.

Source: Universal-International/Photofest.

interesting in spite of this obstacle." Late in life, Cukor reflected, "I came with the talkies, and it took me about three years to learn something about the camera—well, learning what *not* to do. For the first three years, I really didn't know quite where I was, but somehow, even then, I realized that camera movement was very important. You see, on the stage they did not have much movement. People sat on the stage, and then they got up and crossed or made arbitrary movements so that it wasn't static. I felt that in movies you had to have much more real movement."

Cukor had discriminating taste and was able to command top-flight literary properties and some of the wittiest, most acute screenwriters in Hollywood, notably his frequent collaborators Donald Ogden Stewart, Zoë Akins, and Ruth Gordon and Garson Kanin. Cukor helped shape his scripts, without fanfare, by working closely behind the scenes with his writers at every stage of preproduction and production. He demanded frequent rewrites and new writers before he would put a film before the cameras, as, for example, on his 1933 film of Louisa May Alcott's *Little Women*, ultimately adapted by the married team of Sarah Y. Mason and Victor Heerman, who won Oscars for best adaptation. But his reverence for the text, rather than being seen as an asset, has led many critics, typified by Kael, to regard Cukor as an impersonal Hollywood craftsman rather than as an artist whose personality is expressed in his work. In the preconfessional era Cukor inhabited, his public modesty and discretion served him well, enabling him to deal diplomatically with the complicated social and professional position he occupied in Hollywood. But Cukor's habit of not proclaiming the secrets of his private life kept him a shadowy figure, little known to the outside world, and that contributed to the deceptively self-effacing quality of his direction, which has in turn obscured his critical reputation.

Cukor is, however, generally regarded as one of the finest actors' directors in the cinema, a distinction he shares with Bergman, Welles, Renoir, Elia Kazan, and Max Ophüls. I worked as an actor for Welles for more than five years in his satirical drama about Hollywood, *The Other Side of the Wind* (1970–1976; released in 2018), playing a comically exaggerated version of myself as a bumptiously naïve young film critic and historian. That experience has been invaluable for this study of Cukor. Shortly before I began acting for Welles, I asked Renoir for advice on how to become a director, and he wisely said, "Try a little acting." I learned much about directing and screen acting from Welles, who molded my performance from scratch—I had never acted before and had to follow his often intricate instructions without variation. I also saw how a great director of actors works with a cast of widely varied backgrounds. Welles used subtly different approaches with his lead actor, fellow director John Huston, and other veteran and accomplished actors as well as other nonactors like me chosen to play roles modeled somewhat on ourselves.

Welles often would shout at me, "Don't act!," preferring the authenticity of my inexperience to a clumsy attempt to consciously perform without having the tools to do so. But he also let me collaborate with him on my dialogue to shape the character, and as the shooting wore on, I began to pick up more sense of how to behave in front of the camera and found myself easing into the role. I was heartened to read later that Welles would also shout "Don't act!" to young Tim Holt when he played the lead role in *The Magnificent Ambersons*, although Holt, unlike me, was already an experienced and highly skilled actor. (Cukor would give Jack Lemmon similar guidance in his first film, *It Should Happen to You*, as is discussed later in this introduction.) Working for Welles as an actor gave me a rare opportunity as a film critic and historian to understand from the inside the fine points of film acting and the direction of actors.

Welles told an audience of student directors at the Cinémathèque Française in Paris in 1982:

> The most important thing in a movie is the actor. And everything which is in front of the camera. And the decadence of the cinema—and we have a certain decadence—comes from the glorification of the director as being not the servant of the actors but his master. Because the job of a director is to discover in the actor something more than he knew he had. The job of the director is to choose what he sees. And to an extent to create. But a great deal of what is applauded as creation is simply there. It was there, when he put the camera—that actor, that bit of scenery, that veil that hung over the river. It was there. And you're intelligent enough to shoot it. . . . So let us please, since I'm not talking to actors, let us respect and love them and cherish them and help them to be great, because they are the people who have made the cinema unforgettable.

"WOMAN'S DIRECTOR"?

Despite Cukor's acknowledged eminence in directing a wide range of actors, he has been misleadingly and reductively stereotyped as a "woman's director." That label—promoted by the MGM publicity department, particularly when he directed an all-female cast in *The Women* (1939), and glibly adopted by reviewers—serves as thinly veiled, disparaging code for "gay." The longstanding critical condescension toward "women's pictures" by many reviewers and film historians has circumscribed critical perceptions of Cukor over the years. I found that cultural bias dismayingly common when I began to be dedicated to film in the late 1960s. It made many people see films revolving around women's issues as less serious than films dealing with male preoccupations. More recently, however, film scholars have reevaluated that attitude. Thanks to the influence of feminism, women's pictures today (although still sometimes colloquially referred to in retrogressive language, as "chick flicks") are more generally regarded by film scholars as deeply expressive of social undercurrents and psychological complexities.

With his nondoctrinaire, instinctively feminist sensibility, Cukor often placed equal or more prominence on the viewpoint of his female protagonist. That tendency is reflected in his repeated reliance on Zoë Akins, Ruth Gordon, Jane Murfin, and Anita Loos, among other women screenwriters. This is as strikingly evident in his Katharine Hepburn–Spencer Tracy romantic comedy *Adam's Rib* (1949) and the Judy Holliday–Aldo Ray domestic drama *The Marrying Kind* (1952) as it is in more obviously female-centered stories such as the Hepburn version of *Little Women* (1933) and the Ingrid Bergman version of *Gaslight* (1944). Among the many other female stars Cukor guided to major performances included Greta Garbo, Jean Harlow, Rosalind Russell, Joan Crawford, Norma Shearer, Deborah Kerr, Thelma Ritter, Judy Garland, Ava Gardner, Kay Kendall, Claire Bloom, Jane Fonda, Audrey Hepburn, and Anna Karina. Cukor's extraordinary skill in directing women made Clark Gable wary of working with him on *Gone with the Wind*, because of the actor's fear that Cukor would throw the film to Vivien Leigh and Olivia de Havilland, and Gable's reported discomfort over Cukor's homosexuality also helped account for the director's firing from that film by its producer, David O. Selznick, after two years of preparation, including extensive screen testing.

But discerning critics have long recognized that Cukor's body of work contains nearly as many memorable male performances, as he would insist with growing asperity over the years. He drew career-best performances from a wide range of men as well as women, stars as well as supporting actors. Cukor helped reshape the careers of male and female stars and discovered numerous newcomers to the screen while establishing their screen images. Some of the incandescent male performances in Cukor's films include Lowell Sherman's alcoholic director Max Carey in *What Price Hollywood?* (1932); John Barrymore's second-rate actor Larry Renault in *Dinner at Eight* (1933); Cary Grant's insouciant social dropout Johnny Case in *Holiday* (1938); Tracy's affable but exasperated prosecutor Adam Bonner in *Adam's Rib*, perpetually jousting with his wife (Hepburn), a feisty public defender; James Mason's self-destructive movie star Norman Maine in *A Star Is Born* (1954); Rex Harrison's fiercely misogynistic Professor Henry Higgins in *My Fair Lady* (1964); and Laurence Olivier's aging barrister Sir Arthur Granville-Jones in *Love Among the Ruins* (1975), who rekindles his youthful, largely unrequited passion for a flamboyantly flighty retired actress played by Hepburn. All these actors discovered new dimensions to their screen personalities under Cukor's shrewd and sympathetic direction.

Cukor further belied the "woman's director" label by demonstrating his versatility over a wide range of film material. Part of what distinguishes his body of work is his habitual blurring of genre boundaries, making his films difficult to categorize, just as he himself was because of his navigation of complex social roles. Cukor's unusual position in the Hollywood hierarchy made him both an outsider and a quintessential insider—his intimate A-list parties at his West Hollywood home were renowned, but he reserved Sundays for parties with his lesser-known gay friends—and his careful and adept social balancing act is reflected in the creative tension in his films between opposite poles of status. Cukor's work is further characterized by his transgression of traditional gender roles; he was far ahead of his time in exploring what we now call gender fluidity in the astonishing, brilliantly deft 1935 Hepburn-in-drag film *Sylvia Scarlett* as well as his other work.

And Cukor blended comedy and drama with a rare adroitness: he had a natural predilection for seeing the comedy in a situation whenever possible. He said, "I choose my actors well and get to know the quirks of their personalities—and, most of all, I share humor with them. That's how to effect the best collaborations. Then I keep my eyes open when they rehearse and perform, because you never know where the next stimulation comes from." And he declared, "I find it wonderful to take a serious subject and treat it with a kind of impertinence and gaiety." Categorizing is to be avoided when discussing Cukor, for seeing individuals clearly and freshly, without stereotyping blinders, is a major part of the strength and charm of his work.

Is *A Star Is Born* primarily a musical or a drama? Doesn't *Dinner at Eight* (based on the Edna Ferber–George S. Kaufman play about ill-assorted guests at a high-society dinner party) oscillate effortlessly between farce and drama, especially in John Barrymore's absurdly histrionic suicide, adjusting a light on his profile so he will be found in a flattering position? Is Judy Holliday's madly publicity-seeking New Yorker Gladys Glover in *It Should Happen to You* the heroine of a charming romantic comedy or the centerpiece of a sharply pointed social satire? And how to categorize *Heller in Pink Tights*, Cukor's picaresque, visually opulent 1960 Western starring Sophia Loren? McGilligan felicitously describes that improbable adaptation of a Louis L'Amour novel about a troupe of itinerant frontier entertainers as "a handshake between Toulouse-Lautrec and Frederic Remington." Rather than being seen as a virtue, Cukor's directorial versatility often has been held against him, as if it were seen as a crime for an orchestra conductor to be ambidextrous.

"THAT LITTLE SOMETHING EXTRA"

Cukor's self-effacing tendency in working through the text and his actors, coupled with the classical Hollywood "invisible style," helps account for the tendency to regard him more as a metteur-en-scène (the French term for an impersonal journeyman director, literally a "placer in the scene") than an auteur. Cukor's visual style, his mise-en-scène, may not have called attention to itself, at least until his later years when it became increasingly flamboyant, but close analysis shows it to be supple and expressive and elegant.

Cukor paid keen attention to settings, decor, costumes, and cinematography, which became more subtle and sophisticated as his career progressed in the 1930s. His interest in research and art direction intensified in such films as *Little Women, David Copperfield, Sylvia Scarlett*, and *Camille*, and the alluring and authentic visual texture of these films (all set in period except for the picaresque, fantastical *Sylvia*) was accomplished partly through Cukor's insistence on art directors he chose, sometimes over the objections of studios' preference for their own contract staff. Cukor's work was often visually stylized, sometimes subtly, sometimes more daringly, a tendency that complemented the stylized performances he drew from his rich variety of actors and enabled him to provide a unity between their behavior and the atmosphere surrounding them. After making a lavishly mounted semidocumentary World War II drama about the U.S. Army Air Forces, *Winged Victory* (1944), Cukor experimented after the war with neorealism in his extensive location shooting in New York on *A Double Life, Adam's Rib, A Life of Her Own, The Model and the Marriage Broker, The Marrying Kind*, and *It Should Happen to*

0.5. Cukor was always generous in sharing credit with his collaborators, even to a degree that raised questions about his own creative role, but he valued the collaborative nature of filmmaking. Here he confers during the making of *My Fair Lady* (1964) with his editor William Ziegler and art director Gene Allen, a key creative partner in the director's increasingly ambitious mise-en-scène. All three were nominated for Oscars; Cukor and Allen won.

Source: Warner Bros./From the George Cukor Papers of the Margaret Herrick Library, Academy of Motion Picture Arts and Sciences.

You. That postwar trend, inspired by Italian filmmakers, offered another form of stylization that helped reinvigorate Cukor's work and harmonized well with an infusion of new acting talent from the East, most notably including the incandescent Holliday and Lemmon.

Along with that fresh sense of freedom, when studios increasingly responded to public interest in seeing actual locations rather than films shot entirely in studios, Cukor began to develop a more lush and lavish visual style, beginning with *A Star Is Born*, his strikingly adventurous entry into color that boldly disregarded the timid rules the studios were trying to impose about restricted movement within the initially cumbersome CinemaScope format. The early sequence at the Shrine Auditorium film industry benefit, largely filmed from the backstage point of view, is the most spectacularly varied and sustained passage in the film. Nearly surreal imagery of clowns and other kinds of entertainers is beautifully displayed with bold color schemes in the backgrounds and costumes (some of the imagery is borrowed from Degas and other painters) and eccentric choreography, daringly breaking the supposed rules of the day with fast cutting on the wide screen, sometimes using handheld cameras. This bravura sequence and its avant-garde departure from Cukor's black-and-white work made *Cahiers du Cinéma* hyperbolically trumpet, "A DIRECTOR IS BORN!"

Cukor benefited greatly from his collaboration on that film with the color consultant George Hoyningen-Huene, a distinguished international glamour magazine photographer, and his new art director, Gene Allen, both of whom would also serve as major contributors to his work in subsequent years. Besides his work on conceiving and executing set designs, Allen also helped Cukor by suggesting camera setups and doing second-unit directing on their films; Cukor candidly told me that when he began working with Allen, "Maybe that's why my visual sense improved." The heightened flamboyance in Cukor's sophisticated visual style in later years enabled him to move freely between stylization and naturalism, according to the demands of the subjects. Cukor's style always was insufficiently noticed, however, partly because he gave such generous credit to Allen, Huene, his cinematographers, and other art directors for helping him plan scenes and even place the camera, while stressing the role of the director as collaborator rather than taking more of the credit for being the creatively assiduous visual artist he actually was.

Andrew Sarris in his *Village Voice* review of *Travels with My Aunt* (1972) told his audience to read the picaresque source novel by Graham Greene (which reads like a series of short stories), then see the movie, and then "come tell me that you don't know the meaning of mise-en-scène. Even the plot has been changed to weave together relationships on the screen that have become unraveled on the printed page. But, above all, there are the bursts of color amid assured pacing and grading that mark Cukor's mastery of the medium." Sarris observed that Cukor had long been regarded solely as an actors' director and not a visual artist, but in the 1950s and '60s, he "seemed to be reborn as a director in a splash of color and style for its own sake, or rather for the sake of his directorial soul."

Still, while *A Star Is Born* and other late Cukor films are often visually dazzling, the director tends to avoid showiness for its own sake and keeps his visual style at the service of the stories. He does not rely as heavily on montage and conventional "coverage" as other classical Hollywood directors. Cukor's cinematic style is most distinguished (one of his favorite words) by his audacious, virtuosic use of long takes, a tendency that may have struck some critics as overly "theatrical" but in fact is breathtakingly cinematic, going hand in hand with his great respect for actors. His exhilaration in dealing with actors' behavior and their potential for self-revelation shows in the freedom and intensity they are given in exploring sustained scenes. "I think it flows," Cukor told me when I asked about his penchant for long takes. ". . . It's not only that the scenes are long, but you make them more real, more truthful, less *acted*." That virtuosity is more of his directorial sleight of hand: ultimate stylization seeming less acted, less directed, more real.

In addition to allowing the actors to help determine the pacing of a scene while carrying out his elaborate blocking in those long takes, Cukor sometimes displays the rare self-confidence to keep his camera motionless for long stretches of time. That is the case when the feminist lawyer in *Adam's Rib*, Amanda Bonner (Hepburn), plots the defense of a dopey woman (Holliday) who tried to kill her cheating husband. As Hepburn interrogates Holliday, cannily manipulating her into the role of a defensible victim, the actors are allowed, in a five-minute take, to inhabit and explore their roles in all their nuances from ridiculous to sublime (the scene was also planned, with the connivance of both Cukor and Hepburn, as an informal audition to help Holliday win the starring role in the director's 1950 film of the Garson Kanin play *Born Yesterday*, in which she played the lead role onstage). Often the emotions Cukor evoked from his players are delicately shaded; just as often they are raucously comic, as Cukor said he habitually encouraged his actors to be; and sometimes their emotions are raw, anguished, and violent. Cukor excelled above all at exploring the dramatic tensions between people's outer and inner lives. Serving as both a confidant and a cajoler of his actors, he prodded them, usually gently but sometimes with bracing harshness, to delve deeply into emotional areas they tended to keep safely hidden.

Cukor believed that "when you're a director, not only do you direct, you also react, you are the audience. The actors feel it. You must be a discriminating audience, a critical audience, so they will have the courage to try something different. On stage, if an actor does something stupid, the audience would boo him. But, if they do something right, the audience will catch it and encourage it. That's one part of the director's work. The other is the creative part: he is *more* than an audience, he also has to instruct, lead, really direct." Cukor excelled at earning the trust of his actors while being the receptive, encouraging, but keenly judging force who saw clearly from behind the camera what they were doing and selected what they did best. Not every director has that ability to see what an actor is doing and recognize the right moments or takes to incorporate into the film; the best actors' directors, such as Cukor or Welles, are the ones whose ability to do so is most perceptive and decisive.

And as Welles put it:

> I believe that directors are, all of them, actors, just as I believe that most writers are actors. . . . You can't think of a role that a director doesn't have to play. But none of them are really important compared to his real role, which is to be what is absent in the making of a movie—the audience. The director is simply the audience. So the terrible burden of the director is to take the place of that yawning vacuum—to *be* the audience—and to select from what happens during the day which moment shall be a disaster and which a gala night.

Cukor's absorption in show business had begun as a devoted member of the audience at many Broadway plays when he was a boy, usually from the second balcony. His role as the audience when he was directing films was highly interactive. Actors often remarked that he worked in front of the camera in rehearsals, not behind it as many directors do. And during the actual shooting, his empathetic involvement with his actors showed on his lively, expressive face behind the camera. That involved mirroring performances, as if he were playing the roles along with his actors, although in exaggerated ways. He admitted that his expressions often looked "grotesque," sometimes so much that they distracted his actors and made them ask him to stand to the side.

"If I were very handsome, maybe I'd have been an actor," Cukor admitted, and explained, "I don't weep or anything, but there's always some part of me left bloody on the scene I've just directed."

AN EXPERIMENT IN FILM CRITICISM

This book, then, is an experiment in how to study a director primarily through his work with his actors. That approach gets to the heart of Cukor's craft and should enable us to understand his artistic personality more precisely. Studying Cukor through his handling of the people he collaborated with—also including writers, art directors, cinematographers, and others along the way, but principally the actors who served as his instrument—will enable me to range both widely and minutely through his body of work in essayistic portraits of varying lengths. (Cukor films of lesser interest I have not chosen to analyze in detail are discussed in the context of other films.) This approach should illuminate the elusive areas of Cukor's visual style, personal themes, and the characteristic moods and atmosphere he created on the set and on the screen.

Paying close attention to what a director and actor actually *do* in their creative process together, I examine the most intriguing Cukor films through the texture of key performances, by stars or character actors or both. I focus on crucial as well as casual-seeming scenes and on the overall effect of the performances in these films and how they express Cukor's themes and style. Examining the personalities of these actors and comparing their work outside Cukor films also will help illuminate how, as Katharine Hepburn told him, "All the people in your pictures are as goddamned good as they can possibly be, and that's your stamp." It is a challenge to evoke the evanescent nature of screen acting on the page, but I hope I have developed the vocabulary to do so. The task is to pay close and precise attention to subtle, fleeting nuances of behavior and to evoke in words the physical details of the delicate combination of close guidance and freedom Cukor gives his actors, the process through which he enables the audience to comprehend the characters' inner states. Analyzing the theatrical and literary texts Cukor serves with fidelity while he and his writers turn them into cinematic language is also crucial in understanding how he enables his actors to embody the characters.

Not many film books have attempted this kind of close analysis of performance. But valuable exceptions are James Naremore's books *Acting in the Cinema* (1988), the groundbreaking text in this field of film criticism, and *Some Versions of Cary Grant* (2022) and Dan Callahan's incisive studies *The Camera Lies: Acting for Hitchcock* (2020) and *Barbara Stanwyck: The Miracle Woman*

(2012), his 2004 essay on Cukor in *Senses of Cinema*, and his two book collections of essays on *The Art of Screen Acting, 1912–1960* and *1960 to Today* (2018 and 2019). These lively and insightful works have been inspirational for me in approaching Cukor. So has Truffaut's pioneering 1966 interview book with Alfred Hitchcock, which makes extensive use of frame enlargements to help explicate mise-en-scène and, to some extent, acting, while complementing the acutely analytical verbal analysis by Hitchcock and Truffaut.

George Cukor's People: Acting for a Master Director contains a wealth of frame enlargements and other stills illustrating the scenes under discussion as well as the lively way Cukor interacted on the set with his actors. Together, these two ways of looking at Cukor and his work are intended to give us intimate, privileged insights into the particulars of his style and working methods. The frame enlargements are selected to show precise moments of behavior analyzed in the text. Now with the easier availability of frame enlargements, thanks to home video and computers, the Cukor scholar not only can "describe the way Cukor gets from *this* to *this* to *this*" but also "freeze each frame and tell you what *this* is." Tell you and now *show* you.

In many photos from the making of Cukor's films, there are revealing glimpses of his working relationships with his actors in candid shots on sets and locations. We often see him leaning toward the actor or actress to share his thoughts and feelings, confidently and with an intense expression of concentration or an equally intense smile, his right hand characteristically coaxing a point out of the air. The director's palpable intelligence and the actor's or actress's rapt attention convey a shared delight in the moment of artistic creation, and their electric interaction makes for an image of almost sexual cohesion. Eloquent photos of Cukor working with such actresses as Katharine Hepburn, Garbo, Crawford, Angela Lansbury, Audrey Hepburn, and Maggie Smith and such actors as John Barrymore, Grant, Tracy, James Stewart, Olivier, and Harrison show Cukor's passionate, almost priestlike ability to inspire such intimate, confessional moments of onscreen behavior.

THE CRAFT OF SCREEN ACTING: "LESS, LESS"

Cukor was highly talkative on the set, often holding detailed discussions with his actors while rehearsing. When his approach worked—and it sometimes did not, as with Gene Kelly, a fellow director who objected to his "endless chatter" while Kelly was acting with a sullen lack of charm in *Les Girls* (1957)—it made most of his players comfortable. Cukor created a creative space they found conducive to inhabiting their scenes as if in a protective cocoon, despite all the clattering, distracting mechanical apparatus of filmmaking and the crowds of technicians that surrounded their attempts to make moments of cinematic magic. But Cukor told Lambert that with a first-rate actor, a director need not give line readings and not necessarily give overly specific instructions. Instead, he created what he called a "climate" that enabled the actors to relax and feel free while still being subject to the critical and discerning eye of the director.

"Climate" (one of his favorite words) was a concept central to his work. It was the almost indefinable mood and ambiance he conjured up on set with his blend of a commanding presence and his intimately loquacious, often kidding, but intensely, mutually exploratory manner with an actor: "You make a climate in which he can work and find things out for himself. Then you say, 'That's it, you've got it.'" One of the most striking examples is James Mason's climactic scene of emotional breakdown as Norman Maine in *A Star Is Born*. "James is a highly talented man but a reserved, rather enigmatic person," Cukor said, "and I knew that his last scene in the picture, when he breaks down and decides to commit suicide, would be a case of letting him find out things for himself. So I let the camera stay on him for a very long time, and all his feelings came out and he became so involved, in fact, he could hardly stop."

How Cukor expressed himself through his actors and the characters they played will be my principal focus, the lens through which I view and comprehend what he brings to the stories he films. In doing so, I will also interweave analysis of how his mise-en-scène creates a striking visual atmosphere for his characters to inhabit, with his growing sophistication throughout his career from the 1930s onward to the increasing flamboyance and boldly experimental use of color and decor in his later work, from *A Star Is Born* and *Bhowani Junction* (1956) through *Les Girls*, *Heller in Pink Tights*, *My Fair Lady*, *Justine* (1969), *Travels with My Aunt*, *Love Among the Ruins*, and *Rich and Famous*.

Some of Cukor's most elegant and subtly nuanced, wittiest and most mordant work was done in his uneven but fascinating late period from 1954 to the

0.6. What the MGM executive Irving Thalberg called the *"unguarded"* quality Cukor evoked from Greta Garbo while directing her in *Camille* (1936) is evident in this casual glimpse of them on the set. The reclusive actress gives one of her most deeply moving performances in this version of the novel and play *The Lady of the Camellias* by Alexandre Dumas *fils*, about a doomed Parisian courtesan of the nineteenth century.

Source: MGM/Photofest.

end of his career in 1981, as well as his most sexually explicit (yet still somewhat discreet) work in such films as *Justine* and *Rich and Famous*. But the subtle eroticism of Cukor's films had always been a crucial element of his work, such as in his direction of Garbo in *Camille* (1936), her most unguarded and delicately abandoned performance. "It's the uncensored thought the actor flashes to the audience," Cukor said of the scene in which she "didn't touch Armand [her young lover, played by Robert Taylor], but she kissed him all over his face. That's how you create eroticism . . . how you achieve certain moments by really *assaulting* them." And Cukor's direction of Ava Gardner as an Anglo-Indian woman in *Bhowani Junction* gave that ravishingly beautiful but limited actress her most nakedly emotional and vulnerable role, a piquant and scintillating combination. Cukor always knew how to find the most potent combination of suggestion and boldness even within the strictures of the Production Code.

One of the principal reasons Cukor's role as a director is undervalued is that the art of film acting itself is so widely misunderstood. This book aims to help define how it actually works by examining it in close and specific detail. Even in the minds of many film critics and people in the film industry, good film acting is often confused with the *most* acting, "tear[ing] a passion to tatters," as Hamlet says in his speech to the players—overacting, wearing disguises and heavy makeup, or playing someone unlike yourself—the kinds of overwrought, gimmicky performances that tend to win Oscars and Emmys. In contrast, this is how Jack Lemmon recalled making his film debut for Cukor in *It Should Happen to You* after working extensively in theater and television:

> I had just come from a Broadway play, so I'm acting away and *buh-buh-buh*, and I guess unconsciously I'm playing to the balcony. George would say, "Oh, that's good, that scene is good, it's a print, that's a print, but just one more, Jack—one more—and less, *less*, do less." [They rolled the camera again, and] George said, "Oh, that was it, that's perfect, that's wonderful," he said, "but I'd like to do just one more, and, Jack"—and I said, "Are you going to say *less?*" He said, "Yes, yeah, just a little less," and so forth. And—which is uncharacteristic of me, but by then I'd really had it—I said, "Are you trying to tell me *not to act at all?*" And he said, "Oh, yes, *God, yes,*

yes!" . . . I've learned my craft from that advice. It's the hardest thing in the world to be simple, and the easiest thing in the world to act your brains out and make an ass of yourself.

Hitchcock wryly defined for Truffaut this low-key approach to screen acting by adapting an old joke about the British aristocracy: "In my opinion, the chief requisite for an actor is *the ability to do nothing well*, which is by no means as easy as it sounds. He should be willing to be utilized and wholly integrated into the picture by the director and the camera. He must allow the camera to determine the proper emphasis and the most effective dramatic highlights [emphasis added]." While that approach suited Hitchcock's primarily montage-based cinema (the supreme example is *Rear Window*), it obscures the fact that he was actually a highly skilled director of actors and drew eloquent performances from most of his cast members.

Cukor shrewdly doubted whether Hitchcock actually preplanned everything in his films, as he liked to claim. "I've never seen him work," Cukor said, "but his pictures are very clever and adroit and full of talent. However, I'm sure they involve more than just mechanical planning; that would be too simple. . . . He's a master of it, but I'm sure something is left for that moment when he actually does it on the set." Indeed, I found that to be the case when I spent three days in 1975 watching Hitchcock shoot his last film, *Family Plot*, and caught him in the act of improvising with his actors. And though Hitchcock's definition of good screen acting as "the ability to do nothing well" may seem somewhat limiting, like Cukor's advice to Lemmon, it gets to the essence of how the subtleties of facial expressions, body language, and dialogue are more eloquent than the kind of emoting necessary on a stage.

"In films," Cukor said, "it's what you *are* rather than what you *act*."

And yet his films, with their wide range of actors, demonstrate that what makes it possible for him to draw out such outstanding performances is his skill in helping his actors be themselves, enabling them to *find* themselves as actors and as people and the characters they are playing. That is what he did with Lemmon in his engaging comedy-drama performance, enabling the young actor to explore and find the nearly fully formed Jack Lemmon screen persona in his first film. But how exactly does an actor discover what he or she is, and how does a director translate that to the screen? A film actor and director have to *construct* a character together, and a star has to construct a persona, and when those processes work well, they become "what you *are*" onscreen.

Although John Wayne never acted in a Cukor film, and at first glance his rugged demeanor might seem antithetical to the Cukor style, Wayne was a more subtle actor than most people realize. His familiar screen image, which his detractors like to deride as "playing himself," holds a key to the meaning of how good screen acting works and how movie stars are constructed. To say that a star is "playing himself" is one of the most common and pervasive misconceptions about the nature of screen acting, one that skews the whole perspective on the subject.

When I raised that question with Wayne on the set of his last film, Don Siegel's *The Shootist*, in which he gives a masterful, deeply moving performance as a dying gunfighter, he emphatically differed with people who like to say he simply "plays himself" onscreen: "It is quite obvious it can't be done. If you are yourself, you'll be the dullest son of a bitch in the world onscreen. You have to act yourself, you have to project something—a personality. Perhaps I have projected something closer to my personality than other actors have. I have very few tricks. Oh, I'll stop in the middle of a sentence so they'll keep looking at me, and I don't stop at the end, so they don't look away, but that's about the only trick I have." I've always thought Wayne's pausing in the middle of sentences brings a sense of vulnerability to his acting that contrasts with and complements his formidable strength. Wayne could have added that he had carefully worked on putting together his distinctive walk, talk, and other mannerisms while being guided to his best performances by great directors, notably John Ford and Howard Hawks. But ironically, when Wayne developed the great skill to seem at his most natural onscreen, he was criticized for "playing himself," which in fact is what every star must do to become a star.

When Frank Capra appeared on our American Film Institute Life Achievement Award tribute to James Stewart in 1980, he came prepared with a speech that no less an authority than Lee Strasberg, who was watching on television, said was the best definition of motion picture acting he had ever heard:

A film faces the audience with a single thin front line—the actors. If that front line collapses, the show is over. A bad performance can kill the finest story. Yes, there is bad acting and good acting, fine performances and sometimes great performances. But there is a higher level than great performances in acting, a level where there is no acting at all. The actor disappears, and there's only a real live person on the screen, a person audiences care about immediately. There are only a few actors, very few, capable of achieving this highest level of the actor's art. And that tall stringbean sitting right over there, he's one of them.

Cukor directed Stewart to his only competitive Oscar as best actor, for his complex, seriocomic role as the sarcastic but romantic tabloid reporter in *The Philadelphia Story* (1940). As fine as his performance is, many people have considered that award a consolation prize for Stewart's missing out on the best-actor Oscar for Capra's *Mr. Smith Goes to Washington* the year before. One of the few matters I could not figure out how to analyze, try as I might, when I wrote my biography *Frank Capra: The Catastrophe of Success* was Stewart's great performance in *Mr. Smith*. So I was relieved to read much later that Welles said simply, "The performance by Jimmy Stewart is beyond praise." Similarly, Cukor's self-effacing quality as a director, his ability to make his films flow with seeming naturalness of style and authenticity of acting, has caused even many sympathetic writers to face the same kind of conundrum, making them simply finding his work "beyond praise." Or the special quality of his work often escapes the notice of critics and other nonprofessionals and simply seems ineffable or makes his films seem less "directed" than those of more ostentatious, flamboyant directors.

Cukor recognized and philosophically acknowledged, if not accepted, this myopic critical tendency. "The more successful you are as a director, a certain kind of director, the least apparent your hand should appear," Cukor believed. "There are directors who are wonderful, but they don't do it through the actors particularly. I happen to work through the actors." Cukor quickly established himself in Hollywood as a supple, sensitive, and distinctive director of actors after he was brought from the New York theater in the early days of sound as a "dialogue director." Charles Brackett, a novelist and member of the Algonquin Round Table who became a prominent screenwriter in the 1930s, recalled in 1961, "The understatement of great screen acting was mostly George Cukor's invention. He was one of the first to understand the difference between acting for the theater and acting for the camera."

0.7. Cukor's brilliance in making stage plays cinematic while retaining their original dramatic intensity and comedic qualities was a constant in his career and brought him his only Oscar for *My Fair Lady*, based on the musical adaptation of George Bernard Shaw's *Pygmalion*. Part of his deft directorial touch was his ability to modulate the performance of an actor who had played his role many times onstage (Rex Harrison as the linguist Henry Higgins) while easing a veteran film actress into her new part (Audrey Hepburn as Eliza Doolittle).

Source: Warner Bros./Photofest.

The basic need for understatement that Cukor impressed upon Lemmon and others did not prevent the director from allowing and encouraging his actors to perform their roles on a wide range of levels. Cukor's handling of actors is never one-note but always finely shaded; he is a master of *tone*, that most elusive and hard-to-define of qualities in film direction. Knowing that the director is the person who keeps the overall fluctuation of tone in a film in his or her head at all times during production and postproduction—that combination of pacing, relative intensity, size of expression, and interaction with other actors—Cukor demonstrated his rare ability to maintain and shift the elements of tone according to the finely calibrated demands of his highly varied material. His lightness and subtlety in shifting moods and styles within a film is a major part of what makes him a great director. That, more than anything else, might be considered the "Cukor Touch."

But along with encouraging a baseline of restraint, Cukor also would encourage his actors to "go big" and act all-out emotionally when the scene called for it, for as Maggie Smith's Aunt Augusta says in *Travels with My Aunt*, "You must learn to abandon yourself to extravagance!" And throughout his career Cukor excelled at recognizing and bringing out what Mason's Norman Maine tells Garland's Esther Blodgett about her talent in *A Star Is Born* (the screenplay is by Moss Hart). After visiting a nightclub after hours and hearing her sing the electrifying "The Man That Got Away," which Cukor presents in a virtuosically sustained long take, Norman surprises Esther by saying, "You're a great singer. . . . You've got 'that little something extra' that Ellen Terry talked about—Ellen Terry, a great actress long before you were born—she said that that's what star quality was, 'that little something extra.' Well, you've got it."

"That little something extra" is the distinction Cukor brought to his work, the qualities he and his actors and other collaborators contributed over and above the text while still executing it faithfully.

CUKOR'S PERSONAL VISION

Cukor does not flag his characteristic themes as obviously as some other directors tend to do, but his personal preoccupations stand out clearly when one surveys his body of work. That is most evident in the surrogate-director figures, both male and female, who act as Pygmalions to a wide variety of Galateas in films ranging from *What Price Hollywood?*, *Little Women* (1933), and *Sylvia Scarlett* to *Holiday*, *A Woman's Face* (1941), *Born Yesterday*, *The Model and the Marriage Broker* (1951), *Pat and Mike* (1952), *A Star Is Born*, *My Fair Lady*, *Travels with My Aunt*, and *The Corn Is Green* (1979). But most striking and pervasive is Cukor's characteristic gravitation to socially adventurous, subversively rule-breaking, audacious dreamers who are often sexually transgressive and gender fluid in ways that seem far ahead of their time and strikingly modern today. Whether overt or implicit, Cukor's tendencies toward such characters and situations can all be seen as manifestations of a queer artistic sensibility, one that by necessity had to be expressed within the bounds, however inflexible or not, of the commercial system of filmmaking in which he worked.

The most outré example of such transgressiveness is Hepburn's title character in *Sylvia Scarlett*, who masquerades in a traveling theatrical troupe as a boy named Sylvester, attracting the sexual attention of a woman (Dennie Moore) as well as two men (Cary Grant and Brian Aherne). Grant's sly Cockney conman sees through her quickly, but Aherne's dashing, somewhat effete bohemian artist tells Sylvester, "I say! I know what it is that gives me a queer feeling when I look at you." Sylvia's romantic rival, Natalie Paley's Lily Levetsky, exclaims, "The little Pierrot boy! But were you a girl dressed as a boy, or are you a boy dressed as a girl?" Calling her both "How charming!" and "very strong," Lily kisses her.

So advanced in its sensibility that upon its initial release it became the director's most notorious flop, *Sylvia Scarlett* nevertheless has been embraced by modern audiences sympathetic with its piquant and spirited gender-bending drollery. Although Cukor sometimes expressed pain over the harshness of the general critical and audience rejection of *Sylvia Scarlett* on its first release, which forced him to be more circumspect with his gender experimentation onscreen, and though he often called *Little Women* his personal favorite, he told Clarens, "I've been quoted as saying that a good film is a successful film. Well, there was *Sylvia Scarlett*, a flop, and still my favourite picture. Perhaps because we were all so happy while making it. . . . It was like a many-sided love affair."

Other occasional overt traces of Cukor's gay sensibility break through in some of his earliest films in the relatively unbridled pre-Code era. Cukor preferred the word "queer" to "gay." He told the gay publication *The Advocate* in 1982, "I hate that word." Cukor was ahead of the times in preferring the word "queer," which is often used today in boldly reclaiming a former slur for prideful usage; this book will use those words interchangeably. One of the most flamingly queer characters in Hollywood history is a dance instructor named Ernest, played by Tyrell Davis in Cukor's 1933 drawing-room comedy *Our Betters*. Ernest flaunts a brazen appearance, wearing eyeliner as well as lipstick on his bee-stung mouth at the end of the deceptively genteel Somerset Maugham play adaptation. Cukor squeezed that campy performance into the pre-Code film behind the backs of the Hays Office. "Ernest could have taught you *all sorts* of new steps," Constance Bennett's Lady Pearl Grayston tells a matronly duchess (Violet Kemble Cooper) with arch insinuation before Ernest gives her a tango lesson. And he exclaims at the fadeout, "Ah, what an exquisite spectacle, two ladies of title kissing one another!"

After seeing the film, James Wingate of RKO's Studio Relations Department wrote his production chief, Merian C. Cooper, about what he considered the "unfortunate lapse in good taste" in the characterization and makeup of Ernest. Wingate commented, "In the last script submitted, Ernest was described as being dressed like a tailor's dummy, as being overwhelmingly gentlemanly, and speaking in mincing tones, but there was no indication that he would be portrayed as a pansy." Will Hays himself warned RKO that "a script may be entirely proper, yet the material may be handled in such a manner by the director and actor that the final result carries unlooked-for implications. . . . Such a thing, of course, is unthinkable."

As a result of such alarms over the "unthinkable," most often in his subsequent work Cukor had to dial back his overtness and treat gender fluidity more subtly and suggestively. The director did so with David Wayne's gay-coded neighbor, Kip, who continually (and somewhat confusingly) flirts with Hepburn's Amanda Bonner in *Adam's Rib* after the Code office warned against making the character too obviously gay. Kip is even more sexually ambivalent than Douglass Montgomery's effeminate suitor, Laurie, had seemed with Hepburn's Jo March in *Little Women*. Much later, when Code restraints were beginning to relax, Cukor enjoyed playing around with queer innuendos in showing a clueless, hunky beach bum (Ty Hardin) baffled by what to do with the opposite sex when a Southern California housewife (Glynis Johns) giddily but fruitlessly pursues an erotic escapade in *The Chapman Report* (1962). And Cukor is comfortable with the cozy pair of bachelor philologist housemates (Rex Harrison and Wilfrid Hyde-White) in *My Fair Lady*, along with the many other people throughout his films who pursue unconventional single lives, marriages, or partnerships.

They include the Tracy and Hepburn characters who painstakingly and amusingly work out relationships of unusual equality in the Gordon-Kanin screenplays *Adam's Rib* and *Pat and Mike*; the offbeat couple played by Hepburn's tomboy writer and Paul Lukas's mild-mannered, much older Professor Bhaer in *Little Women*; or the couples who negotiate the intricate, often contentious terms of their relationships in such varied films as *Camille, Susan and God* (1940), *The Philadelphia Story*, *Born Yesterday*, *The Marrying Kind*, *It Should Happen to You*, *The Chapman Report*, and *Justine*. Cukor's positive focus on all variety of unconventional relationships and transgressive characters is a function of the enduring queer sensibility in his work, even if it had to be expressed more covertly after *Sylvia Scarlett*. It can be said of Cukor, as it has been of the novelist E. M. Forster, that being queer enabled him to perceive heterosexual relationships more clearly from his sympathetic but critical outsider's perspective.

Like Sylvia Scarlett, many of Cukor's other people role-play by acting for a living. One of his most autobiographical films is *The Actress* (1953), even though, paradoxically, it is the seriocomic story of Ruth Gordon, the frequent Cukor screenwriter, who adapted her own play *Years Ago*, about her youthful obsession with going on the stage. Among the most moving images in Cukor's work are Jean Simmons's wide-eyed, enraptured close-ups as she watches from the second balcony the glamorous actress Hazel Dawn (Kay Williams) and a chorus of tuxedoed men sing "(My) Beautiful Lady" while they waltz and she plays the violin. Those fervent close-ups from the cheap seats memorialize Cukor's own youthful passion for the stage. And Ruth's successful defiance of her initially somewhat skeptical father, Spencer Tracy in a magnificently gruff yet empathetic performance, captures the tenacious, unbeatable nature Cukor displayed throughout his lifetime.

Even if Cukor's characters follow other professions, as do the married lawyers played by Tracy and Hepburn in *Adam's Rib*, they instinctively practice theatricality as a way of life, a means of creating their own individualized roles in the human comedy. Cukor's familiarity with role-playing in his own life enabled him to help his actors glide gracefully, delightfully, and movingly between their public roles and "offstage" moments of more private emotion. His roster of larger-than-life yet always believable characters spans a vast range of life experiences, as disparate as those embodied by Hepburn's adventurous New England writer Jo March in *Little Women*, W. C. Fields's sublimely daffy Mr. Micawber in *David Copperfield* (1935), Greta Garbo's exquisite dying courtesan Marguerite Gautier in *Camille*, Judy Holliday's ignorant but shrewd Billie Dawn in *Born Yesterday*, Tracy's Damon Runyonesque athletic trainer Mike Conovan in *Pat and Mike*, Maggie Smith's defiantly eccentric Aunt Augusta in *Travels with My Aunt*, and Laurence Olivier's lovelorn bachelor barrister in *Love Among the Ruins*.

As Sarris noted in 1968, dreamers of all kinds are omnipresent in Cukor's world: "The director's theme is imagination, with the focus on the imaginer rather than on the thing imagined. . . . Cukor is committed to the dreamer, if not to the content of the dream." And those struck by "impossible dreams" (as Claudette Colbert's stage actress Zaza calls them in Cukor's 1938 film of the same name) can find the dreams liberating or destructive, although usually the former, since Cukor shares the romanticism of his daring characters. He is always keenly aware of the social strictures within which his adventurous characters must function, and Cukor's allegiance is always with the rebels and dreamers whose lives challenge those dictates. In *A Star Is Born*, Garland's abandoning her band for a drunken actor's offer of a screen test after many years of working her way to a modest level of success seems foolish to a fellow band member, but she says with wonderment when she walks out of his motel room as the sun rises, "You think so? Then why do I *feel* like this?" She has taken Norman Maine seriously when he listens to her talk about her hopes of having a number-one hit song but tells her, "The dream isn't big enough."

If the primary virtues of a Cukor character include imaginative self-assurance, poise, and independence, the flip side of those qualities is the self-destructiveness seen in the alcoholics who appear with telling frequency in his films, dreamers whose dreams fly back to strike them in the face. Besides the complex characters played in Cukor films by Barrymore, Mason, and Lowell Sherman, other memorable alcoholics in his work include Lew Ayres's wealthy young lush in *Holiday*, whose speech (by the playwright Philip Barry and screenwriters Donald Ogden Stewart and Sidney Buchman) about the joys of drinking is one of the most finely shaded monologues in screen history; Deborah Kerr's ruined, wraithlike wife of a callous wealthy man (Tracy) in *Edward, My Son* (1948); and Claire Bloom's suburban sex addict Naomi in *The Chapman Report*, a wanton performance of startling intensity and sensual, suicidal abandon, even after the studio's recutting.

Dan Callahan wrote in his insightful 2004 profile of Cukor in *Senses of Cinema*, "This was an artist who understood the deepest kind of pain" but was "fascinated by alcohol and why people needed it, the loosening of social inhibitions that came with it, and the somewhat alluring self-destruction it portended. . . . Cukor solidifies his favorite theme: the glory of alcoholic, lunatic or sexual abandonment and breakdown, the sheer sensuality of it, and, at the end, its high price."

Tracy Lord's (Hepburn) working up the courage over a boozy night to reject her loveless impending marriage in Cukor's film of Barry's high-society play *The Philadelphia Story* is, as Callahan puts it, "a positive re-ordering of her life that could never have been accomplished without the aid of a dozen or so glasses of Champagne. Thus, in Cukor's world, alcohol destroys, but it can also lead to edifying follies. Cukor loves to watch his actors lose control." Cukor's understanding of the dual nature of addiction is what is lacking from the Oscar-winning but one-note portrayal of a morose alcoholic by Ray Milland in Billy Wilder's *The Lost Weekend*. The critic James Agee, an alcoholic himself, acutely observed that Milland's self-pitying would-be writer is so unrelentingly maudlin that the performance misses the "euphoria . . . [and] the many and subtle moods possible in drunkenness" that come along with the deadening effects of the disease. Cukor's alcoholics all partake of "many and subtle moods," a quality that serves as a hallmark of his style.

The quality Ingmar Bergman identified as essential to a film star—danger—is often present in Cukor's characters as they live their lives bravely or recklessly on the margins. That spirit and desperation distinguishes Hepburn's performance as the rebellious socialite Linda Seton in *Holiday* from the sensitive, Oscar-nominated but more contemplative, less headlong performance of Ann Harding in the previous (1930) film version of Barry's play. Hepburn asks her alcoholic brother (Ayres) in *Holiday* to tell her about the appeal of getting "Good and drunk," which he finds necessary to break away, internally at least, from their repressive family. In one of Cukor's greatest scenes, "crammed with" those "little tiny fleeting expressions and motives" Olivia de Havilland highlighted in his work, Ayres's Ned confides to Linda, looking bemused as his heavy-lidded eyes scan her hideaway in their Fifth Avenue mansion, "Well, to begin with, it brings you to life. . . . Mm, and after a while you begin to know *all* about it—you feel, I don't know, important." She asks at the end of his darkly eloquent monologue, "You get beaten though, don't you?" "Sure, but that's good too. Then you don't mind anything, not *an-y-thing* at all. Then you sleep. . . . Other things are worse."

Cukor's preoccupation with the double life of alcoholism, which he often shows as affecting characters of social distinction, has been traced back to his friendship with John Barrymore, whose roistering and hospitalizations provided traits and anecdotes that were adapted for *What Price Hollywood?* and William Wellman's 1937 unofficial remake with Fredric March as Norman Maine, *A Star Is Born*, and made it into Cukor's version of *A Star Is Born* as well. But the theme of alcoholic self-destruction, and Cukor's related interest in states of mental breakdown, are so pervasive in his work that they more likely are metaphors for a disruptive side of his own personality that he managed to hold in balance.

Cukor was sparing in his use of liquor but struggled for much of his life with his weight and was subject to emotional volatility. He had a tendency to veer from diplomacy to fury on the set. He hit Katharine Hepburn during the making of *Little Women* when she misbehaved by spoiling a dress by dropping ice cream on it and laughing after being warned that they didn't have a spare. And he provided a spectacle that Steven Spielberg witnessed when he visited Cukor at work on outdoor shooting on the campus of the University of California, Los Angeles, for *Rich and Famous*. Spielberg reported that the elderly director spent much of his time slumped in his chair, his belt loosened for comfort as old men are wont to do, but once, when he got mad, he jumped up and shouted, and his pants dropped to the ground in front of everyone.

CUKOR'S "WONDERFUL GAMEY QUALITY"

Cukor usually preserved his dignity, however, and he was beloved by most of his collaborators, with whom he tended to work in rare harmony within the studio system. His understanding of the vagaries of the human psyche ensures that people are rarely reduced to stereotypes or treated with censure in his movies. Despite his characteristic emphasis on elegance and charm and sophistication, Cukor also had a fascination with coarseness in human nature. It may have stemmed from what McGilligan calls the less socially respectable side of the "double life" Cukor had to practice in his closeted public life in Hollywood, even though his homosexuality was commonly known and accepted within the industry.

Angela Lansbury, who made her spectacular film debut as a teenager playing the insolent, flirtatious maid in Cukor's *Gaslight*, told the audience at his

0.8. "When we were shooting *Love Among the Ruins* in London, we went out at 8 o'clock one Sunday morning—it was the only time we could work at a certain location—and Kate Hepburn said, 'Aren't we in a wonderful business where we can see these beautiful things and work in these beautiful places?' Well, you'd see that in her face." Cukor and Hepburn making their late masterwork *Love Among the Ruins*, his first film made for television (1975).
Source: ABC Circle Films/ABC-TV/Photofest.

Film Society of Lincoln Center tribute in 1978 that Cukor had "a wonderful gamey quality about him, a wonderful lasciviousness." His late films, such as *Justine*, *Travels with My Aunt*, and *Rich and Famous*, reflect that side of his personality in their often candid and bold explorations of sexual underworlds, behavior, and imagery. Unlike most Hollywood directors from the studio period, Cukor believed in adapting to changing times in the 1960s and beyond. It's notable that one of the modern films Cukor most enjoyed was Paul Morrissey's 1968 film for the Andy Warhol factory about a heroin-addicted male hustler (Joe Dallesandro), *Flesh*. Cukor hailed *Flesh* as "an authentic whiff from the gutter . . . to present this picture of a world, to do it with such original humor—I'm lost in admiration." Such earthiness may have surprised those who pigeonholed Cukor as a gentleman of the old school, missing the fierceness, tenacity, and social and emotional flexibility that enabled him to survive in the Hollywood jungle as a working filmmaker for more than half a century.

Cukor also relaxed a bit late in life in his willingness to talk publicly about queer issues. He virtually "came out" the year before his death, in his 1982 interview with *The Advocate*, included in Robert Emmet Long's book *George Cukor: Interviews*; McGilligan's 1991 biography deals with that aspect of his life in depth. In his later interviews, Cukor often used more candid language than he had in his book with Lambert, whose elegant manner tended to discourage Cukor's penchant for coarseness. Always fond of bawdy language, Cukor used it more openly as he aged and felt more liberated from the restraints of his public image. My and McCarthy's freewheeling 1981 interview with Cukor for *Film Comment* about his later work featured him at his most unbuttoned, capturing his irreverent, often hilariously profane way of commenting on his actors and films. Lambert objected to our not censoring Cukor's off-color language (as he did in their book), but we presented it unapologetically to show how the man really talked, with such endearing candor and ease.

When I asked Cukor about a project he wasn't able to make in his later years, *Vicky*, about the nineteenth-century feminist Victoria Woodhull, Cukor described her and her sister Tennessee Claflin as "so funny. They were real adventuresses." I observed, "Vicky sounds like the kind of role Hepburn could have played in her youth." He said, "Yes, except that it was a little more sluttish than Kate would play. Kate's too intelligent." I countered by pointing out that Victoria Woodhull was the first woman who ran for president of the United States (in 1872). "But that was just nothing," said Cukor with gusto. "She also did a lot of fucking. They were a bad lot, the two of these girls." And when I asked Cukor what he thought of Hollywood extras, he replied in his unbridled language, "Pricks and cunts."

THE ART OF COLLABORATION

George Cukor's People will honor the central importance of collaboration in the art of film. That is what makes a critical study of a generously collaborative director such as Cukor so challenging, since it makes his creative role more difficult to define and has contributed to him being undervalued. But I hope my fresh approach to studying Cukor will offer a fruitful way of defining and honoring what he brought to the filmmaking process in creating his rich and enduring body of work. Rarely do director-centered studies say enough about the director's collaborators, but this focus will help elucidate Cukor's particular approach to filmmaking.

Cukor sometimes suffered setbacks because of his role as part of that system, most egregiously the evisceration of his masterpiece, *A Star Is Born* (later partly restored) but also his notorious firing from *Gone with the Wind* and his assignment to some films started by other directors. But he generally thrived in Hollywood and provides a sterling exemplar of the genius of the system, drawing on the resources MGM and other studios offered him. He directed fifty-five films and kept working until he was eighty-one, the oldest director, at that time, ever to make a Hollywood studio film. And within that system, Cukor, along with some other major directors such as Ford and Hitchcock, managed to put his personal stamp on his work through the strength of his artistic personality and because his interests often coincided congenially with the demands of the system for popular as well as prestigious works of cinematic art.

Cukor's wry wit, his keen sense of psychological and social observation, his charm and irony, and his unbeatable toughness and resilience kept him active long after most of his contemporaries had settled for posh but unhappy retirement. Cukor prided himself on being a "survivor" and not letting setbacks throw him unduly, even managing to joke about most, if not all of them. Cukor prevailed not by pretentious self-dramatization but with humor and unquenchable enthusiasm for his profession. I experienced those qualities firsthand while having lunch with him in 1975 at the Polo Lounge of the Beverly Hills Hotel. I was interviewing him for the Directors Guild of America magazine, *Action*, about one of his most trying experiences, the disastrous Russian-American coproduction of *The Blue Bird*. I brought up other mishaps in his career and asked how it felt to be fired from a film; I was thinking of the 1947 MGM film *Desire Me*, from which Cukor said he had been "removed"; it was partly reshot by other directors and has no directing credit. Cukor reacted by touching my forearm lightly with his right hand, leaning over toward his publicist, and saying, "Notice with what finesse he avoids mentioning the title *Gone with the Wind*."

1

LEW AYRES IN *ALL QUIET ON THE WESTERN FRONT* AND *HOLIDAY*

One of George Cukor's enduring triumphs is a film on which his name does not appear. In the early days of talkies, a "dialogue director" or a "co-director" from the New York theater was often assigned to a picture to ensure that a former silent movie director could handle actors. Even a director as experienced and well regarded as John Ford had to suffer the involvement of co-directors on his early talkies; the result was a needless hodgepodge. When stage directors such as Cukor began making movies of their own, they also had to work with co-directors while learning the basics of cinematic storytelling. But Lewis Milestone, who had won one of the first Oscars for the silent comedy *Two Arabian Knights*, was too prominent to need a "co-director" on *All Quiet on the Western Front* (1930). Universal's ambitious adaptation of the best-selling 1929 German novel by Erich Maria Remarque about the horrors of the Great War was a daringly grand investment of $1.45 million by the second-tier studio.

Enter Cukor. He had been brought to Hollywood as dialogue director on Paramount's *River of Romance*, a 1929 adaptation of a Booth Tarkington play, *Magnolia*, about dueling in antebellum Mississippi. This stilted, cornball melodrama directed by Richard Wallace—redeemed only slightly by an enjoyably hammy performance by Wallace Beery (whom Cukor would later direct in *Dinner at Eight*)—is literally the kind of stagey early talkie Howard Hawks

1.1. George Cukor (standing, center) and Lewis Milestone (to his left), with a group of actors posing while receiving candy bars at work on *All Quiet on the Western Front*, including Lew Ayres, far right. Milestone directed the classic 1930 film version of Erich Maria Remarque's World War I novel. The film's lasting impact was enhanced by Cukor's help in casting the young actors and coaching them while serving as the uncredited "dialogue director."

Source: Universal/Photofest.

had in mind when he said that the dialogue in most of those films "reminded you of a villain talking on a riverboat." Cukor recalled that he was hired to coach the cast in a Southern accent, but he could only manage a "bogus" facsimile, and the qualities of ironic dialogue he found in the play were lost on the producer and director. Next to *River of Romance*, *Gone with the Wind* (which Cukor partially directed) seems like *War and Peace*. Nevertheless, Cukor's early Hollywood champion, the producer David O. Selznick, recommended him to Milestone for *All Quiet*.

The mammoth, uncompromising film was on a different level of importance and a task that would keep Cukor busy for six months. His was the crucial job of screen-testing, helping choose, and then rehearsing the youthful cast members and assisting Milestone in laying out the dialogue scenes.

Remarque's novel follows the disillusionment of an ordinary German soldier, Paul Bäumer, in the hellish experience of trench warfare. A veteran himself, Remarque wrote the book in the first person and present tense, giving a vital immediacy to the punchy, diary-like account of Paul's journey from his militaristic indoctrination as a schoolboy to his moral awakening in combat. Then he is shot by an Allied sniper, becoming another statistic in the vast litany of loss.

Other writers, most prominently Ernest Hemingway (*The Sun Also Rises*, *A Farewell to Arms*) and Robert Graves (*Good-Bye to All That*), also were publishing books that captured the senseless carnage of the war. Gertrude Stein called these former soldiers part of "the lost generation," and their bitter process of enlightenment was memorably defined by Hemingway: "Abstract words such as glory, honor, courage, or hallow were obscene beside the concrete names of villages, the numbers of roads, the names of rivers, the numbers of regiments and the dates." What Hemingway described is what film can do so well, even if neither film version of *Farewell* comes close to the impact of that book; the 1930 version of *All Quiet*, however, in some ways surpasses the power of the book.

Enough time had passed since the Armistice that Hollywood was not only making such gritty war movies as *The Big Parade* (1925) and *What Price Glory* (1926) but had already begun to make films showing the humanity of the former enemy, including D. W. Griffith's *Isn't Life Wonderful?* (1924) and Ford's *Four Sons* (1928). With its mobile camerawork conveying the nightmarish reality of trench warfare with astonishingly visceral impact, and filming in depth by the cinematographer Arthur Edeson to make the settings of both interiors and exteriors (and blends thereof, as in the striking opening of parading soldiers seen through schoolhouse windows) seem almost three-dimensional, *All Quiet* is remarkably free of the stagebound constraints of most early talkies.

And a crucial reason the film maintains its classic status today is that the central performance by the twenty-year-old Lewis Ayres (as he is billed) is so engaging and authentic. The studio wanted Douglas Fairbanks Jr., an established star, for the role but was unable to make a deal for him. They were fortunate to find Ayres, one of many actors who had tested for Paul. After viewing his test again when negotiations for Fairbanks fell through, Milestone urged Universal to cast him in the lead role, but they balked because he was unknown. So Milestone had Cukor direct another test that convinced the film's producer, Carl Laemmle Jr., to hire the young actor.

Ayres's Paul is initially idealistic but increasingly jaded, and his riveting characterization is remarkably natural and relatively free of the theatrical declaiming common to early talkies, aside from a few awkward moments. With his earnest, sensitive demeanor, an aura of sincerity that goes beyond the immediate demands of the role, and as the most handsome of the boys in the cast, Ayres stand out from the less accomplished but still affecting performances of most of the other young actors. Some of them do too much indicating on camera—signaling the audience how to regard their behavior—but Ayres learned the ability to relax into being himself-as-the-character from Cukor, who conveyed his insight that "in films, it's what you *are* rather than what you *act*."

Cukor's creative contribution unfortunately remained uncredited, as it had been on his first film as dialogue director, though here his work went well beyond that limited definition. Milestone deserves credit for blending the blistering spectacle so fluidly with intimate personal scenes and for his expertly balanced and paced handling of Ayres before the camera, but without Cukor's subtly nuanced and intense work with the cast behind the scenes, the film might have become mired in speechifying, as sometimes happens when the screenplay by Maxwell Anderson and George Abbott decides it needs to spell out its humanist, antiwar themes. *All Quiet* demonstrates what Charles Brackett referred to as "the understatement of great screen acting [that] was mostly George Cukor's invention."

All Quiet won the Oscar for best picture and Milestone another for best director. Cukor's extraordinarily disciplined and sensitive training and molding of the young actors, especially Ayres, whom he had recommended for the lead role, did not go unnoticed by the Hollywood studios. Later in 1930, Paramount assigned Cukor to direct a stage adaptation, *Grumpy*, along with a co-director, Cyril Gardner. That stagebound clunker about a doddery old lawyer showed that Cukor (as he readily admitted in later years) initially needed help in understanding the camera, but after two more films that year with co-directors, *The Virtuous Sin* and *The Royal Family of Broadway*, he had made rapid strides in mastering the new medium's steep learning curve. Yet already in *All Quiet*, the performances Cukor helped draw from Ayres and the rest of the predominantly young cast make the film, if not entirely free from gauche, overwrought moments (such as Ayres being called upon twice to lift his head and pray aloud, lapses in the script that he and Cukor could not control), seem remarkably naturalistic today by comparison with most other films of that transition period from silents to sound (*All Quiet* was also released in a silent version for theaters not yet equipped for sound). The 2022 German version of *All Quiet*, though well crafted and welcome in allowing the characters to speak their original language, unfortunately downplays character interchanges in favor of action, as is typical of contemporary filmmaking, and Felix Kammerer's performance as Paul seems pallid and uninvolving next to that of Lew Ayres.

The rapport Cukor achieved through his painstaking work with Ayres and the other young actors showed that before he quite knew what to do with the camera, he quickly grasped the need for it to serve as a quiet observer of human behavior seemingly caught on the fly. Directing actors to be natural is not as easy as it may seem, for as Oscar Wilde put it, "to be natural . . . is such a very difficult pose to keep up." Establishing what natural behavior consisted of in an early talkie called for a rigorous kind of stylization. Ayres was an uncommonly intelligent actor whose expressively low-key face is the kind made for the camera, eloquent in its stillness, supple in its texture, and with soulful eyes, able to communicate thought and emotion in an uncannily empathetic exchange with the viewer, earnest but with little need for demonstrative histrionics.

Ayres's restrained quietude in the classroom as other boys react boisterously to their jingoistic schoolmaster urging them to fight and die for the fatherland singles him out as different, immediately showing that he thinks on a deeper level than his classmates. Praised by his teacher as a promising poet and playwright, and first seen with his bowed head leaning against his clasped hands as the camera tracks in, Paul is not immune to the emotional cajoling and jingoistic fireworks—he becomes the first to stand and say, "I'll go," although in a more subdued voice than the others, and then helps persuade a reluctant classmate to enlist—and before he makes his decision, he is given a close-up to show hesitation while nearly hyperventilating. That instinctive hesitation becomes prophetic when the teacher's frenzied words are proven "obscene" in juxtaposition to the harrowing physical experiences Paul and his classmates undergo in battle.

Paul's gradual processing of the differences between words and action becomes one of the running themes of the film, including in his rueful

1.2. Ayres, at age twenty, gave a startlingly real and heartbreaking performance as the German soldier Paul Bäumer in *All Quiet on the Western Front*. Here, while home on leave from the front, he tells the bitter truth about war to the latest group of schoolboys misled by his jingoistic professor (Arnold Lucy). One of Cukor's first jobs in Hollywood, his work as dialogue director was a vital contribution to this landmark film and helped establish him as a leading actors' director during the transition to sound.

Source: Frame enlargement; Universal.

reaction when he visits the classroom on leave and tries to tell the plain truth about the front to the new boys with quiet conviction, only to be called a "Coward!" by one of them. Paul's mood turns angry and bitter as he denounces the teacher: "You still think it's beautiful and sweet to die for your country, don't you? Well, we used to think you knew. The first bombardment taught us better. It's dirty and painful to die for your country. [*Voice rising*] When it comes to dying for your country, it's better not to die at all." Thanks to Cukor and Milestone's collaboration, the film's strikingly authentic production values, and Edeson's ferociously visceral cinematography, we the audience know the whole truth Paul is vainly trying to convey to those who can neither hear nor see.

A moving father-son relationship develops between Paul and the grizzled Corporal Stanislaus (Kat) Katczinsky, majestically played by Louis Wolheim. Wolheim looks brutish but is warm, humorous, and kindly, as well as keenly intelligent (Wolheim was a mathematics professor as well as an actor). Kat has to calm Paul after he starts losing composure when the boys face their first infantry barrage. Paul puts his arm around the older man as the young soldier begins to learn from Kat how to control his emotions and face danger more stoically. The calmness and wisdom of Wolheim's performance provide a telling dramatic contrast to the vivid battle action and the occasional hysterics of some of the young soldiers, including Paul, as they experience combat and shelter in dugouts to avoid shelling. Paul is the most affected by Kat, and his own force of personality (he is portrayed as a natural leader) enables him to behave more maturely as the story progresses. His personality gradually deadens, however, as Ayres's performance turns even more introverted and melancholy, losing his boyhood earnestness and only rarely showing a vestige of his former joie de vivre.

Kat seems uncannily impervious to danger until he and Paul are strafed by an airplane while walking in a field. Paul carries the wounded Kat on his back in a lengthy tracking shot and takes him to a medical station. But there he learns from another soldier's matter-of-fact report that Kat is dead; Paul's eloquently low-key emotional reaction is shown by his hand trembling slightly as he pulls it back from Kat to find it is covered in blood, and then by his walking away, silently and helplessly. He is soon shot down by a sniper as he extends his hand from a trench, reaching for a butterfly, in one of the cinema's most iconic shots conveying the futility of war. Milestone lent his own hand to double for Ayres in that scene, which is followed by a shot from earlier in the film of Paul and the other boys looking over their shoulders as they march into battle, superimposed on a field of crosses, the soundtrack going completely silent.

Since Ayres's performance is so memorable, it is somewhat surprising to learn that he did not get along with Cukor when they worked on *All Quiet*. Ayres recalled in a 1995 interview, "He was after me all the time, telling me, 'Do this, do that, do this, do this,' because he came from New York [theater], and it bothered me." Cukor's volubility throughout his career rubbed some other actors the wrong way too, but most actors, perhaps tired of working with directors who had little to offer, welcomed his chattering, insightful, often humorous approach. According to Leslie L. Coffin's biography of Ayres,

> Lew felt Cukor was overly critical of him, making him repeat readings dozens of times until they met his approval. . . . Lew, already possessing a certain disdain for authority, found himself hating Cukor, especially when he felt he was being hypercritical and dictated specifics of his performance which should be left to the discretion of an actor. After one particularly difficult day with Cukor, Lew even considered quitting the film. Lew told his [company hotel] roommate [and fellow actor] Billy Bakewell that he thought he would never be able to meet Cukor's standards and he should simply allow them to replace him. Bakewell convinced Lew to sleep on his decision and by the morning the frustration had subsided.

Ayres may have simply been too young and callow (it was only his third film) and too rebellious by nature to put up with so much advice from a dialogue director he found overbearing. But Cukor undoubtedly felt that the young actor needed line readings, and the impressive results bear him out, even if his drilling of Ayres may have been excessive. When I worked with Orson Welles on *The Other Side of the Wind*, he would often say, "It's terrible for a director to give an actor a line reading, but . . ." I would welcome his line readings, because I had no experience and was grateful for any help he could give me. And he would often bawl me out for my failings, once to the point that he stopped shooting for the day because I arrived with the wrong coat; I wept and found myself wandering around the Sunset Strip despondently that night, but all was forgiven the next day. Cukor was like a harsh drill instructor with Ayres and the other boys in *All Quiet*, doing his best to train them to deliver their lines naturally. But Bakewell also complained that Cukor had "a flair for caricaturing a bad dialogue reading so broadly, and with such waspish scorn, that the offender would never dare make that mistake again. His face would become almost gargoyle-like as he avidly mouthed each word along with us and urged us on in a dramatic scene."

Ayres famously became a conscientious objector in World War II, heroically serving as a U.S. Army medic and chaplain's assistant under fire in the Pacific, although he minimized the frequent assumption that his role in *All*

Quiet had inspired him to take that step. Although he was praised by many as time went on and was able to resume his career after the war, his decision initially provoked condemnation and calls for boycotts of his work from some quarters in Hollywood and elsewhere, including even Remarque, who said, "I didn't expect it to have an effect like this. I think we all should fight against Hitlerism." Cukor was one of nine Hollywood figures (also including John Huston, Olivia de Havilland, and Humphrey Bogart) who signed a letter to *Time* magazine in April 1942 calling Ayres's decision "the sad result of a sadder misconception" but came to his support by declaring that

> there was nothing of either a seditious or treasonable nature in his words and action. Such being the case it is not within our conscience to remain silent while so many voices are raised against a man who acted according to dictates of his conscience. As members of the motion picture industry we deny the representation that we are ashamed of Lew Ayres and that we would disclaim him. . . . It is a sorry comment on the rights of democratic life as observed by the motion picture industry, that the public print has been far more understanding and human in its treatment of Lew Ayres than has the industry which he served faithfully and well.

By the time Ayres worked with Cukor for the second time on *Holiday*, eight years after their contentious experience on *All Quiet on the Western Front*, Cukor had learned to become more diplomatic and realized he could take a different tack with the more experienced actor. That sparkling 1938 adaptation of the playwright Philip Barry's romantic seriocomedy rescued Ayres from a busy but mostly unrewarding career in B pictures. As he said of Cukor, though doubtless again with some exaggeration, "When I did *Holiday* with him, he never said a word. And gee, we got on so well. It's very hard to have a director that's directing you all the time. But he was very, very good and very kind to me."

Barry's plays, the epitome of sophisticated Broadway comedy, take an astringent as well as affectionate view on the rich, a balancing act the playwright pulls off with aplomb and that matches Cukor's somewhat ambivalent view of that class. His film version of Barry's 1928 play *Holiday*, starring Katharine Hepburn and Cary Grant, and his 1940 film of the playwright's *The Philadelphia Story* are two of the director's finest works. Cukor told Gavin

Lambert that he found the rich a "great comfort," and his films of Barry's plays partly reflect that admiration, verging on envy, in their luxurious trappings and elegant (if erratically so) style of conduct, even while they are satirizing and critiquing the narrow-minded, selfish, supercilious aspects of the playwright's wealthy characters. The particularly acerbic tone of *Holiday* toward the stuffy Seton family against whom Linda Seton (Hepburn) and her sister's fiancé, Johnny Case (Grant), rebel can also be attributed partly to the film's updated Depression-era setting and the fact that it had two leftist screenwriters, Donald Ogden Stewart and Sidney Buchman, both of whom were later blacklisted (see more on that in chapter 10).

Hepburn is superlative in *Holiday* as the restless heiress bored with her empty Fifth Avenue life and attracted to the idealistic young man played by Grant; he is an early version of what would later be called a dropout. Yet the highlight of the film is Hepburn's scene with Lew Ayres as her disheartened brother, Edward (Ned), when he explains what it's like to be perpetually

1.3.   Avoiding the clichés of movie drunks, Ayres gives another unforgettable performance as Ned Seton, the wryly fatalistic alcoholic brother of Katharine Hepburn's Park Avenue heiress in *Holiday*, Cukor's 1938 film version of the Philip Barry play.

Source: Frame enlargement; Columbia Pictures.

intoxicated as his means of escape. The exquisitely written scene in Barry's play captures that delicate balance of the "many and subtle moods possible in drunkenness" (as James Agee put it) and does so with a memorable mixture of grace, dry wit, and the tragic undertone we sense just below the surface. The poignancy of the scene revealing Ned's cavorting demons in *Holiday* draws from the way the director, writers, and actor avoid descending into maudlin display in their fine-brushed verbal self-portrait Ned sketches with such precision and wryly amused tones and facial expressions.

Ned is introduced in *Holiday* walking with his habitual shakiness through the hall of the absurdly grand Seton residence, obliviously passing a visiting stranger (Grant's Johnny Case) he doesn't know will soon become part of their dysfunctional family and help lift them out of their luxurious rut. Ned is on his way to a Christmas church service, which he clearly regards with consummate boredom as a strictly social obligation, in the presence of his sententious and domineering father (Henry Kolker); we get a sense of Ned's problems through their juxtaposition as they sing a hymn with nearly equal lack of interest and from the bandage Ned wears prominently on his forehead. It covers a wound he pats quizzically from some event the previous night that he cannot quite remember; his careful eye-roll and wince make you viscerally feel his pain, and the bandage serves as a sign of his perpetual psychic damage. This dissolute, pathetic young rich man comes alive as a character only when, after a long absence, he enters the cozy, unpretentious upstairs "playroom" Linda regards as her private preserve away from the corrupting enclosure of her hidebound wealthy family.

Happily recognizing his old piano and drum set, Ned starts playing his long-forsaken musical composition with boyish enthusiasm. Ayres recalled feeling especially comfortable in handling these props because he had given up a brief career as a band musician before achieving his goal of becoming an actor in Hollywood, including as the male lead in a late-silent Garbo movie, *The Kiss* (1929), directed by Jacques Feyder. We find that Ned's relationship with Linda is uncommonly affectionate, though without any trace of incestuous feelings, simply a case of the sister watching out for and trying to revitalize a sibling she knows is in serious trouble that he insists on denying. The drunk scene starts, though, with Linda as the one in trouble. She and Johnny are hiding out in the playroom from the lavish New Year's Eve party downstairs for her father's announcement of Johnny's (foolish) engagement to her shallow and snobbish sister, Julia (Doris Nolan). Johnny and Linda draw closer, but she persuades him to leave him reluctantly to go join the party as the other guests sing "Auld Lang Syne" off-camera.

Ned, resplendent in white tie and tails, makes a wobbly entrance into the playroom holding a glass and a wine bottle. He pours a glass for the disconsolate Linda, who is wandering the room in her elegant black, bejeweled dress. Ned gives a carefully nuanced, thoughtful, but self-defeating answer to Linda's asking, "What's it like—to get drunk, Ned?" His response, "*Grand!*," makes the audience understand the appeal of alcoholic abandon for a man such as Ned, the mixture of heightened perceptions and fatalistic abandon that "brings you to life" and makes you feel "important." But in reality his subjugation to his job as a stockbroker in his father's firm has caused him to abandon any hope of pursuing an independent life or his musical aspirations.

He beckons her with his finger to sit with him on the couch, the camera moving in to frame them in an intimate two-shot. He's stretching out his words with a sly smile, luxuriating in the secretive act of revelation as one hand clasps his bottle and the other is poised with a glass. He leans closer to her as he confides, "And then pretty soon the game starts." Gently swirling his wine and looking around the playroom in quietly gleeful glances, he explains how he succumbs to "the swell game—*ter-ribly* exciting game" of surrendering to drink. "You see, you think *clear-r* as crystal. But every move, every sentence is a problem. That gets pretty interesting."

She responds with a wan smile but a despondent tone, "You get beaten, though, don't you?" And he says, "Sure, but that's good too—" Cukor cuts into the two-shot for the first time with a big close-up of Ned as he tells her that you don't mind anything, "not *an-y-thing* at all. Then you sleep." Eyes glistening with tears, Linda laments how "awful" that is, asking, "Where do you end up?" Ned still covers his underlying gloom with a light manner, half-lidded eyes, a shrug, his mouth widening in a blasé manner: "Where does *everybody* end up? You die—that's all right too." But then Ned's mood abruptly shifts to his belated awareness of Linda's distress.

Ned's supporting-character status, that of providing the tragic subtext for Linda's dilemma, now allows him to stop focusing on himself and become truly supportive of his troubled sister. Half in wonderment, half in sympathy, he says to her, "I *know*—Johnny?" Demanding another glass of wine, she bursts out with the truth that's been hidden beneath all the phony, "noble," civilized, hypocritical Seton family talk: "I love the boy, Neddy." Tears lightly speckle her cheek, and she gives a hollow laugh. This scene is all the more devastating for having been played until the end in an almost offhand manner, balanced between pretending that everything is "all right" and making clear that it's nothing of the sort.

When Johnny finally breaks off the engagement with her crushingly conventional sister, Linda rushes out to catch him as he sails for Europe. She does not fail to beg Ned to come along with them. His hesitation at the doorway when his father forbids him to leave is heartbreaking. "You won't?" she asks. He responds in a low, melancholy voice, looking back toward his father, "Can't." "Caught?" Turning halfway toward Linda but not meeting her eyes, he murmurs, "Maybe." "I'll be back for you, Ned." A pause. He smiles slightly, looks down, telling her: "I'll be—here."

Ned's tragic finale is the counterpoint to the romantic happy ending Philip Barry provides for Linda and Johnny in this elegantly balanced drama of love, manners, and rebellion. That balance represents Cukor and Barry at their best, a portrait of life that is simultaneously satisfying and harsh, depending for its truth on the awareness of finely poised oppositions. Everything in life is perpetually *en marge*.

2

FREDRIC MARCH AND INA CLAIRE IN
THE ROYAL FAMILY OF BROADWAY

Cukor in his youth lived vicariously onstage, watching his favorite actors and actresses perform in Broadway theaters. He was able to savor, sometimes repeatedly, the resplendent performances of theater legends during that rich period of the American theater before the Depression and talking pictures sent it into one of its periodic nose-dives. Paying little attention to his schooling, Cukor was preparing himself for a life backstage, since he recognized, like Shakespeare's Falstaff, that "I am not only witty in myself, but the cause that wit is in other men" (and women). Before long, the young Cukor had talked his way into a succession of minor backstage jobs and found himself running a busy summer stock company in Rochester, New York. He eventually was the director of several Broadway plays, including an adaptation of F. Scott Fitzgerald's *The Great Gatsby* and two vehicles for one of his idols, Laurette Taylor.

Although Cukor's work in the theater did not bring him great success, it was responsible for his being called to Hollywood as part of the influx of stage directors hired to assist in the rocky transition from silents to sound. And his passion for the stage would be reflected not only in the many plays he successfully transferred to film as a director but also in how theatrical influence would stand behind the kinds of characters to which he gravitated, many of whom are actors or directors. Even more so, life as performance, and especially gender as performance, became a central subject of investigation for his long career in movies. Role-playing, in all its variety, would draw from his full range of abilities to create a "climate" that allows his actors to reveal their deepest selves beneath and through the roles they are playing.

So it is fitting that the first truly noteworthy film Cukor directed was all about the theater and how the people in it can never stop acting in what is misleadingly considered "real life." That is the one role for which none of the Cavendish clan is suited. *The Royal Family of Broadway* (1930), based on the 1927 play *The Royal Family* by the Broadway maestros George S. Kaufman and Edna Ferber, is an amusing but somewhat creaky early talkie that looks like a television sitcom, which can be explained by its filming (at Paramount's Astoria Studios in Queens, New York) with multiple, mostly locked-down cameras in soundproof booths and flat lighting brightly illuminating every corner of the principal set. The cinematographer, George J. Folsey, would go on to much finer work in sound films (including Ernst Lubitsch's *The Smiling Lieutenant* and Cukor's *Adam's Rib*) once those technical restrictions were a thing of the past. *The Royal Family* was the last film on which Cukor had a co-director, Cyril Gardner, who had performed that function with him on *Grumpy* as well.

Cukor recalled that the first time he had a strong feeling about what the camera could do was in *The Royal Family*, when he filmed Fredric March's Tony Cavendish (the movie star of the family) walking up a long staircase, trailed by his mother and sister, while undressing for a shower and expounding on his scandalous escape from Hollywood after slugging his director. Cukor instinctively realized that it would be more amusing to sustain the comical

2.1.   Fredric March lampoons the matinee idol John Barrymore in *The Royal Family of Broadway*, the 1930 film of the Edna Ferber–George S. Kaufman play *The Royal Family*, a spoof of the Barrymore acting clan. Co-directed with Cyril Gardner, it was one of Cukor's first films to show his skill at translating theater to the screen with brio; he told Gavin Lambert that this elaborate crane shot was "the beginning of a breakthrough for me, making the camera more mobile." With March from left are Ina Claire and Henrietta Crosman.

Source: Frame enlargement; Paramount.

2.2.   Cukor overcame his feeling of being an awestruck fan and established a warm rapport with John Barrymore while directing him in three films. In the 1933 adaptation of Kaufman and Ferber's play *Dinner at Eight*, Barrymore is the gallant but suicidal fading matinee idol Larry Renault, with Lee Tracy (left) as his beleaguered agent.

Source: MGM/Photofest.

mood of Tony's exhibitionistic action and charismatic attraction to others by filming it in one long take with a crane following him up the stairs. Achieving the shot was difficult with the cumbersome equipment of the time, but Cukor called it a "breakthrough" moment for his career as a filmmaker. Ironically, as Tony pulls off his pants near the end of the shot, he growls, "Ugh, I *hate* pictures!" Long takes would become a signature of Cukor's visual style and work with actors who could handle and appreciate the value of doing a scene "in one."

And in some ways the screenplay of *The Royal Family of Broadway* by Herman J. Mankiewicz and Gertrude Purcell improves on the original material while broadening it here and there beyond the single large drawing-room set of *The Royal Family* but still fittingly presenting the histrionic Cavendishes as performers within their own family stage. The expert screenwriters tighten the focus of the play's scattershot comedy. While reveling in chaotic comedic business and the entrances and exits of its crowded stage, the play lacks the concentration on central characters and situations that makes the playwrights' high-society ensemble comedy-drama *Dinner at Eight* (directed for the screen by Cukor in 1933) and the somewhat similar Kaufman–Moss Hart play about another eccentric New York family, *You Can't Take It with You* (directed by Frank Capra, 1938), resonate more vividly as character pieces. *The Royal Family of Broadway* shows Cukor coming alive as a film director in his third feature (though still learning how to use the camera, with the help of his co-director, Gardner) as the film orchestrates its blend of brightly comedic dialogue and broad parody, smartly acted, with moments of genuine pathos. That tonal blend would distinguish Cukor's more mature film work once he learned to become more adept in handling group scenes with just-right camera placement, deftly orchestrated rhythm of mise-en-scène and cutting, and masterly emotional transitions within and between scenes.

The Royal Family is a barely disguised takeoff on the illustrious Barrymore family. Despite its warm and jolly nature, the play infuriated Ethel Barrymore, who considered a lawsuit, but John Barrymore commented, "Fredric March made me an utterly worthless, conceited hound, and he had my mannerisms, exaggerated but true to life." Barrymore told March, "That's the greatest and funniest performance I ever saw." So the film did no harm to Cukor's eventually close collaboration and friendship with Barrymore, who gleefully parodied himself better than anyone else. Cukor went on to direct him in *A Bill of Divorcement* (1932, as Katharine Hepburn's shellshocked father), *Dinner at Eight* (as a soused film star who kills himself after failing a Broadway comeback), and *Romeo and Juliet* (1936, as a too-old but engagingly rowdy Mercutio). Those roles allowed the aging Barrymore to display his considerable range, even if most of his 1930s film work, including *Dinner at Eight*, shows him engaged in self-parody, gamely sending up his public image as a fading, hammy former Shakespearean star slumming with self-conscious and drunken abandon. Barrymore slyly mocked his own screen persona and the absurd situations that surround his larger-than-life presence. The critic Dan Callahan, in one of his books on cinematic acting, observes, "Watching Barrymore on screen, we are always waiting to see whether he will engage with his material. If he does, he's capable of large-spirited magic, and if he doesn't, he merely moves his face and pops his eyes, wearily, as if he's trying to be amused. . . . Barrymore was the first in a line of outsized American talents who wound up trapped in self-parody."

The Royal Family of Broadway centers on the top-billed Ina Claire's middle-aged star, Julie Cavendish, who is torn about whether to retire and "settle down" to a mundane life with a wealthy suitor. But as sharp as she is, the film is mostly memorable for the parody of a self-parody gaily enacted by March as the outrageously flamboyant Tony Cavendish. Without the pretentious lugubriousness that often mars his film roles, the young March revels under Cukor's adroit handling in his expert takeoff on "The Great Lover" who flees catastrophe in Hollywood to return to the cocoon of his family of oddballs while harboring a probably fleeting impulse to go back on the stage. The play delays Tony's riotous entrance much longer than the film, in which his antics draw most of the attention, even though the stylish, assured Claire provides the quieter, more sensible anchor of the story.

In her early scene after leaving a theater where she's starring in *Romeo and Juliet*, Julie and the august matriarch, Fanny (Henrietta Crosman), are riding in a chauffeured car past the Broadway marquee of one of Tony's movies, *Man Against the Gods*, while Fanny exclaims in dismay, "My son, a Cavendish, in Hollywood! All talking, all color—all terrible!" Then we see a marquee for March's previous film, *Laughter*, with his name billed under Nancy Carroll's. The *Royal Family* play, as Cukor noted, adopted the then-fashionable sneering attitude toward the movies among the denizens of the "legitimate" stage that he did not share. He felt that made the film feel old-fashioned, but its verbal wit still sparkles, and Claire (one of Cukor's favorite stage stars) is sensitive and elegantly nuanced in one of her rare film appearances.

The film draws its vitality from Cukor's close observation of actors' behavior and interaction in long-held two-shots, a trait drawing from his own theatrical background. Such shots enable his actors to explore scenes together at more length than usual in movies; eventually that became a virtuosic hallmark of his cinematic style. The play and screenplay revolve around the ambivalence of this celebrated theatrical clan toward their turbulent profession and the contrary pull of the illusory dream of leading "normal" lives. Two stuffy "civilians," a South American platinum magnate and a stockbroker, try vainly to persuade Claire's Julie and her daughter, Gwen (Mary Brian, who had worked with Cukor on *River of Romance*), to abandon their stage careers. "I'm sick of being a Cavendish! I want to be a human being!" Gwen cries at one point. But inevitably, despite the women's vague feelings of unhappiness about the evanescence of their lives onstage, the stifling nature of traditional marriage repels Cukor's heroines, who, like most women in his films, are too unconventional to abandon their independent destinies.

Claire's Julie, though pronouncing herself tired with the grind of a long-running hit, jumps from her chair automatically during a hiatus from the stage when a maid tells her it's 8 PM, i.e., time for the curtain to rise. Cukor greatly admired Claire's polished, light, assured manner, which made her a leading figure on Broadway in what was then known as "high comedy," before "romantic comedy" became a familiar genre. The best-known of her nine film roles is the imperious but insecure Grand Duchess Swana in Ernst Lubitsch's *Ninotchka* (1939); that casting is a legacy from the period when Cukor had been assigned to the project at MGM before shifting to *The Women* the same year. The actress fit Cukor's penchant for an amused attitude toward human foibles as well as a blend of mature ennui with youthful vitality and love of her craft. Claire provides the equilibrium in what she calls a "family of maniacs," the kind of sensible actress Cukor always respected who did her job with a lack of preening and nonsense. The frantic confusion of the family melodramas that swirl around her in *The Royal Family of Broadway* makes her restrained style in this early talkie represent Cukor's own tolerant but arched-eyebrow view of the zanier aspects of the theater.

Cukor also deeply respects the love of tradition and work-horse nature of the grande dame of the family, Fanny, whose failing health can't keep her from going back on tour in Shakespeare's *Merry Wives of Windsor* (no doubt as Mistress Quickly, who gives the eulogy on the death of Falstaff). An actor dressed as Falstaff says she has been giving one of her best performances, but she dies in her dressing room with her family surrounding her in the film's touching conclusion, which is all the more moving for coming at the end of an essentially comic piece. Henrietta Crosman was another stage veteran who made too few movies; among them is the lead role in John Ford's 1933 *Pilgrimage*, a great performance as the flinty Arkansas farm woman who sends her son to his death in World War I rather than lose him to the girl he loves (I persuaded Twentieth Century-Fox to reissue that neglected gem in its 2007 DVD set *Ford at Fox*). Crosman is given a star monologue in *The Royal Family*, regally perched on a chair holding her cane as she excitedly recalls the ritualistic backstage expressions that precede the start of a play. When Julie, realizing the stage is truly her life, goes on for her mother at the end, she pulls herself together and tells the stage manager, "All right, ring up the curtain!" The light hits her face as she lifts her hand triumphantly and the scene fades out.

The funniest moment in the film is not in the play. It's one of the most droll and outré examples of the queer sensibility in Cukor's work. Tony's niece, Gwen, who's determined to escape the family to get married, is having a meltdown over wanting to quit acting. The heavily made-up Tony is watching quietly from the staircase, wearing a silk dressing gown festooned with palm trees while idly fingering a squash racket he's been strumming like a guitar. Gwen turns to confront him, babbling incoherently about his being a matinee idol for women, and demands: "What have you ever done with *your* life? [*Pointing her finger at him*] Have you ever had babies? Have you ever known what it was to have a home and a husband?"

Tony reacts by rubbing his mustache thoughtfully, looking off into the distance portentously, rolling his eyes, and gesturing in a campy fashion with his hand as if trying to draw out his feelings. Turning his eyes half to the audience as if to take us into his confidence, he exclaims with a leer and sly smile, "You've touched on a secret *dream* of mine, Gwen! I wish you had spared me." Then the butler, carrying a tray, calls, "Lunch!," and Tony slides down the banister and jumps into a chair to eat. March's stylized gestures with his hands—imitating what Callahan calls John Barrymore's "snake-like fingers"—are hilariously combined with statuesque poses and dramatically rolling movements of his head and wavy black hair to mimic Barrymore's sardonic style.

The Royal Family of Broadway is a reflection of the director's transition from the stage to the more congenial world of the movies, where he would spend the rest of his life. Cukor had been an enthralled playgoer and participant in the theater but a less than stellar figure on Broadway. Now he enjoyed parodying John Barrymore's stage image as "The Great Profile" and the Cavendish family's snobbish disdain for Hollywood. Cukor understood their uncertainty over the ultimate worth of their profession and how threatened they felt by the new medium he was entering so enthusiastically.

3

KAY FRANCIS IN *THE VIRTUOUS SIN* AND WITH LILYAN TASHMAN IN *GIRLS ABOUT TOWN*

Cukor's apprentice work as a film director—even in some of his most obscure films—showed signs of motifs and preoccupations he would pursue in his more mature work. Along with his love of theater on display in *The Royal Family of Broadway*, Cukor made two Kay Francis vehicles that explore his passion for masquerading, character transformation, and louche sexual role-playing. *The Virtuous Sin* (1930), set in Russia during World War I, starts as a rather solemn melodrama but takes a surprising and delightful comedic turn when Francis, playing a scientist, transforms herself into a prostitute in order to rescue her worthless husband from execution. In *Girls About Town* (1931), the liveliest cinematic excursion to date in Cukor's budding career, Francis and the effervescent blonde comedian Lilyan Tashman play a team of call girls who share a bed and fleece wealthy saps before Francis falls in love with one of them (Joel McCrea). Cukor's disinclination to judge the women's characters in these racy pre-Code situations is refreshing, and his empathy with sexual outsiders became a hallmark of his work, one reason his films hold up so well today.

Although Francis was one of the major female stars of the thirties, particularly appealing to female audiences for her parading in high-fashion regalia, she was often stuck in routine vehicles and as a result has largely been forgotten today. As Cukor once said, "I think it is pleasing to see attractive people, and that does not mean, because a girl is attractive or beautiful, or a young man handsome, that they're talentless."

Francis is best known now for her incandescently witty and soignée role as a sexually adventurous Parisian perfume company owner in Ernst Lubitsch's masterpiece, *Trouble in Paradise* (1932), the consummate romantic comedy. Her roles for Cukor are quirky and allow her to display her winning, too often neglected bawdy sense of humor in risqué, offbeat situations.

Cukor still had a co-director on the rather lumbering-looking *The Virtuous Sin* (Louis J. Gasnier), based on a play, *The General*, by the Hungarian war veteran and novelist Lajos Zilahy (the play was filmed again three times in 1931, in Sweden, France, and Germany). Cukor graduated as a solo director in 1931 on *Tarnished Lady*, an unsatisfying weepie weighed down by the dead-eyed screen presence of Tallulah Bankhead, whom Cukor felt was more suited to the stage. But *Girls About Town*, his next film, feels truly liberated, opening the door onto Cukor's characteristically light and buoyant style of acting and visuals. Neither of those films is based on a play—Donald Ogden Stewart, who based *Tarnished Lady* on his own short story ("A Story of a New York Lady") and Zoë Akins, the principal writer of *Girls About Town*, became regular Cukor collaborators—and the stories range freely around New York, with a fair amount of lively location work.

The Virtuous Sin, as the title indicates, is about paradoxical behavior and a generous unwillingness on the part of the playwright (and Cukor) to condemn the adulterous and otherwise deceitful behavior of Francis's Marya. She enters into a loveless companionate marriage with a charmless fellow scientist, Victor (Kenneth MacKenna, who in real life would marry Francis the following year), but when he is drafted into the czarist army, his hotheaded insubordination causes him to be sentenced to execution. The drama is heavy going until the film takes its unexpected turn into comedy. Marya masquerades as a prostitute to seduce the gruff General Platoff (Walter Huston), but he is so habitually aloof with women she has a hard time doing so. The film's shifts in tone are often clumsy, but its turn toward comedy is welcome, because that is more Cukor's forte and brings out the best in Francis as well.

Marya disguises herself as a prostitute in an officers' brothel, wearing a spectacular gown, but is repelled by the way men paw her like animals. Then she dresses up in a coquettish outfit—ruffled white dress and parasol, like a tart on holiday (or the renovated and cheeky Eliza Doolittle at Ascot)—and

3.1. Cukor's attraction to the theme of masquerading, a natural subject for a filmmaker who spent his life as both an insider and an outsider, enlivens the somewhat creaky early talkie *The Virtuous Sin* (1930, co-directed with Louis J. Gasnier). The popular romantic star Kay Francis transforms her character from a scientist to a supposed prostitute to barter her husband's freedom from a stern Russian general (Walter Huston). Marya's ruse is so successful she wins the general's love and puts her worthless husband behind her.

Source: Frame enlargement; Paramount.

accosts the general on his horse. He remains suspicious of her behavior, but after he succumbs to spending a night with her, even her revelation of the truth about her mission does not destroy their relationship. Her rigidly moralistic husband condemns her for saving his life, so he deserves her staying with the general, whom she educates in the art of being human.

The masquerades of various kinds that run frequently through Cukor's work, from the influence of his outsider status, make him unusually alert to the deeper issue of identity. That sensitivity underlies the complex psychological process of understanding and maintaining one's social "place" and carrying on in the face of either acceptance or hostility. In these early Cukor films, rough sketches for his later, more accomplished work, role-playing is foregrounded, and identity is overtly questioned. The most fascinating aspect of *The Virtuous Sin* is the unresolved question it raises about who is the true Marya—the loyal wife/sober scientist who tells her ungrateful husband, "To be loyal, I had to be disloyal," or the frisky prostitute/romantic lover?

The film, with its screenplay by Martin Brown and Louise Long, seems to suggest that the truest response is "all of the above." Francis's performance under Cukor's guidance encourages us to accept the different sides of her personality as equally valid and admirable. When the general, trying to figure her out before he learns her secret, compares her personality to a kaleidoscope and says, "You'll be someone else in the morning," she tells him teasingly, "Girls have to act that way—sometimes." But when she realizes she loves him, Francis's playful performance becomes passionately sincere, which takes the amusingly stolid general a while to process: "How many are there of you?" Pondering how he will respond when he learns the truth, she replies, "There's still another one—inside me."

The conflict between impersonal sex and love, and the issues of trust and identity, are given a more frolicsome but still emotionally affecting workout in the pre-Code *Girls About Town*. Cukor gets away with some teasing lesbian humor with the call-girl characters by showing Tashman's Marie and Francis's Wanda briefly in bed together at breakfast time (5:30 in the afternoon). Tashman, a favorite and friend of Cukor's, was a former Ziegfeld Follies dancer who had a busy career in silent films and early talkies, but her life was cut short by cancer in 1934. Garbo was such a fan of Tashman's racy performance as a seductress in Lubitsch's 1926 *So This Is Paris* that it led to them becoming lovers. Francis was known for her uninhibited sex life with both men and women. *Girls About Town*'s screenplay, by Raymond Griffith (the former silent comedian who has a memorable role as the stocky French soldier killed by Paul in *All Quiet on the Western Front*) and Brian Marlow, is based on a story by Zoë Akins, who was also a lesbian. Her partner, the stage veteran Jobyna Howland, overacts grotesquely as a madam in *The Virtuous Sin*, wildly indulged by Cukor, as he sometimes did with older actresses he adored.

Cukor and Akins give *Girls About Town* some weight with an emotional bonding between the two girls, in and out of bed, that makes this a film about female friendship, like Cukor's final film, *Rich and Famous* (1981). The pair of friends in that one is quite different—two literary ladies (Jacqueline Bisset and Candice Bergen) with radically different styles of writing and

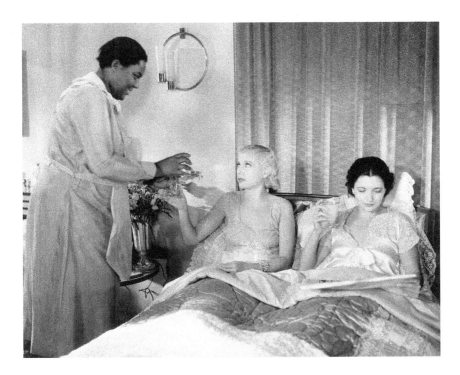

3.2. *Girls About Town* (1931), Cukor's second film with Francis and one of his first solo efforts as a director, is a risqué pre-Code comedy about (thinly disguised) call girls who run a lucrative racket fleecing chumps with the sly help of their maid (Louise Beavers). Francis and another bisexual actress, Lilyan Tashman (middle), get the chance to wink at the audience in this bedroom scene, one of Cukor's frankest escapades into queer humor.

Source: Paramount/Photofest.

behaving—but the last shot of Cukor's career movingly shows them kissing in front of a fireplace on New Year's Eve. The sarcastic attitude toward romance and sex expressed by Tashman's Marie in *Girls About Town*, who enjoys her effervescent game of putting men on, is refreshingly tart in both senses of the word. Tashman's caustic style makes a sparkling complement to Francis's wistful dreaminess. *Girls About Town* even takes time to develop a touching friendship and financial scheme between Marie and the ill-used, frumpy, middle-aged wife (Lucile Gleason) of a comically loathsome "Michigan copper king" (Eugene Pallette).

Wanda and Marie are introduced as disgusted with their life as call girls partying in a Manhattan nightclub with rich codgers from Des Moines: "It's been an evil night" is the film's opening line from Marie. In plain fact onscreen, these two "girls" are high-priced prick-teasers who con suckers out of their money while cleverly avoiding having sex with them. They run this con with the help of their Black maid (Louise Beavers in a less stereotyped role than usual), who impersonates their mother in silhouette in a window (spoofing Whistler's Mother); even pre-Code films had their limits in portraying sex workers frankly, but at least Cukor and these actresses found some fun in the game. The audience is left with no illusions about Wanda and Marie's metier, laying on the innuendo much as Frank Capra did with his more dramatic 1930 Barbara Stanwyck movie about call girls, titled with a similar sense of euphemism, *Ladies of Leisure*. "Doesn't it make you sick to be pawed by a bunch of middle-aged Babbitts?" Marie complains in *Girls About Town* as they fend off the men's clumsy advances. The film's many gags about Midwesterners probably stem from Akins, who was from the region and knew all about its dominant sexual hypocrisy.

Throughout the early scenes showcasing the girls' disenchantment and cynicism, they have to perform phony rituals of romance amid the clinches, another form of elaborate sexual role-playing. But when they take a gig for a sort-of-wild party on a yacht, Wanda is surprised to find herself actually falling in love with her mark, the handsome young Joel McCrea, during a moonlit tryst on deck on a couch strewn with pillows. She warns him, "I might go serious on you, Jim." The film implies through a Lubitschean ellipsis that they have sex on that couch, but Jim drops into a postcoital disenchantment. He stereotypes Wanda by telling this call girl she's just pretending to fall in love: "I gotta hand it to you, though—you've got great technique." But Wanda, wearing only underwear in a cabin below decks, debriefs her girlfriend: "Say, you know, Marie, there are other things in the world besides money." Marie responds suggestively, "Are you going straight on me?" Wanda admits she is ("And I love it!"), but they crawl in bed together again as the scene does a quick fadeout. *Variety*'s review wryly commented, "Kay Francis shows off her figure in undies while explaining [to Tashman] she's through with the gold-digger racket and intends going straight because she's found love with a rich rube. The undie pose and that bit about going straight all in one has its own satirical kick."

But the reviewer's cynicism about Wanda's feelings was not shared by the director, whose lightly humorous edge about a tough dame "going straight" was misinterpreted. Cukor's view of the difficulties of her situation is realistically complex rather than simplistic. He is beginning to use the camera suggestively in this film: he executes a long, gracefully curving tracking shot with Wanda and Jim as they stroll through a zoo, and we watch with a bear and monkeys through the bars of the cages when they kiss, as if to suggest visually that her blithe happiness when he proposes after the end of the shot is another form of entrapment. Before they can go to Michigan, the film puts Wanda and Jim through some (unfortunately tedious) complications involving her previous marriage. But when that business is dispensed with, she's ready to go off with her new husband-to-be while the resilient Marie tells their pimp, "My telephone number is still the same, but from now on I work alone."

4

LOWELL SHERMAN IN
WHAT PRICE HOLLYWOOD?

What Price Hollywood? (1932), the story of an alcoholic director who makes a star of a Brown Derby waitress, is the "rough draft" of Cukor's 1954 masterpiece *A Star Is Born* and the intervening version of *A Star Is Born* directed by William Wellman in 1937 (David O. Selznick was executive producer of *What Price Hollywood?* and produced the Wellman film). The basic plot has the Pygmalion figure committing suicide when his drinking and professional eclipse threaten the career of his protégée. The Wellman version turned the director into an actor; the Cukor remake turned the waitress into a nightclub singer. Probably one reason Cukor wanted to return to the story was the opportunity it gave him to make up for a major flaw in the construction of *What Price Hollywood?*

The dialogue is consistently sharp and intelligent; the source is a story by the journalist-author-screenwriter Adela Rogers St. Johns, and among the people who worked on the script were John Barrymore's biographer Gene Fowler and the director Rowland Brown (who at one point had been expecting to direct the film). But the relationship between Maximillian Carey (Lowell Sherman) and Mary Evans (Constance Bennett) is poorly developed after a promising beginning. Carey is largely absent from the middle section, which chronicles Mary's rise to stardom as "America's Pal" and her unhappy marriage to the wealthy playboy Lonny Borden (Neil Hamilton). Carey's descent into becoming an unemployed lush happens mostly off-screen, and the film's neglect of this more compelling drama is not only a distraction but also a belittling of Mary's character. Although she makes a perfunctory attempt to save her mentor's career and bails him out of jail, the film's concentration in this crucial period on her career and the marriage it imperils makes her seem callously self-centered. That impression of shallowness in Mary's character is highlighted by her haughty behavior upon achieving stardom (the film skips over the transition with a quick symbolic montage), and the scenes after Carey's death also seem superfluous.

By contrast, some of the greatest scenes in Cukor's *A Star Is Born* (written by Moss Hart) occur in the period of James Mason's decline and Judy Garland's desperate attempt to nurse him back to health. Their relationship is much more complex and profoundly emotional than that of Carey and Mary Evans; not only do they become man and wife, but the Garland character, after trying to rescue her husband's career, gains in stature by finally deciding to sacrifice her career to care for him. Ironically, though, that noble but misguided decision prompts Mason's suicide. The scene of Mason sobbing quietly in the darkness of the beach house as he overhears Garland telling Charles Bickford, the studio chief, that she is going to quit the screen is the kind of dramatic interchange that is missing from *What Price Hollywood?*

Bennett, who plays the starring role of Mary, was a box office favorite at the time, but she is little more than adequate with her surface charm; her appeal, circumscribed by period mannerisms, has faded over the years. Bennett also starred for Cukor later that year in *Rockabye*, a slapdash, choppy programmer about a lowborn Broadway star who adopts a child (who might be her own illegitimate child); Cukor reshot an earlier version directed by George Fitzmaurice that RKO considered unreleasable. Aside from an intriguingly bizarre S&M kind of protoscrewball comedy "love scene" with Bennett and Joel McCrea pummeling each other in a kitchen after he chases her with a knife while wearing an apron, the highlight in Cukor's version is a brassy song by Bennett in a speakeasy. She has a similarly stylish musical number in *What Price Hollywood?*, singing "Parlez-moi d'Amour" as Cukor, in dazzling semidocumentary style, shows the complicated mechanics behind the scene. Bennett went on to play the lead role in Cukor's ponderous 1933 adaptation of a Somerset Maugham comedy of manners, *Our Betters*, as Lady Pearl Grayston, an American socialite betrayed by the aristocratic British husband who married her for her money. She also has a supporting role in Cukor's

4.1. Lowell Sherman, a gifted Hollywood director as well as actor, brought verisimilitude to the alcoholic director Max Carey in *What Price Hollywood?* (1932). Constance Bennett plays the waitress given this screen test by Carey before her rise to stardom. *What Price Hollywood?* was the unofficial start of the *Star Is Born* cycle; Cukor would go on to direct the 1954 version as well.

Source: From RKO Radio Pictures photographs of the Margaret Herrick Library, Academy of Motion Picture Arts and Sciences.

1941 Garbo film *Two-Faced Woman* and a cameo in 1954's *It Should Happen to You*.

The most memorable aspect of *What Price Hollywood?* is Sherman's harrowing, utterly convincing performance as the self-destructive director Max Carey. An almost totally forgotten figure today, Sherman was much in demand for sophisticated lecher roles in the twenties and early thirties (he's the city slicker who seduces Lillian Gish in Griffith's silent *Way Down East*). He was a brother-in-law of John Barrymore when he appeared in *What Price Hollywood?*; the stage-trained Sherman had a somewhat similar style in debonair comedy, blending suavity and cynicism. The character of Max Carey clearly is influenced by Barrymore's alcoholic debauchery and jaded approach to his career, but Sherman, with his sharkish demeanor, lacked Barrymore's classic good looks. Cukor felt that despite his talent, Sherman had "a slightly odious quality" that kept him from stardom. Yet that served them well when Carey goes on the skids. Sherman had become somewhat bored with performing and had begun a directing career in 1928, completing thirteen features, sometimes with himself in the cast. He seems to have been briefly revitalized as an actor by Cukor and was beginning to make a name for himself as a director when he died of double pneumonia at age forty-six in December 1934 while directing Miriam Hopkins in *Becky Sharp*, an adaptation of Thackeray's *Vanity Fair*, the first three-color Technicolor feature (the film was finished by Rouben Mamoulian, who scrapped Sherman's footage).

Sherman's early work as a director is visually clumsy and dramatically stilted, though one can detect a directorial touch beginning to surface in *High Stakes*, a high-comedy 1931 piece in which he plays an aging alcoholic playboy. Sherman's forte as a director was a veneer of sardonic humor over risqué material that otherwise could descend into sleaziness. His style grew smoother and more entertaining by the time he made a light comedy about a trio of gold diggers, *The Greeks Had a Word for Them*, from a play by Zoë Akins (released in early 1932, before *What Price Hollywood?* began shooting). But Sherman did not begin to show signs of becoming a major director until he made two noteworthy films released in 1933: Could it have been the experience of working with Cukor that explains his surprising growth in the immediate aftermath? Sherman ranks in the "Expressive Esoterica" section of Andrew Sarris's *The American Cinema* on the strength of Katharine Hepburn's Oscar-winning performance as a theatrical ingénue in *Morning Glory* and Mae West's raffish turn as an 1890s Bowery saloon singer in *She Done Him Wrong*, films backed up with colorful arrays of male supporting characters: "Both as an actor and as a director, Sherman was gifted with the ability to express the poignancy of male lechery when confronted with female longing. His civilized sensibility was ahead of its time, and the sophistication of his sexual humor singularly lacking in malice."

One of the dramatic coups in *What Price Hollywood?*, the contrast between Carey's clumsiness in society and his crisp assurance on the set, is clearly attributable to the shrewd casting of an actual director in the role (the film's working title was *The Truth About Hollywood*). Cukor felt the casting strategy made the character's suicide more moving. He gave Selznick credit for the tone of the film: "Largely through David's influence, we didn't kid the basic idea of Hollywood. Most of the other Hollywood pictures make it a kind of crazy, kooky place, but to David it was absolutely real, he believed in it. I think that's why *What Price Hollywood?* was one of the few successful pictures about the place, in the face of a tradition that they never succeed." Parts of the film's "absolutely real" nature are its depiction of the press as crass, heartless vultures and its pre–*Day of the Locust* sequence of a mob of fans besieging Mary outside the church after her wedding, a scene replicated after Mason's funeral in Cukor's *A Star Is Born*.

Movies about the making of movies usually seem curiously unreal and evasive when it comes down to showing what actually transpires on the set. Perhaps the problem with such scenes is that the director doesn't feel the audience is sufficiently interested in the fine points of moviemaking technique to sit still for realistic documentation. In *What Price Hollywood?*, though, Cukor and Sherman are able to use Carey's directing of Mary Evans for something more than "atmosphere." Like the scenes of Professor Higgins training Eliza's voice in *My Fair Lady*, the moviemaking scenes, with their careful delineation of the creative and technical process, are a meticulously observed process of character transformation. After watching Carey mold Mary from a clumsy neophyte into a polished performer, we feel the tragedy of his loss of control much more acutely than we would if the scenes on set had been conventional and perfunctory.

In addition, these scenes give us revealing insight into the way Cukor himself extracts a performance. The dialogue for Mary's test scene is awful to the point of parody. A stiff in a tuxedo is waiting at the foot of the inevitable staircase for her to walk down and say, "Hello, Buzzy—you haven't proposed to me tonight!" Bennett shrills the line, flounces her arms, fairly hops down the stairs. The stiff is no problem—Sherman just walks over, leans his elbow against the railing, says, "Uh, Mr. Reed—will you, uh, stand here lightly, like . . . y'know? . . . limp, y'know?" Bennett needs a lot of coaxing and cajoling, and Sherman guides her through a rehearsal the way Cukor likes to do it, with a steady stream of chattering commentary, alternating diplomatic suggestion and authoritative sarcasm. He walks her down the stairs (there is a photograph of Cukor doing the same thing with Audrey Hepburn for the ballroom scene of *My Fair Lady*): "Look. Now, when you come down the stairs, come down easily—gracefully—see? He takes a couple of steps, that's all; he doesn't try to act it out for her, just starts her off with a hint. "Lightly there. Now don't put your hand on the railing. You're sober."

Sensing that she is getting flustered, Sherman teasingly buoys her confidence, flatters her in earshot of the "audience" of crew and extras: "Now look here, you remember, you're—you're a pretty girl and this poor sap is going to propose to you. So give it some zip, some *ani*mation. Now come on." He snaps his fingers, beginning to orchestrate the rhythm of the scene: "All right, try it once again. Now come on. [*Snap*] No no, not on your *heels*, and don't clench your hands that way—this is a love scene, not a fight. [*Snap*]" It would be a point for auteurism if one could report that Bennett is instantly transformed into a swan. However, she stinks, and Sherman curtly dismisses her.

That night, she practices on the staircase at home (Cukor believes in work, distrusts "improvisation" that abandons the text). The next day, she is seen on a projection room screen, in close-up, a completely soignée professional. A beautiful cinematic device here: the first thing we see on the screen is the staircase shot, which is smoothly done but not remarkable, and then there is an unexpected cut into the close-up, which we hadn't seen them working on but instantly reveals a surprising depth and subtlety of expression. The studio boss, Julius Saxe (the Russian-born Gregory Ratoff, whom Ben Hecht aptly characterized as "hysterical" and later became a Hollywood director himself), immediately pronounces her a star. This scene verges on being a preposterous cliché about how someone is "discovered" in Hollywood. But when Saxe responds with such excitement to Mary's scene, it plays convincingly because Cukor has so carefully made us see the preparation and false starts that preceded this polished result. Anyone can see Mary's star quality from this footage; it's not something that can be conveyed in words, so Cukor doesn't try to do it—in words.

Playing a drunk was part of Sherman's stock in trade, but it is remarkable how much more convincing his drunkenness is in *What Price Hollywood?* than in, say, *High Stakes*. In the films he directed, Sherman often taxes the viewer's patience with his theatrical mannerisms. In *High Stakes*, the incessant repetition of the bobbing head, the slowly wagging index finger, the rolling eyes, the pursing lips, etc., etc. makes one overly conscious of an actor exercising his repertoire. While toning down Sherman's mannerisms, Cukor makes creative use of his tendency toward hamminess by making that reflect on the character.

The way, for instance, that Cukor varies the meaning of Sherman's characteristic cigarette mannerism—twisting his wrist around and around as he talks, then performing an elaborate rolling wrist flip to position the cigarette in his mouth. The gesture quickly becomes tedious in *High Stakes* because it is nothing more than a device to demonstrate a drunk's ridiculous overelaboration of movement. But in the scene of Ratoff warning Carey that drink is endangering his career, Cukor plays on the gesture to indicate a whole complex of emotional attitudes. As Carey listens to the harangue, he holds his left (noncigarette) hand to his cheek, trying to seem blasé, casts a private glance off-screen without changing his pose, and then, just before the fade-out, lifts the cigarette to chest height, flicking the wrist up and in the same smooth motion flicking the ash down to the floor as the screen begins to darken around him. There's something very devil-may-care about the

4.2. The haggard Max Carey, who describes himself as "all *burned out*" shortly before his suicide in *What Price Hollywood?* Bennett's Mary Evans vainly tries to help him by getting him out of jail.

Source: From RKO Radio Pictures photographs of the Margaret Herrick Library, Academy of Motion Picture Arts and Sciences.

gesture, its tone of contemptuous amusement, its combination of physical grace and emotional curtness, that seems to sum up the character in a flash.

Carey is the first of many powerfully rendered alcoholic characters in Cukor's body of work, his fragility and eventual collapse a thoroughly observed example of Cukor's keen attention to the process of self-destruction. Gary Carey observes in his 1971 book, *Cukor & Co.: The Films of George Cukor and His Collaborators*, "In the drunk scenes, Sherman retains an air of refinement and sensitivity. He plays totally without self-pity and without asking for sympathy." To bring out the squalor and humiliation of an emotional state like alcoholism, the actor and director must take pains to maintain control and distance. If the actor overplays either the pain or the giddiness of alcoholism, he'll quickly become a monotonous drag. And on the other hand, if he's too cautious, too genteel, the torment won't be convincing. Carey's rationale for his drinking is similar to the first explanation Ned gives Linda in *Holiday*, that it "brings you to life. . . . You feel, I don't know, important." Soon after Mary meets Carey and watches him hold his forehead in pain after swilling a drink upon waking, she asks bluntly, "Why do you drink all the time? Can't you cut the heavy swilling?" He replies, "Want to be *bored* all that time?" The element of contrast is all-important: Sherman's infectious, reckless gaiety in the early sections intensifies the effect of his increasingly grave demeanor in the later sections. To see this dapper high-comedy actor turning into a bearded stumblebum is far more shocking than it would be to see a more sobersided actor in the part.

What Price Hollywood? marks a major advance for Cukor in the sophistication of his mise-en-scène. Going beyond the breakthrough of his supple camera style in *Girls About Town*, this heartrending picture about the destructive aspects of his own industry stimulated Cukor's more adventurous use of cinematic tools to create meaning. Now he was surrounding his actors with a "climate" of expressive settings, sound, and camerawork that enhances their characterizations and places them eloquently within a social context, while blending comedy and drama in ways that seem more like real life than simply a theatrical imitation of life. The first seriously disturbing indication of Carey's desperation emerges in a sequence that begins as whimsical—although edgy—comedy. He is stumbling into the garden of Mary's mansion, striking a match on a dimly lit object at the corner of the screen. The camera draws back abruptly as he realizes that the object is the rump of a statue of Venus. The lighting (by Charles Rosher, one of the master cinematographers of F. W. Murnau's *Sunrise* and the longtime house cinematographer to "America's Sweetheart," Mary Pickford) is delicate, whimsical, slightly fantastic: the smoke from the cigarette is backlit to make it into a brilliant cloud, and the statue's face shines brightly out of the gloom.

After Carey tosses pebbles at the bedroom window and lights a newspaper to "burn your house down," Mary and her irritated husband, Lonny, send him to bed. Suddenly in the middle of the night, Carey barges into the couple's bedroom, climbs onto Mary's bed, sits at the side, and tries to tell them something in a blurred, hoarse voice. The quasi-comical aspects of Lonny's outraged bolting out of bed and Carey's brazen disdain for the privacy of the marital chamber intensify the disruptive impact of Carey's boorishness on Mary's life and his own desperation, and Cukor has his face lit from below to make him look drawn and manic. Underneath the couple's bickering, Carey is saying: "Mary, do you mind, both of you, if I become serious for a moment? I—I have something of great importance to tell both of you. . . . Mary, I want to give you some good advice. . . ." We never learn what the advice would have been, because Lonny stomps out of the room (en route to divorce, actually) as Carey mutters: "Nothing's funny to that *bird*" and Mary sits on the edge of the bed, her back to Carey and the camera, sobbing helplessly. The sequence ends with a fadeout on her back, visually consigning Carey to off-screen oblivion.

The suicide sequence is a masterpiece of acting and direction. Carey lies in Mary's bed, completely sober after being sprung from the county jail. His calm, deliberate voice and movements, the illusory warmth and cleanliness of the bed, and Mary's eager solicitude combine to give an impression of tranquility, resignation, and regret: "I'm not the Max Carey that you once knew. I'm all *burned out*, Mary. Don't you see I'm dead inside? I should feel ashamed—degraded—but I just can't feel anything." Rather than cutting to Mary's reaction as Carey speaks, Cukor holds the shot of Carey and lets the audience provide the reactions. Carey's expressions qualify the meaning of his words: as he speaks the word "degraded," his eyes roll slightly inward, reminiscent of the way they'd roll, painfully, when he took a stiff jolt of booze; and when he says, "I just can't feel anything," he leans his head back on the pillow in exhaustion, tired of feeling too much.

Mary tries to cheer him up with brave talk about returning to work. Shaking his head slowly, he replies, "I've stopped kidding myself, Mary. I'm washed up in pictures. Done for." His voice is slow and matter-of-fact. He purses his lips slightly, narrows his eyes in a half-wink, and wags his index finger back and forth, scoldingly. "I haven't got it anymore." He taps the finger to his chest. "It's all gone in *here*. I know." After a few more inconsequential stabs at cheeriness, Mary snaps out the light, wishes him goodnight, and walks toward the door. In the semidarkness, lying perfectly still, he raises his hand and lets the sash of her dress trail through his fingers. It is the slipping away of everything he cares about. The hand lingers a moment in the air and drops to the bed. He calls her name softly, and she stops at the open door. Like Mason in *A Star Is Born* asking Garland to sing as he walks out of the beach house toward the sea, Carey wants to fix her image in his mind for the last time: "I just wanted to hear you speak again, that's all."

She shuts the door, and he sits for a few moments in the gloom, barely visible as he covers his face with his hand, blinks his eyes, looks off left, closes his eyes, looks right, and climbs out of bed. Cukor cuts to a shot inside the adjacent room, heavily shadowed, the perspective vaguely distorted by the lighting. The mise-en-scène makes us share Carey's feeling of dizziness and disorientation. He takes a drink, his eyes open in a terrible stare, and he walks away, tilting his head to one side as if to reestablish his sense of direction.

Looking for a match to light his cigarette, he opens a drawer and, in a close-up taken from his point of view, the camera discovers a revolver. Cukor cuts back to a full shot of Carey slowly looking up from the gun, his face lit by moonlight from the window, the rest of the room dark; the effect is more disturbing than if Cukor had done the conventional thing and cut to a huge close-up of Carey reacting to the gun. This way we first share his feelings by seeing the gun in close-up and then are distanced from his feelings by the cut to full shot; the space around him in the frame keeps him situated firmly in reality, implying that the suicide is a conscious, rational decision rather than the impulsive emotional reaction it would seem if the screen contained nothing but his face.

Closing the drawer, Carey shuffles into yet another room, this one even more heavily shadowed, and stops before a mirror to light the cigarette. At first, as he looks into the mirror, he doesn't notice a framed photograph of himself, suave and assured, on the table. The delay is suspenseful; it allows us time to contemplate the photo and anticipate his reaction. His eyes wander down from the mirror to the photograph, and we see it in close-up. He looks back up at the mirror, the camera shooting over his shoulder toward his anguished reflection, the photograph out of the shot. The cigarette falls from his mouth, and he pushes the photograph away, Cukor cutting back to the wider shot. Again and again, this insistence on critically distancing us from an emotion, rather than just building an effect of hysteria: Carey has never been so sober in his life. No longer a stumbling buffoon, he is now dignified and deliberate, moving toward death almost ceremoniously, almost as if he were directing someone else in the scene, analyzing the actions with a calm, critical eye.

With the last trace of his old self (the photograph) gone, Carey is left with nothing but his twisted alcoholic image, and Cukor cuts, for the first time, to a shot framed completely within the mirror, the face fuzzy and distorted as Carey regards it in horror. What follows is a bravura special-effects sequence by the montage expert Slavko Vorkapich (with Lloyd Knechtel), conveying with images and sound Carey's subjective feeling of frenetic inner torment. Low-angled images of his earlier days as a poised director and debonair social drinker dissolve over his face as the soundtrack resonates with a deafening throbbing noise. Jail bars swim over his face, his eyebrows arching grotesquely. He has no willpower now—there is a cut to a close-up of Carey's feet as they move mechanically into the other room. As if disembodied, his hand, in close-up, raises the gun to his chest and pulls the trigger. Several more images of the past flash by in a subliminal montage before Carey, seen from a low angle, sinks toward the camera in slow motion. When Mary finds his body, she echoes her reaction in the first scene she acted in for Carey, which ended with her discovering a shocking sight below her eyes.

The bravura mise-en-scène of *What Price Hollywood?* not only shows Cukor making a quantum leap in his control of cinematic style but also demonstrates that he had found many new forms of expression to enable an actor to reach deeply into himself onscreen. By doing so, Cukor and Sherman bear out the truth of Jean-Luc Godard's observation that every fictional film is a documentary about its actors.

5

KATHARINE HEPBURN AND JOHN BARRYMORE IN *A BILL OF DIVORCEMENT*

Cukor's camera is now fully, uninhibitedly lyrical as it swoops along to follow the first screen appearance of Katharine Hepburn. The young actress is caught in midflight as she dashes across a balcony and down a staircase and virtually leaps into the arms of her callow boyfriend, gliding into a waltz without any break in the action at a New Year's Eve party. Few screen debuts have been heralded with such rapturous ecstasy. In this breathless panning shot from Cukor's 1932 film *A Bill of Divorcement*, we are made to feel viscerally that something new and rare is being seen, screen history is being made, and, not incidentally, the director's most lasting and fullest relationship with an actress (or any actor, for that matter) is being inaugurated. Fittingly, that was the first shot made for the film.

Over the next four decades and beyond, Hepburn would go on to make a total of ten movies with Cukor, including two for television. He played a key role in shaping her screen persona and helping her guide her own career in most of its varied phases, from raw ingénue to iconic grande dame. Along the way, she enhanced his career with the richest, most collaborative of all his screen partnerships, enabling them to explore the intricate nuances and ambiguities of androgynous femininity. At least six of Cukor's finest films are among those that star Hepburn, and their subject matter and modes are indicative of their mutual dramatic and comedic range: *Little Women, Sylvia*

Scarlett, Holiday, The Philadelphia Story, Pat and Mike, and *Love Among the Ruins.*

When I visited Cukor's home with Todd McCarthy for an interview in 1981, he greeted us in robe and pajamas and told us to look around wherever we wanted while he was getting dressed. Before we went upstairs to his office hideaway, we inspected the impressive array of signed photographs of actors and actresses in a nook on the living-room wall next to the staircase. The photo of Hepburn was signed,

To George—Everything—Kate.

Hepburn's extraordinary entrance in *A Bill of Divorcement*—in the party scene added to the source material—conveyed the director's thrilling sense

5.1.   Katharine Hepburn brought her youthful freshness, candor, and earnest emotion to her film-debut role as Sydney Fairfield in Cukor's 1932 film of Clemence Dane's problem play *A Bill of Divorcement*. Sydney finds a rapport with her mentally ill father, Hilary (John Barrymore), after he unexpectedly returns home from an asylum.

Source: Frame enlargement; RKO.

of discovery. But Cukor and David O. Selznick, who was then RKO's head of production, both felt that the moment when Hepburn's star is born (to borrow a phrase from movies they would make about Hollywood, including Cukor's own masterpiece) is not her entrance but a quieter one after the party. Hepburn enters casually from left of frame and walks toward the fireplace. She arranges a couple of large cushions on the hearth and lies back on them, stretching her lithe, boyish figure. She looks unguarded, at ease, taking a moment to unwind and simply be Katharine Hepburn, almost as if the camera has caught her unawares between takes and given us a good look at her in all her unique dimensions.

This is what François Truffaut called a directorial "privileged moment": a piece of silent business, a short scene that didn't need to be in the film for strictly narrative reasons but captures its underlying poetics while giving us a window into the director's feelings about the story and its characters. Frank Capra put it another way: "Sometimes your story has got to stop and you let the audience just look at your people. You want the audience to like them. The characters have no great worries for the moment. . . . The less guarded they are, the more silly it is, the better. These scenes are quite important to a film. When the audience rests and they look at the people, they begin to smile. They begin to love the characters, and then they'll be worried about what happens to them."

Cukor shrewdly analyzed the audience's process of getting used to Hepburn in her film debut:

At first, the public was taken aback. As the character, she was very sure of herself, and the audience was not quite certain how to take her. But then there was a moment when she flashed this warm, radiant smile for her mother, played adorably by Billie Burke, and the audience could see how very attractive she really was. Then, when she picked up some cushions and lay on the hearth rug, they noticed that she moved beautifully. They realized that something fresh and exciting was happening on the screen. . . . Her odd awkwardness, her odd shifts of emphasis, these were proof of her being alive on the screen.

This brief scene of Hepburn's Sydney Fairfield unwinding and seeming not to have a care in the world is heralded by dissolving a shot of ringing church bells over and out of her reclining on the hearth, as if celebrating her freshly minted stardom. But the scene also has a dramatic purpose, for it serves as punctuation, a moment of illusory calm, before a world of pain comes crashing down on her. *A Bill of Divorcement* is based on a ponderous "problem play" by the British novelist-playwright Clemence Dane, dealing with anxieties about the hereditary nature of mental illness and how underlying genetic problems can be triggered by social circumstances.

In this case, Sydney's father, Hilary (John Barrymore), has been in an asylum for fifteen years since going mad from suffering shell shock in World War I. Initially the issue is how his family should deal with his return as if from the dead; his wife, Meg (Burke), is a one-note, callous villain who all along has simply wanted to forget about him. But his return has a profound effect on Sydney, who realizes forlornly, "So—in our family there's insanity," and is advised by the family doctor not to marry and have children. She turns aside her fiancé (the option of marrying but remaining childless is not considered) and, with histrionic nobility, pledges to devote herself to caring for her father. While psychological studies today support the premise that mental illness can be genetic in origin, triggered by circumstances, or a combination of both, possibilities for treatment have greatly advanced in the years since Dane wrote her play in 1921, making it seem rather archaic now as well as overwrought.

She wrote the play to lobby for passage of a law allowing a married couple to divorce if a partner became insane. The play is set in the future (1933), and Dane notes at the beginning, "The audience is asked to imagine that the recommendations of the *Majority Report of the Royal Commission on Divorce v. Matrimonial Causes* have become the law of the land." But it took until 1937 for the United Kingdom to extend the grounds for divorce beyond adultery and allow it in the case of a partner's incurable insanity. The screenplay by Howard Estabrook and Henry Wagstaff Gribble minimizes the play's debate over the issue, including the freethinking Sydney's forthright attacks on religious scruples over divorce. Instead, the objections to Meg's divorce and remarriage are put in the querulous mouth of Hilary's sister, Hester (Elizabeth Patterson, a favorite Cukor character actress), and are framed predominantly in personal familial terms.

Dane's play proved popular in London in 1921 and when Katharine Cornell starred in that year's Broadway production. A British silent film version

5.2. Cukor shooting *A Bill of Divorcement* at RKO in Hollywood with Billie Burke and John Bar-rymore; Burke plays Hepburn's mother, Margaret. The unexpected return of her former husband disrupts Margaret's plan to remarry.

Source: RKO/Photofest.

appeared in 1922; Cukor's film, his second collaboration with Selznick after *What Price Hollywood?*, was remade by RKO in 1940 with John Farrow direct-ing Adolphe Menjou and the newcomer Maureen O'Hara. The 1932 film is set in contemporary England, mostly on a single large set of the ground floor of the comfortable but not particularly elegant country home of the well-to-do Fairfield family around the New Year's holidays. This stagebound feeling rep-resents something of a regression for Cukor from his more supple *Girls About Town* and *What Price Hollywood?* and mostly lacks the lively sense of nearly constant, well-motivated movement he would introduce into his later play adaptations. Some exceptions to that stodginess come when his direction rises to quiet heights of observation in bravura moments such as Hepburn's introduction and the return home of her father after his escape from the asylum. That development is timed with crashing dramatic convenience to disrupt his wife's remarrriage plans for the following day, although he does not know that at first.

Cukor, the screenwriters, and the actors approach the dubious material uncritically, with what seems utter sincerity. In 1932 Hollywood, the story was considered somewhat edgy, partly because divorce usually was something of a taboo in American films. Although the somber tone makes the film often heavy going today and lacks the leavening comic business Cukor usually would introduce into his direction, the seriousness with which the story is played is mostly salutary for the affecting (but not affected) performances of Hepburn and Barrymore. In the touching scenes they play together, sharing ironically calm and quiet confidences about how their personalities seem to mesh (ominously), the corniness of the plot is less of a hindrance than in Hepburn's more agitated interactions with her mother and her fiancé (David Manners). Then the actors become overly earnest, seeming to feel a need to "sell" scenes they seem to vaguely realize are unconvincing.

Barrymore and Hepburn make a convincing father and daughter (and it's intriguing that both of their characters have androgynous names) because they are histrionic and stylized in their performing styles. But Cukor toned down Hepburn for the screen, keeping her from being what he called "too mannered, highfalutin', actressy" and minimizing her penchant for crying. The director knew the pitfalls of Barrymore's extravagant emoting from spoofing him through Fredric March in *The Royal Family of Broadway*, but Cukor admitted, "When I worked with the Barrymores, the residue remained of having first seen them from the second balcony." Nevertheless, Cukor restrains Barrymore's more flamboyant tendencies other than allowing him brief, intermittent frightening outbursts of rage, since he's mostly distracted in his affect and is making an effort to be gallant. Cukor found Barrymore highly cooperative in their initial collaboration: "When he did the [homecoming] scene the first time, it had the wrong kind of tension. It was too desperate. I said, 'Jack, the man is happy to be home, he doesn't know they don't want him.' He understood this at once and played it the way you see, and that's what made it poignant."

When Barrymore walks briskly into the house as if nothing has happened over the last fifteen years, Cukor gives us a silent sequence of the man exploring the old but rearranged surroundings in a familiar but slightly clumsy way as Sydney, alerted to his presence, watches from the staircase. Sydney has already learned, from a telephone call that comes while she's lying on the hearth, that he's fled the asylum; in the screenplay's overly convenient telescoping of events, he arrives just moments later. Nevertheless, the sequence is touching. Lambert told Cukor, to his surprise, that this scene "seems to me to contain the essence of your style. . . . It's a very kinetic little scene, with a beautiful tension."

Cukor intercuts close-ups of Sydney studying her father, whom she's never known, with piercing looks and what the play calls "a sort of breathless sympathy." The intercutting between them is moving and suspenseful, drawing emotional connections as if through magnetic attraction. Sydney's guileless face, shaped like a porcelain statue, shows no fright but rather curiosity and a growing fascination, mixed with an undertone of anxiety. Hilary bumps into a chair but doesn't seem to notice, while she creeps downstairs and spies on him while hiding behind tall plants. Cukor rhymes panning shots of father and daughter as they move around the sitting room without seeing each other until she reveals herself, asking him, "What are you looking for?" His eyes widen. He calls her "Meg . . . my own darling." Sydney corrects him in a kindly way, her eyes glistening, telling him with simple eloquence, "I think I'm your daughter." His eyes have trouble meeting hers as they wander uncertainly around the room, but hers blaze directly into his with a forthright, welcoming, understanding intensity.

There is some expressively awkward business with his hat coming between them as he leans forward for an embrace; she seems grateful for the obstruction and invites him to sit. He removes his coat, and, watching from behind, she sees a torn seam in his seedy jacket and says reflectively about the situation, "Makes me want to cry." She almost does, but Cukor keeps her from doing so, allowing her to smile as well as looking stricken. They share some relieving laughter about family foibles, and Sydney, seated on the back of a couch, swings down her legs to sit close to him but apprehensively warns that there have been some "changes" he doesn't know about. When he gets up and prowls around, he flashes with anger, and she barks back at him, but he seems oddly reassured, telling her, "You got wild all in a moment—that's my way too. But it means nothing. But Meg, Meg doesn't see that it means nothing." It's no wonder that his talk grows increasingly delusional after the callous Meg enters while Sydney anxiously tries to settle them down.

Hepburn recalled that she felt "shocked" that Barrymore was "giving a very hammy performance" when he first did the scene of his entrance and inspection of the house, but "when the scene was finished, Barrymore came over and looked hard at me; then he went to George and said that he would like to do it again. I think he could tell that this was to me my great moment and he didn't want to let me down. We started again. He was shattering. So sad. So moving. Full of desperation. And always so simple."

The desperation she saw in his performance was the subtext of his surface gaiety that Cukor asked him to play, the man's misguided joy at being home again. That kind of complex nuance would become the hallmark of Cukor's style in handling actors, and here he had Hepburn's tacit help in bringing it out of Barrymore. It was an example of how the "climate" (Cukor's favorite word) on the set and the resulting chemistry between his actors could bring out the deepest meanings of a scene.

Considering Hilary's hopeless predicament and childlike demeanor, Sydney's compassion toward her father seems merited, such as when she says gently, "Poor father, you died." But their relationship is disturbing in ways that probably were not intended or at least are not developed. Incestuous overtones blur some of the problems in the story, which already invites misinterpretation, since Hilary's shell shock is not the entire cause of his illness. His initial confusion of Sydney with Meg is dramatically understandable, since he's confused about time, but the film pours it on by having him exclaiming with a laugh, "Daughter? Daughter! That's good! My wife's not my wife, she's my daughter!" Sydney's vow to forsake her fiancé and spend her life taking care of her father, which becomes the dramatic focus of the rest of the film, also has a vaguely incestuous vibe. And as Lambert points out, the film overdoes the schmaltz by having Hilary happily play his "trashy" unfinished sonata, about which Sydney exudes, "Isn't that lovely, father! Isn't it gay!" That scene is not in the play, which concentrates much more on Hilary's relationship with Meg. Although the veteran actress Billie Burke is billed above Hepburn, her part is secondary in the film. The unintentionally queasy feeling of the ending results partly from the film's dropping Meg's decision in the play to stay with Hilary before Sydney selflessly offers to take care of him for the rest of his life.

David Manners, who plays her rejected fiancé, was a handsome and intelligent young gay actor who became a lifelong friend of Cukor's. Manners had a good run of parts in the early sound period before leaving Hollywood to return to the stage and write novels. He gives a remarkably moving and non-maudlin portrayal of a blind war veteran in Capra's *The Miracle Woman* (1931) and has supporting roles in James Whale's *Journey's End*, Tod Browning's *Dracula*, and Edgar G. Ulmer's *The Black Cat*. But in *A Bill of Divorcement*, Manners and Hepburn have little to do except clinch and debate their problem as she gets maudlin over the impossibility of marriage. Many of Hepburn's other films portray her rejection of marriage as a positive character trait, and if she's cast partly for that independent quality here, it's a further instance of dramatic muddle under the circumstances. Burke is extremely arch as the faithless wife who wants nothing more than to get rid of Hilary so she can remarry; she comes off as a horrid person, but Cukor's inability to draw anything but a wooden performance from her here was rectified in the following year's *Dinner at Eight*, which uses her as the comic foil, a shallow and snobbish woman whose party goes disastrously and hilariously awry.

Cukor was taking a chance in giving what became the lead female role in *A Bill of Divorcement* to such a quirky newcomer as Hepburn, whose boyish figure, gaunt angularity of facial features, coltish mixture of awkwardness and grace in movement, and ambiguous sexual presence were so unlike the attributes of most other female stars of that period. Cukor had to overcome Selznick's objections to cast her, but the director's savvy and enthusiasm triumphantly prevailed. He had seen her in a screen test of a scene from Philip Barry's *Holiday*, a play in which Hepburn had understudied Hope Williams (an actress with whom she was often compared) but was able to go onstage for her only once.

The scene Hepburn chose for the test is the one that's so memorable in the 1938 Cukor film version, when she talks with her brother, Ned, about drinking. The actress wrote in her autobiography, "I knew this scene backwards, as I had understudied it for six months" (the actor-writer Alan Campbell took the role of Ned in the test, and another friend of hers, the talent scout Lillie Messenger, directed it). Cukor found Hepburn's delivery of Barry's stylized dialogue in that early test too high-pitched, but this master of meaningful movement characteristically was struck by a physical gesture: as he remembered it, Hepburn, seen from the back, gracefully swooped down to pick up a highball glass, a bit of behavior he felt made "a sad lyric moment." But in Hepburn's memory of the test, which no longer exists, "She is listening—a glass in her hand. Very slowly she lowers the glass and sets it on the floor" before asking, "What's it like—to get drunk, Ned?"

Cukor's memory generally was more to be trusted than Hepburn's, and he may have consciously been replicating that gesture in his 1936 film *Camille*. Greta Garbo, as the courtesan Marguerite Gautier, gracefully picks up her fan at the opera gala after she drops it and her jealous wealthy patron (Henry Daniell) contemptuously refuses to pick it up. Along with his nurturing of Lew Ayres in *All Quiet on the Western Front*, Cukor's role in helping guide Hepburn into becoming a film star was a further sign of what was becoming celebrated as his keen eye for new talent. But his appreciation for the conventional good looks of Ayres and his intellect and sensitivity were one thing; recognizing that this thoroughly unconventional minor Broadway actress had the makings of stardom was another. As Cukor would recall, "She was quite unlike anybody I'd ever seen." Hepburn in retrospect described herself as "an amateur in the business" when she made her film debut; in a sense she always remained something of an amateur actress, i.e., one who seemed relatively untrained and instead followed her own offbeat instincts, and in that sense "amateur" can be seen as a compliment, since the word comes from the Latin root for "love."

From the first, Cukor was also taken with her uncanny sense of confidence, her devil-may-care, take-me-or-leave-me attitude. That attitude was ingrained from her privileged upbringing and individual defiance. When she argued with her domineering father, a physician of some renown in Hartford, Connecticut, about her ambition to become an actress, he slapped her in the face, but she left home and persisted. That insistence on her independence never left her and enabled her to thrive while navigating the travails of a long career in Hollywood, although she continued to allow her father to manage her financial affairs after she became a movie star.

When I asked Hepburn about her famous speech attacking the incipient Hollywood blacklist in May 1947, she said, "One reason I gave the speech was that I felt, They really can't hurt me. I sort of came over on the *Mayflower*. And I didn't have to depend on movies for my living. . . . I felt very sorry for people who were in a prominent position and depended on the motion picture business, who were desperate for a livelihood and for their family's livelihood." *I didn't have to depend on movies for my living* was a rare status, an integral part of Hepburn's success in getting her way, the kind of fuck-you attitude Hollywood resents yet grudgingly respects. And one of the hallmarks of Cukor's talent was seeing value in what other people rejected as odd, offensive, or strangely endearing and in encouraging actors to embrace those traits onscreen and not sand down their differences to assimilate into the crowd, whether it was a question of physical appearance or unconventional attitudes.

The critical response to Hepburn's film debut was predominantly favorable. As her biographer William J. Mann observes, "All of the most salient traits that would come to define the legend of Katharine Hepburn" were described in Norbert Lusk's review of the film in the *Los Angeles Times*: "Far from being a stencil of anyone else," Hepburn had "a strange beauty that places her apart. . . . Character and intelligence are reflected in every word she utters and every gesture, yet she is human, appealing and girlishly sympathetic . . . forthright, courageous, dignified."

After making such a strong impression in *A Bill of Divorcement*, Hepburn failed to stir audiences with her even quirkier and more androgynous role as an Amelia Earhart–like British aviator, Lady Cynthia Darrington, in Dorothy Arzner's *Christopher Strong* (1933, with Zoë Akins adapting the novel by Gilbert Frankau). Cukor unfairly mocked that uneven yet intriguing film, ostensibly because Hepburn briefly wore a bizarre silvery moth costume, but the film later acquired a feminist following. Hepburn went on to win an Academy Award as best actress of 1933 with *Morning Glory*, her first of a record four Oscars (though none for Cukor films). Her gauche theatrical ingénue in *Morning Glory*, Eva Lovelace, is quite unlike her Sydney Fairfield, since she plays an American for the first time onscreen and is a less challenging figure for audiences to accept in that charming, funny, and endearing film. The shrewd handling of a nascent star by the directors Cukor and Lowell Sherman helped Hepburn catch on quickly with the public, albeit on a somewhat tentative, always somewhat shaky foundation that would be seriously strained by the end of the decade.

Hepburn's Cukor films would remain anchors of both of their careers throughout their various ups and downs. They remained loyal and close friends throughout. "It was as if George and I had been brought up together," she wrote in her autobiography, fittingly titled *Me*. "Total comfort. The same liberal point of view—the same sense of right and wrong."

6

JOHN BARRYMORE AND JEAN HARLOW IN *DINNER AT EIGHT*

One of Cukor's great strengths in his mature work—which was now upon him—was his adroit handling of ensemble pieces. Few other directors could have pulled off the challenging tasks of handling episodic material such as *Little Women*, *David Copperfield*, *The Women*, and *The Model and the Marriage Broker* or of making partial sense of such flawed late films as *Heller in Pink Tights*, *The Chapman Report*, and *Justine* while briskly maintaining a sure hand on the comings and goings of multiple characters and finding a solid through-line in those kaleidoscopic narratives. Key to Cukor's success in orchestrating ensembles was his characteristic skill in blending comedy and drama, his sure command of tone, a skill he made to seem effortless but was actually the result of years of disciplined devotion to his craft.

Dinner at Eight (1933), a highly polished and entertaining MGM "package" based on another play by George S. Kaufman and Edna Ferber (whose *The Royal Family* he had previously filmed), was not a credit Cukor valued highly in retrospect. Cukor felt the film about a group of self-centered, pampered people trying to remain oblivious to the Depression was amusing but on the superficial side. The play opened in October 1932, but the expert screenwriters Frances Marion and Herman J. Mankiewicz sharpened the underlying emphasis on contemporary issues for the film, which began shooting in March 1933. Cukor was given the assignment by David O. Selznick, after following the executive producer from RKO to MGM. *Dinner at Eight* was the studio's prestigious follow-up to its previous year's all-star blockbuster *Grand Hotel.*

But *Dinner at Eight* is the film that enabled Cukor to bring together all he had learned as a theater and film director in the art of, so to speak, herding cats. The play's skillful approach in alternating light comedy with somber drama, often getting unexpected humor out of disastrous situations, was a challenge for a director to finesse on film. What could have seemed a clumsy hodgepodge in lesser hands proved a fast-paced marvel in Cukor's, one that progressed through production remarkably smoothly, with no actorly blow-ups. No doubt Cukor's experience working with Ernst Lubitsch on the 1932 Paramount film *One Hour with You* taught Cukor some valuable lessons about pacing and economy. That film is a musical about adultery, and though it's inferior to Lubitsch's brilliant and more dramatic original version, the 1924 silent *The Marriage Circle*, the comedy in *One Hour with You*, as in most of Lubitsch's work, has serious undertones, dealing with how men should treat women and vice versa.

Lubitsch, who was the producer of *One Hour with You*, took over the direction soon after shooting started, because he felt that his and Cukor's styles were not especially compatible (as did Cukor, who had to sue to get an "Assisted by" credit under Lubitsch's directing credit; the settlement also enabled him to leave Paramount to join Selznick at RKO). But Cukor's opportunity of studying the man David Niven called "the masters' master," humiliating though the circumstances were, proved a priceless learning experience. It advanced the sophistication of Cukor's style and taught him how to use the camera with more precision and economy. As François Truffaut wrote in a 1968 essay on Lubitsch, "If you said to me, 'I have just seen a Lubitsch in which there was one needless shot,' I'd call you a liar. His cinema is the opposite of the vague, the imprecise, the unformulated, the incommunicable. There's not a single shot just for decoration; nothing is included just because it looks good. From beginning to end, we are involved only in what's essential."

Cukor's film directly after his unhappy teaming with Lubitsch, *What Price Hollywood?*, showed a marked improvement in visual storytelling, simultaneously rigorous and imaginative, but it was not until he directed *Dinner at Eight* that Cukor was able to make impeccably efficient use of all he had learned from Lubitsch in blending drama with what was then known as "high comedy." Despite the fact that the Kaufman-Ferber play has several intersecting storylines, numerous star parts, and marked shifts in tone, Cukor and his screenwriters made the story feel all of a piece without making the subplots seem like subplots. Marion and Mankiewicz make smooth shifts from comic detachment to dramatic engagement by eloquently intercutting the characters' frantic maneuvering for social position and sheer survival in the Depression era. Although Cukor somewhat reductively described Kaufman as "quite an astringent writer, [but] not very profound," he admitted that the playwright had "the saving grace of being funny," and the play's smorgasbord of characterizations and mini-dramas enabled Cukor to draw telling contrasts among their particular hypocrisies and often ghastly dilemmas.

While revolving around an upper-crust dinner party thrown by a frivolous society hostess, Millicent Jordan (Billie Burke, in a send-up of the snobbish style she plays so stiffly in *A Bill of Divorcement*), *Dinner at Eight* has a kind of desperate gaiety that constantly qualifies her and the other characters' postures of entitlement. The screenwriters heightened the allusions to the Depression to set the country's economic calamity even more satirically against the frivolity of Millicent's striving for social status. The anxiety provoked by the economic crisis is highlighted in the early reunion scene between the extravagant former stage star Carlotta Vance (Dressler) and Millicent's ailing husband, Oliver (Lionel Barrymore), a shipping magnate, who once had a sort-of romance; both put up a good show but are on the edge of financial collapse.

The crisis was impossible to ignore, and as a result *Dinner at Eight*, despite Cukor's concern about what he considered its superficiality, became one of the most topical films of his career, even though he usually avoided overtly political subject matter. The party is the play and film's satirical symbol of the fragility of the American privileged class: as Mao Zedong put it, "A revolution is not a dinner party." The film began shooting in the absolute depths of the Depression, in the month Franklin D. Roosevelt became president and declared a Bank Holiday. Shortly thereafter, the Hollywood studios and their "company union," the Academy of Motion Picture Arts and Sciences, levied drastic pay cuts on studio employees, causing an uproar during which every studio briefly shut down and the nascent labor movement in Hollywood began joining forces against them.

Cukor's anxious underrating of *Dinner at Eight* in later years may have been a result of his comparing it with more overtly socially conscious films of its period, such as *I Am a Fugitive from a Chain Gang* or *Wild Boys of the Road*. Cukor characteristically approaches social themes more obliquely, with dramatic and comedic irony, and the mixture of modes in *Dinner at Eight* shows his skill in doing so at its most effective. His concern about the ability of light comedy to reflect social values put him in the same camp as the comedy director played by Joel McCrea in Preston Sturges's 1941 satire of Hollywood, *Sullivan's Travels*, who goes on the road as a hobo in search of the Capraesque common man and winds up on a Southern chain gang. After Sullivan and his fellow prisoners escape into joyous laughter at a Mickey Mouse cartoon in a backwoods Black church, he tells the studio chief back in Hollywood, "There's a lot to be said for making people laugh. Did you know that that's all some people have? It isn't much, but it's better than nothing in this cockeyed caravan. Boy!"

Cukor not only had that ability, but he could blend laughter thoughtfully with drama, as he does in *Dinner at Eight*. Most of the characters are living on the edge of ruination, whether financially or socially or in terms of health, and the effects of the Depression provide a constant subtext, a shaky foundation for the goings-on, whether giddy or tragic and despite the film's focus on the privileged classes. The party itself, which Millicent treats as if it were the most important event in the country, becomes something of a comical disaster when Lord and Lady Ferncliffe, the British aristocratic couple in whose honor it is being thrown, casually cancel at the last minute and fly to Florida. Meanwhile, the aspic in the shape of the British Lion that Millicent has planned as the highlight of the dinner is dropped to the floor by quarreling servants.

Not only that, but the most celebrated guest, the down-at-heels movie star Larry Renault (John Barrymore), doesn't show up because he's just committed suicide. The audience feels a sense of schadenfreude as the snobbish Millicent gets her comeuppance and has to improvise a hasty gathering of mismatched guests drawn from various strata of society. When her dying husband tells her just before dinner, "We're broke," she blithely replies, "Oh. But *everybody's* broke, darling. Don't let that worry you. We'll economize." In the play, Millicent shows more social awareness, but the satire is actually more effective when she's clueless.

As the guests go into the dining room, the film ends with the classic exchange of Marie Dressler doing a double-take when Jean Harlow's nouveau riche floozie tells her she's been reading a book. "Yes, it's all about civilization or something," Harlow explains, "a *nutty* kind of a book. Do you know that the guy says that machinery is going to take the place of *every* profession?" Dressler casts her eyes up and down Harlow's spectacular figure in her slinky white silk dress, exclaiming, "Oh, my dear, that's something you need never worry about." This tag, requested by Selznick to give the material a more upbeat ending, was written by Donald Ogden Stewart, who had written *Tarnished Lady* for Cukor and would work with him frequently again. The commercial success of *Dinner at Eight* was a byproduct of its cheeky, seemingly offhand, but up-to-the-minute relevance "all about civilization or something" as well as its brilliance in providing MGM with a livelier follow-up to *Grand Hotel*. Cukor was always proud of the fact that despite the ensemble cast he had to handle like a lion tamer in *Dinner at Eight*, he brought it in remarkably quickly and efficiently, in only twenty-eight shooting days, although he afterward found that cause to regret when studios would ask why he couldn't do so again.

Among the aspects of *Dinner at Eight* that make it seem quintessential Cukor in retrospect are its precursors of other celebrated films by the director. The mixture of humor and poignancy in the reunion of Carlotta and Oliver, who loved her fruitlessly as a young man but lost her to wealthier suitors, uncannily looks forward to the bittersweet romance between the aging actress Jessica Medlicott (Katharine Hepburn) and the lovelorn barrister Sir Arthur Granville-Jones (Laurence Olivier) in Cukor's last great film, and first movie for television, *Love Among the Ruins* (1975). When Carlotta greets Oliver, she brushes his graying hair gently, just as Jessica does with Sir Arthur.

The rowdy relationship between the dizzy platinum blonde Kitty Packard (Harlow) and her wealthy boor of a husband, Dan (Wallace Beery), who has corrupt political ambitions in *Dinner at Eight* is a rehearsal for the dramatically weightier but still comical sparring between the only seemingly scatterbrained ex-showgirl Billie Dawn (Judy Holliday) and the uncouth junk tycoon Harry Brock (Broderick Crawford), who is in Washington to influence politicians in *Born Yesterday* (1950). And the suicide of the drunken has-been of a matinee idol, Larry Renault, as well as the character's futile attempts to hide his despair with humor, look eerily forward to the fate of James Mason's Norman Maine in *A Star Is Born* (1954). When Larry and

6.1. Delighted by Jean Harlow's comic talents in an earlier MGM film, Cukor gave her a plum role in *Dinner at Eight* (1933) as Kitty Packard, the brassy, vulgar, but adorable trophy wife of a boorish businessman played by Wallace Beery.

Source: Frame enlargement; MGM.

Norman succumb to suicidal despair, they are ignoring what Max Carey tells Mary Evans shortly after they meet in *What Price Hollywood?*: "Let me give you a tip about Hollywood—always keep your sense of humor. And you can't miss."

Cukor's fondness for the Barrymore family, including his rollicking parody of them in *The Royal Family of Broadway*, as well as his echoes of John Barrymore's drunkenness through his brother-in-law Lowell Sherman in *What Price Hollywood?*, account for the director's pitch-perfect handling of John's seriocomic character in *Dinner at Eight* as well as his affectionate work with Lionel here, in one of four films the brothers made together. John and Cukor had established a mutually admiring rapport on *A Bill of Divorcement*, so in *Dinner at Eight*, "Although Jack was playing a second-rate actor, he had no vanity as such. He even put things in to make himself hammier, more ignorant. . . . I've always found that if first-rate actors respect you, they'll try anything."

The somewhat seedy Larry Renault is essentially a tragic character. A movie idol on the skids because of the changeover to sound, he's on the verge of being thrown out of his New York hotel suite because he can't pay his bill and is faced with the ignominy of being forced into a bit part in his return to the stage. Bringing out a more subdued performance from Barrymore than in *A Bill of Divorcement*, Cukor brings out Larry's "burned out" quality in his intense but distracted looks and anguished close-ups as he prowls his hotel suite, which he recognizes as his dead end. But the performance is often drolly funny as well. Larry's attempts to posture with dignity are clumsy and mostly met with disdain by his agent, a bellboy, and the hotel manager. The agent, played with more than his usual bite by Lee Tracy, is as destructive to Larry as the studio publicity chief Matt Libby (Jack Carson) is to Norman in *A Star Is Born*, though both characterizations of the flunkies are complex and make us understand why they despise ungrateful colleagues who treat them so shabbily. Barrymore added a witty touch when Larry's agent mentions a prestigious producer who might work with him. Larry woozily postures while leaning against the fireplace, passing his cigarette hand across his brow, briefly shutting his eyes, and misquoting *Ghosts*, the classic Ibsen play about syphilis: "I rather like the idea of going with Stengel. They tell me he does those highbrow plays—Ibsen! 'I want the *Moon*, Mother.'"

When Larry engages in a tawdry romance, even though he knows he shouldn't, with the Jordans' nineteen-year-old daughter, Paula (Madge Evans, who had appeared on Broadway with Barrymore when she was a child actress), he partly redeems himself by gallantly trying to send her away, a move that stirs audience sympathy for this wreck of a man. Larry's capricious behavior, spurred along by his constant drinking, vacillates from self-conscious, self-mocking charm to pathetic wheedling to sudden outbursts of self-destructive rage at people he needs to help him in his comeback. When he begs a hostile bellboy to go out and get him a bottle, confessing "I'm sick," it's as ghastly as Norman Maine at his most abject. Cukor's extraordinary ability to control and shift tone is acute in his handling of Larry's descent. The director's orchestration of the twists and turns of Larry's spinning-out-of-control personality makes it all painfully convincing as well as darkly comedic. When he's finally driven to suicide, even that turns farcical.

6.2. When the has-been matinee idol played by John Barrymore in *Dinner at Eight* commits suicide, he carefully rearranges the lighting in his hotel room for maximum theatrical effect, a seriocomic touch Cukor carried over from the play by George S. Kaufman and Edna Ferber. *Source*: Frame enlargement; MGM.

Barrymore and Cukor worked out a bit of business that undercuts Larry's attempt at a grand theatrical sendoff. At this point the play directs, "His vanity asserts itself. He must make a good exit." But in blocking the first part of the scenes leading to his suicide, they decided, Cukor recalled, that "he should fuck that up, too." So Cukor suggested that after studying his ravaged face in a mirror and dropping his head in anguish onto the chest of drawers beneath it, and then crossing the room while trying to steady himself on a nearby seat, Barrymore should stumble in an "awful middle-aged sprawl," twisting his legs on the carpet and landing with his arm on a footstool.

Lit in silhouette through haunting swaths of gloom by the cinematographer William Daniels, in contrast to the film's overall glossy elegance, Larry rips up a portrait of Paula and tosses it out the window. The wasted-looking former matinee idol preens his hair and tie in a mirror, puts on a smoking jacket, and in a grandiose touch, gives a last little twist to his mustache. He opens a gas vent next to the fireplace and positions himself in a chair along-side it to display for the camera and those who will discover his corpse what is jokingly alluded to in the film as his "Great Profile" (Barrymore's familiar sobriquet). Before he expires, he takes pains to rearrange a standing lamp to cast the most flattering dramatic light on his face, a darkly witty gag carried over from the play. The camera tracks in, we hear a bell from the next scene (it's time for the dinner party), and that's the fadeout as Larry leaves us with a nuanced Cukoresque combination of emotions—regret for his tragic fail-ure and waste of talent along with an indulgent chuckle over an actor's vanity even at the fall of the final curtain. This harrowing but black-comical scene is among the best Cukor ever directed.

Barrymore's willingness to parody his image is endearing, and he and Howard Hawks spoofed the *Dinner at Eight* suicide scene the following year in their raucous film of the Ben Hecht and Charles MacArthur theatrical comedy *Twentieth Century*. When Barrymore's hammy impresario, Oscar Jaffe, summons his former protégée (Carole Lombard) to his train car in an attempt to con her back with him, he pretends to be dying, settling himself at the window and quickly adjusting a lamp to give his face a dramatic glow. Barrymore's third performance in a Cukor film, as Mercutio in MGM's 1936 *Romeo and Juliet*, also approaches that already flamboyant, often facetious role in the spirit of sending up his own familiar mannerisms with tongue-in-cheek glee.

The element of self-parody also permeates the uproariously funny perfor-mance by Jean Harlow in *Dinner at Eight* as the former hat-check girl who's married to the loutish Beery character but is cheating on the side with her doctor, played by the former silent star Edmund Lowe (stiff as usual; even Cukor can't do much with him, but his neglected wife is sensitively played by Karen Morley). Kitty's status as a pampered bauble is displayed in the strik-ing all-white set design of her bedroom and most of her costuming, aside from a funny little black hat she wears indoors. That snow-white setting and Dan-iels's nimbus of soft lighting, ironically contrasting with Kitty's flooziness but adding to the feeling she emanates of creamy sensuality, was a visual device suggested in the play's stage directions. Eleven shades of white and gray were used by Hobe Erwin and Fred Hope, the film's art directors, and Adrian dressed Harlow in slinky white silk gowns. They were so form-fitting that when the crew had trouble keeping the shadow of Harlow's pubic hair from showing, it too was bleached platinum blonde. The visual motif anticipates Cukor's similar staging of the bathroom bailiwick of the kept woman Crystal, played by Joan Crawford in *The Women* with scene-stealing relish but less-sympathetic nastiness.

Kitty affects a ditzy mindlessness but, like Billie Dawn in *Born Yesterday*, is shrewder than she seems. When Dan castigates her for staying in bed all day—a habit that, as Cukor conveys, reflects her state of depression over being a useless sex toy to two men—she retaliates by throwing her adultery in Dan's face. When he threatens to divorce her and leave her without a cent, she reminds him that she has been listening to the particulars of his crooked business deals, and she blackmails him into submission. Both characters have higher but rather delusional aspirations—Dan to become an adviser and even cabinet member to the president, Kitty to be accepted in high society, which the dinner party represents to her—but Kitty wins our heart with her refreshing commonness amid all the pretension and hypocrisy. Her vulgarity and bawdiness are part of her candid nature, and the audience sympathizes with her stifled joie de vivre and unashamed appetites, including her hunger for respectability in the eyes of those she ironically considers "refined people."

Cukor felt Harlow "played comedy as naturally as a hen lays an egg." She had "something vulnerable" that made her attractive: she was "very soft about her toughness." It took a while for those qualities to fully emerge onscreen, however. Harlow had been woefully inept in her earliest pictures, and even Frank Capra couldn't coax much of a performance out of her in his 1931 film *Platinum Blonde*, partly because she was miscast as a snooty society girl. Even though she actually came from a privileged background, she didn't convey that impression with her friends and colleagues or on the screen, who found her refreshingly frank and emotionally direct. She nevertheless made such an impression in Capra's film that Columbia changed the title from *Gallagher* (the name of her romantic rival, played by Loretta Young) to highlight Harlow's physical appeal.

She began to attract more attention as a sexpot in MGM's *Red-Headed Woman* the following year but made an especially strong impression on Cukor in Victor Fleming's *Red Dust*, the studio's racy 1932 comedy set in French Indochina, with Harlow memorably bathing in a rain barrel as Clark Gable inspects her with a sexual candor rivaling her own. When Cukor saw it, "there

6.3. Cukor enjoyed shooting *Dinner at Eight* on a remarkably brisk schedule with his stellar cast. He posed with script pages and Harlow as she reclined on a slant board between takes to keep her satin dress clinging.

Source: MGM.

she was, suddenly marvelous in comedy." Although Fleming, who was good with brassy dames, set the mold, Cukor played an important role in appreciating and showcasing her most appealing qualities. Recognizing that her wisecracking persona paradoxically coexisted with an almost childlike innocence, he helped her relax into the complex comic persona that made her a major star.

As he would do in molding the careers of other actors, Cukor encouraged Harlow's spontaneity. It was an endearing part of her personality that people who knew her often remarked upon, but it had been discouraged by some of the filmmakers who, confronted with her lustrous looks but limited acting training, had made her feel restrained. No longer, after *Red Dust* and *Dinner at Eight*, would she have to feel embarrassed or reserved about acting onscreen the way she felt, even if the persona she created with the encouragement of Cukor, Fleming, et al. diverged from her less raucous off-screen behavior. Her biographer David Stenn described the real Jean Harlow as "a shy, sweet woman-child who wore fuzzy sweaters and flaring slacks, liked to hem-stitch on film sets, and shared a house with her mother. . . . [Harlow was] a glamorous star who was also, according to screenwriter Anita Loos, 'a regular girl' with 'no vanity whatsoever—and no feeling about the sensation she created wherever she went.'"

Cukor drew on the directness of Harlow's personality for her performance as Kitty, who despite her mendacity and sloth (which makes her feel restless) and her intermittent nastiness (including the abusive way she treats her rebellious, slatternly maid, brightly played by Hilda Vaughn), is one of the few honest and, in the end, relatively decent characters in a film filled with hypocrites. When Larry Renault tries to drive Paula away, he confesses that it's "the first decent thing I ever did in my life," but Kitty's instincts in life-changing matters tend more in that direction. When her husband calls her "you little piece of scum," we feel for her all the more, because the description fits him rather than her. The screenwriter Robert Towne observed that movie stars have the ability to "seem to register swift and dramatic mood changes with no discernible change of expression. . . . I think it's because the faces of such actors are like the surface of ponds—the stiller the waters, the more deeply we can see into them. Watching still waters running deep is paradoxical, something of a contradiction at the very least, but then exceptional movie actors inevitably embody paradoxes and contradictions—Marilyn, the child-woman, Marlon, the sensitive brute." Harlow had those paradoxical qualities—she was the brassy child-siren.

While working with Marilyn Monroe even in the highly troubled final stages of her career (in *Let's Make Love* and the unfinished *Something's Got to Give*), Cukor brought out fresh qualities in Monroe that had seldom been seen onscreen. His unequaled ability to control changes of tone in storytelling enabled him to do so with Harlow as well. He adroitly plays on Harlow's dual nature when Dr. Talbot comes to pay a house call, and she switches from cooing baby-talk while her maid is within earshot to a coarse, imploring voice as she scolds her disaffected paramour for ignoring her. Many future performances in Cukor films will benefit as Harlow's does from exploring the contradictions and nuances of actors' personalities and the characters they are playing as well as from their natural offscreen qualities. They benefit greatly from what the MGM executive Irving Thalberg called the *"unguarded"* quality Cukor brought to Garbo's performance in *Camille* (1936). The ability to bring out that sense of abandon in his actors by creating a climate of trust and deep understanding, a sense of being fully seen and accepted, was part of Cukor's special quality as a filmmaker.

7.1. Cukor directing *Little Women*, the 1933 film he sometimes called his favorite, with Katharine Hepburn, Joan Bennett, Frances Dee, and Jean Parker. (He also described *Sylvia Scarlett* as his favorite.)

Source: From RKO Radio Pictures photographs of the Margaret Herrick Library, Academy of Motion Picture Arts and Sciences.

7

KATHARINE HEPBURN IN *LITTLE WOMEN*; THE ENSEMBLE OF *DAVID COPPERFIELD*

"This picture was heaven to do. . . . It was to me my youth!"

So declares Katharine Hepburn in her autobiography, writing of *Little Women*. That and her next picture with Cukor, *Sylvia Scarlett*, are among the greatest and most lasting achievements of their work together and their careers. And both films have been derided at different times and for different reasons, a measure of how challenging these two films are to gender norms. *Sylvia Scarlett*, Cukor's most overtly queer film, featuring Hepburn in male drag for much of the story, provoked an uproar from baffled audiences and reviewers in 1935, and its commercial failure made both star and director more cautious ever after about dealing with androgyny so openly. *Little Women*, on the other hand, was acclaimed in 1933 for what was taken, somewhat misleadingly, as its simply affectionate portrait of New England family life in the 1860s. Cukor sometimes regarded this adaptation of the classic novel *Little Women, or, Meg, Jo, Beth, and Amy* (1868–1869) by Louisa May Alcott as his favorite film, although he told Carlos Clarens that *Sylvia Scarlett*, which he usually publicly disparaged because of the public backlash, was actually his favorite.

Little Women, like *Sylvia Scarlett*, also deals with sexual ambiguity, although more obliquely. The derision sometimes directed at *Little Women* by modern audiences (one film historian who shall be nameless told me in the early 1970s that he found it "a movie for old maids") is based partly on sexism (the kind aimed then at so-called "women's pictures" or what are now known as "chick flicks") and partly on snide superiority toward the film's supposed endorsement of the archaic values of family life in a puritanical time and place. But as Hepburn suggested by drawing a direct link between herself and Alcott's surrogate figure, Josephine (Jo) March, *Little Women* is fundamentally about a young woman's growing sense of independence, establishment of a career, and freedom from the prevailing gender norms of her time.

The social pendulum has swung with "women's pictures," long dismissed by film reviewers as trivial but now recognized by critics and historians as a genre that deals incisively with social and gender issues, and *Sylvia Scarlett* today is a feminist cult favorite. And if *Little Women* seems less radical, even hopelessly "old-fashioned" for those with limited historical perspective and an inability to recognize the film's ambivalence toward the values of the period (the 1860s), it is perhaps more subversive in some ways precisely because its declaration of independence for women is more covert. And its ostensibly fond view of family life in New England is actually one of considerable ambivalence.

Hepburn's Jo is what is called a "tomboy" in *Little Women*, the word long used for girls chafing against the limitations imposed on females by their society. Being a tomboy was usually considered a phase of adolescence that headstrong girls would outgrow. But not in this case, and not in Hepburn's. Today young women who act like boys are more often called, as Hepburn has been, "butch." Hepburn herself as a girl, from at least the age of ten, preferred to be known as "Jimmy." In her unconventional attire, short haircut, and roughhousing, outdoorsy, pugnacious behavior, she created a boyish persona for herself that, unusually for her time, she never fully discarded. Somehow this rare creature made her brand of androgyny popular, to a degree, with movie audiences, under the enthusiastic guidance and indulgence of her fellow free spirit George Cukor. Paradoxically, Hepburn's "feminine" side was also pronounced when she wished it to be and contributed to her appeal to both male and female audiences, and many of the roles she chose emphasized the dual sides of her nature.

Her off-screen image, wearing pants and avoiding marriage (after an early half-hearted attempt fell by the wayside), as well as maintaining what appears to have been a bisexual personal life, was not always accepted by audiences.

So after she and other stars, including Greta Garbo, Mae West, Joan Crawford, and Kay Francis, were declared "poison at the box office" (more famil-
iarly, "box office poison") by Harry Brandt, president of the Independent
Theatre Owners Association, in a May 1938 advertisement in the *Hollywood
Reporter*, Hepburn reinvented her screen image. From Cukor's 1940 film of
Philip Barry's play *The Philadelphia Story* onward, Hepburn took pains to allow
her movie character, while still outspoken about independence and offbeat
in her behavior, to also submit to more conventional gender norms. It was a
career-preserving move that William J. Mann sharply criticizes in his 2006
biography, *Kate: The Woman Who Was Hepburn*, as a hypocritical ploy that sustained her stardom while toning down the riskiness of her appeal:

> It's almost painful to watch today, this humbling of Hepburn, but in 1940,
> mainstream audiences were reassured that she'd no longer pose a threat to
> their conventional values. . . . Yet for all the control she wielded off the
> screen, she had to know how fundamentally she'd compromised herself
> on-screen. David Thomson, having interviewed her, felt she was "doubt-
> less aware" of the irony of being lauded for her post-1940 work while her
> "dazzling achievements" of the 1930s had merely hardened audiences against
> her. Hepburn's close friends agreed that with *The Philadelphia Story* she
> made a very conscious decision to sacrifice, at least on-screen, the prickly
> independence that had once characterized her. "She did it because she knew
> she had to," said [the playwright] James Prideaux. "And she was very smart
> about always knowing what to do to stay on top."

Hepburn's early absorption in her masculine "Jimmy" persona was deeply
rooted and ineradicable psychologically, however, and its enduring force in
helping establish her complex identity has been the subject of much analysis
and speculation among her biographers. She writes in her autobiography that
"being a girl was a torment. I'd always wanted to be a boy." The most mysterious aspect of her life remains her relationship with her brother Tom, who
died under still-uncertain circumstances while he and Kate were visiting one
of their mother's female friends in Greenwich Village during Easter vacation
in 1921. Tom, who was fifteen years old, was found asphyxiated in an attic
early one morning by Kate, although whether it was suicide or some kind of

accidental death has never been conclusively determined; Mann's biography suggests it may have been caused by Tom's experimentation with autoasphyxiation as a risky sexual stimulant.

Vague reports linked Tom's death with despondency over a girlfriend—his father thought that Tom had been vainly trying to "break off [an] affair" with a girl, who had kept "pestering" him along with her mother—but Kate told her friend and biographer A. Scott Berg that Tom "was never really charged up quite like the rest of us. I had heard that maybe a girl had rejected him—who knows, maybe a boy. Whatever it was, he simply could not cope." What's most suggestive about Tom's death in the light of its effect on his sister is that during that visit to Greenwich Village, Tom looked at her and said, "You're my girl, aren't you? You're my favorite girl in the whole world." For her part, she wrote, "I adored him."

Their unusually close relationship, the nature of which has never been entirely clear, lends itself to psychological speculation that in the wake of Tom's death, Kate's enduring life as a "tomboy" into adulthood was a result of a symbiosis with her late brother with whom she shared more than clothes in childhood and that it helped lead her to a career playing daringly androgynous characters onscreen. She felt that "this incident seemed to sort of separate me from the world as I'd known it."

Hence the concentration on Jo's determination in *Little Women* not to settle down in a conventional romantic relationship with a man but to forge a career as a writer. Jo rejects her youthful suitor, a wealthy, sensitive, rather effeminate boy who lives next door, Laurie (Douglass Montgomery), and settles eventually into a sexless-seeming relationship with a considerably older man, the gentle and erudite German-American scholar Professor Bhaer (Paul Lukas), a sort of father figure. That kind of companionate union—with stress on Professor Bhaer's encouragement of Jo's turn from genre writing to more personal fiction, i.e., the book that became *Little Women*—was unorthodox for a woman in nineteenth-century America. Cukor's film follows the throughline of Jo's stubborn pursuit of independent existence on her own terms as a female artist.

The novel's episodic nature and portrait of an insular Concord, Massachusetts, family dominated by women (mother and four sisters), with the father either absent (as a chaplain in the Civil War) or relatively unimportant even

7.2. "This picture was heaven to do," said Hepburn. ". . . It was to me my youth!" Josephine (Jo) March, the character Louisa May Alcott modeled after herself in her novel *Little Women*, is a tomboy like Hepburn, seen here leaping over the fence to her home. Cukor's film of the beloved novel about a budding woman writer is endearing yet often astringent.

Source: Frame enlargement; RKO.

when present, are preserved in the film. While paying considerable attention to all the female members of the family, the screenplay by the married couple Sarah Mason and Victor Heerman nevertheless keeps turning the events around to their primary focus on Jo's development, which is somewhat obscured in the novel by its profusion of incident. Hepburn's autobiography gives great credit to the director in making the film succeed as a living adaptation of the book—"George Cukor [was] perfect. He really caught the atmosphere"—but she stresses the critical importance of the screenplay: "There were a number of scripts done on this. They were all mediocre. Actually bad. Then Sarah Mason and Victor Heerman were hired. They wrote a brilliant script, in my humble opinion. Simple and true and naïve but really believable. It was amazing the difference between this script and its predecessors.

Mason and Heerman believed the book. So did I. The others didn't." (The screenwriters won the Oscar for best adaptation; Cukor received his first of five directing nominations, and the film was nominated for best picture.)

Cukor told Lambert that when he was asked to direct *Little Women*, he hadn't read the novel, thinking it was a book for little girls. "When I came to read it, I was startled. It's not sentimental or saccharine, but very strong-minded, full of character, and a wonderful picture of New England family life. It's full of that admirable New England sternness, about sacrifice and austerity. And then Kate Hepburn cast something over it. Like Garbo in *Camille*, she was born to play this part. She's tender and funny, fiercely loyal, and plays the fool when she feels like it. There's a purity about her."

Cukor in a 1938 essay on directing in the British book *Behind the Screen: How Films Are Made* elaborated on the development of his working relationship with Hepburn:

> When I directed *Little Women* I had to develop a new technique to ensure the best results from the collaboration of Miss Hepburn and myself. . . . This fine actress is more than a personality. She is a human dynamo. Without meaning to be, and simply because of the vigour of her own mind and the intensity of her attitude to her work, she can be, if given the chance, what I would call an artistic bully. . . . I do not say that if I had decided to "lie down" to her from the start, a less good picture would have resulted. But a director with a conscience will fight tooth and nail to get the picture as he wants it. Let me hasten to say that Miss Hepburn and I did not fight at all. I confess freely that I used many weapons in dealing with her— simulated rage, ridicule, and good-humoured cajolery. She has a great sense of humour, and is quite capable of directing it against herself.

From its opening credits—a kind of Currier & Ives image of the moonlit March home in falling snow, framed with woods and flowers (Cukor said he was "very sentimental" about snow)—and with Max Steiner's lovely music played on a harmonium before a full orchestra picks up the main theme, *Little Women* is replete with charm, the most beautifully textured Cukor film to date. He and Hobe Irwin, the New York designer Cukor imported to design the settings, working with the costumer Walter Plunkett and the cinematographer Henry Gerrard, took pains to capture the period in loving detail (this was one of Gerrard's last films before his early death in 1934 as a result of complications from appendix surgery; he had also shot Josef von Sternberg's *Thunderbolt* as well as *Beggars of Life* and *The Most Dangerous Game*). The Alcott home in Concord was studied as the model for the sets, and Plunkett used simple fabrics for the modest means of the March family, as well as repurposing costumes for the characters just as the sisters would do among themselves. Cukor's fondness for research, which came to the fore in this film, gave a new level of depth and texture to his visual storytelling, a pattern he would further in his adaptations of *David Copperfield* (1935) and *Camille* (1936).

Cukor paid tribute in *Little Women*, at least ostensibly, to the idealized portrait of the March family Alcott rendered (with some misgivings) in her book and Hepburn found so enthrallingly reminiscent of her youth. But when you crack the DNA code of Cukor's *Little Women*, a much more ambivalent and disturbing story can be sensed beneath the surface allure and nostalgia. The trees outside the March home in the credits image are stark silhouettes against the night sky, as in a horror movie, and we also see the silhouette of a young woman ambiguously caught in the process of either leaving or returning home. Jo's dilemma is thus suggested almost subliminally from the start.

It's worth recalling that in the nineteenth century, nostalgia was not regarded as it is today, as a warm and fuzzy look back at the past, but as a neurosis, an inability to adjust to change. Hepburn's own home life with her domineering physician father, hard-driving social reformer mother, and dead brother was not as idyllic as she wanted to make it seem. But she was always devoted to her parents and siblings nonetheless and kept returning home to Fenwick, the family's seaside home in Connecticut, all her life. Yet Hepburn had to leave home, over her father's violent opposition, to make something of herself. Cukor left his middle-class home to pursue a bohemian life in the theater and as a closeted gay man in Hollywood, turning his complex fantasies into vivid life onscreen, as Hepburn did with hers. *Little Women* provides a portrait of family life that may seem warm and comfortable but is also a not-so-subtle trap for the restless, rebellious Jo. When you peel off the veneer, her siblings are far less appealing than she is, and her parents seem either demanding (in her mother's case) and almost invisible and all but mute (her father).

Seen from this vantage point, the narrative drive of this version of *Little Women* is about Jo's conflicted attitude toward her family and her desperate

7.3. Jo evades conventional romantic commitment in her native Massachusetts to pursue her life as a writer in New York City. She eventually settles down with a shy, scholarly older man, the German-American Professor Bhaer (Paul Lukas), who is supportive of her career.

Source: Frame enlargement; RKO.

need to escape into her fiercely solitary life as a writer, even while she is continually drawn back (like the silhouetted woman in the credits) to the family homestead for solace in her difficult career and emotional path. She writes her initial stories (tales of horror) secretively in the attic, and when she takes one to offer for publication in a magazine, she literally escapes from the upper story of the house and climbs down the trellis to travel into town with the tale. She has to go to New York to become an author, and when she becomes friendly there with Professor Bhaer, he disparages her stories, as people did with Alcott when she wrote *her* unladylike blood-and-thunder "sensational fiction."

Alcott turned reluctantly to her more acceptable portraits of family life in *Little Women*, its sequel *Good Wives* (used for part of the film story), and other books she tended to disparage as partly compromised by following commercial formulas. Chafing at the compulsions imposed on women to marry for security, Alcott has the mother, called Marmee, wishing that her daughters would "better be happy old maids than unhappy wives, or unmaidenly girls, running about to find husbands." Nina Auerbach observes that in *Little Women*, a book "so dutiful on the surface, only women can build Utopias." The "richness" of Alcott's determined creation of a model of a feminist artistic colony "has to do with the absence from it of controlling men. . . . This underlying faith in the spiritual self-sufficiency of women may explain why the March family has been cherished for decades by women readers."

Cukor's film version, one of numerous film and television adaptations of the novel, portrays the New England society of the 1860s as strictly puritanical, censorious, and highly disciplined. The power of shame is strong in that society and is emphasized in the film as a counterpoint to Jo's rebellion, such as when her father implores his daughters in a letter from the battlefront to always do their "duty" as "my little women." Cukor shows the girls reacting painfully to his letter in an unusual series of close-ups as they make vows to reform. When we see Jo, she is weeping and uncertainly declaring, "I'll try and be what he loves to call me—'a little woman'—and not be rough and wild and do my duty here at home instead of always wanting to go to war to help father." It's clear from Hepburn's troubled look that Jo will be unable to live up to her father's conventional expectations of what a woman should be, and that she and the audience know it.

There's a running motif of Jo showing genuine emotion—often the forbidden kinds of passion, anger, jealousy—but then quickly practicing denial of her feelings and "acting" the dutiful, loyal, generous, selfless sister and daughter. But Hepburn's Jo manages to dominate virtually every scene in which she appears, playing the "male" role in relationships and keeping everyone on her terms. There's little that is truly selfless about Jo, who's preoccupied with making her own unorthodox way in the world at all costs, despite the guilt she often feels about it. Hepburn herself admitted in her autobiography, *Me*, that she was "a totally selfish person . . . a *me me me* person." This follow-up by Cukor to *Dinner at Eight*, a film in which virtually everyone has that flaw, is suffused with a tension between Jo's solipsistic personality and her feeling of duty and love toward her family.

Despite Cukor's sprightly direction of the ensemble cast, Jo's sisters are a pallid bunch compared with the exuberant Hepburn. Whether or not that was intentional, Cukor and his writers don't show much interest in trying to find complexity in the other characters. The family entertain themselves together in the evenings, as people did before radio, movies, and television, but the artistic interests of Amy (drawing) and Beth (music) don't amount to much more than hobbies in contrast with Jo's outsized ambitions. Meg, played by one of the most exquisitely beautiful actresses of the 1930s, Frances Dee, is entirely conventional and hence rather characterless in her femininity. She chastises Jo about her tomboyish manners: "You're old enough to leave off boys' tricks and behave better, Josephine. Now you're so tall and turn up your hair, you must remember you're almost a young lady." Jo, who's writing while Meg is sewing, defiantly declares as she yanks down her hair, "No, I'm not. And if pinning up my hair makes me so, I'll wear it down till I'm a hundred!"

Amy is an airhead, played against type by Joan Bennett without her usual asperity but with frivolity and foolishly unwarranted pretensions of being intellectual (she continually makes malapropisms). Beth, whom Amy says has "an infirmity—she's shy," is so simpleminded that the others treat her as a child, and though some of her scenes are truly touching, the casting of a drippy actress, Jean Parker, makes Beth mostly an irritant. Spring Byington, whose casting Cukor opposed, is actually less cloying than usual as the mother, known as Marmee, although rather one-note in her solid and stolid role as the family rule giver. Neighboring Aunt March, played in lively fashion by the wonderful Edna May Oliver, is a well-off but starchy old skinflint who begrudges every bit of charity she doles out to her threadbare relatives.

In such stifling company, Jo's brazen behavior and exuberant speech and body language make her stand out like a freak, and she revels in her eccentricities, as Cukor does, even if Concord manners dictate she has to keep apologizing for herself. Jo's boyish behavior includes a delightfully graceful leap over a wooden fence in their front yard while wearing her long skirt; heartily playing both male roles, Black Hugo and Roderigo, in the hilariously bollixed play, *The Witch's Curse*, that she writes, directs, and performs with her sisters; throwing snowballs at Laurie's mansion window to make his acquaintance, echoing Roderigo's wooing of a suitor in a castle; taking the lead role as Hamlet while fencing with Laurie; turning down requests to dance at his party before doing a charming waltz all by herself in the hallway; and having her long hair roughly chopped off in a barbershop. She sells her girlish locks to help send her mother to visit their hospitalized father. In a scene that's both poignant and funny, Jo weeps over the lost hair rather than for her ailing father, but she never grows it back, accepting her initial rationalization that "it's boyish, becoming, and easy to keep in order."

Jo's supposed love interest for much of the picture is Laurie, who's played as effete and pretty, almost girlish, a casting choice that reinforces the reversal of gender roles in Jo's orbit. Montgomery's sweet nature keeps Jo devoted to him, but he becomes irate when she rejects his proposal in a long, painful two-shot as she reclines against a tree in the woods, her face a shining oasis in the gloom. A tear slowly makes its way down her face, and her downturned mouth looks as if she has swallowed a lemon: "I *loathe* elegant society, and you like it. And you hate my scribbling, and I can't get on without it." Hepburn's playing of Jo's determination to remain unmarried no matter what others think of her is fully conscious of the loneliness that will entail, although when she meets Professor Bhaer, she finds a companion who offers undemanding, unthreatening affection.

But as admirable as Jo's intransigence is about being entrapped in conventional marriage, her furious reaction to Meg's "horrid" romantic interest in Laurie's tutor, John Brooke (John Davis Lodge), and their decision to marry seems pathological. When Jo begs Meg to let the family stay as it is, her distress is so acute that Cukor emphasizes it in no fewer than three large close-ups. Later, she tells Meg in a fit of panic and rage, "Don't go and marry that man!" After the wedding celebration, Cukor dissolves to a shot of Jo apart from the others, leaning against a tree in the woods, distraught. She refers to the couple's twin children as "the little demons." In this women's world, even the handsome Brooke is a bland male figure of little significance, lacking the devilish charm Lodge exhibits as Count Alexei, Marlene Dietrich's tormented lover, in Sternberg's masterpiece, *The Scarlet Empress* (1934), or the mature gravitas of his Archduke Franz Ferdinand in Max Ophüls's *De Mayerling à Sarajevo* (*From Mayerling to Sarajevo*, 1940). Lodge eventually became governor of Connecticut.

Jo's determination to keep the family together runs the risk of damaging it by not being able to tolerate her sister's differing idea of happiness. As much as we understand Jo's determination to sacrifice conventional happiness for the sake of her career, and as fiercely as she tries to uphold her concept of family, it's hard to disagree with Aunt March when she tells her, "I think you've treated everybody shamefully."

Cukor's camerawork throughout *Little Women* stresses artfully but unpretentiously composed group shots of the mother and the four girls, with unobtrusive camera movements reframing them for emphasis, but he sometimes keeps Jo just outside the cluster or with a contrasting look of distraction. When they all sing the hymn "Abide with Me" with Beth at the piano, Jo lingers apart, not fully participating. Jo's determined aloofness from the family rituals suggests the reasons she must keep fleeing this seemingly heartwarming but actually somewhat chilling and restrictive family. She delivers the film's ending line, "Welcome home!," in the rain on the steps of the Concord homestead as she accepts Professor Bhaer's hesitant proposal. The meek older man who calls her "my little friend" is added to the ranks of the family she keeps simultaneously close but at a safe distance. As Hepburn did with her own New England family, Jo finds comfort and security in being able to retreat to her home whenever she wishes even as she keeps fleeing it for New York City when the warmth inside becomes stifling.

If *Little Women* serves as an example of how to adapt a classic novel satisfyingly into cinematic form without losing its style and dramatic essence, Cukor's subsequent film, *David Copperfield* (1935), offers a negative example. Although it is a popular and beloved film version of the sprawling novel by Charles Dickens and has a memorably apt and colorful cast, it is seriously damaged by being an overly condensed, even rushed adaptation. Only a few scenes play out at sufficient length to allow Cukor to exert his forte, treating behavior and character interplay with subtlety and nuances, and the second half after David grows up is simply uninteresting, a series of disconnected episodes amounting to a total letdown. Another collaboration between Cukor and Selznick, *David Copperfield* was one of the "prestige" films the producer was fond of making from literary classics. He had to coax the New York head office of MGM, Loews Inc., and the studio's production chief, Louis B. Mayer, into letting him make it on a budget of $1 million. The studio was skeptical about the marketplace for such material (wrongly so) and balked at

7.4. W. C. Fields, a Charles Dickens aficionado, effortlessly blended his beloved comic persona with that of Mister Micawber, the eccentric guardian angel who watches over the young orphan David (Freddie Bartholomew) in Cukor's picaresque *David Copperfield* (1935), a film brimming with wonderful character actors.

Source: Frame enlargement; MGM.

Selznick's desire to make *David Copperfield* as a two-part film, which would have solved some of the story problems. The full onscreen title of the film is *The Personal History, Adventures, Experience, & Observation of David Copperfield the Younger.*

What distinguishes the film is its astonishing gallery of character actors, chosen to match the traits and appearance of their characters in the novel; the memorable illustrations by Phiz. were used as guides. W. C. Fields is an endearing Mr. Micawber, doing some of his own physical shtick yet sticking to the script otherwise (Fields was a fervent admirer of Dickens); Edna May Oliver is the gruff yet loving Aunt Betsey Trotwood, her herky-jerky movements providing humor and her commanding presence a complement to her august Aunt March in *Little Women*; Roland Young brings the unctuous Uriah Heep startlingly alive; Basil Rathbone is the quintessence of cruelty as

Mr. Murdstone, with Violet Kemble Cooper as his creepy sister; Jessie Ralph is the warm anchor of David's young life as Nurse Peggotty; and Lennox Pawle is a wondrous creation as the daffy Mr. Dick, an antic figure with uncommon common sense.

But the trouble with these splendid actors is that the impressions they so vividly create don't evolve, a flaw in the novel, which tends to repeat a set of mannerisms for a character for (diminishing) comic effect, a limitation carried over into the overly condensed screenplay by the novelist Hugh Walpole and Howard Estabrook, which plays like a Classics Illustrated comic book. Freddie Bartholomew, an experienced British stage actor, was a find as the sensitive, intelligent young David and became a movie star as a result, but Frank Lawton is bland as the young adult David. Although Cukor & Co. evoke the terrors of child abuse with the hideousness of a horror film—the scene of David being upbraided and flogged by Mr. Murdstone is particularly chilling, with extreme close-ups of the faces of the Murdstones and David and details of their hands intensifying the buildup—the adult David seems strangely unmarked by those experiences the audience has felt strongly through his child's perspective, a major lapse that contributes to the pointless feeling of the second half. The character of David's fallen idol, Steerforth (Hugh Williams), is particularly damaged with the failure to show their scenes at school. But though Maureen O'Sullivan's imbecilic Dora is grating and given too much screen time for her prattling, at least her death scene is handled with admirable restraint.

Cukor and his collaborators—including the cinematographer Oliver T. Marsh, the art directors Merrill Pye and Edwin B. Willis, and the costumer Dolly Tree—lavished considerable artistic effort and research on the look of the film, which captures the texture and feeling of nineteenth-century England. Today the filmmakers would have had the running time for a leisurely rendition of the Dickens novel in a miniseries, as indeed has been done repeatedly more recently. But Cukor and Selznick shared the view that to "improve" a classic is a mistake, since the structural flaws in novels such as *Little Women* (Beth's repeated deathbed scenes) and *David Copperfield* are part of their fabric and that they might unravel if tampered with. This is a minor matter in Cukor's *Little Women*, whose superlative script allows the time and space for letting the central drama of Jo's artistic and personal development play out pleasingly along with side aspects that flesh out her family life. Cukor's reverence for the original texts he filmed is usually a virtue but in the case of *David Copperfield* is a hindrance, making it a series of rushed and literally sketchy scenes and repetitive bits that don't cohere into a satisfying film even before it gradually disintegrates into tedium.

8.1. "To hold, as 'twere, the mirror up to nature": George Cukor, Katharine Hepburn, and Cary Grant on location in Southern California for their 1935 film, *Sylvia Scarlett*. This comedy-drama about gender fluidity draws daringly from the venerable theatrical tradition of cross-dressing.

Source: RKO/From the George Cukor Papers of the Margaret Herrick Library, Academy of Motion Picture Arts and Sciences.

8

KATHARINE HEPBURN AND CARY GRANT IN *SYLVIA SCARLETT*

"The little Pierrot boy! But were you a girl dressed as a boy, or are you a boy dressed as a girl?"

That's the central question, evidently unanswerable, raised by Cukor's most audacious film, *Sylvia Scarlett* (1935). The title character, played by Katharine Hepburn, spends much of the film masquerading as a boy called Sylvester Scarlett. She also makes awkward attempts to behave as a young woman, and both men and women are attracted to her as she explores her gender identity. In this transgressive comedy, Cukor's ode to his favorite actress, Sylvia/Sylvester is closer to what we know of the actual Hepburn than even her Jo March in *Little Women*. While that film dramatizes Jo's quest for independence from restrictive gender norms holding women back from fully satisfying lives, *Sylvia Scarlett* brings the subtexts explored in *Little Women* right out into the open, unmistakably so, as it proved with audiences at the time, who recoiled from this notorious flop. But this deliciously mischievous and profound comedy also layers subtext upon subtext upon subtext and treats the whole subject of gender norms playfully.

By far the most gender-bending film either Cukor or Hepburn ever made and one of the most outré works to ever emerge from a Hollywood studio, the lyrical *Sylvia Scarlett* is all shadings, an endlessly surprising film that twists and turns vertiginously to challenge every aspect of the audience's preconceptions about gender. It leaves us with a portrait of a daringly unconventional young woman whose sexual identity is almost entirely ambiguous, as, this film implies, everyone's is, if the truth be told.

Filmed after *David Copperfield*, *Sylvia Scarlett* was a pet project of Cukor and Hepburn at RKO, made possible by the surprise box office success of *Little Women*, which emboldened them to go further. But their transvestite fling received such a hostile response at the first preview in San Pedro, Cukor recalled, that after it, he and Hepburn told their producer, Pandro S. Berman, "Pan, let's scrap this picture and we'll do a picture for you for nothing." And Berman replied, "perfectly seriously, 'I hope to Christ I never see either of you again!'" Berman eventually cooled down but remained bitter about *Sylvia Scarlett*, calling it "a private promotional deal of Hepburn and Cukor; they conned me into it." The studio salvage job after the preview included tacking on an overly expository prologue of Sylvia and her alcoholic father, Henry (Edmund Gwenn), fleeing their home in Marseilles after her mother dies and Henry confesses he is an embezzler. Cukor and Hepburn filmed this needless scene (nearly five minutes long) in a tongue-in-cheek, singsong, over-wrought style, as if to tell the studio defiantly, "OK, you wanted a treacly, melodramatic opening to rationalize why Sylvia masquerades as a boy, so here goes."

Imagining *Sylvia Scarlett* without the prologue makes you realize what an even bolder film it would have been if it had started instead in medias res, with its foggy long shot of a boat en route to England and introduction of Hepburn on deck in male attire. She's seen at first from behind and in silhouette, acting elusive to conceal her identity. She tries to calm her anxious father under the hawkish gaze of a sinister-looking fellow initially seen in a shadowy full shot inspecting a handbill. He turns out to be a brash Cockney conman, Jimmy Monkley (Cary Grant). Hepburn's face is only gradually revealed after she ducks into a WC labeled "DAMES" and is expelled when a woman screams. It took me many viewings of *Sylvia Scarlett* before I noticed that Monkley, after entering the ship's lounge in the background of the scene and tossing the handbill in the trash, becomes suspicious of Sylvia's disguise as she knocks over some silverware noisily. While she enters the ladies' room in the foreground, he briefly reappears by popping out of the lounge, spying on her. And when they meet in the lounge as Monkley is stealthily pumping her father about his smuggling, Monkley, under the cover of macho bonhomie, tries to feel her up and surreptitiously inspect her chest unsuccessfully.

He doesn't let on to his suspicions for quite a while, the better to manipulate her.

Sylvia Scarlett (a name puckishly playing on the expression "scarlet woman") is an adaptation of a 1918 novel by Compton Mackenzie, *The Early Life and Adventures of Sylvia Scarlett*. Part of a trilogy by the prolific Scottish author and political figure, the novel is set in the nineteenth century and, unlike the film, is meandering, irritatingly twee, and wearyingly long. While updating the story for the screen, the screenwriters cut through the thicket to highlight Sylvia's role-playing and confusion about her gender identity.

The diverse group of writers who brought such wit and panache to the project were Gladys Unger, John Collier, and Mortimer Offner. Unger, an American who also lived in England, was a prolific playwright and screenwriter. Her credits included the mostly lost 1928 Garbo silent film *The Divine Woman*, directed by Victor Sjöström, based on her play *Starlight*. Offner had been a friend of Cukor's from their youth, attending plays with him and acting with the director in a harlequinade Cukor staged at New York's Temple Beth-El during their high school years (from the description in McGilligan's book, it sounds much like the hokey melodrama Hepburn stages in *Little Women*: Cukor played "a skulking villain called Liccoricio"). Offner became a portrait photographer and screenwriter before being blacklisted; he helped write Hepburn's 1935 film *Alice Adams*, based on the Booth Tarkington novel and directed by George Stevens. Collier was a noted British-born writer of often bizarre fantasy fiction (including the 1930 novel *His Monkey Wife, or, Married to a Chimp*) who made his screenwriting debut with the Cukor film. Short stories by Collier were adapted for television on *Alfred Hitchcock Presents* and *The Twilight Zone*, as well as by Orson Welles for his innovative 1956 pilot *The Fountain of Youth*.

Collier recalled his eight weeks working with Cukor as a "delightful experience . . . I'd scarcely seen a motion picture in my life; I didn't know a thing about screenwriting. In point of fact, it was something of a mistake. Hugh Walpole [the novelist who helped adapt *David Copperfield* for Cukor] had told George I'd be right for the job [on *Sylvia Scarlett*]. George thought Hugh was talking about Evelyn Waugh." Together the three screenwriters' disparate talents flowed smoothly into the synthesis of elements that made *Sylvia Scarlett* so quirky, a fitting vehicle for the offbeat fancies of Cukor and Hepburn, whose character is wonderingly described as "you oddity . . .

you freak of nature" by a bohemian artist, Michael Fane (Brian Aherne), who takes a romantic interest in Sylvia after being attracted by her when she is in male drag.

The film's delicate, rather fantastic atmosphere of London and the English countryside owes much to the cinematography by the masterful Joseph H. August (the shipboard scenes recall his expressionistic use of fog that same year in John Ford's *The Informer*). This artificiality of style helps convey the feeling of a wanton, freewheeling adult fairy tale. *Sylvia Scarlett* has much the same whimsical charm of the elevated poetic language of a Shakespearean comedy such as *As You Like It*, which the film evokes with Hepburn masquerading in male garb. That is in the venerable theatrical tradition of the many plays and operas with women in what was known as a breeches role, or *Hosenrolle*. Cukor referred to her characterization by the French term for tomboy, *garçonne*. But films usually are expected to be more "realistic" than the stage, and 1935 audiences already rattled by the sexual ambiguities in *Sylvia Scarlett* were further befuddled by its many and often quicksilver changes of mood.

The film pirouettes from suspenseful and prankish criminality to joyous musical frivolity, sexual game playing, and romantic abandon to the late passage that incongruously follows episodes of delirium tremens, near-drowning, and suicide with a comical car chase in a rather overextended denouement. But for those who can go along with what Cukor and Hepburn are doing here, those dizzying mood changes capture the uneasy nature of Sylvia's existence and the rollercoaster feeling of life being lived, especially the offbeat existence hailed in the film's dedication "To the adventurer, to all who stray from the beaten path . . ."

François Truffaut later pointed out that American audiences often have trouble following a film involving mixed moods. That favorite tendency of the French Nouvelle Vague confused the perennially clueless *New York Times* reviewer Bosley Crowther, who lost his job over his incomprehension of the mixture of comedy and violence in Arthur Penn's *Bonnie and Clyde* (1967). Five years before that film changed the American industry, Crowther wrote of Truffaut's *Tirez sur le pianiste* (*Shoot the Piano Player*), "Why does he scramble his satire with a madly melodramatic plot and have the little piano player kill a man in defense of a girl? It looks, from where we are sitting, as though M. Truffaut went haywire in this film." *Bonnie and Clyde*, however, changed the American film industry when it captivated a youthful audience in tune with the freewheeling spirit inspired by the French (Truffaut had helped Robert Newman and David Benton with their screenplay). And when the women's liberation movement took force in the late sixties, the time came for *Sylvia Scarlett* to be rediscovered as a visionary film about sexual ambiguity and, far ahead of its time, even about what we now call nonbinary identity.

But back in 1935, Cukor and Hepburn were the ones who were thought to have gone haywire. In a telegram to Hepburn after a preview of *Sylvia Scarlett*, Cukor reported that the audience was "interested if a bit confused." The half-hearted studio rescue operation involving the slyly facetious prologue failed to salvage the film's release, which resulted in a heavy financial loss and helped lead to Hepburn's stigmatization as "box office poison." Andre Sennwald's review in the *New York Times* seemed at a loss for how to describe the film, observing that Hepburn "dons trousers, dances gypsy-like on the English countryside and achieves what is customarily if discouragingly referred to as a personal triumph. . . . *Sylvia Scarlett* collects some odd characters and sets them on an odd sort of vagabond odyssey. . . . Something fresh, touching and funny seems to have gone into *Sylvia Scarlett*, but it got caught in the machinery" (Sennwald's review was published two days before he killed himself because of despair over his growing blindness; he also wrote that the film's story and characters "possess the blurred outlines of shapes that are being projected through a veil"). The *Chicago Tribune* called *Sylvia Scarlett* "a queer sort of picture, a fantastic, unhinged sort of thing," and Harry Long in *Modern Screen* wrote of Hepburn's performance, "She looks like a gargoyle on vacation without any makeup."

It's unfortunate that the traumatic effect on Cukor of the unamused, often hostile reception for what he described to Hepburn as "our little love child" caused him to feel defensive about *Sylvia Scarlett*. Despite his sneaking fondness for this *film maudit*, he had trouble publicly accepting the fact that it is one of his handful of greatest films, a masterpiece that became a cult favorite of cinephiles and feminists in later years, a development that caused him some bemusement. Hepburn in her autobiography is entirely dismissive, simply listing the singular *Sylvia Scarlett* as one of "a string of very dull movies" she made in that period. But dullness is the last crime of which the film could be accused.

With all the mercurial mood swings her character undergoes while flirting with or avoiding sexual encounters, Hepburn became somewhat uncertain while filming this valiant but difficult and risky role, confiding to her diary, "This picture makes no sense at all, and I wonder whether George Cukor is aware of the fact, because I certainly don't know what the hell I'm doing." Nevertheless, Cukor maintains a solid control of Sylvia's vicissitudes and brilliantly modulates the tone of the film between comedy and drama, often back and forth even within individual scenes. While giving Hepburn freedom to explore her quicksilver moods, he paradoxically keeps her carefully in hand with technically precise visual and dramatic direction of her hesitations, transitions, and emotional crescendos. Even if she didn't understand or appreciate what she achieved in this triumphant performance, she trusted her friend Cukor enough to let her inner "Jimmy" loose onscreen. One can sense Cukor's creative vitality, excitement, and reckless abandon in every frame of *Sylvia Scarlett*, despite the director's lingering doubts, which made him ask the Museum of Modern Art not to open a 1970 retrospective of his work with it. They started instead with *The Royal Family of Broadway* and moved *Sylvia Scarlett* later in the series.

Both men and women show romantic or sexual interest in Sylvia/Sylvester, and the film wittily and empathetically explores her emotions as a sexually ambiguous young person unsure how to behave in either guise. Jimmy Monkley tries to increase his hold over her by seeming to court her while they are running con games and then cavorting as a troupe of traveling commedia dell'arte performers, the Pink Pierrots. As James Naremore writes in his 2022 critical study, *Some Versions of Cary Grant*, the troupe all wear "nonbinary"-looking clown costumes in this nocturnal performance. Sylvia undergoes exhilarating as well as painful adventures in this picaresque film, which help to gradually but tentatively resolve her emotional conflict between her attraction toward the charming but cynical Monkley and her growing romantic interest in the handsome, rather epicene artist Michael Fane, who comes to see them perform. A running joke in the film is that her attempted confession that she's actually a girl keeps getting interrupted.

While experimenting with male and female costuming and behavior, Sylvia settles on what can be seen as a delicately balanced middle course in dealing with her gender identity. Her conflicts are also a matter of trying to determine her class identity in such a fluid situation. After she and her comrades undergo humiliation at the hands of Michael and his upper-class bohemian friends, Monkley advises her with bitter sarcasm, "Take it from me, it don't do to step outta your *clahs*." Though she initially is put off by Monkley's crass and untrustworthy manner and behavior, finding him a "brute," she becomes drawn to his example as a devil-may-care rule breaker. Her eagerness to join in the con games he teaches her is an implausibly rapid change in her attitude because it contradicts the unfortunately added prologue in which she condemns her father's thievery. But that glitch aside, it makes sense that she allows Monkley to seduce her into crime because she's already aiding and abetting her fugitive father, and their form of crime, like her sexual disguise, is about play-acting. Monkley's suspicions about Sylvia's disguise develop as he tries to increase his hold over her by seeming to court her. But she continues to be put off by his frequent cruelty.

A pivotal scene characteristic of Cukor is the way his characters bond through theatrical performance, in a joyous, marvelously choreographed and enacted little musical skit they spontaneously enact in a London mansion

8.2. A disaster in its time but a cult classic today, *Sylvia Scarlett* is the most daring, gender-bending film Cukor and Hepburn ever made. When Sylvia's mother dies and she escapes to England with her criminal father (Edmund Gwenn), she masquerades as Sylvester Scarlett, a handsome boy who forms a theatrical troupe, the Pink Pierrots, with (from left) Dennie Moore, Gwenn, and Cary Grant.

Source: Frame enlargement; RKO.

before hitting the road. They have invaded the home near Buckingham Palace where Maudie Tilt (Dennie Moore, hilarious in her first film), a comically coarse Cockney friend of Monkley's, works as a maid, a job she is eager to escape. Cukor frames the group's musical gamboling through a doorway that gives the effect of a proscenium; Monkley does a spirited dance with Maudie while Henry sings on the staircase, and the tipsy Sylvia sits on the railing, pretending to play a trombone. The film's cinematographer, Joseph August, casts light from below them, subtly suggesting invisible footlights. When they burst into "By the Beautiful Sea," it's a liberating celebration of their breaking away from conventional society.

The song gives them the idea to become artistes on their seaside summer tour as the scene dissolves to the Pink Pierrots' two caravans rolling through the Cornish countryside. Their transition from con games to theater may seem whimsically motivated, but there are deeper reasons, for as Cukor's biographer Patrick McGilligan observed, in his films "show business is a sanctuary for the misfit, bathing all in a beautiful and forgiving light. His deep feeling for all show people was one that complemented his own interior psychodrama—as someone who (like an actor playing a role) was to live one life onstage and another behind the curtain."

Eventually turned off by Monkley's flippant behavior and amorality, Sylvia finds herself more attracted to Michael after he and his bohemian friends come to watch the Pink Pierrots performing. But when at first they laugh mockingly at Maudie's singing and make her cry, Sylvia erupts in righteous rage, a scene that resembles actual incidents in Hepburn's later life when she would angrily lecture misbehaving theater audiences. Michael wins her over with a gracious apology on the stage. A gentlemanly sort, seductive but in a low-key way, he acts the part of a cynical ladies' man but seems rather fey with his wavy hair and mustache, robes and other dandyish outfits. Michael at heart is dreamily romantic, but he is also narcissistic and fickle and condescending toward her.

In the film's most complex and deftly acted and directed series of scenes, Sylvia cycles through a beguilingly funny and contradictory set of attitudes toward Michael at his country studio as she struggles to deal with her confused sexual feelings for him. Late at night, she comes to see him dressed in a man's suit and bowtie and fedora and climbs into his bedroom window. Despite her boldness, she behaves defensively, in an excessively "girly" manner, alternately flirtatious and shy, almost revealing her secret. "I know what it is that gives me a queer feeling when I look at you," Michael marvels, ostensibly referring to the androgynous impression she gives with the contradiction between her feminine manner and her mannish attire. When he invites her to bed with him for the night (innocently enough, but with subconscious sexual vibes), she gets all giggly, saying with a grin, "No—I *cahn't*," and jumps out the window.

The amusing conceit is that Michael doesn't fully see through her guise until she shows up again the next day at the studio—whose wide doorway and split level make it seem like a theatrical stage—to pose for him in full girlish regalia. Sylvia's shyness as she tries to display her slender figure accented by a flowery dress, while wearing a large sun hat she can hardly handle as it falls from her head as she's coming and going, is among the most touching aspects of the film, since Hepburn in her delightfully witty performance comes off as more awkward being a girl than she is being a boy.

And she may be even lovelier as a boy than as a girl, although it's ironic that in whatever guise, Hepburn is prettier in *Sylvia Scarlett* than perhaps in any other of her 1930s films, thanks in part to August's sensitively molded lighting of her angular features. That helps make her an object of sexual attraction for two women as well, although she pointedly does not reciprocate their advances. Maudie is shamelessly leading on Sylvia's increasingly deluded father, but when she gets the young woman alone, she saucily remarks, "Your face is as smooth as a girl's" and draws a mustache on her with an eyebrow pencil, prompting Sylvia to imitate Ronald Colman. But when Maudie roughly kisses her, the "young man" pushes her away with the excuse, "I've—I've got a girl already." The Code office, which made nearly fifty objections to "sex confusion" in the script, was especially worried about this scene, telling RKO that "such matters should not be treated for light comedy, and nothing suggestively emphasized by any horrified reaction on the part of Sylvia." But the result was Sylvia's relatively mild objection, which, as William J. Mann writes in his book on gay Hollywood, "actually made *Sylvia Scarlett* even gayer." Sylvia goes into what she thinks is her wagon but acts skittish when she finds Monkley undressing for bed and suggesting, "Let's curl up. . . . Hey, you'll make a proper little hot water bottle." Monkley is slyly conniving to test his virtual certitude that "Sylvester" is actually a girl, causing her to panic and jump out of the wagon, dashing into the woods.

The other woman attracted to Sylvia is Lily (Natalie Paley), a sophisticated Russian who is Michael's upper-class lover. Lily regards his odd young companion with mixed emotions of both jealousy and lust. She's the one who provocatively asks Sylvia the vexing question, "But were you a girl dressed as a boy, or are you a boy dressed as a girl?" A friend of Cukor making her American film debut, Natalia Pavlovna Paley was an actual Russian princess, a Romanov. Born in Paris, she was a daughter of Grand Duke Paul Alexandrovich and a first cousin of the last tsar, Nicholas II. One of her half-brothers helped murder Rasputin, and a brother was executed by the Bolsheviks the day after the murder of the ruling Romanov family. Paley before entering films in 1933 was a well-known model, including for the photographer George Hoyningen-Huene, later a close collaborator of Cukor on his color films. Paley adds a further level of exotic sexual flavor to *Sylvia Scarlett* and is an example of Cukor's forte for casting in ways that bring unexpected nuances to his work. He expertly drew a stylized and believable performance from Paley as the exiled aristocrat, suitably snobbish but also pathetic.

The enigmatic Lily coolly sizes up Sylvia as "such a pretty boy! . . . How charming! How *lovely* she is" and kisses her. But Sylvia is shattered when she realizes Michael seems to prefer the more worldly, experienced Lily and has only been dallying with her, calling her "a mere child." Cukor gives Sylvia a series of tightly framed, rawly emotional close-ups in which she tearfully struggles with her emotional confusion over this rebuff. Earlier she had confessed to Michael, "I can't control myself. I never could." Maintaining control is often a challenge for Cukor's characters in their precarious social situations, and some fail disastrously, such as Sylvia's father when he goes mad and leaps to his death, but the tightrope Sylvia/Sylvester is walking demands an extraordinary degree of control, and it takes her most of the film to figure out how to achieve it. Eventually Lily sadly comes to recognize, almost before Michael does, that he is actually enchanted with Sylvia, so she makes a strategic retreat in self-defense.

When Sylvia comes to his studio in women's clothing, she is exaggeratedly coquettish and awkward but pirouettes excitedly by herself while waiting for him, hands to her cheeks, then with arms stretched high. He says, "Good heavens, boy, what are you up to? Oh, I see! You're really a *girl!* I *wondered* why I was talking to you as I did! [*Laughs heartily*] I say, I hope I didn't say something to you I shouldn't have." She sits confusedly with her legs spread, making him laugh and correct her behavior. Cukor gives Hepburn tight close-ups to show Sylvia's agonized reaction, tears brimming, to

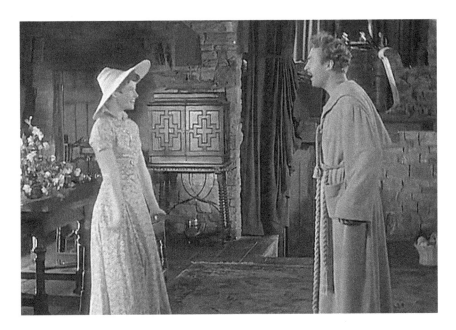

8.3. Brian Aherne's bohemian artist Michael Fane, who earlier told Sylvester, "I know what it is that gives me a queer feeling when I look at you," doesn't realize her full complex identity until she comes to his summer home to bashfully reveal the feminine side of her nature.

Source: Frame enlargement; RKO.

her failed girlishness. Michael pecks her chastely on her cheek but quickly gets stimulated and tries to give her a real kiss, but she pushes him away. Embarrassedly itemizing her supposed bodily flaws—choppy hairdo, lots of freckles, big feet, unmanicured fingernails—she declares, "I—I'm rude and rough and clumsy. I—I should have stayed as a boy. It's all I'm fit for."

Michael teases her by putting on a girlish high-pitched voice before declaring that he will teach her "the tricks of the trade" of femininity, adding suggestively, with "all the funny bits." Acting as a surrogate director, he sends Sylvia outside to reenact her entrance after her first clumsy "rehearsal," and this time her manner is more graceful as she performs femininity but is still exaggeratedly coquettish and artificial. Though Michael seems mostly heterosexual, his bohemian nature and effete side put him at ease with his "queer" attraction to Sylvester, which amuses rather than threatens him and puts her at ease too, ultimately making them a suitable couple. Although Sylvia seemingly has to choose one identity over another at the end of the film (at least temporarily), and that may be in part the film's single concession to the commercial marketplace, it is plausible and meaningful for her to pair up with Michael, since both of them show flexibility about their sexuality.

What makes *Sylvia Scarlett* so enchanting and provocative throughout is not just the cross-dressing but its keen sense—again far ahead of its time—that gender is a performance, one that has to be learned and ultimately should be questioned critically, as Sylvia does throughout the film before trusting Michael enough to run away with him into the woods at the end. The camp sensibility, which often manifests itself in Cukor's work, is at its strongest in *Sylvia Scarlett*, with its unabashed gayness, elaborate role-playing, and sense of theatricality as a way of life (and in the droll tongue-in-cheek mockery of the imposed prologue). The lightly closeted gay director and the more deeply closeted bisexual Hepburn were expert at the rituals and maneuvers of "passing" in their own lives, so Sylvia's masquerade was almost second nature for them, even if it was far more overt than anything else either dared to do before or after on the screen.

Camp had its roots in the dandyism practiced by Oscar Wilde and other "decadent" artists, poets, and dramatists. The *Oxford English Dictionary* first defined camp in 1909 as "ostentatious, exaggerated, affected, theatrical." That approach to life came more into vogue in the 1960s when the gay movement became more assertive and influential. The raison d'être of *Sylvia Scarlett*, treating gender identity as performative, is an insight that has gained currency during the twenty-first century. In her influential 1964 essay "Notes on 'Camp,'" Susan Sontag points out that the phenomenon appeals to those who "constitute themselves as aristocrats of taste . . . [and] homosexuals, by and large, constitute the vanguard—and the most articulate audience—of Camp." Camp, she writes, is an attitude intertwined with sexual avant-gardism and bisexuality: "The androgyne is certainly one of the great images of Camp sensibility. . . . What is most beautiful in virile men is something feminine; what is most beautiful in feminine women is something masculine."

Cukor's penchant for camp is also related to the pervasive sense of theatricality in his work. For as Sontag notes, camp is "the farthest extension, in sensibility, of the metaphor of life as theater," a sensibility "peculiarly suited as a justification and projection of a certain aspect of the situation of homosexuals." And Cukor's penchant for finding comedy wherever possible—as he said of working with actors, "most of all, I share humor with them"—is related to the "detachment" inherent in the camp sensibility: "Camp proposes a comic vision of the world," she writes. ". . . Camp is playful, anti-serious. More precisely, Camp involves a new, more complex relation to 'the serious.' . . . Camp is the modern dandyism."

The American movie-going public in 1935 did not expect something so esoteric as camp from the already eccentric young actress who had come on the scene only three years earlier and already won an Oscar for playing a sweet ingénue. The unusually virulent backlash against Hepburn's dizzyingly complex foray into cross-dressing—which Cukor and Hepburn, misreading the public's appetite for sexual experimentation onscreen, naïvely did not intend to be outrageous, merely provocative—caused both to backtrack to some extent in their approaches to gender and sexuality in their subsequent work. Cukor had already experienced some pushback to his flaming gay scene at the end of *Our Betters*, but that had not discouraged him as much as the reaction to *Sylvia Scarlett* did. He took some advantage of the new sexual freedom of films from the 1960s onward but was not as "out" again as a director until the very last moment of his career in 1981, although the ending of *Rich and Famous* is only tentatively overt in teasing the audience with a quasi-lesbian kiss. Hepburn, after the 1930s, took pains to retool her screen image as more determinedly heterosexual, sometimes even sacrificing her independence to men in her movies and rarely venturing into more than subtly suggestive hints of gender fluidity. The effect was more artistically damaging on her career than Cukor's, since it limited the range of the roles she played even though they kept her safely bankable and eventually made her a beloved iconic figure.

Cukor prided himself on his ability to survive the hard knocks of a long film career, and he maintained his customary discretion in his personal life. He couldn't have masqueraded as heterosexual even if he had tried or if the public had been more interested in directors' lives. And in any case, as a director valued for his versatility and range as a storyteller and adapter of literary material, he had more flexibility than a star in his story choices. Without being so outwardly daring again, he nevertheless adroitly managed to imbue his films with subtextual explorations of gender complexities and to find stories that enabled him to present endlessly supple views of both male and female sexuality.

But as Sontag would put it many years later, what camp taste does is "to find the success in certain passionate failures." And *Sylvia Scarlett* had a much more salutary effect on the career of Cary Grant than on Hepburn's. Grant didn't have the burden of carrying the picture or the blame attached to it. Instead he received highly favorable reviews, *Variety* declaring that he "virtually steals the picture" and Sennwald writing in the *New York Times* that Grant, "whose previous work has too often been that of a charm merchant, turns actor in the role of the unpleasant cockney and is surprisingly good at it."

Playing Monkley with roguish abandon greatly advanced the development of Grant's star persona by enabling him to tap into his roots as a performer. Grant was born Archibald Leach in Bristol, England, joined an acrobatic troupe at age fourteen, and performed in vaudeville and on Broadway before he settled in Hollywood in 1931. Not a genuine Cockney (that refers to a native of east London), Grant picked up Cockney speech patterns and mannerisms from his background in British music halls. Although the accent he developed in his film work tended to be of the posh, amusingly mannered mid-Atlantic kind, Grant occasionally reverted to brash Cockney characterizations again in films, notably in *Gunga Din* (1939) and his personal favorite, *None but the Lonely Heart* (1944). James Naremore writes that "although Grant was intensely serious and even anxious about his job, he liked to amuse people on the set with Cockney imitations and off-color stories from English music halls. This usually relaxed the players, putting them in the right mood and facilitating performance."

Cukor initially resisted casting Grant in *Sylvia Scarlett*, saying he hadn't gone "weak-kneed" over the actor, but it was fortunate that the director gave in to Hepburn's enthusiastic urging to borrow Grant from Paramount (it was the first of four major films the actors would make together; the others are Cukor's *Holiday* [1938] and *The Philadelphia Story* [1940] and Howard Hawks's *Bringing Up Baby* [1938]). Cukor always had a shrewd sense of how to merge an actor's off-camera self with his on-camera role, and in Grant's case the director gave him the freedom to relax and have fun with the part of Jimmy Monkley, exploring facets of his personality that had been stifled by Hollywood filmmakers who didn't know what to do with his diverse talents. "George taught him how to be funny," said Hepburn shrewdly. "He brought out the Archie Leach in Cary Grant." That enabled Grant to go well beyond the stiff "tall, dark, and handsome" secondary roles or leading man he had been stuck with, even when he played a surrogate for the director Josef von Sternberg in the 1932 Marlene Dietrich vehicle *Blonde Venus* or dallied opposite Mae West in two 1933 films, *She Done Him Wrong* and *I'm No Angel.*

Playing Monkley represented a considerable step toward the molding of the suave, dryly humorous, sexually compelling yet emotionally reserved persona that would make Grant one of the most enduring male stars. Grant's raffish character in the Cukor film, who alternately appears sinister and captivating, speaks in drolly rhythmical vaudevillian patter and pursues Sylvia and other women with a flippant, sarcastic manner that barely conceals a deep-seated cynicism toward womanhood. In the 1937 romantic comedy classic *The Awful Truth*, the director Leo McCarey completed the process of creating Grant's star persona by bringing out his more warmhearted, easygoing, vulnerable side, which had been protected by the veneer of his sardonic detachment. His role as a philandering husband who reunites with his ex-wife after they divorce allows Grant's charm to operate in a still somewhat roguish way, but without the fascinating but repellent heartlessness of Monkley's coldly calculating approach to life. When Monkley makes a crass remark about Lily's failed suicide attempt—Sylvia dashes into the ocean to save her, a stunt during which Hepburn almost drowned—Sylvia tells him haughtily, through her tears, "You've got the mind of a pig," and he replies with a gloomy look, almost regretfully, "It's a pig's world."

Monkley is not a total heel, however. He displays some warmth toward Sylvia when her drink-maddened father commits suicide, telling her, "You and me, we suit," the closest he can come to a proposal. And he reacts with humorous grace when she and Michael, finding comfort together in their unorthodox gender roles, form a romantic pair at the end. Monkley is squabbling on a train in his new, misguided relationship with Lily when he sees Sylvia and Michael escaping into the woods. Rather than becoming angry, he collapses with uproarious laughter, drawing his legs up to his chest gleefully as Lily tosses her billowy muff at him on the fadeout.

Cukor fondly recalled that Grant "burst into bloom" in *Sylvia Scarlett.* "In fact, I'm *everything!*," Monkley gaily sings while introducing himself during the performance of the Pink Pierrots, as if to celebrate Grant's newfound opportunity to display many parts of his complex personality. And despite the anguish the negative audience reception for this audacious artistic adventure caused Cukor and Hepburn, the director recalled the filming with pleasure: "Every day was Christmas on the set."

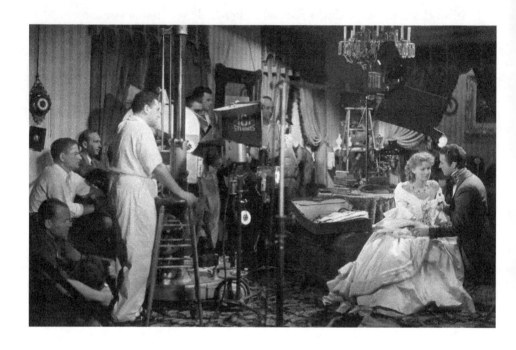

9.1. Cukor filming *Camille* (1936) on an MGM soundstage with Greta Garbo's favorite cinematographer, William Daniels (behind camera in white shirt and glasses). Daniels also shot such other Garbo classics as *Flesh and the Devil*, *Queen Christina*, and *Ninotchka* and four other Cukor films, including *Dinner at Eight* and *Pat and Mike*.

Source: MGM/Alamy.

9

GRETA GARBO IN *CAMILLE*

"Silent film, in my opinion, was truly great for reasons that have nothing to do with talking pictures," Jean Renoir observed in 1961.

I believe silent film was based on hypnotism. It was completely unrelated to the dramatic arts. . . . Silent cinema was a cinema of close-ups. The most effective figures in silent film were those with hypnotic qualities. One of the best was Greta Garbo. You didn't see a Garbo film for the plot. The plots were silly and pointless. . . . But the truth is, a close-up of Greta Garbo looks out imposingly on the audience. . . . The close-up is onscreen, the appropriate music is playing, and the audience is in ecstasy. Suddenly, we feel as if an invisible bridge has been created between this enormous face on the screen and all the people watching.

The "hypnotic" qualities Garbo brought to her work in silent cinema were not always able to find full expression in her talking pictures, which were often of uneven style and quality. Her ability to bring "ecstatic" emotions to the audience could seem diluted and prosaic when she was placed in dramatic situations intended to seem more realistic than her poetically stylized silent work. But her special qualities were carried over into talkies by a few directors who had a close rapport with the actress and were able to integrate her close-ups into storylines that allowed her persona to create that "invisible bridge" with the audience. The best of her talkies before her retirement in 1941—Rouben Mamoulian's *Queen Christina* (1933), Clarence Brown's *Anna Karenina* (1935), Cukor's *Camille* (1936), and Ernst Lubitsch's *Ninotchka* (1939)—equal or surpass the impact of her finest work in silent cinema. But to give a shining example from a Garbo silent, in Brown's *Flesh and the Devil* (1927), a romantic drama costarring her off-screen lover John Gilbert, their startlingly erotic love scenes remain among the most passionate ever filmed. They seem to reveal her soul through her body, in the way, as Renoir put it, Garbo had of making every spectator feel she was in communion directly with him or her.

The story of *Camille*, like those of *Queen Christina* and *Ninotchka*, is not silly and pointless, and the strength of the material given her to work with in those three highly disparate films helps account for the special quality of her performances. Talking pictures needed a more substantial world and set of supporting characters to surround her. Garbo's sublime Marguerite Gautier in *Camille* is often considered her greatest performance, and that is thanks in part to its being based on an enduring literary source, the 1848 novel *La dame aux camélias/The Lady of the Camellias* and the 1852 stage version by Alexandre Dumas *fils*. The venerable tale about a dying French courtesan in love with a romantic young man has been the source of more than forty films and television productions as well as Verdi's opera *La traviata*.

Cukor's *Camille* is the gold standard for this story in cinema, not least because it provides a period setting that is lavish but unostentatiously rendered by her favorite cinematographer, William Daniels, and by the set decorators Henry Grace and Jack D. Moore, whose design helps trap Garbo's tragic woman of uncommon refinement in a lethal marketplace of sexual commerce. The film makes the audience feel the literally suffocating force of that harshly male-dominated environment in its depiction of the withering of the flower Marguerite represents as she dies of tuberculosis after being persuaded to sacrifice her love for a naïve young man, Armand Duval (Robert Taylor), by his father (Lionel Barrymore). The screenplay, primarily by Zoë Akins, revolves around the conflict between the men who buy Camille's favors and the idealistic Armand, who offers her a form of devotion that is, in its way, almost as stifling, while at the same time impossibly exalting.

Cukor's rare ability to turn classic literary works into compelling cinematic productions in this period was first shown in his crucial assistance with *All Quiet on the Western Front* and then with his superb film of *Little Women* and his capturing the spirit of Dickens's *David Copperfield*, despite that film's serious limitations. Those two highly atmospheric adaptations benefited greatly from Cukor's increased absorption in period and location research. Other than for prestige, a motive that carried considerable weight with studios in the Golden Age of Hollywood, the principal reason for delving into a period tale, then as now, is that it has something to say that seems relevant to the audience of the time the film is made. The strength of the female-dominated family under wartime stress in *Little Women* and the outcast boy's travail in the harsh Victorian society of *David Copperfield* had particular resonance with Depression-era audiences.

On the whole, even though many theaters were still racially segregated in that period, filmgoers in the mid-1930s otherwise were more heterogeneous than today's audience for American films, which are mostly spectacles aimed at males between the ages of twelve and twenty-four. Back in the thirties, before the advent of television, films usually had to appeal simultaneously to the whole family, from children to grandparents, and women accordingly had much more influence in the choice of films, which is why so many of the leading stars in that period were female. Today, literary adaptations and films about mature women are mostly the province of the older, more educated and sophisticated audience that watches cable television and streaming services.

Cukor's belief in the kind of faithful adaptation that did not attempt to "improve" the lasting works he filmed by "fixing" their flaws sometimes resulted in uneven quality, most seriously in the second half of his *David Copperfield*, when the boy becomes a dull adult. Cukor's 1936 film of *Romeo and Juliet* was sunk in advance by its absurd MGM star casting, the middle-aged Norma Shearer and Leslie Howard as Shakespeare's star-crossed teenaged lovers. The production is excessively lavish as well, which further deadens its dramatic impact, although the film does have one powerful scene, the long take in which Shearer, unusually focused and intense under Cukor's direction, drinks the fatal potion. *Camille* did not present the same kind of problem as the other classics filmed by Cukor in that period. The author, who was only twenty-five when the novel was published, based it on his romance with an actual ill-fated courtesan, and the story retains its poignancy today, although the dramatic situation in the novel tends toward monotony.

Cukor had enough clout by the time of *Camille* to exert authority over the scriptwriting process, and he and others involved in the production were unhappy with an initial adaptation by the veteran screenwriter Frances Marion (who had adapted the story for a 1915 silent film version of *Camille* starring Clara Kimball Young) and her romantic partner, James Hilton, the younger British author of *Lost Horizon* and *Goodbye, Mr. Chips*. Cukor's stalwart collaborator Akins, with her expert ability to streamline discursive prose into a compelling dramatic structure, came to the rescue. Her screenplay highlights Marguerite's desperate inability to break free from the tragic strictures of her social situation: male dominance, excessive expenditures, crushing indebtedness, and failing health (the script, however, was excessively long at 190 pages but was expertly trimmed by Cukor during production to concentrate on the essentials). The central conflict between Marguerite's cynical wealthy patron, Baron de Varville (Henry Daniell), and her more modestly situated young admirer, Armand, perfectly captures her struggle between commercializing her body and being able to give her love without encumbrance.

The pitfalls that had to be avoided in filming *Camille* in 1936, as Cukor recognized, were the temptation to oversentimentalize the material, the risk of portraying Armand as a hopeless young sap, and the audience's distance from the hypocritical social codes of wealthy men in the nineteenth century who maintain stables of kept women they could not present in polite society. The opening title card sets the story in 1847, when: "In the gay half-world of Paris . . . the code was discretion—but the game was romance." Cukor is eminently suited to bring out all the nuances of a code of discretion, since he lived by one in his own life and was experienced in dramatizing how it could ensnare or liberate people of both sexes.

Furthermore, as MGM's Irving Thalberg mentioned in a story conference for *Camille*, one of the last films he supervised before his untimely death during its production, "We have to live within the mores of the day. Men marry whores in our present society—women who have been promiscuous—and they very often make marvelous wives. In this town you find them all over the place." Cukor knew that milieu and its subtle cruelties and hypocrisies inside and out, as did Akins, so they were able to expertly develop a similar social framework onscreen. Thalberg warned against making Armand "an awful little prig" in his disapproval of Marguerite's way of life, and the writer and director took pains to make the young man's understandable jealousy not only his primary vexation but also emotionally convincing without making him appear overwrought. Thalberg and Cukor addressed the problem partly by stressing the sexual charge between Marguerite and Armand and the desperation of their mutual desire in defiance of social circumstances.

"You know something I've always found frightfully erotic," Cukor said in a 1972 interview with *Esquire* when asked about the trend toward increased eroticism onscreen. "It was in *Camille*, the scene where she leaves the table at the party: that's the most original thing, the way Garbo played it— that sort of hot impatience for each other. She and Armand leave the room. She had a real coughing spell. If you noticed, this is what was erotic: she just leaned over, her body didn't touch him, and she gave him small kisses all around the face. It was so extraordinary." That gesture was suggested by Garbo, who had behaved in the same uninhibited way in a love scene for her 1928 silent film *The Divine Woman*. The forms Garbo's eroticism took were often surprising, the result of sudden dropping of her formidable restraint, displaying a peasant quality underneath, making her seem a force of nature.

And none of her performances is more sensually powerful or emotionally subtle than her Marguerite Gautier. Thalberg told Cukor after seeing one of her early scenes, "She's never been quite like that, she's never been as good!" When Cukor asked how he could say that, since she was simply sitting in a box at the opera, Thalberg said, "I know, but she's *unguarded*." That was one of Cukor's great abilities as a director, to make a climate in which his actors, even the most reserved or private of them, could feel so relaxed that they became unguarded and revealed more of themselves onscreen than they ever had before.

Cukor explained his approach to the film by quoting Henry James about how the enduring quality of *La dame aux camélias* "remains in its combination of freshness and form, of the feeling of the springtime of life and the sense of the conditions of the theatre. . . . It is all champagne and tears—fresh perversity, fresh credulity, fresh passion, fresh pain. We have each seen it both well done and ill done. . . . Nothing makes any difference—it carries with it an April air: some tender young man and some coughing young woman have only to speak the lines to give it a great place among the love-stories of the world." That is the intoxicating mixture Cukor manages to capture, the freshness and the unsettling blend of disparate moods. But as he told Lambert, the material "presented some enormous problems, because you had to make a modern audience understand its conventions."

Most of all, the question of a woman's reputation and social standing in that society in contrast to that of a supposedly well-born young man, however unjustly, was crucial to convey dramatically. The audience needs to know why Marguerite would reluctantly but nobly acquiesce to Armand's father's demand for her to give his son up in order not to destroy his future prospects. All this had to be made both intelligible and affecting while not descending into melodramatic excess. Cukor and Garbo do so in her scene with Lionel Barrymore. Her regretful understanding of his social and financial arguments gives him a growing respect for Marguerite as he shifts from making a demand to "ask this great sacrifice of you as humbly as I'd ask a great favor of a queen." Garbo conveys her intense pain with a piece of behavior she added to the scene: she sinks to her knees and leans against a table, her face pressed against her arm, with her eyes revealing her distress. Cukor's close-ups featuring Garbo's eyes are similar to the close-ups of Jean Simmons leaning on her arms as her eyes watch the stage in *The Actress*, but in this case there is a feeling of devastation rather than enthrallment. The Cukor heroine privately contemplates her distant destiny, whether it be empty or luminous. Marguerite determines to play-act fickle hostility toward Armand, but when she does so, Cukor's camera gives us privileged glimpses of her anguish. And as Cukor put it, "Most ladies cough and splutter their way through this part," but her illness is suggested here with far more delicacy.

Cukor and his collaborators (including the composer Herbert Stothart, whose score is notably restrained) adroitly avoid the pitfalls of the story by treating the charged romantic and dramatic situations as lightly as possible, giving Marguerite a self-defensive air of jocularity and insouciance until she is unable to keep up the pretense. She tries to appear impervious to the pain she is suffering both bodily and socially before her circumstances become overwhelming. Cukor also allows the relatively inexperienced Taylor to play Armand with unadorned sincerity and to express passion, jealousy, and bitterness without descending into bathos.

Especially as he aged, Taylor could be a stiff and sour actor, but his performance here (at age twenty-four and twenty-five) is a marvel of youthful grace and sensitivity, and his male beauty has a luster approaching Garbo's own state of perfection; Cukor's casting of handsome young men often had that kind of appeal. "Armand is historically a terrible part," the director reflected. "I never quite knew why: perhaps because it was usually played by middle-aged men. As a result he seemed stupid doing the things he did. When you get someone really young playing Armand, you understand him; he becomes appealing, with a kind of real youthful passion; whereas if he were thirty-eight years old you'd think, 'Oh, you ass, why did you do that?' So that very crudity, that intensity of young passion made Robert Taylor an extremely good Armand." Armand's impassioned callowness under Cukor's direction is not comical because of the young man's sincerity and how Marguerite is touched by it, even after reflexively mocking him.

9.2. Cukor's direction of Garbo's exquisitely beautiful, quietly moving death scene in *Camille* was influenced by the director's experience of visiting his mother on her deathbed soon before the shooting of that scene. Robert Taylor costars as Armand Duval, the lover of the courtesan Marguerite Gautier in this adaptation of *The Lady of the Camellias* by Alexandre Dumas *fils*.

Source: Frame enlargement; MGM.

Garbo's moments of vulnerability and gradual collapse and descent toward death are beautifully controlled and judged by Cukor. His delicate handling of Garbo and her flawless perception of how to play the character as a tragic heroine without begging the audience for pity vindicate his belief that Marguerite was the role Garbo was meant to play, even if she had misgivings before she committed to doing so. The ultimate effect of *Camille*, in its treating profound emotional situations with restraint and discretion, is akin to Wordsworth's line about "thoughts that do often lie too deep for tears."

"Garbo Laughs"—the celebrated ad line for Ernst Lubitsch's 1939 comedy *Ninotchka*, starring Garbo as an icy Soviet commissar who loosens up romantically on an official visit to Paris—was something of a false tease. Although *Ninotchka* was her first outright comedy, structured around a scene in which her thawing is accomplished with uproarious laughter, she had laughed before in a number of pictures, including *Queen Christina* and, frequently, in *Camille*. And her close friends knew that a mischievous and often droll sensibility accompanied her notoriously distant air of melancholia. From the opening scene in *Camille*, when her older companion/pimp, Prudence (Laura Hope Crews, acting less scatterbrained than usual), is doing her deceptively fluttery but coldly mercenary matchmaking in a carriage, Marguerite regards sexual intrigue with an air of detached amusement. She is jaded about sex and admittedly uncertain if such a thing as love exists, but her sense of humor also enables her to maintain a cautious emotional distance from having her feelings hurt or insulted, as they often are by men in *Camille*. The Dumas story portrays sexual relations in a transactional light, inextricable from monetary considerations of payment or the cost of a life of a kept woman constantly on display for sale (or rent) in social situations at a theater or gambling house or in an expensive carriage on the boulevards.

Marguerite tries to remain above the squalid depths of her milieu, but she can't avoid being tainted by it. When Armand attends her raucous birthday party at her home, he is quietly appalled at the vulgar behavior of her fellow courtesans and their male patrons. Prudence plants a foot on the dinner table while asking Armand's gay friend Gaston (Rex O'Malley) to remove her shoe for comfort, and a crude joke of Gaston's makes the rounds to peals of risqué laughter. The party scene echoes the comedy about call girls and their johns in *Girls About Town* (and both films contain an auction of a woman's belongings), but with more bite this time. Marguerite asks Armand if he's shocked by ribaldry, and when he says he knows all of his friend's jokes but "I'd sooner they weren't repeated at your table," she replies, "Oh, come, come, I'm not a colonel's daughter just out of the convent." And in a line by Akins that Cukor especially admired for its acuity, she tells him, "These are the only friends I have, and I'm no better than they are."

She's trying to tamp down Armand's unrealistic idealism, which the narrative continually threatens to destroy, even as he maintains his admiration for her finer nature. Prudence's loud, crass behavior and the nasty, coarse nature of a rival courtesan, Olympe (Lenore Ulric)—both of them heartlessly mercenary—serve as a counterpoint to Marguerite's quieter, dignified, and caring behavior. These perfectly cast women set off Marguerite's contrasting good taste and the impossible beauty of Garbo. And as the film progresses, Gaston's initial frivolity gives way to a gentle sense of compassion toward Marguerite, causing him to mature and grow in stature, especially in their final scene together.

Cukor's use of Garbo's usually neglected penchant for jollity keeps the drama from being weighed down by the onerous social stigmas surrounding Marguerite and her undisguised acknowledgment of her impending mortality. Early in the film, when a friend compliments her appearance, Marguerite responds, "I always look well when I'm near death." Cukor has Garbo speak the line in a matter-of-fact manner devoid of self-pity, and her light, bantering tone is sustained throughout her early meetings with Armand, in contrast to his earnest sincerity. And yet the changing tone of their love scenes is deftly modulated: a scene the script suggests be played for laughs, Marguerite's telling Armand, "You know, once I had a little dog, and he always looked sad when I was sad, and I loved him so," is played instead as deeply touching by Garbo and Cukor, one of the film's many emotional frissons.

The initial meeting between Armand and Marguerite at a theater is a comical case of mistaken identity—she confuses him with the older, dour, imperious baron, whom she meets a bit later that night but doesn't notice at first—and even Armand, returning to her box after being sent for *marrons glacés*, has a smile and a shrug upon finding the box empty, realizing she's gone with the real baron, with whom he can't compete financially. But Armand sentimentally picks up a handkerchief she has dropped—in the script it's a glove, but the handkerchief is a sign of her illness, discreetly used when her consumption is exacerbated by high emotion—and saves it to return when they meet again months later. It's only when she begins responding more ardently to his overtures that his mood becomes more insistent.

Their relationship escalates when she has a coughing attack at the party as it gets rowdily out of hand, and she takes refuge in a darkened room lit only by candles and a fireplace, collapsing on a divan. He follows, expressing concern for her health. When she calls him a "child," the word is belied by the childlike sound of her own voice as she tells him with a hint of genuine tenderness, "Too much wine has made you sentimental." She draws out the syllables of the last word in an exquisitely lingering manner, ironically showing herself to be filled with what Cukor called "true sentiment. . . . You had to find the real feeling and let it come through," as it does in her intonations. When Armand declares his desire to take care of Camille, the camera tracks in as he grabs her by the arms, insisting, "No one has ever loved you as I love you." She turns her head away and laughs slightly, replying in a mocking tone, "That may be true, but what can I do about it?"

But after he presses his demand for love, and she offends him by laughing again, she has a change of heart, leaning her head against the divan and murmuring to herself with a half-smile, her eyes roaming the darkness, "After all, when one may not have long to live, why shouldn't one have fancies?" She throws her head back in a familiar Garbo gesture of abandon, allowing him to kiss her. To sharpen the contrast between her assumed gaiety and the urgency of the moment, Daniels, the cinematographer, while keeping Armand in shadows, lights her face brightly to convey her incandescent emotions along with the heat of her tubercular condition. As the scene ends with Armand kneeling before her, she leans forward and makes her extraordinary gesture of kissing him greedily all over his face without making other bodily contact, one of the scenes that made Cukor feel "staggered by her lightness of touch— the wantonness, the perversity of the way she played it."

Part of Cukor's ability to draw the best from Garbo was in knowing when *not* to direct her, such as when she strode swiftly through a crowd of men at the theater early in the film, and he resisted an impulse to tell her to parade herself more slowly. He realized that her instinct was correct, that every man would be looking at her without her having to solicit attention. Here, and many times elsewhere in the film, his "code of discretion" as a director meshed with her instincts. She also asked him to keep out of her sight while she was acting, since she found distracting his habit of being so empathetic with his actors while the camera was rolling that he tended to make grotesque faces.

The passion between Armand and Marguerite inevitably becomes untenable and results in their ostracization from high society. The baron cuts her off cruelly, even slapping her after paying her debts, and Armand's father convinces the distraught Marguerite to leave his son after a summer idyll in the country, a self-sacrifice that requires her to play-act being hateful toward him. One of the bravura highlights of the film is the searing scene of the baron, after arriving at her apartment unexpectedly, playing the piano with increasingly vehemence and noise as Armand is ringing her doorbell for a late-night tryst. The suavely menacing Daniell's triumphant grin is chilling as he engages Marguerite in dueling ironic laughter over her remark that the caller might be "the great romance of my life."

Caught in this financial vise, Marguerite undergoes public humiliation as well. Just as harsh as the slap is the scene at the gambling salon when Marguerite, surprised to see Armand again, drops her fan. When the baron tells her twice, "You've dropped your fan," Garbo "did the most unforgettable thing," Cukor recalled: she bent down gracefully, the camera tilting with her, in a gesture that conveys her victimization but is also her elegant way of showing him up as the crude boor he is. She did the gesture "like a dancer . . . Isadora Duncan . . . it was pure grace when she did it," Cukor marveled. Moments later, when the two men are introduced, Marguerite again drops the fan, and Armand shows no hesitation in picking it up, remarking, "Any gentleman would have done the same." The baron instantly steps forward to challenge him, and their public confrontation leads to a duel.

Camille foreshadows similar situations in Max Ophüls's 1953 masterpiece *Madame de . . .* ; in both films the woman is trapped by the self-destructive opulence her society has driven her to choose as a way of life. *Camille* contains numerous references to Marguerite's humble origins—her life on a farm, work in a linen shop, illiteracy until six years earlier, failure to read books—to give us a sharp sense of the limited options available to French women in that period. Dumas, Akins, and Cukor encourage us to see Marguerite's actions not as selfish and callous reflections on the limitations of her love for Armand but as desperate measures for survival in Parisian society as her health continues to fade.

Kenneth Tynan's famous observation "What when drunk, one sees in other women, one sees in Garbo sober" applies nowhere better than in the sublime death sequence that occupies the last seven minutes of *Camille* after Armand's arrival in her bedchamber. The actress was known for never wanting to see rushes or even her completed films, because they always fell short of her expectations, but she made an exception for this passage. It is one of the great operatic death scenes in movies—ranking with Lillian Gish's in King Vidor's silent *La Bohème*, which was so vivid the director briefly thought she had actually died—and its bone-chillingly precise reflection of mortality is based in part on Cukor's experience witnessing the death of his Hungarian immigrant mother.

Helen (Ilona) Gross Cukor died of stomach cancer at age sixty-two in Beverly Hills on June 6, 1936, in the month before filming began on *Camille*, a loss that, according to Cukor's biographer Patrick McGilligan, "devastated" the director. But Cukor admitted, "I use *everything* [for his work]. My mind is always taking notes. . . . I may have passed something on to Garbo, almost without realizing it. You don't tell her how to say 'I'm strong,' but somehow you find yourself creating a climate in which she can say it that way." Garbo's harrowing behavior on her deathbed conveys her extreme weakness, a sense that she is barely there physically. During the shooting, the actress was plagued with a series of illnesses that probably were partly caused by the psychosomatic stress of playing this demanding role, which she initially resisted, ostensibly because its self-sacrificial nature reminded her of her previous film, *Anna Karenina*, although Cukor thought she was born to play Camille, just as Hepburn was to play Jo in *Little Women*.

When Marguerite hears that Armand has come, her eyes are glazed, but she goes into a heartrending state of confused ecstatic panic, begging her maid to lift her to a chair so she can comb her hair and apply rouge. But no sooner does she sit in the chair when she impatiently demands to see him. Armand's abashed behavior, full of shame over misjudging her self-sacrificial reason for rejecting him, makes this as passionate a love scene as any earlier in the story. Marguerite rises unsteadily to greet him but collapses into his arms, her head slipping back, and her breathlessness is manifest in her near-inability to speak. She converses only in a whisper, a direction Cukor drew from his last visits with his mother. Marguerite's last words: "Perhaps it's better if I live in your heart, where the world can't see me. If I'm dead there'll be no stain on our love." As she dies in Armand's arms in a tight two-shot, we see her face when he doesn't, and her eyes briefly roll up into her head as her eyelids close. That is when we realize, before him, that she is gone, but he knows it when her head snaps back. An intense highlight on her silhouette appears at that moment, and a little smile forms on her face as it settles. He rests her head gently back into the chair. As we hear his voice off-screen begging, "Come back," the camera tracks in to fill the screen with her face. Just before the quick fadeout, the eerie lighting effect briefly illuminates the shape of her cheeks and skull against the shadows, making her seem almost translucent.

In that frisson, one of Garbo's most "hypnotic" close-ups, in a scene that stands as a highlight of acting in the cinema, the audience, as Renoir put it, is truly "in ecstasy."

10

KATHARINE HEPBURN AND CARY GRANT IN *HOLIDAY*

C ukor's films often contain little, offbeat worlds inside bigger, more conventional ones. They serve as covert refuges and escape hatches for unconventional characters, and more often than not, Cukor's little worlds are associated with show business. The freedom such enclaves offer and their hidden qualities draw from the same basic source of artistic strength that runs throughout his work, the exploring of nuances and subtexts. The fourth-floor "playroom" that Linda Seton, Katharine Hepburn's character in *Holiday* (1938), makes her own human-sized "home," as she calls it, within her father's large, soulless New York mansion is one of those small worlds.

The upstairs playroom is her hideaway and where much of the film takes place. It is filled with rebellious delight and creative individualism carried out in defiance of restrictive social norms. This place of play is also partly a site of melancholy, carrying the bittersweet memory of Linda's late mother, who decorated it as her hideaway from being a Seton, and the place where Linda and her drunken brother, Ned, have their heartbreaking conversation about his self-destructive form of escape. But it is from this retreat that Linda plots her triumphant departure from the bonds of the Seton household and dashes off to become the romantic partner of a free man, Cary Grant's Johnny Case, on his indefinite "holiday" from a life in the business world.

Philip Barry's plays, also including *The Philadelphia Story*, which Cukor directed with Hepburn and Grant at MGM in 1940, were ideally matched with the director's tastes, style, and themes (Cukor also directed some retakes on the director Edward H. Griffith's 1932 RKO film of Barry's *The Animal Kingdom*, a mildly entertaining but lackluster romantic comedy starring Leslie Howard and Ann Harding; Hepburn had been fired from the stage version of that play during rehearsals). Barry came from a struggling family business background but advanced his writing career with a Yale education, and as a result he had an ambivalent attitude toward wealth, which enlivened his plays and enabled him to capture some of the complex zeitgeist of those unsettled times. Fascinated by the social problems of the privileged, he often dramatized their intramural conflicts over money and position while taking the side of unconventional characters who challenge the attitude expressed by a character in *Holiday* (Linda's sister, Julia, played by Doris Nolan) that "there's no such thrill in the world as making money."

Cukor admired the way Barry deftly intermingles light comedy with darker subtextual issues (epitomized in *Holiday* by the alcoholic despondency of Ned,

10.1. "What's it like—to get drunk, Ned?": While mourning the tragic fate of her alcoholic brother (Lew Ayres), Linda Seton (Hepburn) seeks his help in coping with her own distress over falling in love with her sister's fiancé.

Source: Frame enlargement; Columbia Pictures.

played by Lew Ayres) and the stylized form the dialogue takes, the manner in which, as the director put it, Barry's characters virtually "sing" their lines. Cukor was the ideal director to maintain this masterfully mixed tone, by modulating performances naturally and gracefully staging and blocking scenes with nearly constant, well-motivated, expressive movement to avoid the static feeling of a filmed play.

Cukor's films often take place in the glittering world of high society. Although he told Lambert he found the rich a "great comfort," like Barry he also explored the fissures and despondency inherent in that seemingly solid but actually precarious way of life. Cukor's somewhat contradictory view of the rich was reflected in his comment that Barry "starts to put them down but ends up very cozy with them." Lambert's writings, especially *The Slide Area: Scenes of Hollywood Life*, his 1959 short story collection, often explore the dark underbelly of Hollywood and Los Angeles. So he could not share Cukor's more romantic outlook toward the upper class, diplomatically telling the director he felt that way about "only some of them." Coming from a comfortable middle-class New York City background with immigrant parents, Cukor aspired to a more opulent and socially prominent, though discreetly unpretentious, lifestyle and achieved it as a successful Hollywood director. He functioned remarkably smoothly at the studio most known for depicting luxury, MGM, although his penchant for social criticism, stemming from his status as a gay Jewish outsider, tended to qualify his view of the society people whose posh lives he explored onscreen.

Cukor identifies emotionally with the rebellious natures of Hepburn's Linda, who says she will "go mad" if she doesn't manage to escape her stuffy family surroundings, and Grant's Johnny, a footloose young man who is supposed to marry her sister, whom he fails to realize is shallow and snobbish. Johnny wants to take a "holiday" from business so he can find out why he's been working and who he is. He prefigures what would later be called a "dropout," and though he makes a sufficient living working in a "financial house" (not as a lawyer, as in the play), he scandalizes his stuffy prospective father-in-law (Henry Kolker) and conventionally minded fiancée by declaring that he doesn't believe in making "too much money" but just enough.

Set during the late years of the Great Depression, Cukor's film of *Holiday* is hardly a radical statement, although the screenwriters who adapted the play, Donald Ogden Stewart and Sidney Buchman, were both leftists. Stewart had already become a member of the Communist Party, and Buchman joined the party later in the year *Holiday* was released; both were blacklisted during the post–World War II Red Scare. The utopian social reforms alluded to in the script are left mostly vague, in accordance with restrained Hollywood practice—mentions of "new, exciting ideas running around" that stimulate Johnny and "a spirit of revolt" that dismays the paterfamilias—but the spirit of breakaway idealism Johnny and Linda embody is clear and refreshing. And when it comes to the worst reactionaries in the family, cousin Seton Cram (Henry Daniell) and his wife, Laura (Binnie Barnes), the film gets more sharply pointed, with Linda and her gang mockingly giving the Crams the fascist salute and one of them asking Seton what political system he has in mind when he sneers that America needs "the right kind of government." These topical elements were added in keeping with the late-thirties updating of the play for the screen; Stewart was a prominent member of the Hollywood Anti-Nazi League.

And in a line taken from the play that anticipates the Hollywood studio blacklist prompted by the 1947 hearings of the House Committee on Un-American Activities, Linda's father huffs about Johnny, "I consider his whole attitude un-American" (in the play he says "deliberately un-American"). These political jabs mark a rare foray by Cukor into overt left-liberal rhetoric in his work. The bland liberalism of *Born Yesterday* (1950) is easily digestible Capra-corn, and *Dinner at Eight* skates with mostly light satire around Depression issues. *Keeper of the Flame*, his 1942 Tracy-Hepburn film adapted by Stewart from the novel by I. A. R. (Ida Alexa Ross) Wylie, is something of an exception, an antifascist wartime melodrama about the exposure and killing of a Lindbergh-like would-be American dictator, although its plot suffers from being cautiously vague in specifics. Like most Hollywood liberals, Cukor would largely fail to challenge the blacklist, although he continued to support and employ Judy Holliday, his *Born Yesterday* star and actress in four other films, during her troubles with the witch hunters (see chapter 17). Cukor's self-protective sense of discretion over his private life and desire to sustain his career with the major studios also led him to a degree of political reserve and caution in his public life. Nevertheless, Cukor's films take a broad and pervasive, though largely implicit, political stance in that they usually see the world from the viewpoints of social outsiders.

In any case, Cukor generally prefers to work through nuances of character rather than rhetoric, and he thought Barry especially excelled in that approach to comedy and drama: "Barry had this gift for throwaway candor. . . . The trick is not to play it 'all out.' It's a question of subtle, understated attitudes." Hepburn's Linda Seton in *Holiday* is restless with her pampered lifestyle and is blocked by the pull of luxury and her own self-pitying doldrums until she is goaded by Johnny's example and their growing affection to find a way out. But at first Linda is also blocked by a sense of misguided loyalty to her sister: "My dear girl, do you realize that *life* walked into this house this morning? Oh, darling, don't let him get away!" she tells Julia, pulling her into a private corner and embracing her shortly after meeting Johnny.

The Philadelphia Story, on the other hand, is based on the 1939 play Barry wrote with Hepburn's close involvement to recast her threatened public image of "box office poison" as less unconventional and more submissive to men than she had become while establishing her screen persona with Cukor in the 1930s. *Holiday*, released just three weeks after the independent exhibitors' trade advertisement slapped that label on Hepburn, catches both actress and director on the rebound from the nearly absolute daring of *Sylvia Scarlett* but still reveling in the audacity of nonconformism. When *Holiday* was first performed onstage in 1928, its satire of the rich was more provocative, because the stock market crash and the Depression had not yet occurred. Hepburn understudied its star, Hope Williams, but only managed to go on for her once; however, her screen test of Linda's poignant scene about "the swell game" of drunkenness with Ned helped win her the role in Cukor's *A Bill of Divorcement*.

By the time Cukor filmed *Holiday*, the large-scale social catastrophe outside the Seton mansion made the family seem decadent indeed and grotesquely isolated in their huge, cold fortress from the realities in the streets. We don't see the lower classes except as servants and cab drivers, and though Johnny describes himself as "a plain man of the people," that is his partly self-flattering illusion. Despite his egalitarian nature, his plan to take a holiday and ability to look askance at wealth—to avoid what Thoreau's *Walden* calls the "spending of the best part of one's life earning money in order to enjoy a questionable liberty during the least valuable part of it"—are dependent on his rise from a humble background by working his way through Harvard and socking away a sufficient bankroll through playing the stock market.

Grant's growing relaxation into his low-key, amiable manner since *Sylvia Scarlett* and McCarey's *The Awful Truth* is blended here with a quietly serious tone that gives weight to his process of deciding his future. He explains his plan to Linda by telling her, "I've been working since I was ten—I want to find out *why* I'm working. . . . Now the world's changing out there, there's a lot of new, exciting ideas running around. Some of them might be right, and some might be cockeyed, but they're affecting all our lives. I want to know how I *stand*, where I fit into the picture." In contrast to the Setons, Johnny is a regular guy indeed. "When I find myself in a position like this," he tells the sisters, "I ask myself, What would General Motors do? Then I do the opposite."

Holiday has distinct echoes (literally so, when Johnny tests the acoustics of the marble mansion by yodeling) of two of the best Frank Capra–Robert Riskin films, *Platinum Blonde* (1931) and *Mr. Deeds Goes to Town* (1936), in its challenging of the big-business ethos. Capra, a covert Republican opponent of the New Deal, had his own ambivalent view of wealth, but Riskin, a New Deal liberal, supplied much of those Depression-era films' egalitarian spirit. His brother Everett produced *Holiday* at Capra's home studio, Columbia, where Buchman would write the brilliant screenplay flaying political corruption for Capra's best film, *Mr. Smith Goes to Washington* (1939). Capra knew Buchman was a communist when he wrote that script but informed on him in 1951 when his own loyalty was questioned by the U.S. government.

The playroom in Cukor's *Holiday* is the center of what later would be called countercultural values. Along with its comfy old-fashioned furniture with floral patterns, stone fireplace, books, family knickknacks, and an inconspicuous framed portrait of the late Mrs. Seton, there are a piano and set of drums for Ned to play (Ayres was a band member before he made movies), acrobatic implements in anticipation of Johnny (Grant, who started his career as an acrobat, does backflips in the film), a giraffe doll Linda identifies with, and a puppet theater immediately appropriated by Johnny's intellectual friends Nick and Susan Potter (Edward Everett Horton and Jean Dixon). Asked by Linda to play his unfinished concerto, Ned first starts pounding out the Andrews Sisters' Yiddish pop hit of that period, "Bei Mir Bistu Shein (To Me, You Are Beautiful)," and after noodling a bit of his own melancholy piece, he joyfully plays the banjo as they all celebrate their togetherness by singing Stephen Foster's whimsical minstrel song "Camptown Races."

The screenwriter Donald Stewart, who had originated the role of Nick on Broadway, wanted to play him in the film, but Cukor preferred the more skillful Horton, who was Nick in the first film version of *Holiday*. The Potters, who were socialites in the play and that early (1930) talkie, are turned into

10.2.   While New Year's Eve partygoers off screen sing "Auld Lang Syne," Linda and Johnny Case (Cary Grant) come close to admitting their true feelings. Johnny leans in to kiss her romantically, but Linda still feels compelled to hold him back.

Source: Frame enlargement; Columbia Pictures.

modest academics and made more serious in this version, as bohemian surrogate-parent figures to Johnny who also become close friends of Linda. Dixon, an accomplished stage actress and character actress in films who retired from Hollywood after *Holiday*, is especially endearing as a keenly perceptive observer who soon realizes the depth of Linda's feeling for Johnny. The Potters join them in mocking the pomposities of the New Year's Eve engagement party going on downstairs while Linda, denied the right to hold the party herself in the playroom, gathers her unorthodox little group in protest.

   With the emphasis on life as subversive entertainment in the central playroom sections of the film, Cukor's own values are put on display in stark contrast to the stodgy formality elsewhere in the house. The playroom is a place for dreams—Johnny's dream of a holiday, Linda's of escape, the Potters' of social satire, Ned's of oblivion—and it's no accident that both Linda and Ned are failed artists (her earlier dreams were to be an actress or a painter, as well as a labor organizer). Art is the magic carpet that Cukor's characters can use to fly from their stifling surroundings into a better, if uncertain life. As Carlos Clarens notes in his critical study of Cukor, the playroom is "the refuge of Linda's childhood dreams and longings (like Jo's attic [where she writes] in *Little Women*; but also, tinged with madness and obsession, in the sombre key of [his 1944 film] *Gaslight*)."

Cukor's little-understood ability to make plays seem cinematic—stemming from his recognition that, in contrast to the theater with its often "arbitrary movements" to avoid a static feeling, "in movies you had to have much more real movement"—is exemplified by *Holiday*. Although it is heavy on dialogue, that never seems a burden on this fluid film, because Cukor keeps the characters moving in naturally expressive patterns, with his characteristically graceful but unobtrusive panache. His use of close-ups and intimate two-shots such as in these scenes in the playroom with Johnny and Ned is powerfully restrained, since they stand in contrast with many of the scenes filmed in wider group shots to stress the unified schemes of the central characters. Cukor worked on *Holiday* with the cinematographer Franz Planer, a Czech refugee from Hitler's Germany making his first film in the United States; his masterpiece was Max Ophüls's 1948 Hollywood film *Letter from an Unknown Woman*.

When Cukor's *Holiday* is compared with the early-talkie version directed clumsily for Pathé by the hapless Edward H. Griffith, the difference is a master class on how to transform a play into cinema. Griffith's blocking is clumsy and his mise-en-scène haphazard, while Cukor uses space eloquently to help convey the characters' feelings (such as Johnny's bemused navigation of the mansion, which seems ever-expanding) and moves his people around each other balletically to express their shifting feelings. The earlier film stars Ann Harding, an elegant actress who has some of the offbeat, intelligent qualities of the young Hepburn (Harding was nominated for an Oscar in the role), but the actor who plays Johnny, Robert Ames, is abrasive and lacking in charm, as well as disturbingly puffy-faced and dissipated-looking; he died the following year of delirium tremens. Furthermore, the monotonously lugubrious actor who plays Ned, Monroe Owsley, points up the superior qualities Ayres brings to the role of the alcoholic family scapegoat with his wryly fatalistic manner.

But the earlier film has one strong advantage over the Cukor version: Mary Astor's performance as Julia. Astor is vivacious and sexy in that secondary role while still convincing as a shallow and conventional character. The actress who plays Julia for Cukor, Doris Nolan, on the other hand, is notably unappealing in terms of both her personality and her ordinary appearance. She tends to wear a disapproving frown most of the time, criticizing just about everything about Johnny when we first see them together and forcing him to swap his jaunty bowtie for one of her father's custom-made neckties (proving the wisdom of Thoreau's advice to "beware of all enterprises that require new clothes, and not rather a new wearer of clothes"). Julia is so dreary she makes one wonder how Johnny could have fallen for her, even on their too-short acquaintance, and why he rhapsodizes so much over her, and why, for that matter, Linda professes to be so admiring of her. Nolan is ill-served by her stodgy hairstyle and tacky costuming (including a loosely fitting lamé party dress), in contrast with Linda's gleaming, glamorous image.

Ned's comment to Linda that "most people, including Johnny and yourself, make a big mistake about Julia. You're taken in by her looks. At bottom, she's a very dull girl" comes off as only a half-truth onscreen; the miscasting loads the dice against the character to the point of befuddlement. Cukor had wanted to cast Carole Lombard as Julia, and what a role that would have been for the sexy, larkish actress who was so adept at screwball comedy. But Hepburn disapproved, on the grounds that having two leading ladies in the same movie would be problematical, and she had her way. Most likely her egotism and jealousy were responsible for this unfortunate action on her part; it weakened the film by making the love triangle implausible.

Playing a character described by Barry as "slim, rather boyish, exceedingly fresh," Hepburn is often strikingly dressed in emphatically outlined black, wearing a jaunty little tilted hat like an exclamation point and sporting a brisk-looking pageboy bob. Linda's crisply defined physical appearance and forthright, dryly amused manner of talking and moving make her seem like a knife cutting through the cant of her stifling environment and its deadly hypocrisies she defies. Grant, dressed more comfortably than stylishly, became more and more casually handsome onscreen as he eased into his familiar image, and Hepburn's biographer William J. Mann comments that in *Holiday*, "Hepburn and Grant play together with an intelligence and sexiness Kate never again found with a leading man." With Johnny, Hepburn's Linda also reveals a winning warmth and vulnerability that's nearly bursting to come to the fore. When she shows him her giraffe in the playroom, she warns, "Now don't you say a word about Leopold, he's very sensitive. Looks like me," and turns her freckled face and spindly neck in close-up in parallel with Leopold's spotted visage. As Mann puts it, this bit of clownish play-acting is a "conflation of real and reel life. In that moment, we see more evidence of the softness under her shell."

The playroom is also where Johnny's romance with Linda develops. Feeling increasingly trapped by his engagement to Julia, he insists on bringing in the New Year upstairs with Linda. She persuades him to "step into a waltz" as a music box softly plays "The Blue Danube"; her face, seen over his shoulder, reveals the exquisite anguish of her situation. The delicate scene contrasts musically with the way the party began to an imperial tune by the same composer, Johann Strauss II's "Emperor Waltz." When the noise of the crowd celebrating on the street is heard, Linda throws open the window. She and Johnny are framed from outside in the chilly night as she gives him permission to kiss her on the cheek to mark the festive occasion; the partygoers are

10.3.   Linda's love for Johnny is revealed to us in this close-up as he reluctantly leaves her to go downstairs to his ceremony of engagement to her sister.

Source: Frame enlargement/Columbia Pictures.

singing "Auld Lang Syne" downstairs. The couple make clear their growing affection for each other as Linda turns her eyes toward Johnny fervently yet pushes him away when he leans forward for something more intimate.

As she tells him he must go downstairs, he wanders disconsolately to do his duty, and Cukor gives us a tight, radiant close-up of Hepburn's yearning face watching him at the window, followed by another as he hesitates, and her eyes fill with tears. As Linda is left alone and disconsolate, it's structurally and emotionally right that the great scene with Ned follows, as they talk about his self-destructive addiction. Linda's unusually close relationship with her troubled young brother resembles Hepburn's own involvement with her doomed brother, Tom. It is now that Linda confesses what she cannot tell anyone else: "I love the boy, Neddy."

Linda's stubborn loyalty to her sister evaporates when Julia makes clear that she won't follow him in his iconoclastic path. Unlike Johnny, she is not one of Cukor's dreamers, the people he cares most about. When her father is busy drawing up plans for them to make the rounds of European business contacts during their honeymoon and telling them he's going to lend them a house to begin their married life, Johnny, his hands planted tensely in his pockets, backs away from them in horror and finally declares, "Julia, I'm sorry, but I can't stand it." Cukor intercuts close-ups of Linda's silent suspense as she watches Johnny tell Julia, "I suppose the fact is, I love feeling free inside even better than I love you, Julia."

Julia's scorn for his way of life comes out when she refuses to sail to Europe with him and the Potters. Linda eagerly seizes the opportunity, drawing out Julia's admission about Johnny's departure, "I'm so relieved I could sing with it!" Exultant, and finally freed from her regimented life by Johnny's declaration of independence, Linda bids her sister, brother, and father a spirited farewell at the doorway: "You've got no faith in Johnny, have you, Julia? His little dream may fall flat, you think—well, so it may, what if it should? There'll be another. Oh, I've got all the faith in the world in Johnny. Whatever he does is all right with me. If he wants to dream for a while, he can dream for a while. And if he wants to come back and sell peanuts, oh, how I'll believe in those peanuts!"

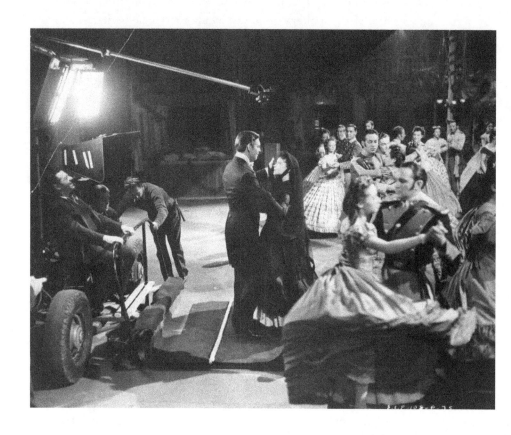

11.1. Riding on the camera dolly following Clark Gable and Vivien Leigh in her widow's garb, Cukor buoyantly reacts to the sweeping dance movements at the bazaar to benefit Atlanta's military hospital in *Gone with the Wind*. After Cukor's firing, this sequence in the 1939 MGM production was reshot by Victor Fleming, but Cukor helped set the tone for the film and continued to direct Leigh and Olivia de Havilland surreptitiously after his firing.

Source: MGM/From the Core Collection, Production Files of the Margaret Herrick Library, Academy of Motion Picture Arts and Sciences.

11

VIVIEN LEIGH, OLIVIA DE HAVILLAND, HATTIE McDANIEL, AND BUTTERFLY McQUEEN IN *GONE WITH THE WIND*

"**N**otice with what finesse he avoids mentioning the title *Gone with the Wind*." That's what Cukor said to his publicist when I asked him what it feels like to be fired from a film. Well, it's time for me to mention that fraught subject.

Cukor intermittently spent more than two years of his life, from October 1936 onward, working on preproduction on the most grandiose film in Hollywood history, David O. Selznick's production of Margaret Mitchell's bestselling novel about the Civil War and the Reconstruction Era. But while under nonexclusive contract to Selznick, Cukor also managed to direct two features, *Camille* and the 1938 Paramount film *Zaza*, starring Claudette Colbert as a nineteenth-century French musical hall performer, an attractive period piece that was severely mutilated by the studio. Cukor also directed unmemorable retakes for *The Prisoner of Zenda*, *I Met My Love Again*, and *The Adventures of Tom Sawyer* and was briefly assigned to direct MGM's *Ninotchka* and *The Wizard of Oz*. When principal photography on *Gone with the Wind* finally began in January 1939, Cukor spent thirteen days directing it before being fired by Selznick.

By all accounts, that humiliation was a heavy blow to the director's pride, but overcoming the setback was also the ultimate tribute to Cukor's remarkable resilience, which enabled him to sustain a long and successful career in Hollywood. In a Hollywood version of musical chairs, he immediately went from Selznick's MGM release to direct MGM's production of Clare Boothe Luce's play *The Women*, a project Ernst Lubitsch swapped for *Ninotchka*. Forever afterward Cukor would manage to joke about his firing and would kindly call other directors who were removed from pictures to reassure them by saying, "I'm phoning to tell you not to worry. It's not going to make the slightest difference to your career, and I should know. . . . If it is any comfort, I was fired from the biggest picture ever made."

Selznick's $4.25 million film version of the Pulitzer Prize–winning but controversial novel by the former Atlanta newspaperwoman was an impossible project for any director. The producer was its true auteur, a megalomaniac who demanded a fanatical degree of control over everyone working on the film, which eventually had several directors. They included its production designer, William Cameron Menzies, whose visual influence was so pervasive that he was virtually the film's co-auteur. Nevertheless, Cukor managed to continue to play a strong creative role in shaping *Gone with the Wind*. He set its tone during strenuous preproduction work with the credited screenwriter, Sidney Howard, and other craftsmen—as Aljean Harmetz writes in her book on the film, Cukor's "eye and sensibility had helped to shape the costumes and the sets"—and by shooting twenty-four hours of test scenes with a myriad of actresses and actors in both black-and-white and color (enough for twelve feature films) during Selznick's much-publicized search for a leading lady.

Among the actresses who coveted the role of Scarlett was Katharine Hepburn, and Cukor loyally pushed for her, even though he realized she wasn't right for the part. Hepburn and Mitchell had both grown up as tomboys, wearing male clothes and calling themselves "Jimmy," but Hepburn was a quintessential Yankee, still in her "box office poison" period, and Selznick didn't think she was sexy. Another Cukor favorite who was more seriously considered was Norma Shearer. Her casting was announced along with Gable's in the *New York Times* in June 1938, along with Cukor as director (next to the paper's review of *Holiday*, with a large picture of Hepburn). But there was a public backlash against Shearer, an actress whose image was thought to be too "nice" for the role, and she also was considered too old for Scarlett, who is sixteen at the start of the story, so she soon withdrew her name from consideration.

The search for the leading lady was so extraordinary that a television movie was made about it, the mildly amusing *The Scarlett O'Hara War*, as part of the

1980 Garson Kanin miniseries *Moviola*, with Tony Curtis convincingly driven as Selznick and George Furth feebly playing Cukor. When I asked Cukor what he thought of the Cukor character, he said with amusement, "He was a dummy, wasn't he? A nice man, but a dummy, always running around after whoever the boss was, saying, 'Oh yes, yes.' He was the shits!" That's not how Cukor behaved with the overbearing Selznick, however. Cukor fought for his creative vision and even after his official departure managed to remain covertly involved in the filming.

Harmetz also writes that Cukor was "in large part responsible for the performances of Vivien Leigh and Olivia de Havilland." When the two female stars learned of Cukor's firing during the shooting of the Atlanta bazaar sequence, they charged into Selznick's office costumed in widows' weeds and vainly implored him to let the director return. At a 1975 tribute to Selznick, de Havilland recalled:

> We were heartsick, Vivien and I, when George left the picture. . . . We stormed David's office dressed in deepest mourning, and for three hours we beseeched him not to let George go. Now all of you who have seen David in his office will remember he had a window seat. Well, he sought the refuge of that window seat, and when we brought out our damp and black-bordered handkerchiefs, he nearly went straight out that window. However, he remained strong, and George did leave the picture, and Victor Fleming came on.
>
> Howard Hughes explained to me the night I heard this terrible news at dinner, "Now, Olivia, disaster does not really lie before you. The talent of George and Victor is the same, but Victor's is strained through a coarser sieve." Now these words reassured me, and Victor proved them true.
>
> However, there were times when I felt the need for the talent strained through the finer sieve. And I would telephone George and ask him for his help, and very generously he would give me black market direction. I did feel guilty toward Vivien about these secret visits to George. Then when the picture was over I found out she had been doing exactly the same thing.

"I was rather touched when I heard about that," Cukor said of the actresses going to beg Selznick to let him stay on the picture. Both actresses felt such loyalty to Cukor and his vision that they secretly made visits to his home on weekends to run scenes with him and benefit from his shadow directing. Leigh wrote her husband after Cukor was fired, "He was my last hope of ever enjoying the picture," and she feuded with Fleming, the principal replacement director. She even enraged him once by demanding that they stop and run one of the test scenes Cukor had shot with her and Ashley Wilkes so they could do it better ("Let's see how George handled it"). John Lee Mahin, who worked on the script briefly with Fleming, told me Fleming became so irate at Leigh at one point that he rolled up his copy of the script and said, "Miss Leigh, why don't you stick this up your royal British arse?"

Cukor's surreptitious involvement with *Gone with the Wind* during production was deeply satisfying for him, not only salving his wounded pride but giving him the pleasure of shaping Leigh's characterization of Scarlett and de Havilland's of Melanie Wilkes. Their two performances remain as a testament to his reputation as Hollywood's finest director of actors in that period. Cukor had been involved in casting and testing Leigh and de Havilland, and as de Havilland recalled of her test at Selznick's home: "George read Scarlett's lines while I read Melanie's. He did this with such passion, such fervor, such dynamism that David was beside himself with enthusiasm. For some reason, George had to stand clutching some velvet curtains. He was absolutely marvelous—I'm sure it was his performance that got me the part." Leigh won the role over the other finalists, Paulette Goddard, Joan Bennett, and Jean Arthur. The uncertain status of Goddard's relationship with the politically controversial Charles Chaplin caused Selznick to drop her from consideration; although the tests show that she captured the minx quality and slyness of Scarlett, Cukor showed some discontent with her acting, interrupting her during a take to say, "Do it once more, more gently, more quietly, more mood. . . . Once more, Paulette, your face is hard . . . relax now."

After Leigh was introduced to Selznick and Cukor on the night they and the second-unit director B. Reeves Eason filmed shots for the burning of Atlanta on the Selznick backlot (December 10, 1938), Cukor filmed tests with Leigh. They included the scenes with Hattie McDaniel lacing up her stays and with Leslie Howard as Ashley Wilkes when Scarlett declares her love for him at the barbecue, with the tone of "indescribable wildness" no other actress gave him, and one in the fields after the war with Douglass Montgomery (Laurie from *Little Women*) playing Ashley when she implores him to run away with her. About the latter, Lambert writes, "Now she presents a woman instead of a girl, hardened by experience, with an underlying panic and desperation; the scene becomes a fierce, disturbing appeal to Ashley to save her life. In fact the performance here is more striking than when she repeats it in the film under Victor Fleming's direction." Both women were nominated for Academy Awards, Leigh winning the Oscar for best actress and de Havilland being bypassed for best supporting actress by Hattie McDaniel, the first Black person to win an Oscar.

McDaniel's groundbreaking performance as Mammy is arguably the greatest feat of acting in the film, transcending the stereotypes implicit in the role to create a fully three-dimensional, deeply moving, and abundantly witty characterization. Mammy is the voice of reason and morality in a film that badly needs it. She doesn't hesitate to scold Gable's Rhett Butler even though they also are relaxed enough to laugh, drink, and kid each other (Rhett also delights her with a gift of a gaudy red petticoat), and her stature is summed

11.2. "George Cukor is the Cellini of directors. . . . Take a look at the scene where Mammy's lacing up Scarlett—it's crammed with tiny fleeting expressions and motives," observed cast member Olivia de Havilland. Among the scenes Cukor directed for *Gone with the Wind* that remain in the film is this early one with Leigh and Hattie McDaniel, who won an Oscar for her supporting role.

Source: Frame enlargement/MGM.

up eloquently when Rhett describes her to Scarlett by saying, "Mammy's a sweet old soul and one of the few people I know whose respect I'd like to have." Perhaps the most powerful single scene in the film is Mammy's monologue about Rhett's grief after the death of his daughter, a long crane shot up a staircase with Melanie (directed by Sam Wood). Though the film criticizes Scarlett's amorality, materialism, and haughty treatment of just about everyone, including her perceived inferiors, and though Mammy's formidable character and some of the visual and dramatic incidents to some extent counteract the film's otherwise skewed racial perspective, *Gone with the Wind* is an often disturbing saga.

It largely romanticizes the Old South: the film never quite recovers from the ghastly introductory title about "a land of Cavaliers and Cotton Fields. . . . Here in this pretty world Gallantry took its last bow. Here was the last ever to be seen of Knights and their Ladies Fair, of Master and of Slave . . ." Ben Hecht, who wrote much of this (probably partly tongue-in-cheek), also described Southerners as "proud, gentle and absurd people," but those words were cut. Even after the ruination caused by slavery and the war, however, Ashley is still nostalgically invoking the memory of "the high soft Negro laughter from the quarters." And despite some gripping human drama depicting the war's consequences, including nightmarish scenes of the horrors of war as experienced by a civilian population (but all blamed on Sherman and the Yankees), the film paints an ugly, ahistorical, and racially charged portrait of Reconstruction in its lugubrious, rushed, and overwrought second half. Leslie Howard, who refused to read the book, disdained the script as "just one climax after another" (reminiscent of the problem with the script of the Cukor-Selznick version of *David Copperfield*).

Cukor had cast McDaniel and helped establish the tone for her performance while directing the early scene of Mammy forcibly lacing up Scarlett for the barbecue at the Wilkes mansion. That scene immediately brings welcome humor to the somewhat ponderous film, imparting Cukor's wry view of life to Mammy's feuding with her headstrong young charge. Mammy scolds Scarlett about how to behave like a lady and bests her with sarcasm, perfectly pointed verbal barbs, and disapproving glances (including a knowing smirk in sidelong close-up) at Scarlett's foolish, unrequited passion for Ashley, the engine that drives her unhinged behavior until almost the end of the film. Mammy keeps trying to pull back Scarlett's bodice to modest proportions, but Scarlett keeps yanking it down, and the mischievous vixen at first resists Mammy's order to have something to eat in private before the barbecue but then mocks her by gobbling mouthfuls from a tray. "If you don't care what folks says about this family, I does," declares Mammy, establishing her as the film's arbiter of sense and sensibility. Cukor drew on McDaniel's unique ability during that Jim Crow period in Hollywood to talk back to white people and get away with it. She controlled situations with her superior wit and endeared herself to the audience with her keen intelligence and expert physical timing.

That scene with Mammy and Scarlett is the one de Havilland cited in commenting on Cukor's "marvelously intricate imagination which works on a very fine scale. . . . It's crammed with tiny fleeting expressions and motives. . . . There's no other scene in the film with so much details, such richness." Within a gargantuan spectacle such as *Gone with the Wind*, with its impressive production values and epic scale, what remains most memorable artistically are those nuances Cukor brought to the human dimensions of the story. Cukor was never especially enamored of Mitchell's 1936 bestseller, whose strong narrative and characterizations are marred by its excessive, rambling length, often melodramatic floridity, and blatant racism. But Cukor got the job because of his expert directing of literary adaptations, including *Little Women* (another film about the Civil War on the home front, though about Yankees) and *David Copperfield* for Selznick and *Camille* for Thalberg.

Yet he chafed at Selznick's increasing interference on *Gone with the Wind*—during the shooting, the producer even demanded to see and approve the rehearsal for each scene before Cukor shot it—and was dissatisfied with the screenplay that went into principal photography on January 26, 1939. Selznick, for his part, was upset with Cukor's stubborn defense of his directorial prerogatives and about the relative slowness and relaxed pacing of his scenes, partly caused by his characteristic elaboration of details to add texture, as well as the producer's worry that Cukor would not handle the large crowd scenes as effectively as the intimate scenes (a concern Lambert thought was belied by Cukor's expert handling of the crowd scenes in *Bhowani Junction*, his 1956 film set in India).

The adaptation of *Gone with the Wind* by Sidney Howard, which Cukor had worked on at length with the distinguished playwright, was tampered with by ten other writers, including Selznick and even, briefly, F. Scott

Fitzgerald. Cukor "groaned and tried to change some parts back to the Howard script," Susan Myrick, a Georgia journalist who was a technical adviser
on Southern dialect and customs, wrote Margaret Mitchell. "But he seldom
could do much with the scene[s]. . . . So George just told David he would not
work any longer if the script was not better and he wanted the Howard script
back. David told George he was a director—not an author and he (David)
was the producer and the judge of what is a good script." After Cukor was
fired on February 13, Selznick acknowledged the script's flaws and shut down
the production to bring in Hollywood's most facile and prolific screenwriter,
Ben Hecht (who notoriously hadn't read the book), to do a frenzied one-week
partial rewrite (a feat that became the subject of an amusing play by Ron
Hutchinson in 2006, *Moonlight and Magnolias*). But in the end, Selznick
mostly went back to Howard's work. He received the sole screenplay credit
and a posthumous Oscar after his death in a tractor accident on his Massachusetts farm in August 1939.

Selznick tried to be faithful to the 1,037-page novel, however chimerical
that ambition was, but he was aware of the controversy over its depiction of
Black characters, and the filming drew protests from the NAACP and Black
journalists over the book's use of the n-word and other problems, including
the scene involving the Ku Klux Klan (not identified as such in the film). Selznick, who considered himself a liberal, softened Mitchell's racism, but not
enough. The casting of Leigh (who had made nine films in England but was
little known in the United States) made the film unfaithful to the opening
words of the novel, "Scarlett O'Hara was not beautiful," though the casting
of such an exquisite young actress seemed inevitable in retrospect.

Besides clashing with Selznick, Cukor also ran afoul of Clark Gable, who
felt uncomfortable with a so-called woman's director guiding him as Rhett
Butler; Gable also was known to be antisemitic and homophobic. Cukor later
reflected, "Perhaps Gable mistakenly thought that because I was supposed to
be a 'woman's director' I would throw the story to Vivien—but if that's so, it
was very naïve of him and not the reaction of a very good or professional actor.
It's not the director who 'throws' things and puts the emphasis the wrong
way. . . . I don't throw anything anywhere at all; there's the truth of the scene
and it states itself." Cukor's biographer Patrick McGilligan reports an awful
incident on the set when Gable exploded and said, "I can't go on with this
picture! I won't be directed by a fairy! I have to work with a *real man!*" Cukor

11.3.   Another scene directed by Cukor has Scarlett receiving a Parisian bonnet from Rhett Butler (Clark Gable), who has to show her how to wear it. This seriocomic romantic scene, the only one with Rhett directed by Cukor to remain in the film, demonstrates how wrong Gable was to believe that Cukor would throw the film to the female stars.

Source: Frame enlargement; MGM.

silently walked off the set. Although Cukor diplomatically told Lambert, "Gable was always very polite with me," McGilligan writes that Cukor "on rare occasions behind closed doors" would tell friends about the homophobic incident.

Despite his bruised feelings, Cukor may well have been glad to be rid of the burden of the troubled production. His replacement, Fleming, who filmed about half the picture but was the only director credited, suffered a breakdown from exhaustion during shooting; additional scenes were directed by Menzies, Wood, Eason, and others. Some of the scenes Cukor directed were reshot (including a day on the bazaar), but Lambert estimates in his book on the film that Cukor's remaining work amounts to about 5 percent of the picture: "Mammy lacing up Scarlett for the barbecue, Rhett arriving at Aunt Pittypat's with the hat for Scarlett, Scarlett and Prissy delivering Melanie's baby, and Scarlett shooting the Union deserter at Tara. The final 'authorship' of the opening porch scene, which was reshot three times, remains in doubt.

It is probably a mixture of Cukor's second version and the Fleming retake." Cukor's scenes were shot by the great cinematographer Lee Garmes, who was criticized by Selznick for his soft and subtle use of Technicolor rather than the bright colors the producer wanted, and Garmes too eventually left the production after shooting most of the first hour of the film without credit.

The anxiety Gable felt about Cukor allegedly throwing the picture in Leigh's direction is belied by the major remaining scene they did together, the one in which Gable brings a stylish green hat to Scarlett to make her gaudy during her mourning for the first husband she frankly never loved. Rife with romantic-comedy humor, including Rhett's having to show Scarlett how to put on the hat facing frontward instead of backward as well as Scarlett's blithe indifference to her widowhood, the scene makes lively use of Gable's virile brand of humor and the air of confidence he winningly exudes in most of his scenes with Scarlett. This helped set the tone for Gable's relaxed performance, perhaps his most complex and appealing, in his cynical pragmatism about both Scarlett and his disdain for the reckless Southern bellicosity. But Fleming deserves considerable credit for bringing out the vulnerability his friend Gable was reluctant to show onscreen. Leslie Howard, in contrast, plays what Hecht and the actor himself felt was a useless character, but that becomes the point of Ashley's weak and melancholy existence. The scene with Scarlett shooting the Union soldier (Paul Hurst) attempting to rape her at the ruined house of her family's plantation, Tara, is suitably shocking and graphic. It dramatically shows that Scarlett meant it when she vowed to kill rather than go destitute and hungry again, even while Cukor works in a shading of her surprise she could actually pull the trigger on a human being.

The memorable but somewhat controversial childbirth scene is an extended tour de force of moody, foreboding cinematography by Garmes, drawing on his experience shooting films for Josef von Sternberg (some of the scene, at dusk, is shot in silhouette to get around the censors, who were skittish about films depicting childbirth), and formidable acting by Leigh as Scarlett having to deliver a baby virtually by herself during the burning of Atlanta, with Yankee soldiers marauding in the streets. Scarlett's fierce resilience comes to the fore in this desperate scene when she rises to Melanie's need despite her own resentment of that duty and her rival's marriage to Ashley.

Her reserves of strength, established here and carried throughout the rest of the film, echo Cukor's own ability to survive a crisis and are what makes Scarlett sympathetic despite her often exasperatingly self-centered, mercurial, haughty, and unabashedly mercenary behavior. It's often been noted that Scarlett's strength in her ordeals of hunger and impoverishment particularly appealed to women and men who had undergone similar ordeals in the late Depression era, and with the Second World War breaking out shortly before the film's premiere, the harrowing scenes of devastation also resonated with the audience's anxieties on that front.

The childbirth scene under fire is the one in which Butterfly McQueen, as the sweet but seemingly simple-minded young slave Prissy, first brags to Scarlett about her ability to deliver babies but then admits under duress in her high-pitched voice, "I don't know *nothin'* about birthin' babies." Nothing about the violence of Southern master-servant relations and Scarlett's cruelty is held back as she hits the hysterical Prissy in the face after warning her, "I'll sell you south, I will!" The fear and agitation both of them feel is very real under the circumstances, and though Prissy is a stereotypical character, Cukor manages to bring her believably and memorably alive in her confrontation with Scarlett and by treating her childlike vulnerability as both comical and pathetic.

The director Paul Morrissey, whose countercultural films in the 1960s and '70s Cukor admired, told Cukor's biographer Emanuel Levy that he should get more credit than he has for the quality of *Gone with the Wind*:

> George did the casting, and he shaped the level of performances. George had this gift of knowing what was good acting. It's not just dialogue; it's performing. In *GWTW*, all the performances belong in history. Hattie McDaniel, Butterfly McQueen, Laura Hope Crews [as Aunt Pittypat] are totally theatrical and artificial, but when you can be funny and artificial and get away with it, that's great acting. George never said, "Now, be realistic, this is a serious movie." There are a lot of dopey, awful directors who smother actors. He could see that Laura Hope Crews was over the top, but she was good.

And Roger Ebert observed in his 1998 review of the film that although Prissy's character is often reduced to the single oft-quoted line, "the character as a whole is engaging and subtly subversive."

Olivia de Havilland's serene, generous, unfailingly kind-hearted Melanie Wilkes can seem at first glance to be too good to be true, but the more one sees *Gone with the Wind*, the more it is apparent that her goodness is, like

Mammy's wisdom, at the heart of the movie. Scarlett herself may be essentially "heartless," as Rhett tells her, albeit fascinatingly so, but Melanie manages to rise above every form of pettiness and jealousy that surrounds her, often at the cost of great draining willpower. Her one serious flaw is her unthinking acceptance of the slavery system that underlies her family's way of life, which seems almost out of character for this genuinely noble woman until it's realized that the system was so insidious it could infect even such an otherwise admirable character. Cukor established de Havilland's performance as quiet and serene but never namby-pamby and followed Mitchell's guidance by making Melanie's endurance, until her death in her second childbirth, as powerful a force in the story as Scarlett's fierce resistance.

During the first childbirth scene, Melanie remains as selfless as always, apologizing for being a burden and expressing gratitude to Scarlett for staying with her, while refusing to take undue alarm at Scarlett's harshness and thinly concealed hysteria while the city burns around them. If Scarlett is, to some extent, similar to Jo March, Marguerite Gautier, and Linda Seton in Cukor's 1930s gallery of strongly independent-minded women who defy convention and defy the consequences, Melanie draws from similar qualities of character even while not acting as overtly rebellious. Melanie withstands every shock and is quintessentially a lady in the best sense of the word. The way de Havilland behaves, conveying her differences with Scarlett with subtle facial reactions of understanding and forbearance, a calm and unhurried manner of speaking, and forthright body language, expresses a fineness of character to which Scarlett could never hope to aspire. We share Rhett's feelings when he says after her death, "She was the only completely kind person I ever knew—a great lady, a very great lady."

De Havilland was one of the few actresses who campaigned to play Melanie rather than Scarlett, and when Cukor told her, "Olivia, there are hairdressers that are true to the period which will make you look pretty. And there are hairdressers that are true to the period which will make you look plain," she said, "It's the plain one I want." And yet her innate beauty is such that her Melanie looks radiant, and her serene behavior seems refreshing in contrast with Scarlett's often frenzied anger, coquetry, and passive-aggressive hostility. In some ways, de Havilland and Gable come off as more appealingly "modern" and more sophisticated in their less-is-more acting styles than Leigh does with her busy, stylized, and sometimes wearying but still compelling performance. De Havilland's taste in choosing to play Melanie showed her rare understanding of what an impact such characters can make on the screen and how playing a good woman can call for more creativity than playing a femme fatale.

As I wrote in my book on Billy Wilder, commenting on de Havilland's rich and complex performance in *Hold Back the Dawn* (1941), written by Wilder and Charles Brackett for the director Mitchell Leisen, which brought her an Oscar nomination for best actress, good women onscreen "are seldom discussed or admired by critics, who tend to consider cynical behavior more honest, not realizing (as the saying goes) that 'the wicked forget the good can be wise.'" When de Havilland was asked in 2004 why she relished the challenge of portraying "good girls" in films, she replied, "I think they're more challenging. Because the general concept is that if you're good, you aren't interesting. And that concept annoys me, frankly. They have the same point of view about girls who are plain. They think that somebody who's intellectual is sexless. Ha. Ha." Molly Haskell wrote in her book on *Gone with the Wind* that de Havilland's Melanie has "a moral majesty," and her "utter sincerity was part of her fineness. She captures the inner security of a perfectly loving woman."

Perhaps it's appropriate to give the last word on Cukor's role in making *Gone with the Wind* one of the great popular successes in film history to the director who replaced him. The screenwriter John Lee Mahin reported to me that Victor Fleming, his close friend and frequent collaborator, told him, "George would have done just as good a job as I. He'd probably have done a lot better on the intimate scenes. I think I did pretty well on some of the bigger stuff. George came from the stage and taught us what directing a dialogue scene was about. He knew. And nobody could direct a dialogue scene like George Cukor. It's bullshit that he's just a woman's director. He's not. He can direct anybody."

12

NORMA SHEARER, JOAN CRAWFORD, ROSALIND RUSSELL, AND JOAN FONTAINE IN *THE WOMEN*

A bitterly misogynistic play by a notorious right-wing snob might not seem, on the face of it, ideal material for a George Cukor film. But the title of *The Women* by Clare Boothe (also known as Clare Boothe Luce from her marriage to Time Inc.'s chief, Henry Luce) fed into Cukor's limiting and somewhat vexatious image as Hollywood's foremost "woman's director" (a label that could cause him to snap, "What the hell do you mean?"). And the play itself has an irresistible gimmick—it's about a group of women who are ostensibly friends but in reality often fierce rivals, and the dramatis personae include no men. The 1939 MGM film version has 135 female roles; the men the women are married to or otherwise involved with are often discussed in the dialogue, ironically enough, but never seen or heard: the studio's ad line for the film was "It's all about Men!"

As for the misogyny, Cukor and his screenwriters Jane Murfin and Anita Loos not only transcended it but turned it on its head by focusing sympathetically on Norma Shearer's character as the betrayed wife, Mary Haines. Luce, in contrast, wrote of Mary in her foreword to the published version of the play, "In spite of her redeeming qualities of faithfulness and sweetness, the difficulty about rooting for Mary is obviously that she is so stupid you hardly give a hoot." Well, Cukor gives a hoot. He and the women screenwriters do not treat Mary as stupid. They give her more time and emotional weight in the story, making her central character believable and worth caring

12.1. The bitter off-screen rivalry between "the Queen of MGM," Norma Shearer (right), and the pretender, Joan Crawford, heightened the resonance of the confrontation between Crawford's predatory gold digger Crystal Allen and Shearer's Mary Haines, whose husband she has seduced in *The Women* (1939). Cukor and the screenwriters Jane Murfin and Anita Loos leavened the harshness of Clare Boothe Luce's misogynistic play for their witty, all-female comedy-drama.

Source: Frame enlargement; MGM.

about. While recognizing that Mary is a sheltered rich woman who at first seems to coast through life and get by on her sweetness—a married life her hateful rival, Sylvia Fowler (Rosalind Russell), calls a "fool's paradise"—Cukor focuses on Mary's feelings of devastation when her husband abandons her and on her growing strength of character as she tries to reconstruct her life.

The director brought out the best in Shearer's decorous persona. Cukor knew her well from their collaboration on *Romeo and Juliet*, and she played a similar role to Mary's in her off-screen life as a wealthy Hollywood socialite. The widow of Irving Thalberg, Shearer was still considered "The Queen of MGM." And as Cukor once observed, "Women in our business are not stupid." Despite her aura of aloofness, even primness, onscreen in her maturity, Shearer could also be a passionate sexual adventuress in real life, as her surprising romance with the randy MGM star Mickey Rooney showed, much to the alarm of the studio chief, Louis B. Mayer, who indignantly broke it up. Although *The Women* has abundant, often raucous humor onscreen, much of it is at the satirical expense of the cynical, nasty characters, and it serves as a counterpoint to the genuinely affecting dramatic emphasis Cukor places on Mary.

The Women is an example of how mise-en-scène and its expression of a director's personality, along with sympathetic screenwriters, can twist, turn, and virtually reverse the thematic slant of the original material. Murfin did the heavy lifting on the adaptation, and Loos, a film industry pioneer and noted wit, was brought in to provide amusing equivalents for Luce's censorable bon mots (F. Scott Fitzgerald and Donald Ogden Stewart were not credited for their substantial contributions to the script; Loos and Stewart often made their contributions on set during the filming). Cukor's admiration for women and deep empathy with them did not preclude a sharp sense of what is often called bitchery. His friends reported that in private, but not in public, Cukor enjoyed gossip (except when it involved Katharine Hepburn) and could be wickedly funny about certain actresses and other women friends, as well as about males. His unvarnished sense of humor served Cukor well in mining for all it is worth, as well as refining, the bitchy comedy that made *The Women* a hit. Though he was clear-minded and sometimes could be harsh in his critical perspective on people, Cukor was also a generous artist with a strongly humanistic perspective on his characters and their foibles.

Because of his prevailing comedic outlook on life, he could enjoy the spectacle of the malicious behavior of Sylvia, the unabashedly vile gossip who sets out to destroy Mary's seemingly happy marriage to Stephen Haines, partly out of envy, because her own marriage is quietly falling apart. And Cukor could enjoy the somewhat campy wickedness of the heartless gold-digging shop girl, Crystal Allen, played with fearsome relish by Joan Crawford, even as she takes Mary's husband away from her and cruelly gloats over her rival's humiliation. But the crucial point about how these characters function in Cukor's film of *The Women* is that they are not the ones we identify with—as the spectator is encouraged to do in Luce's play—but instead are figures of comedy in Cukor's antic view of such goings-on and his acute sense of social satire.

Cukor compared his role in directing *The Women* with that of a "lion tamer." This carnivalesque film is one of his most dazzling directorial achievements in its command of a large and diverse cast of major and minor characters of almost every conceivable (female) type and in the way he takes the caricatures created by Luce and turns them into believable, flesh-and-blood human beings. Not only that, but his command of pacing in this often busy film is breathtaking. The rollercoaster way he shifts from comedy to drama and back to comedy—often within the same scene—is virtuosic and perfectly judged. It's doubtful any other director, even Lubitsch, who was briefly assigned to the project before Cukor was shifted from *Gone with the Wind* to *The Women*, could have pulled off the challenge of handling such material with comparable aplomb. Lubitsch, the master of ellipsis and innuendo, would have had to retool the on-the-nose bluntness of the play's dialogue but would have relished the supreme ellipsis of a world without males, even though as one reviewer put it, men are "the absent presence" in the plot.

With a feeling of utter ease and assurance, Cukor knows just when and how to shift from the busy, even frenetic pacing of group scenes involving the comical gossiping claque of women to the quieter and more deliberately paced scenes involving Mary and her deep, yet restrained, emotional response to her learning of her husband's infidelity and rising to the need of facing who she is without him. The film's often-ferocious pacing seems partly a result of the pent-up creative energy Cukor must have felt following the frustrations of *Gone with the Wind*.

Many in today's audience for *The Women* may feel impatient with Shearer's traditionally ladylike qualities, emotional reserve, and qualities of intelligence and poise in contrast to Crawford's flamboyant amorality, and villainy is often more colorful than goodness. Even Cukor was goaded into taking that attitude by Lambert's criticism of Mary in their interview book as "such a bore . . . a nice, dim woman": Cukor defensively called Mary "so worthy and self-righteous! And with *nobility* on her side!" But Mary is one of his truly good women, like Melanie Wilkes.

If you can get beyond the predictably cynical attitude toward the story, Shearer's performance is finely nuanced and thoughtfully balanced, with a subdued quality of fierceness. Mary's initial reserve is credible and admirable, if self-defeating, until she satisfyingly finds the courage to get her revenge against Crystal, sending her into social banishment and winning back her regretful husband. Lambert changed his view of Mary and of Shearer's performance by the time he wrote his 1990 biography of the actress: "Warned by Cukor that the character could easily appear a wealthy bore, she brings a minimum of weight to the pathos of betrayal and concentrates on the struggle not to betray her feelings. With impeccably restrained technique, she gains sympathy by never playing for it. And when she explains to her daughter that she plans to divorce Daddy, she transforms a potential toe-curler into a persuasive scene and herself into the kind of spontaneous, natural mother that she was unable to be in life."

That Crawford was the hateful rival of Shearer for plum roles at MGM added to the meta-tension of the shooting, a situation that required the command of a director of supreme diplomacy, tact, psychological shrewdness, and discipline, the rare mixture of skills Cukor alone possessed. That enabled studios to trust him with difficult actors and especially with female stars, who understandably tended to be anxious about their standing in the industry, even though in the 1930s, as Molly Haskell points out in her 1973 book, *From Reverence to Rape: The Treatment of Women in the Movies*, leading ladies tended to be dominant at the box office. "At the time Joan's career was less secure than Norma's," however, as Lambert writes in his biography of Shearer, and she was one of the stars who had been stigmatized as "box office poison." Crawford, Lambert relates, "lobbied strenuously for the part of Crystal, seeing it as a reversion to her most successful type, but even tougher, and although Mayer thought it not big enough for her, Cukor was certain she could make it appear very big indeed."

Cukor artfully uses the Crawford-Shearer rivalry to enhance the emotional charge of their confrontation scene in a ladies' dress shop. The general bad taste of the film's costumes and decor befits the subject matter; the costumes were by Adrian, who also supervised the superfluous Technicolor fashion show that interrupts the storyline for four minutes. The action in the dress shop goes back and forth from one fitting room (Mary's) to the other (Crystal's); Cukor conveys the power that Crystal, in a gold-lamé outfit with matching turban, gloatingly exerts until she has to admit that a wife, however humiliated, still has "everything that matters . . . the name, the position, the money" and that she has no chance to keep Stephen in the long run. The seething anger on display from both women makes this seem almost a physical fight scene, complete with an audience of shop girls listening outside the door. Both actresses hold their own, Crystal with her smirking stare and coarse putdowns, Mary with her affronted dignity, restrained comebacks, and struggle to control her vulnerability.

Crystal could have been a one-note heavy, but Crawford, whose career was revitalized by this dazzling performance, gives the character a note of desperation always lurking just below the surface. She keenly feels and resents her déclassé status as a shop girl selling perfume and as the kept woman of a wealthy businessman, a situation that brings her mostly contempt from other women and New York society in general. Crystal seethes with fierce resentment at Shearer's proper but distraught housewife, a kept woman of sorts herself, since she has little to do but appear decorative and supportive whenever her errant husband deigns to come home to their posh but rather desolate Park Avenue apartment or country estate.

Crystal's nastiness is subtly balanced by Cukor with sly shadings of humor so that we can feel a somewhat guilty pleasure over her cruel behavior without giving way to facile moral judgment on a woman who is playing the sexist game the only way she knows. Somehow the character's malice is beyond judgment, an elemental force that is her own enemy and will defeat yet not destroy her. But, as Cukor said in a tribute when Crawford died in 1977, even while playing Crystal, she "made no appeals for audience sympathy; she was not one of those actresses who have to keep popping out from behind their characters signaling, 'Look, it's sweet, lovable me, just pretending to be a tramp.'"

Cukor had earlier directed Crawford in some retakes for the 1935 MGM comedy *No More Ladies* when its director, Edward H. Griffith, was ill. She recalled that Cukor gave her the "roughest time" any director ever had, including telling her after she delivered a speech, "Very fine, Miss Crawford. Now, would you please repeat it? You remembered the words, now let's put some *meaning* into them."

She took his criticism well and revealed previously unseen acting finesse in *The Women* with her bravura display of two-faced behavior while taking a phone call from Stephen in the shop and manipulating him to see her that night instead of Mary ("Say, can you beat him? He almost stood me up for his wife!"). Crystal acts duplicitously lovey-dovey while covering the mouthpiece to snap coarse insults at an amused fellow clerk (Virginia Grey) who's commenting sarcastically on her hypocrisy, both actresses displaying flawless comic timing.

And Crawford's scene in her absurdly gaudy bathroom alternating cooing with a new flame over the phone while swapping hostilities with Mary's daughter (Virginia Weidler), who refuses her demand to call her "Auntie Crystal" (shades of "Mommie Dearest"), is another gem from Crawford and the precociously intelligent Weidler, who is equally good in another Cukor film,

The Philadelphia Story. Crawford would go on to two more unusually good performances in Cukor films for MGM, *Susan and God* (1940) and *A Woman's Face* (1941). All three of these films helped bring new respect to an actress who had been lumped with Katharine Hepburn and others as "poison at the box office" and would help lead Crawford to her Academy Award for Michael Curtiz's *Mildred Pierce* (1945) after she left MGM for Warner Bros.

Luce's highly defensive foreword to *The Women* takes pains to deny that her "rather too roomy" title implies that she is offering a comprehensive overview of the female gender. She calls it "a satirical play about a numerically small group of ladies native to the Park Avenues of America. It was clearly so conceived and patently so executed." But she goes on to contradict herself by claiming that "even history's notably nice women have been notably few" and that "an honest misogynist might conceivably make a case for the title's just applicability to the play's content." She also writes that "the women who inspired this play deserved to be smacked across the head with a meat-axe. And that, I flatter myself, is exactly what I smacked them with. They are vulgar and dirty-minded, and alien to grace."

Though the playwright tries to have it both ways and resentfully attacks Broadway reviewers for their largely negative view of her play as overly nasty (unlike the reviews the film version received for its more balanced perspective on life), Luce's foreword and even more so the play itself gleefully portray women as an often malicious, conniving lot. She is venting her wrath on her gender as a successful career woman who disdained fighting for the rights of less fortunate or less socially prominent women and made no bones about her need to exploit men sexually for social and monetary gain. Her biographer Sylvia Jukes Morris wastes no time getting to the point: "Clare's ambitious mother had always encouraged her drive and taught her how to dissemble and manipulate men."

What redeems the play to some extent is its keen observation of the limited Manhattan high society it portrays, a group of pampered women with too much time on their hands who do little but tear one another apart (making jokes about "Jungle Red" nail polish that gives them claws like bloody animals) and compete ruthlessly for men and money while fretting about their looks and aging bodies in a fancy beauty salon. A more sympathetic observer (such as Cukor) finds these women pitiable, to some extent, for the way they react to a situation of social oppression they can hardly begin to comprehend and that compels them to turn on others of their gender out of a sense of survival of the fittest. The one character in the play who sees the larger picture clearly, a middle-aged writer named Nancy Blake, is partly a Luce alter ego but is portrayed negatively as a resigned virgin whose books barely sell. Her biting remarks about the venality of Park Avenue society are treated with more emotional and intellectual weight in the film, although the adroit actress who plays the role, Florence Nash, still remains too marginal a presence, and it's unclear why Nancy hangs around such people.

The distinguished playwrights Moss Hart and George S. Kaufman invested in the play and gave helpful advice on construction and other matters to Luce when she was rewriting it during out-of-town tryout. Hart (who wrote the screenplay for Cukor's 1954 film *A Star Is Born*) wrote Luce in 1949, "I was filled with an admiration for it that I must confess I didn't have at the time it was produced. . . . It's a great deal more than just a slick, well-constructed play—it's a highly civilized and biting comment on the social manners and morals of our society, and women's place in it." Perhaps Hart was too involved in the genesis of the play, because "highly civilized" it's not, although "biting" is accurate. Above all, it was the filmmakers' artistry and compassion for the characters, particularly for the central character Luce so despised, that enabled them to work their transformation of *The Women* onscreen and make it a truly insightful "comment on the social manners and morals of our society, and women's place in it."

The unholy relish Sylvia Fowler takes in destroying Mary's marriage is so over the top that it becomes ridiculous even though it is actually appalling. Cukor's sensible response to the challenge of handling such an odious character was to ensure that Russell "really grabbed hold of the part and didn't worry about not being sympathetic." Cukor encouraged her to play in the exaggerated, flamboyantly farcical style she demonstrated in a test as one way of doing the role, even though she worried that "the critics will murder me." But he told her that since Sylvia was breaking up a family with a child involved, "If you're a heavy, audiences will hate you. Don't play it like a heavy, just be ridiculous."

The film made Russell's reputation as a comic actor and brought her a career highlight the following year in Howard Hawks's screwball comedy-romance *His Girl Friday*. Cukor recalled that Sylvia "was her first comedy part and she'd never had an audience really like her as a straight leading lady. . . . It

12.2. Rosalind Russell gets her comeuppance as Sylvia Fowler, the nasty gossip in *The Women*.
Cukor told the actress that Sylvia's shameless home-wrecking would make the audience hate her
unless she would come off as comically unsympathetic. Cukor compared himself to a "lion tamer"
while deftly handling his cast of 135 women. This farcical catfight at a Reno divorce ranch pits
Russell against her husband's mistress, Miriam Aarons (Paulette Goddard).
Source: Frame enlargement; MGM.

was broad low comedy, but it was also true. You felt this in the scene when
she went to Reno to get her divorce and had this sudden tantrum, the tantrum of a naughty eleven-year-old girl who'd never been properly slapped."

The catfight between Russell and Paulette Goddard, a Scarlett O'Hara
finalist who conveys both sexiness and relaxed sophistication, makes full play
of the physical ungainliness Russell so hilariously brought to the part of Sylvia. Goddard's Miriam Aarons, a sympathetic Jewish showgirl from New
York, has taken Sylvia's husband away from her, a comeuppance the audience
relishes, and she regards Sylvia's antics with amusement until the rejected wife
goes wild with rage. With her crooked glasses, a facial veil sometimes worn
around her neck, a hat whose load of flowers seems to cause its slant, her
arms all akimbo, and hands that seem to hang uselessly from her wrists,
Sylvia is an agitated mess of a person who exists only to wreak havoc on a
woman she calls "my very dearest friend in all the world."

Carlos Clarens in his book on Cukor refers to the slapstick treatment of Sylvia's "nearly pathological" behavior as making her seem like "a female impersonator trying to crash the powder-room." An upper-class woman who gleefully misbehaves like a lower-class harridan, Sylvia seems to have replaced her sexuality with emotional violence that turns physical in this scene after she's confronted with the showgirl who took her husband away. She even bites Goddard's leg in the donnybrook after they rip each other's clothes off. (*The Scarlett O'Hara War* amusingly shows Cukor thinking ahead to his next movie by checking out Goddard and other actresses for *The Women*. The funniest bit has Joan Crawford mishearing the title as *The Woman* and having to be corrected by Cukor. And oddly enough, Luce's next play, *Kiss the Boys Good-Bye* [1938], was a comical takeoff on the search for Scarlett; it was filmed in 1941 by Paramount as *Kiss the Boys Goodbye*, starring Mary Martin as a singer-actress and Don Ameche as the director of a Broadway show about the South.)

Another actress whose career received a major boost from the film of *The Women* was Joan Fontaine. Telephone scenes abound in *The Women*, since the writers have to get around the inability to show men onscreen, and the actresses expertly convey emotion under Cukor's guidance. The most memorable is Fontaine's call to her husband from the Reno divorce ranch to tell him she is pregnant. Fontaine, who plays the shy, good-natured, naïve Peggy, a young wife mocked by Luce but adored by Cukor, up to that point was a notoriously insecure actress who, he said, "was never really sure she could act." George Stevens told me that when she costarred for him opposite Fred Astaire in the RKO musical *A Damsel in Distress* (1937), she was so weak that Astaire wanted to replace her during shooting, but Stevens refused, saying, "If we take this girl out of this picture, she'll kill herself. . . . We've got to put her though this picture." Stevens explained, "I can understand Freddie, he's a great artist, but she was a girl with problems, you know, she cried and all that. . . . They were right, she was the wrong girl in the wrong spot. She never knew that they wanted her out of the picture, or she would have collapsed."

Cukor knew Fontaine from testing her for *Gone with the Wind*, and when he cast her in *The Women*, he told MGM they should take an option on her, but they declined. When she played the telephone scene, Cukor made such an effective climate for her to allow her to release her emotions in one of his actor-freeing long takes that you can actually see and hear Fontaine's exhilaration as she acquires self-confidence while the scene progresses. By

12.3.   "I really am an actress," Joan Fontaine told Cukor when she completed this long take in *The Women*. As Peggy Day reconciles by telephone with her estranged husband, the audience witnesses the previously insecure young actress blossoming under Cukor's guidance. Fontaine went on to become a polished star in Alfred Hitchcock films, winning an Oscar for the 1941 film *Suspicion*.
Source: Frame enlargement; MGM.

the time the phone call ends, she is ecstatic, both for winning back her husband and for becoming a genuine actress. As Cukor recalled, "She did this scene with the most tremendous force and feeling . . . and after the take she looked at me and said, 'I really am an actress.' She had been acting for four years and not very successfully. Suddenly there was this breakthrough. It was a thrilling moment."

Cukor believed that scene contributed to Alfred Hitchcock and David O. Selznick's choosing Fontaine for the lead role in *Rebecca*, the 1940 film that won the Academy Award for best picture and brought her an Oscar nomination. And in 1941's *Suspicion* for Hitchcock, Fontaine won the Oscar for best actress in one of Hollywood's most notorious rivalries, beating her mutually hostile sister, Olivia de Havilland, despite her brilliant performance in *Hold Back the Dawn*.

The ending of *The Women* has Mary Haines triumphantly heading toward (the still off-screen) Stephen in a nightclub, reaffirming her need for him but this time with a more clear-eyed sense of what marriage means. That may seem a conservative conclusion, yet under the circumstances the affirmation seems reasonable, unless the spectator, unlike the generous-minded gay director, has a fundamental antipathy to the concept of heterosexual marriage. When Mary's mother urges her to accept her husband's infidelity, Mary defines what marriage means to her: "And what if I don't *want* him on those terms? Oh, mother, it's—it's all right for you to talk of another generation when women were chattels and did as men told them to. But this is *today*. Stephen and I are equals. Why, we—we took each other of our own free will for life, because we loved each other. . . . And women that—that stand for such things are just beneath contempt."

Clarens's 1976 book argues that Mary's final lines in the film—that she has "no pride at all! That's a luxury a woman in love can't afford"—have "changed in the intervening years from sheer soap opera to incitement to riot." Indeed, the film changes the ending of the play to put that comment by Mary last, moving a bit earlier her comment (based on Luce's curtain line) about having had "two years to grow claws . . . Jungle Red!" But we don't actually believe that the newly confident, exuberant Mary has no pride. Cukor and his writers' emphasis in shifting the lines reinforces their sympathy with Mary as a positive force for a mature relationship in contrast with the antihuman attitudes of the vultures circling around her.

13

JOAN CRAWFORD IN *SUSAN AND GOD* WITH RITA QUIGLEY AND IN *A WOMAN'S FACE*

In 1982, when I was working as a Hollywood screenwriter, I had a meeting with an MGM executive to propose a contemporary remake of their 1940 Joan Crawford film *Susan and God*. In that adaptation of a 1938 play by Rachel Crothers, directed by Cukor from a screenplay by Anita Loos, Crawford plays a shallow New York society woman who undergoes a religious conversion while visiting England and returns to drive her friends crazy by proselytizing and meddling in their relationships while hypocritically neglecting her own husband and daughter. I wanted to update the Cukor film to make Susan a member of the Religious Right, a fundamentalist Christian bedeviling an agnostic young man caught in her emotional and sexual thrall. I was trying to exorcise the baleful effects of an unfortunate relationship with a religious fanatic Southern belle from whom I had barely managed to rescue myself.

The MGM executive was horrified. She said the studio couldn't make a film satirizing fundamentalist Christians because of the ferocious backlash that would result. Of course, the executive had never heard of *Susan and God* and seemed astonished that MGM had actually made such a film back in the day. In the waning days of my screenwriting career, from which I escaped two years later, gladly retiring to write books full-time, this was an object lesson in how much more daring the Hollywood studios were in the prewar era, the so-called Golden Age. Even when the Production Code exercised often damaging authority over Hollywood productions, the studios had a broader audience in those days and were more willing to deal with social issues than Hollywood in the new, mind-numbing "blockbuster era" that took hold in the mid-1970s. Another way a potentially controversial film such as *Susan and God* could be made in 1940 was that it had the cachet of being based on a Broadway play starring Gertrude Lawrence; MGM bought it for Norma Shearer, but she didn't want to play the mother of a teenager. Modern Hollywood, however, is terminally timid in its choice of material, partly because the audience had become so infantilized but partly also because of the lingering effects of the postwar show business blacklist, which I found had left the film industry in a lasting state of fear over offending powerful groups, especially of the reactionary sort.

So it still seems unusually refreshing to watch *Susan and God* and revel in the biting satire of a ridiculous woman whose religious mania has such ruinous effects. After giving Crawford one of her sharpest roles as a gleeful homewrecker in *The Women*, helping revitalize her career from the label of "box office poison," Cukor overcame MGM's qualms and cast her in two vehicles that allowed her dark side free rein, at least until the films did flip-flops to turn her sympathetic. Hollywood daring had its limits. But *Susan and God* and the 1941 drama *A Woman's Face*—a remake of a 1938 Swedish film starring Ingrid Bergman, with Crawford taking the role of an embittered burn victim who's become a hardened criminal—retain their appeal for connoisseurs of Dark Joan, even though *Susan and God* was a box office bomb (*A Woman's Face* did better business). These stories enable the usually glamorous actress to explore sides of her personality that Hollywood insiders recognized but that did not become publicly known for many years. Both films, in different ways, are about antisocial, warped characters and, significantly, revolve around her characters' troubled relationships with children. Crawford's biographer Bob Thomas, whose book details her "unthinking and sometimes horrid treatment of her children," confirmed to me that the frightening portrait of child abuse painted by her adopted daughter Christina Crawford in *Mommie Dearest*, her 1978 memoir, was accurate and that the star's physical and psychological abuse of her adopted children Christina and Christopher was an open secret in Hollywood.

The 1981 film of *Mommie Dearest*, starring Faye Dunaway and directed by Frank Perry, unconscionably turned the story into a camp laugh riot, encouraging viewers to get off on Crawford beating her little daughter. François

Truffaut told me that project was the only one he seriously considered of the many Hollywood offers he received. He finally turned it down because he felt insecure in his English and because he thought one star could not plausibly play another star onscreen, even though he admired Anne Bancroft, who was attached to the project at that point. If Truffaut, whose films show such deep empathy with children, had directed *Mommie Dearest*, it would have been a far different film, a serious examination of child abuse.

Many people in the film industry have felt it necessary to deny the truth about Crawford's child abuse, whether because of misguided star loyalty or personal guilt for failing to intervene. It's not known whether Cukor, who considered Crawford a friend, ever attempted an intervention on behalf of her children. But his depiction of her onscreen at least indicated an awareness of the darker side of her nature. He also could understand, while taking a critical perspective, the furiously driven nature of Crawford's drive for stardom and how her ambition and class resentment made her capable of monstrous behavior in her personal life even while she was a doggedly dedicated, if sometimes querulous, professional actress. Cukor could admire how she had the guts to play unlikable characters when so many other Hollywood actors refused to sully their images in that way. She needed little persuasion to push beyond her usual creative limitations in *The Women*, *Susan and God*, and *A Woman's Face* with Cukor's shrewd, careful, painstaking, sometimes blunt guidance.

These films in a sense are *about* Joan Crawford, and they stand out in Cukor's career for his adroit handling of an actress who was often poorly used by Hollywood but in their work together managed to transcend her flaws and maximize her potential, expanding her range for her future roles. The extent of her gratitude and friendship is made clear by the inscription she wrote on one of the framed photographs I saw on Cukor's wall of stars when I visited his home to interview him in 1981: "A great actor, a better director—So much devotion, Joan—The marriage offer is still good."

The widespread dismissal of Crawford's acting abilities is evident in comments by F. Scott Fitzgerald while he was working on a script for her at MGM. When Crawford heard of his assignment, she urged him, "Write hard, Mr. Fitzgerald, write hard!" He wrote in a letter to his longtime friend Gerald Murphy:

I am writing a picture called *Infidelity* for Joan Crawford [a project that eventually was shelved because of censorship concerns]. Writing for her is difficult. She can't change her emotions in the middle of a scene without going through a sort of Jekyll and Hyde contortion of the face, so that when one wants to indicate that she is going from joy to sorrow, one must cut away and then cut back. Also, you can never give her such a stage direction as "telling a lie," because if you did, she would practically give a representation of Benedict Arnold selling West Point to the British.

Cukor saw more in Crawford than most people did and knew how to use as well as overcome her limitations. There's a suitably mad gleam in Crawford's large, wide eyes in her giddy early scenes in *Susan and God*. The fanatical intensity, ruthless narcissism, manic chatter, and bitter fury barely contained in her screen image suit her well as Susan Trexel hectors her society friends in an affected mid-Atlantic accent about her newfound commitment to God while passing out inspiring pamphlets. "It's just *love love love—*," she explains, but pauses and adds quizzically, with a tilt of her head as if surprised, "—for other people, not yourself." In scenes Anita Loos effectively amplified from the play, Susan riles up her frivolous but more sensible friends by exposing their hypocrisies and other weaknesses. She causes ruptures in relationships and provokes their growing hostility despite their initial amusement when they think she's putting them on.

Susan is determinedly oblivious to her souse of a husband, Barrie, Fredric March at his most lugubriously unappealing in a jittery performance, as if Norman Maine is wandering in off the set of the first version of *A Star Is Born* (which Cukor passed on directing for Selznick in 1937, even though he would go on to direct the 1954 remake). Barrie is an aimless, wealthy sad sack with a misguided devotion to his estranged wife; it's inexplicable that he is so desperate to get back together with her, since Susan acts as if he hardly exists and is contemptuous when she is compelled to deal with him.

In this grim sort-of-comedy, she's even worse in her brazen neglect of her gawky adolescent daughter, Blossom (Rita Quigley), whose attempts to ingratiate herself with her cold-as-ice mother and sincere expressions of love are painfully shot down as inconveniences. Blossom is the heart of the film. She has come home for a brief visit from being shunted off to boarding school by her self-involved parents. Eventually the gamely chipper but fundamentally depressed girl finds common ground with her drunken father, who's guilty and more sensitive about how they've been neglecting her for years. But Blossom gradually realizes her mother doesn't care for her in the

13.1. Joan Crawford's hilarious, appallingly self-centered religious fanatic in *Susan and God*, Cukor's 1940 film of a satirical play by Rachel Crothers. Susan Trexel's unhinged flirtation with God causes the society woman to blithely ignore her alcoholic husband, Barrie (Fredric March), and to scorn her gawky adolescent daughter, Blossom (Rita Quigley).
Source: Frame enlargement; MGM.

slightest. When they have their reunion, a heartrending scene that's not in the play, Susan does not even look at the bouquet of flowers Blossom hands her. And when Susan comments on Blossom's "ghastly outfit," the girl responds in close-up with a mixture of wistful yearning and confusion, "Mother—you're *funny!*" She eventually can't help feeling that her mother's advice about improving her looks is actually thinly disguised hostility and repugnance. Blossom and her father are both outsiders in the situation, and Cukor always gravitates to outsiders. Letting down her composure, Blossom asks her father, "Why can't we all be together once in a while? Why can't we be some sort of family like other people?"

Blossom is smart and genuinely sweet in Quigley's sensitive portrayal. In her film debut, Quigley is given ample screen time by Cukor and Loos, more than in the play, and has the director's undivided sympathy. Blossom's braces, glasses, and ungainly clothes only make her more appealing to the viewer in this realistically unglamourized teenage role. Her pitiful attempts to win her mother's attention and favor are emphasized in several searing close-ups that turn the prevailing tone of comedy into something approaching tragedy. Her performance is perfectly balanced between the pathos of childlike dependency and the premature adulthood demanded of children of alcoholics. Less known than her younger sister, Juanita, a popular child actress in the 1930s, Rita also appeared for Cukor in his 1942 film *Keeper of the Flame* but retired from acting to raise a family and eventually became corporate secretary of the Petroleum Club of Los Angeles. Cukor's attentive and supportive work with children was rarely recognized, but the delightful performances of Virginia Weidler in *The Women* and his film after *Susan and God*, *The Philadelphia Story*, are further examples of how he responded to intelligent young actresses by treating them like adults, with uncommon respect.

Susan and God reaches its humorous apogee when Susan's guru, Lady Millicent Wigstaff (Constance Collier), shows up from Europe commanding a glee club of loony followers singing supposedly uplifting songs. Given the time period, there's an edge of neofascism in their behavior as they invade the Trexel house. A cowboy singer strumming a guitar warbles an inane song about world betterment, and the group of mostly teenagers parade through the house and out the door like extras in *Triumph of the Will*. The formidable Collier was a friend of Cukor and close to Katharine Hepburn as a longtime companion and acting coach. She scores satirical points against cultism in the film's take-off on the craze for Moral Re-Armament, an international spiritual movement established in 1938 (this element was also in the play). Nevertheless, that organization was antimilitaristic and anti-Nazi and was suppressed in occupied countries by the Hitler regime.

But after this bravely iconoclastic first two-thirds, *Susan and God* takes a misguided turn to mediocrity as MGM tries to make Susan redeemable and repentant. When she begins showing concern for her daughter and doing a makeover on her, it's as if she is becoming a different person. Even then, it's chilling when Susan tells her eager daughter, "Blossom, you look positively *human*. . . . If you're not going to be pretty, then the least we can do is make you interesting." Ironically, Susan is absurdly costumed in the movie, most bizarrely in a hat with a beekeeping veil while she's carrying her purse on a hobo stick. And there's some direct teasing of Crawford's familiar screen image when she tells the girl, "Listen, darling, if there's anything you want to know about this glamour business, just come to your mother. I've been at it lo these many years. You have to make your own success in this life, Blossom. You can't expect anybody else to do it for you." But despite such bracing moments of backsliding to Susan-as-Joan, it's impossible to take seriously her conversion to a loving wife and mother after her sadistic treatment of her family in the early going. *Susan and God* becomes a different film.

Quigley's engaging performance suffers when she is dolled up by Susan and MGM into a pretty but more ordinary-looking teenager having a house party with a bunch of vapid friends. She suddenly becomes a magnet for flirting boys while they are having a taffy pull. The film goes off the rails and enters another genre—can you imagine George Cukor directing a Henry Aldrich movie? The sentimental dramatic revamping of Susan is drawn from the play, but it's disheartening to see Cukor & Co. cop out so foolishly on their promising satirical premise, especially in such an implausible way. The film ends with both Susan and Barrie apologizing to each other with seeming embarrassment and Susan being made to exclaim in all seriousness, "O Dear God, don't let me fall down again!" Nevertheless, the scenes we remember from *Susan and God* are those of the protagonist acting batty and behaving so destructively to her family and supposed friends.

Rose Hobart is suitably frosty and unpleasant as Susan's principal social antagonist, telling her to "leave our souls alone" until the film makes them get all buddy-buddy. But Marjorie Main (who also did a good comic turn for Cukor in *The Women*) is hilarious throughout *Susan and God* as an acerbic servant who responds to Susan's faux-egalitarian order to call her by her first name by drawling it out sarcastically as *"Suuu-sannn."* The rest of the oddly assorted supporting cast includes Rita Hayworth in her budding-star period (doing a solitary rumba as if rehearsing for her pairing with Fred Astaire in *You Were Never Lovelier*), Nigel Bruce as her bizarrely unlikely old crock of a husband, Bruce Cabot and John Carroll as amiable lounge lizards, and Ruth Hussey (so sharp in *The Philadelphia Story*) underused as an attractively sporty gal unwisely carrying a mostly unrequited torch for Barrie.

Much of the film is indifferently staged, blocked without much fluidity, unusually so for a Cukor play adaptation, and it looks like a sitcom. You can feel the director coming alive when Cabot's character, an actor, suggests that they stage a confession scene to see how Susan will react, the kind of play-acting that always enables Cukor to add layers to his scenes. But the best-directed scene, a brief précis of the Cukor style, focuses on Hussey's furtively nuanced reactions as she and March do dancelike, expressively reframed moves around each other in a hotel room before tentatively embracing, and the camera lets us privately in on her ecstatic feelings as glimpsed over his shoulder. As is often the case, most of the problems of this film stem from the uneven original material, but in most other cases, Cukor and his writers manage to overcome such difficulties.

A Woman's Face is a tour de force of unaccustomed underplaying by Crawford in a role that makes her hideously deformed and has her Anna Holm turn her victimized alienation into a life of crime. Made up by the MGM artist Jack Dawn with a ghastly scar covering her right cheek and distorting her eye, Crawford was encouraged by Cukor to walk with a slight hunch and

13.2. Crawford fought Louis B. Mayer to play a disfigured, embittered woman who follows a life of crime in *A Woman's Face* (1941). Her impressive performance brings out depths in Crawford's acting persona other directors did not fathom; her Anna Holm takes especially sadistic pleasure in beating a beautiful woman (the off-screen Osa Massen) during a home invasion.

Source: Frame enlargement; MGM.

limp and to maintain the depressed mask of a lifetime of grief and ostracism. When he felt she was slipping back into her glamour mode, he would pantomime the Hunchback of Notre Dame from behind the camera, and she would get back in character. This is the closest Cukor came to making a horror film. With Anna's quickness to take offense, avoidance of eye contact, defensive sneer, dazed affect, and vicious snapping of her lines, Crawford draws powerfully from her dark emotional depths in conveying how such a victim could turn violently against the world that has cruelly rejected her.

A Woman's Face is a remake of *En kvinnas ansikte*, directed by Gustaf Molander, based on the play *Il etait une fois* (*Once Upon a Time*) by Francis de Croisset. Ingrid Bergman in her bloom of youth before coming to Hollywood from Sweden seems less warped, more pathetic than frightening, not as crazy to the limit of ugliness inside and out as Crawford seems in the early stages of the Cukor remake. Bergman's essential healthiness and physical robustness as a performer make her less intriguing for this kind of deconstruction of a star image that Crawford, a more brittle and on-edge actress, credibly portrays. The MGM film was originally intended by the studio as a Greta Garbo vehicle; her supreme beauty would have made it even more of a paradoxical meditation on the nature of movie glamour and how far the face does and does not reflect the inner workings of the soul. But Garbo rejected the part because of the character's deformity and villainy. And Crawford's casting was furiously opposed by MGM's studio chief, Louis B. Mayer: "Are you crazy?" he asked her. "Do you want the public to see you looking ugly? What kind of foolishness is that?" When she insisted, Mayer told her, "If you want to destroy your career, go ahead."

The result is a stark, almost humorless drama about how "suffering does not ennoble, it embitters," to borrow a line from Cukor's friend Somerset Maugham that President John F. Kennedy liked to quote. Crawford's face as Anna is not as ugly as her fiercely hostile, revengeful personality. Her plastic surgeon, Dr. Gustaf Segert (Melvyn Douglas), tells her that "since the first day I met you, you've presented a perfect picture of the most ruthless, terrifying, cold-blooded creature I've ever met." Cukor and his cinematographer Robert Planck keep Crawford's back to the camera at first, with only brief and partial glimpses of her face in a Stockholm courtroom where she is being tried for murder, before gradually revealing the full extent of her disfigurement. The film has an eerie, dreamlike, German expressionist look with its semiabstract, subtly angled, heavily shadowed, oppressive sets decorated by Edwin B. Willis. The visual style and the casting of Conrad Veidt as the villain sometimes echo *The Cabinet of Dr. Caligari*, the 1920 German nightmarish classic that costars Veidt as Cesare, a somnambulist brainwashed into criminality. *Caligari* clearly seems on the mind of the filmmakers while they portray Veidt's Torsten Barring as the criminal mastermind exercising a mesmeric control over Anna, with his silky voice and imposing face seen in tight close-ups and superimpositions of their two faces. Although the look of *A Woman's Face* effectively complements Anna's warped emotional state, the film sometimes feels more like an admirable technical exercise than a fully satisfying dramatic work.

Like *Susan and God*, *A Woman's Face* raises expectations that it does not fulfill when it softens Anna's character in its second half. Crawford and the film are far more striking before her face is healed by Dr. Segert. In a very Cukorian line, he says when the bandages are removed, "I unveil my Galatea—or my Frankenstein." As she reverts to her familiar Crawford glamorous appearance, it seems to become a different film, even if traces of her inner violence keep recurring. Once again, this Crawford film revolves around the mistreatment of a child, although in *A Woman's Face*, the horrific specter of Crawford as a potential child murderer is dissipated when she has a change of heart. Torsten has sent Anna to the country to become the governess of a four-year-old heir to a fortune, his nephew Lars-Erik Barring (Richard Nichols), so she can kill the boy and Torsten inherit the estate instead.

The screenwriters Donald Ogden Stewart and Elliot Paul, both strongly politically conscious, paint Torsten as a fascist who wants to use the fortune to take over neutral Sweden for Hitler-like ends: "What others have done in other countries, I can do here, because, Anna, the world belongs to the devil." Torsten's evil radiates convincingly from Veidt's cadaverous face, and as his hands nearly choke Anna with excitement while he expounds on his plan, her eyes show us she finally realizes he's insane. It's at this moment that her instinctual unwillingness to harm the boy turns into an urgent need to rescue him.

The latter half of the film is a parade of well-executed but overly obvious MGM special effects involving process screens and miniatures for the Barring rolling mill, ski lift, and waterfall and, at the climax, a race between two sleighs in the snow that serves as a D. W. Griffith-like ride to the rescue. John Waters, the film's second-unit director, shot that sequence in Sun Valley,

Idaho, but despite its technical finesse, the chase and the scenes around the ski lift are so blatantly artificial that they make us feel the boy is never really in jeopardy. The evolution of Crawford's character is not unbelievable, but having her redeem herself makes the second half seem mediocre in comparison with the chilling early scenes.

Cukor has Anna keep her hat slanted in those scenes to shadow her scarred face. She often raises her hand reflexively to touch the scar that has blighted her life. When she invades the home of the Segerts to blackmail the doctor's unfaithful wife (Osa Massen), Anna beats the attractive woman's face so rabidly that her action registers as revenge against beauty itself. And when Anna is called to testify in the courtroom, she tells the story of her childhood injury and turn to crime in a deliberately flat, matter-of-fact tone. To keep Crawford from relating the story with predictable emotion, Cukor had her recite the multiplication tables over and over and recite the lines with similar lack of affect. That shrewd piece of direction enables Crawford to give a remarkably compelling portrayal of a woman so weary of her affliction and the constant damage it has done to her life that she does not need to dramatize it.

Mayer's grudging acquiescence to Crawford's demand to let her make *A Woman's Face* might not have been entirely an indulgence of her creative ambitions. As MGM entered the 1940s, Mayer and other executives felt increasingly burdened by the expensive contracts and slipping box office appeal of some of its longtime female stars, including Crawford, Shearer, and Garbo (the coming of the war in Europe particularly damaged Garbo's box office value). Rather than simply pay them off, the studio put them into inferior vehicles that, whether by design or not, finished the careers of Shearer and Garbo and soon drove Crawford to leave MGM for Warner Bros., where her career took another upturn she attributed partly to what she had learned from working with Cukor. His direction of the last films of Garbo (*Two-Faced Woman*, 1941) and Shearer (*Her Cardboard Lover*, 1942), both commercial disappointments, reflects the dispiriting fact that neither MGM vehicle is remotely worthy of those two grand ladies of the screen.

Two-Faced Woman tried to bring Garbo into the contemporary world in a romantic comedy with her playing "twins" (i.e., masquerading as her own sister to win back her errant husband). But the comedy is labored, and her audience did not want to see her looking so ordinary, playing a ski instructor, wearing an unflattering bathing suit and rubber cap, and doing a rumba in a nightclub, as charming and kinetic as that sequence is. *Her Cardboard Lover* is based on a creaky play by Jacques Deval that Cukor had directed with Laurette Taylor starring in Rochester and had been filmed three times before by MGM. Cukor's film casts Shearer as a wealthy woman who takes on an obnoxiously fervent younger admirer (Robert Taylor) as her "secretary"/faux-boyfriend to ward off an earlier beau (George Sanders) and predictably falls for Taylor romantically. The title is unfortunately apt and off-putting, and the story is simply tired and uninvolving.

"Cukor had noted that Norma's creative energy was lower than usual," Lambert writes in his biography of the star. "Because he knew how to handle her as an actress, and was personally fond of her, he succeeded in recharging it. She worked at the part . . . but 'there were times when she seemed distracted.' By the end of shooting she was nervous and tired." She turned down an offer of a new contract at MGM and "didn't say that she had decided to retire from the screen, only that she needed a long vacation 'to think things over.' As her limousine left the studio, there was no royal farewell, and to the gateman, The Queen of the Lot was simply going home." Her departure, Garbo's retirement, and Crawford's exit for a new creative start at Warners, along with Taylor, James Stewart, and Mickey Rooney going off to war, marked the end of an era at MGM. But Cukor, as was his nature, endured.

The lasting affection and admiration Cukor felt for Joan Crawford after directing her with such rare insight, and his extraordinary skill at critical analysis of actors, were evident in his remarks at a memorial event he organized at the Academy of Motion Picture Arts and Sciences after her death in 1977:

> She was the perfect image of the movie star, and, as such, largely the creation of her own indomitable will. She had, of course, very remarkable material to work with: a quick native intelligence, tremendous animal vitality, a lovely figure and, above all, her face, that extraordinary sculptural construction of line and planes, finely chiseled like the mask of some classical divinity from fifth-century Greece. It caught the light superbly, so that you could photograph her from any angle, and the face moved beautifully. . . . The nearer the camera, the more tender and yielding she became—her eyes glistening, her lips avid in ecstatic acceptance. The camera saw, I suspect, a side of her that no flesh-and-blood lover ever saw.

13.3. Cukor admired the dedication Crawford brought to her work, calling her "the perfect image of the movie star, and, as such, largely the creation of her own indomitable will." Here they confer during the making of *Susan and God*.

Source: MGM.

14

CARY GRANT, KATHARINE HEPBURN, AND JAMES STEWART IN
THE PHILADELPHIA STORY

E ver since I first saw *The Philadelphia Story* (1940) in college in the late 1960s, I've had a hard time getting over the opening sequence of Cary Grant shoving Katharine Hepburn in the face. In this supposedly funny silent opening, the wealthy couple are breaking up. Grant is headed for his convertible with his bags, and Hepburn tosses his pipe rack and golf bag off the porch of their Philadelphia Main Line mansion and breaks one of the clubs over her knee. Grant, turning fierce, charges back toward her, with militaristic drums-and-marching music rearing up on the soundtrack, taps her on the shoulder with his left hand and juts it out as if to hit her in the face. Instead he pushes her through the door with the same hand and stalks away.

The film cuts to a shot of Hepburn lying on the floor just inside the mansion, looking irate and humiliated though not particularly damaged in a physical sense, a way of dismissing her husband's abusiveness as a bit of harmless frolic. *The Philadelphia Story* goes on to give us a great deal of genuine wit and romance, engagingly acted and glamorously photographed, elements that account in large part for the film's widespread popularity among film buffs and its status in some circles as a beloved classic. Yet this romantic allure coexists with Hepburn's character being repeatedly put down and humiliated, if no longer with physical violence after the opening sequence. Why audiences continue to find that opening funny is disturbing to me.

This scene setting up the story of a spoiled socialite being knocked off her pedestal with her complicity is in the screwball comedy tradition. That's one of my least favorite kinds of filmmaking, in which men and women pummel each other around as a substitute for the sexual interplay no longer allowed under the Production Code after 1934. Andrew Sarris defined screwball comedy in 1978 as "the sex comedy without sex . . . [but a] correlation of slapstick and violence with frustration." The rude term used by screenwriters and others for that kind of movie during the thirties and forties was "The Unfinished Fuck." A few genuine classics emerged from that cycle, such as *It Happened One Night*, *My Man Godfrey*, and *The Awful Truth* (part of the subgenre to which *The Philadelphia Story* also belongs, the comedy of remarriage), but most screwball comedies are hard to stomach today. As a result of the more strictly imposed Code, Hollywood's view of romance and sex, in most cases, went from being mature and sophisticated—reaching the apogee with Ernst Lubitsch's *Trouble in Paradise* in 1932—to being crude and juvenile, a trend that persists to the present day.

Although women were roughed around a lot in screwball comedies during the "Golden Age," men took abuse from women too, such as in Howard Hawks's *Bringing Up Baby*, the 1938 screwball comedy with Grant and Hepburn in which her insanely "madcap" heiress ruins the life and work of a distinguished, if shy and stuffy, paleontologist. I find that film acutely and painfully unfunny, since, as Jacques Rivette has written about Hawks's approach to comedy, his raison d'être is to chronicle "gaily, logically, and with an unholy abandon . . . the fatal stages in the degradation of a superior mind." Although *Bringing Up Baby* is considered a beloved classic today in our much coarser cultural environment, in its time it was a massive flop, one of the films that led to Hepburn being stigmatized as "box office poison."

She retreated from the screen to reconsider and revamp her career with the creative help of the playwright Philip Barry, who had served her so well with *Holiday*, and financial support from her improbable romantic partner Howard Hughes. She worked closely with Barry on her comeback vehicle, *The Philadelphia Story*. Hughes bought the film rights to the play for her, and after successfully performing Tracy Lord for a year onstage opposite Joseph Cotten and Van Heflin in the Theatre Guild production, she took the project to Louis B. Mayer at MGM and set up the film version directed by George

14.1. *The Philadelphia Story* was designed by Hepburn and Philip Barry to reshape her image as "box office poison" by bringing her independent nature within more conventional bounds. The play and Cukor's 1940 film succeeded in that goal, although with some detriment to Hepburn's previously challenging persona. James Stewart won the Oscar for best actor as Macauley (Mike) Connor, a quirky reporter who falls under the spell of her haughty Tracy Lord and helps soften her.

Source: Frame enlargement; MGM.

Cukor and produced by Joseph L. Mankiewicz. Hepburn demanded her own terms and mostly got what she wanted, although her first two choices of costars, Clark Gable (for her ex-husband) and Spencer Tracy (for the tabloid reporter), weren't available, so she agreed instead to work with Grant and James Stewart.

Their casting, in any event, seemed ideal for the roles of her once and future spouse, C. K. Dexter Haven, a recovering alcoholic, and Macaulay (Mike) Connor, a writer for *SPY* magazine (read: *Life*) with a touch of the romantic poet. Hepburn surrendered her top billing to Grant, in a sign of her diminished box office drawing power. Under Cukor's empathetic direction, the chemistry between Grant and Hepburn, as well as between Stewart and Hepburn, is droll and endearing enough to distract the viewer much, if not all of the time, from the demoralizing thrust of the storyline.

Both of these appealing men compete for Tracy's hand, once her dull fiancé, the businessman and aspiring politician George Kittredge (John Howard), is safely shunted aside because of his hopeless squareness and stunted view of women. But it's somewhat hypocritical for the film to caricature Kittredge as a male chauvinist while taking a similar, if more sophisticated, overall attitude toward the taming of Hepburn's independence. Kittredge's first scene uses sight gags to telegraph his unsuitability for Tracy when he has elaborately comical trouble mounting his horse for a ride on the Lord estate. Like so many other romantic comedies, the film loads the dice by making the man who is ultimately rejected such an outright loser (Howard also was one of the weakest elements of Capra's *Lost Horizon* with his whiny performance as Ronald Colman's brother). Kittredge indignantly objects to Tracy's sexual tryst with Connor the night before the wedding by saying, "But a man expects his wife to . . ." She fills in his thought, "To behave herself. Naturally," but Dexter slyly adds, "To behave herself naturally." In a neatly suspenseful bit of dramaturgy, it isn't certain until the very end whether the dashing, sardonic Grant or the earnestly romantic Stewart will finally walk down the aisle with Tracy in her improvised wedding ceremony. Even after she decides, Grant has to prompt her about what to say to her guests.

Marxist film historians like to use the word "project" to refer to a film's ideological agenda, and the word usually strikes me as pompous in ascribing a narrowly dedicated purpose to the complex process of cinematic storytelling. But in this case, the film's ideological project is clear and unmistakable. The often-scolding dialogue spells it out over and over just so we have no doubt. Hepburn collaborated with Barry and then with her good friend and mentor Cukor to change her image from a strongly independent woman who doesn't believe in marriage (or constructs an unorthodox partnership) to a more conventional woman whose still-challenging independence needs strenuous taming and domination by a man. It was a dispiriting project, this taming-of-a-pants-wearing-shrew agenda, and it worked. *The Philadelphia Story* was a hit: audiences were relieved to see the high, mighty, and arrogant Kate Hepburn humbled onscreen, her superiority brought down to earth and her independence strictly qualified within more manageable limits. As she tells the wedding guests, "I've made a terrible fool of myself, which isn't unusual."

The Philadelphia Story set the pattern for the rest of Hepburn's career and enabled her to sustain her stardom in films, theater, and television for decades longer, a remarkable achievement when the commercial viability of even a female star was usually brief before the aging process (i.e., turning forty or so) made her unbankable or forced her to end her career in horror movies. Hepburn, born in 1907, made her last theatrical film and last TV movie in 1994, retiring only when she became too infirm to get around and remember her lines. Despite her deliberate process of knuckling under from 1940 onward, she nevertheless played many memorable roles after *The Philadelphia Story*, even if she never again played a woman as eccentrically independent as Sylvia Scarlett and seldom as defiantly rebellious as Jo March or Linda Seton. She won the last of her four Academy Awards as best actress (still a record) in 1982 and kept working with Cukor in films and television until 1979. They made three more features and two TV movies together, including their late masterpiece, *Love Among the Ruins* (1975).

After seeing a stage revival of Barry's *Philadelphia Story* starring the estimable Blythe Danner, Andrew Sarris observed that as good as Danner was in it, the play doesn't work without Katharine Hepburn, because in a quite literal sense, the play is *about* Katharine Hepburn. Unlike *Holiday*, in which Linda is one of a group of characters whose lives intertwine with nearly equal importance, almost all the talk in *The Philadelphia Story* (and there's plenty of it) revolves around Tracy. The play obsessively analyzes her personality and character, criticizing her or rhapsodizing over her, raking over her past and what she did on the night before her wedding, and discussing whether she is or isn't marriage material.

For an actress whose autobiography is titled *Me* and who freely admitted the extent of her narcissism—carried to lengths unusual even for that profession: she writes of dumping her husband, Ludlow Ogden Smith, when her career took precedence, "I was a terrible pig. My aim was ME ME ME"— Hepburn's commissioning of a top playwright to refurbish her image was a determined effort at dramatic psychoanalysis. She even moved into his home to help him work out the story and its details. Rather than taking the occasion to flatter herself, which would have been a further dose of poison for her career, Hepburn encouraged Barry to examine her ruthlessly. The result was paradoxically a mixture of masochism and self-aggrandizement, alternately insightful and blinkered in its view of the subject.

When Hepburn died in 2003, the film historian Molly Haskell discussed with the *Los Angeles Times* this turning point in the actress's career: "She had to do some kind of self-abasement to stay on the good side of the audience. She was beautiful and upper-crust, men felt she was intimidating, she had to give them something. *The Philadelphia Story* was written for and about her, and it's really quite mean. It shows you all the contortions a woman has to go through to have a full life." In *From Reverence to Rape*, Haskell elaborates: "In *The Philadelphia Story*, she is attacked from all sides for her supposed coldness (for real coldness, see Grace Kelly in the fifties' musical version, *High Society*), of which there is not a shred of evidence. This is the furtive revenge of mediocrity on excellence; she is being convicted merely for being a superior creature." And yet, as Haskell adds, even in otherwise demeaning films such as *Bringing Up Baby* and *The Philadelphia Story*, "Her combined integrity, intelligence, and proud, frank beauty rise to the surface, making us feel, with her, the difficulty and joy of being such a woman."

Hepburn's biographer William J. Mann writes, "With *The Philadelphia Story*, however, Hepburn was consciously—even cynically—responding to every fan-magazine criticism she'd endured for the past decade. . . . *The Philadelphia Story*, for all its charm, feels calculated and contrived—because it *is*. If there's anything spiky about Tracy Lord, it's there only so it can be filed down to a smooth, glossy finish." With the success of *The Philadelphia Story* at the box office, as Mann puts it, film "exhibitors hailed the new and improved Kate."

Cukor was one of her enablers in *The Philadelphia Story*, loyally going along with her project of self-reinvention. But as always he brought out as many shadings in her performance as the material allowed—and more. In their long, close, and fertile collaboration, they were simpatico, and he understood how to help her bring out the complexities and nuances of what struck conventionally minded people as her "difficult" screen presence. He was working again with one of his favorite screenwriters, Donald Ogden Stewart, who was too modest in calling *The Philadelphia Story* "the least-deserving-of-praise bit of script writing I have ever done, since Philip Barry had written it so beautifully that my task was mainly an editing one. My chief contribution otherwise consisted in a few added scenes for Jimmy Stewart, and the Oscar which

14.2. *The Philadelphia Story* has Tracy reject her dull fiancé on the morning of their wedding to choose instead between Stewart's Mike Connor and her errant ex-husband, C. K. Dexter Haven (Cary Grant). Although Dexter, a recovering alcoholic, has needled her throughout, she recognizes and accepts his love in the suspenseful finale.

Source: Frame enlargement; MGM.

I received for the screenplay was probably one of the easiest ever obtained." Nevertheless, in this exemplary adaptation of a play into effortlessly fluid cinema, the screenwriter's work included eliminating a minor character (Tracy's brother) who schemes to allow the tabloid reporter and his photographer partner, Liz Imbrie (Ruth Hussey), into the wedding party. The screenwriter much more effectively makes that scheme a blackmailing ploy by Dexter to win back his former wife, who was alienated by his evidently quite serious addiction to drink.

C. K. Dexter Haven is the least showy of the three leading characters, but Grant, so comfortable in tandem with Hepburn after *Sylvia Scarlett* and *Holiday*, gives a by-now-characteristically subtle performance. Dexter is mostly content to remain an amused observer of Tracy's deteriorating relationship with Kittredge and even her affair with Connor, while standing back, literally, and waiting for her to realize she's still in love with him. Grant's quietly vulnerable look in a pair of close-ups as she is choosing between him and Stewart in the suspenseful finale is touching, a sign of Dexter's newfound respect for Tracy.

And yet Dexter fires many of the sharpest darts at her personality earlier, describing "the withering glance of the goddess" she supposedly turned on him during their marriage, when she thought of him as "a kind of high priest to a virgin goddess . . . chaste and virginal," driving him to drink because she was so aloof and narcissistic. When she insists, "I'm not interested in myself for the moment," he retorts, "Not interested in yourself? You're fascinated, Red. You're far and away your favorite person in the world. . . . This goddess must and shall remain intact. There are more of you than people realize. A special class of the American female: The Married Maidens." He tells her she'll "never be a first-class human being or a first-class woman until you've learned to have some regard for human frailty." Thoroughly chastened, she is made to admit just before her wedding, "Oh, Dext! I'm such an unholy mess of a girl."

It's left ambiguous how literally Dexter and Barry—and Hepburn herself, as a collaborator with the playwright—mean their listeners to take all the talk of Tracy's "virgin" nature in marriage or how much they are using such imagery metaphorically to accuse her of what used to be called "frigidity." To give a prominent example of how, before the modern feminist movement took hold, that fraught word was trotted out as an alibi for male misbehavior: When I asked a friend who covered the Kennedy White House for the *Wall Street Journal* if he and his fellow reporters knew of the president's philandering and why they did not write about it, he said they did know but let it go unreported because they were told by the White House press office simply that "Jackie is frigid." That was enough, the reporter said, to stop them from writing about her husband's carrying-on.

Nevertheless, Hepburn's biographer Mann reports of her, "Several friends insisted she had a lifelong aversion to the actual act of intercourse. 'That seemed to be the line she didn't like to cross,' said one. 'She could enjoy the affections of men up to that point, but loathed going any further.'" Mann goes on to suggest that aversion helped explain her "unconscious prerequisite" for relationships with men who had conflicts over their own sexuality: "The suffering of these men, their confusion and anguish, seems to have inspired in Hepburn the caretaker sort of feelings she once brought to her relationship with her brother Tom."

It was unusual for a Hollywood romantic comedy in that era to have a man sneering at a woman as a "virgin goddess." But we come to realize this is a coded male excuse by Haven for his own inadequacies (and, by extension, for those of Kittredge). The language about sex is unusually frank for a 1940 film, as well as the pivotal incident in which Tracy and Connor go off while tipsy and obviously have sex in or around the pool—even if the incident is elliptically portrayed, and Connor gallantly explains it away as "exactly two kisses and a rather late swim"—but the Code always was more lenient in dealing with Broadway hits.

This development disproves the claim that she is a "virgin goddess." When Kittredge says, "There's a kind of beautiful purity about you, Tracy, like— like a statue," she replies softly and hesitantly, registering her disillusion with him, "I—I don't want to be worshipped. I—want to be loved. I mean *really loved*." Near the end, when her father (John Halliday) tells her she looks "like a queen. Like a goddess," she tells him she feels "like a human. Like a human being." But it takes her a long time to get to that point in the movie. And her relationship with her philandering father is the most twisted sexual element in the film. He actually suggests, to her disgust, that the reason he is carrying on with a young ballerina in a show he is backing is that she makes up for his daughter's failure to love him properly as "a devoted young girl . . . full of warmth for him." He berates her as "a prig or a perennial spinster, however many marriages. . . . You have everything it takes to make a lovely woman except the one essential—an understanding heart." At the end, just before getting remarried, Tracy is made to rapturously reassure her father that she loves him: "Never in my life have I been so full of love before." Perhaps in this too we can see traces of Hepburn's ambiguous relationship with her intimidating father and his response to her declaration of intent to become an actress by slapping her in the face.

Barry's stylized dialogue, as Cukor pointed out, has a quality resembling song, and the rhythms of the dialogue exchanged among these splendid actors are elegantly orchestrated by Cukor and his actors. But the playwright also indulges in some overripe romantic dialogue, as pretentious as *Holiday* is offhandedly natural seeming. Despite Cukor's exquisitely intimate direction

14.3.   Although some directors avoid or are not equipped to handle analytical sessions with their actors, Cukor's directing centered around intense, often-lengthy talks and rehearsals with his actors about the script and their characters, such as this session with Hepburn and Stewart on *The Philadelphia Story*.
Source: MGM/Photofest.

and the suitably dreamy romantic music by Franz Waxman, it becomes embarrassing to hear James Stewart gamely rhapsodizing about Tracy as verbal foreplay in the moonlight: "You're lit from within, Tracy, you've got fires banked down in you—hearth fires and holocausts!" Trying to bring him down to earth, she interjects, "I don't seem to you made of bronze?" He rattles on, "No, you're made out of flesh and blood. That's the blank, unholy surprise of it. Why, you're the golden girl, Tracy, full of life and warmth and delight."

Sarris accurately described Stewart as "the most complete actor-personality in the American cinema," but the actor had some trouble with such purple pseudopoetry. With Cukor's help and some encouragement from Noël Coward, who was visiting the set, Stewart rose to the occasion and won the best-actor Academy Award for playing the deceptively diffident young writer. That was widely seen as a "consolation Oscar" for missing out the previous year with his great performance in Frank Capra's *Mr. Smith Goes to Washington*. Stewart himself voted for his good friend Henry Fonda in *The Grapes of Wrath*, which clearly was the most memorable performance of 1940, but Stewart's adroit comic-dramatic performance in Cukor's film is fully deserving of any award. Although Stewart often told me and other interviewers that he preferred directors who didn't give him much dialogue and let him express his feelings visually, he contradicted that claim by being always masterful with dialogue in his range of work for such remarkably diverse directors as Capra, Cukor, Lubitsch, George Stevens, and Billy Wilder, all of whom rely heavily on brilliantly written and spoken language. People forget that Stewart, hardly an inarticulate cowhand even if he liked to pose as one, went to Princeton and could hold his own in any kind of script or situation, whether it demanded haunting pantomime or a torrent of talk (such as his filibuster in *Mr. Smith*) or both (as in Alfred Hitchcock's *Vertigo*).

Connor chafes at his demeaning job as a snoop for the Luce-like picture magazine (edited and published by Cukor's favorite oily heel, Henry Daniell) and thoughtlessly takes his devoted but cautious partner, Liz, for granted while succumbing to the glamorous charms of Tracy Lord. Liz is philosophical about his immaturity and determined to wait it out; Hussey, who previously acted for Cukor in *Susan and God*, was nominated for an Oscar for her deftly urbane performance here. But Connor is also portrayed as something of an intellectual. He is a published short-story writer whose book, which Tracy examines at the local library, is what initially enables her to see past his shambling, cranky, common-man facade to the transgressive cut-up she will find so unexpectedly sexy. Stewart also has a marvelous drunk scene with Grant when they share confidences about Tracy late at night. Grant, a master at the fine and underrated art of listening, adlibbed "Excuse me" when Stewart unexpectedly hiccoughed, a match of those small and endearing character bits Cukor encouraged in loosening up his actors.

Indeed, the whole movie could be described as *The Loosening-Up of Tracy Lord*. Given some of the most glamorous lighting of her career by Joseph Ruttenberg and with her face and form displayed fondly throughout by Cukor, she shows off her trimly athletic figure while doing a graceful dive in her swimsuit before her sexual escapade with Connor. And if that isn't enough to demonstrate that her alleged frigidity is merely a male construct, her jettisoning her fiancé on the morning of the wedding after he says he is willing to take her back if she promises never to drink again shows the men in her life that she is capable of being her own boss. Yet when Dexter gives her a wedding gift of a model of the yacht he designed and built and on which they spent their honeymoon, the *True Love*, she tells Kittredge, "My, she was yar." She defines that nautical term as "easy to handle, quick to the helm. Fast, bright. Everything a boat should be—until she develops dry rot." And when at the end of the film she tells Dexter, "Oh, Dexter, I'll be yar now. I'll *promise* to be yar," it sounds sort of charming as romantic banter until you stop and realize that *Katharine Hepburn* is promising to be easy to handle or, to use another definition of the term, "maneuverable."

Hepburn's next film after *The Philadelphia Story* was her first teaming with Spencer Tracy, MGM's *Woman of the Year* (1942). In a lively and mostly affectionate battle of the sexes, he plays a no-nonsense sportswriter to her sophisticated, soignée international correspondent. She chose George Stevens over Cukor to direct, relating in her autobiography, "I had to explain to Cukor that this script had to be directed by a very macho director from the man's point of view and not the woman's. I'm sure that George was very disappointed." She admitted that this was one of the few times that something "sort of threatened us." Sarris in his *New York Times* review of McGilligan's Cukor biography criticized Hepburn's perpetuation in her autobiography of the "thinly veiled condescension" of Cukor being "demeaned with a wink as a 'woman's director,' a far cry from the womanizing he-men who were generally the rule in Hollywood's directors' chairs. . . . It is a singularly ungracious comment, the reader might think, to make about one's movie mentor, who, along with the producer David O. Selznick, virtually molded Ms. Hepburn in *A Bill of Divorcement* (1932) and who later directed her in nine of her most felicitous performances, among them *Adam's Rib* and *The Philadelphia Story*."

Woman of the Year, for all its qualities, has a finale far more demeaning to Hepburn's image as an independent woman than anything in *The Philadelphia Story* other than its opening gag celebrating spousal abuse. Playing a prominent journalist modeled after Dorothy Thompson, Hepburn is humiliated at inordinate length in an excruciatingly unfunny slapstick routine written by John Lee Mahin showing her failing to make breakfast properly as

Tracy watches her with silently amused dismay. Even Hepburn objected to that retake replacing the original ending after a preview ("That's the biggest bunch of crap I've ever read!"), but in the end she went along with it, and the film became another hit, establishing Tracy and Hepburn as the screen's foremost romantic couple. Joseph L. Mankiewicz, who produced *Woman of the Year* as well as *The Philadelphia Story*, said he devised that new ending for Stevens's film as "the equivalent of her being taken apart in *Philadelphia Story*." Cukor would go on to make two of the best Tracy-Hepburn vehicles, *Adam's Rib* and *Pat and Mike*, whose egalitarian love stories are more truly feminist. And even if Hepburn didn't consider Cukor "very macho," *Pat and Mike* not only gives ample and expertly engineered attention to her athletic prowess but also shows her beating up a hoodlum played by Charles Bronson.

15

INGRID BERGMAN AND ANGELA LANSBURY IN *GASLIGHT*

"Look at the eyes," John Ford said when asked how one should watch a motion picture. "The secret is people's faces, their eye expression, their movements." Priscilla Bonner, who acted for Ford in *3 Bad Men*, his 1926 silent Western, said he told her, "The camera photographs your innermost thoughts and picks them up. If you concentrate, the camera can look into your innermost feelings."

When Ingrid Bergman was preparing to act for George Cukor in *Gaslight* (1944), playing a woman whose husband (Charles Boyer) systematically tries to drive her mad, Cukor suggested she visit a mental institution and study the patients. Bergman focused on one particular woman patient and her eyes. She watched how the woman's eyes moved around, in and out, when she felt uncertain or wasn't sure what was happening to her. Bergman's Academy Award–winning performance in *Gaslight* is a subtle and complex tour de force of varied eye movements and other facial expressions, evanescent and mercurial, reacting to her husband's machinations. The artfully shaded lighting by Joseph Ruttenberg and the superb art direction and set decoration of Victorian London in the 1870s (by Cedric Gibbons, William Ferrari, Edwin B. Willis, and Paul Huldschinsky, who also won Oscars) helped Cukor provide a claustrophobic atmosphere and what he called a "tone" in which Bergman could operate so effectively.

With her face and body language and mostly somnambulistic but occasionally hysterical dialogue, simulating a kind of mental haze with intermittent flashes of lucidity and rage, Bergman through Cukor's methodical pacing and detailing conveys the insidious stages of incipient madness and self-doubt. The film was entirely shot on sound stages at MGM in Culver City, California, a sterling example of the studio system at the height of its craftsmanship and befitting its feeling of claustrophobia.

With this adaptation of the 1938 British play *Gas Light* by Patrick Hamilton (called *Angel Street* when it was a hit on Broadway), Cukor managed to renew his previous luster after a string of so-so assignments at MGM. He had returned to the studio after six frustrating months in the U.S. Army at the Signal Corps Photographic Center at the old Astoria Studios in Queens, New York, where he had shot three of his early talkies for Paramount. Cukor enlisted out of a sense of patriotic duty but had to serve as a private and never won the commission he wanted, which his biographer Patrick McGilligan suggests may have been because of his homosexuality. After going through basic training, which he found especially rigorous at his age (forty-two), Cukor "looked just terrible, physically, arriving in the barracks," recalled Gottfried Reinhardt, who had produced Cukor's *Two-Faced Woman* in 1942. "He was actually too old to go though this and then to be a private. He looked beaten, pathetic."

There was constant hostility between the army officers, with their entrenched way of working, and the Hollywood newcomers. Not only that, but Cukor and others were often lorded over by men who had been junior colleagues in Hollywood. Cukor was mostly relegated to menial duty, such as mopping floors, and making training films, including one about how to build latrines and another called *Electricity and Magnetism, Part II—Ohm's Law* (written by the future Hollywood screenwriter Arthur Laurents; the title usually is mistakenly given as *Resistance and Ohm's Law*). Cukor admitted he knew nothing about the subject, and he tried to improve the technical dialogue with actors on the set. Once Cukor said to Laurents about a humorous classroom scene he had written, "I don't believe it," and the young writer replied, "Did you believe *Her Cardboard Lover?*" Cukor snapped, "You're pretty fresh," but they became friends anyway. Cukor said of his army films, "They were stupid."

But he sometimes had the opportunity to direct musical numbers for entertainment segments of the *Army-Navy Screen Magazine*, including one starring Ingrid Bergman. While directing her, Cukor had an argument with Capt. George Baker, a Hollywood hand who had been commissioned and was functioning as producer. Baker tried to clear the set of army personnel who had crowded around to watch Bergman. Cukor said, "It's OK with Miss Bergman and me. The boys can stay." Baker, enraged, said, "I'm in charge here, Private Cukor! I want them out and they're going! Now!" Cukor turned on him: "Listen, you little pipsqueak: you were a prop boy at Metro before the war, you'll be a prop boy at Metro after the war. The boys can stay!" Cukor achieved his purpose when Baker left the set.

What a pleasure it was, then, for Cukor to return to the expert filmmaking craftsmen and resources of MGM. He worked on *Gaslight* from a script

15.1. Ingrid Bergman's complex, delicate, passionate portrait of Paula Alquist, a woman driven to the brink of madness by her conniving, sociopathic husband (Charles Boyer), in *Gaslight* (1944) won her the Academy Award for best actress. The climax comes when Paula turns the tables on her pleading husband after she manages to have him arrested and placed under restraint in the attic.

Source: Frame enlargement; MGM.

by John Balderston (who had preceded him on the project), Walter Reisch (who worked on construction and visual details), and the British playwright John Van Druten (who specialized in dialogue; Cukor filmed his play *Old Acquaintance* as his 1981 swan song, *Rich and Famous*). Hamilton's thriller is an effective piece of audience-gripping melodrama but is rather thin in its characterization, not as rich as in Cukor's film version, which concretely demonstrates how much a director can do with his material. The dialogue in both play and film is rather blunt as the husband, Gregory Anton (aka Sergius Bauer), manipulates events and the perceptions of his wife, Paula Alquist, to try to convince the susceptible woman that she is losing her mind like her mother, whom he falsely claims died in an asylum.

Gregory is a psychopath who killed her aunt, Alice Alquist, a celebrated opera singer, in the house and returns to it with Paula (called Bella in the play) to search among the victim's belongings in the attic for her missing precious jewels. In effect, the jewels are the Hitchcockian "MacGuffin," the objects that motivate the villain but are of incidental thematic importance, although of great value. They turn out to be hidden in Alice's costume for playing the Byzantine empress Theodora, a former prostitute who would have been played by Ava Gardner in a film project, *The Female*, written for Cukor by John Lee Mahin for Pandro S. Berman to produce at MGM in the 1950s. The search for the jewels is rather preposterous, since the jewel-encrusted costume (in which the valuable gems are mixed with jewels made of paste) is hiding in plain sight among the clothing, furniture, and bric-a-brac in the attic, conveniently in front of a painting of the aunt as Theodora.

But the real theme of the play and film is the situation of a husband manipulating his wife's fragile psyche for his own sinister advantage. Gregory hopes to have Paula committed because she has incriminating information on him and so he can search for the jewels more expeditiously. His frantic, clandestine nocturnal searches cause Paula to hear his footsteps above her bedroom and to see the gaslight dimming as he turns on the lamp in the attic. But he smoothly makes her doubt her own senses while he schemes to portray Paula's increasing paranoia and panic as credible symptoms of the degradation of her personality. Gregory also hides a painting, a brooch, and other objects from Paula to convince her that she has lost or hidden them. Bergman and Boyer are both playing, to some extent, against type. Her robust, tall, healthy figure and strong personality are reduced to the specter of a fragile, dazed, often halting woman in a state of psychological collapse. Boyer, known for playing suave and dashing romantic figures, gives a frighteningly steely performance. His low, harsh, but deceptively matter-of-fact verbal manipulations are accompanied by frozen gazes at Paula, disrupted only by small movements of his face and eyebrows; he is literally supercilious in his disapproving cruelty. Boyer, several inches shorter than Bergman, had to stand on boxes and wear high shoes and boots to act with her, but the result of their interplaying and intricate power struggle is compelling.

Gaslight is a film that starkly analyzes the harsh power imbalance of patriarchy and the sadomasochistic kind of relationship that can beat a woman into psychological submission in marriage. The film is often painful to watch but fascinating in its acute understanding of warped sexual dynamics. In Cukor's body of work, *Gaslight* is a dark reversal of his frequent Pygmalion-Galatea theme. Gregory's behavior, like that of a cruel director mistreating an actress, stems from a similarly extreme form of masculine privilege, akin to the way Professor Henry Higgins obsessively browbeats the Cockney flower girl Eliza Doolittle in Cukor's 1964 film, *My Fair Lady*. But Higgins's behavior is less sinister in that film, a musical comedy based on George Bernard Shaw's *Pygmalion*, because his tutelage is with Eliza's energetic (if often exasperated) collaboration and has a largely positive effect. *Gaslight*, play and film, belatedly introduced the now-popular term "gaslighting" into the language in the 1960s to describe how someone can be fooled into doubting his or her own perceptions or memories. Paula, astonished when she finally comes to understand her manipulation, exclaims that there has been "nothing real from the beginning," including in their seemingly idyllic courtship: "There've been times when I thought I only dreamed those days."

A 1940 British film of *Gaslight* preceded the MGM version, and the Hollywood studio not only bought the rights but, as often happened in those days, tried to destroy all the prints. Yet one survived and has been released with Cukor's film on the Blu-ray edition for comparison (for its British release, the MGM remake was retitled *The Murder in Thornton Square*). Directed by Thorold Dickinson, the 1940 *Gaslight* film is gripping in a quieter and less powerful way, and the expanded elements of the Hollywood version, including scenes of the couple behaving romantically in Italy before their marriage, add depth to the situation. In one piece of foreshadowing as Gregory plays the piano, Paula sings a selection from the Donizetti opera *Lucia di Lammermoor*, which has a celebrated mad scene and deals with a woman who kills her husband.

The husband in the British *Gaslight* is played by Anton Walbrook, who speaks in soft, silky tones as he behaves insidiously but less brutally than Boyer's character. Diana Wynyard, who uses a wispy voice, is softer, paler, more fragile-seeming than Bergman, but as Cukor commented, "Ingrid Bergman had no difficulty in grasping the character of Paula Alquist's essential frailty, but she would complain, 'Oh, I look so *healthy*.' However, I think healthy people *can* be frightened. In fact, very often it's perhaps more moving."

Cukor's film uses more close-ups than the British film, punctuating the exchanges between Paula and her husband with large, intimate glimpses into her feelings and soul, making it seem to be taking place more from the woman's point of view. Bergman's performance is like a river of flowing reactions, not so much a matter of dazzling set pieces—although there are some, including her breakdown as Gregory torments her at a musical recital—but a more measured and incremental series of stages in Paula's victimization. In contrast, the British film, after showing the murder of her aunt (which the remake avoids doing), jumps far more quickly to Gregory's scheming against his wife's mental health, and the Cukor film is more psychologically convincing for being so chillingly methodical.

The mood is brilliantly sustained, paced, and varied by Cukor and Ruttenberg with their mesmerizing mise-en-scène. A further sign of the director's advancing ease, fluidity, and mastery in the cinematic medium, *Gaslight* perhaps most resembles *Camille* in its exquisitely chosen settings and integration of the lead actress into a period milieu. Cukor and Ruttenberg frequently use low angles, deep-focus photography, and a dense interplay of light and shade to increase the sense of menace and foreboding and to make the ceilings and other objects in the house seem to weigh down and squeeze in on the beleaguered heroine. *Gaslight* is a highly sophisticated example of the Old Dark House horror/noir genre, and the use of multiple levels in the house on Thornton Square, with ascending degrees of dread up to the mysteriously blocked-off attic, is orchestrated dramatically and through escalating use of deep shadows. As usual with Cukor, he is not doing so to show off his facility with the camera but rather to serve his performers. The house becomes virtually the third character in this unholy triangle. At one point Paula says, "I am afraid of this house."

Bergman eloquently uses her body language to express her sense of intimidation. We often see her sneaking fearful looks above herself to try to understand the noises and the changes in the gas lighting, cringing in abject terror on her bed and elsewhere to fend off the assaults on her sanity, and walking in twisting and contorting ways. When she contrastingly flashes her famously magnetic, life-embracing smile or, in a particularly liberating scene, dances gaily around the sitting room in long shot as Gregory plays a waltz from Johann Strauss II's *Die Fledermaus* on the piano, the contrast with her generally oppressed mood is enhanced. The many inventive and intuitive ways Bergman uses her eyes like the mental patient she observed, as Paula desperately seeks answers from Gregory and the decor while the camera burrows in extraordinarily close to her, make us share her feeling of confusion and disorientation and her search for clarity. Even when we realize what Gregory is doing to her (Cukor lets the audience in on the actual threat in the manner of Alfred Hitchcock's suspense films), the panic inherent in her situation and Bergman's controlled performance is viscerally conveyed, beyond our rational sense of the goings-on.

As the film progresses, we realize that it is a dual study of madness, both the alleged insanity that Paula fiercely resists but sometimes feels she is succumbing to and the genuine and more frightening madness of Gregory, the ruthless psychopath who so smoothly controls her. His low, even tone is punctuated only with rare outbursts when he feels his game is close to being exposed. But for the most part he speaks like a hypnotist, in a deceptively soothing tone and with maddening repetitions of her first name, usually a flaw in screenwriting but fitting here because of his condescending, peremptory, incantatory tone. Not only a strange man for failing to value and instead abusing his beautiful wife, Gregory has an obsession with the jewels (which can't be sold in any case, since they are too famous) that is a sign of his mania and a deranged continuation of his hidden guilt and subconscious need for exposure as a man who murdered out of greed.

Paula's fearful descent into a chaotic state of mental breakdown precedes her gradual rebirth in the latter part of the film. One glaring flaw in the film is the casting of Joseph Cotten as the Scotland Yard detective who takes an interest in the cold case of Alice's murder and a romantic interest in Paula. The unexplained presence of this American in London makes him seem like a participant in a precursor of a law enforcement exchange program between the U.S. government and Scotland Yard ("MISS BERGMAN AND MR. COTTEN Through Courtesy of DAVID O. SELZNICK," as the opening credits put it; Selznick owned both of their contracts, accounting for the improbable casting, but he otherwise did not interfere unduly in the production). In the original play, the detective is a sixtyish retired bloke called Mr. Rough, a hearty sort who functions in a more no-nonsense, less polished way than Cotten's Brian Cameron.

But as in any melodrama, we are relieved when the doggedly devoted but gentlemanly investigator becomes involved in the life of the tormented woman and becomes her rescuer, eventually invading the house to confront her husband. The detective clears her mind of the fear of madness by reassuring her that she has not been imagining the odd things that have been going on around the house. The elements of romance between them are kept minimal, since they barely know each other, but a quick coda suggests a future relationship, with Dame May Whitty as an inquisitive neighbor exclaiming "Well!" while seeing them together on the roof at the fadeout. Whitty's involvement is another clumsy contrivance; she meets Paula on a train journey, like her Miss Froy in Hitchcock's *The Lady Vanishes*, but improbably turns out to live across the square from her in London, turning up periodically to provide busybody comic relief.

Bergman initially chafed at Cukor's method of working. She recalled, "Cukor explains everything in such detail that sometimes you feel like saying, 'Please don't say any more because my mind is so full of explanations.' I used to tease him by saying if it were a little line like 'Have a cup of tea,' he would say what kind of a cup it was and what kind of tea it was until you got so worried you couldn't say the line." She may have felt overwhelmed at first with a husband driving her crazy with his constant needling remarks before the camera and a director seeming to hector her with constant chatter behind the camera, even if all that contributed to the extraordinary quality of her performance. Cukor commented:

> Between setups I try to compensate for the absence of an audience, and the special tone and excitement that an audience can lend a performance, by going in and talking to the actors about all sorts of things. I'm really not quite sure what I say, but it's just to keep them stimulated, on edge. . . . When I did this with Ingrid, she'd look at me with those cool Swedish

eyes and say, "You've already told me that. I'm not stupid, I remember it." So I thought: "Oh dear, well, well, well, I mustn't say that." Then, when I wanted to say something, I thought: "I'd better not." And then: "Oh, the hell with this. That's the way I work and she may as well get used to it." She did, and we became good friends.

Bergman's performance shows the benefit of Cukor's mesmerizing conveyance of "tone" and his minute attention to coaxing the subtlest nuances out of his actors. She finally lashes out at the climax when she takes her revenge against her husband for torturing her. Subdued by the detective, Gregory is tied to a chair in the attic. As Paula looms over him for a change, he tries to convince her that the detective has been telling lies about him and that his deceptions were innocent. He begs for another chance, telling her to find a knife to free him, and we fear that she might succumb again to his deception. At first she teases him and us by pretending to still wonder if she might be mad.

But after seizing and throwing away the knife, she moves closer, behaving "savagely," as the playwright puts it. In a sustained outburst of satisfying fury, Paula becomes what the film's co-screenwriter Walter Reisch called "a goddess of vengeance," turning Gregory's game against him by saying: "How can a madwoman help her husband to escape? . . . If I were not mad, I could have helped you. Whatever you had done, I could have pitied and protected you. But because I am mad, I *hate* you. Because I am mad, I have betrayed you, and because I am mad [*raising her voice*] I'm rejoicing in my heart without a shred of pity, without a shred of regret, watching you go with glory in my heart!"

An equally remarkable performance was given in *Gaslight* by Angela Lansbury, an Anglo-Irish newcomer to movies. She was only seventeen when she was cast as Nancy, the sullen and impudent Cockney maid who behaves seductively toward Gregory, and she received a best-supporting-actress Oscar nomination. In what Cukor aptly called a Cinderella story, Lansbury had come to Los Angeles with her mother, Moyna Macgill, a prominent Irish stage actress who was trying to break into the Hollywood studios. The co-screenwriter Van Druten told Cukor that the mother and daughter, whom he had met at a party, had been wrapping Christmas packages at the Bullocks Wilshire department store and suggested they bring in Angela for a screen

15.2. "Suddenly, I was watching real movie acting," Cukor said of the film newcomer Angela Lansbury, doing a music-hall song as the seductive Cockney maid in *Gaslight* (1944) opposite Charles Boyer. "She *became* this rather disagreeable little housemaid—even her face seemed to change, it became somehow lopsided."
Source: Frame enlargement; MGM.

test. Her performing experience had been limited to working in music halls and nightclubs, but she looked older than her age and was emotionally mature; "I was ready," she recalled.

Cukor saw Lansbury's potential right away when she did an audition; he wanted to cast her but first had to convince MGM that she was sexy enough for the role. She proved it when he started her off with the important scene of Gregory flirting outrageously with Nancy in front of Paula after insisting that the maid bring in coal for the fire. The scene is a key stage in Gregory's manipulation of his wife's feelings. And as Lansbury put it, "I was my immediate naughty and rather cheeky self."

Cukor was startled by just *how* immediate her confidence before the camera was: "Suddenly, I was watching real movie acting. She *became* this rather disagreeable little housemaid—even her face seemed to change, it became somehow lopsided." Lansbury said Cukor "laughed uproariously when I did my Cockney accent. Then he would goad me into being saucy and sexy with Ingrid and Charles." Lansbury remembered Cukor as a "marvelous" director to launch her career in such spectacular fashion: "George had a wonderfully mobile face. . . . He would never give me a reading, you understand, but he certainly would indicate to me how he felt she might react or what a slut she was. . . . I had it all—it was all there. Somebody just had to say to me, 'Think about that—Use this—She's so-and-so—Don't you agree she's this and this?' And this is the way George would help and encourage me to give the performance that I did."

Nancy in the play and the earlier film version of *Gaslight* is portrayed as a rather stupid girl, but Lansbury's Nancy is sharp as a dagger. She is in fact used as a weapon by Gregory against his wife as well as a plaything for his own sexual pleasure. The overt sexual action happens implicitly, off-camera, however. The more openly intimate behavior in the play between Nancy and her master is eliminated from Cukor's film, to its benefit. The saucy interplay between Lansbury and Boyer is far more provocative. Perhaps the scene that made her a star is the one at the midpoint of the film when she makes her availability frankly clear to him through sexual innuendos and bawdy body language. As he prepares to go out on the town, she appears in a mirror behind him, wearing her black maid's uniform dress, white apron, and frilly white mob cap with two long white ribbons trailing down her back. She looks rather like a depraved nun. As she helps him into his dress coat and overcoat, tapping his shoulder twice, he asks what she is doing that night. She says she's going to a music hall and tosses her head, her eyes rolling heavenward as she lifts both hands above her, giving him a sideways glance and a sly smile as she sings a racy-sounding music-hall ditty and does a little galloping dance around him, waving her left hand airily.

She's made her impression, and the camera moves slightly closer as she tells him she's going with a "gentleman friend." He facetiously warns her, wagging his cigarette hand scoldingly, about how "gentlemen friends are sometimes inclined to take liberties with young ladies." She laughs slightly, sardonically, as she says, "Oh no, sir. Not with *me*. I can take care of myself. [*Pause*] When I want to." She moves almost imperceptibly toward him, staring boldly into his eyes. Then, with a wry grin, he pretends to chastise her as "not at all the kind of girl that your mistress should have for a housemaid."

15.3. Cukor's "wonderfully mobile face" and subtle way in conversation of letting her know "how he felt [her character] might react or what a slut she was" helped Lansbury quickly adapt to film acting and create a memorable character in *Gaslight*.

Source: MGM.

Now Nancy laughs more heartily and says slyly, "No sir? She's not the only one in the house, [*lowers her voice*] is she?" With a frank and serious look in her eyes, her jaw set, she sways forward toward him with her young but already formidable figure. Cukor cuts to a close-up of Gregory matching her gaze silently, putting his cigarette in his mouth with a nod of appreciation and leaving, suitably enthralled but also perhaps a bit intimidated by her forthright sexuality.

The crowning touch comes when Gregory is led away by the police at the end, past the servants. As he glances at Nancy, she dips her body in a tentative little curtsy, following him solemnly with her eyes with a stare of mingled complicity and insolent condemnation for his foolishness in getting caught. This magnificent performance was the eye-opening introduction to Lansbury's long, versatile, and formidable career in films and stage musicals as the mother of the Manchurian Candidate and Gypsy Rose Lee and the monstrous seller of meat pies in *Sweeney Todd: The Demon Barber of Fleet Street*.

16

SPENCER TRACY AND KATHARINE HEPBURN IN *ADAM'S RIB* WITH JUDY HOLLIDAY AND IN *PAT AND MIKE*

Cukor's mastery of directing dialogue took a fresh leap forward with his work on seven films written by Ruth Gordon and/or Garson Kanin. The married team brought a new style of naturalistic banter to their postwar screenplays, often filmed on location with the greater flexibility afforded Hollywood filmmakers under the influence of the neorealist movement in Europe and New York. Spencer Tracy and Katharine Hepburn spoke together and otherwise interacted with such casual, offhand ease in *Adam's Rib* (1949) and *Pat and Mike* (1952) that they established themselves as the leading modern romantic team in movies while seeming to give audiences an intimate glimpse of who they were off-camera.

That was partly an artful illusion, since their love life and personalities were far more complex and unorthodox than the characters they played. But they continue to captivate audiences with their remarkably real-sounding, breezy, and elliptical exchanges. These are actually highly stylized, as much as Cukor's earlier work with the more obviously artificial Philip Barry, and his expert direction brought out the special qualities of the Gordon-Kanin screenplays. Cukor worked remarkably closely with the writers and stars of these films (also including Judy Holliday with her offbeat charm) to create sparkling works of joint authorship.

Their films resonate even more with audiences today, who delight in the way these films were ahead of their time in capturing modern relationships between men and women. In more sophisticated ways than *The Philadelphia Story*, *Adam's Rib* and *Pat and Mike* reinvigorated Hepburn's independent nature onscreen to some extent while managing to sustain her public appeal, even while remaining within certain circumscribed limits. *Adam's Rib* offers a delightfully witty take on the clash between husband and wife attorneys in court—assistant district attorney Adam Bonner (Tracy) for the prosecution, attorney Amanda Bonner (Hepburn) for the defense—arguing the fate of a rather dopey wife, Doris Attinger (Holliday), who attempted to kill her philandering husband, Warren (Tom Ewell). *Adam's Rib* has become a more accepted classic, with its lively discussion of the rights of women and gender equality, but the lesser-known *Pat and Mike* is actually the superior film. Rather than laying out its themes so explicitly with rhetorical dialogue and an allegorical plot, the unpretentious, undidactic *Pat and Mike* takes a lighter approach to the theme of equality. It relies more on behavior and action in conveying the mutual respect that develops between Tracy's raffish sports promoter, Mike Conovan, and Hepburn's all-around star athlete, Pat Pemberton. Not only that, *Adam's Rib* lets down its promise by attempting to refute the arguments of Hepburn's crusading feminist attorney at the end, while in *Pat and Mike* she and Tracy evolve and maintain a truly refreshing "five-oh, five-oh" relationship throughout.

Garson Kanin, who began as an actor, directed seven films at RKO before his World War II service in the U.S. Army, in which he made several documentaries. After the war, Kanin turned his focus to writing plays, screenplays, and books (including the 1971 *Tracy and Hepburn: An Intimate Memoir*, which outraged Hepburn and Cukor, who felt it violated confidences). Kanin partnered with his wife, the actress, journalist, and playwright Ruth Gordon, on a string of remarkable screenplays before they tired of bickering when they wrote together and went their separate ways professionally. As Patrick McGilligan writes in one of his *Backstory* collections of interviews with screenwriters, the team

> was probably the greatest pure screenwriting collaboration in all Hollywood history—pure because no one rewrote their scripts; because their screen stories were all original; because they never worked under contract; and because director Cukor, a close friend, filmed their scripts as written. The films the Kanins wrote together signaled, to a large extent, the high tide

of American sophisticated comedy. No films were (are) more admired by other Hollywood comedy writers—few films play as well today, without embarrassing concessions to yesteryear's artificialities.

Kanin helped establish the Tracy-Hepburn screen relationship with his uncredited contribution to their first of nine films together, *Woman of the Year*. Before entering the army, he worked with his brother, Michael, and Ring Lardner Jr., the credited screenwriters on that George Stevens film. Cukor directed Tracy and Hepburn together for the first time in *Keeper of the Flame*, the lugubrious 1942 MGM drama written by the leftist screenwriter Donald Ogden Stewart from the novel by I. A. R. Wylie, whose works include the short stories on which John Ford based his World War I films *Four Sons* (1928) and *Pilgrimage* (1933). Cukor's most overtly political film, *Keeper of the Flame* is set during World War II and deals with an incipient fascist movement in the United States organized by a late national hero, whose widow (Hepburn) secretly helped kill him to stop his plot against the country. A reporter (Tracy) discovers that something is amiss with the hero's public image. But wouldn't he know that about the movement from reading the papers? He's less credible in this heavy-handed film than she is. And as usual with the rare Hollywood films about domestic fascist plots, the details are left rather vague, in this case even more so than in *Meet John Doe*, the somewhat muddled 1941 Frank Capra–Robert Riskin film.

Cukor directed Ruth Gordon as Melvyn Douglas's secretary in *Two-Faced Woman* before he began working with her and her husband as a screenwriting team on the 1947 backstage drama *A Double Life*. Ronald Colman won an Oscar for playing a stage star whose unstable personality is taken over by the character of Othello. That leads to his murdering a young waitress (Shelley Winters) and almost strangling his ex-wife (Signe Hasso) onstage while she is playing Desdemona before he stabs himself with a dagger. The restrained, dignified Colman is hopelessly out of his range in playing the Shakespearean character, and despite Cukor's theatrical background, the scenes onstage are clumsy. The one-note, simplistic, and corny plot twist is heavily telegraphed in this film noir. Deficient in genuine mystery and unable to bring itself to risk any humor about the deranged character, it lacks the best qualities of Gordon and Kanin's subsequent screenplays.

A Double Life is partly redeemed by Cukor's inspired work with Winters, whose lackluster career in minor films up to that point was given a major boost by her sensitive and poignant playing of the forlorn, rather cheap young woman whose life is snuffed out after she becomes besotted with the distinguished older man. Her character somewhat resembles Angela Lansbury's sluttish maid in *Gaslight*, although Lansbury's character is smarter and more in control of her life. Cukor's work with these two young actresses demonstrated his remarkable ability to discover and nurture new talent and send them on to long and fruitful careers. And *A Double Life* provided McGilligan with an evocative title for his insightful biography of Cukor, which explores his discreet gay life alongside his more visible professional career.

16.1. The naturalistic screenplay of *Adam's Rib* (1949) by Ruth Gordon and Garson Kanin is enhanced by the way Spencer Tracy and Katharine Hepburn appear to be improvising as they handle a morning bedroom scene. The case that will pit this pair of married lawyers against each other in court is touched off here by Hepburn's Amanda Bonner discovering that a woman has shot her errant husband. Amanda's spouse, Assistant District Attorney Adam Bonner, fails to share her glee. *Source*: Frame enlargement; MGM.

Adam's Rib draws on intimations audiences already had of the off-screen relationship between Tracy and Hepburn, which was more of an open secret than some writers have claimed. I remember in 1964, when I learned from Pat O'Brien's autobiography that he and Tracy had gone to my high school, Marquette University High School in Milwaukee, I excitedly told my favorite priest, who scowled, "Spencer Tracy—he's shacked up with that Hepburn woman, and he's never given a penny to the school."

As Hepburn's biographer William J. Mann writes, *Adam's Rib* "would be the film that defined Hepburn and Tracy as a couple in the public mind, the picture that convinced the world their lives were the same off the screen as they were on.... After five films together, they'd finally gotten their rhythms down right." Hepburn commented, "I think on film we came to represent the perfect American couple. Certainly the ideal man is Spencer: sports-loving, a man's man.... And I think I represent a woman. I needle a man. I irritate him ... yet if he put a big paw out, he could squash me. I think this is sort of the romantic, ideal picture of the male and female in the United States." And Mann notes that by fostering that Tracy-Hepburn relationship onscreen, she was also "disempowering her offscreen image. That strident woman in the red dress? Don't worry about her. Underneath, she's just a pussycat." Hepburn famously wore a red dress while boldly attacking the House Committee on Un-American Activities' investigation of Hollywood, the Motion Picture Alliance for the Preservation of American Ideals, President Truman, and other redbaiters at a May 1947 Los Angeles Henry Wallace for President rally.

Mann's incisive, iconoclastic biography paints the Tracy-Hepburn offscreen relationship as something of a sham, a devoted but mostly platonic union after its early days and more fractious and off-and-on than is usually imagined from most accounts, including Kanin's mythmaking memoir. Mann is on firmer ground characterizing Hepburn as a bisexual with mostly lesbian leanings than he is in speculating on the basis of sketchy accounts that Tracy was a closeted gay man tormented by conflicts over his bisexuality. But it's clear enough that the portrait of the idealized Tracy-Hepburn married couple in *Adam's Rib*, despite its feminist rhetorical byplay, is something of a romanticized construct fabricated to appeal to but not unduly trouble American movie audiences about the stars' extramarital, unorthodox relationship off-camera.

Hepburn's niece Katharine Houghton, who plays her daughter in the final Tracy-Hepburn film, *Guess Who's Coming to Dinner* (1967), said she thought *Adam's Rib*

> represents a fairly accurate dynamic—for one aspect of their relationship, anyway. The banter and the flirtation seem very genuine. . . . Yet Kate, especially in the early years of their relationship, was never confident that she was good enough or beautiful enough to keep Spencer's interest. . . . Amanda is more confident than Kate of her spouse. I doubt that Kanin or Gordon ever suspected the depth of Kate's insecurity, or maybe they simply chose not to address it. . . . Perhaps one could say that the Bonners were a couple they would have liked the world to think they were.

The extraordinary sense of intimacy *Adam's Rib* achieves is partly owed to the seemingly effortless skill of the two stars to behave so casually in their acting that it appears to replicate a genuine personal rapport. Their s naturalistic overlapping of dialogue, with the kind of shorthand married couples achieve, is mostly present in the script, however. The script (later published) is full of exchanges that play beautifully onscreen, with intricate comedic rhythms, yet look odd on the page because they are so fragmentary, often made up of incomplete sentences, seemingly meandering banter, and mere hints of meaning. Even the running gag of Tracy getting his words mixed up under stress is written into the script. Reflecting Kanin's own expertise as a director, visual aspects of many scenes are also suggested in the screenplay, and though Cukor follows some of those suggestions, such as shooting Tracy and Hepburn running in and out of a static frame as they get dressed for a dinner party, he disregards others, such as by turning a fragmented scene into a memorably long uninterrupted take (Hepburn interrogating her client, Holliday, in jail).

Gordon and Kanin have an uncanny knack of capturing the way a couple talk when they know each other inside and out and can complete each other's thoughts—although the conflict in the film comes when they begin to think they *don't* know each other as well as they thought they did. That contrast makes for scintillating tensions between them and an ability of both characters to get under each other's skin in and out of the courtroom.

Although Hepburn was known for her constant chatting on set, like Cukor, Tracy was notably taciturn when it came to discussing his characters or taking direction. Cukor directed Tracy six times, including an atypically unsympathetic, chilling, but one-note role as a ruthless businessman in that same year's British-made film *Edward, My Son*, which is mostly memorable for its harrowing performance by Deborah Kerr as his wife, who destroys herself with alcohol. With unusual candor, Tracy told Cukor about his role (drawn from the play by Robert Morley and Noel Langley), "It's rather disconcerting to me to find how easily I play a heel. I'm a better actor than I thought I was. When I was doing Father Flanagan [in *Boys Town* and *Men of Boys Town*], that was acting. This is not acting."

Mostly when they worked together, as Cukor recalled, Tracy would say, "Well, I certainly learned those lines, spoke those eight pages down to every 'if,' 'and,' and 'but'; I knew every word." "That's all he would tell you," the director added. "Now there was a great deal else that went on with him, but he wasn't telling it to you. That would have taken the magic out of it somehow, to have chewed it all over beforehand." What people didn't see was Tracy doing his own private rehearsing at home while learning his lines, or sometimes running his lines with Hepburn. Tracy's mastery of acting was partly a matter of hiding the mechanics and making it all seem natural, off the cuff, and Cukor's role was to help him relax so he could do just that. Tracy's running conversations with Hepburn in *Adam's Rib* are among their best moments onscreen together and most effective examples of his antimethod method, with the two of them perfectly in rhythm together, using their intimate knowledge of each other's vocal mannerisms, emotional ploys, and character traits.

An early example comes as they are reading the morning papers in bed, not looking at each other. Tracy puts on his glasses and drinks coffee while Hepburn learns that Doris Attinger has shot her husband: "Hot dog!—What, what?—Wait a second.—[*He scratches his face, rubs it*] What is it?—Woman shot her husband.—Ahhhh, kill 'im?—Wait, just a second—I think she, uh, let's see—[*She's disappointed*] Nope, no.—That's a shame.—[*She smiles brightly*] Condition critical, though.—[*After shooting her a brief look, he tells her,*] Umm, umm, congratulations." These line readings include small interpolations and alterations they made on the set. Tracy and Hepburn expertly anticipate or react to each other's lines in the film, including the occasional adlib of an entire line, such as when he sees her in a hat he bought and quips, "Yeah, you look kinda like Grandma Moses." She comes back with, "I'm a lucky girl." Cukor generally discouraged improvisation and would even call Gordon and Kanin on the phone back east to ask them for additional dialogue, but he allowed his actors the space to play with their lines to fit their mouths more easily and make it all flow.

The explicitly feminist slant of *Adam's Rib*—earlier titled *Love Is Legal* and *Man and Wife*—comes from the legal clash of the husband and wife in court while Amanda tries to turn the attempted murder case into a cause célèbre, as indeed it becomes in New York's tabloid newspapers. She tells the judge, "I submit that my entire line of defense is based on the proposition that persons of the female sex should be dealt with before the law as equals of persons of the male sex." But her defense is predicated on the so-called unwritten law allowing men to kill their cheating wives. In the case of a woman shooting her cheating husband, Amanda's argument is that if men can get away with murder in court by shooting a cheating spouse, why shouldn't a woman? That position deeply offends Adam with his reverence for legal principles. It also rankles his rather old-fashioned patriarchal nature, which expresses itself in his somewhat condescending tolerance of his wife's career until he considers that she pushes it and him too far in court.

Although she thinks Adam agrees in principle with the concept of women's equality, he becomes incensed by what he repeatedly calls her "contempt for the law" and accuses her of trying to "turn a court of law into a Punch and Judy show." While the film makes hay with the fact that any trial is a form of theater, and this is one by explicit design, *Adam's Rib* also shows its modernity by exploring the nature of gender as a performance, with its definitions remaining fluid, "male" and "female" shifting in application from moment to moment. Adam's veneer as a sophisticated modern urban male begins to disintegrate under the pressure of the feminist challenge of the jousting with his wife in court, and his inner sexism comes out at the height of his duress: "I'm old-fashioned. I like two sexes! And another thing, all of a sudden I don't like being married to what is known as a 'new woman.' I want a wife, not a competitor."

This conflict turns the Attinger attempted murder case into a prototypical battle of the sexes Anno 1949, a conflict between love and professional antagonism. But the case and the ideological differences that emerge between the

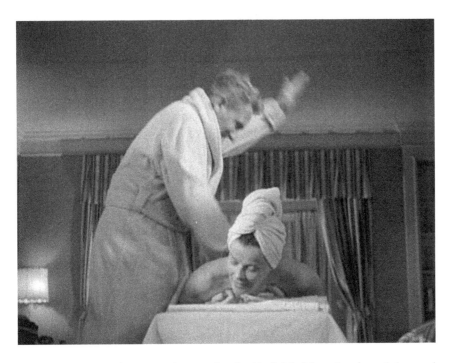

16.2. During a time of tension in their marriage in *Adam's Rib*, Adam gives Amanda her usual massage but provokes her outrage by concluding it with a decidedly unfriendly slap on the rear. *Source*: Frame enlargement; MGM.

married lawyers seem archly contrived to make the film a gender allegory. That is amusing and accounts for the film's latter-day status but also gives it a relatively bloodless feeling in contrast with the more relaxed and sensual, and less overtly rhetorical, *Pat and Mike*. Nevertheless, *Adam's Rib* glides along wittily and emotionally engaging the audience until the film has to tie up the issues. It's satisfying that the jury returns a verdict of not guilty, since Amanda's case that Doris was acting in defense of her family—and the unstated argument that it was a crime of passion involving a woman not behaving entirely rationally—are arguable and partly convincing. But the idea that two wrongs make a right—the male double standard being turned into a defense by women—is indefensible from a legal standpoint, even if Amanda believes it a necessary form of righting an imbalance in the system. Adam is infuriated by the sophistry of that argument by the wronged wife's advocate.

When Amanda turns the courtroom into a literal circus by calling a female weightlifter as a witness and having her lift Adam into the air and by inviting the jury to imagine sexual role changes for the members of the love triangle (Holliday and her rival, Jean Hagen, turning into attractive men, the foolish husband [Ewell] turning into a grotesque woman), the film takes a turn into absurdism. That enables Amanda and the film to make a sharp satirical point about male supremacy. And as Molly Haskell observes in *From Reverence to Rape*, by making Adam into a laughingstock in court, Amanda "goes *too* far and humiliates him, while he remains a gentleman. She stoops to unscrupulous methods while he maintains strict honor and decorum. But, then, he can afford to, since the law was created by and for him."

In the film's overly protracted finale, Amanda is made to admit the flaw in that argument. Adam, seething over his loss in court, bursts in on her and her male friend Kip Lurie (David Wayne), a songwriter who lives across the hall and is passionately devoted to Amanda even though he is also coded as gay, making him something of a Cukor surrogate figure (the song he composes, a retooled trunk number entitled "Farewell, Amanda," was written by none other than Cole Porter). Although it's hard to "read" Kip entirely coherently, part of his contradictory nature is attributable to censorship, since the Breen office warned the filmmakers about making him seem too gay. When Adam accosts them together and pulls out a gun, pretending to threaten them, Amanda shouts, "No one has a right to—," but stops, "suddenly realizing what she has said," as the script puts it. Adam, grinning, eats the gun—it's made of licorice—and gloats over her admission that the double-standard defense is false.

This rather smug gag always gets a big laugh. But it's one of numerous points when the film becomes too cutesy, such as having Amanda call Adam "Pinky" and him call her "Pinkie," or the couple playing lovey-dovey games under the table in court. The film goes on to stage a long, tediously "comical" brawl between Adam and Kip, which has the uncomfortable feeling of gay-bashing. Cukor also may have been conflicted about Kip because he tended to disapprove of men who flaunted their gayness, as Kip does in the film, rather than behaving discreetly, like him.

The film ends with two scenes of Adam showing he can fake tears just like a woman. That redundant stunt helps win back his wife, and though it can be seen as a sexist joke, Haskell interprets it more positively:

Tracy only half-playfully cries. The beauty of the marriage of true minds is that it allows the man to expose the feminine side of his nature and the woman to act on the masculine side of hers. . . . Even the slightly coy happy ending testifies to the fact that the film strikes deeper into the question of sexual roles than its comic surface would indicate and raises more questions than it can possibly answer. . . .

The success of their union derives from the preservation of their individuality, not rigidly but through a fluctuating balance of concession and assertion. . . . A purely political-feminist logic would demand that she be given Tracy's head, in unqualified triumph (an ending that some small part of us would like to see), rather than make an equivocal, "feminine" concession to his masculinity. But marriage and love do not flourish according to such logic. Their love is the admission of their incompleteness, of their need and willingness to listen to each other, and their marriage is the certification—indeed, the celebration—of that compromise.

One of the highlights of *Adam's Rib* (an MGM film) is the Judy Holliday "screen test" inserted into the movie by Hepburn and Cukor as a plot to persuade Harry Cohn of Columbia Pictures to cast Holliday in *Born Yesterday*. Holliday was still starring in that hit play by Garson Kanin (which debuted in 1946) while filming *Adam's Rib*. She was captivating audiences as the ditzy but unexpectedly shrewd Billie Dawn, the mistress of a coarse junk dealer visiting Washington, DC, to make a corrupt deal. But Cohn was refusing to cast her in the film version, responding to the idea with, "That fat Jewish broad?"

Cukor had appreciated Holliday's unusual talent since she played a small dramatic role as one of the wives in a San Francisco hotel room watching their husbands fly off to war at dawn in his film *Winged Victory* (1944). That is the best scene in an otherwise impersonal semidocumentary feature written by Moss Hart, an overwhelmingly male wartime morale-booster Cukor directed for the U.S. Army Air Forces and Twentieth Century-Fox. Holliday plays Ruth Miller, a woman from Brooklyn married to the average-guy character played by Edmond O'Brien. She touches the heart in an understated, authentic way, with no sentimentality but an honest foreboding of loss and grief.

Hepburn had the idea of filming Amanda's five-minute interview with Doris Attinger in *Adam's Rib* in an unbroken long take in the women's jail to

16.3. This long take in *Adam's Rib* was part of a scheme by Hepburn to convince Columbia's Harry Cohn to let Judy Holliday play her acclaimed stage role of Billie Dawn from Kanin's play *Born Yesterday* in Cukor's upcoming film version. The uncouth Cohn, who had scorned Holliday as a "fat Jewish broad," was won over by Cukor's filming of this comical scene of Hepburn's attorney interrogating her client about her shooting her husband. Hepburn and Cukor gave Holliday the best angle while the star and her regular stand-in, Eve March, were less prominently placed.

Source: Frame enlargement; MGM.

show off Holliday's acting skills. Cukor eagerly agreed and placed the lawyer and client at a table with Hepburn in self-effacing profile at the left of the frame and Holliday sitting sideways, her face seen more fully, twisting a hand-kerchief as she talks. Eve March, Hepburn's longtime friend and lookalike stand-in, plays Amanda's secretary, partly visible as she takes notes in side view at the far right. That gives the scene a subtle mirror effect while still keeping the audience's focus on Holliday. When Amanda calls the shooting of Doris's husband an accident, she guilelessly replies, "Oh, no accident—I *wanted* to shoot 'im." Amanda cautions, "Suppose we decide later just what you *wanted* to do." Asked when she decided to shoot her husband, she says, "I didn't decide nothin'—I was doin' everything like in a dream. Like I was watchin' myself but I couldn't help it. It was like a dream."

Holliday is hilariously deadpan and self-incriminating as Hepburn, throwing the entire scene to her, questions her softly, trying her lawyerly best to coax Doris into being a bit more cagey. This rather dumb but victimized woman is showing how incapable she is of protecting herself in a hostile legal system unless she has a sympathetic and scheming female lawyer directing her behavior. Like all of Holliday's acting, the scene is a mixture of wide-eyed comic ingenuousness and unexpected poignancy; a highly intelligent woman, she often played against her own personality with complex effectiveness.

Holliday's delightful performance in *Adam's Rib* also included the film's bravura opening scene, shot on crowded New York street locations, as she comically stalks her unsuspecting husband with a gun. When Cohn saw the long take of Holliday's interrogation scene, it finally convinced him to cast her in *Born Yesterday*. She won the best-actress Oscar over formidable veteran competition, Gloria Swanson in *Sunset Blvd.* and Bette Davis in *All About Eve*—the two may have canceled each other out. Holliday went on to star in two more movies for Cukor, *The Marrying Kind* and *It Should Happen to You*, becoming one of his quintessential stars and most simpatico actresses.

Pat and Mike was built by Gordon and Kanin around Hepburn's extraordinary athletic prowess. She was a superb tennis player and golfer as well as an avid swimmer, fond of what she considered character-building swims in the cold Atlantic Ocean off her home in Connecticut. She declared in her old age, "In the next life I plan to be a Wimbledon champion." The film's semidocumentary visual style is a special pleasure for Hepburn admirers because it gives her an exhilaratingly authentic and spacious showcase for her golf and tennis skills. But this romantic comedy, with Hepburn playing a women's sports phenomenon, gives a vigorous workout to other sides of her personality as well.

Its loose, seemingly casual narrative, actually finely and tightly structured, enables her and Tracy to play their most endearing couple. It's an odd love match that shows how a male-female partnership can work best when based on complementary qualities rather than similarity. Her Pat Pemberton and his Mike Conovan embody the equality that the married couple in *Adam's*

Rib do more talking about than exemplifying. The dialogue in *Pat and Mike* is more organic, without undue soapboxing or pretension. And it's a story told as much in visuals—looks and exchanges, body language, and athletic feats—as it is in dialogue.

The authenticity of the sports scenes in *Pat and Mike* is remarkable. Unlike most movies about sports, which resort to a lot of fakery in the shooting and editing, the scenes with Hepburn and other women athletes—including some long, successful putts and other spectacular golfing shots—are often filmed by Cukor and his cinematographer William Daniels in single takes to make clear that these exploits are not the result of montage or special effects. The result is sheer joy to watch, pure cinematic oxygen. Hepburn is also competing with several top professionals, most notably the legendary Babe Didrikson Zaharias, on whom Pat's character appears to have been based. Zaharias was considered the world's greatest women's athlete and was nicknamed "Babe" after the similarly multitalented Babe Ruth. When Zaharias, Hepburn, and other women play in a champion golf match, their camaraderie is refreshing to watch as they congratulate one another on good shots and victories, a form of unstressed feminist solidarity.

In stark contrast is the running motif of Pat getting spooked whenever her smugly sexist fiancé, Collier Weld (William Ching), watches her play. He is a vice president of the Oakland, California, college where she is director of women's sports. Right away we know he's wrong for Katharine Hepburn when he chastises her for wearing pants after honking his horn angrily and picking her up for a fundraising golf game with a conservative donor. When the admiring golf pro at Pat's country club (Jim Backus) asks her handicap, she replies, "A fella." Collier's baleful influence causes her to lose her self-confidence and flub golf shots or tennis returns and make errant serves whenever their eyes meet during matches. His hex on her even leads to a nightmarish fantasy sequence of a tennis match with outsized net and distorted rackets when Pat plays the celebrated glamour queen Gussie Moran at San Francisco's Cow Palace.

The patronizing Collier makes it worse by continually belittling Pat verbally and trying to convince her to let him control their relationship and, as women were expected to do in those days, settle down as a housewife and put her dream of independent achievement behind her. When he demands, "Why won't you just let me take charge?," she mutters uneasily, "Have to be in charge of myself." Slickly handsome and conformist in every way, Collier is the worst nightmare of early-1950s male supremacy. Pat's masochistic attraction to him is comprehensible as a sign of her insecurity and lack of self-esteem before she learns *how* to be in charge of herself.

In an earlier draft she had a husband who owned a car dealership, but in the film she is a widow who quits her job at the college under Mike Conovan's influence and turns professional, touring the country while trying to avoid seeing Collier as he follows her around, shattering her confidence. The irony of *Pat and Mike* is that her tutor in self-assurance is a seemingly domineering but actually more egalitarian male. Mike is a raffish New York sports promoter straight from the Damon Runyon playbook. He hangs out at Lindy's, makes deals with underworld partners, and his stable also includes a childlike heavyweight boxer (Aldo Ray) and a horse. Pat has a charming scene with Ray's Davie Hucko in which she encourages him to fight his own lack of confidence rather than focusing his antagonism on other people. As an easygoing handler of diverse talent, Mike instinctively, and credibly, believes in equality between the sexes, even if his masculine ego has to overcome a blow from Pat's prowess when she physically protects him from his unsavory cronies with a quick barrage of judo moves and karate chops. The hoods include future tough-guy star Charles Bronson, then billed as Charles Buchinski in a winning performance as a rugged-looking but rather gentle persuader.

The best-remembered moment in *Pat and Mike* comes when Tracy adds a New Yorkese twist to a line expressing appreciation for Hepburn's lithe middle-aged figure. As he's about to take a drink from a water fountain at the golf course and she's walking away from the camera, he tells his crony, Barney (Sammy White), in an almost throwaway fashion, "Not much meat on her, but what there is is cherce." Kanin went to the location to hear that line spoken but was dismayed that Tracy changed it from "choice" to "cherce," which of course is what helps make it so memorable. "I was horrified," Kanin writes in *Tracy and Hepburn*. "I felt that with all this the line would surely fail and that the moment would be wrecked. I mentioned it to George, who, in turn, spoke to Spencer. Take two. Exactly like the first, only more so. I left."

Months later, at the New York preview, Kanin "tensed" when Tracy's line was coming, but then, "the theater exploded. I learned a lot from him. So did Kate. So did we all. He claimed *he* had learned most from his idol, George

16.4. "Not much meat on her, but what there is is cherce," Mike Conovan (Spencer Tracy) tells a crony after this chat with Hepburn's Pat Pemberton about the possibility of her joining his stable of athletes, including a lunkheaded boxer and a horse. The offbeat pairing of the raffish sports promoter and the independent-minded female sports star in *Pat and Mike*(1952) makes for one of Cukor's most endearing romantic comedies and a dazzling showcase for Hepburn's athletic talents.

Source: Frame enlargement; MGM.

M. Cohan, who once said to him, 'Whatever you do, kid, always serve it with a little dressing.'" MGM used Mike's line as the tag in its trailer for the film, which is oddly hosted by Aldo Ray, whom MGM (like Columbia, which made his previous film with Cukor, 1952's *The Marrying Kind*) was giving a buildup for stardom that unfortunately never quite panned out for him.

Much of the humor, and the nicely underplayed point, of *Pat and Mike* is its reversal of clichéd gender and class expectations. Mike may seem like a gruff, uneducated, somewhat uncouth character (he makes his first appearance climbing through a window in Pat's hotel room), and he admits that their romantic teaming is unlikely since it involves "an upper-cruster like you and a—and my kind of type that can't even speak left-handed English yet." Pat turns her back on her academic institution and stifling relationship with her personally controlling fiancé when she recognizes that Mike's straightforward nature is genuinely egalitarian.

After she loses a golf match, he tells her, "I don't think you ever been properly handled," and she agrees with a self-deprecatory laugh, "That's right. Not even by myself." But she is taken aback in a deliciously busy scene when they are eating at Lindy's, and he irks her and the frazzled waiter by changing all her orders—with his eyes widening in alarm when she puts a cigarette in her mouth and he takes it out—and telling her that while she's in training, she can't drink or smoke or spend time with men. Pat asks with escalating unease, "Well, you don't expect to be watching me every minute—out of every twenty-four hours—out of every *day*—do you?" Nodding vigorously, Mike casually shoots back, "If I have to, sure," and she says, "Not sure I'll like that." But he explains himself in a matter-of-fact way, as if their setup is the most natural thing in the world: "Hmm. Not asking you to like it. But you'll see, pretty soon—pretty soon, I'll trust you, because you'll trust me. Because what's good for you is good for me. And you for me, see? We're the same. We're equal. We're partners, see? Five-oh, five-oh."

Gradually, as she ponders the situation, she realizes this kind of partnership, with its basis in mutual respect, shared needs, and complementary qualities, is different from the bogus sort of partnership Collier is offering her in his patriarchal form of marriage. But given the unorthodoxy of the relationship between Pat and Mike, it takes a while for both of them to accept that "five-oh, five-oh" can be interpreted in many ways, including physical intimacy. That creeps up on them without the film stressing the matter, such as when Mike is giving her a stretching workout at their training camp. It's unlike the massage Adam and Amanda give each other in *Adam's Rib*, which results in an angry confrontation when he slaps her rear end. This workout is less controlling and hierarchical, and it ends with their faces coming close but not quite touching as they stare into each other's eyes, assessing each other and progressing to mutual acceptance. Cukor's deceptively casual-seeming direction, as was the case in *Adam's Rib* as well, tends to minimize editorializing montage fragmentation in favor of two-shots allowing both performers equal weight and taking a balanced perspective on their points of view, however comically unlikely this balance may seem at first in *Pat and Mike*.

The incongruity and surprisingly complementary nature of the couple's teaming is what is most refreshing about *Pat and Mike*. And it perhaps accounts for why the film tends to be somewhat undervalued in contrast with the more intellectualized, more highbrow *Adam's Rib*, with its highly educated, upper-class married couple urbanely and explicitly thrashing out gender issues and never quite reaching the satisfactory resolution the later, more perfect film gives us. *Pat and Mike* has a feeling of discovery throughout, keeping us constantly off-guard and, if we go along with the game it plays, delighting us with the way it shakes up and makes us reevaluate complacent expectations about gender and class roles.

After Pat rescues Mike by beating up the hoods who want to renegotiate their deal, the script indicates how Mike now looks at her with the kind of complex feelings the Gordon-Kanin scripts always brought to their characters: "His face blends humiliation, surprise, fury, victory, defeat, awe, love and hate." As the screenwriters knew, Cukor and Tracy are up to the challenge of conveying such an intricate mixture of moods. Mike tells Pat with a new asperity, "I like everything to be five-oh, five-oh. I like a he to be a he and a she to be a she." That bespeaks a male anxiety akin to the trepidation much

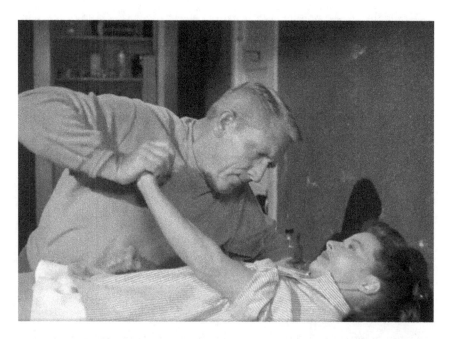

16.5. The stretching workout Mike gives Pat as part of their athletic training ritual winds up having unexpected erotic overtones.

Source: Frame enlargement; MGM.

of the American movie-going audience expressed by rejecting Cukor and Hepburn's blurring of the conventional lines between "she" and "he" in *Sylvia Scarlett*. Even though nothing either did after that was quite so overtly daring, they found ways of subtly balancing their need to express unorthodox gender fluidity with the state of heterosexual romance in American films.

That is what happens in the climactic yet still understated love scene of *Pat and Mike*, one of those long takes with an intricate exchange of dialogue that Cukor favors to draw his audience into the intimacy of his characters without tipping his hand aesthetically—except to those who comprehend the art of directing. To chase the ever-demanding Collier out of her hotel room, Pat has called for help, reassuring Mike's wounded ego without demeaning her own personality or their sense of equality, which has proven a bit fragile. And now, in this romantic comedy that conjures up passion between the sexes without showing overt sexual contact, Pat and Mike manage to square away matters between them. She's sitting up in bed, leaning forward, dropping the blanket she's pulled up around her chest, while he stands there in his pajamas and trench coat, looking stunned. Lapsing into his kind of left-handed English, she asks, "I mean, wh-what would I have did if you hadn't been around. Done." He responds with a chuckle,

"I figure you can take care of yourself."

"No, I can't."

"Ah, yeah, bet you could even lick me if you tried."

She leans toward him earnestly.

". . . No, I couldn't. I need someone to look after me."

"Yeah? What about me?"

"Why not?"

Mike is looking pensively at his pajamas under his coat and then up at her with surprise. After a pause, his face relaxing with satisfaction, he says,

"Well, I don't know if I can lick you or you can lick me, but I'll tell you one thing I do know—"

"What?"

The ultimate Tracy-Hepburn exchange:

"Together we can lick them all."

"You bet."

And now Cukor's camera starts moving in to frame them more closely as Mike sits on the bed, and Pat leans even nearer with a rapt, confident smile.

17

JUDY HOLLIDAY IN *BORN YESTERDAY,* *THE MARRYING KIND* WITH ALDO RAY, AND *IT SHOULD HAPPEN TO YOU* WITH JACK LEMMON

G uiding established stars such as Tracy and Hepburn into the radically changed postwar filmmaking environment was one part of a leading director's job. Discovering and developing new stars who fit that zeitgeist was another. From the beginning of Cukor's career in Hollywood, he had always proved unusually skillful at both tasks. Judy Holliday was a fresh new kind of star in postwar Hollywood, a pretty and charming but realistically deglamorized leading lady who could handle comedy as well as drama with aplomb and blended both with offbeat originality. And this young actress from the New York stage was unabashedly Jewish (though not named or directly identified as such) in an industry that had usually been skittish about allowing Jewish stars to assert their ethnic identity onscreen. Cukor had given Holliday two of her early breaks in movies, including her first important showcase in *Adam's Rib,* which convinced Columbia's Harry Cohn to give her the starring role in the director's 1950 film version of Garson Kanin's play *Born Yesterday,* which she had made a success onstage. The film won her the best-actress Oscar. So Cukor was ideally suited to help launch the accomplished actress as a popular leading lady of the 1950s.

Holliday was born Judith Tuvim before she went to Hollywood as a member of a nightclub act to appear in movies and had to change her last name, deriving it from "yom tovim," Hebrew for *holiday.* Judy's first job as a teenager had been working as an assistant switchboard operator and receptionist for the

17.1. "A true artist" Cukor called Judy Holliday. ". . . She could interpret a text with the subtlest detail." Their creative relationship brought out the qualities that made her a new kind of star for the postwar period, luminous and witty and conveying an extraordinary range while playing "ordinary" women instead of conventional glamour queens. They made four movies together in her all-too-brief Hollywood career, including this one, the 1954 romantic comedy *It Should Happen to You*. *Source*: Columbia Pictures; Photofest.

Mercury Theatre, run by Orson Welles and John Houseman; it's speculated, but hasn't been proven, that she was an extra in *Too Much Johnson*, Welles's uncompleted 1938 silent film. Holliday's career-transforming break came when she replaced my favorite actress, the anxious Hollywood veteran Jean Arthur, who left *Born Yesterday* just before the out-of-town tryouts.

Arthur told me she fled Hollywood and her contract with Columbia after seriously considering murdering Cohn, who she said would enter the women's dressing rooms surreptitiously to attack his female stars. She thought she could shoot him in the shadowy corridor connecting the dressing rooms and get away with it. But after spending three hours walking the streets of the backlot, Arthur decided instead to leave movies behind. She appeared in only two more, Billy Wilder's *A Foreign Affair* and George Stevens's *Shane*, and had a bumpy stage career, often quitting shows because of stage fright before retreating as a recluse to her home in the Northern California town of Carmel.

Holliday, two decades younger than the miscast Arthur, turned the dazzling role in *Born Yesterday* of the brassy but surprisingly savvy former showgirl Billie Dawn, the restless mistress of a domineering junk magnate, into a personal triumph. Directed by the playwright, the show opened on Broadway in February 1946, costarring Paul Douglas, and Holliday had a run of more than 1,200 performances. The film version was adapted by Kanin without credit. Cukor had found that Albert Mannheimer's adaptation and a rewrite by Julius and Philip Epstein still needed reworking, and Cohn wouldn't pay any more on the script or give Kanin adaptation credit, so Mannheimer received sole screen credit and an Oscar nomination. Holliday's Oscar should have resulted in a steady succession of starring roles. But she lost work when she ran afoul of the post–World War II Red Scare for her socialist family background and her casual leftist activities. She appeared in the infamous anticommunist pamphlet *Red Channels* (1950), which meant automatic blacklisting until a person managed to "clear" himself or herself.

Holliday was cleared, nominally at least, after appearing in executive session before the U.S. Senate Internal Security Committee in March 1952. Despite her principled opposition to the witch hunt and her fervent desire before her testimony to avoid naming names, she acknowledged to the committee that a late uncle had been "a very radical Communist" before "he had a change of heart and became a rabid anti-Communist," and, when questioned about a woman she described as her "best friend" and asked whether her friend was involved "in any respect with your signatures and affiliations with these Communist-front organizations," Holliday denied it but nervously blurted out, "I was told that she was a Communist." Even after that hesitant degree of cooperation with the committee, Holliday's career was blighted by graylisting, partly because of further smearing in the press when her testimony was publicly released; she spent much of her subsequent career back on Broadway. Cohn, whose attitude toward blacklisting was flexible, remained mostly supportive, casting her in four more Columbia films after *The Marrying Kind*, which had been released shortly before her testimony. She followed it with the lead in Cukor's *It Should Happen to You* (1954). But Holliday's film career was less active than it should have been—she worked only once with another studio, MGM, in her last film, Vincente Minnelli's

1960 version of the stage musical *Bells Are Ringing*, in which she had won a Tony Award—until her death from cancer at age forty-three in 1965.

Audience expectations for films changed after World War II, with more extensive use of location shooting as well as more stories about ordinary people with actors who were not always expected to be conventionally beautiful. The Italian neorealist movement influenced Hollywood and led to shooting in the streets of New York and other locations with gritty films about working-class characters. Actors felt freer to present themselves candidly, without disguising or distorting their identities. Previously, there had been relatively few overtly Jewish stars (Eddie Cantor, John Garfield, Sylvia Sidney, Danny Kaye, and the Marx Bros. among them); other Jewish stars (such as Theda Bara, Edward G. Robinson, Paulette Goddard, Melvyn Douglas, and Lauren Bacall) had often passed for Gentile.

Even though Holliday had been compelled to change her name, she benefited from these cultural advances thanks to the decline in antisemitic prejudice as a result of the war, and her lovable persona and unusual acting range were embraced when she played Billie Dawn in the film of *Born Yesterday*. But she was also an unpredictable actress with a protean image the public loved but found hard to grasp. She had an androgynous look, highly feminine yet with a stocky build and a somewhat mannish short hairstyle, and Hollywood found it hard to fit her into established modes.

In its early, frolicky scenes, *Born Yesterday* established her screen image as a zany comedian with a high-pitched, amusingly screechy voice, but even in that film she evolves into a more serious personality with an unexpected intelligence and aptitude for learning. *The Marrying Kind*, given its often somber subject matter and rollercoaster emotional impact, is a hard-to-categorize film and unsurprisingly was not the commercial success that *Born Yesterday* was. The tragicomic original screenplay by Ruth Gordon and Kanin is the story of an ordinary New York couple, Florence and Chet Keefer (Aldo Ray), who relate their troubles to a sympathetic family court judge (Madge Kennedy, a silent film actress friend of Cukor's who hadn't made a film since 1928 but was launched on a new career as a character actress by this role). *The Marrying Kind* is a richer and more complex character study than the broad comedy mixed with pseudo-Capra political drama in *Born Yesterday* or the gimmicky satire of the modern cult of celebrity in Kanin's original comedy *It Should Happen to You*.

The convincingly low-key performances by Holliday and Ray in *The Marrying Kind* combine with extensive New York location work in a modest, affecting film that forms part of Cukor's adventurous neorealist period, along with *Adam's Rib*, *It Should Happen to You*, and *The Model and the Marriage Broker* (his 1951 comedy-drama featuring Thelma Ritter). The novelty and freshness of these films advanced Cukor's career stylistically while the old studio system that supported him was starting to crumble. And Holliday's Flo Keefer in *The Marrying Kind* endures as her major performance for Cukor.

Cukor defined for Lambert the actress's unique qualities:

> Like all the great clowns, Judy Holliday could also move you. She made you laugh, she was a supreme technician, and then suddenly you were touched. She could interpret a text with the subtlest detail, her pauses would

17.2. Judy Holliday's brassy ex-showgirl Billie Dawn in *Born Yesterday* (1950), a role she originated in Garson Kanin's stage play, has an intellectual side she brings out with the help of her Pygmalion figure, the political journalist Paul Verrall (William Holden). Holliday won the Oscar for best actress in a field crowded with strong competition.

Source: Frame enlargement; Columbia Pictures.

give you every comma—she'd even give the author a semicolon if he'd written one. And vocally she was fascinating, she had a way of hitting the note like a bull's-eye, and the slightest distortion in the recording meant that you lost something. If you lost any of the highs you lost a moment of comedy, and if you lost any of the lows you lost a moment of emotion. A true artist.

Billie Dawn as incarnated by Holliday onscreen behaves not as a caricature but as a real person, endlessly surprising everyone and defying expectations. Someone whose opening line is a hilariously high-pitched, screechy *"Whaaat?"* initially acts like the "dumb broad" she is called by her crass boyfriend, Harry Brock (Broderick Crawford). Billie gradually reveals an eagerness for self-improvement that rivals Eliza Doolittle's. As George Bernard Shaw did with his Eliza in *Pygmalion*, Kanin provides Billie with a Henry Higgins, a political journalist, Paul Verrall (William Holden). He is hired by Harry to tutor her in the ways of the world and make her less embarrassing, more presentable. The important people she meets in a Washington, DC, hotel while Harry is bribing a congressman and worming his way into political influence are taken aback by Billie's malapropisms and general ignorance. But she has her own emotional and intellectual needs, starting with, "I'd like to learn how to talk good," just like Eliza.

She also gets an immediate romantic charge from Paul—taking him aback by asking bluntly, "Are you one of these *taaallkers* or would you be interested in a little *action?*"—but their liaison is slow to develop under Harry's wary eye. Holden, earnest, bespectacled, and well mannered, is somewhat pallid in the secondary role (it was the year of *Sunset Blvd.*, after which his career as a leading man finally took off). The script sanitizes some of the risqué dialogue and costuming in the play, and Crawford unfortunately delivers Harry as a one-note, bellowing heavy without any of the complexity Paul Douglas reportedly brought to the role onstage. Cukor's usual ability to find nuances in his characters was in abeyance where Harry was concerned; he took too literally a line by Harry's long-suffering, jaded lawyer, Jim Devery (Howard St. John), "He's always lived at the top of his voice." But Cohn, who knew that Harry was largely based on his own blustering personality, roguishly enjoyed that resemblance and had Crawford under contract. The actor had just won the best-actor Oscar for his role as the political demagogue in the film of Robert Penn Warren's *All the King's Men*, a much more nuanced performance.

The Pygmalion-Galatea kind of relationship Paul and Billie enjoy is Cukor's way of dealing with his fascination with class mobility and mutable personalities as well as a representation of the actor-director relationship in molding character. Billie also has affinities with the raucous but shrewd blonde gold digger played by Jean Harlow in *Dinner at Eight*, who rebels against her coarse husband and manages to outwit snobs and hypocrites who underestimate her. Billie's yen for learning is part of her compulsion to rise in society but even more an attempt to achieve self-esteem and win the respect of people she values. She despises her brutal boyfriend, who exploits her as a tool in his criminal activities until she wises up and decides no longer to cooperate.

The screenplay opens up the play effectively beyond the hotel suites Harry and Billie inhabit, and the film's production designer, Harry Horner, one of the best in the business, makes the expensive hotel's decor look suitably garish and vulgar (the play calls it "a masterpiece of offensive good taste," but in the film it's simply bad taste). Paul's tutoring mostly involves teaching Billie the democratic principles on which the country was founded, getting her to read books, and giving her an inspirational tour of Washington monuments and other buildings; the script gets preachy but unsatisfyingly so, because its political discussions are so vague and shallow. After Paul takes her to see the Declaration of Independence, the Constitution, and the Bill of Rights, he says, "I think a lot of the original inspiration's been neglected and forgotten." But as urgent a problem as that obliviousness was at the time, he doesn't explain how. He considers Brock fascistic and a "menace" and helps Billie block his crooked scheme, but that's about it.

Frank Capra's 1939 classic, *Mr. Smith Goes to Washington*, is an obvious model for *Born Yesterday*, which engages in similar rhetoric and repeats much of the earlier film's tour of Washington while substituting the Jefferson Memorial for the Lincoln Memorial. Kanin once said, "I'd rather be Capra than God, if there is a Capra." That witty remark suggests awareness of Capra's fraudulence as a political satirist and commentator. The so-called champion of the "common man" in 1930s movies was actually a reactionary Republican who borrowed liberal ideas, largely without acknowledgment, from his screenwriters, including Sidney Buchman, the writer of *Mr. Smith* and the co-screenwriter of *Holiday*. Capra later blamed his writers when his loyalty was questioned during the Red Scare; my 1992 biography *Frank Capra: The Catastrophe of Success* exposed Capra's duplicity and his informing on colleagues, including Buchman, to the U.S. government.

The vaguely liberal platitudes expressed in *Born Yesterday* are weaker than the themes of Capra's best films, muddled though those films are, and reveal a timidity in the play and film, stemming from the anxious political climate of 1950. And though the film shows Harry bribing a weak and guilt-ridden congressman, Hedges (Larry Oliver), it cops out in a way that was augmented for the screen. The film has the morally conflicted Devery tell Harry about members of Congress, "These guys are honest, sincerely trying to do a job. Once in a while you find a rotten apple, like Hedges, and then you can have him—but just once in a while—in a *great* while," instead of the play's cover-your-ass line, "That's the trouble with this town—too many honest men in it." Even taking the Red Scare into effect, Cukor's films are far more insightful about the sociopolitical dynamics of interpersonal relationships than they are with generalized political commentary. But *Mr. Smith Goes to Washington* is politically a far gutsier film than *Born Yesterday*: it paints most of Congress as corrupt. The timid *Born Yesterday* does not subscribe to Mark Twain's comment that "it could probably be shown by facts and figures that there is no distinctly native American criminal class except Congress."

Despite the deficiencies of the material, Holliday's Billie is always winning. Holliday's most famous set piece, her gin game with the sullen, mostly silent Harry, demonstrates her innate shrewdness early in the film with few words. Cukor's filming the droll scene mostly in a long take enables the audience to savor her expert card-playing technique and timing and her gleefully matter-of-fact humming and other mannerisms as she triumphantly beats the seething bully. Cukor's quietly observational style makes the most of Holliday's long practice in honing the material onstage, and he helps her find new business to express her feelings in the film, such as a lovely moment after she and Paul kiss and she tries to turn off a light but keeps waving her hand blindly at the switch.

As Billie's initially ditzy detachment from mundane reality gradually turns into focused ambition, she is such a formidable character that she virtually controls the relationship with her Henry Higgins figure while simultaneously getting the upper hand on the brutish Harry, especially after he shockingly strikes her in the face. As happens with Hepburn in *Pat and Mike*, Billie eventually declares that she's nobody's to own, and her delight in her new-found learning manifests itself most cleverly when she forces Harry's hesitating lawyer to explain some papers she is asked to sign, and she exclaims, "A *cartel!*" As the front-page obituary of Holliday in the *New York Times* observed, "Where such a role was usually characterized merely by gum-chewing, sinuosity and unalloyed brassiness, she made it not only funny but also human and moving."

The Marrying Kind shows Cukor's strengths in implying the impact of class issues and sociopolitical stresses on ordinary people without preachment or oversimplification. The marriage of Florence (Florrie) and Chet Keefer is constantly threatened by economic problems. They live in a quintessentially sterile and soulless modern housing development, Manhattan's Peter Cooper Village, part of a massive and controversial project spearheaded by Robert Moses. And the Keefers never get ahead even though Chet dreams up get-rich-quick schemes that seem rigged to disappoint them. His job at the main post office sorting facility, though stable, is a dead end, and Cukor said he wanted to portray the setting as stale, claustrophobic, and empty, if not hellish at least purgatorial (the film's fantasy about the president of the United States paying Chet a visit in the post office, to ill effect, is clumsy). The couple's apartment is drab and mostly unfurnished for quite a while before they get some depressing furniture. They never even get around to sleeping in a double bed, because of the continuing strictures of censorship, which Cukor deplored.

Joseph Walker's cinematography is deliberately devoid of the romantic sheen he brought to twenty Capra movies, including *It's a Wonderful Life*, which this film somewhat resembles in theme, along with other harshly realistic films of the period about the travails of ordinary couples. They include Vittorio De Sica's Italian neorealist classic *Bicycle Thieves* (1948), as well as William Wyler's *The Best Years of Our Lives* (1946), Akira Kurosawa's *One Wonderful Sunday* (1947), George Stevens's *A Place in the Sun* (1951, based on Theodore Dreiser's novel *An American Tragedy*), and the 1954 blacklisted film by Michael Wilson, *Salt of the Earth*.

Perhaps the most deleterious effect of the Keefers' marginal economic status is how it causes Chet to feel a constant sense of inadequacy as a man in the terms of the American system of that period, stemming from his perceived failure to succeed and provide a better life for his wife and two children. He angrily tries to convince Florence not to go back to work, because it makes him feel unmanly. When Florence gets a modest inheritance from a former employer, Chet can't accept it, believing irrationally that she must have slept with the boss. The Keefers, though not stupid, are portrayed as inarticulate and limited in their understanding of their situation, though they at least try (unsuccessfully) to avoid blaming each other.

People who knew Holliday reported that she was highly intelligent even though she became known for playing what were reductively described as "dumb blonde" roles. Her sensitivity and the sense of nonintellectual intelligence with which she imbues Florence help make the role nuanced. The script and Cukor make some cleverly ironic points about marital disagreement by having the couple misdescribe to the judge in opposite ways their memories of their courtship and the early years of their marriage.

Aldo Ray, whose publicity buildup by Columbia included getting a special plug at the end of *The Marrying Kind*, was an untrained actor who had been discovered in an audition while serving as a constable in a small town in California. Cukor worked with him energetically, and he delivers a convincing enough performance as Chet, even if his scratchy voice and the character's irascible, hardheaded ignorance seem somewhat off-putting. Ray was another of the new kind of quirky postwar Hollywood stars, but his promising career eventually fizzled as he became typecast in tough-guy roles and suffered from a drinking problem.

The screenplay of *The Marrying Kind* has been criticized for condescension toward the working class. But that seems more of an intermittent limitation in the writers' approach than an outright insult, given their attempting a darker, more detached view of the American Dream than usually seen on American screens. Gordon, Kanin, and Cukor show compassion toward their characters and keen insights into the couple's malaise. Furthermore, the film thoughtfully critiques the usual Hollywood approach to portraying courtship and marriage in an unrealistically romantic manner. As the title itself seems to suggest, this film portrays the Keefers as part of a separate category from that of the gay director and remains skeptical that their marriage will work out, even when they decide to give it another try at the end, after telling their tales of woe to the judge.

17.3. The sequence of the boy drowning in *The Marrying Kind* (1952) starts with the family—including his working-class parents Florrie and Chet Keefer (Judy Holliday and Aldo Ray)—enjoying a Decoration Day picnic before Joey (Barry Curtis) runs off. A blend of domestic comedy and harrowing drama, this film written by Ruth Gordon and Garson Kanin shows Cukor's skill at turning from one mode of storytelling to another, giving his films the feeling of real life being lived.

Source: Frame enlargement; Columbia Pictures.

Most strikingly, the Keefers' marriage is almost destroyed by their grief over the loss of a child. Americans generally try to evade feelings of grief, given social pressure for illusory "closure," but this film unflinchingly shows the devastating impact of the grieving process, as have two other notable American films involving a couple whose child dies, King Vidor's masterpiece *The Crowd* (1928) and Stevens's *Penny Serenade* (1941). The brilliantly directed sequence in *The Marrying Kind* of the drowning of their six-year-old son, Joey (Barry Curtis), at a Decoration Day picnic, is a haunting shock that reverses the mostly comic momentum of the film, and it is one of Cukor's most powerful and memorable achievements. Earlier, the son's name was mentioned by Florrie in a flat, affectless tone to the judge, "We told you about Joey, didn't we? Our boy?" In retrospect, that line and her way of delivering it seem eerily expressive of her deadened emotional state.

The fatal sequence begins, like so many unexpected catastrophes, in a breezy, casual manner. The Keefers are sitting and reclining on a blanket in a park near a lake, seen in the near distance behind them, as Florence has another futile get-rich inspiration (flavored postage stamps). She cheerfully strums a ukulele and warbles a romantic song ("Dolores" by Frank Loesser and Louis Alter) in Holliday's sweetly captivating singing voice (the song is a subtle premonition: Dolores, derived from the Latin *dolor*, is a Spanish name that means pain, sorrow, or grief). Joey runs off with friends to go swimming, Florence shouting a brief, almost subconscious warning to go only to the edge, since he just ate.

As she sings with blissful obliviousness ("How I love the kisses of Dolores / . . . I would die to be with my Dolores"), we see the feet of people moving back and forth behind them, without seeing the rest of their bodies, until the pace accelerates of more and more feet running mostly in a leftward direction toward the lake. Just after Florence sings the line about death, a man's voice calls out, "Where's the mother?," and Cukor cuts to a wide shot showing the lake. But the Keefers don't notice until a boy runs up, pointing and shouting incoherently that their son, Joey, is "in the water." With stunning force, Cukor follows Chet in a tracking shot as he runs toward the lake through tall rushes and uses a whip pan to show him plunging into the water as another man carries Joey's lifeless body out of the lake. Chet lifts him to the grass and frantically tries to revive him with Florence's help. Cukor said he knew that Ray had been a U.S. Navy frogman in World War II, which made his actions seem more violent and desperate.

The sequence abruptly dissolves to a long take of sustained emotion as Florence breaks down and collapses her head onto her arm on the table in the judge's office, helplessly pounding her fist as the judge tries to console her; Chet also breaks into tears, going to a window and turning his back to the camera. This series of images is a devastatingly effective cinematic depiction of the helpless, inconsolable agony of grief and the irrational guilt that often afflicts a couple who have lost a child. "I don't know how we lived through it," Florence tells the judge, incongruously smiling and laughing as people sometimes do in moments of uncontrollable emotion. "Maybe we didn't."

17.4. During Cukor's neorealist period, the New York–set *It Should Happen to You*, a satire of American success mania, gave Jack Lemmon his first film role. Drawing on his stars' musical talent, Cukor let Lemmon and Holliday sing as he noodled on the piano in a seemingly impromptu scene that is part of the film's casual charms.

Source: Frame enlargement; Columbia Pictures.

Cukor told Lambert that he was inspired for the drowning sequence by his memory of a 1928 New York stage production of Chekhov's *The Cherry Orchard*. Alla Nazimova, as Madame Ranevskyaya, saw the tutor of her son, who drowned years earlier, and suddenly threw herself on him, violently sobbing as she relived the moment. Discussing the tentative ending of *The Marrying Kind*, when the couple reconciles in a shadowy room in the courthouse, Lambert told Cukor, "On the surface it looks conventionally happy. . . . But you can't help feeling they're going back to a kind of hell." Cukor "emphatically" responded, "Yes, yes! If you believe the picture up to then, it's the only way it can hit you."

After this high point in Cukor's career and his work with Kanin and Holliday, *It Should Happen to You* came as something of a letdown. The meaningless title imposed by Columbia in postproduction irritated Kanin. He had titled his script *A Name for Herself* and wanted to direct the film but couldn't come to terms with Cohn, so he walked away from it.

The film's satirical point is on target, if not ahead of its time, anticipating Andy Warhol's famous comment that "in the future, everyone will be world-famous for fifteen minutes." In a role Kanin originally intended for Danny Kaye but that Gordon insisted would work better with Holliday, she plays the lovable goofball Gladys Glover, an out-of-work girdle model in New York City who splurges her savings on a giant billboard in Columbus Circle, displaying only her name.

Gladys is one of Cukor's quintessential dreamers, and her desperate desire to be somebody works beyond her imagining, making her a minor celebrity famous for being famous on more billboards, print advertisements, and TV shows. The film, like others from Hollywood when it became threatened by the new medium, mocks the inanity of early TV in scenes of Gladys preening on a vapid talk show and reading from cue cards on a variety program. The film's premise is amusing in a Preston Sturges way, and even endearing as Holliday plays it, but the film is directed in rather lackluster fashion by Cukor, a sign of his emotional disengagement from its dismayingly conventional message.

It Should Happen to You is not content with having Gladys feel frustrated by the hollowness of her fame. Instead, her boyfriend, a documentary film-maker named Pete Sheppard (Jack Lemmon in his feature debut), constantly berates her for her egomania and presumption for wanting to stand out of the crowd. Why that's such a bad thing is not made clear in Kanin's script, although Cukor gives Gladys plenty of time to enjoy her fame and allow herself to be wooed by a flighty playboy (Peter Lawford), largely to escape Pete's censorious kvetching.

That negative aspect of Pete's character is somewhat at odds with Lemmon's personality, but his natural charm and seemingly effortless versatility as an actor were already fully on view in *It Should Happen to You*. Cukor was in his element guiding Lemmon to his debut as an effectively restrained screen actor after his beginnings in the broader media of theater and television. The film seems confused, however, about what a documentary filmmaker does to make a living. When we see the film that Pete is making when he meets Gladys, about ordinary people lazing around or bickering in Central Park, it turns out to be shot slickly with a tripod, even though Pete has been shooting it with a handheld 16mm camera. Clearly the world of documentary filmmaking was as alien to a Hollywood studio veteran such as Cukor as it must have seemed to many in the audience of the time.

Pete also becomes a somewhat thankless and irritating character with his spoilsport nature as he lectures Gladys about conformism. That theme did not come out of the blue but was anticipated by a secondary character in the Gordon-Kanin script for *The Marrying Kind*, Chet's brother-in-law, Pat Bundy (Mickey Shaughnessy). Pat works as a butcher, and when Chet goes to his butcher shop for marital advice, complaining about Florence's inheritance, Cukor films the scene in a long take with Pat giving a virtuosic monologue while making an entire elaborate pâté from scratch. Letting us observe Pat's craftsmanship is a tribute from Cukor to an accomplished workman (and to Shaughnessy for this acting tour de force), but Pat does not tell Chet what he needs to hear. Pat points out, "You got a bad attitude to money," which is true enough. Pat is satisfied with what he has, a steady job with good working conditions, and he says he can put the job behind him when he goes home contentedly each evening: "I don't want to be a big man. . . . So what's wrong with my point of view? All right, so I'm a stick-in-the-mud. No ambition." He gestures to his completed creation and says, "Is that beautiful, or am I prejudiced?"

But despite the director's affection for Pat and the actor who plays him, the writers' message is for Chet to be content with his humdrum life. The scene is jarring, although it is of a piece with the repeated emphasis in *The Marrying Kind* on the futility of the Keefers' aspirations to break out of their financial rut, which contributes to the collapse of their marriage. In *It Should Happen to You*, Kanin as solo screenwriter has Pete lecture Gladys in the same vein. Pete discourages Gladys's aspirations in an offensive way that seems churlish and simply stifling of her dreamy personality, as well as strangely out of keeping with his supposedly avant-garde profession, though he always wears a tweed sport coat and tie while making his documentaries, even during a summer heat wave.

"What is the point of it?" Pete demands at her dinner table. "Where is it gettin' you? No place. . . . What is this craze to get so well known? . . . Well, you think everybody is so anxious to be above the crowd?" He rises, leans over her intimidatingly, and asks, "But why isn't it more important to learn to be a *part* of the crowd?" Her face, in close-up at the left side of the fame, maintains her resolute, quixotic look. There's a charming moment when he complains, "I can't seem to get you down to Earth," and she looks up and laughingly replies with her ditzy kind of sense, "What's so wonderful about

Earth?" But under Pete's baleful influence, Gladys comes to think of herself as a "freak."

She even makes a climactic patriotic ode to Cold War militarism, declaring to a bunch of Air Force men that she's done nothing to warrant having them name an airplane after her. "I don't stand for anything," she confesses in front of newsreel cameras. "You fellas do." This follows the formula of what Andrew Sarris calls the "obligatory scene" from Capra films of "the confession of folly in the most public manner possible." And Gladys asks the military to rename the plane "*One of the Crowd.*" This dispiriting, quintessentially 1950s paean to conformism seems strangely incongruent with Cukor's fondness for dreamers—even in this film—and makes it seem fortunate that he stopped working with Kanin after this.

But he made a delightful and touching film in 1953, *The Actress*, from an autobiographical play by Ruth Gordon, *Years Ago*, about her youth in New England, when she was dreaming of going to New York and becoming an actress.

18.1. The great character actress Thelma Ritter is endearing and funny in a rare leading role as Mae Swasey, a lonely but resourceful New Yorker who sets up other people's romances in *The Model and the Marriage Broker* (1951). At the end of the film, Mae unexpectedly finds her own partner for more than their regular card game when her raffish pal Doberman (Michael O'Shea) proposes to her.

Source: Frame enlargement; Twentieth Century-Fox.

18

THELMA RITTER AND COMPANY IN
THE MODEL AND THE MARRIAGE BROKER

C ukor's films are festivals of great character actors. The wealth of character actors available to the studios in Golden Age Hollywood—and his deep knowledge of theater and film actors and loyalty toward them, especially toward aging actresses—enable actors who aren't stars to find roles that stand out as among their finest. Thelma Ritter is a superlative example. Her multifaceted performance in *The Model and the Marriage Broker*, a lesser-known but charming Cukor film from 1951, is among her rare opportunities to play what is in effect a leading role onscreen, even though she is billed after the putative stars, Jeanne Crain and Scott Brady.

Ritter was always good and was regarded highly by her peers. She appeared in stock companies and vaudeville before coming to films late after raising a family, with an attention-getting unbilled role in *Miracle on 34th Street* (1947). Her six Academy Award nominations for best supporting actress (between 1950 and 1962) remain a record, even though she never won an Oscar. Fondly remembered for her homely, pleasing mug (like "a squashed cabbage leaf," as Henry Higgins calls Eliza Doolittle), gravelly voice, and wry, no-nonsense, down-to-earth, often wisecracking manner, she demonstrated a remarkably wide range onscreen, including key roles in *All About Eve*, *Rear Window*, and *The Misfits*. Her apotheosis is as Moe, the police informant with principles she barely comprehends in Samuel Fuller's 1953 *Pickup on South Street*, with her bitterly resigned death scene that's one of the high points of acting in the cinema. As the romantic French song "Mam'selle" winds down on her Victrola, she tells the hit man who's come to take care of her, "Look, mister, I'm so tired, you'd be doin' me a big favor if you'd blow my head off."

Ritter is such an authentic actress that she can break your heart without reaching for sympathy. And she can make you laugh with seemingly effortless ease, sometimes simultaneously, as she does in a previous 1951 film that gave her a sizeable if hackneyed role, Mitchell Leisen's *The Mating Season*, as a working-class cook who masquerades as a servant when her son marries a rich woman. Both that film and *The Model and the Marriage Broker* were produced by Charles Brackett and written by him with Walter Reisch and Richard Breen. All three writers had worked with Billy Wilder, especially Brackett, whose long partnership with Wilder had broken up the year before. In *The Model and the Marriage Broker*, Ritter plays a goodhearted but world-weary and scheming Manhattan matchmaker, Mae Swasey. It's a glorious opportunity Cukor gave Ritter, a comedy-drama that revolves around one of her most endearing performances. Jeanne Crain, an actress under contract to Fox, is the department store model Kitty Bennett, who becomes Mae's surrogate daughter. A bland actress who behaves like an actual mannequin, Crain is the star to carry the marquee billing for the younger audience while fronting for the actual leading lady. Cukor wanted Joanne Dru for the role; she shines in such films as Howard Hawks's *Red River* (1948) and John Ford's *Wagon Master* (1950) and would have been smarter and sexier than Crain, but Fox unfortunately overruled him.

The superlative screenplay of *The Model and the Marriage Broker* offers a truthful slice of working-class life, part of Cukor's lively neorealistic string of films using New York locations. The financially struggling Mae, who often takes cases pro bono and has to overcome the social stigma that was attached to the matchmaking profession in those days, has a modest office in the historic Flatiron Building on Fifth Avenue. The settings throughout the film, including her apartment, are realistically modest and cramped, even byzantine, in their odd angles that give the feeling of living and working in a maze. The affectionate slice-of-life screenplay has none of the condescension that somewhat mars the Gordon-Kanin scripts for Cukor. Brackett and his collaborators concentrate, in a poignant and unpreachy way, on the theme of loneliness and how it can be overcome. Although *The Marrying Kind* the following year expresses a profound skepticism about the institution of marriage, Cukor's worldview is broad enough to see it in a more positive, if still somewhat quizzical, light in *The Model and the Marriage Broker*.

The empathy Mae feels with her clients stems from painful personal experience. Her profession is her refuge from feeling abandoned in marriage long ago and her loneliness without a partner. The person who knows her best is a raffish card-playing pal named Doberman (Michael O'Shea), who visits her office regularly to chat as they casually relax together. He keeps popping in unannounced, pulling out a pack of cards from her desk, usually without taking off his hat. At the end, hatless for a change, he surprises Mae, and us, by offhandedly proposing to her as "somebody more suave-ah, like me for instance," than another man who's been courting her. It seems absolutely right that Mae's quietly unremarked-upon relationship with Doberman comes to this understanding. But Mae reacts in amazement when he makes his pitch, taking off her glasses to stare at him as her secretary provides additional comic relief by kibitzing in the background, and he just says at the fadeout, "Come on, come on, play already."

One way we know they're right for each other is that when Mae and her way of life needed defending earlier, Doberman eloquently came to her rescue. Kitty didn't realize Mae was in the matchmaking business and hurts her deeply by saying it's "awful" she's been interfering with her life trying to set her up with a man. She cruelly leaves her with, "Go find yourself another daughter." But Doberman tells Kitty about Mae's occupation, "Look, you wouldn't know the score—you got a pretty face. [*He opens Mae's cabinet of files on clients*] These people here, they don't *have* pretty faces. Go ahead, check. Know what you'll find? Lot of plain Janes. Lot of guys startin' in to be bald, have to be led and pushed around, haven't got the guts to say what should come natural to 'em. Lonely? Shy? Sounds kinda comical when you read it in an ad, don't it? Ain't so comical when it happens to you."

Doberman heatedly tells her that when another woman took away Mae's husband, "that was the loneliest woman on the face of this Earth." He walks back to the file cabinet and leans on it, saying, "I—I don't think you catch on that only somebody as lonely as she was could know how many more there are of the same kind. You won't find your name on any of these cards. Uh-uh. She filed your card away in here [*touches his heart*]." Cukor, as a bachelor who had to treat his personal life with discretion and compartmentalize it, could easily relate to Mae and the crucial importance she places on the value of friendship, as well as the vicarious satisfaction she takes from her benevolent manipulation of other people's lives.

Although the film gets sidetracked from time to time on the less compelling, obligatory love story between Kitty and an X-ray technician, Matt Hornbeck (Brady), it is mostly *about* the character actors who surround them. It exudes Cukor's compassion and love for offbeat, unconventional social outsiders, such as the inept, the homely, the wallflowers, eccentrics, and social rejects whom people meanly dismiss as "losers." He gives us a heartwarming and funny gallery of engagingly offbeat performers with everyday pathos and believability. They include O'Shea, a former vaudevillian and a versatile actor whose final feature film role was as Gladys's promoter in *It Should Happen to You*; Nancy Kulp, a Cukor discovery in her film debut as Hazel Gingras, a shy and gawky spinster painfully insecure around men; Dennie Moore, a Cukor favorite from *Sylvia Scarlett* and *The Women* in her last film as the sister-in-law trying discreetly to get Kulp out of her home; Zero Mostel (before his blacklisting) as a cranky optometrist grudgingly playing the dating game; and Jay C. Flippen as a misogynistic middle-aged ladies' man who courts Mae unsuccessfully at an upstate health spa for lonely older women before she realizes how deadly dull he is.

The only misfire in the cast, and a surprising exception to the film's compassionate spirit, is Frank Fontaine overdoing the almost imbecilic simplemindedness of a shy Swedish man, Hjalmer Johannson, before Fontaine achieved television fame in a similar but marginally more compos mentis role as the boozer "Crazy Guggenheim." When the singer-songwriter Tom Lehrer introduced his satirical song "National Brotherhood Week" at a 1965 concert, he said, "This is just one of many such weeks honoring various worthy causes. One of my favorites is National Make-Fun-of-the-Handicapped Week, which Frank Fontaine and Jerry Lewis are in charge of, as you know."

The first person we see in *The Model and the Marriage Broker* is a frantic, blowsy woman in her fifties outside the Flatiron Building hesitating about whether to go in to see Mae. This is Emmy Swasey, played by Helen Ford, a faded Broadway musical comedy star of the 1920s. She backs off but returns later in the film. Emmy is the woman who stole Mae's husband long ago, but she comes back to see Mae as a widow, desperately seeking her help in finding another man, telling her, "You don't know what it's like to be so alone."

Mae retorts, "You taught me all about that twenty years ago, Emmy." Ironically given her occupation, Mae became disillusioned with marriage because of her husband leaving her. She tells Kitty that when a woman is abandoned, "right then her pride is gone for good." But when her old enemy comes to her apartment, Emmy is a pathetic ruin offering Mae the opportunity for schadenfreude. Mae can't resist a little smile at how Emmy has aged, but otherwise she is too kind to succumb to that impulse, feeling protective of the poor woman and perhaps recognizing that she herself has been better off all those years being unmarried. Their scene together is a biting, acerbic highlight of the film.

A major reason we love and remember character actors is that they don't look like stars but seem like real people onscreen, quirky, often homely or funny-looking, but with recognizably lived-in faces and reliably wise or foolish ways of behaving. They stand out as colorful figures we come to know like friends, like the characters in Dickens novels (Ritter in her offscreen life was a devotee of Dickens) and Cukor's richly cast adaptation of *David Copperfield*. They are unlike the conventionally good-looking kind of second-rate stars who often populated films in the studio contract system, such as Jeanne Crain, whose blank features defeat Cukor's attempts to find emotion in her face (he called her a "flat tire"). Frequently as Cukor is blocking a scene with Kitty, he characteristically will bring her into an imbalanced foreground closeup at the right or left of the screen to give us her point of view on what we are seeing, and although we can feel him off-camera strenuously making his usual faces trying to coax some expression out of Crain, the effort is only intermittently successful. On the other hand, when Cukor's blocking moves Ritter into the foreground, as he often does while keeping other actors in the frame for context, she can let pain or amusement or duplicity show on her face without apparent effort, by subtly changing her way of looking.

Even Crain is warmer when Ritter brings out her humanity in their intimate scenes showing Mae's motherly nature as the older woman tries to guide her with men and protect her from them. Kitty tells her, "It's hard to find a man that you can *like*." That seems borne out when Mae unwisely maneuvers her ("No commission") into a relationship with Matt, whom she likes for reasons that seem rather misguided. Brady, who was Cukor's choice for that role, is a much more focused, sharper kind of actor than Crain, a tough-guy brother of the notoriously aberrant actor Lawrence Tierney. Brady later made a strong impression as the outlaw called the Dancin' Kid in *Johnny Guitar*, Nicholas Ray's expressionistic 1954 Western classic.

Although Brady has a relaxed, unshowy, adroit five-minute take at a bowling alley with Ritter in *The Model and the Marriage Broker* as they edge around each other while parrying casually about his reluctance to settle down, his behavior with Kitty when Mae matches them somewhat incongruously becomes a form of stalking. Matt repeatedly pushes his way into her apartment against her wishes and pitches woo by murmuring menacingly, "If I had you I'd keep you locked up in a closet." Although this unpleasant relationship drags down the film by distracting us from the far more interesting scenes with Mae and her clients, it at least goes to suggest the risky side of the matchmaking business, even if that was not the fully conscious intent of the script but a reflection of the sexual mores of the time that Cukor brings out more starkly in the direction.

Perhaps this unexpected overtone is a sign of Cukor's jaundiced view of the modeling racket. He had already made a film acerbically dissecting that milieu, MGM's *A Life of Her Own* (1950), portraying it as an impersonal, frantic business with a youth obsession (much like Hollywood) that barely pays attention to the individuality of models but treats them as disposable objects. One ex-model in *A Life of Her Own* (Ann Dvorak in a harrowing performance) commits suicide because she's considered over the hill and has turned to alcohol for solace. Despite the trenchant screenplay by Isobel Lennart, Lana Turner unfortunately is her wooden self in the lead role. She plays an ambitious woman from Kansas who comes to New York and succeeds as a model but winds up so disenchanted in middle age that in Cukor's original version of the film she kills herself after having to work as a maid. To Cukor's dismay, MGM cut that, among substantial amounts of other footage, leaving Turner to walk away down a street at night after rejecting the option of suicide.

Modeling is a form of acting, and *A Life of Her Own* displays the side of Cukor that often faced up to the harshly inhuman side of the media and various forms of show business. *The Model and the Marriage Broker*, although giving Crain a job like that of the models in *The Women*'s high-fashion dress shop, is not cutting about the trade but treats modeling as dully matter of fact and unglamorous, perhaps because of Kitty's lower-scale, more mundane work environment. The heart of *The Model and the Marriage Broker* is in Mae's kindly but sometimes sarcastic interactions with her "family" of lovable but quirky clients. The film is an example of Cukor's penchant for stories about performing, since Mae's job too is a form of acting and directing, setting up her little dramas and hyping her clients, sometimes nearly out of recognition but usually as an expression of her fundamental benevolent optimism. Much of the humor comes from her attempts to jolly these sad sacks out of their ruts and into some hope about their condition. Mae resembles Cukor with his love for people, especially actors and outcasts, and especially aging women who have been virtually forgotten and neglected by the film industry and the public.

Some of them can be spotted as extras or in bit parts throughout his work; when Mae goes to the health spa, one of the elderly ladies chatting on a porch is Mae Marsh, who was the leading lady of D. W. Griffith's *The Birth of a Nation* and *Intolerance* and had become a member of the Cukor and John Ford stock companies. I once attended a luncheon at Universal that Cukor held in honor of Gertrude Astor, a former silent-film actress in Ford and Frank Capra movies and a onetime Universal contract actor who had become a bit player in talking pictures. Cukor invited Universal's current young contract players along with the silent-film director Allan Dwan and others who had known Astor long before. When the touching event was over, I saw Astor standing on a corner outside waiting for her chauffeur-driven car, clutching the bouquet of red roses Cukor had given her and weeping.

Mae's weekly party at her apartment with her motley crew on a rainy Sunday afternoon is the hilarious centerpiece of *The Model and the Marriage Broker*. The scene begins poignantly, however, with Hazel playing Robert Schumann's "Traumerei" ("Dreaming") on the piano, a haunting piece of music Ernst Lubitsch has his romantic couple play on the violin and piano for the ending of his tragic 1932 film *The Man I Killed/Broken Lullaby*. But Mae's party turns comical when she mischievously ties string to connect her bashful bunch with one another so they can twist around and get entangled, a goofy ploy that actually breaks the ice. When she orders the antisocial, cigar-smoking George Wixted (Mostel) to stop watching a Western on her little TV screen and steers the almost terminally introverted Hazel from her piano into a chair, Hazel automatically pops up when George sits next to her, but Hazel's sister-in-law pushes her back down as George continues to stuff his

18.2. The Cukor discovery Nancy Kulp, who went on to a long career as an engaging comic actress, playing Hazel Gingras, one of the socially maladroit clients of Mae Swasey in *The Model and the Marriage Broker* at a getting-acquainted party in Mae's home. To Kulp's left, as a relative trying to find her a husband, is Dennie Moore. Mae is trying to set up Hazel with an awkward fellow played by Zero Mostel (back to camera at right, with Frank Fontaine).

Source: Frame enlargement; Twentieth Century-Fox.

face, ignoring his seatmate. Against all odds, that pairing leads to marriage, and we see Hazel in Kitty's dress shop, preening with almost uncontrollable pride as she picks out her trousseau.

With her lanky, gaunt appearance and elongated face, Kulp has an endearing, touching, yet oddly funny way of looking away from people when she reluctantly engages with them in this film. She was discovered by the keen-eyed, uncommonly perspicacious Cukor while working as a publicist at MGM; she may have reminded him of the equally equine but more extroverted Edna May Oliver, who is so memorable as Aunt March in *Little Women*, Betsey Trotwood in *David Copperfield*, and the nurse in his *Romeo and Juliet*. Before Cukor gave Kulp her break, she had been a journalist and a member of the U.S. Naval Reserve in World War II. She went on to a busy career as a character actress, including roles in *The Marrying Kind* and Cukor's *A Star Is Born* (unfortunately cut from that film when the studio shortened it) and was best known for her delightful role as the bank secretary Miss Jane Hathaway in the long-running TV comedy series *The Beverly Hillbillies*. She left Hollywood and ran unsuccessfully for Congress as a Democrat from Pennsylvania before finishing her career as an acting teacher.

As George, the sour and myopic misanthrope, Mostel effectively plays against his natural exuberance in Cukor's film. He was a versatile and busy actor before that but was soon fired by the studio he called "18th Century-Fox" because of growing scrutiny of his leftist activities. He was blacklisted after the screenwriter Martin Berkeley, the most prolific HUAC informer, accused him in 1952 of being a communist, and he refused to name names in his appearance before the committee in 1955. Mostel was spectacular in the hit 1960s Broadway musicals *A Funny Thing Happened on the Way to the Forum* and *Fiddler on the Roof* and after returning to movies had another triumph as the crooked Broadway producer in Mel Brooks's 1967 comedy, *The Producers*. Mostel's last role before the camera, the year before his death, was in *The Front*, a 1976 film full of former blacklistees before and behind the camera. His suicidal comedian Hecky Brown is a tragicomic commentary on the toll the witch hunt took on actors in the postwar era.

Much of the courage and originality went out of Hollywood during that period with the banishment of hundreds of talented actors, writers, and others. The extraordinary talent pool of character actors that made even such modest films as *The Model and the Marriage Broker* so enduring was severely diminished. If most of these actors never won an Oscar, even the great Thelma Ritter, they brought a depth of humanity to classic Hollywood filmmaking that the industry mostly lacks in today's corporate climate. The kind of role she plays in *The Model and the Marriage Broker* and that modest, humane kind of film are no longer being made and were something of an anomaly even in 1951.

19.1. "The director's theme is imagination, with the focus on the imaginer. . . . Cukor is committed to the dreamer," writes Andrew Sarris. Jean Simmons as *The Actress* (1953) is one of Cukor's quintessential dreamers, gazing enraptured from the second balcony at the world of theater she wants to join. Although *The Actress* is a biopic of Cukor's frequent screenwriter Ruth Gordon, it also may be the director's most autobiographical film.

Source: Frame enlargement; MGM.

19

SPENCER TRACY AND JEAN SIMMONS IN *THE ACTRESS*

S creen-filling close-ups of Jean Simmons watching enraptured from the second balcony of a theater in 1914 Boston set the tone from the beginning of *The Actress*, Cukor's film about the stagestruck youth of the playwright and screenwriter Ruth Gordon. These sublime images echo Cukor's own early days skipping high school in New York to attend every Broadway play he could, usually also from the second balcony. As Ruth Gordon Jones (whose first line in the film is "I hate Jones for a name"), Simmons is swaying gently and murmuring along with the music, leaning her head on her gloved hand, the camera featuring her large, luminous eyes.

She is watching a glamorous actress named Hazel Dawn (Kay Williams) onstage in a 1911 Edwardian musical comedy called *The Pink Lady*. Hazel and a male chorus are performing a novelty number while waltzing to the song "(My) Beautiful Lady." She plays the violin, enchantingly statuesque in a resplendent white gown and billowing hat, while the men in tuxedos sing and dance around her ("Dream, dream, dream and forget / Care, pain, useless regret"). Although the routine sounds silly, it doesn't strike us that way, for Cukor puts us in the body and soul of the yearning young woman dreaming that she will become a Hazel Dawn herself. Ruth is a quintessential Cukor dreamer, someone consumed with the ferocious, unstoppable determination to escape her hometown (the Wollaston neighborhood of Quincy, Massachusetts) and make something of herself.

The Actress (1953) is based on Gordon's 1946 autobiographical play, *Years Ago*, adapted for the screen by the author. But it's not so much about Ruth herself as it is about her father, Clinton Jones. Fredric March won a Tony Award for playing the role on Broadway. In Cukor's film, Clinton is majestically played by Spencer Tracy. It's one of Tracy's greatest roles, even if it is not one of his best-remembered or most celebrated, since the film was a flop. MGM lost faith along the way and recut it after previews (when it was titled *Fame and Fortune*). Not the clichéd stifling father figure we might expect in a seemingly familiar kind of story about an ambitious girl struggling to escape her circumstances, Clinton Jones has a gruff facade as a frustrated former seaman marooned in his modest home and his humdrum job as a foreman in a food factory. But his thwarted sense of adventure and freedom, and a secret past in the theater he reveals belatedly to his restless daughter and his wife, Annie (played by Teresa Wright, who was only thirty-four to Tracy's fifty-three), are what allow him to encourage and support Ruth's ambition, an unexpected development that makes this film deeply moving.

Cukor's identification with Ruth makes this one of the films closest to his heart, for as he told Lambert, "I'm lost in admiration for people who come to New York or Hollywood with no money, only hopes. I had the enormous advantage of being born in New York and living at home when I first went out to fend for jobs in the theater. . . . After I graduated from high school. I said to my family, 'I want to go into the theater.' Nothing can shock parents today, of course, but then it was as if I'd said, 'Well, Mom and Dad, I'm going to become a pusher.'"

Tracy's Clinton Jones navigates uncomfortably with his weighty anchor of an aging body—smoking a pipe and wearing "hair short for 'youth,' so they told me, since mother is played by Shirley Temple," he wrote Garson Kanin while the film was shooting—in the oddly shaped, cramped house that replicates Gordon's own home in Wollaston. One of the happy byproducts of the director's passion for research, it's a mazelike setting, designed by Arthur Lonergan and decorated by Emile Kuri and Edwin B. Willis, that helps express the claustrophobia that Clinton and his daughter feel and her need to escape. *The Actress* epitomizes the subtly evocative visual style Cukor had developed by this stage of his career, with his peripatetic blocking bringing actors into the foreground for emphasis and intricate but unobtrusive tracking shots reframing actors' movements on the tight set dexterously planned for that purpose.

The quietly masterful black-and-white cinematography is by Harold Rosson, who had worked with Tracy on *Captains Courageous* and ten other films, as well as shooting three silent films for Josef von Sternberg and such other films as *The Garden of Allah* (which won him an Oscar for his color work), John Huston's *The Red Badge of Courage*, *The Wizard of Oz*, and *Singin' in the Rain*. Rosson also shot the "Born in a Trunk" medley for Cukor's *A Star Is Born*, but that was directed by the film's choreographer, Richard Barstow, and the MGM songwriter Roger Edens, so *The Actress* was Rosson's only filming with Cukor, whose work benefited greatly from his collaboration with many of Hollywood's top cinematographers at MGM and other studios.

Distant sounds of trains headed for New York subtly punctuate the action of *The Actress* throughout, suggesting the inevitability of Ruth's urge to leave home. Her father is not just the domestic tyrant he first appears, however, but a tender and sensitive man. Carping at his circumstances and poverty to his perpetually anxious and placating wife, Clinton terrifies his daughter into hiding her ambition, since she assumes he will oppose it for the conventionally moralistic reasons of that period. But Clinton believes that "a woman should be independent" and make her own living, and he empathizes with Ruth's ambitions. He surprises her and us by making her dream possible, as unrealistic as it may seem.

Her ambition should have seemed more *believably* unrealistic, however, since Gordon had to overcome the handicap of her plain appearance, which made her success as an actress, against all odds, an especially remarkable achievement. When the film's Ruth finally musters up the courage to tell her father, in close-up but in a soft, diffident voice, "I want to go on the stage," he doesn't erupt but reacts quietly and quizzically: "Well, what makes you think you got the stuff it takes? . . . What makes you think you're an actress? . . . I seen actors and actresses all my life, pretty nearly, but I never seen nobody look like you." He takes her chin in his hand gently and studies her appearance with concern.

The moment is moving but does not make sense, however, because Simmons is miscast; the twenty-three-year-old British actress, playing seventeen,

manages a credible American accent, but her beauty throws the film askew. Cukor admitted the problem in retrospect:

> If a girl like Jean Simmons says, "I want to go on the stage," it's no great surprise. Obviously she's lovely, and she probably should. I'm sure with Ruth it was much more difficult. Of course, this was the Hollywood tradition at the time. Nobody was ever *really* plain—either plain girls were played by Olivia de Havilland or they wore glasses, and then someone took the glasses off and they were ravishing beauties. I suppose there were no actresses, or no name-actresses, anyway, around at the time who were absolutely right.

As Tracy stares into Simmons's eyes and holds her chin while frankly assessing her chances as a professional actress, we have to mentally super-impose the image of the homely Ruth Gordon over the actress who plays her. That would make believable the young woman's ferocity of ambition to overcome her limited physical attributes through sheer willpower and intelligence. The youthful Gordon did become a star onstage in lead roles, and after making her film debut in 1915, she had a modest early career as a screen actress, including as Mary Todd Lincoln in *Abe Lincoln in Illinois* and as Melvyn Douglas's secretary in Cukor's *Two-Faced Woman*, before she made a greater name for herself as a playwright and leading screen-writer, including on the Cukor films with her husband, Garson Kanin.

Remarkably, it was in her old age that Gordon finally became an actual movie star. She received an Academy Award nomination for best supporting actress in *Inside Daisy Clover* (1965) and won the Oscar in that category for playing a modern witch in *Rosemary's Baby*, Roman Polanski's 1968 horror

19.2. The moment when Ruth Gordon Jones finally musters up the courage to tell her father shyly, "I want to go on the stage." A moving representation of what Cukor told his chronicler Gavin Lambert: "I'm lost in admiration for people who come to New York or Hollywood with no money, only hopes."

Source: Frame enlargement; MGM.

19.3. Ruth's father, Clinton Jones (Spencer Tracy), is naturally stunned by his daughter's declaration of intent to go on the stage. But as Cukor recalled, Tracy "looked at her with this eloquent face of his" and afterward told the director he was remembering how his father looked at him in similar circumstances and said, "Oh that poor little son of a bitch; he's going to go through an awful lot."

Source: Frame enlargement; MGM.

classic. Gordon brought down the house when she said in her acceptance speech, "I can't tell you how encouraging a thing like this is." Her roles in *Where's Poppa?* and *Harold and Maude* established her as a leading lady, a funny new kind of star. Her often bizarre, sophisticated approach to comedy made her unexpectedly popular at the time of the youth movement taking over Hollywood.

Simmons, on the other hand, was a precocious beginner in British films at age fourteen in 1944 and became a star while playing Estella as a girl in David Lean's classic 1946 film of Dickens's *Great Expectations*. She received her first Oscar nomination for her supporting role as Ophelia opposite Laurence Olivier in his 1948 *Hamlet* and had many starring roles in Hollywood after migrating there in 1951 with her husband, the actor Stewart Granger (who starred opposite Ava Gardner in Cukor's 1956 epic romance set in India, *Bhowani Junction*). Simmons always regarded *The Actress* and Cukor with fondness and named her daughter Tracy Granger, a film editor, after her costar. Cukor, who had considered and rejected Debbie Reynolds to play Ruth even though she would have been distractingly cute for the role, loyally thought Simmons was "wonderful" as Ruth; the director's being "lost in admiration" for the character's determination seemed to override everything in his mind.

But in fact, for all her talent, Simmons is not only miscast; the role is badly misconceived by both actress and director. Part of the fault lies with the play and script. It's a common failing when writers write autobiographically to make their youthful selves seem less promising and talented than they really were and to mock their early aspirations and struggles. As Graham Greene put it in *A Sort of Life*, his 1971 autobiography:

> There is a fashion today among many of my contemporaries to treat the events of their past with irony. It is a legitimate method of self-defense. "Look how absurd I was when I was young" forestalls cruel criticism, but it falsifies history. . . . Those emotions were real when we felt them. Why should we be more ashamed of them than of the indifference of old age? I have tried, however unsuccessfully, to live again the follies and sentimentalities and exaggerations of the distant time, and to feel them, as I felt them then, without irony.

The only way to take Simmons as Gordon with any seriousness would be with a heavy dose of irony, for the character Simmons plays is not only gorgeous but seemingly without talent as an actress when she puts on a show for her parents. That may not have been what Gordon, Cukor, or Simmons fully intended, but it's impossible to avoid that judgment while watching her painfully inept "recital" when Clinton asks her to demonstrate why she wants to pursue an acting career. She quickly draws up a pair of chairs for them and, using a door frame as a proscenium and standing on the staircase "so it would look more like a theater," she announces, "I'll do one comical and one tragical."

Part of what made Tracy a great actor was that he "never acted listening," as Simmons put it, "which is what a lot of actors do—they 'act' listening." Clinton watches Ruth's recital earnestly but with understandable incredulity, shooting a glance at his wife's desperate look of rapt admiration as Ruth declaims a speech from Shakespeare's *Twelfth Night* (delivered in the play by Viola in drag as Cesario, to Olivia) with histrionic excess, head thrown back and arms waving. Her father has to ask, without meaning to be rude, "Uh, uh, hold on, hold on just a minute, uh—is this the c-comical one or the tragical?" Ruth is momentarily chagrined after doing the "tragical" part, but showing what he later calls the "gumption" that convinces him she could succeed, she launches into a "comical" musical number that's only slightly less embarrassing. She gallops back and forth in and out of the improvised proscenium, singing a ditty from *The Pink Lady*, "Bring Along the Camera," while pulling a black hood over her head and making corny hand gestures like a photographer (perhaps hinting at her future film career). She may be cute and energetic, although rather frantic, but her musical routine is also rankly amateurish. Her father comments, "You can be heard, all right, but—uh, do you think folks'd shell out money to see it?"

Cukor recalled that Tracy "loved and respected" Jean Simmons, and that in this scene, Ruth

was starting things off rather badly. And Spencer looked at her and he did something very funny: for no reason at all, he looked at the mother as though she had talked this girl into doing something. But then he looked at her with this eloquent face of his and his face changed color. And I said, "That was lovely." He said, "Well, I remember when I told my father that I wanted to be an actor and he looked at me, this skinny kid with big ears, and he said, 'Oh that poor little son of a bitch; he's going to go through an awful lot.'" He drew out of his own experiences.

This was one of the many times that Tracy, as was his habit, surprised Cukor with his acting. Cukor and others related that unlike most other actors, Tracy usually would resist if the director tried talking to him too much, preferring to keep his own counsel about how he would play a scene. "He didn't seem intense at all," Simmons recalled. "It just seemed like rolling off him, easy. Obviously, he'd be up half the night—working, working, working, and then would come on totally prepared. He would say to me, 'Listen, kid, just know your lines and get on with it.' . . . I had to rely totally on George Cukor, who was so funny because he would get up and play my character—and it was oh so much better than I could possibly do. . . . George would say, 'This is how you do it.' And then he would go up to Spence—and they were great friends—and start to do it and Spencer would just walk away. He'd say, 'Shut up, George!'"

"With Spencer," Cukor explained, "we would rehearse and occasionally he would let you in on what he thought, and he was also creative, but neither he nor Katharine Hepburn do all this business of going into things and exaggerating and examining themselves, which I think lets a lot of the magic out. Spencer would, I'm sure, be preoccupied with the part. I'm sure he would be mulling it over. But he didn't articulate it because he felt that 'if I talk about it an awful lot, then when I do it it won't have the freshness.'" So Cukor learned to step back and do as little directing as possible with Tracy, trusting him to know the role thoroughly and do it meticulously and brilliantly. Their work together is a supreme example of how Cukor created what he called a "climate" for the set that enabled an actor to relax and ease his way into the part.

That wonderfully concerned, quizzical, yet loving close-up as Clinton Jones watches and listens to his daughter traipse through their hallway doing her pathetically bad routine shows that, despite it all, he has faith in her and feels she has the right to get her chance in life. Even if Ruth in the film shows no obvious talent, we understand from whence her histrionic drive and ambitions came by watching and listening to this fascinating man with his secret past and his entirely natural acting-out of his complex feelings in front of the family that serves as his small captive audience. The Wollaston home is Clinton's stage. The quirky layout and planes and angles of the set, with doorways leading off in various unpredictable directions to suggest "offstage" spaces, help give the sense that the action always seems to revolve around Clinton's emoting. He is a practiced storyteller who acts out his feelings, even though

the self-centered Ruth is lost in her dreamy fantasies or chattering and competing for attention. When she expresses her dreams, they mostly revolve
around lavish costumes and a luxurious life; that materialism is a reflection
of how marred she has become by her family's impoverishment.

Her father's early complaining about his wife's expenditures, nitpicking
about what he considers household extravagances, running battle with the
family cat, and stream of nostalgic reminiscences of his happier life as a seaman strike a humorous note but with an underlying sense of pain and resentment of his circumstances that dominate his frustrated life. Cukor, as the film
goes on, makes breathtaking use of several long takes with Tracy, redirecting
the audience's attention to him and away from his bombastic daughter while
allowing him to reveal his previously hidden feelings to her and Annie. In
one scene, Clinton surprises them as he walks back and forth in the sitting
room, the camera following as he recalls his theatergoing habit while visiting
foreign countries in his seafaring days. He tells of his admiration for such
storied figures as Helena Modjeska, Lawrence Barrett, "Lotta" (Crabtree),
and Edwin Booth and how he spent time as a stagehand so he could observe
Crabtree and Booth up close. Later he tells Annie how he used to wear gold
hoop earrings and a sash for a belt and changed his name to something more
suitable (as Ruth soon will too).

The fact that Clinton has withheld these colorful aspects of his personality from them all these years, letting them out only when he has to explain
why he does not oppose Ruth taking a "pretty rough voyage" by going on the
stage, is powerful dramaturgy and allows Tracy stunning moments of character revelation. Among the universal truths in *The Actress* is how seldom we
bother to learn who our parents were before we came along. Clinton's theatrical side also comes out in a delightful comic interlude as he performs in an
exhibition by the married men's gymnastic group at the Boston Young Men's
Christian Union, thoroughly mortifying his daughter as she watches from a
balcony with her mother. Tracy has a big silly grin as he trots into the gym
with the other men and goes through a series of routines climaxing with a
human pyramid. While serving as the stalwart base of the pyramid to the
tune of Sousa's "Washington Post March," he loses his pants for a second time
in front of the crowd, much to Ruth's horror. The aging child star Jackie
Coogan (the title character in Chaplin's silent classic *The Kid*) makes wise-
cracks behind them, further shaming Ruth and dismaying Annie.

But we admire Clinton's pluck, aging dexterity, and above all his game quality, which outweigh his tendency to cause embarrassment as a performer; in that combination of traits as well he and Ruth are similar. And the other serious element of this interlude (which is only alluded to in the play) is that it crystallizes for Ruth why she is so adamantly opposed to her father's ambition for her to become a physical culture instructor like the spinsterish woman (Mary Wickes) who puts on an exhibition of juggling Indian clubs, a show that's not much to look forward to in life compared with the risk of going on the New York stage.

The most virtuosic scene in *The Actress* is a bravura, breathtaking long take near the end of the film in which Clinton unloads his previously hidden feelings about his painful upbringing. He's explaining why he's willing to stake Ruth to her start in the theater. He does so while making and eating a sandwich as he moves back and forth in their tiny kitchen, at first sitting with Ruth and Annie as they bring him plates and food, then going into the pantry and to another room to get more food and drink while the camera follows him partway, letting him exit from view briefly but moving closer and pulling out while he delivers a three-and-a-half-minute monologue. His righteous anger builds as he reveals the secret trauma he has been carrying around of how his mother killed herself when he was two and how he became an abused child raised by cruel relatives ("They was *awful* people") before running away to sea as a cabin boy at the age of eight. In a moving, low-key, but powerful touch, his daughter's hand reaches into frame onto his arm during this account, a key turning point in the film, since it represents a break from her narcissism and self-centeredness. The camera tracks back to reframe Clinton through the eyes of his wife and daughter listening in the foreground so we can see them all together. That Ruth and her father can share their seemingly unlikely sense of empathy with each other is the spine of the play and screenplay.

I've never forgotten a simple but profound lesson about Tracy that my father, Raymond McBride, learned from Cary Grant when he interviewed him for the *Milwaukee Journal*. My father asked Grant what actor he most admired, and he said Tracy. When asked why, Grant picked up a glass of water and demonstrated. Grant showed how difficult it is to talk in a scene while drinking a glass of water in a way that seems natural. He told my father that Tracy was the actor who showed them all how to play a scene with such a seemingly effortless, flawless combination of talk and gestures.

Richard Burton, while speaking of Tracy's acting on *The Dick Cavett Show* in 1980, described what he called the

> tremendous effort and tremendous art that went into that, deliberately hiding from the audience any technique whatsoever, so that it seemed that it was there by accident. I went to watch him work once at MGM when he was doing a film called *The Actress*. . . . I'd read the script, and he had a very long speech about poverty and the bitterness that poverty makes in people and so on, and it was a really eloquent piece of writing. The actor's gums, as 'twere, *ached* to get my teeth onto the speech. And I wanted to see how Spencer Tracy would do it. And so I sat there . . . and he started munching a piece of bread, I think it was, as the speech started. [*Mimics his action*] And he spoke the speech chewing all the time. At one time he left the room, and so [for what seemed to Burton like] a good third of the speech he wasn't onscreen. And he walked back into the room still chewing. And it was devastating. Devastating. . . . And it was extraordinary because it was the exact opposite of what I *thought* he would do with it.

As one of Cukor's quintessential dreamers, Ruth makes up for her deficiency of talent with her earnestness, idealism, relentless drive, and flinty New England determination to succeed, a quality she shares with Hepburn's Jo in Cukor's *Little Women*. Cukor suggests that will be enough to carry Ruth through to ultimate success, hard though it may be along the way. We admire her drive even though she is constantly on the edge of being impossible and irritating in the film, which at least helps counteract any tendency toward sentimentality. But we have to take her on faith, as her parents do, and that works in this hardscrabble context. And we never forget those establishing images of her watching Hazel Dawn with enchantment, which keep us identifying with her no matter how critical of her immaturity the film (inadvertently or not) encourages us to be.

Although Teresa Wright is youngish to play Tracy's wife and didn't think she carried off the role, she looks suitably beaten-down and bedraggled and riddled with grim self-denial in the presence of her overbearing husband and flighty daughter. Annie's constant anxiety to appease her husband goes hand in hand with quietly supporting her daughter's ambitions but concealing them from him as long as they can. An important subplot in the film is Ruth's rejection of an offer of marriage to the gawky but charming young Anthony Perkins, making his film debut as Fred Whitmarsh, a well-off Harvard student hopelessly courting her. She accompanies her rejection of his proposal at a stage door with a self-consciously theatrical gesture, throwing out her arm and accepting a chaste kiss as she declares, "I'm going through that door, and behind it's my whole life. . . . From an actress—almost."

Before leaving home, she tells Fred that she must not marry him, "because if I did, then I myself might not want to be an actress." He asks her, "Aren't you ever gonna get interested in a fella?," and she replies, "Not unless they live in New York City or just outside." As he drives away forever, she goes inside the house, passing through a dark shadow and moving into the foreground of the shot, leaning against a doorway in evident pain, facing the realization that a career in show business involves sacrificing a conventional life and happiness. She leaves Fred behind in her Massachusetts hometown just as Jo leaves Laurie to pursue her artistic destiny in New York.

Cukor himself had devoted himself to that kind of life, so Ruth is another of his gender-bending surrogate figures; casting a gay actor as Fred helps emphasize the personal connections. And when Clinton fills out an application for her to be trained as a gym teacher and comes to the question "Sex," he studies his daughter before declaring after a long pause, "Female." "Oh, dear, you had to go and be so *different*," her mother sighs, vainly asking, "Would you just for all our sakes please consider being normal?" We can see in Annie's self-abnegating personality in marriage the kind of unfulfilled life Ruth must reject to become a truly independent woman in a time when helping a workman carry her own trunk makes Fred think of her as "some kind of a suffragette or something." The legacy from father to daughter of their restless nonconformity, being "different," and their subsequent sense of entrapment, along with his gift of his most precious possession (a spyglass) for her to sell in New York, is what helps ensure that her quirky creativity will eventually blossom, as it did for the playwright. The only advice the old salt gives her is: "Don't ever act in no place where they sell hard liquor."

MGM's lack of faith in *The Actress* led to some recutting by its producer, Lawrence Weingarten, that Cukor thought hurt the film, as well as battles over sound recording, partly because the studio worried that Simmons sounded "irritating if she uses the higher register" and that Tracy was throwing away some of the dialogue he muttered with a pipe in his mouth. That was part of his naturalistic playing, since Clinton, like any other father, often expects not to be listened to. Cukor was able to reach a rapprochement on the sound with Weingarten, though not on the cuts, which left the release version at only ninety minutes. Studio attempts to "improve" a picture with recutting often result in its dying at the box office, which happened with *The Actress*. But Cukor was able to write Gordon and Kanin after a public preview in Inglewood, near Los Angeles, that was largely a success: "At first they think they're seeing a 'homey' sentimental comedy. They dote on Spence, laugh at his jokes. Then they're taken aback by the strength of his feelings and his occasional bursts of violence. They're gradually forced to the realization that he isn't quite the old peach they'd first taken him for. But when the picture is over, the audience feels that they've met an extraordinary human being."

20.1. Judy Garland's electrifying song number "The Man That Got Away" was filmed in a single take in *A Star Is Born*, sustaining the mood and the atmosphere of a little jazz club on the Sunset Strip during an after-hours jam session. James Mason's Norman Maine, who is off-screen watching along with us, is moved to tell Esther afterward, "You're a great singer," and we believe him, even if she is initially doubtful.

Source: Frame enlargement; Warner Bros.

20.2. In this haunting scene from his masterpiece, the 1954 musical drama *A Star Is Born*, Cukor alluded to his removing heavy makeup and a wig from Garland's Dorothy Gale while he was briefly assigned by MGM to the 1939 fantasy *The Wizard of Oz*. When Mason's troubled movie star Norman Maine in *A Star Is Born* finds Garland's neophyte actress Esther Blodgett all gussied up by their film studio in her new identity as Vicki Lester, he cleans her off and restores her face to its natural beauty.

Source: Frame enlargement; Warner Bros.

20

JUDY GARLAND AND JAMES MASON IN *A STAR IS BORN*

In his brief time in preproduction as the director of *The Wizard of Oz*, Cukor made one decision that was vital to the success of that classic 1939 MGM musical fantasy. Confronted with the sight of young Judy Garland in garish makeup and a blonde wig, Cukor ordered the wig removed and more naturally subdued makeup applied to bring out the teenage Judy's wholesome qualities as the Kansas farm girl Dorothy Gale. Cukor did not work with Garland again until his first musical and first finished and completely in color film, the lavish 1954 dramatic remake of *A Star Is Born*, Garland's comeback vehicle for Warner Bros. after a series of personal and professional disasters, including her firing from her longtime studio, MGM.

For a crucial scene in *A Star Is Born*, Cukor harked back to *The Wizard of Oz* and had James Mason haul Judy into his dressing room and humorously but tenderly remove the grotesque makeup and blonde wig the studio in the film had used to turn her Esther Blodgett into a conventional starlet. Cukor dissolves to Esther in a mirror, with Mason's Norman Maine peering over her shoulder lovingly as her natural good looks miraculously are restored (with the aid of subtle pink lighting), making her years of turmoil disappear and turning her almost girlish again, as the musical score poignantly accompanies her transformation. That scene encapsulates the film, with its removal of her self-protective mask and revelation of her true personality under Norman's creative ministration. "What difference does it make how well I sing if my face is so awful?" she asks Norman as he rubs cold cream all over it, but he assures her, "Your face is just dandy," and she laughs with relief and delight.

"Once more unto the breach, dear friends," says Norman when he shows Esther her genuine appearance, quoting a speech by the king rallying his troops in Shakespeare's *Henry V.* Norman is a hopeless alcoholic hell-bent on self-destruction, his career as a movie star collapsing as his discovery, Esther, rises to stardom as "Vicki Lester," but he is ennobled by his belief in her talents, selfless in never doubting but encouraging her and aiding her ascent. And he is gallant, if bitterly ironic, amid his own ruination and the events leading up to his suicide by walking into the ocean from his Malibu beach home at sunset. Cukor had dealt with this theme in *What Price Hollywood?*, the 1932 David O. Selznick production starring Lowell Sherman and Constance Bennett that had launched the durable string of films about this archetypal Hollywood rise-and-fall saga. While remaking William Wellman's 1937 version of *A Star Is Born*, the Selznick film starring Fredric March and Janet Gaynor, Cukor and the screenwriter Moss Hart deepened the story's emotions, stripping away its inherent clichés to dig down into the heartbreaking realities it is exploring.

As well as being among the finest and most honest films about Hollywood, Cukor's *A Star Is Born* is one of the most emotionally powerful and aesthetically brilliant films ever made. Garland's Esther is portrayed as older and more experienced than Gaynor's character (they were actually about the same age when they made their versions, but Gaynor still looked girlish). Esther is an itinerant band singer lured by the often illusory promises of the film industry but wary at the same time of the irresponsible Norman. Yet she is transformed by his faith in her ability to succeed in that ruthless business. The film achieves its veracity in paradoxical ways, capturing the irresolvable conflicts inherent in the industry. The portrait it offers is simultaneously operatic and intimate, romantic and jaded, optimistic and bitter about how Hollywood grinds up and destroys people, and a virtuosic and subtle work of art with a rich but subdued color scheme and central characters who are both tragic and resilient. And like other great but overweeningly ambitious Hollywood films, including *Greed* and *The Magnificent Ambersons*, *A Star Is Born* was severely mutilated by its studio, existing today as only a partly restored work, fragmented and somewhat ruined, like the industry itself, with its casually destructive attitude toward its traditions and legacy.

A Star Is Born is both the crowning glory of Garland's career and one that encapsulates her own ruination. It's a bitter irony that her triumphant but expensive CinemaScope production with her husband, Sidney Luft ($6 million, considerably over budget), destroyed her status as a movie star and drove her out of the business for years. And for Cukor, the ultimate Hollywood survivor, it was a far more painful experience than even his firing from *Gone with the Wind* but also a work in which he took considerable artistic pride, despite the trauma. Although his career was uneven after this landmark, that was mostly a result of the upheavals in the industry that disrupted the system in which he had long flourished, but the blow did seem to have a disruptive effect on his career. Nevertheless, while his later years were erratic, they still brought forth some of his finest films.

A Star Is Born arguably remains Cukor's greatest achievement, even if it was shortsightedly and crassly hacked up by Warners after its critical success and promising early runs. The studio, which had shoehorned in some extraneous musical numbers over Cukor's objections, made the cuts to squeeze in more daily runs for the long movie (shortening it from 181 to 154 minutes). That reckless and foolish move caused such damage that many ordinary viewers found the storyline somewhat incoherent or stayed away because of negative publicity and word-of-mouth about the recutting. Despite its disappointing playoff and Garland's failure to win her expected and well-deserved Oscar (Grace Kelly won instead for *The Country Girl*), *A Star Is Born* acquired cult status over the years with cinephiles and Garland aficionados. The lost complete version became a Holy Grail, eventually the subject of a strenuous search by the film historian Ronald Haver with the support of Warners and the Academy of Motion Picture Arts and Sciences. Haver wrote a fascinating 1988 book drawn from his archaeological research into this saga, *A Star Is Born: The Making of the 1954 Movie and Its 1983 Restoration*.

Haver managed to locate the entire original soundtrack and some but not all of the missing visual material, filling in other parts with stills. Warners released his 176-minute version, which gives a much fuller sense of the richness and texture of the extraordinary work of Cukor and his collaborators (the reason the restoration is five minutes shorter than the original is that Haver, in yet another irony, felt it necessary to cut parts of the soundtrack because he didn't have enough stills covering those scenes). Besides Hart and the cast, Cukor's coworkers, at the top of their games, included the art director Gene Allen, the cinematographer Sam Leavitt, and the color consultant George Hoyningen-Huene, the celebrated fashion photographer recruited by Cukor to work on this and his subsequent color films, all of which are stylistically lavish and daring. The affinity Cukor displayed with his use of the widescreen format here and in subsequent work such as *Bhowani Junction*, *My Fair Lady*, and *Travels with My Aunt* allowed the director to mount lavishly textured tapestries, both lush and intimate, drawing visually alluring dramatic impact from the most extravagant cinematic resources.

Garland's film career before *A Star Is Born* largely was in musical comedies. But with his keen sense of performers' hidden qualities, Cukor recognized her potential as a dramatic actress. He was aware of the emotional *Sturm und Drang* in her difficult private life and how she had been turned into a drug addict by MGM as a callous means of reducing her weight and keeping her hyperactive at work. Those elements would feed into her deep

20.3.   Cukor supervising Garland's makeup for *A Star Is Born*.

Source: Warner Bros./From the George Cukor Papers of the Margaret Herrick Library, Academy of Motion Picture Arts and Sciences.

understanding of the story dynamics in *A Star Is Born*, including Norman's addiction. Cukor also appreciated a quality that was crucial to him: "She could talk about the most devastating experiences of her childhood—this over-weight little girl with the enormous talent—and have you screaming with laughter. She had an absolutely devastating eye, and while making fun of her-self, she could also zero in on the other person being talked about with great humor and style." And he recalled that it was in 1949, shortly before her fir-ing by MGM, that "I gave a birthday party for Ethel Barrymore—it was her seventieth—and Judy came and sang 'Happy Birthday' to her. She did it with such feeling and emotion that I thought Ethel would dissolve in tears. Any-one who could sing like that, I thought, had the emotional ability to be a great dramatic actress. That was the first time I got the idea I wanted to direct Judy."

Hollywood's classic Pygmalion-Galatea story, with one partner going uphill while the other goes down, *A Star Is Born* draws from Cukor's use of Norman Maine as a director figure of sorts as he discovers, guides, nurtures, and encourages his actress protégée, even sacrificing his life to preserve her career. That is a large part of what makes Cukor's second version of the story so dramatically meaningful, and it is far deeper than his first run at it in *What Price Hollywood?* Unlike Sherman's more disinterested Max Carey in his benevolent nurturing of Mary Evans through the shoals of the studio system before he kills himself as a result of his alcoholism, Norman is also the roman-tic partner of Esther. When the studio renames her Vicki Lester, it reminds us that Frances Gumm was renamed Judy Garland and that part of her per-sonality was transformed and obliterated.

The first *A Star Is Born*, which Cukor passed on directing because he found it too similar to the film he had made only five years earlier, rectified that story problem. The Oscar-winning story of the 1937 film was by the director Wellman and Robert Carson; the screenplay was by Alan Campbell, Car-son, and Dorothy Parker. Ring Lardner Jr. and Budd Schulberg contributed Esther's famous line, "This is Mrs. Norman Maine," which was cut from the script of that version but restored by John Lee Mahin; it is used in Cukor's film as well. With it Esther pointedly shames the hypocritical Hollywood crowd who rejected Norman, while the serenity she displays beneath her tears shows she is beginning to cope with his loss.

Expanding the scope of the story in the 1954 remake by allowing Esther to express her feelings through music strongly enhanced the role and brought forth the whole range of Garland's talents. One of the odd ironies of the first three versions of the story is that the leading lady "discovery" is played by an already famous star, and in the cases of Gaynor and Garland, by one who has been on a career downslide. People argue about whether the woman's role eclipses the man's in some of the *A Star Is Born* cycle (including the later remakes with Barbra Streisand and Lady Gaga), but despite Garland's prominence as a musical performer, which makes her a more central figure than Gaynor is in her film, Mason is so moving and his character so compelling that the two roles in Cukor's film feel of equal weight and importance, regardless of relative screen time. His Norman, who is further ennobled by sacrificing himself for Esther, also seems superior to the trashy roles he evidently plays, even if we never see any of them. A brief outtake from a hokey stunt he performs on a studio-bound Chinese junk, à la Errol Flynn and Douglas Fairbanks, is one of the extras on the Blu-ray edition, but otherwise we mostly hear Maine disparaging his own work. Norman's pain and despondency, we can infer, stems partly from his own sense of squandering his talent in Hollywood.

John Barrymore, one of Cukor's favorite actors, was one of the models he had in mind for the male role, with his self-mocking, tragicomic displays of alcoholic dissipation, partly to show contempt for his fall in stature. Barrymore did receive some good parts in Hollywood talkies from Cukor and others, but his glory days were mostly behind him in the theater, and Cukor and Fredric March satirized his descent into silly talkies in *The Royal Family of Broadway*. The scene in the 1937 *A Star Is Born* with Norman in a sanitarium was based on Cukor's visit with Barrymore when MGM put him into a sanitarium near the studio to dry him out for *Romeo and Juliet*. Cukor told Selznick about that eerie visit, and he wound up directing the same scene seventeen years later. Cukor's treatment of the scene with the studio chief Oliver Niles (Charles Bickford) visiting Norman is considerably more disturbing than its equivalent in the earlier film, partly because of its more visceral verisimilitude, Norman's heightened degree of shakiness, and his gallows humor, some imported from the Wellman film and some nuances added by Cukor.

As a recovering alcoholic myself and someone who was dangerously overmedicated as a youth, I've always found that much in the Cukor film strikes a resonant chord with me. I especially relate to a line (based on one that

Dorothy Parker originally wrote for Norman in the 1937 film), "We dine here at 5:30—makes the nights longer." I remember exactly that feeling, down to the hour and minute, when I was incarcerated in a mental hospital when I had a physical and psychological breakdown as a teenager, a period I wrote about in my memoir *The Broken Places*. The many alcoholics in Cukor's films have frequent moments of lucid introspection, and their awareness of their powerlessness over addiction adds to the poignancy of those roles. They allow Cukor to dramatize the dilemma of alcoholism while exploring in depth a more pervasive issue, the mingled highs and lows of reckless gaiety and despondency in bipolar personalities and human beings in general.

Ingmar Bergman once observed that the quality of danger is essential for a film actor to become a star. Not every good male actor has that quality, but Cukor could zero in on those he knew had it in them. Cukor wanted Cary Grant for Norman, recognizing the moodier side of the usually debonair Grant that James Naremore, in his critical study of the star, calls the "Dark Cary." But after a prolonged hesitation, Grant passed on playing Norman. Cukor was particularly chagrined because he had helped develop Grant's stardom through three of his best early roles and because he thought Grant's refusal stemmed from his reluctance to fully reveal his inner self on film. Grant had done a powerful script reading with the director, "but when he finished," Cukor recalled, "I was filled with a great, great sadness. Because I knew Cary would never do the role. He would never expose himself like that in public."

Mason was a distinguished British stage and film actor whose major roles had included the leads as the Irish revolutionary in *Odd Man Out* (1947), the German field marshal Erwin Rommel in *The Desert Fox: The Story of Rommel* (1951), and Brutus in *Julius Caesar* (1953). He knew he was further down the list of male stars. But with his haunted quality, keen intelligence, Shakespearean eloquence, and mordant wit, Mason was perfect for Norman, playing with more sardonic humor than the often-lugubrious March but not dissimilar to Sherman's version for Cukor, although Sherman is more brittle in his humor and Mason more soulful as well as younger-seeming and more vital. Mason brings to the role a surface gaiety, joie de vivre, and self-mockery that keeps the character appealing despite the addiction and crudities of behavior that bring Norman down. Mason crucially had what Cukor called a "reserved, rather enigmatic" quality that contributed to Norman's ironic recognition of his failings but also made his breakdown leading up to his suicide even more powerful. Unlike Grant, Mason was unafraid to explore his own psychological depths onscreen when it was required. As he listens in bed to Esther telling Niles she is going to give up her career to care for Norman, the prolonged agony we witness is a tremendously powerful expression of Norman's despair and the guilt that leads plausibly to his self-sacrifice for Esther's sake.

As Haver writes, Mason's casting was "a blessing for the film, for few performers of his caliber would have had the maturity to allow themselves to be subordinate to Judy Garland, to sit and react while she sang to them, and generally be upstaged by her. This prospect is probably what kept Cary Grant from accepting the role." But that description somewhat underrates the importance of the role of Norman, who indeed feels "upstaged" by his wife but acts on his mingled feelings of pride and resentment in complex ways throughout the film. Even Mason found it difficult to sit and react for long shooting days in response to Garland's virtuosic "Someone at Last" number, in which she comes back home from filming her big production number to lift Norman's spirits by imitating it in a seemingly improvised way, with Cukor using two cameras for added spontaneity. But Norman's varied and genuine reactions of amusement are touching, because we realize why she is knocking herself out, ingeniously using household objects as props, to distract Norman from his agony over being unable to find a job. The light touch both Mason and Garland bring to their roles, a hallmark of Cukor's films, is the self-defensive facade they share; it covers the desperation just underneath that lets them slide naturally into their times of torment. That mélange of feelings is the key quality of acting that makes Cukor's film superior to the 1937 version. Mason also received an Oscar nomination for *A Star Is Born*.

Norman's often-appalling behavior in the Cukor film begins with his drunken rampage backstage at a Shrine Auditorium industry benefit, the most spectacularly varied and sustained passage in the film. Nearly surreal imagery of clowns and other kinds of entertainers is beautifully displayed with bold color schemes in the backgrounds and costumes (some of the imagery is borrowed from Degas and other painters) and eccentric blocking and choreography, daringly breaking the supposed rules of the day with fast cutting on the wide screen, sometimes using a handheld camera. This bravura sequence and its avant-garde departure from Cukor's black-and-white work made *Cahiers du Cinéma* hyperbolically trumpet, "A DIRECTOR IS BORN!" The sequence climaxes in Esther's quick thinking as she cleverly incorporates the woozy Norman into her big-band act, pulling him into the spotlight as he staggers onto the stage, thus putting him in debt to her. But the seeds of his self-destruction and the danger he poses to Esther are palpable in this early sequence, which includes physically attacking photographers and the studio publicity chief Matt Libby (Jack Carson), whose understandable contempt for the abusive, out-of-control Norman eventually makes him cruelly gloat over his downfall.

Nevertheless, what follows this scandalous calamity at the benefit makes us view Norman in ways that linger throughout the rest of the film. We soon become aware of his fine taste and appreciation of Esther's talents that other people cannot recognize. Those abilities emerge when he visits the modest after-hours nightclub where she and the boys in her band are jamming. Norman has an epiphany when he hears her electrifying rendition of "The Man That Got Away," an instant classic torch song written for the film by Harold Arlen (music) and Ira Gershwin (lyrics) after Hart requested what he called a "dive" song for Garland.

One of the most visually stunning and emotionally moving musical numbers ever put on film, the song is performed in a long take, composed for the CinemaScope image to give a feeling of roving and spontaneity as the camera moves in, out, and around with Esther in the half-darkened club. She delivers the song full-throated but with a wistful smile that balances the raw-nerved energy and vulnerability she puts into her passionate singing about a lost romance. Her piano player and good friend Danny McGuire (Tom Noonan) accompanies her, and the other musicians are mostly visible at the sides and in the foreground of the picture, their instruments glinting in the dark. They are often silhouetted as Leavitt's cinematography and the visual setting by Allen and Hoyningen-Huene give a smoky feeling of nocturnal, clandestine intimacy. What makes the scene look particularly romantic is a semitransparent scrim Allen put between the musicians and the bar to make it seem less realistic and give it what he called a "slightly impressionistic look."

Three separate attempts and many takes of the final version were required to get this number to look right as Cukor & Co. experimented with the new wide screen and different color stocks, set decoration, and costuming. The film's original cinematographer, Winton C. Hoch, who had won three Oscars for his masterful Technicolor work, was fired after he could not get the look Cukor wanted for this shot. The final effect after all this effort to tame the initially daunting CinemaScope process is among the most stunning scenes Cukor ever put on the screen, with overwhelming visual and emotional resonance.

Norman has been listening transfixed from a table in the shadows. As the film scholar Joe McElhaney points out, Cukor's use of an unbroken take of Esther's song implicitly puts us in Norman's position as spectator, always an important place to be in a Cukor film, like Ruth's second-balcony seat at the theater in *The Actress*: "So many moments in Cukor where a character does not simply watch a performance but is enraptured by it, as though their entire perception of the world is being altered. One of the greatest moments in Cukor in this regard is one we don't even literally see: James Mason watching Judy Garland sing 'The Man That Got Away' in *A Star Is Born*."

After hearing her, Norman takes Esther outside to a noisy alleyway over-looking the Sunset Strip to explain why, to her surprise, he expertly discerns that "you're a great singer." Insisting he is "as sober as a judge, and I know *exactly* what I'm saying," he tells her she gave him the "little jabs of pleasure" one gets from watching a great prizefighter or bullfighter or dancer. "You've got 'that little something extra' that Ellen Terry talked about—Ellen Terry, a great actress long before you were born—she said that that's what star quality was, 'that little something extra.' Well, you've got it." Esther considers her current job with the band a major step in her career and has only a modest opinion of her own talents, so she is thrown by what Norman says but instinctively believes it, and the realization entirely disrupts her life. She is another of Cukor's quintessential dreamers, and Norman convinces her that her dream of having a number-one hit record is not big enough. "Don't settle for the little dream," he tells her. "Go for the big one."

Norman makes that possible by tracking her down later and getting her a screen test, although that part of the film, their offbeat courtship, was the most severely damaged by the studio recutting. His frantic attempts to locate her after he's shanghaied off to sea for a film shoot while hungover and her struggles to survive in a crummy rooming house while working as a carhop (after vowing she will never again become a waitress) and doing singing commercials remain incomplete and are covered in Haver's restoration by stills interspersed with brief clips found in the Warners stock film library. Although it's exciting to get glimpses of those long-lost, often humorous scenes, as well as a greater sense of Norman's sincerity in trying to help her career rather just being on the make, the damage done to this section is particularly unfortunate.

In the script it's a bracingly realistic demonstration of the grueling perils actresses and other newcomers face in Hollywood and the dreamlike improbability of Esther/Vicki achieving what's misleadingly known as "overnight" stardom. Despite the butchery of this lengthy sequence, Garland's talent and Cukor's direction make her rise to stardom plausible even in the shortened version. The humiliating daily existence of most Hollywood hopefuls in the fragmented modern industry was knowingly and compassionately conveyed by Hart and Cukor during this period of transition, when the studios were beginning to collapse as the industry was disrupted by drastic economic and technological change.

Those realistic elements are introduced into Norman's story as well, which helps explain why even such a sympathetic studio chief as Oliver Niles has to let him go. When Niles fires Norman at the actor's newly built home in Malibu, he explains that it is partly because the changes in the industry have made him too expensive to afford anymore. Using the CinemaScope frame with pointed dialectical effect, Cukor frames their discussion between the threat to movies at the far left of the frame (a television showing a boxing match and Esther's shampoo commercial) and the traditional Hollywood at the far right (a screen showing a movie to Norman's guests). Niles delivers his unwelcome message as kindly as he can, and Norman is gracious in return: "Oh, we had a long roll of the dice, didn't we, Oliver?" Some commentators have wondered why the film portrays the studio chief in such a benignly paternal light. Cukor and Selznick had a grudging fondness for the moguls, which resulted in reversing the clichés about their monstrous behavior from most films about Hollywood, even if those clichés in many cases had a substantial foundation in truth.

That three-dimensional portrait of Niles pays off dramatically in his empathetic relationships with Norman and Esther. Partly because Esther has become such a valued star, but also against his and the studio's best interests, Niles compassionately tries to help her deal with her husband's addiction. The film's most dramatically intense scene is the long take of the two of them talking in Esther's dressing room, with an unconventional use of the wide screen. Niles is only partly visible at far left, and Esther is at far right with a vast space between them (her table with makeup, a mirror and wall behind it, and a funereal batch of lilies at far right), a space that represents the gulf of their mutually admitted lack of understanding how to help Norman.

On the verge of collapse, Esther pours out her conflicted feelings of love and hate for Norman in a powerfully written monologue as Niles mostly listens. Esther is wearing clownish makeup with freckles (blurring as she cries) and a childish straw hat. She is playing a New Orleans newsgirl in a musical number (on a pastel set borrowed from *A Streetcar Named Desire*) that serves as a wraparound for this harrowing scene. Esther's ability to perform under such duress demonstrates what a trouper she is, as Garland and Cukor were when they suffered their grievous setbacks. Garland's speech in the dressing room is halting and often nearly breathless as she struggles to keep herself together. She finally can't succeed and lays herself emotionally bare before her friend and employer. "Love isn't enough," she tells him despondently. "I thought it was. . . . And I'm—I'm afraid of what's beginning to happen within me [*taps her chest*] . . . because . . . sometimes—I—hate—him. . . . I [*hand to mouth*] hate him for *failing*. I hate *me*, too [*pointing at her chest*]. I hate me 'cause I've failed too."

The part of the musical number that follows this scene, the finale of "Lose That Long Face," was one of Haver's rediscoveries. It was first directed in lackluster fashion by the Warners dance director Jack Donohue after Cukor tried to have it cancelled; when Garland protested the new director, Cukor came back to watch the film's choreographer, Richard Barstow, reshoot it. The fact is that this number is second-rate, and it could have been cut along with some other scenes Cukor thought were expendable, such as the proposal scene on the soundstage. Another rediscovery, amusing though it is, the proposal seems anticlimactic after the love scene on a nightclub terrace when Norman unsuccessfully begs the loyal Esther to let him go because "it's too late. . . . I destroy everything I touch, I always have. Forget me, I'm a bad lot."

Cukor said if cuts were needed, he and Hart could have "sweat[ed] out" twenty minutes from the 181-minute running time "and they'd never miss them. They refused, just went ahead with these lethal cuts and threw all the material away." Cukor also did not direct, and vehemently opposed the inclusion of, the fifteen-minute musical medley that literally stops the film at midpoint, the "Born in a Trunk" number directed by Barstow and the MGM songwriter Roger Edens and photographed by Harold Rosson. Although this garishly overblown number, which resembles a parody of an Arthur Freed musical, remains a favorite with many Garland fans, its inclusion in an already riskily lengthy film wound up causing more germane scenes to be cut.

Cukor's fellow director Elia Kazan, one of the leading actors' directors in the cinema, candidly wrote Hart after a small studio preview of *A Star Is Born* that he thought Cukor had directed the film "without a sense of proportion. . . . Numbers which were supposed to be the essence of informality were informal on such a huge scale! I also thought he had put too much self-pity into the feelings of the two leads. On the other hand, there is some magnificent work in it and Judy has superb moments." Kazan wrote the studio chief Jack L. Warner that Cukor and Garland had done the dressing-room scene "beautifully." But Kazan's criticism of the use of the new CinemaScope format in that scene, in which he felt Cukor "had to rely upon a close two shot" rather than using close-ups, seems misguidedly old-fashioned and blind to the power of Cukor's filming both Garland and Bickford together but widely separated with his eloquent widescreen composition.

And Cukor does indeed bring a "sense of proportion," a dual dramatic perspective, to this story about a movie-star couple that is both intimate and glaringly amplified for the scrutiny of the public. That dual vision conveys a complex emotional response to the material as well as making admirably experimental use of the new possibilities of the medium in ways people had not expected from Cukor. They had not been paying close attention to his increasingly virtuosic use of long takes and the extensive location work in his recent films that had broken away from studio confines, signs of his flexibility and the adventurous side of his creative personality.

Another of the numerous emotional high points of *A Star Is Born*, and the most appalling behavior by Norman, is his interruption of Esther's acceptance speech for the Oscar. The oddly anachronistic setting is the relatively intimate Cocoanut Grove nightclub at the Ambassador Hotel, where the Oscars had not been held since 1943. The film shows a TV hookup, since the show had begun being nationally televised from theaters in Hollywood and New York in March 1953, almost seven months before *A Star Is Born* began shooting. Norman, who before marrying Esther had been shown prowling the nightclub for starlets, staggers into the ceremony and pushes his way through the formal crowd tipsily, dressed in street clothing, applauding loudly. He appropriates her moment of triumph for a tirade against the studio chiefs in the audience with the maudlin, repeated theme of "I need a job!"

After the drunken Norman plants a kiss on Esther, she watches with a shocked poker face, uncertain how to act, as he makes an utter fool of himself. Cukor shot this scene twelve times to get the full visceral impact of "seeing a proud man humbled." After Norman sits on a step and slips, Mason added the business of having Norman step up and down the stairs on the stage as he speaks, because he had seen a child do that once, and "I thought that Norman was very childlike" (Libby at another point describes him as being like "a child with a blowtorch").

While bringing out the full ugliness of the most disgraceful conduct at the Oscars until Will Smith slapped Chris Rock on camera in 2022, Mason's acting and Cukor's direction masterfully avoid what the director told Warner was the pitfall of possible "bad laughs." The most horrifying moment, directed for maximum impact through staging and cutting, makes the viewer recoil from the physical sensation. It comes when, as Hart's script puts it, Norman "gestures to the orchestra in back of him and inadvertently strikes Vicki sharply across the face. He stares at her wildly, his eyes not focusing, and starts to sway slightly. He is beginning to come apart. He makes no effort to resist as Vicki pilots him from the stage and through the shocked crowd. Oliver [Libby in the film] pulls out a chair for him and he almost collapses into it. His hands

20.4. "You really scared the hell out of me," Cukor told Garland after she let loose Esther's bottled-up emotions about her husband's death in this scene near the end of *A Star Is Born*. She has been nearly catatonic at her shadowy, cave-like Malibu beach home but is jarred out of her silent grieving by her old friend and musical partner, Danny McGuire (Tom Noonan).
Source: Frame enlargement; Warner Bros.

go over his eyes as the realization of what he has done begins to come over him; in anguish he begs, 'Somebody give me a drink . . . please . . .'" (in the film he says, "A drink, somebody.").

Garland's acting reaches an emotional crescendo when she is in her library after Norman's suicide. At first she seems almost catatonic with grief while sitting before the fireplace, her mostly brown outfit blending into the dark and shadowy tones of the room, helping to visually express her feeling of being lost. When her old friend and colleague Danny enters to remind her that this is the night she has committed to attend another annual benefit at the Shrine, she refuses to go. She erupts in long-pent-up pain and fury, telling him to leave her alone and that she doesn't want any sympathy. Cukor told her quietly before the take, "You know what this is about. You really know this." She gave him a look that showed she understood he wanted her to draw emotions from her own turbulent life.

Garland's outburst, like the rest of her acting in the film, transcends melodrama because it feels so true to her character and her situation. But Cukor had not reckoned on just how *"absolutely* terrifying" Garland's acting would be in this scene and how strong the relatively inexperienced Tommy Noonan was in confronting her. He makes her face up to her selfishness in giving up

20.5. "This is Mrs. Norman Maine": One of the most famous ending lines in film history, this moment at the Shrine Auditorium in *A Star Is Born* is Esther's way of reminding her Hollywood colleagues of what they lost when Norman died, how badly they mistreated him, and how much he gave to her.

Source: Frame enlargement; Warner Bros.

her life, in "tossing aside the one thing [Norman] had left. . . . You're the only thing that remains of him now. And if you just kick it away, it's like he never existed, like there never was a Norman Maine at all."

As Danny berates her in this long unbroken take, she turns her back to him, but he and the camera circle around her relentlessly while he continues to face her down. She walks away toward the door, and the camera pushes in slightly. Then it holds on her back in a long pause before she turns around, totally changed and softened, as she squeezes his hand and agrees to go to the benefit. There she will pay her tribute to Norman. The staging of this cathartic confrontation is an echo, in reverse, of Norman's change in behavior from joy to utter gloom when he turned around following a long pause at the door of their home, following his humiliation with a delivery man (Strother Martin) not recognizing him ("Sign right here, Mr. Lester"), after Esther has knocked herself out to entertain him with her improvised musical number. Norman, like Esther in the library, is wearing a somber brown outfit, and when he returns from the door he tells her about her invitation to the industry benefit at the Shrine Auditorium. Now after her meltdown in the library, the grieving Esther is headed to reclaim his name at that benefit by announcing herself as "Mrs. Norman Maine."

Cukor quickly had Garland do her scene with Noonan one more time for protection in case of some technical mishap. Then the director said to her, "You really scared the hell out of me," and she joked, "Oh, that's nothing. Come over to my house any afternoon. I do it every afternoon." She gave him a look and added, "But I only do it *once* at home."

21

AVA GARDNER IN *BHOWANI JUNCTION*,
KAY KENDALL IN *LES GIRLS*,
AND SOPHIA LOREN AND ANTHONY QUINN
IN *HELLER IN PINK TIGHTS*

After reaching the artistic pinnacle of *A Star Is Born* and then seeing his masterpiece shattered into fragments, Cukor's career, probably not coincidentally, went into a period of disarray. The impact of that calamity on its director bore some resemblance to how the butchery of *Greed* and *The Magnificent Ambersons* affected the careers of Erich von Stroheim and Orson Welles. As tends to happen with projects that challenge industry conventions and stretch formal limits, the system pushed back against the Promethean efforts of all three directors. The lingering effects of the trauma on Cukor, personally and professionally, marked the next few years of his peripatetic, somewhat scattered, fragmentary career. But he persisted, eventually won an Oscar for best director (for his masterful 1964 film version of *My Fair Lady*), and in his final years in the industry, despite further setbacks and periods of enforced idleness, made some remarkably fresh, exuberant, and moving films. When I said to Cukor in 1981, "Older directors seem to have a kind of . . .," he completed the thought: "Wisdom?"

When *A Star Is Born* was being mutilated in Hollywood, Cukor was far away in Pakistan, busy with preproduction on the intimate epic *Bhowani Junction*, another ambitious CinemaScope project he undertook as a creative adventure to expand his artistic range beyond what Hollywood expected of him. Set during the chaotic post–World War II period of the British exit from India, the MGM film mixes political intrigue with the romantic entanglements of an Anglo-Indian woman (Ava Gardner). But *Bhowani Junction* was also badly mangled by its studio, and it was not released until May 1956. Like other veteran Hollywood directors in that period when the studio system in which they had prospered was beginning to disintegrate around them, Cukor was not particularly adept at coming up with projects on his own. He mostly had to take what he could get during the late 1950s and early '60s, and most of his fancied projects fell through. Under contract to MGM but available for loan-out, he replaced directors on troubled films or accepted uncongenial casting or had to deal with other forms of studio interference. Cukor was still in demand to work with major actresses, including Gardner, Kay Kendall, Anna Magnani, and Sophia Loren, and they stimulated his creativity, even if their vehicles were often uneven.

Cukor's failed attempts to launch some of his personal projects in this period are documented sadly in the biographies by Patrick McGilligan and Emanuel Levy. One that would have been intriguing was *Laurette*, a biopic of the great stage actress Laurette Taylor, most celebrated for playing, late in her career, the mother in Tennessee Williams's *The Glass Menagerie*. Cukor directed Taylor in plays in the 1920s and was a fervid admirer, and he thought Judy Garland would be right to play her onscreen. But after *A Star Is Born*, which was conventionally seen in those days as a dubious debacle, they were not a duo any Hollywood studio wanted to reunite. The most eye-opening aspect of the *Laurette* project was Cukor's notion of building up his own character in the story to leading-man status and fantasizing about casting either Marlon Brando or Burt Lancaster as himself. But Cukor was skittish about autobiographical revelations, and the time had not yet come for a closeted gay director to edge his way out for at least limited forms of public scrutiny either onscreen or in print. Fortunately, that time would arrive while Cukor was still making pictures, although it came very belatedly and with conditions attached.

With *Laurette* in limbo, Cukor, whose creative energies felt stymied if he wasn't working on a film, made himself available as a relief pitcher on two directorless productions, *Wild Is the Wind* (1957) and *Song Without End* (1960); he also shot some scenes for Vincente Minnelli's *Lust for Life* (1956) and Daniel Mann's *Hot Spell* (1958). Following the release of *Bhowani Junction*, Cukor was assigned to direct another MGM film, *Les Girls*, which came at the end of the studio's musical cycle in 1957. Although visually alluring and with a glorious comic performance by Kay Kendall, *Les Girls* is a creative disappointment overall, largely because of its feeble storyline. Cukor had more artistic success with an unlikely project he initiated at Paramount based on a Western novel owned by that studio. Cukor's lone adventure into the Western genre, the picaresque *Heller in Pink Tights* (1960) is a lively and sensual vehicle for Sophia Loren. The offbeat *Heller* is a highlight among his work in that period, even if it too was somewhat compromised by studio interference.

After *Les Girls*, Cukor's hiring on the Paramount film *Wild Is the Wind* resulted from a round of directorial musical chairs. When Fred Zinnemann bailed on the foundering Warner Bros. film adaptation of Ernest Hemingway's *The Old Man and the Sea*, *Wild Is the Wind* lost John Sturges as its director. So Cukor stepped in to direct Anna Magnani and Anthony Quinn in one of numerous uncredited retoolings of *They Knew What They Wanted*, Sidney Howard's Pulitzer Prize–winning 1924 play. The screenwriter Arnold Schulman's contemporary version, whose setting and predictable plot dynamics do not lend themselves to Cukor's strengths, is about an Italian-American sheep rancher in Nevada who sends away for a mail-order bride, his late wife's sister.

It's enjoyable, up to a point, to see Quinn chewing scenery, but here he is a poster boy against toxic masculinity run amok, without much sensitivity to make his character bearable. The great Italian actress Magnani is tough enough to keep up with Quinn (both received Oscar nominations), and Cukor, always fond of outsiders, does a good job in capturing the immigrant woman's painful frustrations and feeling of alienation. The film's highlight is a song Magnani gets to sing in Italian at her birthday party. When she and Quinn (on the guitar) perform a duet, you can feel the actress's joy in finally getting to cut loose under Cukor's encouraging direction before things go wrong again for her and her out-of-control husband, in a relationship so repellent that the viewer wants to call out "Basta!" at the contrived happy ending.

On *Song Without End*, a hopelessly trite biopic of Franz Liszt starring Dirk Bogarde, Cukor was sent for when the film's director, Charles Vidor, died of a heart attack after three weeks of shooting on location in Vienna. As Bogarde wrote in one of his witty memoirs, Cukor "was not about to be dismayed by taking over a shipwreck with an almost, to him, unknown, crew. He was a working professional from the tip of his fingers to the crown of his splendid head, and he expected and demanded no less from us. He rallied our forlorn band together swiftly. . . . The only thing he couldn't do much about was the script, although he [and the uncredited Walter Bernstein] did manage to clear up quite a number of 'Hi! Liszt . . . meet my friend, Schubert, he's a pal of Chopin's.' Which was a relief. However, none of us was under any illusion."

Cukor's adventurous, post–*A Star Is Born* foray into the genre of historical spectacle, *Bhowani Junction*, was made in Pakistan and England because India put up barriers against the politically fraught production. The lavish CinemaScope film has the kind of epic sweep that later would be associated with David Lean pictures. Although the project is an outlier in Cukor's career for various reasons, including its concentration on political turmoil and its extensive crowd scenes, the exotic setting is not as anomalous as might be thought when you realize that Cukor was returning to the part of the world that, according to family lore, may have been his ancestral homeland.

According to McGilligan's biography, the Cukor family, who were Jewish, thought they were "descended from sons of the tribe of Joseph who journeyed to India some three or four hundred years before the birth of Christ." The family name was said to have originally been Chukor, which means "partridge" in Hindi and Sanskrit, but it became Czukor when the

21.1.   Ava Gardner's Anglo-Indian character, Victoria Jones, in *Bhowani Junction* (1956) is among many people in Cukor films with conflicting identities. In this adaptation of the novel by John Masters set during the tumultuous postwar period when India won its independence from the British Empire, Victoria is confronted about her ambivalence by an Indian patriot, the Sardarni (i.e., the Leader): Freda Jackson.

Source: Frame enlargement; MGM.

family migrated to the area of the Caspian Sea and then to Hungary before being simplified to Cukor when George's grandfather Joseph came to the United States in 1884. "Czukor" is Hungarian for "sugar"; the German equivalent is Zucker. Adolph Zukor, the principal founder of Paramount Pictures, was born in Hungary as Adolph Czukor in 1873 and changed his name after coming to America. McGilligan reports that Cukor "liked to say that because of his last name he suffered amiable confusions [with Zukor] when he directed films in the early sound era for Paramount. . . . Though otherwise they were unrelated; perhaps, said Cukor jokingly, he would have had 'an easier time' at Paramount altogether if the *C* had been dropped instead."

Joseph Cukor's son Victor (whose name in Hungarian was Farkas, meaning "Wolf") married the Hungarian native Ilona Gross (called Helen in the United States) in 1894. They had two children, Elsie and the younger George, who was born at the family home in New York City on July 6, 1899. That date is listed on his state of New York birth certificate, not July 7 or 14, as have often been reported. Although most sources give his middle name as Dewey, said in family lore to be their tribute to the naval hero Admiral George Dewey, only an initial, I., is listed as a middle name on Cukor's birth certificate, for reasons that are unclear (perhaps the Dewey was later bestowed on George as an informal honorific); Cukor later had a production company called by his supposed initials, G-D-C. Cukor was raised in comfortable but not luxurious surroundings. His father, listed as a merchant on his son's birth certificate, was graduated from New York University Law School and became an assistant district attorney. George's uncle Morris, also a lawyer, became even more prominent and prosperous as president of the Municipal Civil Service Commission and an officer in Hungarian cultural societies.

Along with the possible family connection for Cukor with its Indian setting, *Bhowani Junction* was even more closely connected to the director's personality through its heroine, Victoria Jones (Gardner), who is torn by her mixed identity and marginal status when she returns to her home in India after World War II. The British she serves as a WAC and railway clerk are preparing to leave India, their longtime colony, in turmoil. Based on the 1954 novel by John Masters, a former British army officer who served with the Indian army during the war, the film has Victoria symbolically fought over by men who represent her three different identities. They are another Anglo-Indian, Patrick Taylor (Bill Travers); an Indian, Ranjit Kasel (Francis

Matthews); and a British army officer, Col. Rodney Savage (Stewart Granger). But the casting of the central characters gives short shrift to actual Indians; Gardner, a white woman from North Carolina, seems to have won the role because of her "exotic" looks and because she played the mulatto, Julie, in the 1951 version of *Show Boat*. Abraham Sofaer, who plays an important supporting role with authority, was Burmese and Jewish; the other leading "Indian" roles are played by English actors.

And unfortunately for the film adaptation, the romantic and political themes are awkwardly blended. The depiction of the clash between Gandhi's pacifistic Congress Party and the Communist Party is predictably loaded to make the latter seem like raving madmen (a reflection to some extent of American domestic politics during the Cold War era). The novel is more politically sophisticated than that, but the film is essentially a muddled narrative, treating the complexities of the "Quit India" movement in broad, simplistic terms. It is better when it shows events without much comment rather than debating the issues, but Cukor is out of his league with this kind of foreign political saga, particularly one whose stabs at complexity keep getting bogged down by the residue of old Hollywood stereotypes about India and the British Raj. The film ends with a corny chase sequence reminiscent of a silent serial, a thwarted assassination attempt on Gandhi. A more powerfully filmed set piece is the passive resistance by Gandhi supporters lying in front of a train and dispersed by Col. Savage by having sewage tossed on them (in the novel, his Gurkha troops urinate on them). The scene conveys the ugliness of the political struggle in the waning days of empire and the harshness of the departing British as they tried to cope with the turmoil they had caused.

The script by Sonya Levien and Ivan Moffat was further damaged when MGM rearranged the footage to get to Gardner's romance with Granger from the beginning and following with flashbacks while adding a superfluous narration by Granger that laboriously explains the political situation. Often the narration even fills us in on what a character is thinking or feeling, a deadly mistake in screenwriting. The remaining dialogue is often flatly expository as well. Granger's stiffness is not entirely caused by his role, which was softened from the book, and the character's underlying humanity takes too long to evolve. Cukor had wanted the grittier Trevor Howard for Col. Savage but was overruled by MGM, while Travers gives a hysterical performance as Taylor (Cukor had preferred John Mills), and Matthews's subtle acting as Kasel suffers from reduction in his screen time. Cukor felt the film was also hurt by the studio's excision of what, for that time, were racy sexual elements. They included a cunnilingus scene between Gardner and Travers that Cukor said anticipated the groundbreaking depiction of sexuality in Louis Malle's *Les amants/The Lovers* (1958), with Jeanne Moreau.

Once more Cukor was ahead of his time and, in his newly provocative mood, daring to push beyond the bounds the censors would allow. What remains of value in *Bhowani Junction* is mostly the sumptuous imagery of surging crowds and the gorgeous widescreen cinematography, much in muted brown and tan tones, by Freddie Young (later Lean's cinematographer on *Lawrence of Arabia* and other epics). Although Cukor is not known for spectacle, he handles the crowd scenes with aplomb, with the help of the veteran second-unit director Andrew Marton (for some reason uncredited), but they seem somewhat disconnected from the personal story. *Bhowani Junction* bears some resemblance to *Gone with the Wind* in looking at historical conflict through the viewpoint of a complex female character, but the 1939 film has a much stronger storyline.

Cukor and Young have a resplendent camera subject in Gardner at the height of her sensual beauty, and her performance has both delicacy and intensity in its anguish and her attempts to understand and come to terms with her complex social status. But unlike in her delightfully relaxed and comical performance in John Ford's *Mogambo* (1953), which seems to capture who she really was, Gardner's performance as Victoria Jones is so tightly wound as well as fragmented by recutting that it does not manage to sustain the kind of emotional involvement Garland brought to *A Star Is Born*. Although that performance was also chopped up to some extent, Garland shows a much greater range, depth, and ability to develop a scene fully than Gardner is able to do here. Since the writing and staging of Gardner's scenes with men is largely inert, she gives the impression of acting mostly by herself. Although her personal struggle is intended to make her somewhat enigmatic, she remains a stubbornly mysterious or confused character. *Bhowani Junction*, a rather daring, if compromised, attempt by Cukor to go beyond his usual boundaries, was a major disappointment, and he did not work again for almost a year and a half.

As well as the last gasp of the MGM musical in an era increasingly dominated by rock 'n' roll, *Les Girls* (1957) marks the finale of Gene Kelly's distinguished career for that studio. The story is somewhat tinged with melancholy, too, since it deals with a Parisian musical act of Kelly and three female dancers that has broken up by the time the film starts. The hard times for movie musicals are indicated by Kelly's Barry Nichols being stuck with a TV show and a string of orange-juice stands. *Les Girls* is told in flashback, not because of recutting this time but by design, revolving around a libel trial in London by one of the women, Angèle Ducros (Taina Elg), against another, Lady Sybil Wren (Kay Kendall), who has written a racy memoir of their time as chorines.

But the attempted *Rashomon* structure doesn't amount to much, and the screenplay by John Patrick, based on a story by Vera Caspary (who joked she was paid a sizeable sum for writing only two words, i.e., the title), is not only emotionally uninvolving but so frivolous it would make a bonbon seem filling. The glossy CinemaScope surface makes the film watchable, thanks to Cukor's team: the color coordinator George Hoyningen-Huene, the art directors Gene Allen and William A. Horning, the cinematographer Robert Surtees, and the costume designer Orry-Kelly (who won an Oscar for the drolly sumptuous, sometimes risqué outfits). But as Cukor's second attempt at a musical, it pales in comparison with *A Star Is Born*—but then, doesn't every musical? That's the trouble when a filmmaker tackles a routine job in the shadow of a masterpiece.

What makes *Les Girls* so dispiriting, besides the dumb title (perhaps intended as a double or triple entendre, although the trailer helpfully points out, "*Rhymes with 'Playgirls'*"), feeble plot, and second-rate songs by the ailing Cole Porter (his last full set for a film), is the lackluster presence of Gene Kelly. *Les Girls* is far inferior to his classics *On the Town*, *An American in Paris*, *Singin' in the Rain*, and *It's Always Fair Weather*. Manny Farber summed up Kelly's screen personality in two words, "histrionic conceit," which applies here. In *Les Girls*, he is so hammy, smug, and unctuous that Mitzi Gaynor seems to be speaking for Cukor when she says of Kelly's character, "Barry fell in love with himself the first time he looked in a mirror, and he's been faithful ever since." The casting of the bland Gaynor was imposed by the studio on Cukor, who protested to no avail, but his discovery, the Finnish actress and dancer Taina Elg, as the playgirl Angèle, is not much better. Gaynor's straitlaced American, Joy, winds up married to Barry after their romance in the last of the three flashbacks, a development that seems hard to fathom except as a requirement of the plotline of his carrying on with each woman in turn.

The movie is stolen by Kendall, the sparkling and highly intelligent British actress who has the one memorable, sustained sequence, a riotous drunk scene in the girls' eccentrically designed, labyrinthine apartment that ends with Sybil doing an operatic aria (her singing was dubbed by Betty Wand). Kendall is an ideal Cukor actress, as witty and sophisticated as she is elegantly beautiful, tall, and regal. Cukor called her "a natural clown with a marvelous comedic instinct." Her Sybil carries on with paradoxically graceful clumsiness, stumbling and sprawling repeatedly on the floor of the tiny two-level apartment, while having a jolly time doing so. Cukor and Kendall talked about doing more films together, but she died of leukemia at age thirty-two in 1959 while married to Rex Harrison, Cukor's future leading man in *My Fair Lady*.

Kelly had clashes of temperament with Cukor, chafing at the director's habitually involved discussions of scenes and line readings as "endless chatter." Kenneth Tynan reported after interviewing Kelly that he considered Cukor "basically . . . a theater man who neither cares about nor understands the camera." But that was a shortsighted view of Cukor, and the egotistical

21.2. The British comic actress Kay Kendall in her uproarious drunk scene as Sybil Wren in Cukor's 1957 musical, *Les Girls*, starring Gene Kelly. The tall, limber Kendall's balletic cavorting in her Paris apartment is the highlight of this uneven but visually flamboyant film that came at the end of MGM's long cycle of stylish musicals.

Source: Frame enlargement; MGM.

Kelly was used to directing himself, though his work in that department was far more deft and refined when he teamed on features with Stanley Donen. Kelly predictably feuded with Cukor's gifted choreographer, Jack Cole, but took over that function when Cole fell ill during production. The songs in any case give little room for inspired treatment in dance or visual style, and Kelly often falls back on imitating his earlier, better work, making eyes and grinning at the camera while admiring his own charm in its mirror. The film's last major number, a weak takeoff on the delightful "Girl Hunt Ballet" by Fred Astaire and Cyd Charisse in Minnelli's 1953 MGM musical, *The Band Wagon*, has Kelly doing a painfully bad imitation of Brando wearing a black leather jacket in *The Wild One*. He strips off his jacket for a so-so dance with Gaynor in their black outfits on a stylized barroom set that looks like a dashed-off red-and-white sketch. Kendall's inspired clowning aside, *Les Girls* is one Cukor film in which the sets tend to outact the performers.

McGilligan calls Cukor's 1960 Western, *Heller in Pink Tights*, a "colorful Wild West comedy done as if a handshake between Toulouse-Lautrec and Frederic Remington." Nothing demonstrates Cukor's spirit of gallant adventurousness in his later years more than his wholehearted plunge into that unfamiliar (for him) genre. This charmingly picaresque Sophia Loren film was based on the 1955 Louis L'Amour Western novel *Heller with a Gun*. Although somewhat manhandled by Paramount before its release, *Heller in Pink Tights* became one of Cukor's most personal projects, an affectionate tribute to the raffish touring companies of the nineteenth-century American theater.

Drawing on his nostalgic memories of running a stock company in Rochester as a young man and on his admiration for the film pioneer D. W. Griffith, Cukor was partly inspired by a film treatment Griffith had written in 1945 dealing with his own touring days. Griffith also introduced elements from the life of the celebrated stage actor-manager Joseph Jefferson (1829–1905), whose career began in his childhood and lasted into the early days of silent films. Jefferson was best known for touring in his own adaptation of Washington Irving's short story "Rip Van Winkle." Cukor's meetings with Griffith led to a script by Maxwell Anderson for a musical called *Troupers West*, with songs to have been written by Kurt Weill, but it found no takers. Even after touching on similar material with *Heller in Pink Tights*, Cukor tried to raise interest in a film about Griffith from 1964 through 1972, now called *Twilight Revelers*, that would have starred Gregory Peck.

Cukor worked with Loren's husband, the Italian producer Carlo Ponti, in shaping *Heller* for her, enlisting Walter Bernstein to rewrite a screenplay by the terminally ill Dudley Nichols, the writer of many John Ford films, including his classic 1939 Western *Stagecoach*. Loren's swanky performance as a professionally flirtatious actress named Angela Rossini gave her and Cukor ample opportunity for whipping up offbeat Western atmosphere in a film that is part genre parody and part serious drama about her tenuous romance with her actor-manager lover, Tom Healy (Anthony Quinn).

This time around, Quinn is uncharacteristically subdued in the role of the financially and emotionally insecure Healy, who plays the producer-director role in Angela's life and career. Cukor had wanted to cast the dashing young British actor Roger Moore, but Paramount wouldn't go along with his hunch about the actor who eventually would become James Bond. Quinn is visibly uncomfortable in the role, which he complained made him feel this was "an unfortunate film" in which "I was basically playing a homosexual." But Cukor brings out a tender, vulnerable side the actor too seldom displayed. Healy's gentle quality contributes to the film's pervasive reversals of Western clichés in favor of more intriguing twists on masculine-feminine relationships and other aspects of the genre.

Cukor's gender-bending sensibility with the "Pink Pierrots" traveling show troupe in *Sylvia Scarlett* and other films of various kinds is reflected here in the staging of the venerable hippodrama *Mazeppa*, based on the poem by Lord Byron. The play features a Ukrainian warrior tortured by being strapped to the back of a horse. (The young John Ford borrowed from *Mazeppa* by having Harry Carey strapped to a horse in his recently restored 1918 Western *Hell Bent*.) The nineteenth-century actress Adah Menken caused a sensation with her Katharine Hepburn-like "breeches [male] role" in *Mazeppa* and her seeming "nude" costuming (an abbreviated white tunic over pink tights). The gag is replicated with Loren early in *Heller in Pink Tights* and later with the ruggedly macho gunfighter Clint Mabry (Steve Forrest) dressed as a woman to save him from the villains as the horse carries him out of the theater.

Angela's sexual attraction to Mabry is made clear the moment they first see each other, when Healy is displaying the troupe's wares on a muddy western street. In a time when actresses were regarded as the equivalent of prostitutes—"We're all actresses, aren't we?," a madam asks her—Angela is expected to tease (at least) various males the troupe needs to cajole. She even allows Mabry to win her in a poker game, but that adds to the skittish tension between Angela and Healy until he is seriously wounded in a gunfight. She finally realizes she has more in common with him than with the suave hired killer. Cukor praised Loren's "light and humorous" qualities and has fun with what Lambert called the "fiendish, sly ingénue" played by Margaret O'Brien, the former child star whose ripening Della pushes herself forward as a romantic rival to Angela. Cukor portrays the voluptuous Angela's mischievous flirtations without judging her character, and even after her sexual fling with Mabry, she and Healy accept each other without further question. Although Healy is not entirely a disciple of nonviolence (he holds his own in a backstage brawl with Mabry over Angela), his is essentially an artistic soul, a trait she belatedly comes to appreciate by using her ill-gotten gains to buy them a theater as a wedding present.

The film's many droll riffs on Western tropes are matched by the whimsical and often flamboyantly colorful art direction by Gene Allen and Hal Pereira, color coordination by George Hoyningen-Huene, cinematography by Harold Lipstein, and costuming by Edith Head, smartly integrated here into Cukor's personal stamp on a new genre. When a painting of a nude woman in a saloon/casino (conveniently in widescreen format in this VistaVision film) opens to reveal Angela's face peering from the nude's midsection, it is the kind of bawdy touch that wouldn't have been possible in a Western even a few years earlier but helps give *Heller* its flavorful period atmosphere.

Cukor's loving recreations of cornball melodramas with gaudily multihued stage settings and costumes are of a piece with other stylized elements of the film. The tongue-in-cheek theatrical lettering of the credits sequence sets the flamboyant tone. In similarly gaudy style are the two rickety red wagons festooned with posters advertising the troupe that house them as they race ahead of creditors from town to town (the locations were filmed in Arizona, including at the Old Tucson Studios, where Howard Hawks made *Rio Bravo* and his other late Westerns). But this somewhat avant-garde film's closest affinities are to foreign classics about touring theatrical troupes, Federico Fellini's *La strada* and Ingmar Bergman's *Sawdust and Tinsel*.

Cukor was proudest of a flamboyant scene in *Heller in Pink Tights* borrowed from Jefferson's autobiography. It shows a band of Native Americans—dressed not in stereotypical feathers and bonnets but in a motley, mismatched array of period costumes—having a gay old time as they tear into the costume trunks of the abandoned wagons, dress in women's gowns, and gleefully fling the colored fabrics into the air, swirling them close to the camera. The scene turns into an impromptu musical number when these men find instruments and dance, celebrating their anarchic moments of joy before they have to go back to being "Indians."

Paramount was nonplussed by this most unconventional Western, the screenwriter Bernstein told McGilligan, so the studio "cut it their way—which was to cut out all the quality of the characterizations, and go to plot—the plot was ridiculous! I know they made [Cukor] shoot a couple of action scenes that weren't in the original script. He had no interest in doing that, but he was very much a company guy; he knew he didn't have control; that was it and on to the next thing."

22.1. Cukor trying his best to evoke a performance from Marilyn Monroe in *Something's Got to Give*. He said she seemed to be "acting underwater" in their unfinished 1962 film, which he and the studio had to abandon not long before her death.

Source: Twentieth Century-Fox/From the Core Collection, Production Files of the Margaret Herrick Library, Academy of Motion Picture Arts and Sciences.

22

MARILYN MONROE IN *LET'S MAKE LOVE* AND *SOMETHING'S GOT TO GIVE*

How do you make Marilyn Monroe relax and be herself onscreen, whatever "herself" was in the supremely anxious final stage of her life? Somehow George Cukor managed to do that. The two vehicles he directed Monroe in hardly mattered; they were shabby and unworthy of both of them. The second film was not finished, and she died soon after being fired from it, after Cukor and everyone else had given up on trying to get her to concentrate on a job she eventually found impossible. This actress, whom Cukor called "a miraculous phenomenon of the screen," had become terrified of facing the camera, in the view of Henry Weinstein, the producer of her abortive final film, Cukor's romantic comedy *Something's Got to Give*. The machine that created her was now trying to devour her. Cukor had found he couldn't really communicate with this profoundly disturbed actress, who was off in her own dazed world, impervious to even his direction. But if this supreme communicator couldn't reach her, he did try his damnedest to provide his "climate" for her to be herself. And that proved enough for at least some semblances of Monroe's fractured identity to be preserved onscreen, with refreshingly relaxed intimacy, in the films they worked on together, *Let's Make Love* (1960) and the uncompleted *Something's Got to Give* (1962).

Only four directors managed to suffer through the experience of directing Monroe twice. John Huston, Billy Wilder, and Howard Hawks also did so.

Hawks, who experienced the least mishegoss with Marilyn, told me about directing her in *Monkey Business* and *Gentlemen Prefer Blondes*, "Marilyn Monroe was the most frightened little girl who had no confidence in her ability. She was afraid to come on the screen. Very strange girl. And yet she had this strange effect when she was photographed. . . . There were a lot of times when I was ready to give up the ghost. . . . But I had an easy time compared to some of the directors who worked with her afterward. Because after she got very important she became more and more frightened, and she just didn't want to come out and do a scene." Hawks felt, "There wasn't a real thing about her. Everything was completely unreal. They tried to make her play real parts in a couple of pictures, and the pictures were disasters."

Not quite. Monroe's performance as the 1920s band singer Sugar Cane in Wilder's *Some Like It Hot* (1959) is touchingly real in its vulnerability and the sweet, forlorn, natural sexiness she incarnates of a lovely woman who constantly finds herself victimized by men, always winding up with "the fuzzy end of the lollipop." She drove Wilder around the bend with her chronic lateness and frequent disorientation: "It demoralizes the whole company. . . . [*Sighs*] On the other hand, I have an Aunt Ida in Vienna who is always on time, but I wouldn't put her in a movie." Wilder brought out a tenderness in her that had been glimpsed from time to time in earlier roles but now helped define her character. Sugar may be treated by callous men as if she doesn't have "a real thing about her," but that's not who the film shows us she is. The vulnerability that people who knew her saw in her, her childlike quality, and the scattered nature of her personality—elements that helped make her such a splendid comedian—seemed to capture much of what we know about Monroe's "real" self, at least from people who saw her with sympathy rather than used her with contempt.

The year after playing an off-Broadway actress and singer in Cukor's musical comedy *Let's Make Love*, Monroe gave another strong, touching, and constantly vulnerable performance in her last completed film, Huston's *The Misfits* (1961), written for her by her then-husband, the playwright Arthur Miller. She plays Roslyn, a woman whose still-beautiful face and body nevertheless reflect how she has been kicked around by life. After she extricates herself from a hollow marriage on a visit to the divorce capital of Reno, Nevada, she reluctantly finds solace in the arms of a far more weathered partner, Clark Gable's aging cowboy, literally at the end of his rope. He is hoping to catch a little time before dying to settle down in a truly intimate way he has never before wanted or been able to manage, and though Roslyn has misgivings about his way of life, she finds that prospect appealing.

Despite the depth of such late characterizations, so many years in Hollywood participating in creating an illusory image, combined with Monroe's deep-seated psychological problems and the predatory behavior of many people around her, made it difficult for her to continue working in "the business of creating illusions," as Irving Thalberg called the process of making movies. With *Some Like It Hot* and while playing another showgirl for Cukor the following year in *Let's Make Love*, Monroe was almost hopelessly trapped in the wilderness of mirrors her personality had become. Hers was an endlessly multiplying and constantly mutable image that seemed to make her life race out of gear beyond her futile attempts at controlling it. Her dependence on drugs and alcohol exacerbated her dazed condition. Although Cukor considered her "quite mad," he felt that Hollywood, though it was often criticized for causing her problems, was the only place a person in her condition could have continued to function at all.

What did Monroe have to say about working with Cukor? "He cherishes the actor," she told Kenneth Tynan after making *Let's Make Love*. In the somewhat patronizing fashion that unfortunately was typical for those who dealt with her, Tynan added in his 1961 *Holiday* profile of Cukor that she offered that comment with "her pink, vulnerable face reflecting hard thought." But she went on regardless, "He and John Huston are directors who honestly respect actors. The first day on the set, he told me not to be nervous. I said I was born nervous. He told me, 'If I don't sleep tonight, it'll be because I'm worrying about *you* not sleeping.'" Perhaps telling her "Don't be nervous" was an inadequate admonition, but she seemed to appreciate his speaking with genuine empathy, which she more than most people could tell from pseudo caring. Even though Cukor had his temperamental outbursts, he also had the rare ability to remain calm on set while things were collapsing around him, which must have radiated into her consciousness. As their work together progressed, his handling of the childlike but willful actress called on all of his considerable resources for patience and concern, which were in short supply on their second film but, as Miller wrote Cukor during the shooting of *Let's Make Love*, made that film an unusually happy working experience for her.

22.2. Cukor felt he "really had very little influence" on Monroe while directing her in the 1960 comedy *Let's Make Love*; he thought she was "quite mad." But in making "a climate that was agreeable for her," he brought out her natural vivacity in unguarded moments, such as when her off-Broadway actress sings Cole Porter's "My Heart Belongs to Daddy."
Source: Frame enlargement; Twentieth Century-Fox.

Monroe as seen through Cukor's lens is as frankly bawdy as she had ever been onscreen—thanks to his pushing the envelope of fast-eroding Hollywood censorship strictures—while exhibiting a softer, more mature sexuality. Like some of her last photo shoots, that quality actually makes her more appealing than in her younger days, when she often seemed encased in gaudy makeup and tight costuming, as if for merchandising as a plastic Marilyn Monroe Doll. Her photo shoot with the *Vogue* photographer Bert Stern in June 1962 (published posthumously as "The Last Sitting" that September) shows her torso and face peeking through veils, her figure undisguisedly a bit worn and realistically aging, by Hollywood standards at thirty-six, with a ripe sensuality I've always found preferable to her youthfully voluptuous but cartoonlike self. Tynan wrote, "While unquestionably sincere, Cukor's admiration for Miss Monroe does not prevent him from being playful at her expense. Once, in a party game, he was asked what food she most reminded him of. He immediately replied: 'A three-day-old Van de Kamp Bakery angel cake.'"

In *Let's Make Love*, it's mostly the casual side of Monroe on view in her quiet dialogue scenes as her Amanda Dell gets to know a French billionaire,

Jean-Marc Clément (Yves Montand), and tries to figure out what this mysterious man is doing in her life. Her face is most beautiful in relative repose, when she is being unemphatic yet conveying her thoughts and feelings with a constant subtle interplay as only the most eloquent of film faces can do. As Cukor told Tynan, "Her face *moves*—it catches the light—it's genuinely photogenic. And she *thinks boldly*. She thinks as a dog thinks. *Au fond*, her mind is wonderfully unclouded—she doesn't censor her thoughts. She's like Elvis Presley, like all the great performers—whenever she enters, it's an occasion."

Cukor makes Monroe's entrance in *Let's Make Love* such an occasion, a spectacular display of her electrified eroticism, somewhat modified for her maturing image. She makes her entrance rehearsing in a small Greenwich Village theater while sliding down a pole in a blue sweater and black tights as a group of men in light brown outfits cavort around her and she sings Cole Porter's "My Heart Belongs to Daddy." Colored lights bathe her half-clad form as she moves in and out of the dark, confined space, a minimal set composed of a few poles set against a background of foil and a bank of spotlights. After a while she strips off her sweater and wears only a low-cut black bustier with the tights, in a lush number as genuinely erotic as her final song in *Some Like It Hot*, "I'm Thru with Love," which she delivers in a clinging see-through dress. But that number has a much different effect, since it's the heartbreaking climax of the picture, and Cukor's more lighthearted romp seems to be designed to have Monroe announce, "I'm not through yet," while being relaxed enough to appear her own age (thirty-four) rather than trying to maintain Hollywood's false image of the perpetual starlet.

But in a peculiar way, the "Daddy" number, going well beyond its incestuous lyrics and her declaration that "My name is Lolita," is also somewhat disturbing, especially if one has seen the devastating gang rape sequence Cukor would go on to film in *The Chapman Report* (1962), with a group of jazz musicians encircling and pawing the elegant but masochistic Claire Bloom in a frenetically cut orgy. The graceful Jack Cole dancers in the "Daddy" number also pass Monroe around and twist her in suggestive poses, in a similarly filmed but stylized, nonviolent representation of a group sexual encounter.

Unfortunately, Marilyn's rendition of Porter's standard is the musical highlight of *Let's Make Love*. The rest of the songs (by Sammy Cahn and James Van Heusen) are duds, and too many feature an appallingly smarmy British pop singer named Frankie Vaughan, part of Cukor's misguided attempt to tap into the jukebox scene. The storyline had some promise—a billionaire playboy, curious about his portrayal in an off-Broadway satirical revue, winds up impersonating himself in the show while attempting to romance the lead showgirl under a false identity. Cukor could have done something with the layered situation of a man having to be coached about how to play himself and learning who he might actually become. But the script by Norman Krasna, with additional material by Hal Kanter, is mostly witless.

Montand is embarrassingly bad, miscast as the wealthy roué. He had to learn his English dialogue phonetically, which spoils his arch attempts at humor, and his actual singing talent was wasted. Originally the role was conceived by Krasna for a stolid all-American "shit-kicker," and Gregory Peck was cast before wisely bowing out when Miller began rewriting the script to augment Monroe's role. Cukor turned to Rock Hudson, who would have been right for the role, but Universal refused to lend him to Twentieth Century-Fox. Monroe in fact has surprisingly little to do in the film, and one suspects Miller's heavy hand in some incongruously pretentious lines in which Amanda, who's going to night school because "I got tired of being ignorant," expresses political concern for the Third World and other liberal causes.

Monroe's scenes with Montand (with whom she was carrying on a much-publicized affair during the filming) have a sweetness that contrasts with her brassy image in the show, also titled *Let's Make Love*. As Amanda, with unconscious irony, tries to coach Clément to be more like himself, she impresses him because, he says, she's the first person who has treated him like a regular human being. By concentrating on her co-star, Monroe becomes less self-conscious and more unguarded, and though their dialogue is mundane, her gentleness toward this awkward fellow makes her seem more attractive than in her brassy sex-symbol antics in films such as *Gentlemen Prefer Blondes* or Wilder's *The Seven Year Itch*, when she plays cartoonish comical exaggerations of her image. Cukor admitted that on *Let's Make Love*, "As a director, I really had very little influence on her. All I could do was make a climate that was agreeable for her." But she reminded him of Jean Harlow in her quality of "enchantment" and her ability to do comedy adroitly yet with seeming innocence: "She had this absolute, unerring touch with comedy. . . . She acted as if she didn't quite understand why it was funny, which is what made it so funny." She also conveys a sense of innocence about sexuality that makes it all the more erotic. In the last shot of the film, when Monroe is alone with Montand in an elevator, she suddenly opens her blouse to expose her black brassiere with unabashed delight.

The visual schema in CinemaScope by Gene Allen, George Hoyningen-Huene, and the cinematographer Daniel L. Fapp makes Monroe stand out from backgrounds mostly drained of color, so she is always extraordinarily vivid, but Cukor was unable to shoot in the long-take style he favored because "she couldn't sustain scenes. She'd do three lines and then forget the rest, she'd do another line and then forget everything again. You had to shoot it piecemeal. . . . Her performance was done in very minute bits and yet, when you put them all together, they fitted together, perfectly smooth." This can be seen most clearly in the scene of the couple dining in a Chinese restaurant, which is filmed in a shot-reverse-shot style uncharacteristic of Cukor that makes his direction seem impersonal or overly detached but still enables Monroe to appear appealingly warm, vulnerable, and understandably baffled in this intimate encounter. She quizzes Clément about his life, kindly urging him to become more ambitious, but laughs uneasily when he proposes to her and runs away after he confesses his true identity, since she thinks he is delusional.

One could never have predicted, however, that a Marilyn Monroe movie directed by George Cukor would be stolen by . . . Milton Berle (a development so remarkable that the *New York Times* headlined Bosley Crowther's review of "this listless romance" "Milton Berle Steals Show in 'Let's Make Love'"). Out of desperation, Montand's billionaire hires experts to coach him in comedy (Berle), singing (Bing Crosby), and dancing (Gene Kelly). Berle dazzles in his thirteen-minute low-comedy tour de force. Acting as a surrogate director, he tries to show the painfully inept Clément how to walk funny (on his ankles) and talk funny (while vainly squeezing the billionaire's face and slapping him) and how to do a *Sylvia Scarlett* kind of routine: "I'll be the girl, and you be the boy." In another modest sign that the Production Code was beginning to loosen up to Cukor's benefit, Berle does a hilariously campy swish act while advancing on Clément lasciviously and making eyes at him; female impersonation had been a staple of Uncle Milty's act when he ruled over the wild early days of network TV. Wilfrid Hyde-White, as Clément's punctilious secretary, watches with raised eyebrows followed by a comical "we are not amused" frown. And when Kelly coaches Clément in a romantic dance to physically express the sentiment "darling, I love you," Hyde-White chuckles slyly from the sidelines and does a double-take at the disgruntled Kelly;

this film won the veteran British actor the part of Colonel Pickering in Cukor's *My Fair Lady*.

Berle is acting in a vacuum, since the "joke" is that Clément can't get how to be funny. And yet all this shtick works for the film, since Berle is allowed to constantly express disgust through his expert repertoire of throwaway grimaces and by following up his purchased praise ("Wonderful, wonderful") with an aside to kibitzing cronies from NBC, "The worst thing I've ever seen." Crosby and Kelly, in contrast, phone in their wasted cameo appearances, but they don't deserve the license to trash *Let's Make Love* that Cukor gives Berle. In the comedian's delightful stretch of the film, Cukor finds a way to send up his own detachment from the lousy material he's been handed in this dispiriting phase of his career as the studio system was collapsing.

The spectacle of a major star imploding lends grim fascination to the saga of *Something's Got to Give*. Much has been written about the debacle of Monroe's unfinished final film, chronicling how she failed to show up for most of the seven weeks of shooting from April through early June in 1962. She repeatedly called in sick but angered Fox by flying to New York to sing her notoriously risqué "Happy Birthday, Mr. President" to John F. Kennedy on May 19, which helped precipitate her firing on June 8. At the JFK event, his brother-in-law Peter Lawford, alluding to her problems at work, introduced her as "the late Marilyn Monroe." Fox was already in a state of crisis with the runaway production of *Cleopatra* in Rome, and the studio had to sell its backlot, which eventually became the commercial and housing development Century City.

Through it all, Cukor tried vainly to provide the "climate" for his seriously troubled star to keep working in the only film still shooting on the lot, but most of the time he had to shoot around her with the co-stars Dean Martin and Cyd Charisse and supporting players Phil Silvers, Steve Allen, John McGiver, and Wally Cox. The film's art director, Gene Allen, recalled that Cukor was Monroe's "greatest fan—he saw things in her that to this day I would argue with him about. He leaned over backwards not to hurt her. . . . But I had to tell George Cukor that it was strange . . . she had no focus." Cukor found she could no longer remember lines. The studio said it had managed only five days of shooting with Monroe. Cukor finally agreed that she should be fired and replaced by Lee Remick (after Kim Novak and Shirley MacLaine turned down the role). But when Martin exercised his contractual right to leave the production if Monroe was no longer in the film, Cukor also quit.

Following a legal battle, Fox quixotically made plans to restart the project with Jean Negulesco directing Monroe, but before that could happen, she died at her Brentwood home on August 4 or 5, in mysterious circumstances that have never been adequately explained. When production finally resumed on the story, it was retooled as *Move Over, Darling* (1963), directed by Michael Gordon and starring Doris Day, James Garner, and Polly Bergen.

The reputation of Monroe's final project could not have been lower for many years. But in 2001, a narrative version of the eight-plus hours of material shot for the film was assembled by Fox and American Movie Classics. Running thirty-eight minutes, as part of a TV documentary called *Marilyn Monroe: The Final Days*, the CinemaScope condensation is something of a revelation. A remake of the 1940 film *My Favorite Wife*, starring Irene Dunne and Cary Grant and directed by Garson Kanin, *Something's Got to Give* is also loosely based on the 1864 poem "Enoch Arden" by Alfred, Lord Tennyson about a man thought lost at sea who returns to find his wife married to another man; Enoch doesn't reveal to her that he's still alive but dies of a broken heart. The

22.3. Despite her problems working on *Something's Got to Give*, Monroe's scene as a mother coming back from a long absence to reunite with her children (including Robert Christopher Morley) draws poignantly from the actress's regret over her own childlessness. This frame enlargement is from a 2001 reconstruction of some of the surviving footage as part of the documentary *Marilyn: The Final Days*.

Source: Twentieth Century-Fox/American Movie Classics.

poem or variations of it have been filmed several times, beginning with D. W. Griffith's short *Enoch Arden* in 1911 and continuing in various uncredited iterations.

Kanin's RKO version makes the castaway a woman (a more provocative slant, especially under Code strictures) and has a happy ending. The screenplay by Bella and Samuel Spewack from a story they wrote with the film's producer, Leo McCarey, went through various hands at Fox for the remake, with Walter Bernstein retooling Nunnally Johnson's script under Cukor's supervision. Though a fragmentary and incomplete representation of the calamitous project, the 2001 assembly shows Monroe in a charming light, beginning with a tender scene of her Ellen Arden returning to her home and encountering her two children, who are five years older and don't remember her. Before her husband (Martin) can bring himself to reveal the truth to his new wife (Charisse), Ellen passes herself off as the children's nanny, a Swedish woman named Ingrid, while putting on a Garboesque accent. Knowing Monroe's sadness about not being able to have children, Cukor brought out her sensitivity and sweetness, along with intimations of repressed pain, in her tight close-ups watching the children before she crouches next to the pool and chats with them while comforting them incognito.

The poignant yet relaxed scene was filmed on a Fox sound stage modeled on Cukor's own home and pool, his comfortable private retreat above the Sunset Strip. In the last piece of finished footage shot for the film, filmed on her birthday, June 1, and also shot beside the pool, she appears to be her classically beautiful, provocative, deceptively but professionally confident self. After presenting the nebbishy Wally Cox (her casting idea) to Martin's Nick Arden as the man she spent five years on a desert island with, instead of her actual paramour, hunky Tom Tryon, she is filmed with Martin and Cox in a strikingly low-angled three-shot that displays her to advantage. As Cox exits the frame, she advances a bit toward Martin, gazing into his eyes as if she owns him, her lips breaking into a triumphant smile. Monroe and Martin turn to the camera and laugh as Cukor's voice is heard calling out "Thank you," and the shot fades off the screen.

Monroe's most famous scene in *Something's Got to Give*, her nocturnal nude swim in the pool, is also included in the assembly. She was supposed to be wearing a flesh-colored bikini but took it off in the water and, under the eyes of photographers she had invited, romped in the nude, splashing and laughing and then perching on the side of the pool. Her nudity is partially blocked by her arms as she twists and smiles up toward Martin, who was filmed separately, watching her cavorting from a window but looking anxious because Nick is still trying to figure out how to explain her presence back home to his new wife. When Monroe rises and puts on a blue bathrobe, we see her naked backside briefly but clearly. Monroe's unabashedly sensual, blithely merry display of her body was a culmination of her exhibitionism, which resulted in her famous 1949 nude calendar shot that became the first *Playboy* centerfold in 1953. She had a dream from childhood of walking naked through a church congregation "with a sense of freedom, over their prostrate forms, being careful not to step on anyone," as she recalled to *Time* for her 1956 cover story. Her display of nudity intended for *Something's Got to Give* conveys a charge of liberation even today, especially when it is seen in the context of that period just before the sexual liberation movement.

It's doubtful much of this groundbreaking display of nudity—the first by a Hollywood star since the Code was tightened in 1934—would have survived onscreen (Fox included a sanitized clip in its 1963 documentary, *Marilyn*). But Cukor showed that he was willing to go along with Monroe's attempt to push the envelope of sexual frankness in this film, a sign of his refreshing candor about sexuality as the country and the industry evolved, partly under the influence of foreign filmmakers. That she was willing to unveil herself before Cukor's camera shows the special kind of trust she (like other actresses) had for the director. Her nude swim was seen around the world in photographs before the film was shut down for other reasons.

The prescient, well-written *Time* profile quoted her as declaring when she left Hollywood for New York in 1955, "I want some respect. I don't care about money. I want better parts and better directors. I want to be an actress." As the uncredited writer, Ezra Goodman, put it, "Hollywood snickered." But Goodman took her ambitions seriously and quoted a friend of hers as saying that was her "absolute, desperate attempt to find out what she was and what she wanted." The article frankly discussed her Dickensian childhood in and out of orphanages and foster homes, including her rape when she was six by an adult male she bitterly remembered as "a friend of the family," and how those experiences fueled her emotional problems and drive to be an actress: "What she needed, Marilyn felt in a confused way, was not success so much as salvation. . . . And yet, curiously, life in its deepest expressions was on

Norma Jeane's side—perhaps had always been on her side. The sensitivity which made her feel so deeply the shocks of her childhood was countered by a set of instincts as solid as an anvil. She took blows that would have smashed many people, and she cracked a little, but she did not fall apart."

Until she did. Despite the disarray her problems had caused, Cukor perhaps could be faulted for the lack of compassion he showed when he spoke to the gossip columnist Hedda Hopper on June 6 about Monroe's imminent firing. He had tried his hardest to guide her through her final attempt to find "salvation" through acting for one of the "better directors." But now, having given up on her after their last harrowing experience working together, he spoke bluntly and without attribution as "one of the most knowledgeable men in the industry." What he told Hopper was, "I believe it is the end of her career. She wants to do the picture, but she has no control of herself. Her performance is not good. It's as tho [sic] she's acting underwater. And she's intelligent enough to realize this."

Two days later Cukor received a telegram:

DEAR GEORGE PLEASE BELIEVE ME IT WAS NOT
MY DOING I HAD SO LOOKED FORWARD TO
WORKING WITH YOU WARMLY=
                    MARILYN.

It's unclear whether or not Cukor realized that Monroe had sent similar telegrams to the other 103 members of the company of *Something's Got to Give*.

23

CLAIRE BLOOM, JANE FONDA, GLYNIS JOHNS, AND SHELLEY WINTERS IN *THE CHAPMAN REPORT*

W hat Angela Lansbury called Cukor's "wonderful gamey quality . . . a wonderful lasciviousness" helps account for his willingness in his advancing years to delve frankly into the depths of sexuality. That included filming *The Chapman Report*, a prurient and pretentious 1960 bestselling novel by Irving Wallace that sensationalizes a sexual survey of American married women. Although the framework of the story is laughably presented with a straight face in the novel, Cukor's interest is not in the pair of male sexologists conducting the survey—whom he portrays as doltish and unethical, among other failings—but in the opportunity the film gave for some extraordinary portrayals of women struggling to escape from the oppressive sexual conventions of the time (1962). Cukor felt the story offered potential for a film that was "lively, kinky, and very much of today."

Unfortunately, *The Chapman Report* was another Cukor *film maudit*, perhaps predictably hacked up by the censors and by Darryl Zanuck of Twentieth Century-Fox, who retained producing control even after the financially strapped studio unloaded the project onto Warner Bros. (Zanuck's son, the Fox executive Richard D. Zanuck, was the credited producer). More than twenty minutes were cut for the expurgated release version, and as Cukor warned Warners executives, "The picture was delicate enough. Now [it] has been hurt with the sledgehammer, ruthless and brutal treatment; these cuts will be fatal and disastrous to the picture." But Jack L. Warner ruled in favor of Zanuck's cuts, calling Cukor an "obstinate putz."

Although the director felt the film had been "ruined," he still thought it has "some of the best scenes I've ever had anything to do with," including extraordinary performances by Claire Bloom and Jane Fonda. Glynis Johns is also superb as the comic relief, but since her scenes were less affected by the cutting, Cukor felt they imbalance the picture. And because of the clumsy reediting, some of the transitions between harrowing drama and frolicsome sex farce seem jarring.

"Had we been able to make this picture say, in France, it would have remained intact . . . and made a sensation," Cukor said in a 1964 interview conducted in Paris with Richard Overstreet for *Film Culture*. "As it was, we were the victims of stupid censorship, lack of courage and lack of taste. As I conceived it *and filmed it* the picture would have gone over. It would have been a sensation. . . . In any case, on the next film I do I don't plan to pull any punches." As it happened, though, Cukor's next film was *My Fair Lady*, set in Edwardian England. He had to wait until 1969 and his salvage job on the troubled production *Justine* to put his more advanced views of sexuality into practice.

The Chapman Report was simultaneously too subtle and too daring for its moment. It's easy to get distracted by the introductory scenes featuring the pompous Dr. George Chapman (Andrew Duggan) and his writing assistant, Paul Radford (Efrem Zimbalist Jr.), as they arrive in Los Angeles to examine the libidos of married women in an upper-middle-class suburb. Coming years after the Kinsey reports on sexual behavior in the American male (1948) and female (1953), their investigation and attitudes are retrograde even by 1962 standards, even if the trailer calls "the intimate life of the modern woman . . . a field never even talked about before." It takes a while for the viewer to become alert to how the film slyly mocks and subverts these two poseurs who are actually just a pair of sexist quacks. Their attitudes toward female sexuality strike a viewer today as virtually medieval, which might lead to the mistaken impression that the film shares their viewpoint. That helps account for *The Chapman Report* being seldom seen today or being regarded as a strange artifact from a quaint and ugly past. But the sexologists' benighted viewpoints were the norm among American men at the time.

Dr. Chapman's oracular pronouncements and solemn lecturing to the press and a women's club condemn the pervasiveness of American prudery but attempt to counteract it with sanitizing twaddle about how "sex is decent, clean, and dignified." Despite such rhetoric, he and his colleague Radford are mired in old-fashioned, fatuous attitudes that treat women's sexual desire as scandalous. The sexologists regard the problems of the four women presented in the film as deviant behavior rather than how viewers today would see it, as these women's rebellious acting-out of their desperation and confusion in a sexist time and place. Released the year before Betty Friedan's groundbreaking book *The Feminine Mystique*, *The Chapman Report* is a window onto that transitional period when the country was on the verge of the women's liberation and sexual freedom movements but not yet ready for the kind of candor Cukor attempted onscreen. The women's anguish about sexuality is a symptom of their and the culture's urgent need for revolutionary change in sexual mores and gender roles, a need with which Cukor thoroughly sympathizes.

The "gamey" situations in which Cukor's women place themselves, though they stop just short of the book's explicitness, are redolent of familiar tropes of pornography: an alcoholic divorcée (Bloom) whose promiscuous pickups

23.1.   Jane Fonda's Kathleen Barclay, discussing her sex life with a man surveying the sexual habits of suburban women, captures the torment of a woman unfairly blamed as "frigid" because of her husband's aloofness in *The Chapman Report* (1962). Although mutilated by the censors and Darryl F. Zanuck, Cukor's film of a trashy novel by Irving Wallace explores the dilemmas of American women before the feminist movement combated the hypocrisies of traditional gender roles.

Source: Frame enlargement; Twentieth Century-Fox.

end in disaster, a young widow (Fonda) maligned as "frigid" because of her late husband's sexual inadequacy, a lascivious housewife (Johns) seducing a young jock who is clueless about how to give women sexual pleasure, and an unhappily married woman (Shelley Winters, who gives a more ordinary performance) carrying on a doomed clandestine affair with an obvious cad. But the "lurid" nature of the book, as Cukor called it, is transcended by the director's intense concentration on the personalities of these women. He manages to tap into the subconscious of each of his four lead actresses; he stages the action, wherever possible, in his favored long and/or intricately blocked takes, to allow them to explore much deeper and more complex feelings than are evident in the often clumsy or overly obvious dialogue. This is a Cukor film in which the actresses play the subtext as much if not more than the text.

Cukor involves us viscerally in their emotional responses to sexuality as well as to love or its absence in their lives. In another subversive touch, the director's longtime character actor Henry Daniell (the sinister baron in *Camille*) appears as a rival sexologist, Dr. Jonas. He deplores the Chapman study for neglecting the role of love in favor of analyzing only the physical aspects of sexuality. But everything about the man and his sepulchral demeanor is off-putting. This deliberate distancing conveys Cukor's more sophisticated and nonjudgmental recognition that love and physicality are inextricable in women's sexual behavior. That viewpoint is reflected in his critical portrayals not only of Chapman and Radford but also in Daniell's utter lack of humor and warmth when he talks about love while looking as severe as Colin Clive in *Bride of Frankenstein*.

Cukor was forced to shoot, under duress, an absurd, falsely "reassuring" ending in which Dr. Chapman smugly summarizes their report to Radford by claiming that 87 percent of American married women are in love with their husbands: "But the bad [marriages] are so vivid that we lose sight of the fact that the vast majority falls right into this column, 'Happily Married Women—and Men.'" This obscenely cheery conclusion contradicts what the film has shown us with its case studies of female torment or unrequited longing, which are actually fairly representative of American sexual hang-ups in that period.

Working from a script with a final draft by his trusted colleague Gene Allen (but credited to three other writers as well, Wyatt Cooper and Don M.

Mankiewicz, from an adaptation by Grant Stuart, a pseudonym for Arthur Sheekman, along with Allen, who was also the film's production designer), Cukor approaches each of the women with compassion and understanding that are lacking in the sexologists' impersonal, benighted report. He also shows a bracing lack of sentimental condescension toward them as simply victims. Instead he sees them realistically as attempting to take control of their lives and desires, however clumsily, absurdly, or tragically, and as being unfortunately complicit in their social problems.

Dr. Chapman's survey supposedly is nationwide in scope but as portrayed here reflects sociopolitical prejudices of that period by its severe limitations, concentrating exclusively on privileged but unhappy white women in the fictitious suburb of Briarwood, which represents Brentwood or Pacific Palisades. It shows the women as entrapped by empty, oppressive privilege in ways they, like the sexologists studying them, do not clearly fathom. Allen's production design, George Hoyningen-Huene's color coordination, and Harold Lipstein's heavily shadowed lighting pointedly make the women's expensive ranch homes look like dark, gloomy tombs, with suitably ghastly bad taste in design and furnishings. The costumes by Orry-Kelly, on the other hand, give each woman a distinctive color scheme, with the stylish Fonda almost entirely in virginal white and the sporty Johns in beige and white sharply standing out from their settings but Bloom in earth tones and Winters in mostly dark blue blending morosely into theirs.

Zimbalist's slick operator, Paul Radford, behaves with a blatant lack of ethics by almost immediately violating the survey's promise of confidentiality. After interrogating Fonda's Kathleen Barclay from behind a screen in his office, he goes to her home and courts her. Despite her initial anger at this betrayal, she gradually responds and opens up her hidden feelings and sexuality. But today's viewer is more aware of his transgression, which was unfortunately common in that period among therapists and other authority figures and usually damaging to the women involved. It's telling that the smarmy Dr. Chapman reacts in a blasé fashion when he learns of Radford's dalliance with a subject, finding it amusing and titillating and congratulating him rather than firing him. Even Dr. Jonas adds his congratulations and tells Paul that's what Kathleen needs. The film presents these incongruities without comment or apparent criticism, just as symptoms of the way even supposedly professional men viewed women's sexuality in that period (the script hedges somewhat by making Paul a writer rather than a doctor, yet that distinction is mostly irrelevant).

Once the survey gets underway, the film minimizes that obligatory framework and gives the actresses the opportunity to explore their characters, their coping strategies, and their relationships with the men in their lives, who are mostly fools or heels. Some of the most striking scenes are the long takes (which were even longer before the recutting) of the women's initial interrogation sessions, which Cukor called "what was really first class in the picture." He keeps his camera almost entirely on the women and their discomfort at the mechanical ways the sexologists treat them as statistics and case studies rather than as human beings with complex feelings about their sexual issues. Cukor was especially proud of the way that Fonda, who was still a relatively inexperienced actress in transition from her ingénue period, explored her screen personality with a remarkable range and depth.

Her character, the widowed Kathleen Barclay, has been stigmatized as "frigid . . . [a] *femme de glace*" by her late husband, a celebrated test pilot who is actually known as "Boy." His bizarre name seems allegorical in the film, sending up a large red flag about his immaturity (the book indicates his first name was Boynton, a detail the script omits). It's clearly suggested in an overheated flashback that Boy (John Baer) was projecting onto Kathleen his own inability to function with her, with an implication that he may have been homosexual. More than two decades after *The Philadelphia Story*, men were still stigmatizing women with the charge of "frigidity" to sidestep responsibility for their own sexual dysfunction, and Kathleen has internalized that form of brainwashing.

In a primarily cool-blue setting, she sits in the grilling chair with anxious vulnerability, legs carefully crossed. She is struggling to maintain a skittish and "adult" poise in her girlish white dress and oversized white hat, her hair swept high and face made up like a Kabuki performer, her hand balancing a cigarette shakily. But she loses her false, defensive smile and falls apart as she fails to lie convincingly about her marriage. Asked if she enjoyed sex with her husband, she responds after a significant pause, "Very much," with tears coming to her eyes, "Isn't that normal?" After a nervous laugh, she runs out of the office, refusing to listen anymore to what she calls "sickening" questions about their physical relationship and none about love. She later insists, agitatedly, to Paul, "I'm not one of your pathological cases—Boy and I had a wonderful life together."

Kathleen acts terrified about sex during her initially chaste relationship with Paul, partly because of his inappropriate behavior but also a carryover from her emotionally abusive relationship with "Boy." Her personality as an adult woman is further blighted by her unnatural relationship with her father (Roy Roberts, known for playing authority figures and heavies), a domineering man who irrationally expects her to remain faithful to her dead husband, who is considered a national hero. Kathleen's father treats her like a teenager, expecting a quasi-incestuous goodnight hug and kiss each evening and looking askance at Paul for dating his daughter. Underneath her "cold" facade, Kathleen has been seething, holding herself rigidly together with damaging difficulty, and the process of having her sex life interrogated begins to free the suppressed anger she feels at both her late husband and her father. Fonda may have been channeling some emotions from her relationship with her own father, Henry, a cold and distant authority figure she only later came to terms with; Cukor would have known about her issues and helped her incorporate them into the performance.

Paul takes advantage of his developing romantic relationship with Kathleen by persuading her that it is a form of mature sexuality; she needs to shake her neurotic attachments to Boy and Daddy, but Paul may not be much of an improvement. When he first comes to her home, she is wearing another white outfit but with a large gray, inverted "V" bow strategically placed over her groin area, like a "Do Not Enter" sign. The frustrated Paul eventually treats her with unfeeling emotional harshness, shouting, "You're driving me up the wall! . . . I am, and I'm sure your friends are, bored with your problems!" He does so to wean her away from "Boy" and her father in his highly unprofessional manner, even while he claims, without seeming to recognize the irony, "Boy was insensitive." Nevertheless, they finally achieve a long, soulful kiss. Fonda's performance as her prefeminist character torn between the demands of various insensitive men is agonizingly convincing.

Claire Bloom's great performance as Naomi Shields is the most powerful aspect of the film. She gives a devastating portrait of a self-destructive woman desperate for physical and emotional contact who sees no alternative to

23.2. Claire Bloom's searing performance as Naomi Shields, an alcoholic woman addicted to risky sexual habits and brutalized by a vicious musician (Corey Allen, to her left), is the most memorable aspect of *The Chapman Report*. This gang rape sequence was chopped up before the film's release but still conveys the horror of her tragic situation.

Source: Frame enlargement; Twentieth Century-Fox.

recklessly acting out on her sexual addiction. Unable to control herself, she makes herself a raw-nerved victim to male cruelty. Her alcoholism and eventual suicide are among the most moving of the many portrayals of alcoholics in Cukor's work. Although her character has often been reflexively described by critics with the sexist term "nymphomaniac," the film doesn't use that demeaning word or reduce her to any simplistic categorization.

Naomi's succumbing to her self-destructive impulses by playing with sexual fire is one of the most searing examples of what Dan Callahan identifies as Cukor's "favorite theme: the glory of alcoholic, lunatic or sexual abandonment and breakdown, the sheer sensuality of it, and, at the end, its high price." Cukor cast the British actress against her image as a proper lady in order to make her sexually voracious character seem more shockingly contrary to cliché, and her portrayal is utterly convincing in its desperate wantonness and abandon. Her gang rape at the hands of a sleazy, drugged-out jazz clarinet player named Wash Dillon (Corey Allen) and three of his fellow band members was severely cut by Darryl Zanuck but still conveys the stark horror of the scene with its brevity and rapid editing, jagged angles, and tight framing as Naomi is pulled down among them and mauled.

Naomi is introduced in the film lying face down in bed at her home, a fore-shadowing of her ultimate suicide. Wearing a sheer top, her hair disheveled, she gets up and moves in and out of the shadows restlessly. She tries to seduce a clean-cut young water delivery man (Chad Everett) in a classically quasi-porno movie scene, but after they share a passionate kiss in silhouette, she throws him out instead. After shooting her first take in the film, Cukor asked Bloom to remove her brassiere in her low-cut brown blouse when she moved around. Bloom commented, "I was kind of surprised, but I thought, well, if Cukor wants me to take my bra off, I'll take my bra off, take my *knickers* off too—anything he wants! [*Laughs*] So I did, and he's right. It encouraged a kind of louche, different way of moving, and a different way of looking. . . . The difference between George and other directors was that he was an extremely sophisticated European gentleman, with irony, wit, and delicacy."

When Wash comes to Naomi's home on a pretext, leering at her as they stare at each other through the gauze-like pattern of the screen door, she hesitates before he talks his way inside and makes double entendres about her sexual hunger. After she cries out, "I don't like that kind of talk!," he tries to attack her before his young son interrupts them by ringing the doorbell. The camera follows her around throughout the film, from her interrogation scene to her death, as she prowls like a hungry animal. She gazes at her predator with helpless lust even while knowing he will help her destroy herself.

Cukor is not succumbing to "blaming the victim" but dealing with self-destruction on a higher and subtler dramatic level, as he often does with his alcoholic characters and as he did with the similarly refined Greta Garbo's characterization of the courtesan suffering from her fatal illness in *Camille*. What Cukor said of Garbo's performance after he watched that film late in his life could apply to his handling of Bloom's performance as well: He said he was "staggered" at "the wantonness, the perversity" of Garbo's approach. "That usually is a sort of a sobbing part, a victim part, but she played it—she was the author of her own misery. And it had enormous eroticism and bold-ness." By transcending sentimentality, Bloom also reaches the level of classical tragedy.

Bloom gives an uninhibited performance of such startling intensity and sensual, suicidal abandon (even after the recutting) that it suggests how powerfully Cukor could have responded if he had not been censored here and had been given more opportunities than he intermittently found in such late films as *Justine* and *Rich and Famous* to further explore "the wantonness, the perversity" offered by the increasing sexual freedom in films. But even some fairly explicit sexual scenes in Cukor's last film, *Rich and Famous*, show that he always viewed that area of filmmaking, to some extent, with the same quality he valued so strongly in his private life—discretion—and believed in emotionally involving the audience rather than being as visually explicit as some other filmmakers were during that period.

The monologues of the women under interrogation that distinguish *The Chapman Report* show how powerfully Cukor could use dialogue and suggestiveness, rather than explicit imagery, to explore female sexuality. Naomi's free-associating, self-contradictory, often broken monologue about the course of her sex addiction while being interrogated for the sex survey is brilliantly delivered by Bloom with an unsettling blend of reminiscing excitement and guilt-ridden agony while she roams the cage-like office, moving toward and away from the camera, crossing over into Paul's space behind their barrier. She tells how at first "I was discreet" while picking up strange men to have sex with, but her clipped, angry tone reaches a masochistic crescendo when she talks about abandoning her earlier discretion so she could have sex with a young man in her home. That caused a confrontation with her husband about the truth of her desires: "I wanted him to beat me. I wanted him to kill me." Instead, she reports, "He cried."

After Naomi is brought back home after the gang rape, brutally tossed onto the street by Wash like a pile of garbage, torn and bruised and bleeding, she is comforted and taken inside her home by Kathleen, her neighbor, but roughly orders her to leave when Kathleen tries to dissuade her from drinking. Later, although Naomi had tried and failed to escape the attack, she slides to the floor of her home and places a drunken phone call to Wash at his nightclub, inviting him and the other band members over for another round of humiliation: "I'll leave the door open."

After making that invitation, Naomi is aghast at herself, weeping. She turns on a lamp, tears away the lampshade, and contemplates her face in a mirror, her lips gradually forming a faint smile. As the camera moves in to an extreme close-up of her image in the mirror in one of the most extraordinarily moving and disturbing shots of Cukor's career, her face looks drained

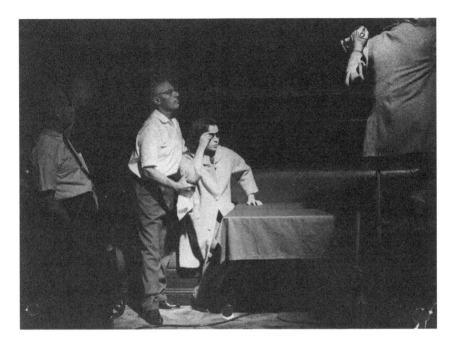

23.3. Cukor directs Bloom in a nightclub scene as her self-destructive character seeks out the man who will destroy her.

Source: Twentieth Century-Fox/From the George Cukor Papers of the Margaret Herrick Library, Academy of Motion Picture Arts and Sciences.

of blood and too wasted to fully express the terror she feels, while she pushes back her disheveled hair and touches her cheeks with her fingers, staring distraughtly and laughing at herself, her eyes dark and haunted. Then, without a cut, the camera follows her to the bedroom as she moves with sudden decisiveness, grabbing a bunch of pills and pouring a drink while the camera lingers on her disappearance into deep shadow before she slides onto the bed, counting out pills carefully before the camera moves in as she swallows just the right quantity with booze, her head slumping onto the pillow. The camera now is pulling back from her. She looks solemn and decisive, but also fearful, as she embraces the pillow and finds the rest she has been craving.

When Dr. Jonas learns of Naomi's death, he chastises the Chapman survey and Paul for helping cause it: "Your interview was a contributing factor." But Paul reassures him callously, "That girl was doomed." Case closed, heartlessly, though not by Cukor.

Another British actress, Glynis Johns, as Teresa Harnish, the sexy middle-aged comic relief, tapes her interrogation session for the entertainment of her husband. He is a pseudosophisticated but rather complacent record producer (John Dehner), with whom she has a loving but unadventurous sexual relationship. Johns livens up this otherwise somber film with her delightfully racy portrayal, a woman several years ahead of her time. Her quest for what she sees as avant-garde sexual liberation ("to give myself to a primitive force") is thwarted by male sexual ineptitude as well. When she finds a dumb jock playing football with his pals on a beach, her blue eyes peering lasciviously from under her hooded eyelids, Teresa murmurs, "What a magnificent animal!" She unabashedly ogles Ed Kraski (Ty Hardin), a buff second-string pro football player. But it seems that Ed is sexually blocked, like Boy Barclay, by an unacknowledged case of latent homosexuality.

Teresa tries to seduce Ed by hiring him to pose for a painting, encouraging him with, "Ed, you'd be surprised what good sport this can be." But when she asks him to pose nude in imitation of Myron's *Diskobolos* while holding a can of beer instead of a discus, Ed reacts in shock: "Wait a minute, lady [*laughs uneasily*]—you don't expect me to take off all my clothes [*laughs*] in front of a *woman?*" Cukor's protracted enjoyment of filming Hardin and his fellow jocks frolicking on the beach in front of the sexually agitated Teresa irritated Jack Warner, who complained to Richard Zanuck after watching the rushes that "Cukor shot enough football for the complete schedule of USC, UCLA, Notre Dame, and the University of Oregon. . . . You can tell George I am disappointed."

But we are not: the director's flaunting of the latent gay overtones of the beach bums' physical camaraderie and the voraciousness of the svelte and maturely sexy Johns (who was thirty-nine at the time) are among the film's highlights. When she and Ed are awkwardly carrying on in his apartment, we hear an oil well outside suggestively "pumping, pumping, *pumping!*," to quote what Norma Desmond tells her gigolo about the wells that are the source of her wealth in Billy Wilder's *Sunset Blvd*. Eventually Teresa has to tell her own rent-a-stud, "Kiss me, Eddie—you might enjoy it!" But when he finally reciprocates by bending her over and pushing her to the floor in Neanderthal fashion, she runs away. She expected something more romantic, which he and other macho men like him in 1962 fail to comprehend: "I can't breathe, Ed! . . . Things like this should take *time*—you can't just toss me about like a football!"

Johns is not only funny but unexpectedly touching in her buoyant eagerness about sex and childlike in her innocence. The film deals in various ways with the naïveté of that preawakened period on the cusp of women's liberation when women were expected to behave like children but were chafing at restrictions they could hardly articulate.

Shelley Winters credited her career takeoff to Cukor's transformative direction of her small but important role as the thoughtlessly flirtatious waitress murdered by Ronald Colman's deranged actor in the 1947 film *A Double Life*. She returns here in a thankless role that would have been better suited to an actress cast against her victim type. Her performance as Sarah Garnell, the least surprising in a film marked by three constantly surprising performances, is sincere but little better than workmanlike.

Yet Winters stirs some sympathy with her painful blundering through her sterile marriage and foolish extramarital affair, even though she is acting in what the critic Glenn Erickson calls "her full dumbbell mode (which began to wear thin back in George Stevens' great [1951 film] *A Place in the Sun*). . . . Sarah's delusion that the ostentatiously creepy Fred [Ray Danton] loves her is almost as funny [as Teresa's behavior], especially when he won't take her anywhere but his boat and insists that she not show up without making an appointment." Sarah's affair, and her making up with her wounded husband (the stolidly loyal Harold J. Stone) after Fred spurns her, are the only parts of these women's stories that descend into the level of soap opera triteness.

Virtually all the men in *The Chapman Report* are venal or foolish, and it's been pointed out that, perhaps to emphasize their backward sexual nature in contrast to the richer and more sympathetic personalities of the four women, several of the men cast in the film are best known for having played screen heavies, including Danton and Stone. Danton is the Prohibition-era gangster Legs Diamond in *The Rise and Fall of Legs Diamond*, Budd Boetticher's 1960 noir, and the thug-turned-movie star George Raft in *The George Raft Story* (1961). Danton and most of the other men in *The Chapman Report* were cut-rate pragmatic choices from among Warners' stock company, including the bland TV actor Zimbalist (who co-starred as a detective in *77 Sunset Strip* and later became best known for his lead role in *The F.B.I.* series), but some are standouts. Hardin, who starred in the TV series *Bronco,* gave a gripping performance as a GI in *Merrill's Marauders,* Samuel Fuller's 1962 World War II film, before stripping down to play the hunky blockhead in *The Chapman Report.*

Cukor remembered what a warm reception *The Chapman Report* received from a preview audience in San Francisco, perhaps the most sexually sophisticated city in the country. But censorship had already "emasculated" the film of some of the qualities Cukor and his actresses had put into it, and he felt the audience in the theater "was ahead of it and wanted more rather than less." Still, that was before Darryl Zanuck began laying his heavy hand in recutting the picture. So the mood was upbeat when Cukor and Richard Zanuck and Jack Warner gathered in the projection booth to celebrate the audience reception. The younger Zanuck recalled, "After we got through talking about the picture, Jack Warner right then and there offered *My Fair Lady* to Cukor. George was very excited; it was something he had really desired."

24

REX HARRISON AND AUDREY HEPBURN IN *MY FAIR LADY*

eorge Cukor's 1964 film of *My Fair Lady*, though disparaged by snobs and even by some Cukor admirers, is in fact a quintessence of his work. To appreciate the film on that level requires a fairly detailed knowledge of his career and a lack of prejudice against the masterful play adaptations that comprise much of his work, including several of his classics, such as *Dinner at Eight*, *Camille*, *Holiday*, *The Philadelphia Story*, *Gaslight*, *Born Yesterday*, and *Love Among the Ruins*. But even more than that, it must be seen why Cukor's *My Fair Lady* is the epitome of a personal film, even if it came with more preexisting constraints than some other Cukor classics and does not reach the emotional heights and depths that make his musical *A Star Is Born* his masterpiece, mutilated though it may be.

Nevertheless, seeing *My Fair Lady* as one of his most personal films goes to the heart of the much-misunderstood auteur theory and a recognition, as the original French proponents of *la politique des auteurs* proposed, that a skillful director can take a celebrated property that has been worked over by many other accomplished hands and mold it to please not only spectators who revere the play (and stage musical) versions but also to express himself or herself.

A director such as Cukor, who thrived for so long in the Hollywood studio system—of which *My Fair Lady* is among the last of its kind, as well as the culmination of the classical musical genre and the system itself—did not always select his own material. He could lobby to be chosen to direct a property the studio owned and help shape it to meet his artistic needs, as he often did by working with his writers and other collaborators. Or just as often, he was selected by a studio as their best possible choice, for one reason or another, to turn out the kind of adaptation they expected. Often in Cukor's later career, he did not have the kind of discretion in choosing material he had tended to enjoy during his long tenure at MGM but had to take the most workable property that was offered to him, while sometimes having to make do with dubious material. And then his finished work sometimes was run through the studio meat grinder before its release (as with *Bhowani Junction* and *The Chapman Report*) or even afterward (as with *A Star Is Born*).

My Fair Lady, however, escaped being mutilated by Warner Bros., even at its length of 170 minutes, because it fulfills its goals splendidly, with classical Hollywood elegance. Aside from the controversial casting and dubbing issues involving the lead actress, Audrey Hepburn, the film of *My Fair Lady* is a seamless match of this Pygmalion-like director with his material, the hit musical adaptation by Alan Jay Lerner (book and lyrics) and Frederick Loewe (music) of George Bernard Shaw's classic 1913 play, *Pygmalion*. Not only did the film come to Cukor with the weighty demands of the fidelity the public expected to those revered works, but his *My Fair Lady* followed an excellent 1938 British film adaptation of *Pygmalion* with an Oscar-winning screenplay by Shaw himself. Lerner wrote the screenplay for Cukor's film, some of which was borrowed from Shaw's, which was directed by Anthony Asquith and Leslie Howard, who played Professor Henry Higgins. Harry Stradling Sr. photographed both that black-and-white film and the Technicolor *My Fair Lady*.

Much has been written about all the peregrinations the story of Higgins—a pedantic and misogynistic professor of phonetics in Edwardian-era London who wins a bet to turn a Cockney flower girl ("this draggle-tailed guttersnipe") into a lady, a pseudo-"princess"—took in all its various dramatic and musical incarnations. The creative problems and pressures upon Cukor and his filmmaking colleagues, who did not always see eye to eye, have been thoroughly chronicled. But Cukor's contributions to *My Fair Lady*, his success in navigating the many risky shoals of the massive production to give it a unified and eloquent stylistic tone, and his personal investment in its themes, characterizations, and what he liked to call a film's creative and emotional "climate" have received surprisingly scant attention.

24.1. Audrey Hepburn's performance as Eliza Doolittle in *My Fair Lady* (1964) was compared unfavorably to earlier incarnations of the character by Julie Andrews and Wendy Hiller, but under Cukor's guidance she brought her own charm and sensitivity to the role. Here he conveys his intense empathy to Hepburn in her most challenging task, playing the "squashed cabbage leaf" Professor Henry Higgins encounters selling flowers at Covent Garden.

Source: Warner Bros./From the George Cukor Papers of the Margaret Herrick Library, Academy of Motion Picture Arts and Sciences.

Even dedicated Cukor scholars have often written off or slighted *My Fair Lady*, the only film to win him an Academy Award as best director, as an impersonal assignment executed with his expected professional skill but an overly detached style that owed more to others than to him. If it had been only that, however, the film probably would not have endured as such a deeply beloved popular success, as it remains decades after its release. Gavin Lambert, Cukor's sympathetic and insightful chronicler, starts the section on the film in their interview book by asking the director, "Would you say that *My Fair Lady* was more prepackaged than most of your films?" Cukor responded by "*bristling slightly*" and snapping, "That's what you intellectuals are pleased

to say." Lambert half-apologizes but explains that he thought Jack L. Warner, who personally took producer credit on his studio's mammoth financial
gamble, "must have assembled the major creative elements in advance."

That should have gone without saying, although Cukor was able to influence the choice of some of his collaborators and deserves full credit for tying
everyone's work together, the first task of any successful director. But Cukor
takes it upon himself to school Lambert on the basics of how a director
approaches a sacred text from the theater, a subject one would have thought
the interviewer would have understood by that point in his extended conversation with Cukor. When Cukor received his Oscar for directing the film,
the first piece of gratitude he expressed, characteristically, was, "I had
wonderful material to work with."

Yet even Lambert seemed biased by the prevailing condescension directed
at the film. Andrew Sarris lambasted it in his *Village Voice* review as "an
evening of disenchantment. As a long-time admirer of George Cukor's
directorial style, I had expected something more in the way of creative adaptation." This attitude persisted: Jeanine Basinger claims in the 2000 documentary based on Lambert's book, "There's so much irony in the fact that
George Cukor, who made so many of Hollywood's best-remembered and
most-loved movies, would get his only Oscar for *My Fair Lady*, a movie that
really doesn't represent the warmth, the nuance, the subtlety, you know, of
his work."

On the other hand, Cukor's longtime collaborator Gene Allen, who served
as the film's art director (and de facto production designer under Cecil Beaton, who mainly designed the extravagant costumes), says in that documentary, "It was interesting for somebody like George Cukor to have an assignment
to do *My Fair Lady*, [which] has some built-in problems. First of all, it's a
great hit on the stage. So right away the director has the problem of, How
much do you open it up? You'll be criticized as the director if you open it up
too much, if you change it too much, or it loses the flavor of the theater. On
the other hand, if you don't add to it, they'll just say it's a photographed play.
Look at that, and you'll see that Cukor solved all those problems."

Cukor explained to Lambert that he approached *My Fair Lady* by not violating the text, which he would not have been allowed to do in any case
("Not that I wanted to pull it apart at the seams"), but respecting it while
being unafraid of transforming it into cinematic scenes. He keeps the film

continually moving with natural fluidity and strikes the right tone in handling the dialogue and visuals in terms of how stylized this major example of a stylized film genre needs to be. As Cukor said of the dazzling "Ascot Gavotte" sequence, a blend of extreme theatricality and color design but using actual horses in a stylized way, "There's a big number sung during the sequence, so it couldn't be realistic. Nor could the picture as a whole. It had to take place in a kind of dream world."

The warmth, the nuance, the subtlety of his work can all be found in abundance in *My Fair Lady*.

No director was better suited to explore the emotional and intellectual nuances of that musical with the subtlety of Cukor, whose entire career made him the closest equivalent in the movies to the better parts of Pygmalion, the figure from Greek mythology and Ovid's *Metamorphoses*, the sculptor who creates a female statue and falls in love with it before it is transformed into a real woman. The many instances of Cukor lovingly guiding, discovering, and shaping the potential of his actresses and transforming them into stars no doubt played a strong role in persuading Jack Warner to hire him for the job (Vincente Minnelli was the first choice but asked for too rich a deal; Cukor was in no such position but was eager to take on the task for a flat fee of $300,000, without the percentage Minnelli demanded). The greatest controversy surrounding the film version of *My Fair Lady* was Jack Warner's decision, before hiring a director, to give the female lead to Audrey Hepburn, a major international star of long standing, over Julie Andrews, the vivacious young British singer and actress who had starred in the musical on Broadway and had appeared on television but was a relative unknown to the film audience.

Hepburn lacked Andrews's sublime singing voice. Even though Hepburn recorded some of the songs for the film, she was bitterly disappointed when her only intermittently suitable singing voice, which had trouble hitting high notes, was not used but rather the lovely soprano voice of Marni Nixon (who had dubbed, among others, Deborah Kerr in *The King and I* and Natalie Wood in *West Side Story*). It's impossible to know how Andrews would have fared under Cukor's direction, although she soon went on to become a major film star, winning an Oscar for her first picture, Disney's charming fantasy *Mary Poppins* (1964), while Hepburn was snubbed by not being nominated. But the cast album from Broadway's *My Fair Lady* and video clips that survive of

Andrews singing some of the songs tend to suggest she may have been too sprightly and cheerful for the more stringent emotional demands Cukor made on Hepburn.

The warmth and delicacy Cukor drew from that older, more experienced actress, and a sense of melancholia that underlies her performance, even the jollier parts, tend to indicate her casting was a benefit to the film. This despite cinematographer Stradling's need to use filters to make Hepburn seem younger (she was thirty-four at the time, but the film says Eliza is twenty-one; Andrews was twenty-seven then) and the incongruity of hearing another woman's voice emanating from Eliza. To further complicate matters, Hepburn's own singing voice is heard in the lead-ins to some of the songs, particularly when Eliza is exasperated or angry.

As Higgins and his companion, fellow linguist Colonel Hugh Pickering (Wilfrid Hyde-White), wait anxiously for Eliza to come downstairs begowned for the crucial test of her speech and manners at an embassy ball, Pickering chides Higgins for what appears to be his "confounded complacency." But Higgins, as is his habit, is concealing his deeper feelings beneath his veneer of harshness and mockery. As Pickering, walking toward him, confronts him anxiously about his seeming not to care about Eliza, Cukor positions Higgins in a pose of seeming relaxation but actual tension, in a shadowy corner seated on a divan. "You act as if she doesn't matter at all," Pickering tells him, and Higgins replies, "Oh, rubbish, Pickering, of course she *matters*. What do you think I've been doing all these months? What could possibly matter more than to take a human being and change her into a different human being by creating a new speech for her? It's filling up the deepest gulf that separates class from class, and soul from soul. No, she matters *immensely*." Cukor briefly holds on Higgins reflecting before his attention turns to Eliza appearing on the staircase.

Cukor spent his career conducting what Pickering calls "an experiment in teaching," coaxing performances from actors and actresses with his stream of adroit, if occasionally infuriating, analysis of their characters and hints about how to play them. His concentration on how actors speak was particularly and painstakingly acute—as one can hear by listening to an audio recording of Cukor coaching a nonactress to speak her brief lines in *My Fair Lady*. He cast an actual member of the European aristocracy, the German Baroness Veronika (Bina) von Goldschmidt-Rothschild, in the pivotal role of the Queen of Transylvania, who is, as he tells her, "the last word" on Eliza's social transformation at the embassy ball. Cukor gives rapid-fire direction as he makes the baroness say her few lines, including her principal one ("My child, my son would like to dance with you," changed in the film to "Miss Doolittle, my son would like to dance with you") over and over. She does so with varying inflections and, eventually, an ideal balance between grace and authority. This is fascinating to hear and revealing of Cukor's method with actors in a way unlike any other record of him at work.

Cukor knew just how much to be demanding and how much to be kindly cajoling, but in the case of this dignified yet unprofessional player, he needed to convey firmness by transferring his way of speaking to her. When the baroness seemed nervous at first, he said, "No, no, no, don't criticize yourself, Bina. I'll tell you how to do it." As she speaks the "My child" line repeatedly, he tells her, with increasing briskness, sometimes giving her line readings, "Now say it with a smile. —Now with more authority and speak up more. —Now a little faster. . . .—Now say it with more authority and with good humor. . . .—Now say it a little faster with *just* the same authority. You're the last word!"

It works beautifully in the film, with the line dubbed over a long shot of the baroness before her son takes her to the dance floor, the camera pulling back to display their triumphant waltz in full figure, with the other guests watching and then dancing around them. Cukor cuts to Higgins nudging Pickering as they silently celebrate what they see as their (not Eliza's) triumph.

Higgins's similarly demanding style is edged, for comedic effect, with a frequent tone of meanness, even contempt, toward Eliza's coarse Cockney lingo. Nowhere is this tone more amusing, in a heartlessly satirical way, than when he encounters Eliza in the first scene in the film, on a rainy night when he takes down her dialect as she sells flowers in Covent Garden. After she complains in her grating voice, he explodes, "A woman who utters such disgusting and depressing noises has no right to be anywhere. No right to live. Remember that you're a human being with a soul and the divine gift of articulate speech. That your native language is the language of Shakespeare and Milton and the Bible. Don't sit there crooning like a bilious pigeon."

Part of the amusement we take from Higgins's outbursts is the rhythm of Shaw's language, so musically and majestically delivered by Harrison. Cukor was working with a polished film veteran who had played Higgins onstage for more than two and a half years in New York and London, so Harrison knew his lines thoroughly, but he also tended to be insecure beneath his smooth, cocky veneer. He admittedly needed help in finding the right levels of delivery for the camera and to renew his performance with a fresh aura, as if he has just thought of his words. Cukor was a master at that kind of guidance and took the unusual step, at Harrison's suggestion, of letting him do his songs live with a wireless microphone concealed under his tie.

Lerner realized that the role of Higgins needed to be written for a dramatic actor, not a singer, and Harrison, with the help of a vocal coach, Bill Low, developed a distinctive style of *Sprechstimme*, "speak-singing" or "talking on pitch," that preserves the sensibility of Shaw while taking advantage of Harrison's musically inflected baritone. Lerner observes in his screenplay that despite Higgins's rudeness and penchant for insulting people, he remains likeable because of his sense of humor. Cukor makes ample use of Harrison's sly, mischievous quality that makes him such a superb actor in high comedy and partly redeems Higgins's negative qualities.

If Higgins, in the Shaw play and the Cukor film, seems pathological, there might be a hidden psychological explanation that wouldn't have occurred to Shaw or anyone connected with *My Fair Lady* but draws on more modern psychology. The British actor Harry Hadden-Paton, who played Higgins in the 2018 Lincoln Center Theater revival of the play, recalled his discussions with its director, Bartlett Sher: "Bart and I very early on had conversations about Higgins's psychology. We wondered whether he were around today if he wouldn't be diagnosed with autistic spectrum disorder. He has a lot of symptoms. He's very focused on the specifics of language. He doesn't necessarily communicate very well. He doesn't understand other people's emotions. He's sensitive to noise. I'm not saying Higgins is autistic or isn't. But it's useful from our point of view to give him a reason for why he is the way he is."

Cukor recognized something akin to an autistic streak in Higgins, though, when he observed that the difference between *My Fair Lady* and most productions of *Pygmalion* "lay in the casting of Rex Harrison. Eliza was usually played by one of those overpowering actresses, and Higgins became an almost subsidiary, rather weak character. In the British film Leslie Howard did him charmingly as a romantic, but Rex hit the fanaticism, the possessed quality, and this made him infinitely touching and original." Harrison brought to the film his rather diabolical look—and infamously bad temper—which give his Higgins a sense of danger. That frightens Eliza and proves as intimidating as Shaw intends but is modulated by the quietly gentlemanly behavior of Hyde-White's Pickering (another Cukor surrogate onscreen, a replacement for the younger and heartier Robert Coote, who played the role onstage) and by the perfectly timed humor of the many witty lines Harrison utters and "sings."

Harrison in the various iterations of *My Fair Lady* also gives Higgins more sexual vitality than the wispy Howard does in *Pygmalion*, even at his more advanced age in the film, which gave Warners pause. The studio and Cukor considered Cary Grant and Peter O'Toole for the role before wisely settling on Harrison. Grant was older than Harrison, however, and famously told Jack Warner, "Not only will I not play Higgins, but if you don't use Rex Harrison, I won't even go to the film." An offer was made to O'Toole, who was Cukor's first choice, but negotiations fell apart when his demands were considered excessive by Warners. O'Toole eventually played Higgins onstage in *Pygmalion* in the 1980s in London and New York; he hollers and romps through the role distractingly in a 1983 made-for-cable movie opposite Margot Kidder. His erratic exuberance makes you appreciate all the more the subtlety with which Harrison plays Higgins in Cukor's film. But Cukor probably could have worked with the younger O'Toole to better modulate his approach to the role.

As heard in the New York and London cast albums of the stage version of *My Fair Lady*, Harrison played Higgins in a brisk, more cerebral and detached way, relishing the sound of his voice but not bringing much emotion to his songs beyond his habitual tone of brittle contempt. Although it's hard at this distance to tell what Harrison brought to his interchanges with other actors onstage, he seems more self-contained in his songs in the theater than in the film. Cukor slowed down, to some extent, Harrison's rapid, crisp delivery and brought out a deeper sense of feeling and spontaneity, more concern (however intermittent and obtuse on Higgins's part) with how people react to his bluster, as well as a more pensive, subtly vulnerable approach.

The nuances Harrison and Cukor find in Higgins work wonderfully in the heightened intimacy of film, and Harrison won an Oscar as best actor. For all his brilliance as a performer, he relied considerably on the skill of his director in pacing his speech and the emotional highs and lows of his performance. The words Higgins so rapturously uses to describe the English language to Eliza apply to Harrison's delivery of them: its "extraordinary, imaginative, and musical mixtures of sounds," a line he delivers while letting his fingers play around his mouth when he talks about music, as if conducting the sounds with an orchestra.

The only time I had the experience of seeing a Cukor actor do his or her character onstage was when I saw Harrison do his umpteenth performance as Higgins in a touring production of *My Fair Lady* during its 1980–1981 run at the Pantages Theater in Hollywood. He was ghastly. Doubtless just doing the show for his sizeable star salary, Harrison literally walked through the performance, seeming to have no emotional connection left with the character, perhaps understandably after having done it so often. But it was a severe letdown to see him, as well as a lesson in how much a director can affect a film performance. (That tour and Harrison's terrible behavior on it are chronicled by its director, Patrick Garland, in *The Incomparable Rex*, his often hilarious yet also appalling 1998 memoir.)

The biting, sarcastic tone Harrison brings to Higgins's early scenes needed careful modulation onscreen by Cukor to avoid being heavy-handed, lacking humor, and seeming monotonous. So Cukor varies it with moments of Harrison lowering his voice and delivering his directions of Eliza in a more relaxed manner that may not be exactly kindly but displays more forbearance. At times Higgins is actually warm and gentle; those moments are manipulative on his part to some extent, but they also reveal the emotional side he takes such pains to keep hidden from the world. Higgins is a master of the spoken word, delivering the magnificent Bernard Shaw dialogue with the mellifluous voice of Rex Harrison, under the guidance of a director whose work celebrates language. Higgins convinces us, and Eliza, of the transformative power of speech. And he is molding her personality with elements of genuine kindness and collaboration and with the understanding that, for all his egomania, he is not doing it alone but relying on her to perform well under his direction, just as Cukor does with his actors.

Just before her epiphany in the thrilling musical number "The Rain in Spain," when she suddenly breaks through and talks like a lady, Higgins takes her aside and speaks with true commiseration, as a good director will do when an actor is faltering and despondent. Because she tells him her head aches, he takes the ice pack he has been selfishly using on his own head and plunks it against her forehead, telling her without a trace of condescension but as a

24.2. Cukor's career-long attraction to the Pygmalion theme is about the joy accompanying character transformation. This is the moment when Eliza learns to express herself in a more articulate way through the guidance of her director figure, Professor Higgins (Rex Harrison). *My Fair Lady* goes on to explore Eliza's anxiety over her change in social status now that she can speak "proper" English.

Source: Frame enlargement; Warner Bros.

real collaborator, "I know your head aches; I know you're tired; I know your nerves are as raw as meat in a butcher's window. But *think* what you're trying to accomplish. [*Sits next to her*] Just *think* what you're dealing with. The *majesty* and *grandeur* of the English language, it's the greatest possession we have. The noblest thoughts that ever flowed through the hearts of men are contained in its extraordinary, imaginative, and musical mixtures of sounds. And that's what you've set yourself out to conquer, Eliza. And conquer it you *will*."

Eliza looks stunned, pensive, and more mature after he speaks. She is one of the dreamers who abound in Cukor's work. Her hostess at the ball, the ambassador's wife (Lillian Kemble-Cooper), remarks (as part of an exchange added during filming) that she has "such a faraway look, as if she's always lived in—in a garden." Higgins replies, "So she has—a sort of garden." But this young woman, like Ruth Gordon Jones in *The Actress*, is also feisty and determined and stands up to her gruff but ultimately sympathetic father figure.

Despite her fragile appearance, Hepburn was a tough survivor, having lived through the Nazi occupation of the Netherlands as an adolescent. She was born in Belgium but was of Dutch and British descent. According to her authoritative biographer Alexander Walker, "She helped distribute anti-Nazi propaganda leaflets and copies of clandestine broadcasts by the BBC or secret Dutch radio stations. She carried them concealed in her shoes." Although, as Walker notes, overblown mythology has accreted around Hepburn's other activities during the war, it is established that she raised money for the Resistance by giving solo ballet concerts and at least in one documented incident served as a courier: "In 1943, an English parachutist landed and went into hiding in the wooded hills of the Klarenbeeksche, not far from Arnhem. Audrey agreed to carry a message to this contact from the Resistance."

Eliza's spunky self-determination manifests itself when she hears Higgins make his bet with Pickering. She takes her hard-earned money, dresses up in her best slum finery, and goes to Higgins's posh home to become his pupil. He huffily refuses to talk with her, since he already has annotated her lingo in his notebook, but she tells Pickering when he courteously inquires what she is seeking from lessons, "I—I want to be a lady in a flower shop instead of selling at the corner of Tottenham Court Road. But they won't take me unless I can talk more genteel. He said he could teach me."

Shaw's satire of the rigid British class system plays seriously with the fact that it rests partly on attributes that are *not* innate—ways of talking, social manners, proper clothing—but can be learned. In short, the class system is based on illusion, on theater, even though it is a very real and cruel barrier to human growth. Higgins, who has the virtue of showing contempt for the system and the biases that underlie it, takes on the challenge of transforming Eliza partly as a joke to fool the snobs who take the system seriously and whose own social standing, despite what they think, does not make them worthy of looking down on her.

But as Higgins comes to see Eliza as a human being and not simply an "experiment in teaching," he realizes that by playing with illusion he is tampering with a person's soul as well as her social standing, a responsibility he had not reckoned with but comes to accept. He is a dreamer too, an unworldly intellectual and artist of sorts who, like the mythological Pygmalion, fantasizes about his ability to create a new person out of a "squashed cabbage leaf . . . condemned by every syllable she utters . . . for the cold-blooded murder of the English tongue!"

Cukor's career-long concentration on stories that deal with the molding and transformation of character through performance gives him keen insight into all the nuances of that process. His guidance of Hepburn's Eliza, in parallel with Higgins but often at odds with that tyrannical "director," is delicate and touching, showing the respect he had for hardworking actresses who take their transformations seriously. Cukor always understood the paradox of film acting, that playing a part often entails revealing deeper truths about an actor's own personality and that the director's task is to help the actor learn more about herself and bring that deeper understanding into the character she is playing.

One of the major differences between *My Fair Lady* and both the Shaw play and the British film of *Pygmalion* is the time and detailed attention Cukor gives to the laborious, often painful steps Eliza suffers through under Higgins's mostly ruthless guidance. This welcome emphasis replicates the discipline Cukor believed necessary to a credible performance and the hard work involved in what too many people consider the frivolous profession of acting. Much of Eliza's learning process seems comical—being hooked up to Higgins's colorful machines to measure and guide her speech—but the comedy has a serious subtext as her personality changes. And her pain and exhaustion are palpable in Hepburn's performance, through which Eliza is seen winning the grudging respect of her demanding tutor. In the British film, this is accomplished too swiftly, with time-compressing montages by its editor, David Lean, but Cukor, as always, makes character transformation viscerally felt by the audience.

Cukor's leisurely narrative style and widescreen (Super Panavision 70) canvas for *My Fair Lady* gives him plenty of room to explore that learning process and to deploy his characteristic attention to subtle nuances of character and behavior, this time without his work being chopped up. *My Fair Lady* is a good example of how his unobtrusive style functions so well for the material that its finesse mostly escapes notice. His camera is always in the right place in this film, and the action keeps flowing smoothly and naturally, with the actors moved around, toward, away from the camera, with two-shots and close-ups intercut with just the right tempo by William Ziegler, the film's editor. The rhythms of performance and narrative serve the material with the emphases demanded by each scene and the overall flow of the picture. Cukor's is the style that conceals style. Jean Renoir was another director who believed in this kind of style: "Technique," he said, "that's a terrible word in art! You have to have it, but so completely that you know how to disguise it." Cukor's fellow directors understood and appreciated the subtlety of his self-effacing style more than most reviewers and film scholars have.

Martin Scorsese said in a documentary about the making of *My Fair Lady* that deals extensively with the director's collaborators:

> We also have to remember too that there was a great director named George Cukor, and this was one of his last really great works. And I think Cukor was a remarkable director who dealt in the thirties and in the forties with films that seem to come from theater, like *The Philadelphia Story*, and pictures like that were actually plays. And yet even though literally most of the film had people talking in rooms, they were always movies. And I don't know how he did it. I think it was the pacing of the actors, where the position of the camera [was], and that sort of thing. But I've always been a great fan of Cukor's.

To examine a central scene in *My Fair Lady*, the "Rain in Spain" musical number, is to understand how his expert yet unobtrusive blocking and

24.3. "The Rain in Spain" number celebrating Eliza's transformation. Harrison's misogynistic philologist lets down his guard with his pupil and his fellow linguist, Colonel Pickering (Wilfrid Hyde-White). *My Fair Lady*, a masterful adaptation of the stage musical based on George Bernard Shaw's play *Pygmalion*, has been underrated by film historians.

Source: Frame enlargement; Warner Bros.

pacing, his sensitive handling of his actors, and his consummate skill in shifting tones from comedy to poignancy help bring this scene to life with such seemingly nonchalant naturalness. Cukor does this even though the scene is the height of artificiality, with three characters in a room breaking spontaneously into song and dance. He treats the scene mostly as drama rather than comedy; he always said he preferred a drama with music to a straight musical, although the distinction often blurs.

Six servants upstairs precede the intimate drama of "The Rain in Spain" with a chorus, begging Higgins to stop his work with Eliza (it's early morning) and let them sleep. This device, borrowed from the play, is one of the numerous Lubitsch touches in *My Fair Lady*. Cukor follows the example of the director who virtually invented the romantic comedy, shared his ambivalent view of riches and luxury, always involved the servants in the story, and loved to undercut the pretensions of nobility.

Although Lubitsch sparred with Cukor when they tried to work together on *One Hour with You*, his influence permeates Cukor's satirical view of high society and the conventions of romantic comedy. Lubitsch was a German-born immigrant to the United States and Cukor the son of Hungarian immigrants, so they naturally gravitated in their work to outsiders and drew comedy and drama from the fascination with the complex process of assimilation that immigrants all face as they transform their way of speaking, manners, and clothing to fit into their alien new societies, as Eliza tries to do in *My Fair Lady*. Most importantly, Cukor's work in this and other films shares the central theme in Lubitsch (as I have defined it in my 2018 critical study, *How Did Lubitsch Do It?*): how men should treat women and vice versa.

From the chorus of servants, Cukor goes to a shadowy shot of Higgins slumped wearily in his chair with the ice pack on his head, laboriously commanding Eliza to speak her exercise line once again. Now comes the moment when she speaks correctly, wondrously, the vexing line Higgins has been hammering into her head as a feat of proper diction: "The rain in Spain stays mainly in the plain." Eliza's breakthrough follows the painstaking buildup of her and Higgins's suffering through her repeated failure. The buildup is crucial to the dramatic and emotional effect of her exuberant delivery of the line and the joyous song and dance of celebration with Higgins and Pickering that follow her achievement. Higgins's compassionate speech beforehand as he takes a seat next to her on the sofa, bidding her to *"think* what you're trying to accomplish" and rhapsodizing about "the *majesty* and *grandeur* of the English language" has helped give her a newfound sense of complicity with her teacher, as Cukor's pep talks did with his actors.

Just before she speaks the line, Cukor lets the camera linger for a long pause on Eliza sitting silently on the sofa, motionless, puzzling over her task in a wide shot with Higgins slumped wearily behind his desk in the background, his hand over his face. Cukor holds on them in the wide shot to downplay the feeling of predictability it would have had if he had cut to a close-up of Eliza. After a while she speaks the line slowly and precisely. Higgins says in a low voice, "What was that?"

Only then does Cukor give her a close-up when she turns toward Higgins and slowly speaks the line perfectly again, her mouth dropping in wonderment, following it with a quick series of ecstatic matching close-ups of her and Higgins as she recites the line again and again with mounting elation. The effect is that of a miracle but a believably human one, like the discovery of language in Arthur Penn's 1962 film of William Gibson's *The Miracle Worker*, when the previously mute Helen Keller (Patty Duke) has her breakthrough and speaks the word "Water." After that, Helen runs ecstatically around the yard of her Alabama home, touching things while her teacher, Annie Sullivan (Anne Bancroft), signs their names to her, and she signs back to her. Helen triumphantly rings a bell and gives thanks to her "Teacher." Higgins may have been less benevolent-minded than Annie Sullivan, but their sometimes harsh-seeming methods have a similar result. *My Fair Lady* is not often talked about as a movie about teaching, but that's what it is, and Shaw's words on the subject in Higgins's mouth convey a passion for learning and for character transformation similar to Sullivan's passionate hope for Helen. Cukor heightens the element of delighted surprise in Harrison's performance as well as in Hepburn's.

The emotional impact of Helen's dancelike epiphany in *The Miracle Worker* is similar to Eliza's epiphany as she speaks the words that convey her becoming a "lady" and as her voice makes its rapturous rise into song, with Higgins matching her in a joyous duet. The scene was worked out by Cukor with the film's choreographer, Hermes Pan, who served in that role in a long partnership with Fred Astaire. Astaire and Pan even shared an uncanny physical resemblance; they would dance together while working out their numbers before Fred's female partner would step in and rehearse with him.

Higgins, Eliza, and Pickering rise and come together in their celebratory ersatz-Spanish dance after she perfects her "rain in Spain" line, and the camera tracks in to frame them more closely before Higgins slaps her on the back, driving her roughly into the foreground as he accepts congratulations from Pickering, shaking hands. Higgins plays a xylophone for rhythm as she walks up to him and speaks another exercise line, then enunciates yet another with the same precision. Cukor follows them into a widening shot as all three do a kind of flamenco dance and waltz, Higgins using a large red handkerchief as a flag in front of Pickering charging like a bull. We keep noticing Eliza being excluded from the men's reverie, but she is so pleased with herself at this moment that she doesn't care. That point will come later in the film.

The camera pulls farther back in the same shot as Higgins abruptly but gracefully sweeps her into a lively, romantic-looking waltz—Hepburn displaying her ease as a dancer, her original profession in show business—as Cukor cuts to an even wider perspective, their full bodies visible, as Astaire insisted in dances with his partners. Eliza stands on a chair and claps the rhythm before she descends into Higgins's arms, and they briefly waltz again. Their energies spent, all three fall back into their seats, shouting "Olé!" and laughing in delighted release.

Higgins proposes that they should try out Eliza in society at the upcoming Ascot race. The housekeeper, Mrs. Pearce (Mona Washbourne), enters in her robe, protesting the noise. The men leave, ignoring Eliza and having a jolly talk in the hall and on the staircase about buying a gown for her. Higgins pantomimes how it would look on Pickering, one of the film's relaxed, irresistible bits of gay humor that accompany the men's contented living arrangement. Later in the film, after Eliza runs away, Higgins harrumphs in his ostensibly most misogynistic but actually somewhat facetious rant, "A Hymn to Him," which includes his lines to Pickering, "Why can't a woman be more like a man?," "Well, why can't a woman be like *you?*," and "Would you complain if I took out another fellow?" Pickering responds, "Never!" And Higgins concludes with a flourish, "Well, why can't a woman be like *us?*"

When Higgins tells Eliza that she might marry, he explains, "You see, Eliza, all men are not confirmed old bachelors like me and the Colonel. Most men are the marrying sort—poor devils. Anyway, you're not bad-looking. You're really quite a pleasure to look at sometimes. Well, not now, of course, when you've been crying, you look like the very devil." Cukor's sly humor about queer overtones in his work, coming out more as the sixties progressed, was simultaneously able to convey both his fondness for male companionship and his inarguable bona fides as perhaps the least misogynistic director in Hollywood other than Dorothy Arzner and Ida Lupino.

Following the "Rain in Spain" number, Eliza lingers in the room with Mrs. Pearce after the men leave her, savoring her triumph with her head tilted sideways in wonderment and singing one of the most beautiful songs in the musical, "I Could Have Danced All Night." Its placement suggests an infatuation with Higgins, as the film does in various subtle ways to prepare us to accept its unlikely romantic ending, which Cukor makes work despite all our misgivings. Before Eliza sings, she is sitting on the edge of the sofa, contemplating her miraculous transformation.

Dancing and singing by herself in the parlor and up the stairs, she is shepherded to bed by Mrs. Pearce. The servant women prepare Eliza in her bed gown, a ritual she interrupts by dancing into the bathroom as the camera tracks back with her and using a towel like the red flag in a bullfight before washing her face. After they coax her into the covers and leave her in the dark, Eliza is still too excited to sleep, so she continues singing, sitting up in bed and hugging the pillow, rising to a crescendo of happiness before the scene fades out. This is her gayest moment before events that follow, her tests in high society and battles with Higgins, take away most of her joy and make her reexamine the perilous situation she has entered with her new, unfamiliar personality.

The warmth of these scenes lingers even when, in the wake of her triumph at the ball, Eliza is callously ignored by the two men while Pickering and the servants serenade Higgins. Cukor continually emphasizes her quietly seething in the background of shots, glaring with pain in a solo closer shot, and eventually retreating into a shadow against the wall. At one point, Pickering approaches her and, while reenacting the ball, seems about to take her arm, and she smiles at him hopefully, but he is still ignoring her, and her face sinks at the men treating her as nothing more than a prop in their performances.

She erupts against Higgins when he thoughtlessly asks her for his slippers, which she throws at him, stripping off her jewelry, including some that's rented and a ring he bought her at Brighton, which triggers his nearly violent rage. Her fierce outcries to Higgins—"Why didn't you leave me where you picked me out of, in the gutter? . . . What's to become of me?"—and his complacent responses make them almost come to blows. As Cukor said of Eliza's despondency in this scene (a point that's also true of Higgins's rage), "There's a savagery in Shaw's directions which is usually omitted." When Higgins leaves the room, Cukor has her fall to her knees against his chair and pound the arm with her fist, holding the other fist to her face before throwing the slippers at him.

Suicidal at first—like so many other Cukor characters when their identity is threatened with destruction—she escapes to her old haunt at Covent Garden ("where I belong") with her hapless high-society suitor, Freddy Eynsford-Hill (Jeremy Brett). Freddy has been lingering outside her house for much of the movie hoping for a moment with her. Freddy, another dreamer, is not treated by Cukor with the mere mockery, verging on contempt, that he receives in the plays by Shaw and Lerner. Cukor, unusually for him, engages in very few long takes in this movie, preferring the more conventional shot/countershot method, which seems appropriate to emphasize the constant disjunction and confrontations between Eliza and Higgins and to subtly suggest their lack of genuine emotional partnership. But Cukor breaks his self-imposed stylistic rule by giving the blithely romantic Freddy a series of long takes in which he sings "On the Street Where You Live," some of the film's most movingly wistful interludes (Brett was also dubbed, by Bill Shirley). Cukor's Freddy, a paragon of male beauty, has a certain nobility in his devoted, sincere, mostly solitary romanticism; although he often may seem silly, this film, even with its abundant humor, is not one that ridicules romanticism. He tells Eliza when she finds him lingering outside her home near the end of the film, "Don't laugh at me, Miss." In its wryly sophisticated yet unabashed romanticism, *My Fair Lady* seems an end to an era in Hollywood. Romanticism was rapidly becoming a dirty word in the sexual revolution, which stressed sex without love or other emotional entanglements.

As Eliza moves slowly through the early-morning crowds of costermongers and flower girls at Covent Garden, looking inquiringly at the kind of young woman she used to be, Cukor turns this into one of the film's most poignant sequences. We hear the strains of "Wouldn't It Be Loverly?," Eliza's introductory song of aspiration when she was a common flower girl, as his camera follows the lady Eliza walking pensively off by herself in a wide shot from a dramatic low angle. She is wearing a striking peach-colored outfit that further emphasizes her alienation. When Freddy finally asks if she's "all finished here," Eliza says quietly, "Yes, Freddy, I'm finished here," in a tone that indicates her final acceptance of whatever her new identity may be. This sequence is perhaps the most suffused of all with Cukor's personal touch, for he identifies keenly with Eliza's isolation and bravery in facing an uncertain future, as he had long been doing and so many of his other characters do. His visual filming style here, mixed with the echo of her early song, enables the audience to share those bittersweet feelings. She strides to their cab with Freddy and allows herself just a brief momentary look back before she moves on forever. We might wonder if Eliza would wind up running a flower shop with Freddy after all, as Shaw rudely suggests in his epilogue, but with a more satisfying result for her emotionally, given Cukor's more engaging view of Freddy, and even financially as a woman in charge of a small business.

Cukor shared the view of most critics that Hepburn was not fully credible as the dirty flower girl in the opening of the film, straining somewhat to put on a Cockney accent. He accepted Lambert's observation that Wendy Hiller, who gives a magnificent performance in the earlier *Pygmalion* film, is one of the few actresses who could pull off the Cockney parts of the role, with her sturdy peasant features and stalwart manner. Andrews, in the surviving fragments of her stage performance, although thoroughly British unlike Hepburn, seems too fresh and sunny for the early sections' establishment of the "verbal class distinction" that ruthlessly governs English society.

But repeated viewings of *My Fair Lady*, while watching it for what it is rather than as it could have been with another actress, make clear that Hepburn gives an honorable performance as the flower girl. The musical stylization and Cukor's guidance of her badinage with Higgins help us accept her skillful impersonation. Nevertheless, it's inescapable that Hepburn, an actual aristocrat by birth, is better suited for the delicate, regal appearance she assumes at the ball as her new personality shines through. Rex Harrison, who tended to disparage both Andrews and Hepburn ungenerously, later said, "Eliza Doolittle is intended to be distinctly ill at ease in European ballrooms. Bloody Audrey has never spent a day of her life *out* of European ballrooms." Hiller carries off the transformation with a strain believably evident in her appearance and manner during those parts of the *Pygmalion* film.

Undoubtedly, the ideal Eliza in *My Fair Lady* would speak and sing with the same voice and be equally convincing in both guises, but that's almost too much to ask of any one actress, even Julie Andrews. As a result, the film of *My Fair Lady* gives us a dual sense of the character that is never entirely resolved and to some extent works against the film. Having two women, in effect, play the same part subtly undercuts Eliza's transformation into a different person; part of her sings as beautifully as Marni Nixon all along, although that surreal condition could be read as Eliza, through Higgins, managing to liberate her inner Marni Nixon, if not her inner Julie Andrews. In any case, while watching the film of *My Fair Lady*, I can't help thinking of a comment Jean Renoir made in 1968: "I hate dubbing. I even believe that in a period of high civilisation, like the twelfth century, if people had done dubbing in films they would have been burned in the public square for pretending that man may have one body and two souls."

And yet in that transformation theme is a deeply moving idea, taken directly from Shaw, that stresses how human personality, though mutable, exists in its social context and how that determines how we regard people. Eliza shares that insight when she goes to visit Higgins's mother (Gladys Cooper). The elegant and tolerant elderly woman's wide, bright, and spacious drawing room, as Shaw indicates, indicates her good taste in furnishings, unlike her childish son's penchant for living amid clutter and knickknacks. When Mrs. Higgins commiserates at tea with Eliza about how she has been so crudely treated by her son after her triumph at the ball, Eliza, serenely in close-up and intercut with Henry glaring from across the room, gives her the benefit of the wisdom she has gained: "You see, Mrs. Higgins, apart from the things one can pick up, the difference between a lady and a flower girl is not how she behaves but how she is treated."

When Higgins makes his blustering entry into his mother's abode and remonstrates with Eliza, he is vainly attempting, less successfully than before, to hide his need for her. His torrent of mixed flattery and peevish abuse does not convince her to return to him. She has learned to become independent and is considering teaching phonetics and/or marrying Freddy, the latter a nod to Shaw's mischievous epilogue about how that fate awaits her as a comforting if inadequate consolation for her entry into society.

Shaw mightily resisted ending his play with the conventional romantic resolution, but he went along with a "happy ending" for the 1938 film. When I interviewed the veteran British actor Bramwell Fletcher, who knew Shaw and was doing a one-man show based on him in 1967, I asked what Shaw would have thought of the ending of *My Fair Lady*, in which Fletcher under-studied Harrison and Edward Mulhare. "It wasn't what Shaw intended," he replied. "Would he have liked it?" I asked. And Fletcher replied, "Of course he wouldn't. But he would have liked the money." So too did Jack Warner, whose company invested more money in the film of *My Fair Lady* than any other screen musical had cost to date, $17 million (the equivalent of $171 million in 2024), including a record $5.5 million for the rights to the show. And Cukor, being pragmatic, didn't fight him over the ending.

But I don't think he would have been inclined to do so if he had the chance, even if that compromise ending predictably gave cannon fodder to the snobs who disparaged the film. The British film ends rather coldly and somewhat ambiguously with Higgins turning his back to Eliza and the camera, block-ing his face from view in close-up and showing us only his hat, as he demands to know where his slippers are. Cukor stages the scene more emotionally: Hig-gins, by himself, turns on his recording of her voice from her first visit to his home and walks slowly to a chair. He sits facing us, leaning forward pen-sively, hands clasped, as the camera slowly moves in to a close-up of him at a rare loss.

Cukor cuts to Eliza entering the room in a pink gown and hat, fully a lady now. She listens to herself quizzically and looks on Higgins with kind amuse-ment as she takes in his absorption in the recording. Then she turns off the machine and says, in an echo of the old flower-girl self that still partly exists within her, "I washed my face and 'ands before I come, I did."

Higgins responds by lifting his head slowly, murmuring "Eliza?" and smil-ing privately, straightening up in his chair, but he doesn't turn around to let her see his feelings. He says with his now-transparent bluff, "Where the devil are my slippers?" while tilting his hat over his eyes and leaning back with pleasure. Cukor ends the film in a wide two-shot of both of them facing for-ward, but with Higgins's eyes covered, as she walks toward him, smiling, on the fadeout. The orchestra is playing a reprise of "I Could Have Danced All Night" as the end title appears over a bank of red carnations, a reprise of the floral montage behind the main title credits.

With the warmth, the nuance, the subtlety that characterize his best work, Cukor took a stage show that managed to make a hit of a love story without a love scene or overt love song and carefully prepared the audience to accept Eliza Doolittle and Henry Higgins as partners, however unconventional and uncertain their partnership may be. Cukor spent a lifetime living unconventionally while necessarily respecting the conventions of heterosexual love onscreen yet also subtly countering them with a myriad of nuances and variations he found in human relationships that question the conventions. Cukor's definition of "partners" was not simply sexual or romantic, not exclusively physical, intellectual, or emotional, but volatile and stimulating blends of those ingredients.

If the "confirmed old bachelors" Higgins and Colonel Pickering and their Galatea-turned-real woman Eliza can all share a home and a profession and be partners with one another, Cukor accepts that as what Noël Coward would make of it, a natural design for living. *Two* human beings are transformed in *My Fair Lady*, Eliza Doolittle and Henry Higgins, a pair of dreamers in the finest Cukor tradition, and the film is, among other things, a tribute to the artful workings of his métier and a testament to the value of collaboration.

25

ANNA KARINA AND DIRK BOGARDE
IN *JUSTINE*

I always have a special place in my heart for a *film maudit*. What Jean Cocteau defined as a "cursed film" is one that has been damaged in some way and snubbed or worse by reviewers. Such films are often among the most daring, most personal works of their directors and have suffered because of that very audacity or from the tragic or tragicomic circumstances of their making or release, such as Cukor's *Sylvia Scarlett*, *A Star Is Born*, and *The Chapman Report*. Another such film is his *Justine*, based on parts of Lawrence Durrell's poetic tetralogy of novels, the Alexandria Quartet, *Justine*, *Balthazar*, *Mountolive*, and *Clea* (1960–1961). Molly Haskell, in one of the few sympathetic reviews the film received on its release in 1969 (another was from Vincent Canby in the *New York Times*), noted parenthetically in the *Village Voice*, "Incidentally, I am proceeding on the foregone and needless-to-belabor conclusion that any attempt to adapt the Alexandria Quartet is categorically insane."

The seemingly impossible project had already defeated the writer-director Joseph L. Mankiewicz, who was renowned for the literary nature of his screenplays, and numerous other writers, including Ivan Moffat (who had co-scripted *Bhowani Junction*) and even the critic Andrew Sarris (who had panned *My Fair Lady* and married Haskell in 1969, after *Justine* was released). Cukor came aboard the troubled project after Joseph Strick, who had begun directing it on location in Tunis in September 1968 from a screenplay by

Lawrence B. Marcus, was fired by Twentieth Century-Fox's president, Richard D. Zanuck.

Zanuck recalled the company and turned to the director he had worked with on *The Chapman Report* to finish *Justine* at the West Los Angeles studio as a patchwork rescue job incorporating and trying to match some of Strick's footage with its largely inherited cast. *Justine* was produced by Cukor's old frenemy Pandro S. Berman, who had recoiled in horror from the gender-bending *Sylvia Scarlett* but now was supervising a much gamier project in the permissive period following the collapse of the Production Code.

Cukor badly needed a job at that point in his career, despite the fact that his last film had won him the Oscar as best director in 1965. He had chosen an inopportune time to try to launch himself as a producer-director with a company he formed in 1963, G-D-C. The studio system was in a terminal state in the late sixties, with the major studios foundering amid chaotic social change and barely functioning. They were turning to younger, largely untried talent while being swallowed up by corporate conglomerates. Cukor's skills had been honed in that collapsing system and were not attuned to doing business in the New Hollywood. Most veteran Hollywood directors were struggling or retiring, but Cukor valiantly soldiered on regardless, since film-making was his raison d'être, and kept working until 1981, although only intermittently.

Numerous projects he tried to float in the wake of *My Fair Lady* found no takers, although a couple came close. His most cherished were an adaptation of James M. Barrie's *Peter Pan* to star Audrey Hepburn; *The Nine Tiger Man*, a satirical romance from a novel by Lesley Blanch largely set during the Indian rebellion of 1857; Cukor's biopic of D. W. Griffith, *Twilight Revelers*, with Gregory Peck; and *The Bloomer Girl*, the story of the nineteenth-century feminist Amelia Bloomer, the inventor of bloomers for women and a crusader for women's suffrage. That was a film Cukor hoped Katharine Hepburn would star in along with Shirley MacLaine and Harry Belafonte. Cukor even considered doing a tragicomic behind-the-scenes making-of film about his abortive Marilyn Monroe project *Something's Got to Give*, to be jokingly titled *It's What's on the Screen That Counts*.

His project *Vicky*, about Victoria Woodhull, the free love advocate and first woman to run for president of the United States, from a script by James Costigan, author of *Love Among the Ruins*, with a rewrite by James Toback, also failed to happen. Toback thought *Vicky* fell through in 1977 because of Cukor's depression after the debacle of his 1976 Russian film, *The Blue Bird*, a leaden fantasy based on the 1908 play by Maurice Maeterlinck made under extremely trying conditions in the USSR. Cukor "was not ready emotionally to do another movie," Toback told Patrick McGilligan. "The critics were able to convince him that perhaps he should never make another movie. He could dismiss the critics as morons and ignoramuses, yet on more than just a practical level, he needed them."

Fascinating as Cukor's unmade late projects sound, and regrettable as it was that they fell through, his staying available even for a patchwork job enabled him to keep his hand in for films that did come to fruition. His late work included his eccentric but endearing and stylish film loosely based on Graham Greene's novel *Travels with My Aunt* (1972) and one final masterpiece, the TV movie *Love Among the Ruins* (1975). And despite his setback with *The Blue Bird*, he became active again with his relatively routine TV movie version of Emlyn Williams's autobiographical play about a schoolteacher and her young Welsh coalminer protégé, *The Corn Is Green* (1979, starring Katharine Hepburn), and his spotty but sporadically engaging final film, *Rich and Famous* (1981), made when he was eighty-one, the oldest director up to that time ever to make a film for a major Hollywood studio.

Cukor's adventurousness and adaptability in his old age was the happy byproduct of his lifelong resilience in the face of turmoil and changing times. He also benefited from a rare quality Lesley Blanch astutely commented on in a 1961 letter to Kenneth Tynan for his *Holiday* profile of Cukor: "I think he has not, or has passed, *ambition*, in the destructive sense. This makes him utterly free. And being perfectly sure of who he is, what he is, he does not envy—is not eaten up by competition." When he returned to Hollywood from the nightmarish experience of *The Blue Bird*, I asked him how he had learned to cope, and he said,

> First of all, to go into the theater or the movies is folly and madness. But there is something that urges us to go and do it, and if that urge is strong enough it should sustain us. I don't go on about things; I don't luxuriate in suffering. You can't. People are nattering at you, they bring their problems to you, and you have to very charmingly say, "Fuck that." . . . When we were shooting *Love Among the Ruins* in London, we went out at 8 o'clock one

Sunday morning—it was the only time we could work at a certain location—
and Kate Hepburn said, "Aren't we in a wonderful business where we can
see these beautiful things and work in these beautiful places?" Well, you'd
see that in her face. It renewed *her* enthusiasm. I think sour, disillusioned
people are just bores.

Cukor was happy to step in with only a week's preparation to take over the
reins of *Justine*, since it was the kind of sophisticated literary material that
stimulated his creativity, and he welcomed the chance to work again with Dirk
Bogarde, with whom he had become friends on another emergency operation, *Song Without End*. *Justine* also gave Cukor the opportunity to plunge
into the new freedom directors were allowed in handling the kind of sexual

25.1.   Dirk Bogarde and Anna Karina are standouts in the motley cast of *Justine* (1969), a troubled
production inherited by Cukor from Joseph Strick, who had been fired after location work in
Tunis. Cukor had a close rapport with these two actors playing doomed characters in the visually
lush adaptation of Lawrence Durrell's Alexandria Quartet. Karina is the tubercular belly dancer,
Melissa, the most open-hearted character in the mazelike story, and Bogarde is the British con-
sular official, Pursewarden, who almost inadvertently becomes a traitor to the empire.

Source: Twentieth Century-Fox.

material that only a few years earlier would have been impossible to deal with. There still were some censorship restrictions on what Cukor could shoot, and he intended the film to run about three hours, although the release version runs 116 minutes. It shows the results of being worked over roughly with its often jagged continuity, gaping story holes in the byzantine Durrell adaptation plugged with heavy-handed voiceover narration, and jarring shifts between Strick's slack location work and Cukor's lively studio shooting. Cukor and his visual staff did their best to try to blend the mishmash into something resembling coherence.

He was working under a considerable handicap in having to use Strick's location footage for about a quarter of the film. When François Truffaut was asked by the *New York Times* in 1970 what his least favorite recent American film was, he replied, any film directed by Joseph Strick, from *Ulysses* to *Tropic of Cancer*: "I loathe Strick. He has done the most damaging thing a moviemaker can do with his career, with his morality. He has tried to conceal his weaknesses by choosing the great literature of the world to put on the screen, a task for which he is easily the world's least qualified person." (Strick also directed film versions of Jean Genet's play *The Balcony* and the James Joyce novel that preceded *Ulysses*, *A Portrait of the Artist as a Young Man*.)

Although it was no surprise when *Justine* resulted in a colossal box office bomb, few people in the know placed the primary blame on Cukor, and a few discerning cinephiles recognized the quality of what he had achieved under such duress. Ragged and fragmentary though it is, *Justine* is a lush, beautifully textured film, ravishingly shot by Leon Shamroy, one of the masters of color cinematography, particularly renowned for his work with women (he tied with Joseph Ruttenberg for the most Oscars for cinematography, four, including for *Leave Her to Heaven* and *Cleopatra*). *Justine* is startling in its modernity even today for a film by a director who had come up through the system and was and still is by most people regarded as a classical, if not conventional, stylist. Aside from Orson Welles with his independent project *The Other Side of the Wind*, no other veteran Hollywood director among the few who continued working in the waning days of the studio system made such an outré, racy, sexually and stylistically adventurous film during that transitional period. The audacious visual gambles Cukor had begun taking with his postwar neorealist films and expressionistic color films paid off again as he managed against all odds to put his artistic stamp on a film that, *maudit* or not, remains enchanting and harrowing, often simultaneously, in its louche mixture of decadence and despondent moods, characterizations, and visual atmosphere.

Cukor and Shamroy (who had long been known for his willingness to experiment) freely use handheld, prowling cameras, subtly disguised uses of the newly fashionable zoom lens, and montages blending group shots with tight close-ups, some using image-compressing long lenses, to immerse the viewer in the decadent, disorienting atmosphere of Alexandria. The film achieves what Canby in his *Times* review called "an exquisite cinematic beauty. . . . *Justine* is a movie of so much opulence that the eye and ear are constantly persuading the mind to take a rest."

The camera follows the audience surrogate figure, the young Irish writer and teacher Darley (Michael York), through the labyrinthine streets and shabby nightclubs and dwellings of 1936 Alexandria as he becomes immersed in the polyglot Egyptian city's alluring but appalling corruption. Haskell felt that Cukor's grafting of new studio footage onto another director's location work succeeded against the odds in "conjuring up a sense of place, that wholly real and wholly imaginary city of the senses, Alexandria. . . . Cukor's interiors are brilliantly detailed, aged, lustrous." The art direction, with its delicate blend of fantasy and stark naturalism, was by William J. Creber, whose credits included *The Greatest Story Ever Told* and *Planet of the Apes*, and Jack Martin Smith, who was known for his work on classic MGM musicals for the Arthur Freed unit. The film's assistant art director, Fred Harpman, worked again for Cukor on *Rich and Famous*; the set decoration for *Justine* was by Raphael Bretton and Walter M. Scott.

Following a crudely cobbled-together expository opening with Darley introducing us to some of the characters, including screen-filling shots of the sphinx-like face of the enigmatic Justine (Anouk Aimée), the film rivets our attention with a pulsating nightclub scene in which a sickly belly dancer, Melissa (Anna Karina), performs frenetically with an entourage of drag queens. The cutting is unusually fast for a Cukor film, the camera angles intimate and disturbingly voyeuristic. Melissa freaks out after being drugged with Spanish fly in her champagne by a group of rowdy sailors pawing her (a scene reminiscent of the gang rape of Naomi in *The Chapman Report*) and runs out screaming through the packed slum streets, collapsing outside

Darley's apartment. He rescues her, enlisting the help of Pursewarden (Bogarde), an intoxicated British diplomatic official who is another of the desperate figures providing Darley with his unsentimental education.

York's Darley is largely a passive character, something of a cipher; the actor is adequate in his underwritten role, which is similar to his more appealing Christopher Isherwood surrogate figure in Bob Fosse's 1972 *Cabaret*, similarly set in a decadent prewar environment (in that case Weimar Berlin during the period of the rise of Nazism). The script process was burdened with the plethora of characters who intersect in Durrell's overlapping narratives from differing points of view. The film retains many but not all of the featured characters and does not attempt to emulate the multiple viewpoints, opting instead for a simpler, unsatisfying, but perhaps inevitably linear storyline. Cukor's primary interest goes to two lost souls, Melissa and Pursewarden, played by simpatico actors he found "really lent themselves" to their self-destructive roles. Like similarly tragic characters in previous Cukor films, they are captives of their addictions and ruinous sexual involvements, making gallant but doomed attempts to survive the corrupting influences that enmesh them.

Cukor found the leading lady he inherited, Anouk Aimée, to be a "blank, boring wall. She didn't try and she was indomitably refined—wouldn't do the coarseness of it." Aimée, a Parisian who had become an international star in Claude Lelouch's awful piece of romantic schlock, *Un homme et une femme/A Man and a Woman* (1966), was one of the few actresses Cukor openly despised. She earned that status with her intransigence and her attempt to bail out of the film before it was finished to pursue her love affair with Albert Finney, but a threat of a lawsuit by Fox persuaded her to stick around for the finish.

Nevertheless, although a better, more committed actress would have dug deeper into the complex role, Aimée is a stunning camera subject who lends herself well to playing an enigma, albeit one without much logic or sense of agency who has to carry more weight thematically than her performance merits. Justine Hosnani is a nonpracticing Jew who believes in Zionism. By sleeping with various men, she works with her wealthy husband, Nessim (John Vernon), a Coptic Christian banker, in their arms smuggling to Palestine for the Jewish insurgency against the British. That subplot is barely sketched in and holds little interest for Cukor. The political intrigue is mostly relegated to the clumsy and inadequate voiceovers, much like the way the political conflicts in India were treated in the studio makeover of Cukor's *Bhowani Junction*.

But on a visual level and through Jerry Goldsmith's haunting score, Cukor intermittently succeeds in making Justine seem dangerously alluring to Darley. She uses him as she does other men, while claiming at the end in a sop to his youthful naïveté, "There were times I simply adored you." The director's genuine romanticism was always tempered with a shrewd understanding of the disillusioning ways of the world, and with this decadent material and at this stage of his career, Cukor was mostly interested in examining the illusory nature of romantic entanglements. His camera explores the sexual underground of Alexandria, including a child brothel (which he had to

25.2. Cukor with Karina relaxing between takes of *Justine*. The Danish actress was the muse of Jean-Luc Godard, with whom she made eight films and became an icon of the French Nouvelle Vague. She continued her career in European films after working on *Justine* in Hollywood but looked back on her work with Cukor fondly.

Source: Twentieth Century-Fox.

suggest, with difficulty, by using little people) in which Justine searches for her possibly mythical lost child, who represents her own vanished sense of self.

The uneducated Melissa, who is called the simplest of the characters and the only one who is "exactly what she seemed to be," is poignantly devoted to Darley despite his reckless attraction to Justine, who resembles Dietrich's Lola Lola in drawing men seductively to her "like moths around a flame." Karina, the Danish actress who had been Jean-Luc Godard's muse in numerous films earlier in the decade, plays the tubercular, drug-addicted part-time prostitute Melissa as a badly used woman who is resigned to her victimhood yet continually hopes vainly for someone to help her escape her entrapment. Haskell singled out Karina's performance for praise: "Cukor enables us, if not to respond deeply, at least to almost smell her cheap perfume and feel the dead weight of her cheerful exhaustion."

Cukor's heart goes out to Melissa, with her shabby attempts at glamour in cheap yellow clothing and floral decorations, her desperate simulation of gaiety as she feigns a sexually alluring persona in the nightclub, and her emaciated look as she plays sweet but pathetic sexual games with Darley, inscribing love messages on each other's bodies with lipstick. Those were the first nude scenes shot by Cukor to reach the screen; Strick had shot the formulaic sequence of Aimée, with her spindly, modelish figure, romping naked in the surf with Darley watching. Melissa's innocent involvement in the arms-smuggling plot, whose workings she guilelessly reveals to Pursewarden after Darley abandons her for Justine, leads to the suicide of that British official.

Bogarde's expertise at playing tormented characters is at its most acute under Cukor's trusted guidance. Soon after he first appears in the film dancing in drunken revelry, he is shown in silhouette in his hotel room, with a muezzin chanting outside at dusk. Pursewarden murmurs with a catch in his voice an ambiguous self-judgment: "the perfection of him who chooseth not male or female for his partner, nor any like him." The camera follows him through a deep shadow and tracks in to a mirror, his image sliding woozily back into view as he swallows a drink and studies himself with disgust before spitting at his face in the mirror. When Darley silently enters the shot in the mirror behind him, Pursewarden, an inconsolably lonely man, tells him wisely, "Go to bed, Brother Ass."

Pursewarden's jaded nature can't eradicate his feelings, and he seeks temporary refuge with Darley's castaway, asking her imploringly, "Melissa, tell me, how do you defend yourself against loneliness, Melissa?" She replies with flat, unselfpitying resignation, "I have become loneliness itself." When Justine later asks Pursewarden teasingly whether he is a homosexual, he nonchalantly answers yes, his voice indicating that such categorization is too simplistic, but she taunts him because he shows insufficient interest in her sexual favors. Pursewarden regards her manipulation of men from various social strata with a mixture of revulsion, amusement, and helpless fascination. He is a character made for Cukor: his existence is a set of clashing "half-tones, suggested and never over-stressed," as Henri Langlois described the director's approach to portraying the nuances of human existence.

Another Cukor alcoholic, Pursewarden turns to the bottle to blur the guilt he feels because of his longtime incestuous affair with his blind sister (Elaine Church, another actress Cukor regretted inheriting, who plays her scenes with a dimwitted smile). When his sister tries vainly to become betrothed to his British governmental superior, Mountolive (George Baker), whom he serves as first secretary, Pursewarden is shattered, an emotion he struggles movingly to disguise. Part of Pursewarden's tragedy is that his intelligence makes him acutely aware of the foolishness of his actions. He allows his compulsions to destroy his public life when his indiscreet involvement with Justine and her anti-British plot makes him, if only peripherally, a traitor to the British Empire. Melissa, relaxing in a bathtub, has innocently revealed to him the extent of this plot "to butcher John Bull," while wondering with a little childish laugh, "Why does everybody hate the English? I think the king and queen are *so* dignified."

Pursewarden's suicide while on the telephone to Justine in his hotel room, in the half-light of dawn to the sound of another muezzin's chant, is as moving as anything in Cukor. Gradually breaking into tears, he bitterly reveals his awareness of how she has used him and tells her he has turned her and her husband in to Mountolive, ending their intrigue. "Ah! What a filthy world," he murmurs before biting on a cyanide capsule, grimacing and making a faint cry as he plummets to the floor.

More than any of his other films to date, *Justine* partakes of both sides of Cukor, the man of worldly elegance and the man acquainted with the secretive, louche side of life. His late films allow us glimpses of how this artist, whose dreams and dreads were both public and private, was able to portray those varied shadings while keeping his emotional equilibrium, in large part through his aesthetic sense. For all its unevenness, unfinished state, and sense of gathering darkness, the lush texture of *Justine* shows how Cukor could find a paradoxical beauty in portraying even the most squalid parts of life. Lesley Blanch called him "a voluptuary in the true classical sense—able to enjoy the greatest luxuries and the smallest toys; finds exquisite pleasures in many ways; which is probably the secret of living."

26

MAGGIE SMITH, ALEC McCOWEN, LOU GOSSETT, ROBERT STEPHENS, AND CINDY WILLIAMS IN *TRAVELS WITH MY AUNT*

n Cukor's later, liberated years, like other aging artists in times of change, he was freer to be himself than he had ever been before. Going his own way blithely indifferent to contemporary trends, like Duke Ellington, Georgia O'Keeffe, and John Ford, yet drawing inspiration from exciting new developments throughout the world of cinema, Cukor often seemed avant-garde in his mischievous audacity and stylistic flamboyance, even if his films were sometimes erratic. This period brought us the louche and often lovely, campy, and whimsically morbid *Travels with My Aunt*; his raunchy and tender celebration of female sexuality and friendship, *Rich and Famous*; and his impeccably crafted and deeply felt final masterpiece about a long-interrupted but enduring romance, *Love Among the Ruins*. In these films he explored recherché realms of sensuality and romance and furthered his career-long concentration on sexual unconventionality and fluidity. Cukor's late journey of self-revelation met approval from knowledgeable critics even if his films were not always widely noticed or accepted.

Hollywood figures are often anxious about accepting career achievement awards because they think it signifies their careers are over in the eyes of their peers. Cukor's struggling to find work after his Oscar for *My Fair Lady*—widely seen as both a tribute to the impeccable craftsmanship of that film and as a belated award for his entire body of work—showed the melancholy truth of that concern. But this indefatigably doughty survivor plowed ahead and put his distinct, if not always recognized, personal signature on the disparate "go" projects that came his way. Cukor's enthusiastic willingness to work for television at a time when that medium was still thoughtlessly looked down upon in Hollywood as inferior to feature films was a sign of his eagerness to keep working but also a measure of his pragmatism about change in the industry. He showed a cheerful resilience in the face of setbacks that would have driven most old directors into embittered retirement.

As it turned out, *Love Among the Ruins*, a collaboration with two old friends who had never worked together before, Katharine Hepburn and Laurence Olivier, was a triumph for all three of them. Not only did they all win Emmy Awards for that 1975 TV movie, but it showed Cukor as ahead of his time in appreciating the value of that medium. Television (and later cable TV and streaming) was taking over the function of making literate drama—dialogue-driven movies about people rather than robots, superheroes, and special effects—for an adult audience when the American feature-film industry was devolving into a medium of tent-pole spectacles primarily aimed at the juvenile demographic. (This book will break chronology to end with that splendid film Cukor made for television, since *Love Among the Ruins* showed him at the peak of his creative strengths toward the end of his career and is a better way to go out with Cukor than his uneven final feature, *Rich and Famous*.)

Cukor's return to his old studio, MGM, with *Travels with My Aunt* (1972) was supposed to have reunited him with Hepburn, whom he hadn't directed since *Pat and Mike* at MGM twenty years earlier. *Travels* is based on the idiosyncratic, highly uneven 1969 grab-bag of Graham Greene stories masquerading as a picaresque novel. Jay Presson Allen, the screenwriter of *Marnie* and *The Prime of Miss Jean Brodie*, shares screenplay credit on the Cukor film with Hugh Wheeler, who did a discarded earlier draft. Allen told Patrick McGilligan that *Travels with My Aunt* only came together for Cukor because of the fierce efforts of Hepburn to find him a job at a time when he was in another career trough. But Allen explained the travails that resulted as the project foundered because the box office and critical failure of Hepburn's 1969 film *The Madwoman of Chaillot* made her not want "to play another crazy old lady. . . . However, she would never admit it. She was loyal to George and reluctant to let him down. George wanted desperately to work, and as she began to withdraw or find problems, he became frantic. . . . He couldn't afford to deal with Kate, the real problem, because he would lose the project." Allen kept working on the script, ostensibly to satisfy Hepburn's demands, but felt the actress actually wanted to get out of the project. The screenplay Hepburn herself wrote, Allen said, was "pretty good. . . . but she *still* didn't want to play it. . . . The script they went with had one big speech of mine. Otherwise, it was all Kate's."

When James Aubrey, the notoriously destructive head of MGM at the time, eventually fired Hepburn, Cukor wanted to quit in solidarity, but Hepburn insisted he continue. Allen said the Writers Guild of America in its credit arbitration disregarded her own disavowal of script authorship and support of Hepburn's, not wanting to award credit to a nonmember of the guild. So *Travels with My Aunt* is a Cukor-Hepburn collaboration without Hepburn in the cast but with Maggie Smith playing a sort of camp parody of a Hepburn-style septuagenarian grande dame mixed with her own formidable theatrical mannerisms in blatantly unreal old-lady makeup.

Smith was thirty-seven at the time and had won an Oscar as best actress for her arch and biting portrayal of a haughty, fascistic Scottish schoolteacher in 1969's *Jean Brodie*. The casting of a middle-aged actress as the flamboyant, dotty, criminally nonconformist adventurer Augusta Bertram in *Travels with My Aunt* allowed Cukor the opportunity for three visually sumptuous flash-backs, two of which are the highlights of the film emotionally as well. That would not have been possible had Hepburn played the role, although Allen reported that she and Cukor clashed over his desire to have Hepburn play her younger self in flashbacks. That would only have worked if it had been done in a sketchy, highly stylized way, as the young actress Jessica Medlicott (Hepburn) is suggested in brief snippets of fantasy imagery in the courtroom in *Love Among the Ruins*. On balance, it is fortunate that Smith played Aunt Augusta rather than Hepburn, although the extremely campy style of her per-formance is the major aesthetic question raised by the film.

A not-unsympathetic but understandably nonplussed reaction to the spec-tacle of Smith swanning with abandon around Cukor's lavishly appointed Panavision frames was offered by Roger Greenspun in his *New York Times* review. Although Smith "seems to have surrounded her character rather than to have inhabited it," Greenspun felt that Cukor's deceptively light film not only has "great charm" but "surprising emotional complexity." *Travels with*

My Aunt, he wrote, is "full of privileged moments, lucid, controlled and grace-ful, and any of them might serve to epitomize the style and the meaning of the valuable cinema of George Cukor."

The picaresque misadventures of Augusta and her timid, bourgeois "nephew" (actually a secret son) Henry Pulling in some characteristically seedy precincts of Greeneland struck some observers as something of a private joke by the great novelist. The novel not only lacks coherence even as a series of interconnecting stories but lurches from heavily tongue-in-cheek, dilatory epi-sodes in its first half to a jarring excursion in the second part into dark realms less suited to one of Greene's so-called entertainments than to his more overtly serious fiction involving bleak and treacherous international journeys. Trans-porting the lightly portrayed, mildly amusing characters over from the first section to the second, more violent part doesn't work well.

The screenwriters and director wisely jettison the grimmest elements of Greene's rickety, rather random plot structure, such as the murder in Para-guay of Augusta's slippery but charmingly roguish Black companion, Wordsworth (Lou Gossett), and the involvement of Henry (Alec McCowen) in a smuggling operation. Instead they concentrate on two intersecting threads that follow Henry's emotional liberation and Augusta's romantic disillusion-ment. In the process, the aunt who is really Henry's mother (a secret it takes him a comically long time to recognize) forms a bond with him that enriches both of their personalities, enabling them to discard the dead weight of their pasts while pointing the way to a more vital, but unknown, new direction together. "It's the *traveling* that's interesting," she explains to Henry, calling it a means for "the accumulation of memories."

Travels with My Aunt is partly a film *about* the past and its deceptive roman-tic allure and the need to let old illusions go; it is simultaneously an old man's film and an exhilaratingly youthful film. Few directors of Cukor's generation were making such vital work in that era; Billy Wilder was one who did. He made a film with some similar concerns and story patterns that same year, *Avanti!* Both films were shot extensively on European locations and deal with sexual liberation, the bracing impact of foreign adventure and criminality shaking up a conventional life for the better, and a complicated relationship between contemporary hedonism and past conceptions of romanticism. It was fascinating to see how Cukor and Wilder, who had both become regarded as passé in the United States as a result of the youth movement of that period, transformed themselves partly by necessity and partly by choice into European filmmakers, Wilder in a flight back to his personal and professional roots and the equally cosmopolitan Cukor escaping to the continent of his ancestors. Cukor in those years enjoyed hosting an annual luncheon at his home for the directors of films nominated for the best-foreign-language film Academy Award. His role as a sage and bon vivant living in splendidly continental style and receiving distinguished foreign guests, writers as well as directors, in his villa off Sunset Boulevard helped redefine his image as a man far more au courant than most of his aging peers.

Travels with My Aunt "creates a feeling of a dream-like labyrinth through life," Andrew Sarris wrote in his *Village Voice* review, praising the film's sumptuous mise-en-scène with its "bursts of color amid assured pacing and grading that mark Cukor's mastery of the medium." Cukor introduces Augusta

26.1. The younger Augusta Bertram (Maggie Smith) in the most sumptuously filmed scene of *Travels with My Aunt* (1972), the flashback in which she meets Mr. Visconti (Robert Stephens), the con man who will break her heart. Their waltz in the Buffet de la Gare de Lyon/Le Train Bleu is already bittersweet, since it shows the schoolgirl's loss of innocence to the predatory roué.

Source: MGM/Alamy.

to us under the credits as a youthful aesthetic object, the model for a faux Modigliani nude lovingly caressed by the camera as it tracks closely along her body under the credits (we don't get to see the full painting, resplendent with red pubic hair, a display that causes Henry some humorous embarrassment, until it is sold on the black market at the climax of the movie). The elderly, disreputable Augusta reencounters Henry for the first time since his baptism when she barges into his (putative) mother's cremation ceremony, a farcical event in this whimsically morbid film that is obsessed with death and decay but is at heart Cukor's cocking a snook at mortality.

Augusta has spent her life pining for the rogue she considers "the only man I have ever really loved," the man who in fact seduced her as a schoolgirl and has been her emotional abuser and user ever since (we have to suspend disbelief to accept Smith as a schoolgirl, which we are easily able to do because that flashback is so visually and emotionally ravishing). Ercole Visconti (Robert Stephens, Smith's husband at that time), a suave Italian cad, pimp, and thief who appears from the start to everyone but Augusta an obvious creature of artifice, is a con man and ladies' man, a dandy with carefully waved hair, florid mustache, elegant attire, and a musical lisp he uses in his practiced seduction song routine.

Visconti and Augusta share a memorable, sumptuously filmed dance in the iconic Buffet de la Gare de Lyon (now the Le Train Bleu) restaurant of that historic Paris train station. Elaborating considerably with richness of texture and detail on the sequence as it is laid out in the script, Cukor and his cinematographer, Douglas Slocombe, film the period flashback sequence with a briskly flowing, breathlessly romantic feeling, using quick cuts of tight two-shots swooping and gliding through the restaurant, often using long lenses and diffusion to stylize the imagery of Augusta's cherished moment from her past.

The entrée to the flashback is a shot of the elderly woman reminiscing while seated in the restaurant, a slow zoom in to a close-up that becomes a magical panning shot (apparently seamless though joined via optical effects) as it picks up Visconti, decades earlier, prowling the floor for a new conquest. The camera gracefully zooms back from a violinist to a wide shot of dancers as Visconti passes among them, and then it tracks in from an overhead view and cranes down, following him to a station window. He spots the youthful Augusta with her group of schoolgirls headed for a train. She stands out amid their gray uniforms because of her height and flowing red hair. Two bright red lights in the gloom of the tracks, together with her hair, provide signs of danger: Visconti is the devil come to tempt her.

With a wordless interchange of shots accompanied by the film's graceful waltz theme by Tony Hatch, Visconti with his charming grin and repeated waves of the head seduces Augusta to flee her reserved life and run to the train station restaurant, where she joins him in a waltz, the beginning of a long erratic affair that includes his installing her in a series of brothels. As she enters the rococo fin de siècle restaurant, Cukor's camera rushes in with a rapturous movement to capture her bedazzled look as she takes in the glamorous setting, her hands covering her mouth in awe. Visconti's outstretched hand enters the frame and takes hers, turning her head as he draws her into the waltz with seductive skill as the scene widens. The tight shots of their dancing are excitedly intercut by Cukor and John Bloom, the film's editor, as we see other dancers swirling around them. Augusta stares at ceiling frescoes of foreign adventures Visconti describes as they dance, holding out the prospect of life in "the company of kings and courtesans," the visual tour a precursor of the rambling but adventurous life she will lead, intermittently, with him. During their waltz, she loses her schoolgirl hat, which causes her to gasp but laugh.

With practiced technique, Visconti reaches behind his head and hands a bill to the violinist/orchestra leader, who knows exactly what romantic song to play next, "Serenade of Love" (by Jackie Trent and Hatch), the film's theme song and Visconti's regular seduction tool. He sings to Augusta as she stares at him enraptured in flowing two-shots ("Each time you smile at me, / I know that we should be / Together making dreams come true"). By the end of the sequence, the seduction is complete: her voice is joining his in a refrain about being together "making dreams come true."

An epitome of classical cinematic romanticism and the visual splendor of Cukor's late style, the sequence has a bittersweet Ophulsian feeling that, like the lyrical passages of dancing in *Letter from an Unknown Woman* and *Madame de . . .*, makes it at the same time a celebration and a critique of romanticism. Like Ophüls's master of ceremonies in *La ronde*, Cukor could say, "J'adore le passé," yet this film shows that he also scrutinizes Augusta's past and her deluded memories with a healthy skepticism. And the name Visconti (supplied by Greene but resonating cinematically) suggests echoes of the sumptuous ball and the aura of decadence and sense of mortality in Luchino Visconti's 1963 film, *The Leopard*.

One of the most exquisite and lyrical passages in Cukor's career, this waltz sequence in *Travels with My Aunt* would have been enough to make the whole project, with its checkered history, worthwhile. Although a lighter-than-air feeling is imparted by the flowing, intimate camerawork and the rapid cutting as young Augusta is swept along by her seducer, the undertone is melancholy. When we hear her voice joining his romantic song on the soundtrack, it turns out to be the aged voice of Aunt Augusta, whom we see on the dissolve back to 1972 remembering with mingled pleasure and pain as she sits with Henry in the restaurant. Henry's look of compassionate curiosity as he gazes at her in close-up is the warmest yet from this younger man who until now has viewed her with a jumble of emotions mostly highlighted by dread and contempt. The progression of Henry's understanding of this woman, who initially seems so alien to his puritanical, socially backward nature, is a major thread of the film, entwined with his own sentimental education through the often bawdy, dangerous events she guides him into experiencing for the first time. She tells him late in the film with passionate sadness, "Sometimes I get the awful feeling that I'm the only one left, anywhere, who finds any fun in [*clasping her fist*]—*life*."

Since the man she calls Mr. Visconti took her innocence, Augusta is perpetually fooled by the aging cad and is sent on a reckless mission to rescue him from a fabricated kidnapping attempt. Desperate to save the man she considers her inamorata, she drags Henry along, hoping to foster some kind of relationship with her son. He is an emotionally and sexually repressed, socially inept yet charmingly gentlemanly assistant bank manager. Calling herself "your last chance at life," she feels the need to rescue him from his life of terminal dullness in a London suburb. When she asks at the cemetery what he does besides work at the bank, he says primly, "I cultivate dahlias," a line followed by an exquisitely prolonged Maggie Smith pause as she takes in its direly absurd implications. The contrast Cukor draws throughout between McCowen's expertly droll low-key manner and precision of speech and Smith's wild flamboyance conveys much of the thematic importance of her transference of life to his initially deadly shell. McCowen's keen actorly intelligence and embodiment of his "dull" character without condescending to Henry

makes him a delicious counterpart to Augusta and a reactive audience identification figure throughout.

But Henry's comical failings as a human being urgently require Augusta's
intervention. His timid insularity is not the worst of his problems; his greatest flaw is the bourgeois contempt he expresses for the louche lifestyle of the
woman he does not realize is his mother, a moralistic sense of judgment Cukor,
Greene, and Hepburn (as screenwriter) do not share. But even so, the worst
opprobrium a Cukor character can hurl at another is that he or she has failed
to dream. In a mutually bitter long take in Wordsworth's apartment about
the fate of the stolen Modigliani, Henry declares to Augusta, "I have done
nothing wrong," tells her he despises Visconti, and berates her for "immoral-
ity." She grips Henry by the lapels and, as the camera holds on her anguished,
contorted face, explodes in her most passionate outburst, "You have done
nothing at all! Nothing, absolutely nothing. Oho! My poor Henry, you have
lived so—ooh, so *meagerly*. . . . I have always looked the world straight in
the eyes and I have never despised anyone. . . . You—you *risk* nothing—
[you've] *given* nothing—*suffered* nothing—*lost* nothing—*loved* nothing!
You even *dream* nothing! You—you take care, Henry. I am your last chance
at life; take me or leave me!"

Smith is an expert farceur, and her body language throughout the film is
balletic, her long arms and famously expressive wrists flailing for punctuation as her slender torso responds instinctively to the dramatic or comedic
needs of each situation; her interactions with McCowen, playing an ultrare-
served square with eloquent minimalism, are almost like Laurel and Hardy
comedy routines. The exquisite, justly celebrated way Smith puts elaborate
nuances on her lines of dialogue and the witty timing of her pauses are given
a thorough workout here along with her fluttery, wing-like gestures and the
almost liquid quality she imparts to her bodily movements.

The viewer may wonder, as many have, why Cukor and his team allowed
Smith to put on such extravagant makeup, encasing her face in a rubbery
old-lady mask, brazenly accented eye shadow and rouge, mouth garishly lip-
sticked, and flaming orange-red hair. Anthony Powell's ravishingly soignée,
Oscar-winning costuming sometimes garbs her in understated black and
white, as Cukor is fond of doing with his characters for contrast to heighten
the impact of the other colors in his scenes, but Powell sometimes goes all

26.2. The camp aspect of *Travels with My Aunt* is highlighted in the flamboyant old-age makeup worn by Smith. Here the outré Aunt Augusta in this adaptation of Graham Greene's picaresque novel is embarking on a hazardous mission abroad with her supposed nephew/secret son, the sexually repressed Englishman Henry Pulling (Alec McCowen).

Source: MGM.

out for fire-engine-red impact with her capes and gowns. It would have been possible to display a more subdued Aunt Augusta who still would have possessed sufficient wildness for the role.

But I believe Cukor was going for a camp style with Smith and the film in general. *Travels with My Aunt* is among the least naturalistic of his many stylistic experiments, one of his most extravagantly stylized films. In so doing, Cukor in his old age is boldly returning to the mode of his outré 1935 film *Sylvia Scarlett*, a similarly picaresque film that had become a cult classic over the years. As Susan Sontag noted in her 1964 essay on camp, "Camp is esoteric—something of a private code, a badge of identity even, among small urban cliques. . . . To camp is a mode of seduction—one which employs flamboyant mannerisms susceptible of a double interpretation; gestures full of duplicity, with a witty meaning for cognoscenti and another, more impersonal, for outsiders."

Cukor's direction of Smith's performance as such an artificial, highly theatrical form of role-playing is the essence of camp as well as consistent, in an exaggerated way, with his approach to character throughout his long body of work, "seeing the world as an aesthetic phenomenon," as Sontag writes of camp. *Travels* has particular affinities with the androgynous hero-ines of *Sylvia Scarlett* and *Camille*; Hepburn and Garbo could be considered sisters of Aunt Augusta. The metaphor of life as theater governs Cukor's entire body of work and was foregrounded increasingly as he aged and became more artistically self-conscious. So it is not surprising that Augus-ta's life is one long outré performance in high style, her every utterance and every move italicized, since she is living a life of commingled deceit, self-conscious mysteriousness, habitually seductive allure, and emotional eva-siveness. All of these are characteristics of the camp aesthetic that Cukor thoroughly enjoys, with his predominantly comic sensibility and fascination with exploring the interplay between genuine emotion and the manner of performing it.

Maggie Smith's tendency toward extravagant mannerisms and comple-mentary ability to imbue her playing with the subtlest nuances and ironies through her musically modulated voice and demonstrative body language makes her the perfect actress to embody a woman who lives her life as a self-conscious performance. With her large, saucer-like eyes, lithe, angular, almost cubistic figure, riotous fluidity of movement, and strikingly feminine yet also sharply vulpine appearance, Smith is physically ideal for the camp aesthetic. Sontag could have been describing that actress while commenting that one of the great images of camp sensibility is the androgyne, such as seen in the "swooning, slim, sinuous figures" of pre-Raphaelite painting and the "thin, flowing, sexless bodies" of art nouveau. The masklike makeup and the sensuous fabrics and outlandish colorings that surround Aunt Augusta are part of Cukor's way of ironizing both her ultrachic femininity and her mannish independence and aggressiveness, a collection of paradoxes Cukor relishes in a female character who often seems like a drag queen "perform-ing" femininity.

Aunt Augusta flaunts her audaciously unconventional blend of gender atti-tudes while gaudily displaying a quenchless sexual vitality and adventurism. At her advanced age, her appetites seem scandalous to square people such as Henry, as does her blithe attachment to a younger lover in an interracial sex-ual relationship, although Henry is too polite to say everything he is think-ing, and Cukor has McCowen reveal his subdued shock mostly in his subtle facial expressions. A more subdued Aunt Augusta was not on Cukor's palette as he approached this outsized, amoral, sensual creature of Greene's

26.3. Maggie Smith confers with Cukor while filming the flashback in the lavish Belle Epoque restaurant of the Paris train station.

Source: MGM.

imagination and the magnificently flamboyant actress he engaged to play her. As Alec McCowen saw it while filming, "Cukor should have been a little more controlled [with Smith], but he simply fell in love with her. Every time she did something, he loved it."

Perhaps in Cukor's eyes encouraging Smith to go big and play Aunt Augusta with the utmost panache is a sign of the defiant attitude toward old age the director shared with William Butler Yeats, who wrote in his poem "Sailing to Byzantium":

> An aged [wo]man is but a paltry thing,
> A tattered coat upon a stick, unless
> Soul clap its hands and sing, and louder sing
> For every tatter in its mortal dress . . .

Cukor's sensibility with boldly, self-consciously stylized contrasts of color and other elements of cinematic visual style had become increasingly heightened since he began working in color on *A Star Is Born* with George Hoyningen-Huene and Gene Allen. Cukor's adventurous visual advances on other films led to his modernist approach to the shooting of *Justine* and his sumptuous work here with his production designer and second-unit director, John Box, who had won Oscars for his production design of David Lean's *Lawrence of Arabia* and *Doctor Zhivago* and was nominated for *Travels with My Aunt*. Cukor, Box, and Slocombe approach avant-garde levels of style with their dazzling flashbacks. They also include a risqué romp punctuated with time-compressing jump cuts of a languidly decadent Augusta in a brothel, imbued with strong lesbian associations, and a Feydeau-style farcical episode of her time as one of two kept women of a homely but wealthy industrialist ensconced in the same lavish Parisian hotel.

Although the end credits somewhat misleadingly list a series of foreign locations, *Travels with My Aunt* was mostly based in Spain because of budget limitations, along with shooting in England and Paris. The production team employs the settings with versatility, benefiting from the script's tightening of Greene's sprawlingly episodic novel to a few major episodes. The film moves quickly and easily in Cukor's refreshing modern vein through its briskly deployed locations and stylized studio sets emphasizing old-world luxury reminiscent of Cukor's days at MGM in the 1930s.

And it recalls, farther back, the self-conscious artifice of silent days, such as when Visconti spirits Augusta away to an outdoor grotto on the brothel grounds, dripping water from its rocks. Visconti scoops up water, tosses it on her face repeatedly, and wipes away her whorish makeup as he remakes her with perverted delight into a facsimile of her schoolgirl days. Then he kisses her. She is alternately laughing, beaming, closing her eyes, and staring intently in intercut close-ups, her expression a mixture of rapture and pain at this belated reunion. While Visconti is doing all this to her, she lifts a yellow flower to her mouth; it is matched by a yellow flower she presses to her face as the film cuts to the elderly Augusta on the train remembering, her eyes closed in mingled reverie and grief. The scene in the grotto simultaneously seems to return her to purity while also having Visconti, her lover and pimp, manipulating her in his malign fantasy image.

The scene at the end of Augusta reuniting with Visconti on an African beach is devastating to the old woman. She achieves what she believes will be her lover's rescue only to find him taking her ransom money and callously rising from his wheelchair, stripping off his bandages and sling, removing his disguise and annihilating her romantic dream before her gaping eyes. Augusta is one of the most assiduous of Cukor's many dreamers, and it's characteristic that although the director never mocks her romantic devotion to her false and destructive dream image of Visconti, Cukor takes a clear-eyed look at her necessary disillusionment.

While empathizing with her shattered reaction to the realization that she has wasted much of her life on a false idol—leading her into a life as a prostitute, kept woman, and smuggler, a life that Cukor pointedly does not portray as purely negative but as filled with jolly delights—he shows the old woman, in an embrace with Henry in a ruined village, summoning up the emotional energy to regroup and recover from this tremendous blow. Visconti represents the folly yet poignant attraction of the romantic impulse, the dream of monogamy she is forced to forgo in life. She is one of the quintessential Cukor dreamers and, despite her battering by her romantic illusions, the ultimate Cukor survivor. She would agree with his approach to life's nuisances: "I don't luxuriate in suffering. You can't. . . . You have to very charmingly say, 'Fuck that.'"

McGilligan observes that the director identifies both with Augusta's wildly unconventional, sensual, irrepressibly bold "drag queen" adventuress and

Henry's carefully bottled-up bachelor. He seems asexual rather than gay, but when Wordsworth offers him some hookers for what he calls a bout of "jig-jig," he proclaims a trifle too insistently, "I don't *want* a girl!" The director also finds elements of himself in Gossett's Wordsworth, as Augusta calls him (his real name is Zachary). Augusta's loyal companion, sexual and otherwise, is an exotic man from Sierra Leone who blithely enjoys life in utter disregard of accepted social conventions and whose wisdom and savoir faire Henry, initially disdainful, comes to respect. A straight but sexually adventurous man, Wordsworth can be seen as Augusta's "trade," while resembling the many tenderly devoted gay friends who met Cukor's emotional needs and provided him with companionship, however socially disreputable they would seem to square society.

Henry's coming-out as a sexual creature is mostly thanks to his prolonged exposure to his unconventional mother and her lover yet is not complete until he encounters another character on the Orient Express. Cindy Williams's Tooley, a young American hippie, initiates Henry sexually, in what one could call "a little touch of Harry in the night." Tooley is an adventurer as well, pursuing a casually rambling life, yet she is also a lost soul. She shows flashes of the pain, fear, and loneliness that accompany her peripatetic existence. But in her youthful sense of freedom whatever the consequences, she represents the open, blossoming side of Cukor that enabled him to evolve with the times in the 1970s; she is like a younger version of Aunt Augusta. Williams's long-take scene with McCowen in her train compartment as they get stoned and discover a temperamental affinity is among the emotional high points of the film.

Cukor frames the scene with his wide screen through the doorway between their compartments and has Williams suddenly rush forward in the frame and clutch the partition as her manic laugh turns to a sob when she breaks down while talking about her feckless boyfriend and her anxiety about pregnancy. Her moment of emotional vulnerability leads to the tenderly elliptical love scene that helps change Henry into a mensch; one wonders if Aunt Augusta deliberately encouraged Tooley to teach her son the facts of life (she left her a bottle of champagne). Tooley, who majors in English literature, compares the shy but pliable Henry to a Dickens character and quickly divines the truth about Augusta being his mother, even though he doesn't realize it yet. The only cut in the scene comes naturally, when Tooley and Henry lie back on the bed in her compartment and begin snuggling.

In that early stage of her career when she was a promising young actress in such films as *American Graffiti* and *The Conversation*, Cindy Williams often showed a touching moodiness and glumness that was unusual for her generation of actresses and counterbalanced her sprightly façade, before she flattened out her acting style by going cutesy in a long-term TV series, *Laverne & Shirley*. Cukor told me in 1975 that he had found Williams "a very gifted girl, a serious girl, a nice girl, a strange private little girl; I don't know her very well. She was easy to direct within her scope. She had limited scope, which I'm sure is much wider now." He said he had tried cutting up the long take on the train but found that it played beautifully with just the single cut: "That was carried by this very expert actor, Alec McCowen. It's the kind of thing that can sustain itself. That's the way the scene was written; I think it should be unobtrusive, but it flowed. It was a virtuoso scene."

With all its style and charm, *Travels with My Aunt* was not a commercial success. It did not appeal to the predominantly youthful 1972 film audience because its blend of the disparate sides of Cukor's personality and his paradoxical strengths didn't fit into any conventional niche and, most of all, because this freewheeling jeu d'esprit was about old age and mortality in a period of the frenzied chauvinism of youth. Perhaps it was a private joke on his part as well and a covertly personal meditation on the kaleidoscopic nature of sexuality by his old friend Katharine Hepburn. Cukor's late work often had undercurrents that were as intriguing if not more so than the actual storylines of those pictures.

While most veteran Hollywood directors were struggling or retiring, Cukor valiantly soldiered on regardless, since filmmaking was his raison d'être, and kept working until 1981, although only intermittently. But Cukor kept vigorously and adventurously creating whenever he found the opportunity, and he exemplified Augusta's declaration that "age, Henry, may a little modify our emotions—it does not destroy them."

27.1. When he directed the romantic comedy-drama *Rich and Famous* (1981) at age eighty-one, Cukor was the oldest director ever to make a major-studio Hollywood film up to that time. Pleased to return to MGM for his twenty-second film there, Cukor posed graciously for this publicity shot in front of the Thalberg Building with the stars of *Rich and Famous*, Candice Bergen and Jacqueline Bisset, even though he and Bisset clashed during the filming.

Source: MGM.

27

JACQUELINE BISSET AND CANDICE BERGEN IN *RICH AND FAMOUS*

"**F**eelings of great depth and poignancy surface unpredictably in this film by George Cukor, though they have little to do with the ostensible subject: the director seems to be responding to the material in private, wholly personal ways completely divorced from the concerns of his collaborators." So wrote Dave Kehr in a retrospective 1985 review of *Rich and Famous* for the *Chicago Reader*. Kehr's astute observation accounts for the 1981 film's jarring mixtures of tone and why it makes only little sense as what Gerald Ayres's screenplay sets out to be, a study of a tumultuous lifelong friendship between two female literary rivals.

Based on a 1941 play by John Van Druten, *Old Acquaintance*, which became a creaky 1943 Bette Davis–Miriam Hopkins vehicle the playwright wrote with Lenore Coffee for the director Vincent Sherman, *Rich and Famous* is sometimes startlingly candid and fresh in its concentration on erotic matters. It is particularly strong on the fraught relationships between middle-aged and much younger lovers and what Jacqueline Bisset's character calls the "obsession with young flesh." Such matters, as Cukor put it, were "in the air" when the director's final film appeared.

The frenemies played by Bisset and Candice Bergen are novelists with starkly different audiences and reputations. Bisset's Liz Hamilton (renamed from the character of Katherine [Kit] Markham in the play and Kit Marlowe in the earlier film) is a winner of the "National Writers Award" who has become blocked after her first novel (never quoted or clearly described in the film, although her conversation is pretentiously filled with quotes from other writers); she narcissistically dramatizes her problem with everyone she meets. Bisset gives a finely wrought, passionate performance of a woman seething with repressed anger and tormented by her sexual conflicts, but Liz's kvetching about her writer's block becomes so irritating you wish she'd go into another line of work.

The archly renamed Merry Noel Blake, a character wildly overplayed by Bergen for much of the movie (the trashy novelist was called Mildred [Millie] Drake in the previous incarnations), is consumed with envy over Liz's literary success but exceeds her fame (and wealth) with her slick facility and low taste. Merry cranks out a series of bestsellers, starting with a roman à clef about her fellow Malibu dwellers that causes such enmity it makes her and her scientist husband, Doug (David Selby), flee the trendy colony after one of the neighbors sets fire to their car (an off-screen scene that would have been funnier if the film had shown it).

Cukor avoided mentioning models for the film's two novelists, but the film's producer, William Allyn, who developed the project with Bisset over more than a decade at Universal and finally at Cukor's old studio, MGM, told me he thought of Liz as akin to Joan Didion or Joyce Carol Oates (the latter a strange comparison in light of Oates's vastly prolific career) and Merry as resembling Jacqueline Susann or Judith Krantz.

Incredibly, *Rich and Famous* has Merry somehow eventually writing a novel that ties for the prestigious literary prize with a book by a fellow author who sounds like Toni Morrison or Alice Walker. This is only the most preposterous of the literary aspects of the story, which also fails to make clear how Liz, after writing one *succès d'estime*, survives comfortably for years on an advance for a second unfinished novel and how she's able to afford a picturesque mill in Connecticut, let alone what it was about her first book that made her so important. That's especially baffling, since Liz tells a UCLA student audience in a scene set in 1969, "Perhaps it is true . . . that I do not involve myself specifically in feminist politics." She appears evasive and defensive about that stance when challenged by one of the students, a young Black woman, with "Why not?" She deflects the question by talking about her "paralysis" as a writer and how her lifelong "love for old men" led her to base her first novel on her father.

How Merry and Doug can live in Malibu on an alcoholic scientist's salary while she writes her first book is also a mystery. Ultimately, the literary rivalry in *Rich and Famous* seems relatively meaningless because of its contrived unreality and because most of the conversation in the film is about eroticism and the evolving nature of women's love lives in the wake of the women's liberation movement. Cukor admitted to me and Todd McCarthy about the literary rivalry in the story, "I think that was Van Druten's phantasmagoria."

The script by Ayres is so banal, arch, and pretentious that the film's commentary on changing sexual mores is far more compelling visually than verbally, if not always entirely illuminating of the women's characters. Cukor stages a remarkably erotic scene of Liz taking Jim, an eighteen-year-old male hustler with cocksure male-model prettiness (Matt Lattanzi), to her suite at New York's Algonquin Hotel for an afternoon tryst. That genuinely provocative scene caused critical controversy of a homophobic nature after MGM had almost cut it from the film. Cukor first shows Liz gazing in lingering, intense close-ups at Jim undressing himself. Then Cukor's camera holds on extended close-ups of her kissing and caressing the young man's buffed torso while she

27.2. The sex scene in a hotel room between Liz Hamilton (Bisset) and a much younger male hustler (Matt Latanzi) in *Rich and Famous* was frank enough to inspire homophobic backlash from Pauline Kael. Her *New Yorker* review calling the sex scenes "creepy" while alluding to Cukor's homosexuality proved controversial.

Source: Frame enlargement; MGM.

sits on the bed as he stands naked before her, lifting her head so their eyes can meet; we also see his naked backside at length as she stares at him sensually.

Bisset argued to MGM executives, "God, don't cut that scene, that's what the film is about. She does things like this. She's full of self-loathing and she has to be humiliated." Bisset told McCarthy and me in our interview with her, "Sometimes people *are* unsympathetic. Maybe I *like* being unsympathetic. I don't know. . . . This film for me is as European a part as I could find. There are things in it where I allowed myself not to let anybody get in there, between me and the camera. I think a lot of American films de-sexualize women. I'm talking about letting the guts come out in the face." (Part of what gives the film its European tone is the delicately romantic score by Georges Delerue, who had composed the music for Bisset's 1973 François Truffaut film, *Day for Night.*)

Pauline Kael sparked an angry response when her *New Yorker* review called Cukor's film "a hopelessly demented movie . . . a tawdry self-parody. . . . *Rich and Famous* isn't camp, exactly; it's more like a homosexual fantasy. Bisset's affairs, with their masochistic overtones, are creepy, because they don't seem like what a woman would get into. And Bergen is used almost as if she were a big, goosey, female impersonator." She mocked the way in one scene while Bisset is on the phone in a hotel room with a young *Rolling Stone* reporter, Chris Adams, played by Hart Bochner, "the focus is held snugly on his blue-jeaned rear. (Are we in the audience supposed to be turned on *for* her?)" And in the sex scene with the hustler, "poor distinguished, sex-starved Bisset can't resist his smooth young flesh. She begins to kiss his abdomen passionately, gratefully. It's gruesomely silly. . . . This picture might have been *made* by young hustlers."

The gay critic Stuart Byron attacked Kael in the *Village Voice* for the way the review fits into her history of indulging in the "tiredest homophobic myths. . . . However much male gay life has followed promiscuous patterns not available to straights until the advent of the postpill paradise, the gay fantasy has always been exactly the same as the straight fantasy: love and happiness with one person forever. . . . It is apparent that Kael, like the straight men who seem to have shaped her romantic consciousness, won't accept that Bisset has one-night stands and sometimes enjoys them—and yet is not viewed as a sick nymphomaniac."

Kael was not alone in expressing that kind of reaction to this scene. David Denby wrote in *New York* magazine, "As the jabbering movie falls into silence and the camera, unmoving, passes into a trance, the naked young man holds Liz's face against his muscular, hairless chest, and she's mightily aroused. The scene is peculiar because Cukor treats the man rather than the woman as a sex object, and the man himself looks and operates like a gay hustler rather than a gigolo." McGilligan comments in his biography, "As proud as he was of the film, Cukor, who knew that he would never have the stamina to direct again, felt mortally wounded by Kael's and other negative reviews."

Part of what perturbed these reviewers is that Cukor presents the scene quite differently from the way Bisset herself regarded it: he does not see it as an example of Liz's "self-loathing" or judge her for going along with the casual pickup but makes us feel her desire for loveless sexual abandon. Even if some viewers, like the actress, might find this a "humiliation," Cukor does not. The unusual nature and intensity of the scene resonate with the director's lively creative and personal involvement; the film often seems distracted or sluggish elsewhere, but not in this passage. *Rich and Famous* also has some intimate bedroom scenes between the two women and other partners and a comically lewd sequence of Liz and a pickup (Michael Brandon) joining the "mile-high club" as their plane comes in for a landing at New York's JFK International Airport.

The sexually anxious Liz becomes emotionally entangled with Merry's husband, a dull plot thread with a tedious male actor that mostly exists to give Merry opportunities to rant at Liz with her overblown sense of betrayal. Another mystery: What does Liz see in Doug, this pompous sad sack? Despite Liz's principled insistence that she rejected Doug's advances out of respect for her friendship with Merry (who moans about her marital breakup, "It's the times—what ugly times we live in—another broken home—I never wanted to be a statistic"), Merry rejects her friend's denial in a scene that leads to a physical brawl. Liz more seriously undertakes a romance with the *Rolling Stone* reporter, Bochner's Chris, who interviews her and stays on for an unsatisfactory relationship marred by miscommunication and mutual discomfiture.

Cukor is handicapped by the clumsy script and by allowing Bochner to give an overly smug, self-righteous performance; occasionally in his films, Cukor will seem so enamored of a male supporting actor's blandly handsome appeal that he lets him coast on his looks, a problem that similarly afflicts heterosexual directors with actresses who are cast as much for their looks as for their talent. Nevertheless, in Cukor's dramatization of the tormented Liz's sexual conflicts through his intimate concentration on Bisset's facial expressions and body language, the director is grappling intelligently with the dilemmas faced by a single woman trying to navigate the unsettled customs of modern sexuality and attempting to work out her own way of coping with sex and love in middle age.

Rich and Famous spends much of its second half dealing with sexual relationships that are perilously unbalanced because of age discrepancies or social status: after her bout with the teenaged hustler (identified in the credits as "The Boy, Jim"), Liz praises his beauty and endurance but complains about how young men are often so inarticulate. She half-jokingly says she is considering writing a novel called *Young Flesh*, another instance of how *Rich and Famous* teeters slyly on the boundary between studio entertainment and softcore porno film, as *The Chapman Report* had almost two decades earlier. Cukor's filming of the sex scene between Liz and Jim was influenced by his fondness for *Flesh* (1968) and the other funky, laidback, casually raunchy bisexual softcore films of Paul Morrissey, including *Lonesome Cowboys* and *Trash*. Cukor praised Morrissey for "a marvelous kind of mischief, holding nothing back and just watching it happen. . . . Nobody has any kind of guilt in these pictures. None of the attitudes are conventional, you never see a tear—that's extremely refreshing! I don't like sordid things, but these pictures I luxuriate in. They're so bold and undiluted and really new."

Since at age eighty-one Cukor was the oldest director ever to make a Hollywood studio film up to that point (he was eighty-two when *Rich and Famous* was released), I wrote an article about that milestone in *Daily Variety*. Cukor told me that distinction "thrilled" him, and *Rich and Famous* shows how au courant he was up to the end of his career. He unabashedly examines issues about the conflict between love and sex that caused debate within the gay community at the time as well as among liberated women who, like Liz, were struggling to find satisfying new models for heterosexual relationships. Some reviewers complained about how Bochner and Lattanzi look so alike that they are confusingly interchangeable, but they miss the point that Liz, with her difficulty in sustaining a relationship of emotional intimacy, is attracted to these two partly for that very reason, as the editing makes clear visually when she is talking about Lattanzi but Cukor cuts to Bochner. Liz goes for a certain shallow type of male adulator, Lattanzi for (presumably paid) impersonal sex and Bochner for an attempted romance that doesn't live up to her desires.

Rich and Famous sometimes seems retro in its sexual attitudes, with Liz expressing the desire for an old-fashioned marriage and family while also admitting her hesitancy about romance with a younger man. Brave as the elderly director was with this film about evolving sexual mores and comfortable as he was with themes of decadence and self-destruction—as the thematically related *Chapman Report* and many of his other films had shown—he had his own longstanding conflicts about relationships, including still feeling the need to be discreet about his sexual orientation. And when Gavin Lambert asked him, "During all those years in the closet, did you suffer very much when you realized that you could never have a complete, out-in-the-open love affair?" Lambert later wrote of their private discussion, "After thinking this over, George supposed that 'many of us suffered.' But when there's no choice, he pointed out, you either make the best of it or suffer even more. And during any affair, out-in-the-open or secret for whatever reason, same or opposite sex, didn't lovers *always* suffer? 'I certainly hope so,' George said with the same deflecting smile. 'After all, it's what many of my pictures that you like so much are about.'" Cukor's familiarity with such tormenting sexual issues enabled him to reflect in *Rich and Famous* the conflicts many American women in that period of evolving mores had in trying to reconcile their mixed desires about committed relationships and impersonal sexuality.

Liz's boyfriend Chris is not a dumb stud but a well-read twenty-two-year-old journalist who admires her writing and tells her vaguely, "You have political anger, but reason keeps it cool." But Bochner's smooth, block-like handsomeness and stolid demeanor make Chris's supposedly precocious pronouncements about modern sexuality seem even more wooden and trite in their tendency to tie up almost intractable problems into neat aphorisms. When he makes one of several proposals to Liz and she commits the faux pas of joking about it out of (admitted) fear and defensiveness, he becomes irate. He storms out of bed as she turns toward the camera and rises from the bed while Cukor tracks in to her stunned face, which is more eloquent than any of the dialogue in the scene. That's the abrupt end of their relationship, and his hurt reaction shows that despite his confident façade, he is no more at ease with intimacy than the highly neurotic, self-defeating Liz.

The supposedly highbrow Chris runs off on a Fleetwood Mac tour with Merry's teenaged daughter, Debby (Meg Ryan in her first film), who's portrayed as silly and flighty. In Van Druten's rather stolid play, the equivalent character and her romantic problems are the centerpiece of much of the action, with the two novelists' careers seeming relatively insignificant, their rivalry more a clever plot gimmick than a seriously explored or bitingly satirized theme. The 1943 film version, no doubt because of the demands of the star system, elevates the two mature women's relationship into the foreground, as does Cukor's remake.

Cukor's penchant to find comedy wherever possible made him more appreciative of Bergen's broad style of acting than Bisset's brittle approach to character. When McCarthy and I interviewed Cukor about his late work, he rhapsodized at length about Bergen and her playing of what he fondly called "an eccentric," telling us that "she is intelligent, and she plays a dummy in this. Certainly Candice gives a brilliant performance. I like the casting. It gives a freshness and originality. . . . Because she was pretty, she always had to play lovely, sad ladies. She said her father [the ventriloquist Edgar Bergen] told her to play comedy, but they gave her these pretty, dull parts." But Bergen's performance is strained, her Atlanta accent clumsy, her body language often awkward and flailing, and her mannerisms so vulgar that the character is a walking display of florid acting. Furthermore, to stress Merry's ostentatious wealth and bad taste, her costuming is often intentionally ridiculous on the filmmakers' part, although sometimes a certain uncharacteristic elegance creeps in nonetheless.

Cukor is playing up Merry-as-"dummy" with such gusto that the performance, like Maggie Smith's in *Travels with My Aunt*, becomes camp. Perhaps he also was influenced by Miriam Hopkins's screwball comedy–style portrayal of the character in *Old Acquaintance*, which is so shrill and absurd that it is often hailed as a camp classic. It's especially renowned for the hilarious moment (adapted from the play) in which Bette Davis grabs Hopkins by the shoulders, shakes her vigorously, pushes her down into a chair, snaps off a clipped "Sorry," and strides out of the room, satisfied. Too bad that piece of business was not lifted for *Rich and Famous*. But Bergen's performance improves considerably when she settles down, relaxes into her contrived persona, and stops being such a wild overactor in the second half of the film.

Although her performance is still marred by her accent and other shtick Cukor encourages from her, Bergen manages some genuinely touching moments, including her childish breakdown in Central Park when her husband finally abandons her and a beautiful full shot of her in profile, wearing her most tasteful blue dress while standing stock-still in a bedroom looking out at her guests at a New Year's Eve party with a hard-won serenity before leaving with a bottle of champagne to go see Liz. They have just had an all-out screaming and hitting argument that transcends the cliché about catfights in women's pictures (as does the raucously funny one at the Reno divorce ranch in *The Women*) because the two actresses' intense viciousness toward each other feels so authentic.

Cukor in our conversation did not hide the animosity he felt toward Bisset during the making of the film: "She's very anxious. Also, she has to be held down, because she doesn't know the whole goddam thing. She can't run the show. She *thinks* she can." I learned that Cukor was furious at her mostly because, as her producing partner Allyn told me, the veteran director was not used to having an actress being in charge of his film, whether nominally or not. I mentioned to Cukor that in the old days actresses such as Garbo had a similar kind of power, but he said, "Yes, but there was also good manners. You deferred; she deferred. It was very civilized. I would find it very difficult to be under the thumb of the actress."

As had happened with *Justine*, Cukor inherited *Rich and Famous* from another director. Robert Mulligan shot for four days before the production shut down because of a Screen Actors Guild strike. Mulligan exited (his footage was reshot) because, Bisset told us, they disagreed on the way the cinematographer (Adam Holender) was shooting the film: "It was rather *more* dramatic lighting than I felt we should have. Candy and I had to go through a twenty-year span and needed a little help at times, especially in winter. . . . And in a comedy, dark lighting can really spoil the picture. I stuck to my guns, and when Cukor came in and looked at the stuff, he felt it wasn't right for the concept of the film either."

They hired Don Peterman, a little-known cinematographer who, along with the art director Fred Harpman, gave the film a cool, softly diffused, more glamorous look. Paradoxically, even though Cukor is loosening up further here with the new sexual freedom available onscreen, his mise-en-scène is more traditional than his freewheeling style on *Justine* and *Travels with My Aunt* and even feels subdued for 1981 yet still fluid and graceful. Evidently he felt that pushing the envelope with what he showed onscreen was more effective within an unostentatious and indeed classical cinematic framework.

Bisset also complained of Mulligan that she found him "very closed" in his approach to directing actors. "Mr. Cukor is much more constant in personality. He didn't over-direct. He left us a lot of freedom in places. Certain places he was very particular about, the timing and stuff, but there were scenes where he hardly said anything at all." The tension Todd McCarthy and I noticed on the set between Cukor and Bisset was diplomatically addressed by the actress, who mentioned his occasional irascibility and elaborated on how he worked:

> There were places where I would have liked to have been allowed to play it with more depth. The pace works for the movie overall in a comedic sense, but at times I felt there were comments that I would have played a little more internally. But there's a great *joie de vivre* in him, and you can pick up on that. He really got me worried at one point. He kept saying, "Very funny, very funny." I thought, "Does he really think this is that funny?" And then he'd say, "Hmmm. Hokey. Hokey, but funny. Print." *Hokey?* What the hell is that?! But it's his way. Sometimes "hokey" and "funny" can mean tantalizing, slightly offbeat, maybe. It threw me for a loop in the beginning, but then I started to know that if he said "Hokey, but funny," we were in good shape.

Perhaps "hokey" was also a subtle dig at Bisset, but what Cukor may have meant in a positive sense by using the word "hokey" was conveyed in his telling us, "There were a lot of plays that I did before, serious plays, that now I think are funny. . . . John Van Druten was a skillful playwright [and one of the screenwriters on Cukor's *Gaslight*], but to me he was rather stodgy and old-fashioned. [*Old Acquaintance*] was all rather ladylike and very nice, you know. . . . [Ayres] changed the whole thing. He makes it really funny, and much more naughty. . . . I'm perfectly comfortable with it. I'm not prudish. I'm not easily shocked." However, Bisset told us about the scene in which she has sex in an airplane bathroom with a man she has met on the flight, "I hated doing this orgasm thing. God knows, it's difficult. I'm not an exhibitionist. I directed myself. [Cukor is] very shy about sex scenes. He really doesn't enjoy directing those things. He holds back. Physically stays quite back and doesn't come up close. Which I must say is just fine by me, because you have to have as few people around as possible. Otherwise you don't stand a chance of being able to relax."

When I transcribed our interview with Cukor, I realized that he had given Bisset short shrift. The most he begrudged in her favor came when we said, "Bisset's gallant but self-destructive character recalls others in your work, such as Norman Maine in *A Star Is Born* or Garbo in *Camille*. She gives a very striking performance." That may have been overenthusiastic in the heat of the moment to compare her performance to two of the greatest in his body of work, yet hers is an intensely controlled depiction of the character's anguish and desperation, counterbalanced with a generous, adventurous approach to life. Cukor responded to our comment by saying, "It's all due to the writing. She's very good, but the writing is very good. The other one is a scream. She tickled me." It is noticeable when seeing the film today that while Cukor's camera views Bergen's Merry with abundant warmth and indulgence, he is contrastingly restrained and detached in dealing with Liz. But that makes his observation of the character acutely analytical, which in the long run makes Liz far more compelling than the exuberant Merry. When it is appropriate to the story, Cukor also dwells on larger and longer-held close-ups of Liz, such as in the bedroom scenes.

Although he did not like Bisset personally, his professionalism and artistry enabled him to deal with her performance with the care and respect it demanded. As McCarthy and I wrote, it is remarkable that their personality clash "did not work to the detriment of the film, but may actually have enhanced the tensions underlying her deeply felt characterization, which emotionally dominates the film, despite Cukor's preference for Bergen and his stated intentions to keep the film light and comical." Ironically, Cukor has far more in common with Liz than with Merry, since Liz is an artist coping with a single life and the perennial absence of a romantic relationship, leading her to a lonely dedication to her career, along with the limited compensations of secret promiscuity.

As Dave Kehr put it in discussing how Cukor's "private" concerns "surface unpredictability" in *Rich and Famous*, "the film stays in the mind for its dark asides on aging, loneliness, and the troubling survival of sexual needs." Cukor's clash with Bisset may have stemmed in part from this uncomfortable similarity he felt with her character. So after our interview, I called him and spent fully half an hour on the phone trying every way I could to coax something more out of him, something positive, about Bisset, but I was met with a fiercely impressive yet calm display of just how stubborn George Cukor could be.

Although an enduring friendship, despite all odds, is the overriding unifying factor in *Rich and Famous*, and the film shows the difficulty of sustaining one in the face of competition, envy, and suspicion, the film, as indeed was the case with the source material, leaves the viewer with a question Millie's husband asks Kit in the film *Old Acquaintance*, "Why are you and Millie such friends?" *Rich and Famous* never satisfactorily answers that basic question about these two extremely disparate women. Even if life provides examples of similar cases of unlikely friends, such a random level of verisimilitude is insufficiently convincing for a drama. In that regard, this story may be a failure, but the deeply moving ending of Cukor's film redeems everything that had gone before in leaving us with one of his most memorable scenes, a fitting, wry, affectionate way of concluding his long career.

Merry flees her party on a snowy night to find Liz curled up in a chair in her high-collared white bathrobe, drinking whiskey in front of a blazing fireplace in her Connecticut retreat. In long shot the old mill resembles the novelist Jo March's New England home in *Little Women*, and as Cukor told Lambert about that film, "Snow is something I'm very sentimental about." Apologetic for once, Merry, looking vulnerable in her sleeveless party dress, haltingly expresses appreciation for their long, if imperfect, friendship, an affirmation Liz echoes wholeheartedly. She brings glasses so they can share the champagne Merry has brought from New York. Liz tells her, "We've accomplished one hell of a lot in one lifetime. What we deserve is a rest."

Then as the clock strikes midnight, with the light from the fire flickering up at them, Liz turns longingly toward Merry and says, "Kiss me." Ever the more conventional of the pair, Merry smiles apprehensively and asks, "After all these years, are you going to tell me that there's something strange about you?" Liz shakes her head and tells her, "It's New Year's Eve. I want the press of human flesh." She reaches toward her friend, her head entering Merry's close-up and turning it into a tight two-shot as her right arm wraps around Merry's shoulder and they tightly embrace. Cukor cuts to an angle from the

27.3. "Are they lesbians? That's meant to be," Cukor said of the ending of his last film, *Rich and Famous*. When longtime friends Liz (Bisset) and Merry Noel Blake (Bergen) spend New Year's Eve together, they share what Bisset called "a friendship kiss" before toasting their relationship in front of a fire. Katharine Hepburn felt they should have gone further, as she said she would have done. Cukor maintained his discreet style up to the end, but while taking advantage of the new sexual freedom in films, pushed it as far as he felt he could.

Source: MGM/Photofest.

other side, favoring Liz, as she kisses Merry fervently but still chastely on the cheek.

Then he gives us a reverse two-shot from behind the women, facing the fireplace, as they clink glasses and drink their toast. By showing the fire in back of them in the scene as they come out of their embrace, Cukor mischievously employs the old Production Code–era shorthand for a sexual encounter. The film—and Cukor's career—ends with a fadeout as the two old friends gaze into each other's eyes with something resembling love.

The closest Cukor approached to "coming out" in his personal life was in an interview with the gay publication *The Advocate* in 1982, the year before he died. He discussed, in somewhat guarded terms, the limited progress that had been made in dealing with gay subject matter onscreen and off-, while making his own sexual orientation implicitly clear. Cukor told his interviewers, Douglas W. Edwards and David B. Goodstein, that "in twenty-five years—I won't be here then—I'm sure there will be candor there too [in depicting gay sex onscreen]. As of now I think they're scared to death of it." Asked what gay people could do to accelerate the process, he said, "Behave themselves." He explained that he considered it necessary to avoid the stereotypical image "that if you're queer, you're ridiculous. . . . The audience is accepting things by leaps and bounds, but I don't think that they're yet ready to accept a frankly gay—I hate that word—relationship seriously." Asked, "What do you think it's going to take?" he replied, "Time."

Cukor's true "coming out" was not journalistic but cinematic, in the career-concluding kiss he shows at the end of *Rich and Famous*. I told him in 1981 that "people are sure to find provocative" this ending that "crystallizes the theme of the picture: the men in the story come and go, but the women's friendship endures."

"Yes," he said, "that's rather touching. It's romantic and truthful. I think friendship is very, very important. We all appear at our best in a good friendship."

"It certainly means a lot in your life."

"Yes. All these ladies. All these ladies . . ."

"There's something teasing about the women kissing, because you wonder . . ."

"Are they lesbians? That's meant to be."

"What did you tell the actresses when they did the scene?"

"They were scared to be thought to be lesbians. And they're not, surely. What did I tell them? It should be done with a light touch. That's the trick of doing things. I don't think you're supposed to take the kiss very seriously."

Confirming what Cukor said about the actresses' reluctance, Bisset said, "I didn't want to kiss her on the mouth. Knowing the way the public is, they could say, 'Oh, that was the point, they were two dykes.' Candy and I both felt that it was a friendship kiss. They *do* love each other. Basically, that's all they've got left. Though I think Liz is still ready to try again." But after seeing the film at a private screening with Cukor, Katharine Hepburn said, "If I had done that scene, I would have taken her by the shoulders, pulled her toward me, and *really* kissed her."

The tentative nature of the kiss—expressed most movingly in Merry's shy, somewhat anxious but still eager smile as she responds to Liz's invitation—is part of what makes this such a meaningful ending to Cukor's career. His life-long sense of discretion, which helped lead him to approach his art with a light touch whenever possible, gives the women's kiss a teasing dimension that makes it seem like a wink to the audience. It invites us to a shared understanding of the importance of the emotions we don't always expose directly but keep within us. Cukor's art is a play between those poles of exposure and careful concealment, an interchange in which profoundly felt passion often bursts forth, as it does in life itself.

28.1. On location in London for *Love Among the Ruins,* Cukor directed Katharine Hepburn for the tenth time and their old friend Laurence Olivier for the first time, drawing performances from these two magnificent actors that rank with the finest in their late careers. Made from an eloquent and witty script by James Costigan, the director's 1975 television debut was also his final masterwork.

Source: ABC Circle Films/ABC-TV.

28

KATHARINE HEPBURN AND LAURENCE OLIVIER IN *LOVE AMONG THE RUINS*

G eorge Cukor's last masterwork, though not his final film, *Love Among the Ruins* (1975), is a graceful précis of his themes and approach to creating characterization. A deeply personal work, this seriocomic romance between two elderly people is Cukor's valentine to his longtime friend and collaborator Katharine Hepburn and a wry reflection of the bachelor director being a "disappointed romantic," as Laurence Olivier's character describes himself. James Costigan's superb screenplay was originally written in 1966 as a television play intended for Alfred Lunt and Lynn Fontanne, but after initial interest, they turned it down. Costigan's agent, Audrey Wood, wrote, "Perhaps it had something to do with the title; that word ruins did not appeal to two people of such advanced age." The script contains many other humorous references to the lady being "of a certain age," but Hepburn was refreshingly undaunted by such matters.

Once again she came through to keep Cukor active in his craft and because she wanted to appear in lighter, more romantic material than she had been doing lately. She spearheaded the making of *Love Among the Ruins* for television, a medium she already had enthusiastically embraced (starting with *The Glass Menagerie* in 1973) as her box office appeal waned. *Love Among the Ruins* was Cukor's first work for TV, and he reveled in the glorious opportunity to pair his favorite actress for the first time with Olivier, who was a longtime friend of theirs. In his book *On Acting*, Olivier describes *Love Among the Ruins* as "my happiest professional film experience." The idea for their teaming came after Hepburn appeared in 1973 on *The Dick Cavett Show*. The host asked, "Are you sorry you never acted with Olivier?" She replied, "Well, neither of us is dead yet, even though you may think so [*laughs uproariously*]."

Wood brought Hepburn and Cukor together with Costigan, with backing by ABC Circle Films, which allowed the director artistic freedom. The Edwardian London setting of this exquisitely produced film is of the same comfortable vintage for Cukor as that of *My Fair Lady*. The material was an "evergreen" just waiting for the right combination of actors and beautifully suited to two outsized talents whose lively interactions are not in the nature of rivalry but the result of mutual admiration and artistic nourishment.

Hepburn's role as the long-retired stage actress Jessica Medlicott is the gaudier of the two, an encapsulation of her stature by that point in her career as an icon of personality acting, a grande dame relishing her theatrical eccentricities for the delight of her devoted public. As her shy but doggedly devoted suitor, Olivier's Sir Arthur Granville-Jones, K.C., is a distinguished barrister whose romantic fixation on the youthful Jessica, with whom he had a brief affair decades earlier, has made this "patriarchal" figure (as she admiringly calls him) appear somewhat ridiculous as well as emotionally stunted. But Sir Arthur is the director's surrogate character, a consummate Cukor dreamer who has forsaken romantic involvement and poured his vitality and brilliance into his career. Oliver seizes the opportunity for an acting tour de force that gradually reveals how the seeming dottiness of the man whose colleagues patronizingly call "Granny" becomes a glorious resurgence of his youthful exuberance and passion, a vindication of his much-deferred romantic obsession.

With delicious irony that Sir Arthur finds vexing, he is hired to represent Jessica in a breach of promise suit brought by a much younger man, a handsome but flagrantly fortune-hunting cad, Alfred Pratt (Leigh Lawson). The two protagonists' professions and the theatrical nature of the courtroom setting allow Cukor a luxurious opportunity to exercise his career-long approach to human interaction, and romance in particular, as a form of performance. And the achieving of justice in this trial is a tribute to the importance of theatrical revelation. Costigan's witty screenplay elicits humor and sentiment by having the cast play on two levels at once, with the subtext of Sir Arthur's yearning for Jessica evident mostly to him and the audience, not to the other characters until toward the end. Jessica eventually realizes and reciprocates the depths of his feelings, and her solicitor, George Druce (Richard Pearson), also gets some inkling of why Sir Arthur has been, as he puts it, guilty of "woolgathering" throughout the story.

Sir Arthur, in fact, is a walking, living subtext. As is shown humorously in his initial consultation with Jessica when his mind wanders back in time, his dialogue is often on a different track from that of his baffled client and the disconcerted members of the court. When he stares fixedly at her at their reunion, the camera slowly zooming in to a tight close-up of his face, the shot answered by an intimate close-up of Jessica with the background out of focus, she becomes so nonplussed that she waves her black-gloved hands in front of her face with a nervous laugh, turns her back on him, and walks to a rain-spattered window. Cukor and his cinematographer, Douglas Slocombe, effectively employ a variety of cinematic methods throughout the film—zoom and tracking shots, shifts to hazy vignette effects, fantasy imagery, and stylized use of color—to allow us access to his subjective state.

Sir Arthur frequently lapses into a lovestruck trance while others around him are acting normally, a dreamy condition that causes some measure of alarm but stops a bit short of making him seem disqualified to function in court. That tendency, which Cukor treats with both humor and compassion, is an extreme function of a character's emotional compulsion to reshape the world according to his dreams and desires. Sir Arthur, who has a mellifluous voice and a charmingly schoolmasterish penchant for quotation, borrows from Dryden at his reunion with Jessica—"Old as I am, for ladies' love unfit, / The power of beauty I remember yet"—and later, perhaps suitably under the circumstances, misquotes that poet as having written that "Love is the finest frailty of the mind" (what Dryden actually wrote was "And love's the noblest frailty of the mind"). The very first quotation Sir Arthur murmurs in the film, wryly employed as he contemplates his thinning hair in a mirror while primping for his reunion with Jessica ("the site once of a city great and gay. . . . / The country now does not even boast a tree"), is slightly altered from the 1855 Robert Browning poem that gives the film its title. Sir Arthur defensively calls his fondness for quotation "the legal profession's common alternative to an original mind," yet his tendency to poeticize his situation is a key to his stubbornly romantic view of life.

Along with its elements of romantic comedy and drama, the lovestruck aspect of *Love Among the Ruins* is the film's thematic essence for Cukor, an expressionistic approach to character that allows Sir Arthur's romanticism to triumph over the mundane reality of his legal occupation. The coincidental reemergence of Jessica into his life after a gap of so many years (even if he has deliberately taken a home near hers) comes to seem like a magical apparition akin to the fantasy images of her as Portia in *The Merchant of Venice* (the play in which he first saw her, with her character masquerading as a male lawyer) that he conjures up in his head during the trial (her name, Jessica, is Shakespearean as well, that of Shylock's daughter in the play). The truism that the victor in a trial is not necessarily the person with the best factual case but the one who tells the most compelling story governs the outcome of this legal case, a fact about which Sir Arthur takes pains to remind Jessica.

Sir Arthur's histrionic ability (with Jessica's covert cooperation) allows him to vindicate her from her human failings as well as to metaphorically transform her back into the youthful actress he loved as a struggling law student when she was on a theatrical tour through Toronto. *Love Among the Ruins* thus serves as one of the purest expressions of Cukor's career-long dedication to the transcendent power of the dreamer and the role of theater in heightening and improving upon reality. Sir Arthur also assumes the role of a director in his attempts to stage scenes with Jessica to reenact their earlier time together, including a luncheon in a German restaurant for which he orders the same food they ate back then (much to his chagrin, she rejects the sauerbraten and the schaum torte dessert) and has the orchestra play the same music, Schubert's Waltz No. 1, Opus 9. That waltz serves as the basis for John Barry's lovely score, helping govern the tone of the mise-en-scène on which Cukor collaborates with Sir Arthur, both dramatically and comedically.

Love Among the Ruins takes place simultaneously in two planes of reality, the framing story in 1911 (the year after the death of King Edward VII, but a date still considered to be in the era named after him) and Sir Arthur's memory of his romance with Jessica forty years earlier. Their three-day fling was so passionate that it led to a promise of marriage she broke to marry instead a wealthy man she did not love. The fallible nature of memory gives the piece much of its humor and poignancy as Sir Arthur desperately struggles to stir Jessica's reminiscence of the brief romance and his having been "jilted by Jessica Jerrold," as she puts it in commiseration. That blow, he furiously tells George Druce, "ruined my life" (the phrase is echoed deceitfully by Alfred Pratt in his court testimony about her). *Love Among the Ruins* takes a bittersweet view of nostalgia, as Sir Arthur's inability to adjust to the reality that his life had changed. Costigan and Cukor carefully maintain ambiguity about two crucial elements of the story: how much Jessica remembers and when it begins to come back to her, and when and how much she decides to play-act the hysterical outbursts that help him win her case in court.

Sir Arthur is compelled by Jessica's vanity and vulnerability to blackmail to mock and humiliate her in court to win sympathy for her case, an ambivalent process in which his unholy relish in doing so at her expense is his exorcism of the lifelong anger, humiliation, and shame he has endured at her hands after their initial fling. But she is so adept in the tricks of her theatrical trade—like many a Cukor heroine—that at some point she sees through the ordeal to which he subjects her and aids and abets his charade. Although Sir Arthur demands that she present a dignified elderly front to the courtroom, she defies him by wearing a spectacularly theatrical red-and-white dress, white feather boa, and a grandly designed hat similarly festooned with feathers. But does part of him expect her to defy his edict? He sighs, "Good heavens," but does not seem entirely surprised when she makes her appearance.

The emotionally fragile but defiantly brazen old lady is manipulated by her barrister into outbursts that are calculated to show her to the audience (judge, jury, spectators, press, and we the film audience) as a ridiculous figure no young man would dream of romancing other than for money. She does not appear to cotton on to Sir Arthur's strategy until he mocks her relentlessly in court ("this crumbled, pathetic ruin of a once-great lady . . . trembling on the threshold of senility"), causing her to erupt in outrage and help him win the case by appealing to the jury's sympathy. And yet she later insists that her overreactions were play-acting, including forcing the bailiff to drag her out of the courtroom screaming abuse, to the merriment of the spectators. The ambiguity with which Costigan and Cukor present her behavior—even though George Druce after the verdict calls her "You devil! . . . You *actress*, you!"—renders the truth of her claim of calculation deliberately unknowable. Perhaps it even is unknowable, to some extent, to Jessica herself, who may be exaggerating to deny her earlier sense of humiliation and insist on her own greater sense of agency. And perhaps both elements of her response are true simultaneously. When Sir Arthur asks at the end when she began to remember, she admits with some agitation, "I'm not sure—a, a little patch here and there."

What we know for sure is that in Cukor's dramatic world, displays of theatrics—by Sir Arthur as well as by Jessica—are the best way to discover the true motivations of characters, even if some aspects of human nature remain partly mysterious. Cukor's approach to his actors, like Jean Renoir's, enabling them to express feelings "on the margin of so many things," has seldom been more evident than with the intricate expressions of moods that pass between Hepburn and Olivier in *Love Among the Ruins*.

Over the course of Jessica's trial, she ultimately respects, admires, and falls back in love with Sir Arthur as much for his virtuosity as a courtroom performer as for his undying, though sorely tested, emotional devotion. During most of Sir Arthur's defense, Cukor shows her angry reactions in amusing three-shots featuring her and George (trying to calm her) in foreground profile with Sir Arthur speaking behind them. In those shots her outrage seems genuine, just as the calculated flattery of the rival barrister, John Francis Devine, K.C. (Colin Blakely), a sly Anglo-Irish charmer with the

28.2. One of the most touching moments in *Love Among the Ruins* comes when the aging barrister played by Olivier, Sir Arthur Granville-Jones, gives his spirited courtroom defense of Jessica Medlicott (Hepburn) and inadvertently refers to her as "Jessie" before adding the syllable "-ca." He thereby almost betrays in public that he has loved his client unrequitedly ever since their brief affair in his youth.

Source: Frame enlargement; ABC Circle Films/ABC-TV.

"common touch," seems to stir her vanity to genuine delight, much to Sir Arthur's disgust. Cukor shrewdly withholds a screen-filling close-up of Sir Arthur in his final argument until the barrister is roused to his most passionate tribute to Jessica's qualities of character, not only in her old age but as a young woman (this part of his speech was a late addition to the shooting script).

Talking to the jury of "that most precious of words in the language—love, love. . . . It's love that is on trial here, gentlemen," he evokes, ostensibly metaphorically, a young man who would have loved her in her youth with the sincerity her accuser so grossly lacks. Olivier's gifts for full-throated theatrical oratory are given full rein here in a magnificent three-minute peroration he delivers in close-up with fierce concentration, carried away with the kind of emotion that uses heightened acting to transcend acting. His speech carries a sense of double meaning his immediate audience would not fully comprehend, including with its eloquent midcourse pause and correction of his client's name to avoid betraying the privacy of his memory:

The girl—ah—the girl that Jessie . . . ca Medlicott once was is gone and will not come again. The day when she might have joined her life with that of a young man her contemporary is past. Like her, such a youth can be young no longer, but were he here, he would remember for us the wonder of that young girl, of their young love, and he would say to us, "Yes, she was doting, she was passionate, she was a thousand times more exciting and dynamic than ever this ignominious little Pratt could have suspected and let alone understood. She had more dignity, more delicacy, and pride than any of you could know."

After breaking down, overcome by the "humiliation" he and others have put her through, Sir Arthur concludes by quoting two of Shakespeare's sonnets (slightly revising them in the process): "To me, fair friend, you never can be old, / For as you were when first your eye I eyed, / Such seems your beauty now. . . . And ruined love, when that it grows anew, / Shows fairer than at first, more strong, far greater." Olivier's acting is so truly felt, so compellingly passionate, that it rises to a height that many of his other film performances, which tend to be overly fussy and emptily virtuosic, never achieve. Cukor's sensitive guidance of Olivier's performance perfectly controls his shifting tones, his gliding surely yet almost indistinctly between absurdity and deep feeling, and his sense of when to underplay and when to play up his expressions of emotion. These are all areas in which the director excelled in handling his actors as he created what he liked to call the "climate" in which they inhabited their characters.

What Sir Arthur means by telling George that Jessica "ruined his life" is partly his excuse for his diffidence around women. Although this theme is integral to the serious heart of the story, Costigan and Cukor also play with it by having Sir Arthur tell Jessica about his "rotten luck with women," not only over his mother's death when he was a child but also about a beloved aunt running away with a mounted policeman at "the worst possible time. My voice was just beginning to change, if you see what I mean." This humorous suggestion of a lifelong sexual immaturity in Sir Arthur does not negate his devotion to Jessica but heightens the tone in Olivier's performance that brings out his boyish vulnerability, his arrested development made more enduring because of her abandoning him after their romance in Toronto. But from her point of view, *he* abandoned *her* by making her wait a year because of his inability to support a wife; during that time, struggling in her career and terrified of poverty, she left the theater and married for money rather than love. That traumatic series of events is part of the running undercurrent of Costigan's depiction of Sir Arthur reverting to the lovestruck young man he was so long ago, a side he has kept alive beneath his imposing eminence as a barrister. When the youthful Arthur keeps popping through the old man's veneer, it makes him both absurd and lovable in equal measure, in Jessica's eyes and in ours, and it brings him even closer to Cukor.

In the same vein, the joshing friendship between Sir Arthur and George Druce (who is so thoughtfully and wryly played by Pearson) has echoes of the jolly semi-gay humor surrounding the Henry Higgins–Colonel Pickering palship in *My Fair Lady*. So does Jessica's asking George about Sir Arthur, "Have you never felt that he wants to thrash you and caress you all at once, like some cruel, fond parent?" To which the calmly heterosexual George responds, "Good heavens, no." There's a further inside gag when her solicitor tries to mollify her while she becomes agitated during her first conference with Sir Arthur, and she snaps, "Oh, stop fussing, George!," a line one can easily imagine her saying frequently to her old friend and colleague Cukor.

Costigan's script deliberately evokes many aspects of Hepburn's screen persona, including her bold sense of independence, defiance of convention, narcissistic self-display, susceptibility to romantic involvement with a "patriarchal" man, and androgynous Sylvia Scarlett side, which is evoked when Jessica gamely quotes a critic in Toronto who wrote of her, "Miss Jerrold has that boyish quality which in France is called 'gamin' or 'gamine.' Miss Jerrold's voice, alas, is as flat as her figure, and her figure is as flat as the Interior Plains, which is the flattest place in Canada." As a showcase for the actress in her ninth role for the director (they would go on to make another TV movie together, the less distinguished adaptation of Emlyn Williams's play *The Corn Is Green*, in 1979, scripted by Costigan under a pseudonym), *Love Among the Ruins* is filled with the kind of professional respect, admiration, and affection that can best be seen through the craft with which the director frames her performance and that of Olivier.

When I asked Cukor, "Did you try to accommodate your shooting style to television?," he said, "I asked them, and they said, 'Just do it the way you would in a movie.'" Although Cukor and Slocombe, with whom he previously worked on *Travels with My Aunt*, did make more frequent and supple use of zooms in *Love Among the Ruins* than Cukor had in his theatrical films, taking advantage of the intimacy of the television experience, they also spectacularly employed one of the director's favorite techniques from throughout his long career in films, the long take. There are several in *Love Among the Ruins* that rank with Cukor's most audacious and expressive, including the bravura one with Olivier and Pearson turning two street corners as they take a lengthy walk to a pub while Sir Arthur vents his outrage about Jessica's not remembering him, but most impressive is the eight-minute take in her flat with Sir Arthur.

She has summoned him for what he imagines will be her admission that she does indeed remember their ancient tryst but instead infuriates him anew by insisting on telling him about how and why she fell for the blandishments of Alfred Pratt (a physically appealing young man she admits had "no conversation," the same complaint Liz makes about the young hustler in *Rich and Famous*). Sir Arthur and Jessica move around each other warily in her drawing room, the camera continually shifting positions and encircling them while she relates her wrenching story. Sir Arthur does his best to appear gentlemanly and interested. That comes at considerable and comical emotional expense on his part and hers, for she feels ashamed to confess her romantic folly. She frequently turns away from Sir Arthur toward the camera to reveal her most painful emotions, another hallmark of Cukor's style.

Cukor said to me about his use of long takes in this television film, "It depends on if the actor has the capability of doing it. And also on the style of the thing. If the actor can do it and if it suits the piece, then it's good. Others can't sustain it. I like to do it. I think it flows. Olivier and Kate Hepburn can do long, sustained scenes and do them perfectly naturally. It's not only that the scenes are long, but you make them more real, more truthful, less *acted*." When I suggested that the long takes contributed to making Olivier's performance one of the finest on film he had delivered in recent years, Cukor said, "Maybe that, and also Hepburn is a most accomplished actress, and they're very generous with each other. We were lucky."

The most poignant scene in *Love Among the Ruins* comes at the end, when Sir Arthur and Jessica reenact their first meeting. He pretends to accost her as she exits through a doorway in the court building, just as he had at the

26.3. As Jessica had done during their romance many years earlier, she poignantly caresses Arthur's hair outside the courtroom after they win their case. They are nostalgically reenacting their ancient love affair while simultaneously rekindling it.

Source: Frame enlargement; ABC Circle Films/ABC-TV.

stage door in Toronto. Pretending to be his gauche boyish self, he expresses the same kind of lovestruck endearment as they seal their reborn relationship with play-acting: "Excuse me—I do hope you don't think me too bold, but I—I saw the play tonight, and I thought you were most awfully good in it." She responds with alacrity and agrees to have supper with him, and when she sees that his hair is (again) mussed, she brushes it back with her white-gloved hand in a lingering caress whose tenderness and grace gives it the feeling of a first kiss. Sir Arthur offers a most suitable quotation that encapsulates their belated relationship as well as the theme of the film: "Grow old along with me! / The best is yet to be." "Dryden?" she asks. "Browning," he says. She takes his arm and responds, "I accept."

Cukor's people in this finale have long lines of his other characters walking behind them, metaphorically, as they stroll away from his camera down a tree-lined road in a park lovingly set back in time, in a more romantic age. *Love Among the Ruins*, with its mingled themes of love, loss, and rebirth, carries a freshness and joyful feeling of play in its mastery of a new form and its meeting anew of two great actors under the eyes of a cinematic master operating at his full undiminished capacity.

ACKNOWLEDGMENTS

G eorge Cukor's work has always presented a challenge to film critics and scholars. As I wrote about it in 1971, my first attempt, his work is "more difficult to evoke or analyze than that of almost any other major director." The challenge is how to deal with his actor-centric approach, the complexity of the dramatic and comedic moods and character shadings he creates with his people, his subtle and unobtrusive visual style, his expressive blend of theatrical and cinematic style, and his self-effacing tendencies as a director. And so I commented then that "what we want from a book on Cukor, ideally, is a sensitive exploration of how he takes a situation and floods it with dozens of insights and impulses; how he makes human instruments, his actors, resonate with the richest possible timbre."

Since I wrote those words for *Film Quarterly* while reviewing an earlier book on Cukor, I have written other articles about the director and had the benefit of interviewing him repeatedly, as well as spending a day in 1981 watching him at work on an MGM soundstage on his last film, *Rich and Famous*. But during those years I never felt I had solved the vexing challenge of how to write about him, so I have made a more thorough and in-depth attempt in this study by approaching his films largely through his work with actors, an unusual, somewhat experimental, and fitting way to study a director, especially this director. I began sketching out my approach in my May–June 1973 *Film Comment* essay on *What Price Hollywood?* Parts of that close study of

Lowell Sherman's performance as the alcoholic director have been woven into my section on Sherman in *George Cukor's People*.

Many other experiences have also flowed into my approach to Cukor and film acting over the past fifty years. Most importantly, I had the opportunity to spend more than five years working as an actor for another of the greatest actors' directors in the cinema, Orson Welles, in *The Other Side of the Wind*. As a nonactor meticulously guided by Welles while performing my satirical role as a film critic and historian among a rich and diverse cast of actors of varying degrees of experience, I had a firsthand education about what film acting really is. On the first day of shooting, I sighed when the seventh take of a shot went wrong while I was trying to handle several props at once, and Welles told me, "Now you appreciate what actors go through." After my first three years of acting under Welles's alternatively cross and benevolent tutelage, I found that I was learning much about the craft. Appreciating what actors go through is part of it, and doing so with Welles has helped me immensely as a film critic.

Film acting is an art that is still widely misunderstood, not only by the public but also by many critics and film historians. But I have learned from some of the most perceptive critics of film acting as well, including James Naremore, Dan Callahan, Simon Callow, and my collaborator on my critical study *John Ford*, the late Michael Wilmington. A superb actor whom I directed in a play and a film, Mike taught me valuable lessons about how to understand and appreciate actors. I have also benefited from interviewing many actors, directors, screenwriters, and others during my years of work on *Daily Variety* in Hollywood and as a film historian and biographer. My time as a screenwriter also enlightened me about acting, especially when I had the rare opportunity for a young writer to write speeches for and with many stars from Hollywood's classic era and rehearse them while serving as the co-writer of five American Film Institute Life Achievement Award tributes with the producer George Stevens Jr. on CBS-TV. Visiting many film sets to watch actors at work with directors also has been an extraordinary privilege and has further enhanced my perspective.

I even had the benefit of being directed by proxy by Cukor himself. While I was appearing in various films as a bit player or extra, which were further learning experiences for me as a film historian and screenwriter, I spent two days playing a tuxedoed guest at a 1920s Hollywood party in a 1975 James

Ivory film, *The Wild Party*. James Coco stars as a character loosely based on the ill-fated Roscoe (Fatty) Arbuckle. Ivory told me he and his partner, Ismail Merchant, had gone to Cukor for advice on how to recreate the atmosphere of a Hollywood party in that period. Cukor confirmed to me that he had suggested that Ivory should have his assistant director give each actor or extra a personal history so they would know why they were at the party and give them a sense of how they should act.

So the AD on *The Wild Party* told me that my tuxedoed young party guest was the son of a studio executive and that I was on the make to succeed on my own in the film industry. That level of character detail was part of what Cukor liked to call the "climate" of a scene, his favorite word for how he liked to go about creating his films with his actors and technicians. As a result of that helpful piece of direction channeled via Cukor, I brashly grabbed Coco's hand as he entered the party, circulating through the crowd at his mansion, greeting his guests. Coco reacted gamely and graciously to my chutzpah, reciprocating my gesture with a smile. In my audacity I was behaving much as the social-climbing high-society party guests do while grabbing the hand of Katharine Hepburn's renegade heiress even as she sweeps contrarily down a staircase through a New Year's Eve gathering in Cukor's classic *Holiday*.

I have been fond of Cukor's movies since I was introduced to his work through *My Fair Lady* in 1965, during its road-show engagement at the Towne Theatre in downtown Milwaukee. That film meant a great deal to me in my formative years. I saw it on weekend passes from a mental hospital where I was sent after suffering a physical and psychological breakdown during my senior year at Marquette University High School caused by the pressures of school, my dysfunctional family, and a crisis over my religion and sexuality. I chronicled these events in my memoir *The Broken Places* (2015), which tells the story of how my life was saved by a troubled young Native American woman I fell in love with at the hospital. She liberated me from my delusions and repression; she was the Henry Higgins to my Eliza Doolittle.

Though I also identified with Professor Higgins in *My Fair Lady*, since one of my hobbies in high school was the study of etymology, I more deeply identified with Eliza and her transformation from a flower girl into a lady, from a wild unmotivated creature to a determined and civilized person. I remember being unexpectedly moved when Eliza told Higgins's mother, "You see, Mrs. Higgins, apart from the things one can pick up, the difference

between a lady and a flower girl is not how she behaves but how she is treated."
I went to see *My Fair Lady* five times that winter and spring and was profoundly inspired by its echo of my ongoing transformation. I luxuriated in
the beautiful road-show presentation of this exhilarating story of how one
person can save another and how someone can remake his or her life. It's no
exaggeration that the film helped save my life and further my own transformation into a more enlightened human being. As I watched more Cukor films
and experienced his frequent return to the Pygmalion-Galatea theme, especially his emotionally devastating treatment of such a relationship in *A Star
Is Born*, I came to be enamored of his work and appreciative of his humanity,
grace, style, and humor.

Getting to know Cukor personally after I moved to Hollywood also was
invaluable for my understanding of his creative personality. I became as fond
of him as I was of his films. My interviews with Cukor in 1975 for *Action*
magazine about how he survived the disastrous filming of *The Blue Bird* in
the Soviet Union, and in 1981 about *Rich and Famous* and his other late work
for *Film Comment* (with Todd McCarthy), as well as my follow-up interview
trying vainly to get him to say something positive about Jacqueline Bisset's
performance, were comprehensive and revealing in many ways. With Todd,
whom I thank for his collaboration on our interview and the sidebar interview we did with Bisset to make up for Cukor's reticence about her, I was
able to visit Cukor's stylish home in West Hollywood during our interview.
He told us to look around wherever we wanted (including not only his elegant library and his wall of inscribed photographs of his actors but even in
cupboards and drawers in his private second-floor study!), as we did with fascination while he was dressing for our interview.

My day-long visit with Todd to the set of *Rich and Famous* at MGM was
somewhat less revealing than my up-close encounters, since I was kept far
back from the action and Cukor spoke so quietly with his actresses, but that
in itself provided insights into his style of directing, as did witnessing the
elderly director's still-imposing command of his set. I also saw him on other
social occasions in Hollywood while covering the industry for *Daily Variety*.
They included the Writers Guild of America, West, awards show at which
Cukor happily accepted our award to him for his respect for writers, which
was so rare for a director and so gratifying to the members of our craft; the
ceremony at which the Academy of Motion Picture Arts and Sciences accepted

Cukor's donation of his extensive collection of papers to the Margaret Herrick Library; the premiere of *Love Among the Ruins* at the Los Angeles International Film Festival (Filmex); and the preview party at the American Film Institute for François Truffaut's *The Story of Adele H.*, at which I had the pleasure of eavesdropping on a meeting between Cukor and Truffaut. The French director had expressed his great admiration for Cukor while writing film reviews for *Cahiers du Cinéma* and other publications in the 1950s.

At my first meeting with Cukor in 1975, I was impressed by the perception he showed when he analyzed my character. He said, "You're a very determined young man but deceptively mild-mannered. Keep that." That accurate insight into levels of my personality that were not apparent to many people helped demonstrate his characteristically shrewd perception of actors' personalities and why he was such a remarkably insightful director of actors in both large and small parts.

For the writing of this critical study of Cukor, I benefited from the thorough research and thoughtful observations in my longtime friend Patrick McGilligan's 1991 biography, *George Cukor: A Double Life*, which I have relied on as a key source of biographical information. Pat's diligent research elucidates Cukor's previously hidden personal life with sympathy and complexity and details the progress of his career with Pat's characteristically close attention to the work of screenwriters. Pat and I have exchanged many mutually helpful pieces of advice and information during our friendship, which dates back to our college days at the University of Wisconsin, Madison. Pat and another longtime friend, James Naremore, whose books *Acting in the Cinema* and *Some Versions of Cary Grant* were role models for this study, were careful readers of my manuscript for Columbia University Press, and I appreciate their helpful and constructive suggestions and enthusiasm.

Other valuable sources included *George Cukor: Hollywood Master*, the diverse collection of critical pieces edited by Murray Pomerance and R. Barton Palmer; *George Cukor: Interviews*, the collection edited by Robert Emmet Long, which contains my two published interviews with Cukor; William J. Mann's astute, iconoclastic biography *Kate: The Woman Who Was Hepburn*; Carlos Clarens's perceptive critical study *Cukor*; Emanuel Levy's biography *George Cukor: Master of Elegance*; the wise critical writings of Truffaut and Andrew Sarris; and the Alexander Street online collection of film scripts, which contains many screenplays of Cukor films. Dan Callahan's *The Camera*

Lies: Acting for Hitchcock, his two collections of essays about modern actors, and his essay on Cukor for *Senses of Cinema* provided guidance and insights, as have Simon Callow's books on Charles Laughton and Orson Welles, and Truffaut's *Hitchcock*, the book that has taught me the most about film.

The late Ronald Haver, curator of film at the Los Angeles County Museum of Art, gave me free passes to movies for years and deserves thanks from all of us for his tireless work on the partial restoration of Cukor's *A Star Is Born*, which he chronicled in a lively and informative book on the subject. In the early 1970s, I had thought of writing a book on that film and proposed it for the British Film Institute's Cinema One series in 1972 to no avail, so I am grateful that Ron wrote his. Ron's grandly produced volume *David O. Selznick's Hollywood*, about one of Cukor's key producing collaborators, also served as an example, like Truffaut's *Hitchcock*, of how to blend illuminating illustrations with text in a book of film history and criticism.

Another special note of gratitude goes to the late Gavin Lambert, the distinguished British novelist, critic, biographer, and screenwriter who spent his later years in Los Angeles. We became friends, partly thanks to our shared fondness for Ford and my gratitude for Gavin's impassioned defense against the vituperation of his close friend Lindsay Anderson of what Wilmington and I wrote about *The Searchers* in our critical study. For a 2005 career profile of Gavin, "Sketches from the Slide Area: Gavin Lambert and the Business of Illusions," that unfortunately ran posthumously in *Written By*, the magazine of the Writers Guild of America, West, I had the pleasure of interviewing him, reading all his books, and watching the films he had written. Gavin deserves the gratitude of all Cukor scholars for his delightful 1972 book of interviews, *On Cukor*, the closest that guarded director ever came to an autobiography. Gavin's sharp insights and provocative, empathetic conversations with Cukor were a crucial resource for my study, backed up as they were with Gavin's close acquaintance with his films and wide knowledge of the social context in which Cukor flourished. As a review of the 2000 edition of Gavin's book, I wrote a lengthy essay on the director's work, "George Cukor: The Valor of Discretion," for Gary Morris's *Bright Lights* magazine, to which I was a grateful longtime contributor.

I am grateful to San Francisco State University for giving me a sabbatical to work on this book. My thanks go to Amy Sueyoshi, our provost and vice president for Academic Affairs; President Lynn Mahoney; Interim Dean

Sophie Clavier of the College of Liberal and Creative Arts; Carleen Mandolfo, associate vice president for Faculty Affairs and Professional Development; and Professor Aaron Kerner, director of our School of Cinema. Aaron has been supportive of my teaching plans and needs, especially during the pandemic, and his empathy has been a boon to my work and health. I have been teaching at San Francisco State since 2002 and am pleased to have an academic home in which I can share my dialogue on cinema with our lively students. I especially thank my longtime friend and colleague Professor Steven Kovacs, filmmaker and film historian. He helped bring me to SFSU and has always been supportive in every way, including giving his smiling approval as Roger Corman's head of production on the night we blew up the school in *Rock 'n' Roll High School*, the 1979 film I co-wrote. And as a native of Hungary, Steve advised me on Hungarian names and cultural traditions for this book.

It is a pleasure to work again with Columbia University Press, which previously published my critical studies *How Did Lubitsch Do It?* (2018) and *Billy Wilder: Dancing on the Edge* (2021). John Belton and Philip Leventhal acquired this book for the Film and Culture series, as they did the others. John, my longtime friend and colleague, is a major film historian and a thoughtful and sympathetic editor. Philip, as executive editor, is always helpful, responsive, and encouraging. He and John are ideal collaborators on film books. Their suggestions on this one were beneficial. Caitlin Hurst has publicized my books assiduously and with keen intelligence. This book benefited from the careful and wise copyediting by Robert Fellman and the expert indexing by Silvia Benvenuto. Thanks to Elliott Scott Cairns for his excellent design of the book and to production editor Michael Haskell, assistant editor Emily Simon, and copywriter Zachary Friedman. I also am grateful to Drew Davidson of Films by Humans for his expert work with me on frame enlargements from Cukor films.

My beloved partner, Ann Weiser Cornell, an internationally known teacher and writer, has always been supportive in our life together and as a brilliant critic and editor of my writing. We have had a wonderful time these past few years watching Cukor films together, most of them repeatedly, and our discussions and Ann's keen comments have been invaluable. When I completed a draft of the manuscript, she read it with her customary acuity, making many suggestions for cutting, sharpening of language, and clarification of analysis.

Our shared love of film helped bring us together in the first place, and it was a pleasure to see and hear her responding with such enthusiasm and joy to Cukor's work. I always trust her judgment and almost invariably follow her reactions to my work. No more delightful companion could I have expected to have than Ann, who makes our daily lives so happy and fulfilling.

Berkeley, California

March 17, 2024

FILMOGRAPHY

George I. Cukor
Born: July 6, 1899, New York, New York
Died: January 23, 1983, Los Angeles, California

Although Cukor's date of birth is given incorrectly in various sources, often as July 7 or 14, 1899, his New York State birth certificate (No. 27202), filled out by Dr. Louis Friedman, states that Cukor was born at home (329 E. Fourth Street, New York City) on July 6. Furthermore, although his middle name is usually given as "Dewey" (supposedly a family tribute to the naval hero Admiral George Dewey), his birth certificate lists only an initial, I., as a middle name.

FILMOGRAPHY KEY

GC	George Cukor
DIST	Distributor
P	Producer or Executive Producer or Associate Producer (most prominent listed)
D	Director
S	Screenwriter(s) and source material
C	Principal cast members
L	Length (in minutes)
R	Release date

FILMS AS DIALOGUE DIRECTOR (UNCREDITED)

1929

River of Romance. DIST: Paramount; P: [none credited]; D: Richard Wallace; S: Ethel Doherty, Dan Totheroh, John V. A. Weaver, from the play *Magnolia* by Booth Tarkington; C: Charles (Buddy) Rogers, Mary Brian, June Collyer, Wallace Beery, Henry B. Walthall; L: 78; R: June 29, 1929.

1930

All Quiet on the Western Front. DIST: Universal; P: Carl Laemmle Jr.; D: Lewis Milestone; S: Maxwell Anderson, George Abbott, Del Andrews, from the novel *Im Westen nichts Neues/All Quiet on the Western Front* by Erich Maria Remarque; C: Louis Wolheim, Lew Ayres, John Wray, Ben Alexander, Slim Summerville; L: 152 [later cut; restored version, 133]; R: April 21, 1930.

FILMS AS CO-DIRECTOR

1930

Grumpy. DIST: Paramount; P [none listed]; D: GC, Cyril Gardner; S: Doris Anderson, from the play by Horace Hodges and Thomas Wigney Percyval; C: Cyril Maude, Phillips Holmes, Frances Dade, Paul Lukas, Halliwell Hobbes; L: 74; R: August 1, 1930.

The Virtuous Sin. DIST: Paramount: P: [none listed]; D: GC, Louis J. Gasnier; S: Martin Brown, Louise Long, from the play *The General* by Lajos Zilahy; C: Walter Huston, Kay Francis, Kenneth McKenna, Jobyna Howland, Paul Cavanaugh; L: 80; R: October 24, 1930.

The Royal Family of Broadway. DIST: Paramount; P: [none listed]; D: GC, Cyril Gardner; S: Herman J. Mankiewicz, Gertrude Purcell, from the play *The Royal Family* by Edna Ferber and George S. Kaufman; C: Ina Claire, Fredric March, Mary Brian, Henrietta Crosman, Arnold Korff; L: 82; R: December 22, 1930.

1932

One Hour with You. DIST: Paramount. P: Ernst Lubitsch; D: Lubitsch, "Assisted by" GC; S: Samson Raphaelson, from the play *Nur ein Traum/Only a Dream* by Lothar Schmidt [a musical remake of Lubitsch's 1924 silent film *The Marriage Circle*]; C: Maurice Chevalier, Jeanette MacDonald, Genevieve Tobin, Charles Ruggles, Roland Young; L: 78; R: March 23, 1932. Also released in a French-language version, *Une heure près de toi*.

FILMS AS DIRECTOR

1931

Tarnished Lady. DIST: Paramount; P: Walter Wanger; D: GC; S: Donald Ogden Stewart, from his story "New York Lady"; C: Tallulah Bankhead, Clive Brook, Phoebe Foster, Alexander Kirkland, Elizabeth Patterson; L: 83; R: May 2, 1931.

Girls About Town. DIST: Paramount; P: Raymond Griffith; D: GC; S: Griffith, Brian Marlow, from a story by Zoë Akins; C: Kay Francis, Joel McCrea, Lilyan Tashman, Eugene Pallette, Lucile Gleason; L: 80; R: November 7, 1931.

1932

What Price Hollywood? DIST: RKO; P: David O. Selznick; D: GC; S: Jane Murfin, Ben Markson, Gene Fowler, Rowland Brown, from a story by Adela Rogers St. Johns; C: Constance Bennett, Lowell Sherman, Neil Hamilton, Gregory Ratoff, Louise Beavers; L: 88; R: June 23, 1932.

A Bill of Divorcement. DIST: RKO; P: David O. Selznick; D: GC; S: Howard Estabrook, Harry Wagstaff Gribble, from the play by Clemence Dane; C: John Barrymore, Billie Burke, Katharine Hepburn, David Manners, Elizabeth Patterson; L: 70; R: September 28, 1932.

Rockabye. DIST: RKO; P: David O. Selznick; D: GC [who reshot a version directed by George Fitzmaurice]; S: Jane Murfin, from the play by Lucia Bronder, based on her short story "Our Judy"; C: Constance Bennett, Joel McCrea, Paul Lukas, Jobyna Howland, Walter Pidgeon; L: 68; R: November 25, 1932.

1933

Our Betters. DIST: RKO; P: David O. Selznick; D: GC; S: Jane Murfin, Harry Wagstaff Gribble, from the play by W. Somerset Maugham; C: Constance Bennett, Violet Kemble Cooper, Phoebe Foster, Grant Mitchell, Gilbert Roland; L: 83; R: February 23, 1933.

Dinner at Eight. DIST: MGM; P: David O. Selznick; D: GC; S: Frances Marion, Herman J. Mankiewicz [with additional dialogue by Donald Ogden Stewart, uncredited], from the play by George S. Kaufman and Edna Ferber; C: Marie Dressler, John Barrymore, Wallace Beery, Jean Harlow, Lionel Barrymore; L: 111; R: August 23, 1933.

Little Women. DIST: RKO; P: Merian C. Cooper; D: GC; S: Sarah Y. Mason and Victor Heerman, from the novel *Little Women, or, Meg, Jo, Beth and Amy* by Louisa May Alcott; C: Katharine Hepburn, Joan Bennett, Paul Lukas, Edna May Oliver, Jean Parker; L: 115; R: November 16, 1933.

1935

The Personal History, Adventures, Experience, & Observation of David Copperfield the Younger, aka *David Copperfield.* DIST: MGM; P: David O. Selznick; D: GC; S: Hugh

Walpole, Howard Estabrook, from the novel by Charles Dickens; C: Edna May Oliver, Elizabeth Allen, Jessie Ralph, Freddie Bartholomew, W. C. Fields; L: 130; R: January 18, 1935.

Sylvia Scarlett. DIST: RKO; P: Pandro S. Berman; D: GC; S: Gladys Unger, John Collier, Mortimer Offner, from the novel *The Early Life and Adventures of Sylvia Scarlett* by Compton Mackenzie; C: Katharine Hepburn, Cary Grant, Brian Aherne, Edmund Gwenn, Dennie Moore; L: 95; R: December 25, 1935.

1936

Romeo and Juliet. DIST: MGM; P: [Irving Thalberg, uncredited]; D: GC; S: Talbot Jennings, from the play by William Shakespeare; C: Norma Shearer, Leslie Howard, John Barrymore, Basil Rathbone, Edna May Oliver; L: 125; R: August 20, 1936.

Camille. DIST: MGM; P: David Lewis [and Irving Thalberg, Bernard H. Hyman, uncredited]; D: GC; S: Zoë Akins, Frances Marion, James Hilton, from the novel *La dame aux camélias/The Lady of the Camellias* by Alexandre Dumas *fils* and his stage version; C: Greta Garbo, Robert Taylor, Lionel Barrymore, Lenore Ulric, Henry Daniell; L: 109; R: December 12, 1936.

1938

Holiday. DIST: Columbia; P: Everett Riskin; D: GC; S: Donald Ogden Stewart, Sidney Buchman, from the play by Philip Barry; C: Katharine Hepburn, Cary Grant, Doris Nolan, Lew Ayres, Edward Everett Horton; L: 95; R: May 24, 1938.

Zaza. DIST: Paramount; P: Albert Lewin; D: GC; S: Zoë Akins, from the play by Pierre Berton and Charles Simon; C: Claudette Colbert, Herbert Marshall, Bert Lahr, Helen Westley, Constance Collier; L: 83; R: December 29, 1938.

1939

The Women. DIST: MGM; P: Hunt Stromberg; D: GC [with Technicolor fashion show sequence supervised by Adrian, the film's costume designer]; S: Anita Loos, Jane Murfin, from the play by Clare Boothe [Luce]; C: Norma Shearer, Joan Crawford, Rosalind Russell, Mary Boland, Joan Fontaine; L: 133; R: August 29, 1939. Partly in color.

Gone with the Wind. DIST: MGM; P. David O. Selznick; D: Victor Fleming [and GC, Sam Wood, William Cameron Menzies, B. Reeves Eason, uncredited]; S: Sidney Howard [and Ben Hecht et al., uncredited], from the novel by Margaret Mitchell; C: Clark Gable, Vivien Leigh, Olivia de Havilland, Thomas Mitchell, Hattie McDaniel; L: 238; R: December 15, 1939. Color.

1940

Susan and God. DIST: MGM; P: Hunt Stromberg; D: GC; S: Anita Loos, from the play by Rachel Crothers; C: Joan Crawford, Fredric March, Ruth Hussey, Rita Hayworth, Rita Quigley; L: 117; R: June 7, 1940.

The Philadelphia Story. DIST: MGM; P: Joseph L. Mankiewicz; D: GC; S: Donald Ogden Stewart, from the play by Philip Barry; C: Cary Grant, Katharine Hepburn, James Stewart, Ruth Hussey, Virginia Weidler; L: 112; R: December 5, 1940.

1941

A Woman's Face. DIST: MGM; P: Victor Saville; D: GC; S: Donald Ogden Stewart, Elliot Paul, from the play *Il était une fois . . . /Once Upon a Time* by Francis de Croisset; C: Joan Crawford, Melvyn Douglas, Conrad Veidt, Osa Massen, Reginald Owen; L: 106; R: May 9, 1941.

Two-Faced Woman. DIST: MGM; P: Gottfried Reinhardt; D: GC; S: S. N. Behrman, Salka Viertel, George Oppenheimer, from the play *Die Zwillingsschwester/The Twin Sister* by Ludwig Fulda; C: Greta Garbo, Melvyn Douglas, Constance Bennett, Roland Young, Ruth Gordon; L: 90; R: November 30, 1941 [and censored/revised version: December 31, 1941].

1942

Her Cardboard Lover. DIST: MGM; P: J. Walter Ruben; D: GC; S: Jacques Deval, John Collier, Anthony Veiller, William H. Wright, from the play *Dans sa candeur naïve/In His Naïve Candor* by Jacques Deval and the English version, *Her Cardboard Lover*, by P. G. Wodehouse and Valerie Wyngate; C: Norma Shearer, Robert Taylor, George Sanders, Frank McHugh, Elizabeth Patterson; L: 93; R: July 16, 1942.

Keeper of the Flame. DIST: MGM; P: Victor Saville; D: GC; S: Donald Ogden Stewart, from the novel by I. A. R. Wylie; C: Spencer Tracy, Katharine Hepburn, Richard Whorf, Margaret Wycherly, Forrest Tucker; L: 100; R: December 1942.

1943

Electricity and Magnetism, Part II—Ohm's Law. DIST: U.S. Army War Department (Signal Corps training film); D: GC; S: Arthur Laurents; L: 19; R: 1943. Cukor served as a private in the U.S. Army Signal Corps, making training and other films at the Signal Corps Photographic Center in the Astoria Studios in Queens, New York, from October 7, 1942, to May 8, 1943.

1944

Gaslight. DIST: MGM; P: Arthur Hornblow Jr. D: GC; S: John Van Druten, Walter Reisch, John L. Balderston, from the play *Gas Light* [aka *Angel Street*] by Patrick Hamilton; C: Charles Boyer, Ingrid Bergman, Joseph Cotten, May Whitty, Angela Lansbury; L: 114; R: May 4, 1944.

Winged Victory. DIST: Twentieth Century-Fox; P: Darryl F. Zanuck in association with the U.S. Army Air Forces; D: GC; S: Moss Hart, from his play; C: Mark Daniels, Edmond O'Brien, Lon McCallister, Don Taylor, Judy Holliday; L: 130; R: December 20, 1944.

1947

Desire Me. DIST: MGM; P: Arthur Hornblow Jr.; D: [GC, Jack Conway, Mervyn LeRoy, Victor Saville, all uncredited]; S: Marguerite Roberts, Zoë Akins, Casey Robinson, from the novella *Karl und Anna/Karl and Anna* by Leonhard Frank; C: Greer Garson, Robert Mitchum, Richard Hart, Morris Ankrum, George Zucco; L: 91; R: October 31, 1947.

A Double Life. DIST: Universal-International; P: Michael Kanin; D: GC; S: Ruth Gordon, Garson Kanin (with excerpts from the play *Othello* by William Shakespeare); C: Ronald Colman, Signe Hasso, Edmond O'Brien, Shelley Winters, Ray Collins; L: 104; R: December 25, 1947.

1949

Edward, My Son. DIST: MGM; P: Edwin H. Knopf; D: GC; S: Donald Ogden Stewart, from the play by Robert Morley and Noel Langley; C: Spencer Tracy, Deborah Kerr, Ian Hunter, James Donald, Leueen MacGrath; L: 112; R: March 1, 1949.

Adam's Rib. DIST: MGM; P: Lawrence Weingarten; D: GC; S: Ruth Gordon, Garson Kanin; C: Spencer Tracy, Katharine Hepburn, Judy Holliday, Tom Ewell, David Wayne; L: 101; R: November 16, 1949.

1950

A Life of Her Own. DIST: MGM; P: Voldemar Vetlugin; D: GC; S: Isobel Lennart; C: Lana Turner, Ray Milland, Tom Ewell, Ann Dvorak, Margaret Phillips; L: 108; R: September 1, 1950.

Born Yesterday. DIST: Columbia; P: S. Sylvan Simon; D: GC; S: Albert Mannheimer [and Garson Kanin, uncredited], from the play by Kanin; C: Judy Holliday, Broderick Crawford, William Holden, Howard St. John, Frank Otto; L: 103; R: December 25, 1950.

1951

The Model and the Marriage Broker. DIST: Twentieth Century-Fox; P: Charles Brackett; D: GC; S: Brackett, Walter Reisch, Richard L. Breen; C: Jeanne Crain, Scott Brady, Thelma Ritter, Zero Mostel, Michael O'Shea; L: 103; R: November 1951.

1952

The Marrying Kind. DIST: Columbia; P: Bert Granet; D: GC; S: Ruth Gordon, Garson Kanin; C: Judy Holliday, Aldo Ray, Madge Kennedy, Sheila Bond, John Alexander; L: 92; R: March 13, 1952.

Pat and Mike. DIST: MGM; P: Lawrence Weingarten; D: GC; S: Ruth Gordon, Garson Kanin; C: Spencer Tracy, Katharine Hepburn, Aldo Ray, William Ching, Sammy White; L: 95; R: June 5, 1952.

1953

The Actress. DIST: MGM; P: Lawrence Weingarten; D: GC; S: Ruth Gordon, from her play *Years Ago*; C: Spencer Tracy, Jean Simmons, Teresa Wright, Anthony Perkins, Kay Williams; L: 90; R: September 25, 1953.

1954

It Should Happen to You. DIST: Columbia; P: Fred Kohlmar; D: GC; S: Garson Kanin; C: Judy Holliday, Peter Lawford, Jack Lemmon, Michael O'Shea, Vaughn Taylor; L: 86; R: January 15, 1954.

A Star Is Born. DIST: Warner Bros.; P: Sidney Luft; D: GC [and the film's choreographer, Richard Barstow, and Roger Edens, for the "Born in a Trunk" medley and Barstow for "Lose That Long Face" number]; S: Moss Hart, from the 1937 screenplay by Dorothy Parker, Alan Campbell, and Robert Carson, based on the story by William A. Wellman and Carson; C: Judy Garland, James Mason, Jack Carson, Charles Bickford, Tom Noonan; L: 181 [cut to 154 after premiere; restored to 176 in 1983, including film footage and stills]; R: September 29, 1954 [and July 7, 1983, for the restored version]. Color.

1956

Bhowani Junction. DIST: MGM; P: Pandro S. Berman; D: GC; S: Sonya Levien, Ivan Moffat, from the novel by John Masters; C: Ava Gardner, Stewart Granger, Bill Travers, Abraham Sofaer, Francis Matthews; L: 110; R: May 1, 1956. Color.

1957

Les Girls. DIST: MGM; P: Sol C. Siegel; D: GC; S: John Patrick, from a story by Vera Caspary; C: Gene Kelly, Mitzi Gaynor, Kay Kendall, Taina Elg, Jacques Bergerac; L: 114; R: October 3, 1957. Color.

Wild Is the Wind. DIST: Paramount; P: Hal B. Wallis; D: GC; S: Arnold Schulman, from a story by Vittorio Nino Novarese; C: Anna Magnani, Anthony Quinn, Anthony Franciosa, Joseph Calleia, Dolores Hart; L: 114; R: December 11, 1957.

1960

Heller in Pink Tights. DIST: Paramount; P: Marcello Girosi, Carlo Ponti; D: GC; S: Dudley Nichols, Walter Bernstein, from the novel *Heller with a Gun* by Louis L'Amour; C: Sophia Loren, Anthony Quinn, Margaret O'Brien, Steve Forrest, Eileen Heckart; L: 100; R: January 1, 1960. Color.

Song Without End. DIST: Columbia; P: William Goetz; D: Charles Vidor [GC finished the film after Vidor died three weeks into shooting; GC receives a screen-filling credit of "GRATEFUL RECOGNITION OF HIS GENEROUS CONTRIBUTION TO THIS FILM"]; S: Oscar Millard [and Walter Bernstein, uncredited]; C: Dirk

Bogarde, Geneviève Page, Patricia Morison, Ivan Desny, Capucine; L: 141; R: August 11, 1960. Color.

Let's Make Love. DIST: Twentieth Century-Fox; P: Jerry Wald; D: GC; S: Norman Krasna, Hal Kanter [and Arthur Miller, uncredited]; C: Marilyn Monroe, Yves Montand, Tony Randall, Frankie Vaughan, Wilfrid Hyde-White; L: 119; R: September 8, 1960. Color.

1962

The Chapman Report. DIST: Warner Bros.; P: Darryl F. Zanuck, Richard D. Zanuck; D: GC; S: Wyatt Cooper, Don Mankiewicz, Grant Stuart [pseudonym for Arthur Sheekman], Gene Allen, from the novel by Irving Wallace; C: Efrem Zimbalist Jr., Shelley Winters, Jane Fonda, Claire Bloom. Glynis Johns; L: 125; R: October 5, 1962. Color.

Something's Got to Give. DIST: Twentieth Century-Fox [unfinished]; P: Henry Weinstein; D: GC; S: Arnold Schulman, Nunnally Johnson, Walter Bernstein, from the 1940 screenplay *My Favorite Wife* by Bella Spewack, Sam Spewack, based on a story by the Spewacks and Leo McCarey; C: Marilyn Monroe, Dean Martin, Cyd Charisse, Tom Tryon, Wally Cox; L: 38 [reconstruction]; R: 2001 [reconstructed version shown in TV documentary *Marilyn Monroe: The Final Days*]. Color.

1964

My Fair Lady. DIST: Warner Bros.; P: Jack L. Warner; D: GC; S: Alan Jay Lerner, from his musical play adapted from George Bernard Shaw's play *Pygmalion*; C: Audrey Hepburn, Rex Harrison, Stanley Holloway, Wilfrid Hyde-White, Gladys Cooper; L: 170; R: October 21, 1964. Color.

1969

Justine. DIST: Twentieth Century-Fox; P: Pandro S. Berman ["A Pandro S. Berman-George Cukor production"]; D: GC [and Joseph Strick, who was fired while on location but some of whose footage was retained for the release version]; S: Lawrence B. Marcus, from the Alexandria Quartet of novels, *Justine*, *Balthazar*, *Mountolive*, and *Clea*, by Lawrence Durrell; C: Anouk Aimée, Dirk Bogarde, Anna Karina, Michael York, John Vernon: L: 116; R: August 6, 1969. Color.

1972

Travels with My Aunt. DIST: MGM; P: James Cresson, Robert Fryer; D: GC; S: Jay Presson Allen, Hugh Wheeler [and Katharine Hepburn, uncredited]; C: Maggie Smith, Alec McCowen, Lou Gossett, Robert Stephens, Cindy Williams; L: 108; R: December 17, 1972. Color.

1975

Love Among the Ruins. DIST: ABC Circle Films/ABC-TV; P: Allan Davis; D: GC; S: James Costigan; C: Katharine Hepburn, Laurence Olivier, Colin Blakely, Richard Pearson, Leigh Lawson; L: 100; R: March 6, 1975. Color.

1976

The Blue Bird. DIST: Twentieth Century-Fox; P: Harry N. Blum, Robert H. Greenberg, Paul Maslansky; D: GC; S: Hugh Whitemore, Alfred Hayes, Aleksei Kapler, from the play *L'oiseau bleu/The Blue Bird* by Maurice Maeterlinck; C: Elizabeth Taylor, Jane Fonda, Cicely Tyson, Todd Lookinland, Patsy Kensit; L: 99; R: April 5, 1976. Color.

1979

The Corn Is Green. DIST: Warner Bros. Television/CBS-TV; P: Neil Hartley; D: GC; S: Ivan Davis [pseudonym for James Costigan], based on the play by Emlyn Williams; C: Katharine Hepburn, Ian Saynor, Bill Fraser, Anna Massey, Toyah Willcox; L: 93; R: January 29, 1979. Color.

1981

Rich and Famous. DIST: MGM; P: William Allyn; D: GC; S: Gerald Ayres, from the play *Old Acquaintance* by John Van Druten; C: Jacqueline Bisset, Candice Bergen, David Selby, Hart Bochner, Matt Lattanzi; L: 117; R: October 9, 1981. Color.

Like other directors in the era when the Hollywood studios dominated American filmmaking, Cukor directed some reshoots and added scenes for other directors' films. In addition to films listed above for which he did more substantial renovations, these films he contributed to (with their principal directors listed) include *The Animal Kingdom* (d. Edward H. Griffith, 1932), *Manhattan Melodrama* (d. W. S. Van Dyke, 1934), *No More Ladies* (d. Edward H. Griffith, 1935), *The Prisoner of Zenda* (d. John Cromwell, 1937), *I Met My Love Again* (d. Arthur Ripley and Joshua Logan, 1938), *The Adventures of Tom Sawyer* (d. Norman Taurog, 1938), *Escape* (d. Mervyn LeRoy, 1940), *I'll Be Seeing You* (d. William Dieterle, 1944), *Lust for Life* (d. Vincente Minnelli, 1956), and *Hot Spell* (d. Daniel Mann, 1958). Cukor also shot many screen tests over the years, including a large number for *Gone with the Wind*. That additional work enabled him to become familiar with many actors he would later direct in his own features. Further details on these films are in the Cukor biographies by Patrick McGilligan and Emanuel Levy.

NOTES ON SOURCES

ABBREVIATIONS

AMPAS	Academy of Motion Picture Arts and Sciences' Margaret Herrick Library
EL	Emanuel Levy, *George Cukor: Master of Elegance: Hollywood's Legendary Director and His Stars*
FT	François Truffaut
GC	George Cukor
GL	Gavin Lambert, *On Cukor*
JM	Joseph McBride
KH	Katharine Hepburn
NYT	*New York Times*
PM	Patrick McGilligan, *George Cukor: A Double Life: A Biography of the Gentleman Director*
WM	William J. Mann, *Kate: The Woman Who Was Hepburn*

SELECTED BOOKS

Cecil Beaton, *Cecil Beaton's Fair Lady*, New York: Holt, 1964.

James Bernardoni, *George Cukor: A Critical Study and Filmography*, Jefferson, NC: McFarland, 1985.

Peter Bogdanovich, *Who the Devil Made It* (interviews with GC and other directors), New York: Knopf, 1997.

Dan Callahan, *The Camera Lies: Acting for Hitchcock*, New York: Oxford University Press, 2020.

Gary Carey, *Cukor & Co.: The Films of George Cukor and His Collaborators*, New York: Museum of Modern Art, 1971.

——, *Katharine Hepburn: A Hollywood Yankee*, New York: Pocket Books, 1975, and revised edition, 1984.

Carlos Clarens, *Cukor*, British Film Institute Cinema One series, London: Secker & Warburg, 1976.

James Curtis, *Spencer Tracy: A Biography*, New York: Knopf, 2011.

David Ehrenstein, *Open Secret: Gay Hollywood: 1928–1998*, New York: Morrow, 1998, and updated edition, *Open Secret: Gay Hollywood: 1928–2000*, New York: Harper Perennial, 2000.

Keith Garebian, *The Making of "My Fair Lady,"* Toronto: ECW Press, 1993.

Aljean Harmetz, *On the Road to Tara*, New York: Harry N. Abrams, 1996 (on the making of *Gone with the Wind*).

Molly Haskell, *From Reverence to Rape: The Treatment of Women in the Movies*, New York: Holt, Rinehart and Winston, 1974, and third edition, with foreword by Manohla Dargis, Chicago: University of Chicago Press, 2016.

——, *Frankly, My Dear: "Gone with the Wind" Revisited*, New Haven, CT: Yale University Press, 2009.

Ronald Haver, *David O. Selznick's Hollywood*, New York: Knopf, 1980.

——, *A Star Is Born: The Making of the 1954 Movie and Its 1983 Restoration*, New York: Knopf, 1988.

Elyce Rae Helford, *What Price Hollywood? Gender and Sex in the Films of George Cukor*, Lexington: University Press of Kentucky, 2020.

Katharine Hepburn, *Me: Stories of My Life*, New York: Knopf, 1991.

Charles Higham and Joel Greenberg, *The Celluloid Muse: Hollywood Directors Speak*, London: Angus & Robertson, 1969, and Chicago: Regnery, 1971.

Higham, *Kate: The Life of Katharine Hepburn*, New York: Norton, 1975, and revised edition, 1981.

George Houle, *The George Cukor Collection*, Los Angeles: Houle Rare Books & Autographs, 1986 (on GC's book collection).

Garson Kanin, *Tracy and Hepburn: An Intimate Memoir*, New York: Viking, 1971.

Gavin Lambert, *On Cukor*, New York: Putnam, 1972; updated edition, ed. Robert Trachtenberg, New York: Rizzoli, 2000.

——, *GWTW: The Making of "Gone with the Wind,"* Boston: Little, Brown, 1973.

Emanuel Levy, *George Cukor, Master of Elegance: Hollywood's Legendary Director and His Stars*, New York: Morrow, 1994.

Robert Emmet Long, ed., *George Cukor: Interviews*, Jackson: University Press of Mississippi, 2001.

Lorna Luft and Jeffrey Vance, *A Star Is Born: Judy Garland and the Film That Got Away*, Philadelphia: Running Press, 2018.

Sid Luft, *Judy and I: My Life with Judy Garland*, Chicago: Chicago Review Press, 2017.

William J. Mann, *Behind the Screen: How Gays and Lesbians Shaped Hollywood 1910–1969*, New York: Viking Penguin, 2001.

——, *Kate: The Woman Who Was Hepburn*, New York: Holt, 2006.

Samuel Marx, *Mayer and Thalberg: The Make-Believe Saints*, New York: Random House, 1975.

Joseph McBride, *Two Cheers for Hollywood: Joseph McBride on Movies*, Berkeley: Hightower Press, 2017.

Patrick McGilligan, *George Cukor: A Double Life: A Biography of the Gentleman Director*, New York: St. Martin's, 1991.

James Naremore, *Acting in the Cinema*, Berkeley: University of California Press, 1988 (includes chapter on KH in *Holiday*).

——, *Some Versions of Cary Grant*, New York: Oxford University Press, 2022.

Gene D. Phillips, *George Cukor*, Boston: Twayne, 1982.

Murray Pomerance and R. Barton Palmer, eds., *George Cukor: Hollywood Master*, Edinburgh: Edinburgh University Press, 2015.

Andrew Sarris, *The American Cinema: Directors and Directions, 1929–1968*, New York: Dutton, 1968.

Richard Schickel, *The Men Who Made the Movies*, New York: Atheneum, 1975 (includes GC interview for Schickel's TV documentary series of the same title).

David O. Selznick, ed. Rudy Behlmer, *Memo from David O. Selznick*, New York: Viking, 1972.

George Stevens Jr., ed. and introduction, *Conversations with the Great Moviemakers of Hollywood's Golden Age at the American Film Institute*, New York: Knopf, 2006, and paperback edition, New York: Vintage, 2007 (contains edited transcript from seminars with GC at the AFI in 1972, 1977, 1978, and 1979).

François Truffaut, *Hitchcock/Truffaut*, first published as *Le cinéma selon Alfred Hitchcock*, Paris: Éditions Robert Laffont, Paris, 1966; published in English, New York: Simon & Schuster, 1967, and revised edition, 1985.

Mark A. Viera, *Irving Thalberg: Boy Wonder to Producer Prince*, Berkeley: University of California Press, 2009.

Steve Wilson, introduction by Robert Osborne, *The Making of "Gone with the Wind,"* Austin: University of Texas Press, 2014.

PUBLISHED SCREENPLAYS

Film Scripts Online, Alexander Street database, Alexander Street Press, 2023. Contains numerous screenplays and continuity scripts of Cukor films.

Gene Fowler and Rowland Brown (and Jane Murfin and Ben Markson, based on a story by Adela Rogers St. Johns), *What Price Hollywood?*, New York: Frederick Ungar, 1985.

Ruth Gordon and Garson Kanin, *Adam's Rib*, New York: Viking, 1972.

Sarah Y. Mason and Victor Heerman, *Little Women*, n.d., in Lorraine Noble, ed., *Four-Star Scripts*, New York: Doubleday, Doran, 1936.

SELECTED DOCUMENTARY FILMS AND TELEVISION INTERVIEWS (CHRONOLOGICAL ORDER)

Cineastes de notre temps: Conversation avec George Cukor/Filmmakers of Our Time: Conversation with George Cukor, written and produced by Janine Bazin and André S. Labarthe, directed by Hubert Knapp and Labarthe, May 12, 1969.

GC on *The Dick Cavett Show*, ABC, 1972; PBS, 1981.

The Men Who Made the Movies: George Cukor, written and directed by Richard Schickel, PBS, 1973, revised version, TCM, 2001.

The Film Society of Lincoln Center Tribute to George Cukor, CBS, 1978.

The Making of a Legend: "Gone with the Wind," directed by David Hinton, written by David Thomson, TNT, 1988.

Marilyn: Something's Got to Give (on Marilyn Monroe and the making of Cukor's unfinished 1962 film *Something's Got to Give*), Henry Schipper, producer-writer-narrator, Fox Entertainment News, 1990.

All About Me (on KH), directed by David Heeley, written by Heeley, KH, and Joan Kramer, Top Hat Productions/Turner Pictures, TNT, 1993.

More Loverly Than Ever: The Making of "My Fair Lady" Then & Now, directed by Suzie Galler, Galler West/CBS Video, 1994.

American Masters: George Cukor: On Cukor (based on GL), documentary, written and directed by Robert Trachtenberg, PBS, November 22, 2000.

Marilyn Monroe: The Final Days (deals with the making of *Something's Got to Give* and includes a partial reconstruction of the unfinished film), Patty Ivins Specht, director; Monica Bider, writer; narrator, James Coburn, American Movie Classics/Fox Television Studios/Prometheus Entertainment/Van Ness Films/Foxstar Productions, 2001.

Reflections on "Gaslight," directed by John Mulholland, MODA Entertainment, 2003.

In Search of Tracy Lord, produced by Issa Clubb, Criterion Collection, about *The Philadelphia Story*, 2017.

EPIGRAPH

KH, "You never had," is quoted by GL. She makes a similar comment in the documentary *George Cukor: On Cukor*.

INTRODUCTION: IS GEORGE CUKOR AN AUTEUR?
AND WHY DOES THAT MATTER?

Books

GC flirted with autobiography; GL; PM; Lambert on GC wanting him to write his biography: *Mainly About Lindsay Anderson*, New York: Knopf, 2000. Background on *la politique des auteurs* and the auteur theory: Sarris, *The American Cinema*; and John Caughie, ed., *Theories of Authorship: A Reader*, London: British Film Institute, 1981. Ernst Lubitsch working with writers: JM, *How Did Lubitsch Do It?*, New York: Columbia University Press, 2018. GC, "not a writer," "We worked very closely," "The more successful," on director as "the audience," "In films, it's what you *are*": Clarens, *Cukor*. GC's firing from *Gone with the Wind:* sources including PM, GL, Lambert, *GWTW*; Harmetz, *On the Road to Tara*; also GC background, ibid.

GC, "I'm not an *auteur*": GL, original edition only; GC, "My work really begins," "I find it wonderful," on interest in research and art direction, on hitting KH, "removed" from *Desire Me*, "climate," James Mason, and Garbo kissing Robert Taylor: GL. Henri Langlois on GC, KH, "All the people": GL. PM on GC's "double life," including his social life, and on *Heller in Pink Tights*. King Vidor to GC on staging plays: letter quoted in PM, February 24, 1933, from GC collection at AMPAS. Multiple writers on *Little Women:* KH, *Me*; PM.

JM in *The Other Side of the Wind* including Orson Welles to Tim Holt: JM, *What Ever Happened to Orson Welles? A Portrait of an Independent Career*, Lexington: University Press of Kentucky, 2006 and revised edition, 2022. GC, "I choose my actors": Bill Davidson, "George Cukor: 'Just Being Witty and Stylish Isn't Enough,'" *NYT*, April 30, 1978, the director told *NYT* when he received the Film Society of Lincoln Center award in 1978.

James Naremore, *Acting in the Cinema*, Berkeley: University of California Press, 1988, and *Some Versions of Cary Grant*, New York: Oxford University Press, 2022; Dan Callahan, *The Camera Lies: Acting for Hitchcock*, New York: Oxford University Press, 2020, and *Barbara Stanwyck: The Miracle Woman*, Jackson: University Press of Mississippi, 2012, and his two collections of essays, *The Art of Screen Acting, 1912–1960* and *1960 to Today*, Jefferson, NC: McFarland, 2018 and 2019. FT, *Hitchcock/Truffaut*. Hamlet "tear[ing] a passion to tatters": Shakespeare, *Hamlet*, London: first quarto edition, 1603. Alfred Hitchcock on screen acting: FT, *Hitchcock/Truffaut*. GC on Hitchcock: Higham and Greenberg. JM, *Frank Capra: The Catastrophe of Success*, New York: Simon & Schuster, 1992, and revised edition, New York: St. Martin's, 2000.

Welles on James Stewart: Welles and Peter Bogdanovich, ed. Jonathan Rosenbaum, *This Is Orson Welles*, New York: HarperCollins, 1992. GC, Objections by RKO's James Wingate and Will Hays objection to Tyrell Davis performance in *Our Betters*: Mann, *Behind the Screen*, including Wingate to Merian C. Cooper, February 20, 1933, and Hays to Wingate, March 1, 1933; warning by Code office about Kip in *Adam's Rib*: EL. Sarris on "dreamer" theme in GC's work: *The American Cinema*. GC on Paul Morrissey's *Flesh*, "an authentic": PM; "to present": GL. Suicide ending cut from *A Life of Her Own*: GC in Clarens; Jeremy Arnold, *"A Life of Her Own,"* Turner Classic Movies website, July 27, 2005.

Articles

JM, *"Cukor & Co.,"* Autumn 1971 *Film Quarterly* review of Carey, *Cukor & Co*. JM, "George Cukor: *The Blue Bird*" (interview), *Action*, November–December 1975; reprinted in Long. JM article on GC as oldest Hollywood studio director: *Variety*, October 17, 1980. JM and Todd McCarthy, "Carry On, Cukor" (interview with comments on visiting set of *Rich and Famous*), *Film Comment*, September–October 1981, with JM and McCarthy, "Jacqueline Bisset on *Rich and Famous*," ibid.; GC interview reprinted in Long and in JM, *Two Cheers for Hollywood*. JM, "George Cukor: The Valor of Discretion," *Bright Lights*, April 2001, reprinted in *Two Cheers for Hollywood*.

GC, "If I were very handsome": Mary Rourke, "George Cukor—a Magnificent Obsession," *Women's Wear Daily*, April 25, 1978, quoted in Callahan, "Cukor, George," *Senses of Cinema*, October 2004. Background on *la politique des auteurs* and the auteur theory: FT, "Une certain tendance du cinéma français," *Cahiers du Cinéma*, January 1954; Sarris, "Notes on the Auteur Theory in 1962," *Film Culture*, Winter 1962/1963. Alexandre Astruc on the "caméra-stylo": "Du Stylo à la caméra et de la caméra au stylo"/"The Birth of a New Avant-Garde: La Caméra-Stylo," *L'Écran Française*, March 30, 1948. Roland Barthes on "the death of the author": from his essay first published in English as "The Death of the Author" in *Aspen*, nos. 5–6, 1967, and then in French as "La mort d'auteur" in *Manteia*, no. 5, 1968.

André Bazin on "the genius of the system": "De la politique des auteurs," *Cahiers du Cinéma*, April 1957, reprinted in translation, "On the *politique des auteurs*," in Jim Hillier, ed., *Cahiers du Cinéma: The 1950s: Neo-Realism, Hollywood, New Wave*, Cambridge, MA: Harvard University Press, 1985, and Thomas Schatz, *The Genius of the System: Hollywood Filmmaking in the Studio Era*, New York: Pantheon Books, 1989. Pauline Kael's criticisms of GC are from her essay "Circles and Squares," *Film Quarterly*, Spring 1963, reprinted in her collection *I Lost It at the Movies*, Boston: Little, Brown, 1965. Ernest Callenbach (as E. C.), "The result certainly shows": review of GL, *Film Quarterly*, July 1973.

FT on "this admirable film" and "the beauty of Cukor's work" in his review of *A Life of Her Own*, "Notes sur d'autres films," *Cahiers du Cinéma*, December 1953, Wheeler Winston Dixon, with translations by Ruth Cassel Hoffman, Sonja Kropp, and Brigitte Formentin-Humbert, *The Early Film Criticism of François Truffaut*, Bloomington: Indiana University Press, 1993. FT on *It Should Happen to You*: 1954 review included in FT, trans. Leonard Mayhew, *The Films in My Life*, Paris: Flammarion, 1975, and New York: Simon & Schuster, 1978. Edward Buscombe on GC: "On Cukor," *Screen*, Autumn 1973; quoted in EL, "Cukor, George: Director of Classic Hollywood Cinema—Part 1," emanuellevy .com, June 29, 2015.

Charles Brackett, "The understatement," and Gene Kelly, "endless chatter": Kenneth Tynan, "George Cukor," *Holiday*, February 1961, reprinted in Tynan, *Profiles*, selected and ed. by Kathleen Tynan and Ernie Eban, London: Nick Hern Books, 1989, and New York: HarperCollins, 1990. Olivia de Havilland on GC: Ronald Bryden, "Epic," *The Observer* (London), January 7, 1968, quoted in Carey, *Cukor & Co*. *Cahiers du Cinéma*, "A DIRECTOR IS BORN!": quoted by Sarris in his latter-day upgrading of GC, "Cukor," *Film Comment*, March–April 1978. Sarris review of *Travels with My Aunt*, *Village Voice*, January 4, 1973. GC on long takes: JM-McCarthy interview. JM, "'Nothing Will Ever Stop Hitch,'" *Daily Variety* 42nd Annual Issue, Fall 1975, on the shooting of *Family Plot*, reprinted in *Two Cheers for Hollywood*. John Wayne to JM interview: "Wayne, Stewart and 'Shootist'—a Sense of History-in-the-Making," *Daily Variety*, January 29, 1976, reprinted in *Two Cheers for Hollywood* as "Wayne, Stewart and 'The Shootist'—a Sense of History-in-the-Making."

GC, "I came with the talkies" and his preference for "queer" to "gay" and how GC virtually "came out": Douglas W. Edwards and David B. Goodstein, "A Conversation with George Cukor," *The Advocate*, April 29, 1982, reprinted in Long. Callahan, "This was an artist": "Cukor, George." James Agee review of *The Lost Weekend*: *The Nation*, December 22, 1945. Angela Lansbury on GC's "wonderful gamey quality" to Film Society of Lincoln Center tribute 1978 and GC, *Little Women* his "secret favorite": Judy Klemesrud, "His Living Legends Salute Cukor," *NYT*, May 1, 1978 (Lambert tells him in GL, "I can well understand why it's your own favorite picture"). GC's profane language in "Carry On, Cukor" and Lambert's objection: GL to JM. GC on *Vicky* project: "Carry On, Cukor"; also see PM.

Other Sources

Comments by GC, Sidney Poitier, and the announcer at April 10, 1968, Academy Awards ceremony: video clip at oscar.org. GC papers at AMPAS, Beverly Hills, donated 1979. GC, "bum's laugh": JM heard this at Academy screening of *Little Women*. Naremore on books about GC not doing him "full critical justice": Naremore to JM, 2023. Jane Murfin and Harry Wagstaff Gribble, *Our Betters* screenplay, n.d. Frank Capra on acting: *The American Film Institute Salute to James Stewart*, CBS-TV, 1980; also Lee Strasberg on the speech: JM, *Frankly: Unmasking Frank Capra*, Berkeley: Hightower Press, 2019, and *Frank Capra: The Catastrophe of Success*. Jean Renoir and Marcel Dalio: "Renoir preferred to explore feelings en marge" (on the margin): the February 8, 1967, episode "La règle de l'exception" in *Jean Renoir, le patron/Jean Renoir, The Boss*, a filmed series by Jacques Rivette for *Cineastes de notre temps*, 1966–1967.

GC, "Maybe that's why" on Gene Allen: from unpublished notes of JM's interview "George Cukor: *The Blue Bird*." Welles on director as audience: *Remembering Orson . . .* , videotape of the November 2, 1985, Welles memorial at the Directors Guild of America; he made the remarks in November 1981 at a luncheon honoring him by the Hollywood

Foreign Press Association. Welles to students in Paris on February 24, 1982, "The most important thing": *Orson Welles a la Cinémathèque française/Orson Welles at the Cinémathèque française*, a 1983 documentary by Pierre-André Boutang and Guy Seligmann. Jack Lemmon on working with GC: *On Cukor* documentary. GC, "Pricks and cunts" as description of Hollywood extras: in conversation with JM. GC remark about JM to publicist during interview on *The Blue Bird*.

1. LEW AYRES IN *ALL QUIET ON THE WESTERN FRONT* AND *HOLIDAY*

Books

Erich Maria Remarque novel, *All Quiet on the Western Front*, originally published as *Im Westen Nichts Neues*, Berlin: Propylaen/Ullstein-Verlag, 1929, trans. A. H. Wheen, as *All Quiet on the Western Front*, Boston: Little, Brown, 1929. GC on "bogus" Southern accent in *River of Romance* and GC on *All Quiet*: GL. Howard Hawks on typical early-talkie dialogue: JM, *Hawks on Hawks*, Berkeley: University of California Press, 1982. Lew Ayres: production of *All Quiet* 1930 film version, working with GC on that film and *Holiday*, his conscientious objector status in World War II and service as medic and chaplain's assistant: Lesley L. Coffin, *Lew Ayres: Hollywood's Conscientious Objector*, Jackson: University Press of Mississippi, 2012.

William Bakewell on GC: *Hollywood Be Thy Name: Random Recollections of a Movie Veteran from Silents to Talkies to TV*, Metuchen, NJ: Scarecrow, 1991. Gertrude Stein, "lost generation": from epigraph for Ernest Hemingway, *The Sun Also Rises*, New York: Scribner, 1926; Hemingway, "Abstract words": *A Farewell to Arms*, New York: Scribner, 1929. Oscar Wilde, "to be natural": his play *An Ideal Husband*, London: Smithers, 1899.

Philip Barry play *Holiday*, New York: Samuel French, 1929. GC, the rich a "great comfort": GL. Donald Ogden Stewart was a communist and later was blacklisted: Stewart, with note by KH, *By a Stroke of Luck! An Autobiography*, London: Paddington, 1975. Capra and Sidney Buchman, who became a member of the Communist Party by late 1938, was later blacklisted, and was informed on by Capra: JM, *Frank Capra: The Catastrophe of Success*.

Articles

Brackett on GC: Tynan, "George Cukor." Remarque, "I didn't expect": "Remarque 'Sorry for Lew Ayres,'" *Los Angeles Evening Herald and Express*, March 31, 1942. "Pacifist Ayres," telegram to *Time* magazine from GC, John Huston, Mary Astor, Franchot Tone, Olivia de Havilland, George Oppenheimer, Walter Huston, Charles Lederer, and Humphrey Bogart: *Time*, April 20, 1942. Agee on drunkenness: review of *The Lost Weekend*, *The Nation*.

Other Sources

Ayres on GC's directing in *All Quiet* and *Holiday:* TCM archival interview 1995, Turner Classic Movies, YouTube. Buchman joined Communist Party in late 1938: Buchman testimony to House Committee on Un-American Activities (HUAC), September 25, 1951, from *Communist Infiltration of Motion-Picture Industry*, 82nd Congress, vol. 7, House Committee on Un-American Activities, U.S. Government Printing Office, Washington, DC.

2. FREDRIC MARCH AND INA CLAIRE IN *THE ROYAL FAMILY OF BROADWAY*

Books

GC's youthful theatergoing and directing: PM; GL. "I am not only witty": Sir John Falstaff in William Shakespeare, *Henry IV, Part II*, act 1, scene 2. George S. Kaufman and Edna Ferber play, *The Royal Family*, first produced in 1927, published in Garden City, NY: Doubleday, Doran, 1928; also in *Kaufman & Co.: Broadway Comedies*, New York: Library of America, 2004. GC recalled crane shot "breakthrough" in *The Royal Family of Broadway*: GL. Callahan on John Barrymore: "John Barrymore—Sweet Prince of Irony" in *The Art of American Screen Acting, 1912–1960*.

Article

John Barrymore on March's performance is from his article "Those Incredible Barrymores," *The American Magazine*, February 1933.

Other Sources

Claudette Colbert told JM that romantic comedy in the early days of sound was referred to as "high comedy" before the other term came into use.

3. KAY FRANCIS IN *THE VIRTUOUS SIN* AND WITH LILYAN TASHMAN IN *GIRLS ABOUT TOWN*

Books

Kay Francis's career and sex life: Lynn Kear and John Rossman, *Kay Francis: A Passionate Life and Career*, Jefferson, NC: McFarland, 2006.

GC, "I think it is pleasing": Schickel, *The Men Who Made the Movies*. Lajos Zilahy play *A tábornok/The General*, 1928. Lilyan Tashman and Garbo relationship: Barry Paris, *Garbo*, New York: Knopf, 1994.

Articles

Variety review of *Girls About Town*, November 3, 1931.

4. LOWELL SHERMAN IN *WHAT PRICE HOLLYWOOD?*

Books

Screenplay by Gene Fowler and Rowland Brown (and Jane Murfin and Ben Markson, based on a story by Adela Rogers St. Johns), *What Price Hollywood?* GC reshot earlier version of *Rockabye*: PM. Sarris on Sherman: *The American Cinema*. GC, "slightly odious" and why he thought *What Price Hollywood?* was "absolutely real": GL. Ben Hecht on Gregory Ratoff: *A Child of the Century*, New York: Simon & Schuster, 1954. Carey writes on Sherman in *Cukor & Co*. GC re creating "climate" for actors: GL.

Articles

JM, "*What Price Hollywood?*," *Film Comment*, May–June 1973 (parts included in this section of the book). Rowland Brown had been expecting to direct the film: Philip K. Scheuer, "Principle of the Thing Makes Directors Quit," *LAT*, July 17, 1932. Jean-Luc Godard, every fictional film is a documentary on the actors: Dennis Lim, "It's Actual Life. No, It's Drama. No, It's Both," *NYT*, August 20, 2010.

5. KATHARINE HEPBURN AND JOHN BARRYMORE IN *A BILL OF DIVORCEMENT*

Books

Clemence Dane play *A Bill of Divorcement*, London: Heinemann, 1921.

KH entrance was first shot made for film, KH on John Barrymore's entrance scene, screen test from *Holiday*, "an amateur," and "It was as if": *Me*. GC and David O. Selznick agreed on the moment KH became a star, GC on screen test and filming *A Bill of Divorcement*: PM. FT, "privileged moment": FT, *Hitchcock/Truffaut*. Frank Capra, "Sometimes your story": 1973 interview with Richard Glatzer, in Glatzer and John Raeburn, eds., *Frank Capra: The Man and His Films*, Ann Arbor: University of Michigan Press, 1975.

GC on KH, "Her odd awkwardness," "too mannered": Higham, *Kate*. GC, "When I worked with the Barrymores," "When he did the scene," and "She was quite unlike" and Lambert, "seems to me": GL. KH slap from her father, acting in *Holiday* onstage, and "all of the most salient": WM. KH, "One reason": JM, *Frank Capra: The Catastrophe of Success*.

Articles

KH photo inscription: JM-McCarthy interview. Norbert Lusk review of *A Bill of Divorcement* in *LAT*, October 9, 1932, quoted in WM.

Other Sources

GC on KH, "At first" and "a sad lyric moment": PM from BBC interview transcript with GC from his collection at AMPAS.

6. JOHN BARRYMORE AND JEAN HARLOW IN *DINNER AT EIGHT*

Books

George S. Kaufman and Edna Ferber play *Dinner at Eight*: Garden City, NY: Doubleday, Doran, 1928; also in *Kaufman & Co.: Broadway Comedies*. GC and *One Hour with You* and David Niven on Lubitsch, "the masters' master": JM, *How Did Lubitsch Do It?*; PM on the shooting and lawsuit by GC. FT on Lubitsch: 1968 essay in *The Films in My Life*.

   GC, *Dinner at Eight* material not "profound," on John Barrymore as Larry Renault, and on staging suicide scene, and Thalberg on "*unguarded*" quality GC brought to Garbo's performance in *Camille*: GL. GC proud of speed of shooting: PM; GL. Hollywood studios pay cuts, shutdown, and labor movement: Larry Ceplair and Steven Englund, *The Inquisition in Hollywood: Politics in the Film Community, 1930–1960*, New York: Anchor/Doubleday, 1980. Comical tag written by Donald Ogden Stewart: David Stenn, *Bombshell: The Life and Death of Jean Harlow*, New York: Doubleday, 1993; also background of Harlow and information on shooting. GC, Harlow "played comedy": Stenn, from GC 1964 statement (AMPAS); comments by Stenn on Harlow's personality. Other comments by GC on Harlow are from GL. Harlow and *Platinum Blonde*: JM, *Frank Capra: The Catastrophe of Success*. Robert Towne on movie stars: "On Moving Pictures," introduction (originally published in *Scenario*, Winter 1995) to *"Chinatown"; "The Last Detail": Screenplays by Robert Towne*, New York: Grove, 1997.

Articles

Mao Zedong, "A revolution is not a dinner party": his essay "Report on an Investigation of the Peasant Movement in Hunan," 1927.

7. KATHARINE HEPBURN IN *LITTLE WOMEN*; THE ENSEMBLE OF *DAVID COPPERFIELD*

Books

Louisa May Alcott, *Little Women, or Meg, Jo, Beth and Amy*, Boston: Roberts Brothers, Parts One and Two, 1868, 1869. Sarah Y. Mason and Victor Heerman screenplay, *Little Women*. KH, "heaven to do" and comments on the screenplay drafts: *Me*. GC sometimes regarded *Little Women* as his favorite film: GL; Klemesrud; GC told Clarens *Sylvia Scarlett* was his favorite.

KH was a tomboy who called herself "Jimmy" and on "being a girl": WM; KH, *Me*; WM on her evidently bisexual life and his criticism of KH for making her image more conventional. KH calling herself "totally selfish" and GC "caught the atmosphere": *Me*. KH relationship with brother Tom and "this incident seemed": KH, *Me*; also on KH and Tom: WM; KH in A. Scott Berg, *Kate Remembered*, New York: Putnam, 2003. KH's father thought Tom was trying to "break off [an] affair" with a girl: WM, citing report of the office of the chief medical examiner of New York; Tom possibly was involved with a boy: Berg.

GC, "When I directed *Little Women*," from his essay "The Director" in Stephen Watts, ed., *Behind the Screen: How Films Are Made*, London: Arthur Barker, and New York: Dodge Publishing, 1938. GC, "When I came to read it" and "sentimental" about snow: GL. GC's interest in design of the film and his fondness for research: GL; PM. Alcott's "sensational fiction" and turn to more acceptable writing: Nina Auerbach, "Afterword" to *Little Women* by Louisa May Alcott, Bantam, New York, 1983.

Selznick coaxed MGM/Loews to make *David Copperfield*: EL; PM. W. C. Fields an admirer of Dickens: EL; Carlotta Monti, with Cy Rice, *W. C. Fields and Me*, Englewood Cliffs, NJ: Prentice-Hall, 1971. GC and Selznick did not believe in "improving" classics: GC in GL; Selznick, *Memo from David O. Selznick*; GL; Higham and Greenberg. Guerric DeBona, OSB, "Dickens, the Depression, and MGM's *David Copperfield*," in Naremore, ed., *Film Adaptation*, New Brunswick, NJ: Rutgers University Press, 2000.

Articles

KH et al. "poison at the box office": Harry Brandt, Independent Theatre Owners Association, "WAKE UP! HOLLYWOOD PRODUCERS," advertisement in *Hollywood Reporter*, May 4, 1938. "Dr. Hepburn's Son, 15, Hangs Himself While Visiting in New York," *Hartford* [CT] *Courant*, April 4, 1921. Henry Gerrard career and death: George E. Turner, "Hunting *The Most Dangerous Game*," *American Cinematographer*, October 2, 2020.

Other Sources

Howard Estabrook, adapted by Hugh Walpole, *The Personal History, Adventures, Experience, & Observation of David Copperfield the Younger* screenplay, 1934.

8. KATHARINE HEPBURN AND CARY GRANT IN *SYLVIA SCARLETT*

Books

Compton Mackenzie, *The Early Life and Adventures of Sylvia Scarlett*, London: Martin Secker, 1918. Production and audience response of *Sylvia Scarlett*, GC asked Museum of

Modern Art not to open retrospective with the film, Mortimer Offner and GC, "show business is a sanctuary," "burst into bloom," "every day": PM. Producer Pandro S. Berman, "a private promotional deal": Higham, *Kate*; Berman upset by film: PM; Higham, *Kate*; EL; prologue added and GC, KH characterization "*garçonne*": EL. John Collier, "Delightful experience" working on the film: Max Wilk, *Schmucks with Under-woods: Conversations with Hollywood's Classic Screenwriters*, New York: Applause Theatre & Cinema Books, 2004. FT and *Bonnie and Clyde*: Antoine de Baecque and Serge Tou-biana, *François Truffaut*, Paris: Editions Gallimard, 1996, and English version trans. Catherine Temerson, *Truffaut*, New York: Knopf, 1999.

KH dismissive of *Sylvia Scarlett*: KH, *Me*; KH diary, "This picture makes no sense": quoted in PM from interview with KH by David Robinson in the *Times* of London, November 24, 1973. Censorship concerns: Mann, *Behind the Screen*, quoting censor Joseph Breen letter to RKO president B. B. Kahane, August 5, 1935, Production Code Administration files, AMPAS. Naremore on *Sylvia Scarlett* and GC not "weak-kneed" about Cary Grant: *Some Versions of Cary Grant*. Definition of "camp": *Oxford English Dictionary*, 1909. Grant background: Naremore; Scott Eyman, *Cary Grant: A Brilliant Disguise*, New York: Simon & Schuster, 2020. KH on Grant, "George taught him": Tynan, "George Cukor."

Articles

GC on discussion he and KH had with Berman after *Sylvia Scarlett* preview: Tim Hunter, "George Cukor: 50 Years of Feisty Filmmaking," *Washington Post*, September 20, 1981. Bosley Crowther review of *Tirez sur le pianiste* (*Shoot the Piano Player*): "Scrambled Satire: Truffaut's 'Shoot the Piano Player' Opens," *NYT*, July 24, 1962. GC, "most of all": Davidson. Reviews of *Sylvia Scarlett*: Andre Sennwald, "Katharine Hepburn and Edmund Gwenn in 'Sylvia Scarlett,' at the Radio City Music Hall," *NYT*, January 10, 1936; *Chicago Tribune*, December 31, 1935; Harry Long, *Modern Screen*, June 1936; *Variety*, Jan-uary 15, 1936. Sennwald's suicide: "Sennwald's Death Laid to Gas Fumes," *NYT*, Janu-ary 13, 1936; "Frank S. Nugent '29J Succeeds Sennwald '30J," *Columbia Daily Spectator*, January 16, 1936; JM, "The Pathological Hero's Conscience: Screenwriter Frank S. Nugent was the quiet man behind director John Ford" (profile of Nugent), *Written By*, May 2001, reprinted in JM, *Two Cheers for Hollywood*, as "Screenwriter Frank S. Nugent: The Quiet Man Behind John Ford." Susan Sontag, "Notes on 'Camp,'" *Parti-san Review*, Fall 1964, reprinted in her collection *Against Interpretation and Other Essays*, New York: Farrar, Straus & Giroux, 1966. Natalie Paley background: Wikipedia.

Other Sources

GC telegram to KH, December 9, 1935.

9. GRETA GARBO IN *CAMILLE*

Books

Alexandre Dumas *fils*, *La dame aux camélias/The Lady of the Camellias*, 1848, and his 1852 stage version. GC unhappy with Frances Marion-James Hilton script, turned to Zoë Akins: Viera; Karen Swenson, *Greta Garbo: A Life Apart*, New York: Scribner, 1997. Irving Thalberg on storyline of *Camille*, "We have to" and "awful little prig": Swenson, quoting associate producer David Lewis's recollection of what Thalberg told the writers. Thalberg, "She's never been" and "*unguarded*": GC in GL. Thalberg death: Viera. GC quotes Henry James, "presented some enormous," "Most ladies cough," Akins line GC admired, "true sentiment," directing Garbo in theater scene, and thought Garbo born to play Camille and KH to play Jo March: GL; James on *La dame aux camélias*, "Dumas the Younger" (1895) reprinted in his collection *Notes on Novelists with Some Other Notes*, New York: Scribner, 1914.

GC on Armand role: Higham and Greenberg. Garbo in *Ninotchka*: JM, *How Did Lubitsch Do It?* Garbo jollity recognized by close friends: Swenson; Paris, *Garbo*. GC, "staggered": Paris. Garbo watched death scene: Swenson. Death of Helen Gross Cukor and GC using details of her death for *Camille*: PM; GL; findagrave.com. Garbo's illnesses: Swenson; her initial resistance to playing Camille: Garbo letter to Salka Viertel, November 22, 1935, quoted in Swenson. William Wordsworth, "Thoughts": "Ode: Intimations of Immortality from Recollections of Early Childhood," in *Poems, in Two Volumes*, London: Longman, Hurst, Rees, and Orme, 1807, edited and revised, 1815.

Articles

GC on sexual charge between characters in *Camille*: Noel Berggren, "Arsenic and Old Directors," *Esquire*, April 1972. GC on Garbo picking up fan: Richard Overstreet interview, "George Cukor," *Film Culture*, Autumn 1964, reprinted in Long. Tynan on Garbo: "The ecstacy of existing," *Sight and Sound*, Spring 1954.

Other Sources

Jean Renoir on acting in silent film: *Jean Renoir parle de son art/Jean Renoir Talks About His Art*, part I, an interview with Jacques Rivette, produced by Janin Bazin and Jean-Marie Coldefy, ORTF, France, 1961, in *Stage & Spectacle: Three Films by Jean Renoir*, Criterion Collection, 2004. Zoë Akins, Frances Marion, and James Hilton screenplay, *Camille*, 1936.

10. KATHARINE HEPBURN AND CARY GRANT IN *HOLIDAY*

Books

Philip Barry play *Holiday*, New York: Samuel French, 1929. Donald Ogden Stewart, *By a Stroke of Luck!* KH firing from *The Animal Kingdom* play, KH understudy to Hope Williams in *Holiday*, and her screen test of scene from that play: KH, *Me*; WM. GC, "Barry had this gift" and debate with Lambert about the rich: GL. Lambert, *The Slide Area: Scenes of Hollywood Life*, London: Hamish Hamilton, and New York: Viking, 1959. GC family background, Stewart wanted to play Nick in film: PM. Political orientations of Stewart and Sidney Buchman and their later blacklisting: see notes for chapter 1. Barry play *The Philadelphia Story*, New York: Coward-McCann, 1939. Hollywood blacklist and Judy Holliday: See notes for chapter 17. KH et al., "box office poison": see notes for chapter 7.

Capra-Robert Riskin films and Capra's relationship with Buchman: JM, *Frank Capra: The Catastrophe of Success*. Ayres's background as band member and KH disapproval of GC's idea of casting Carole Lombard: Coffin, *Lew Ayres*. Grant's background as acrobat: Eyman, *Cary Grant*. Clarens on *Holiday* and other GC films. Henry David Thoreau, "spending of the best part" and "beware of all enterprises": *Walden, or Life in the Woods*, Boston: Ticknor & Fields, 1854. WM on *Holiday*.

Articles

GC, "arbitrary movements" and "in movies": Edwards and Goodstein.

11. VIVIEN LEIGH, OLIVIA DE HAVILLAND, HATTIE McDANIEL, AND BUTTERFLY McQUEEN IN *GONE WITH THE WIND*

Books

Margaret Mitchell, *Gone with the Wind*, New York: Macmillan, 1936. GC's work on the film version and production histories of filming and reception: Selznick, *Memo from David O. Selznick*; GL, *GWTW*; Haver, *David O. Selznick's Hollywood*; Harmetz, *On the Road to Tara*; Haskell, *Frankly, My Dear: "Gone with the Wind" Revisited*; Wilson, *The Making of "Gone with the Wind"*; David Thomson, *Showman: The Life of David O. Selznick*, New York: Knopf, 1992; GL; and the PM and EL biographies. Scenes in film directed by GC, B. Reeves Eason as the film's second-unit director, Lee Garmes shot almost one-third of the film: Lambert, *GWTW*.

GC working on other films in that period: PM; EL; GL. GC calling other directors removed from films: PM. Mitchell grew up as tomboy calling herself "Jimmy": Marianne Walker, *Margaret Mitchell and John Marsh: The Love Story Behind "Gone with the Wind,"* Atlanta: Peachtree, 1993.

KH and Norma Shearer considered for Scarlett: Lambert books *GWTW* and *Norma Shearer: A Biography*, New York: Knopf, 1990; Harmetz. Vivien Leigh and Olivia de Havilland begging for GC's reinstatement and working with him surreptitiously: Lambert, *GWTW*; GC, "I was rather touched": GL; also booklet *The Producer Prince: A Celebration of David Oliver Selznick*, Los Angeles: Friends of the USC Libraries, University of Southern California, 1976 (transcript of a tribute at USC, April 6, 1975). Leigh on GC and Victor Fleming: her letter to husband, Leigh Holman, cited by Lambert, *GWTW*. De Havilland, "George read": Lambert, *GWTW*, except for line "He did this with such," quoted by PM from TV interview transcribed in GC papers at AMPAS, also the source of GC-de Havilland discussion on Melanie's appearance. GC on Leigh, "indescribable wildness" and "now she presents" and "Perhaps Gable": Lambert, *GWTW*. Hecht working on script: *A Child of the Century*; Harmetz; and Ron Hutchinson's play *Moonlight and Magnolias*, New York: Dramatists Play Service, 2006. Hecht opening intertitle originally described Southerners as "absurd": Harmetz reproduces Hecht memo with that line crossed out, February 26, 1939.

Leslie Howard called script "Just one climax" and Susan Myrick wrote Mitchell about GC's complaints: Harmetz. Clark Gable's attitude toward GC: PM (quoting Gable) and books on the film. Paul Morrissey on GC's direction of actors in film: EL. De Havilland in *Hold Back the Dawn*: JM, *Billy Wilder: Dancing on the Edge*, New York: Columbia University Press, 2021. Haskell on Melanie: *Frankly, My Dear.*

Articles

KH and Norma Shearer considered for Scarlett: "Shearer To Star in 'Gone with Wind,'" *NYT*, June 24, 1938, article appearing next to Frank S. Nugent's review of *Holiday*; and "Shearer Gives Up Role of Scarlett," *NYT*, August 1, 1938, which mentions that GC "has been holding out for Miss Hepburn for months but was overruled." De Havilland on GC's "marvelously intricate imagination": Ronald Bryden, "Epic," *The Observer* (London), January 7, 1968, quoted in Carey, *Cukor & Co.* Eason directing burning of Atlanta: Ezra Goodman, "Step Right Up and Call Him 'Breezy,'" *NYT*, April 19, 1942. Roger Ebert review: "*Gone with the Wind*," rogerebert.com, June 21, 1998. De Havilland on playing "good girls": Anita Gates, "The Good Girl Gets the Last Word," *NYT*, November 7, 2004.

Other Sources

GC to publicist about JM, during 1975 on *The Blue Bird*. Sidney Howard, *Gone with the Wind*, screenplay, January 24, 1939. *The Scarlett O'Hara War*, 1980 NBC-TV movie, written by William Hanley from the novel *Moviola* by Kanin, directed by John Erman, with George Furth as GC; part of 1980 miniseries *Moviola: A Hollywood Saga*; GC to

JM-McCarthy about his character in the TV movie. John Lee Mahin quoting Fleming to Leigh and Fleming on GC: McCarthy and JM, "Bombshell Days in the Golden Age," *Film Comment*, March–April 1980, reprinted in Patrick McGilligan, ed., *Backstory 1: Interviews with Screenwriters of Hollywood's Golden Age*, Berkeley: University of California Press, 1986, and JM, *Two Cheers for Hollywood*. GC directing Pauline Goddard screen test: *The Making of a Legend: "Gone with the Wind."*

12. NORMA SHEARER, JOAN CRAWFORD, ROSALIND RUSSELL, AND JOAN FONTAINE IN *THE WOMEN*

Books

Clare Boothe [Luce], with foreword, play *The Women*, New York: Random House, 1937. Norma Shearer's career and personality: Lambert, *Norma Shearer: A Biography*, New York: Knopf, 1990. GC enjoyed gossip in private except when it involved KH: WM. GC, "lion tamer" and on Rosalind Russell, Fontaine "was never really sure," GC criticized Mary and GL agreed: GL. Unspecified reviewer on "the absent presence" of men in *The Women*: Sylvia Jukes Morris, *Rage for Fame: The Ascent of Clare Boothe Luce*, New York: Random House, 1997, also see Morris, *Price of Fame: The Honorable Clare Boothe Luce*, New York: Random House, 2014. Haskell on Joan Crawford and Shearer: *From Reverence to Rape*. GC, Crawford and GC and filming of *No More Ladies*: Bob Thomas, *Joan Crawford: A Biography*, New York: Simon and Schuster, 1978; Crawford, "roughest time": PM. Crawford's family life: Christina Crawford, *Mommie Dearest*, New York: Harper-Collins, 1978; Thomas.

Moss Hart and George S. Kaufman advised Boothe on play: Morris, who quotes Hart's 1949 letter to her. F. Scott Fitzgerald and Donald Ogden Stewart contributed to script: GC in Clarens; Morris; PM. Russell in test and film, her comment "the critics," and GC, "If you're a heavy": Russell and Chris Chase, preface by Frederick Brisson, *Life Is a Banquet*, New York: Random House, 1977. Clarens on Russell in the film and on the ending. Boothe play *Kiss the Boys Good-Bye*, first produced in 1938, published in 1939, New York: Random House.

Articles

GC snaps "What the hell": Edwards and Goodstein. GC, Crawford "made no appeals" in her role: GC, "She Was Consistently Joan Crawford, Star," *NYT*, May 22, 1977. George Stevens on Fontaine: JM and McGilligan, "A Piece of the Rock: George Stevens" (interview), *Bright Lights*, no. 8, 1979, reprinted in McGilligan, *Film Crazy: Interviews with Hollywood Legends*, New York: St. Martin's, 2000, and in part in Paul Cronin, ed., *George Stevens: Interviews*, Jackson: University Press of Mississippi, 2004, and in JM, *Two Cheers for Hollywood*. GC on Fontaine's telephone scene: Overstreet.

Other Sources

Anita Loos and Jane Murfin, *The Women*, screenplay, n.d. TV movie *The Scarlett O'Hara War*.

13. JOAN CRAWFORD IN *SUSAN AND GOD* WITH RITA QUIGLEY AND IN *A WOMAN'S FACE*

Books

Rachel Crothers play *Susan and God*, New York: Random House, 1938. MGM bought it for Norma Shearer, MGM easing out Garbo, Shearer, and Crawford in early 1940s with inferior vehicles, Crawford's work on GC films, her makeup for *A Woman's Face*, and Louis B. Mayer's objections to her casting in that film: Thomas, *Joan Crawford*. Crawford career and personality: Thomas; Christina Crawford, *Mommie Dearest*. Joan Crawford to Fitzgerald, "Write hard" and her letter to Gerald Murphy in Aaron Latham, *Crazy Sundays: F. Scott Fitzgerald in Hollywood*, New York: Viking, 1971; Thomas. Constance Collier friend of GC and KH: KH, *Me*; WM.

How GC directed Crawford in *A Woman's Face:* GL; Thomas. *A Woman's Face* originally intended by MGM as a Garbo film and her rejection of it: Paris, *Garbo*. Jacques Deval play *Her Cardboard Lover: Dans sa candeur naïve/In His Naive Candor*, first performed 1926, published in Paris: Librairie Théatrale, 1927, and the English version, *Her Cardboard Lover*, by P. G. Wodehouse and Valerie Wyngate, 1927; GC had directed the play with Laurette Taylor: PM. Lambert on Shearer in the film version and her retirement: Lambert, *Norma Shearer*. GC remarks on Crawford at AMPAS memorial, 1977: Thomas (a longer version of GC's remarks published in GC, "She Was Consistently Joan Crawford, Star").

Articles

Crawford inscription to GC on photograph: JM-McCarthy interview.

Other Sources

Thomas to JM on Crawford's abuse of her children; FT to JM on his interest in directing the film version of *Mommie Dearest*. Moral Re-Armament movement: Wikipedia.

14. CARY GRANT, KATHARINE HEPBURN, AND JAMES STEWART IN *THE PHILADELPHIA STORY*

Books

Philip Barry play *The Philadelphia Story*. Screwball comedy was called "The Unfinished Fuck": Maurice Zolotow, *Billy Wilder in Hollywood*, New York: Putnam, 1977. KH worked closely on *Philadelphia Story* play with Barry, background on how project was planned to change KH's image, her setting up production at MGM, how play and film reflect her relationships with men: WM. KH, "I was a terrible pig": *Me*. Donald Ogden Stewart on his screenplay for the film version: Stewart, *By a Stroke of Luck!*

Sarris on James Stewart: *The American Cinema*; Noël Coward visit to *Philadelphia Story* set and encouraging Stewart: PM. Grant adlibbed "Excuse me": Naremore, *Some Versions of Cary Grant*. KH teaming with Spencer Tracy in *Woman of the Year*: KH, *Me*; WM; retake of ending, KH's objection, Joseph L. Mankiewicz's comment: Curtis, *Spencer Tracy*.

Articles

Sarris on screwball comedy: "The Sex Comedy Without Sex," *American Film*, March 1978. Sarris on Blythe Danner in *Philadelphia Story* onstage: *The Village Voice*, quoted in Robert B. Ray, *The ABCs of Classic Hollywood*, New York: Oxford University Press, 2008. Haskell, "She had to do": Mary McNamara, "It was her defining role: life," *LAT*, July 1, 2003. Jacques Rivette on Hawks: "The Genius of Howard Hawks," trans. Russell Campbell and Marvin Pister (pen name for JM), adapted from a translation by Adrian Brine, *Cahiers du Cinéma*, May 1953, reprinted in JM, ed., *Focus on Howard Hawks*, Englewood Cliffs, NJ: Prentice-Hall, 1972, and in Hillier, *Cahiers du Cinéma*.

Stewart voted for Henry Fonda in 1940 Oscar competition: n.a., "The Philadelphia Story," tcm.com, February 27, 2003. Stewart claimed to prefer directors who didn't give him much dialogue: JM, "Aren't You . . . Jimmy Stewart?," *American Film*, June 1976, reprinted in *Two Cheers for Hollywood*. Sarris on KH's "singularly ungracious comment" about GC in *Me*: "The Man in the Glass Closet," *NYT*, December 15, 1991 (review of PM). Mahin interview by McCarthy and JM, "Bombshell Days in the Golden Age."

Other Sources

Background on production of *Philadelphia Story* play and film: *In Search of Tracy Lord* documentary.

15. INGRID BERGMAN AND ANGELA LANSBURY IN *GASLIGHT*

Books

Patrick Hamilton play *Gas Light* first published: London: Constable, 1939. John Ford to Priscilla Bonner: her interview in JM, *Searching for John Ford*, New York: St. Martin's, 2001. GC in Signal Corps, U.S. Army, World War II: PM and EL biographies; GC argument with Capt. George Baker: Arthur Laurents, *Original Story By*, New York: Knopf, 2000. Breakdown of screenwriters' work on *Gaslight* and GC, "Between setups": Higham and Greenberg.

Ingrid Bergman, "Cukor explains everything": John Kobal, *People Will Talk*, New York: Knopf, 1986. Bergman in climactic scene "a goddess of vengeance": Walter Reisch in PM. Angela Lansbury background, casting and acting in *Gaslight*, GC "laughed uproariously": Martin Gottfried, *Balancing Act: The Authorized Biography of Angela Lansbury*, Boston: Little, Brown, 1999; GL, including GC on Lansbury, "Suddenly, I was watching."

Articles

Ford, "Look at the eyes": "John Ford" (interview), *Focus!*, October 1969. MGM bought and tried to destroy 1940 British *Gaslight* film, Philip Horne, "Something happened," *The Guardian* [UK], October 3, 2008. GC at Signal Corps Photographic Center and Gottfried Reinhardt on GC: Richard Koszarski, "Subway Commandos: Hollywood Filmmakers at the Signal Corps Photographic Center," *Film History* 14, nos. 3/4, War and Militarism, 2002. GC's Empress Theodora project, *The Female:* McCarthy-JM, Mahin interview.

Other Sources

John Van Druten & Walter Reisch, and John L. Balderston, *Gaslight*, screenplay, August 10, 25, 1943, with changes September 13. Ingrid Bergman studying mental patient: Pia Lindstrom (Bergman's daughter) in *Reflections on "Gaslight,"* with Lansbury's other quotes about the film and GC. *The Female*: GC papers at AMPAS. U.S. Army Certificate of Service: George D. Cukor, Private 3926008, Company A, 846th Signal Service Photographic Battalion, Signal Corps Photographical Center, Long Island, New York, October 7, 1942 to May 8, 1943. GC also served as a private with the U.S. Army at the Students Army Teaching College of the City of New York: Abstract of World War I Military Service, October 7 to December 7, 1918. GC's 1943 short film for the U.S. Army Signal Corps, *Electricity and Magnetism, Part II—Ohm's Law*, is listed in the U.S. War Department field manual FM 21-7, *War Department Films, Film Strips, and Recognition Film Slides*, Washington, D.C.: U.S. Government Printing Office, January 1945 (in some sources, the film is erroneously called *Resistance and Ohm's Law*).

16. SPENCER TRACY AND KATHARINE HEPBURN IN *ADAM'S RIB* WITH JUDY HOLLIDAY AND IN *PAT AND MIKE*

Books

Garson Kanin, *Tracy and Hepburn: An Intimate Memoir*, New York: Viking, 1971 (the book outraged GC: PM). Kanin interview and comments by McGilligan on Ruth

Gordon-Kanin scripts: McGilligan, *Backstory 2: Interviews with Screenwriters of the 1940s and 1950s,* Berkeley: University of California Press, 1991. Gordon-Kanin screenplay *Adam's Rib:* New York: Viking, 1972. *Adam's Rib* "would be the film": WM. KH speech at Henry Wallace rally 1947: WM; JM, *Frank Capra: The Catastrophe of Success.* WM on Tracy-KH relationship and their sexuality, Katharine Houghton on *Adam's Rib*'s portrayal of Tracy-KH relationship: Curtis, *Spencer Tracy.*

Tracy to GC about his role in *Edward, My Son*: Schickel, *The Men Who Made the Movies.* GC quoting Tracy, "Well, I certainly learned" and comment on his working methods: Higham and Greenberg. Tracy's private rehearsals: Curtis; GL. Tracy and KH adlibs in *Adam's Rib:* GL; also compare film with published screenplay (and Curtis citing Tynan, "Katharine Hepburn," *Everybody's Magazine,* June 28, 1952). Haskell on *Adam's Rib: From Reverence to Rape.* Censors warned about making Kip seem too gay: EL; GC tended to disapprove of flaunting gayness: PM.

Judy Holliday "screen test" in *Adam's Rib:* Will Holtzman, *Judy Holliday: A Biography,* New York: Putnam, 1982; EL; *Tracy and Hepburn;* Eve March and KH: WM. Harry Cohn saying of Holliday, "That fat Jewish broad?": Holtzman; PM. KH's sports skills: WM; *Me.* "Choice" changed to "cherce" in *Pat and Mike: Tracy and Hepburn.*

Other Sources

Marquette University High School (Milwaukee, Wisconsin) priest to JM on Tracy: Father Charles Shinners, SJ, 1964; Tracy and Pat O'Brien attended Marquette Academy (predecessor school): O'Brien, *The Wind at My Back: The Life and Times of Pat O'Brien,* Garden City, NY: Doubleday, 1964. KH on her sports skills and "In the next life": *All About Me.* Gordon and Kanin, *Pat and Mike* screenplay, November 28, 1951, with changes December 27, 1951 (includes line reading "choice"); earlier draft in which Pat had a husband: description by Walter Reuben, Inc., seller, and first page of June 5, 1951, draft, abebooks.com. Trailer for *Pat and Mike.*

17. JUDY HOLLIDAY IN *BORN YESTERDAY, THE MARRYING KIND* WITH ALDO RAY, AND *IT SHOULD HAPPEN TO YOU* WITH JACK LEMMON

Books

Judy Holliday background and work with GC: Holtzman, *Judy Holliday.* Holliday working for Mercury Theatre: McGilligan, *Young Orson: The Years of Luck and Genius on the Path to "Citizen Kane,"* New York: HarperCollins, 2015. GC to GL on Holliday; also in GL, drowning sequence in *The Marrying Kind* influenced by GC seeing production of *The Cherry Orchard.* Kanin play *Born Yesterday:* New York: Viking, 1946; Kanin wrote shooting script of film version without credit: GL; PM. Kanin interview:

McGilligan, *Backstory 2*. Capra, his writers, and the post–World War II Red Scare: JM, *Frank Capra: The Catastrophe of Success*. American Business Consultants, *Red Channels: The Report of Communist Influence in Radio and Television*, New York: Counterattack, 1950.

Mark Twain on Congress: Samuel L. Clemens, *Pudd'nhead Wilson's New Calendar*, in *Following the Equator: A Journey Around the World*, Hartford, CT: American Publishing Company and New York: Doubleday & McLure, 1897. Peter Cooper Village project spearheaded by Robert Moses: Robert A. Caro, *The Power Broker: Robert Moses and the Fall of New York*, New York: Knopf, 1974. Kanin wanted to direct *It Should Happen to You*, film originally intended for Danny Kaye, and Kanin disliked film's title: Holtzman; PM. Sarris on "obligatory" scene in most Capra films: *The American Cinema*. Gordon play *Years Ago*, New York: Viking, 1947.

Articles

Holliday obituary, "Judy Holliday, 42 [*sic*: 43], Is Dead of Cancer," *NYT*, June 8, 1965. Kanin, "I'd rather be Capra": Marilyn Berger, "Garson Kanin, a Writer and Director of Classic Movies and Plays, Is Dead at 86," *NYT*, March 15, 1999.

Other Sources

Albert Mannheimer (and Kanin, uncredited), *Born Yesterday* screenplay, June 20, 1950. Jean Arthur to JM about why she left Hollywood. Holliday appearance and testimony before U.S. Senate committee and her graylisting: Holtzman; U.S. Senate Subcommittee to Investigate the Administration of the Internal Security Act and Other Internal Security Laws of the Committee on the Judiciary, *Subversive Infiltration of Radio, Television, and the Entertainment Industry: Hearings*, 82nd Congress, U.S. Government Printing Office, March 26, 1952. Song "Dolores" by Frank Loesser and Louis Alter. Andy Warhol, "In the future": Catalogue of an exhibition of his art in Stockholm, Sweden, 1968.

18. THELMA RITTER AND COMPANY IN *THE MODEL AND THE MARRIAGE BROKER*

Books

George Bernard Shaw, *Pygmalion*, London: Constable, and New York: Henry Holt, 1913. Brackett and Wilder: JM, *Billy Wilder: Dancing on the Edge*. GC wanted Joanne Dru to play the model in *The Model and the Marriage Broker* and called Jeanne Crain "flat tire": EL. Thelma Ritter background and fondness for Dickens: Sam Staggs, *All About "All About Eve": The Complete Behind-the-Scenes Story of the Bitchiest Movie Ever Made!*,

New York: St. Martin's, 2000. MGM mutilated GC's *A Life of Her Own*: Clarens; Arnold, *"A Life of Her Own."* Zero Mostel background and blacklisting: Jared Brown, *Zero Mostel: A Biography*, New York: Atheneum, 1989; Ceplair and Englund, *The Inquisition in Hollywood*.

Articles

Nancy Kulp discovered by GC: Hank Grant, "Frustrated Spinster Nancy Kulp Type-Cast," syndicated column, June 22, 1963.

Other Sources

Ritter's Oscar nominations: oscars.org. Sam (Zero) Mostel testimony, *Government of the United States Investigation of Communist Activities, New York Area—Part VIII (Entertainment)*, House Committee on Un-American Activities, 84th Congress, First Session, U.S. Government Printing Office, Washington, DC, October 14, 1955. Tom Lehrer on Frank Fontaine: Introduction to his song "National Brotherhood Week" on his album *That Was the Year That Was*, Reprise Records, 1965. Kulp's career: Wikipedia.

19. SPENCER TRACY AND JEAN SIMMONS IN *THE ACTRESS*

Books

Ruth Gordon play *Years Ago*. The musical comedy play *The Pink Lady*, book and lyrics by C. M. S. McLellan, music by Ivan Caryll, from the French farce *Le satyre* by Georges Berr and Marcel Guillemaud, published in London: Chappell, 1911, including lyrics for the songs "(My) Beautiful Lady" and "Bring Along the Camera." GC, "I'm lost in admiration" and on Jean Simmons as Ruth Gordon Jones: GL. Spencer Tracy, "hair short": Tracy to Kanin, December 21, 1952, quoted in Curtis, *Spencer Tracy*. GC research for the film: Higham and Greenberg.

GC considered and rejected Debbie Reynolds: PM; EL. GC called Simmons "wonderful" in *The Actress*; also, Simmons on Tracy and his working relationship with GC: Curtis. Graham Greene, "There is a fashion": *A Sort of Life*, London: Bodley Head, 1971. Tracy usually kept his own counsel about acting: GC in GL; Curtis. *Twelfth Night* speech delivered by Ruth in *The Actress*: Viola as Cesario in Shakespeare, act 1, scene 5. GC on Tracy in Ruth's recital scene and on how he worked with Tracy: Schickel, *The Men Who Made the Movies*. MGM's lack of faith in *The Actress* and battles over sound recording and performances: Curtis citing MGM's Sidney Franklin (Simmons's voice "irritating"); Lawrence Weingarten to GC, February 25, 1953; and GC to Weingarten, March 2, 1953. GC's report on preview to Gordon and Garson Kanin, letter, April 24, 1953, quoted in Curtis.

Other Sources

Gordon Oscar acceptance speech for *Rosemary's Baby*, 1969, aaspeechesdb.oscars.org. Simmons named her daughter Tracy after her costar: Tracy Granger to JM. Grant on Spencer Tracy to Raymond E. McBride [JM's father]. Richard Burton on watching Tracy work on *The Actress: The Dick Cavett Show*, PBS, August 4, 1980, YouTube.

20. JUDY GARLAND AND JAMES MASON IN *A STAR IS BORN*

History of *A Star Is Born* development, production, mutilation, and partial restoration: Haver, *A Star Is Born: The Making of the 1954 Movie and Its 1983 Restoration* (the fullest source of information on these subjects); Lorna Luft and Jeffrey Vance, *A Star Is Born: Judy Garland and the Film That Got Away*; Sid Luft, *Judy and I*. History of *What Price Hollywood?* and 1937 version of *A Star Is Born*: Selznick, *Memo from David O. Selznick*; Haver, *David O. Selznick's Hollywood*; Thomson, *Showman*.

GC's work on *The Wizard of Oz* with Garland: PM; EL; GC responses to her personality and problems: PM. GC, "She could talk about": Haver, *Star*. Writing of the line, "This is Mrs. Norman Maine": Haver, *Star*; Thomson. John Barrymore an influence on Norman Maine character: PM. JM vouching for veracity of "We dine here" line (attributed to Dorothy Parker in Haver, *Star*); similarity to JM, *The Broken Places: A Memoir*, Berkeley, CA, Hightower, 2015, Naremore, "Dark Cary": *Some Versions of Cary Grant*.

Cited from GL about the film: original shape of film and mutilation of film; GC on Barrymore as a model for Norman; GC on Mason's reserve and directing his breakdown; GC on directing Garland in sequence with Tom Noonan convincing Esther to pay tribute to Norman. GC said he and Moss Hart could have made more cuts: Higham and Greenberg. Elia Kazan to Hart on *Star Is Born:* letter after May 17, 1954, preview; Kazan memo to Jack L. Warner after the preview: both quoted in Haver, *Star*.

Articles

GC, "But when he finished." *Cahiers du Cinéma*, "A DIRECTOR": quoted by Sarris in "Cukor."

Other Sources

Hart, screenplay, *A Star Is Born*, October 7, 1953 (quoted from Haver, *Star*). History of Academy Award venues: oscars.org. Joe McElhaney on Mason listening to Garland singing: Facebook post, October 2, 2023. Souvenir program, theatrical presentations of restored version, *A Star Is Born*: AMPAS and the Academy Foundation in cooperation with Warner Bros., July 1983. Mahin to JM and McCarthy about "This is Mrs. Norman Maine" line.

21. AVA GARDNER IN *BHOWANI JUNCTION*, KAY KENDALL IN *LES GIRLS*, AND SOPHIA LOREN AND ANTHONY QUINN IN *HELLER IN PINK TIGHTS*

Books

Problems in making *Bhowani Junction* and *Les Girls* and GC's career difficulties in late 1950s and early 1960s: PM, EL. *Laurette* project: PM. Louis L'Amour, *Heller with a Gun*, Greenwich, CT: Fawcett Gold Medal, 1955. *Song Without End* production problems: PM; Dirk Bogarde on GC and that film: Bogarde, *Snakes and Ladders: A Memoir*, London: Chatto & Windus, 1978.

Cukor family history and name: PM; Steven Kovacs to JM. John Masters novel *Bhowani Junction*, London: Michael Joseph, 1954, and New York: Viking, 1954. History behind *Bhowani Junction* and other films about India and British colonialism: Dror Izhar, *"Quit India": The Image of the Indian Patriot on Commercial British Film and Television, 1956–1985*, Newcastle: Cambridge Scholars Publishing, 2011. GC on sexual elements excised: Overstreet; Higham and Greenberg; PM; GL.

Production of *Les Girls*: Vera Caspary comment on the script: PM; Gene Kelly on GC: Tynan, "George Cukor"; also Kelly criticisms of GC and how Kelly took over choreography in EL. Manny Farber on Kelly: "Underground Films: A Bit of Male Truth," *Commentary*, November 1957, reprinted in his collection *Negative Space: Manny Farber on the Movies*, New York: Praeger, 1971. Kelly's career: Clive Hirschhorn, *Gene Kelly: A Biography*, Chicago: Regnery, 1975. Kay Kendall's death: Alexander Walker, *Fatal Charm: The Life of Rex Harrison*, London: Weidenfeld and Nicolson, 1992.

PM description of *Heller in Pink Tights* and on its inspiration by his film projects dealing with D. W. Griffith and Joseph Jefferson; Jefferson, *The Autobiography of Joseph Jefferson*, New York: Century Company, 1890. GC wanted to cast Roger Moore, screenwriter Walter Bernstein's comments on the film: PM. Anthony Quinn's complaints about his role: EL. *Mazeppa* and Lord Byron: H. M. Milner play *Mazeppa*, London: Dicks' Standard Plays, 1831, based on Byron's 1819 narrative poem "Mazeppa," London: John Murray, based on a legend about Ukrainian military leader Ivan Mazepa. Adah Isaacs Menken acting in *Mazeppa*: biography by Alan Ackerman, *The Shalvi/Hyman Encyclopedia of Jewish Women*, Jewish Women's Archive, Auburndale, MA, jwa.org. GC's praise of Sophia Loren and Lambert's of Margaret O'Brien: GL. Filming in Arizona: EL; IMDb.

Articles

JM exchange with GC in 1981: JM-McCarthy interview.

Other Sources

GC Certificate and Record of Birth, State of New York, no. 2702, New York City Department of Records and Information Services, Municipal Archives, as George I. Cukor, July 6, 1899, born at home in New York City, submitted and signed by Dr. Louis Friedman. Andrew Marton second-unit director of *Bhowani Junction* (uncredited): AFI Catalog, aficatalog.afi.com; IMDb [his work is mentioned in PM, but he is not identified]. Trailer, *Les Girls*. GC project *Laurette*: documents in GC papers, AMPAS, 1951–68. GC's *Troupers West* project: script material and notes in GC papers, AMPAS, 1945–47, and GC's Griffith biopic project *Twilight Revelers* script and research material in GC papers, AMPAS, 1964–72.

22. MARILYN MONROE IN *LET'S MAKE LOVE* AND *SOMETHING'S GOT TO GIVE*

Books

GC on Marilyn Monroe, "miraculous": Clarens. Hawks on Monroe: JM, *Hawks on Hawks*. Wilder on Monroe: Zolotow, *Billy Wilder in Hollywood*. Monroe's background and personality and production history of GC's *Something's Got to Give*: PM; Donald Spoto, *Marilyn Monroe: The Biography*, New York: HarperCollins, 1993; Gary Vitacco-Robles, *Icon: The Life, Times, and Films of Marilyn Monroe*, vol. 2: *1956 to 1962 & Beyond*, Albany, GA: BearManor Media, 2014; and Anthony Summers, *Goddess: The Secret Lives of Marilyn Monroe*, New York: Macmillan, and London: Victor Gollancz, 1985, and updated edition, London: Weidenfeld & Nicolson, 2022; those books also provide accounts of her death, though their authors often disagree, and the case remains somewhat mysterious. Monroe's date of death uncertain: Dr. Thomas Noguchi, Autopsy report, Office of County Coroner, Los Angeles, August 5, 1962 (lists August 5 as date of death) and related documents, Office of County Coroner, August 1962; Summers (lists August 4 as probable date of death); Vitacco-Robles (lists "between" August 4 and 5).

Irving Thalberg, "the business of creating illusions": Samuel Marx, *Mayer and Thalberg: The Make-Believe Saints*. GC considered Monroe "quite mad," said she "couldn't sustain scenes," "very little influence," "She acted as if," "She had this absolute": GL. GC, "Her performance": Clarens. Monroe and Tynan on GC; GC on Monroe, "Her face moves": Tynan, "George Cukor." Arthur Miller to GC about *Let's Make Love* happy experience for Monroe, GC on Harlow and Monroe: EL. Yves Montand had to learn dialogue phonetically for *Let's Make Love*: Vitacco-Robles. Previous casting plans, Miller worked on script, Gene Allen on GC as Monroe's "greatest fan": PM. Monroe affair with Montand: Spoto; Vitacco-Robles; Summers. Alfred, Lord Tennyson poem "Enoch Arden": London: Edward Moxon, 1864.

Articles

Bosley Crowther review, "Milton Berle Steals Show in 'Let's Make Love,'" *NYT*, September 9, 1960. Bert Stern, "The Last Sitting" (photo shoot with Monroe), *Vogue*, September 1962. Monroe's childhood dream and other quotes from *Time* cover story: Ezra Goodman [uncredited], "To Aristophanes & Back," May 14, 1956. GC to Hedda Hopper about Monroe: Hopper, "Marilyn to Be Replaced; Is She Finished?," syndicated column, June 7, 1962, shown in *Marilyn Monroe: The Final Days*, quote identified by PM as being from GC.

Other Sources

Montand on filming of *Let's Make Love*: *Late Night with David Letterman*, NBC-TV, June 17, 1987, YouTube. Fox documentary *Marilyn*, 1963. Documentaries on the filming of *Something's Got to Give*: *Marilyn: Something's Got to Give*, 1990, and *Marilyn Monroe: The Final Days*, 2001 (including 38-minute assembly of scenes from the uncompleted feature). Monroe had become terrified of facing the camera: producer Henry T. Weinstein in *Marilyn: Something's Got to Give*. Telegram from Monroe to GC, June 8, 1962, reproduced in the documentary *On Cukor*; similar telegram sent by Monroe to other members of *Something's Got to Give* company: Summers; Vitacco-Robles.

23. CLAIRE BLOOM, JANE FONDA, GLYNIS JOHNS, AND SHELLEY WINTERS IN *THE CHAPMAN REPORT*

Books

Irving Wallace novel *The Chapman Report*, New York: Simon and Schuster, 1960. Production history of film version: PM; EL; GC forced to shoot absurd ending: EL. GC on potential for "lively, kinky" film, Claire Bloom on GC, "The difference": EL. GC, "The picture was delicate": PM quotes transcript of phone call between GC and Warner Bros. executives, February 28, 1962, Warners collection in Cinema-Television Archives at the University of Southern California; Jack L. Warner called GC an "obstinate putz": telegram from Warner to Darryl Zanuck, February 15, 1962; Warner memo to Richard Zanuck about football scenes: October 13, 1961: quoted in PM.

Alfred C. Kinsey, Wardell B. Pomeroy, Clyde E. Martin, *Sexual Behavior in the Human Male*, Philadelphia: W. B. Saunders, 1948, and Kinsey, Pomeroy, Martin, and Paul H. Gebhard, *Sexual Behavior in the Human Female*, Saunders, 1953. Betty Friedan, *The Feminine Mystique*, New York: Norton, 1963. Final draft of *Chapman Report* script by Gene Allen; Grant Stuart pseudonym for Arthur Sheekman: PM. GC interrogation sessions "what was really": GL. Jane Fonda's troubled relationship with father: her book *My Life So Far*, New York: Random House, 2005. Shelley Winters credited her career takeoff to

GC: Winters, *Shelley II: The Middle of My Century*, New York: Simon and Schuster, 1989; EL. Richard Zanuck on Jack Warner offering *My Fair Lady* to GC: EL.

Articles

Lansbury, "wonderful gamey quality": Klemesrud. GC on San Francisco preview and felt film "ruined" and "emasculated" but had "some of the best scenes"; "Had we been able": Overstreet. Callahan on pain and self-destruction in GC characters, "Cukor, George." Glenn Erickson, review of *The Chapman Report* DVD, dvdtalk.com, August 7, 2012.

Other Sources

Trailer for *The Chapman Report*. Bloom, "I was kind of surprised": *On Cukor* documentary. GC on Garbo in *Camille: The Men Who Made the Movies: George Cukor* documentary.

24. REX HARRISON AND AUDREY HEPBURN IN *MY FAIR LADY*

Books

Shaw, *Pygmalion*. Alan Jay Lerner musical play with lyrics, *My Fair Lady*, New York, Coward-McCann, 1956. Production history of film version: PM; Beaton, *Cecil Beaton's Fair Lady*; Harrison, *An Autobiography*, New York: Morrow, 1975; Harrison, *A Damned Serious Business: My Life in Comedy*, New York: Bantam, 1991; Garebian, *The Making of "My Fair Lady"*; Walker, *Fatal Charm*; Walker, *Audrey: Her Real Story*, London: Weidenfeld & Nicolson, 1994. Lambert-GC exchange on *My Fair Lady* as "prepackaged"; GC, "lay in the casting"; "Not that I wanted"; "There's a big number"; "There's a savagery"; and discussion of Wendy Hiller in 1938 *Pygmalion* film: GL. Grant and Peter O'Toole considered for Henry Higgins; Grant's response to Jack L. Warner: Walker, *Fatal Charm*.

Patrick Garland on Harrison touring in *My Fair Lady* (including the actor's "Bloody Audrey" comment): *The Incomparable Rex: A Memoir of Rex Harrison in the 1980s*, London: Macmillan, 1998, reprinted as *Rex Harrison: The Last of the High Comedians*, introduction by Simon Callow, London: Dean Street, 2019. Audrey Hepburn in World War II: Walker, *Audrey*. Jean Renoir on technique: GL. Lubitsch and GC: JM, *How Did Lubitsch Do It?* Hermes Pan and Fred Astaire working relationship: Thomas, *Astaire: The Man, The Dancer*, New York: St. Martin's, 1987; John Franceschina, *Hermes Pan: The Man Who Danced with Fred Astaire*, New York: Oxford University Press, 2012.

Articles

Sarris review, "My Faded Lady," *Village Voice*, December 17 and 24, 1964. Renoir on dubbing: Rui Nogueira and François Truchaud, "Interview with Jean Renoir," *Sight and Sound*,

Spring 1968. Bramwell Fletcher interview by JM: "Shaw Impersonated," *The Shavian*, Spring–Summer 1967, reprinted in *Two Cheers for Hollywood*. Harry Hadden-Paton on Higgins: Brendan Lemon, "Here's Harry's Henry Higgins," *Lincoln Center Theater Blog*, December 13, 2018, lct.org.

Other Sources

Lerner, screenplay of *My Fair Lady*, June 24, 1963. GC's Academy Award acceptance speech: April 5, 1965, oscars.org. Jeanine Basinger and Gene Allen in *On Cukor* documentary, 2000. Hepburn's singing voice is heard in extras on DVD and Blu-ray editions of *My Fair Lady*. Cast albums, *My Fair Lady* (stage version), 1956 (Broadway) and 1959 (London): Columbia Broadway Masterworks, produced by Goddard Lieberson. Video clips of Julie Andrews as Eliza: YouTube. Audio recording of GC directing Baroness Veronika (Bina) von Goldschmidt-Rothschild: *George Cukor directs Baroness Bina Rothschild in the ballroom scene*: extra on the DVD and Blu-ray editions.

Harrison tended to be insecure: "Ronald Neame, Cinematographer/writer/producer/director" (video interview), Criterion Channel, producer Karen Stetler, 2010. Nancy Olson Livingston reports Lerner and Frederick Loewe wrote Higgins for a dramatic actor, not a singer; Martin Scorsese on *My Fair Lady*; Jeremy Brett's singing dubbed by Bill Shirley: documentary *More Loverly Than Ever*. O'Toole in *Pygmalion* onstage: theatricalia.com (as Higgins, 1984 and 1987; as Alfred Doolittle, 1957); and as Higgins in Showtime film of *Pygmalion*, 1983.

25. ANNA KARINA AND DIRK BOGARDE IN *JUSTINE*

Books

Lawrence Durrell's Alexandria Quartet: *Justine, Balthazar, Mountolive, Clea*, London: Faber and Faber, 1960–1961. Production history of film version, *Justine*: PM; EL; Clarens. Joseph L. Mankiewicz had worked on film adaptation: PM; Kenneth Geist, *Pictures Will Talk: The Life and Films of Joseph L. Mankiewicz*, New York: Scribner, 1978. GC's production company, G-D-C and abortive projects, including James Toback on *Vicky* project: PM. Censorship restrictions on *Justine*: GL; Dirk Bogarde, *Snakes and Ladders*. GC intended *Justine* to run about an hour longer than release version: Clarens. GC, Anna Karina and Bogarde "really lent themselves" and on Anouk Aimée, Langlois on "halftones": GL; Aimée tried to leave the film: EL.

Articles

Jean Cocteau defined "*film maudit*": inspired by Paul Verlaine's reference to Les poètes maudits in 1888, Cocteau used "*film maudit*" to describe Welles's *Macbeth* (1948) and with

Bazin organized a Festival du Film Maudit, July–August 1949, in Biarritz: J. Hoberman, "No success like failure—a natural history of the film maudit," *Sight & Sound*, April 2021. Molly Haskell review of *Justine*, *Village Voice*, September 18, 1969, with Sarris column mentioning that hers was the first by another writer as part of his column, "films in focus." Sarris worked on *Justine* screenplay without credit: Hillel Italie, AP obituary of Sarris, 2012 (died June 20). Vincent Canby, "Screen: 'Justine,' a Chronicle of Mysticism and Masquerade," *NYT*, August 7, 1969. Lesley Blanch on GC: Tynan, "George Cukor." GC to JM, "First of all": "George Cukor: *The Blue Bird*." FT comment on Strick: Guy Flatley, "So Truffaut Decided to Work His Own Miracle," *NYT*, September 27, 1970.

26. MAGGIE SMITH, ALEC McCOWEN, LOU GOSSETT, ROBERT STEPHENS, AND CINDY WILLIAMS IN *TRAVELS WITH MY AUNT*

Books

Graham Greene, *Travels with My Aunt*, London: Bodley Head, 1969; background on novel: Norman Sherry, *The Life of Graham Greene*, vol. 3: *1955–1991*, New York: Viking Penguin, 2004. GC's late career history, including preproduction and production of *Travels with My Aunt*: PM; EL. Jay Presson Allen on *Travels*, GC, and KH, including the actress's work on the script: Allen interview in McGilligan, ed., *Backstory 3: Interviews with Screenwriters of the 1960s*, Berkeley: University of California Press, 1997.

Maggie Smith's career and Alec McCowen on GC directing her: Michael Coveney, *Maggie Smith: A Biography*, London: Weidenfeld and Nicolson, 2015. Wilder and *Avanti!*: JM, *Billy Wilder: Dancing on the Edge*. GC's annual luncheons for directors of films nominated for best foreign-language film Academy Award: PM; EL. W. B. Yeats, "Sailing to Byzantium": in his book *Stories of Red Hanrahan and the Secret Rose*, London: Macmillan, 1927 edition. "A little touch of Harry": the Chorus in the Prologue to William Shakespeare, *Henry V*, act 4.

Articles

Roger Greenspun review, "George Cukor Brings Graham Greene's 'Travels with My Aunt' to the Screen," *NYT*, December 18, 1972. Sarris review, *Village Voice*, January 4, 1973. Sontag, "Notes on 'Camp.'" GC, "I don't luxuriate in suffering": JM, "George Cukor: *The Blue Bird*." GC luncheons for directors: JM-McCarthy interview.

Other Sources

Hugh Wheeler and Jay [Presson] Allen screenplay draft, *Travels with My Aunt*, February 25, 1972. GC to JM on Cindy Williams: notes of material not included in published version of JM's 1975 interview "George Cukor: *The Blue Bird*."

27. JACQUELINE BISSET AND CANDICE BERGEN
IN *RICH AND FAMOUS*

Books

Source play for *Rich and Famous:* John Van Druten, *Old Acquaintance*, New York: Random House, 1941. GC's emotional response to negative reviews of *Rich and Famous*: PM. GC fondness for *Flesh* and other Paul Morrissey films, "sentimental" about snow: GL. GC-Gavin Lambert discussion about love affairs: Lambert, *Mostly About Lindsay Anderson*, New York: Knopf, 2000.

Articles

Dave Kehr, review of *Rich and Famous*, *Chicago Reader*, October 26, 1985. GC, sexual matters "in the air" and his limited "coming out": Edwards and Goodstein interview, *The Advocate*. Pauline Kael review, *New Yorker*, October 26, 1981; Stuart Byron reply to Kael, *Village Voice*, November 11–17, 1981; *Salon* staff, "The Gay Attacks on Pauline Kael," *Salon*, June 25, 2004. David Denby review, "Taking Off," *New York*, October 19, 1981. JM on GC as oldest director to make Hollywood studio film to that point (GC told JM he was "thrilled" by that distinction): *Variety*, October 17, 1980. Comments by GC on *Rich and Famous*, "There were a lot of plays," and on Morrissey films in JM-McCarthy interview; JM-McCarthy, "Jacqueline Bisset on *Rich and Famous*" (interview; includes KH quote on ending of *Rich and Famous*).

Other Sources

Screenplay of *Rich and Famous* by Gerald Ayres, n.d. JM's visit to MGM set during filming. William Allyn to JM about the film, GC's fury at Bisset, and models for characters. Bisset on directing herself in airplane sex scene: JM's unpublished notes from JM-McCarthy interview. JM telephone call to GC to try to coax positive comment about Bisset's performance (before JM-McCarthy interview ran in *Film Comment*, 1981).

28. KATHARINE HEPBURN AND LAURENCE OLIVIER
IN *LOVE AMONG THE RUINS*

Books

James Costigan's screenplay originally written as a television play intended for Alfred Lunt and Lynn Fontanne and brought to KH by Audrey Wood: Wood with Max Wilk, *Represented by Audrey Wood*, Garden City, NY: Doubleday, 1981. Laurence Olivier, "my happiest": his book *On Acting*, New York: Simon and Schuster, 1986; see also *Confessions of an Actor*, New York: Simon and Schuster, 1982.

John Dryden, "Old as I am" from "Cymon and Iphigenia," in *Fables Ancient and Modern; Translated Into Verse, from Homer, Ovid, Boccace, and Chaucer: with Original Poems*, London: Jacob Tonson, 1721; Dryden, "And love's the noblest": from his play *The Indian Emperour; Or, the Conquest of Mexico by the Spaniards, being the Sequel of The Indian Queen*, act 2, scene 2, first performed 1665, London: Henry Herringman, 1667. Robert Browning, "Love Among the Ruins," from his collection *Men and Women*, London: Chapman and Hall, 1855 (the line Sir Arthur slightly misquotes is actually "Now the country does not even boast a tree"); Browning, "Grow old," from his poem "Rabbi Ben Ezra," *Dramatis Personae*, London: Chapman and Hall, 1864. Shakespeare, *The Merchant of Venice*, London: first quarto edition, 1600. Shakespeare sonnets quoted by Sir Arthur: "To me, fair friend" and "And ruin'd love": Sonnets 104 ("now" quoted instead of "still") and 119 (the original lines are, "And ruined love, when it is built anew, / Grows fairer than at first, more strong, far greater").

Articles

GC on origins of *Love Among the Ruins* project and his shooting style in his first movie for TV: JM-McCarthy interview. Peter B. Flint, "George Cukor, 83, Film Director, Dies," *NYT*, January 26, 1983.

Other Sources

James Costigan screenplay *Love Among the Ruins*, April 29, 1974. KH interview on *The Dick Cavett Show* that inspired her teaming with Olivier on the film: October 3, 1973, ABC-TV. Wood involvement discussed by Stephen Vagg in audio commentary for the film: Kino Lorber Blu-ray edition, 2020. Renoir, "on the margin": see notes for introduction.

INDEX

Abbott, George, 46

ABC Circle Films, 428

Abe Lincoln in Illinois (Cromwell, 1940), 289

Academy Awards: *Born Yesterday* (Cukor, 1950) and, 249, 259; Box and, 405; Crawford and, 189, 262–63; *A Double Life* (Cukor, 1947) and, 239; Fontaine and, 193; Garland and, 303; *Gaslight* (Cukor, 1944) and, 223, 231; *Gone with the Wind* (Fleming, 1939) and, 173, 176; Gordon and, 289–90; Hepburn and, 213; Hoch and, 309; *Hold Back the Dawn* (Leisen, 1941) and, 181; *Holiday* (E. Griffith, 1930) and, 164; Holliday and, 249, 257; *Les Girls* (Cukor, 1957) and, 324; *Little Women* (Cukor, 1933) and, 116; *My Fair Lady* (Cukor, 1964) and, 1, *3*, 317, 359, 360, 393; *The Philadelphia Story* (Cukor, 1940) and, 218–19; Ritter and, 275; Rosson and, 287; Simmons and, 290; Smith slapping Rock (2022) at, 314; in *A Star Is Born* (Cukor, 1954), 313–14; *A Star Is Born* (Cukor) and, 308; Stewart and, 30; *Wild Is the Wind* (Cukor, 1957) and, 319

Academy of Motion Picture Arts and Sciences, 2, 99, 206, 303

Acting in the Cinema (Naremore), 23–24

Action (magazine), 41

Actress, The (Cukor, 1953): cinematic style of, 286–87; queer artistic sensibility in, 296; screenplay for, 272, 289–91; Simmons in, 35, 148, *284*, 285–86, 287–94, *288*, 295–96, 310; Tracy in, 286, 287–89, *288*, 291–97

Adam's Rib (Cukor, 1949): auteur theory and, 5–7; cinematic style of, 18–19, 21; critical and commercial reception of, 246–47; Cukor as "woman's director" and, 16; Folsey and, 58; Gordon-Kanin screenplay for, 237–38, 242; Hepburn in, 16, 21, 221, 237–38, *240*, 241–49, *245*, *248*, 253–54; Holliday in, 21, 237–38, 247–49, *248*, 257; neorealism and, 261; queer sensibility in, 34–35, 246; Tracy in, 16–17, 221, 237–38, *240*, 241–47, *245*, 253–54

Adrian, 105–6, 187

Advocate, The (magazine), 33, 40, 423–24

Agee, James, 37, 53

Aherne, Brian, 33, 129–30, 134–35, 136–38, *137*

Aimée, Anouk, 387–89

Akins, Zoë: *Camille* (Cukor, 1936) and, 144, 146–47, 151; *Christopher Strong* (Arzner, 1933) and, 95; Cukor and, 13–14, 16; *Girls About Town* (Cukor, 1931) and, 66, 68; Sherman and, 76

Alcott, Louisa May, 14, 111, 118–19

Alexandria Quartet (Durrell), 381

Algonquin Round Table, 30

Alice Adams (Stevens, 1935), 129

All About Eve (Mankiewicz, 1950), 249, 275

Allen, Corey, 350–51, *350*

Allen, Gene: Cukor on, 20; *The Chapman Report* (Cukor, 1962) and, 346–47; *Heller in Pink Tights* (Cukor, 1960) and, 328; *Les Girls* (Cukor, 1957) and, 324; *Let's Make Love* (Cukor, 1960) and, 337; *My Fair Lady* (Cukor, 1964) and, *19*, 360; *Something's Got to Give* (Cukor, 1962) and, 338; *A Star Is Born* (Cukor, 1954) and, 303–4, 309, 405

Allen, Jay Presson, 394–95, 396

Allen, Steve, 338

Allen, Woody, 9

All Quiet on the Western Front (Berger, 2022), 47

All Quiet on the Western Front (Milestone, 1930): Ayres in, 43–52, *44*, *48*, 94; Cukor and, 145; R. Griffith in, 68

All Quiet on the Western Front (Remarque), 43, 45

All the King's Men (Warren), 262–63

Allyn, William, 412, 419

Ameche, Don, 192

American Cinema, The (Sarris), 8–9, 76

American Graffiti (Lucas, 1973), 408

American Movie Classics, 339

American Tragedy, An (Dreiser), 265

Ames, Robert, 164

Anderson, Maxwell, 46, 326

Andrews, Julie, 361–62, 376–77

Animal Kingdom, The (Barry), 158

Animal Kingdom, The (E. Griffith, 1932), 158

Anna Karenina (Brown, 1935), 144, 154

Arlen, Harold, 309

Army–Navy Screen Magazine (short film series), 225

Art of Screen Acting, 1912–1960, The (Callahan), 23–24

Art of Screen Acting, 1960 to Today, The (Callahan), 23–24

Arthur, Jean, 172, 258–59

Arzner, Dorothy, 374; *Christopher Strong* (1933), 95

As You Like It (Shakespeare), 130

Ashby, Hal: *Harold and Maude* (1971), 290

Asquith, Anthony: *Pygmalion* (with Howard, 1938), 358, 369, 376, 378

Astaire, Fred, 192, 326, 372

Astor, Gertrude, 281

Astor, Mary, 164–65

Astruc, Alexandre, 5

Aubrey, James, 395

Auerbach, Nina, 119

August, Joseph H., 130, 135

auteur theory, 5–10, 357–58. See also *politique des auteurs* and Sarris, Andrew

Avanti! (Wilder, 1972), 396–97

Awful Truth, The (McCarey, 1937), 141, 161, 210

Ayres, Gerald, 225–26, 411, 413, 415–16

Ayres, Lew: in *All Quiet on the Western Front* (Milestone, 1930), 43–52, *44*, *48*,

94; in *Holiday* (Cukor, 1938), 36, 51–55, 52, 158–59, *158*, 164

Baker, George, 225
Bakewell, William, 50
Balcony, The (Genet), 385
Balderston, John, 225–26
Balthazar (Durrell), 381
Bancroft, Anne, 197
Band Wagon, The (Minnelli, 1953), 326
Bankhead, Tallulah, 66
Barbara Stanwyck (Callahan), 23–24
Barrie, James M., 382
Barry, John, 430
Barry, Philip: Cukor and, 157–59, 160–61, 237; Hepburn and, 210, 212, 213–14. See also *Animal Kingdom, The* (Barry); *Holiday* (Barry); *Philadelphia Story, The* (Barry)
Barrymore, Ethel, 60
Barrymore, John: in *A Bill of Divorcement* (Cukor, 1932), 60–61, *89*, 90–93, 102–3; Cukor and, 37–38, 60–61, 63–64; in *Dinner at Eight* (Cukor, 1933), 16–18, 59, 100, 102–5, *104*; drinking and, 37–38, 102, 306; in *Romeo and Juliet* (Cukor, 1936), 105; Sherman and, 75–76; *A Star Is Born* (Cukor, 1954) and, 306; in *Twentieth Century* (Hawks, 1934), 105
Barrymore, Lionel: in *Camille* (Cukor, 1936), 148
Barstow, Richard, 287, 312
Barthes, Roland, 7
Bartholomew, Freddie, *123*, 124
Basinger, Jeanine, 360
Bazin, André, 7
Beaton, Cecil, 360
Beavers, Louise, *69*, 70
Becky Sharp, 76
Beery, Wallace, 43, *102*

Beggars of Life (Wellman, 1928), 116–17
Behind the Screen (Watts), 116
Belafonte, Harry, 382
Bells Are Ringing (Minnelli, 1960), 259–60
Bennett, Constance: in *Our Betters* (Cukor, 1933), 33–34; in *What Price Hollywood?* (Cukor, 1932), 73–75, *75*, 77–78, *79*, 81–82
Bennett, Joan, 120, 172
Benton, David, 130–31
Berg, A. Scott, 114
Bergen, Candice, 2–4, 68–69, 411–13, 418–19, 421, 422–25, *423*
Bergen, Polly, 339
Berger, Edward: *All Quiet on the Western Front* (2022), 47
Bergman, Ingmar, 9, 14, 37, 307; *Sawdust and Tinsel* (1953), 328
Bergman, Ingrid: *Army–Navy Screen Magazine* (short film series) and, 225; in *Gaslight* (Cukor, 1944), 223–24, *225*, 226–31, 232–35; in *A Woman's Face* (Molander, 1938), 196, 203
Berkeley, Martin, 283
Berle, Milton, 337–38
Berman, Pandro S., 128, 226, 382
Bernstein, Walter, 327, 329, 340
Best Years of Our Lives, The (Wyler, 1946), 265
Beverly Hillbillies, The (television series), 283
Bhowani Junction (Cukor, 1956): cinematic style of, 323; crowd scenes in, 175, 320, 323; Gardner in, 27, 317–18, *320*, 321–24; Granger in, 290, 321–23; mise-en-scène in, 25; political plot in, 387–88; production of, 320–21; screenplay for, 322, 381; sexuality in, 27, 323
Bhowani Junction (Masters), 321
Bickford, Charles, 311–12, 313
Bicycle Thieves (De Sica, 1948), 265

Big Parade, The (K. Vidor, 1925), 45

Bill of Divorcement, A (Clift, 1922), 89

Bill of Divorcement, A (Cukor, 1932): Barrymore in, 60–61, *89*, 90–93, 102–3; Burke in, *89*, 92–93, 99; critical and commercial reception of, 95; divorce in, 88, 89–90; Hepburn in, 85, 86–88, *86*, 89–93, 95, 161; Selznick and, 87, 88–89, 93

Bill of Divorcement, A (Dane), 88–89

Bill of Divorcement, A (Farrow, 1940), 88–89

Birth of a Nation, The (D. W. Griffith, 1915), 281

Bisset, Jacqueline: in *Day for Night* (Truffaut, 1973), 414; in *Rich and Famous* (Cukor, 1981), 2–4, 68–69, 411–25, *413*, *423*, 435

Black Cat, The (Ulmer, 1934), 93

Blanch, Lesley, 382, 383, 390

Blonde Venus (Sternberg, 1932), 140

Bloom, Claire: in *The Chapman Report* (Cukor, 1962), 36, 335, 344, 345–46, 347, 349–53, *350*, *353*; Cukor and, 16

Bloom, John, 399

Bloomer, Amelia, 382

Blue Bird, The (Cukor, 1976), 41, 383

Bochner, Hart, 414, 415–18

Boetticher, Budd: *The Rise and Fall of Legs Diamond* (1960), 355

Bogarde, Dirk: in *Justine* (Cukor, 1969), 384, *384*, 389–90; in *Song Without End* (C. Vidor, 1960), 319–20

Bogart, Humphrey, 51

Boleslawski, Richard: *The Garden of Allah* (1936), 287

Bonner, Priscilla, 223

Bonnie and Clyde (Penn, 1967), 130–31

Born Yesterday (Cukor, 1950): Crawford in, 101; Holliday in, 35, 101, 247, 249, 257, 258, 259, 260, 261–63, *261*, 264–65;

Mr. Smith Goes to Washington (Capra, 1939) and, 263–64; political drama in, 160, 260; queer sensibility in, 34–35; screenplay for, 259, 262, 263; surrogate-director figure in, 32, 263

Born Yesterday (Kanin), 21, 247, 257

Box, John, 405

Boyer, Charles, *225*, 226–31, 232–35, *232*, *234*

Brackett, Charles, 30, 46, 181, 276–77

Brady, Scott, 275, 279–80

Brando, Marlon, 318

Brandt, Harry, 113

Breen, Richard, 276–77

Brett, Jeremy, 375–76

Bretton, Raphael, 386

Brian, Mary, 62

Bride of Frankenstein (Whale, 1935), 346

Bringing Up Baby (Hawks, 1938), 140, 210, 214

British Film Institute, 9

Broken Lullaby (*The Man I Killed*) (Lubitsch, 1932), 281

Bronco (television series), 356

Bronson, Charles (Charles Buchinski), 221, 251

Brooks, Mel: *The Producers* (1967), 283

Brown, Clarence: *Anna Karenina* (1935), 144, 154; *Flesh and the Devil* (1927), 144

Brown, Martin, 68

Brown, Rowland, 73

Browning, Tod: *Dracula* (1931), 93

Bruce, Nigel, 201

Buchinski, Charles. *See* Bronson, Charles

Buchman, Sidney, 36, 52, 159–60, 162, 263–64

Burke, Billie: in *A Bill of Divorcement* (Cukor, 1932), *89*, 92–93, 99; in *Dinner at Eight* (Cukor, 1933), 99

Burton, Richard, 295
Buscombe, Edward, 10
Byron, George Gordon, 327
Byron, Stuart, 414

Cabaret (Fosse, 1972), 387
Cabinet of Dr. Caligari, The (Wiene, 1920), 204
Cabot, Bruce, 201–2
Cahiers du Cinéma (journal), 20
Cahn, Sammy, 335–36
Callahan, Dan, 23–24, 36, 61, 63–64, 350
Callenbach, Ernest, 8
Camera Lies, The (Callahan), 23–24
caméra-stylo (camera-pen), 5
Camille (Capellani, 1915), 146
Camille (Cukor, 1936): auteur theory and, 5–7; Barrymore in, 148; camp style in, 403; cinematic style of, 18, 117, 144; Daniell in, 346; Garbo in, 26, 27, 35, 94, 109, 142, 144, 147–55, 149, 351, 403; mise-en-scène in, 228; queer sensibility in, 34–35; screenplay for, 144, 145–47, 151–52; sexuality in, 27, 147; Taylor in, 148–49, 149, 151–55; Thalberg and, 109, 175
camp style: in Camille (Cukor, 1936), 403; concept and history of, 138, 402–3; in Let's Make Love (Cukor, 1960), 337; in Mommie Dearest (Perry, 1981), 196–97; in Old Acquaintance (Sherman, 1943), 418; in Rich and Famous (Cukor, 1981), 418; in Sylvia Scarlett (Cukor, 1935), 138–40, 402, 403; in Travels with My Aunt (Cukor, 1972), 393, 395, 402–3, 418; in The Women (Cukor, 1939), 185
Campbell, Alan, 93, 305
Canby, Vincent, 381, 386
Capellani, Albert: Camille (1915), 146
Capra, Frank: G. Astor and, 281; on characters, 87; Red Scare and, 263–64;

Sarris on, 272; tribute to Stewart (1980) and, 29–30
Capra, Frank—films: It Happened One Night (1934), 210; It's a Wonderful Life (1946), 265; Ladies of Leisure (1930), 70; Lost Horizon (1937), 212; Meet John Doe (1941), 239; The Miracle Woman (1931), 93; Mr. Deeds Goes to Town (1936), 162; Mr. Smith Goes to Washington (1939), 30, 162, 219, 263–64; Platinum Blonde (1931), 106, 162; You Can't Take It with You (1938), 60
Captains Courageous (Fleming, 1937), 287
Carey, Gary, 80
Carey, Harry, 327
Carroll, John, 201
Carson, Jack, 103
Carson, Robert, 305
Caspary, Vera, 324
censorship. See Motion Picture Production Code (Hays Code)
Chaplin, Charles, 172
Chapman Report, The (Cukor, 1962): Bloom in, 36, 335, 344, 345–46, 347, 349–53, 350, 353; critical and commercial reception of, 97, 350, 355, 356; Daniell in, 346; drinking in, 36, 350; as film maudit (cursed film), 343–44, 381; Fonda in, 344, 345–46, 345, 347–49; gang rape in, 335, 350–51, 350, 352–53, 386–87; Johns in, 344, 345–46, 347, 354–55; male actors in, 355–56; queer sensibility in, 34–35, 354; screenplay for, 346–48; sexuality in, 343–56, 416, 417; suicide in, 350, 353; Winters in, 346, 347, 355; Zanuck and, 382
Chapman Report, The (Wallace), 343
character actors: in David Copperfield (Cukor, 1935), 123–24, 123, 279; in The Model and the Marriage Broker (Cukor, 1951), 97, 275, 278–79, 281–83, 282

Charisse, Cyd, 326, 338

Chekhov, Anton, 269

Cherry Orchard, The (Chekhov), 269

Chicago Reader (newspaper), 411

Chicago Tribune (newspaper), 131

chick flicks (a.k.a. women's pictures), 15–16, 111–12, 419

child abuse, 196–97, 204

Ching, William, 250–51

Christopher Strong (Arzner, 1933), 95

Cinémathèque Française, 11

Claflin, Tennessee, 40

Claire, Ina, 61–62

Clarens, Carlos, 9, 111, 164, 192, 194

Clea (Durrell), 381

Cleopatra, 385

Clift, Denison: *A Bill of Divorcement* (1922), 89

"climate," Cukor's directorial technique: 25, 58, 80, 92, 109, 147, 154, 192, 292, 331, 334, 336, 338, 358, 434

Clive, Colin, 346

Cocteau, Jean, 381

co-directors: Cukor and, 43, 46, 58, 60, 66

Coffee, Lenore, 411

Coffin, Leslie L., 50

Cohan, George M., 251–52

Cohn, Harry: *Born Yesterday* (Cukor, 1950) and, 247, 249, 257, 258, 259; *It Should Happen to You* (Cukor, 1954) and, 269

Colbert, Claudette, 169

Cole, Jack, 326, 335

Collier, Constance, 200

Collier, John, 129

Colman, Ronald, *13*, 239, 355

Columbia Pictures: *Born Yesterday* (Cukor, 1950) and, 247, 249, 257–59; *Holiday* (Cukor, 1938) and, 162; *It Should Happen to You* (Cukor, 1954)

and, 269–70; Kanin and, 269; A. Ray and, 252, 266

Conversation, The (Coppola, 1974), 408

Conway, Jack: *Red-Headed Woman* (1932), 106

Cooke, Alan: *Pygmalion* (1983), 365

Cooper, Gladys, 377

Cooper, Merian C., 34

Cooper, Violet Kemble, 123–24

Cooper, Wyatt, 346–47

Coote, Robert, 365

Coppola, Francis Ford: *The Conversation* (1974), 408

Corn Is Green, The (Cukor, 1979), 32, 383, 435

Corn Is Green, The (Williams), 383, 435

Cornell, Katharine, 88–89

Costigan, James: *The Corn Is Green* (Cukor, 1979) and, 435; *Love Among the Ruins* (Cukor, 1975) and, 427, 428, 431, 434–35; *Vicky* project and, 382–83

Cotten, Joseph, 210, 229–30

Country Girl, The (Seaton, 1954), 303

Coward, Noël, 218–19, 379

Cox, Wally, 338, 340

Crain, Jeanne, 275, 276, 277–78, 279–81

Crawford, Broderick, 101, 262–63

Crawford, Christina, 196

Crawford, Christopher, 196

Crawford, Joan: as "box office poison," 113, 187, 189, 196; Cukor and, 16, 197–98, 206; life and career of, 189, 196–98, 205; in *No More Ladies* (E. Griffith, 1935), 188; in *Susan and God* (Cukor, 1940), 189, 196, 197, 198–201, *199*, 207; in *A Woman's Face* (Cukor, 1941), 189, 196, 197, 202–5, *202*; in *The Women* (Cukor, 1939), 106, *184*, 185, 186–89, 197

Creber, William J., 386

Crews, Laura Hope, 150, 151

Croisset, Francis de, 203

Cromwell, John: *Abe Lincoln in Illinois* (1940), 289

Crosby, Bing, 338

Crosman, Henrietta, 63

Crothers, Rachel, 195

Crowd, The (K. Vidor, 1928), 267

Crowther, Bosley, 130–31, 337

Cukor, Elsie, 321

Cukor, George: art directors and, 18–19, *19*, 20; auteur theory and, 5–10, 357–58; Broadway theater and, 57–58; cinematic style of, 4, 11–15, 18–22, 24–32; as co-director, 43, 46, 58, 60, 66; collaboration and, 40–41; critical reception and public recognition of, 1–10, 14, 30, 393–94; *Desire Me* (uncredited, 1947) and, 41; as dialogue director, 30, 43–50; family and background of, 320–21; *Gone with the Wind* (Fleming, 1939) and, 11, 16, 41, 169–81, 186, 192, 303; Lubitsch and, 98–99, 371; military service and, 224–25; name, 320–21; new approach to, 23–24; as partially closeted gay man, 12, 16, 40, 139, 176–77, 224, 318, 417, 423–25. *See also* queer sensibility; personal vision of, 32–38; photographs of, *3, 6, 19, 24, 39, 44, 107, 126, 207, 218, 258, 304, 359, 388, 404*; *The Scarlett O'Hara War* (Erman, 1980) and, 171; screenwriters and, 9, 12–14, 16. *See also specific screenwriters*; sense of humor of, 17, 185; *Song Without End* (C. Vidor, 1960) and, 318, 319–20; television and, 394. See also *Corn Is Green, The* (Cukor, 1979); *Love Among the Ruins* (Cukor, 1975); unmade projects of, 40, 226, 318, 326, 382–83; *The Wizard of Oz* (Fleming, 1939) and, 301; as "woman's director," 15–18, 176–77, 181, 182, 220;

"wonderful gamey quality" of, 38–40, 343. *See also specific films and actors*

Cukor, Helen (Ilona) Gross, 154, 321

Cukor, Joseph, 321

Cukor, Morris, 321

Cukor, Victor (Farkas), 321

Cukor & Co. (Carey), 80

Cukor Touch, 32

Curtis, Tony, 170–71

Curtiz, Michael: *Mildred Pierce* (1945), 189

Daily Variety (newspaper), 416

Dalio, Marcel, 11–12

Damsel in Distress, A (Stevens, 1937), 192

Dane, Clemence, 88–89

Daniell, Henry, 219, 346

Daniels, William, 104, *142*, 144, 152, 250

Danner, Blythe, 213

Danton, Ray, 355

David Copperfield (Cukor, 1935): character actors in, 123–24, *123*, 279; cinematic style of, 12, 18, 117, 124; directing of literary adaptations and, 97, 145, 175; Oliver in, 282; queer sensibility in, 35; screenplay for, 122–23, 124–25, 174

Davis, Bette, 249, 418

Davis, Tyrell, 33–34

Dawn, Jack, 202–3

Day, Doris, 339

Day for Night (Truffaut, 1973), 414

Dee, Frances, 120

Delerue, Georges, 414

De Mayerling à Sarajevo (*From Mayerling to Sarajevo*) (Ophüls, 1940), 121

Denby, David, 415

Depression, 99

Desert Fox, The (Hathaway, 1951), 307

De Sica, Vittorio: *Bicycle Thieves* (1948), 265

Desire Me (uncredited, 1947), 41

Deval, Jacques, 206

Dewey, George, 321

dialogue director: Cukor as, 30, 43–50

Dick Cavett Show, The (talk show), 295, 428

Dickens, Charles, 279, 290. See also *David Copperfield* (Cukor, 1935)

Dickinson, Thorold: *Gaslight* (1940), 227–28

Didion, Joan, 412

Dietrich, Marlene, 121

Dinner at Eight (Cukor, 1933): auteur theory and, 5–7; J. Barrymore in, 16–18, *59*, 100, 102–5, *104*; cinematic style of, 104–6; comedy and drama in, 17–18, 60–61; critical and commercial reception of, 101; drinking in, 103; Harlow in, 100–101, *102*, 105–9, *107*, 263; light satire in, 160; screenplay for, 97–100, 119; suicide in, 17–18, 100, 101, 103, *104*

Dinner at Eight (Kaufman and Ferber), 60, 97, 99

Directors Guild of America, 41

Divine Woman, The (Sjöström, 1928), 129, 147

divorce: in *A Bill of Divorcement* (Cukor, 1932), 88, 89–90; *A Bill of Divorcement* (Dane) and, 88–89; in *The Women* (Cukor, 1939), 187, 191

Dixon, Jean, 162–63

Doctor Zhivago (Lean, 1965), 405

Donen, Stanley, 326; *Singin' in the Rain* (with Kelly, 1952), 287

Donohue, Jack, 312

Double Life, A (Cukor, 1947), *13*, 18–19, 239–40, 355

Douglas, Melvyn, 203–4

Douglas, Paul, 259

Dracula (Browning, 1931), 93

Dreiser, Theodore, 265

Dressler, Marie: in *Dinner at Eight* (Cukor, 1933), 100–101

drinking: Barrymore and, 37–38, 102, 306; in *The Chapman Report* (Cukor, 1962), 36, 350; Cukor's preoccupation with and representation of, 36–38, 350; in *Dinner at Eight* (Cukor, 1933), 103; in *Edward, My Son* (Cukor, 1948), 36, 243; in *Holiday* (Cukor, 1938), 36, 37, 80, 158–59; in *Justine* (Cukor, 1969), 389–90; *in A Life of Her Own* (Cukor, 1950), 280; in *The Lost Weekend* (Wilder, 1945), 37; Monroe and, 333; in *The Philadelphia Story* (Cukor, 1940), 37; in *A Star Is Born* (Cukor, 1954), 37–38, 306–7; in *What Price Hollywood?* (Cukor, 1932), 78–80

Dru, Joanne, 276

Duggan, Andrew, 344–45

Dumas *fils*, Alexandre, 25, 144, 145–46, 147–48, 153

Dunaway, Faye, 196–97

Dunne, Irene, 339

Durrell, Lawrence, 381

Dvorak, Ann, 10, 280

Dwan, Allan, 281

Early Life and Adventures of Sylvia Scarlett, The (Mackenzie), 129

Eason, B. Reeves, 172, 177

Ebert, Roger, 179

Edens, Roger, 287, 312

Edeson, Arthur, 45, 48

Edward, My Son (Cukor, 1948), 36, 243

Edwards, Douglas W., 424

Elg, Taina, 324–25

Ellington, Duke, 393

Emmy Awards, 394

Enoch Arden (D. W. Griffith, 1911), 340

"Enoch Arden" (Tennyson), 339

Epstein, Julius, 259

Epstein, Philip, 259

Erickson, Glenn, 355

Erman, John: *The Scarlett O'Hara War*
(1980), 170–71, 192

Erwin, Hobe, 105–6

Esquire (magazine), 147

Estabrook, Howard, 88, 124

Evans, Madge, 103

Fairbanks, Douglas, Jr., 45

Family Plot (Hitchcock, 1975), 28

Fapp, Daniel L., 337

Farber, Manny, 324

Farrow, John: *A Bill of Divorcement* (1940),
88–89

F.B.I., The (television series), 355–56

Fellini, Federico: *La strada* (1954), 328

Feminine Mystique, The (Friedan), 345

Ferber, Edna, 58–60

Ferrari, William, 223

Feyder, Jacques: *The Kiss* (1929), 53

Fiddler on the Roof (musical comedy-
drama), 283

Fields, W. C., 35, 123–24, *123*

Film Comment (magazine), 2, 40

Film Culture (journal), 344

Film Quarterly (journal), 4, 8

Finney, Albert, 387

Fitzgerald, F. Scott, 57, 175–76, 185,
197–98

Fitzmaurice, George, 74

Fleming, Victor: *Captains Courageous*
(1937), 287; *Red Dust* (1932), 106–8;
The Wizard of Oz (1939), 169, 287, 301.
See also *Gone with the Wind* (Fleming,
1939)

Flesh (Morrissey, 1968), 39–40, 416

Flesh and the Devil (Brown, 1927), 144

Fletcher, Bramwell, 377–78

Flippen, Jay C., 278

Folsey, George J., 58

Fonda, Henry, 219

Fonda, Jane, 16, 344, 345–46, *345*,
347–49

Fontaine, Frank, 278

Fontaine, Joan, 192–93, *193*

Fontanne, Lynn, 427

Forbes, Bryan: *The Madwoman of Chaillot*
(1969), 394–95

Ford, Helen, 278–79

Ford, John: G. Astor and, 281;
co-directors and, 43; Cukor and, 393;
on filmmaking, 223; Marsh and, 281;
Wayne and, 29

Ford, John—films: *Four Sons* (1928), 45,
239; *The Grapes of Wrath* (1940), 219;
Hell Bent (1918), 327; *The Informer*
(1935), 130; *Mogambo* (1953), 323;
Pilgrimage (1933), 63, 239; *Stagecoach*
(1939), 327; *3 Bad Men* (1926), 223;
Wagon Master (1950), 276

Foreign Affair, A (Wilder, 1948),
258–59

Forrest, Steve, 327–28

Fosse, Bob: *Cabaret* (1972), 387

Fountain of Youth, The (Welles, 1956), 129

Four Sons (Ford, 1928), 45, 239

Fowler, Gene, 73

Francis, Kay, 65–71, *67*, *69*, 113

Frankau, Gilbert, 95

Freed, Arthur, 312–13, 386

Friedan, Betty, 345

From Reverence to Rape (Haskell), 187,
214, 246–47

Front, The (Ritt, 1976), 283

Fuller, Samuel: *Merrill's Marauders*
(1962), 356; *Pickup on South Street*
(1953), 275–76

*Funny Thing Happened on the Way to the
Forum, A* (musical comedy), 283

Furth, George, 170–71

Gable, Clark: Cukor and, 16, 176–77; in *Gone with the Wind* (Fleming, 1939), 16, *168*, 173–74, 176–77, *177*, 178, 180–81; *The Philadelphia Story* (Cukor, 1940) and, 211

Garbo, Greta: as "box office poison," 113; in *Camille* (Cukor, 1936), 26, 27, 35, 94, 109, *142*, 144, 147–55, *149*, 351, 403; Cukor and, 16; life and career of, 68, 143–44, 205–6; in *Two-Faced Woman* (Cukor, 1941), 205–6; *A Woman's Face* (Cukor, 1941) and, 203

Garden of Allah, The (Boleslawski, 1936), 287

Gardner, Ava: in *Bhowani Junction* (Cukor, 1956), 27, 317–18, *320*, 321–24; Cukor and, 16, 226; in *Mogambo* (Ford, 1953), 323; in *Show Boat* (Sidney, 1951), 322

Gardner, Cyril, 46, 58, 60; *Grumpy* (with Cukor, 1930), 46, 58

Garland, Judy: Cukor and, 16; life and career of, 74; in *A Star Is Born* (Cukor, 1954), 74, 301–3, 304–6, *304*, 308, 309–16, *314–15*, 318, 323; in *The Wizard of Oz* (Fleming, 1939), 301

Garland, Patrick, 366

Garmes, Lee, 178

Garner, James, 339

Gas Light (Hamilton), 224, 226

Gaslight (Cukor, 1944): Bergman in, 223–24, *225*, 226–31, 232–35; Boyer in, *225*, 226–31, 232–35, *232*, *234*; cinematic style of, 223; Cotten in, 229–30; Cukor as "woman's director" and, 16; Lansbury in, 38–39, 231–35, *232*, *234*, 240; mise-en-scène in, 228; screenplay for, 225–26; surrogate-director figure in, 227

Gaslight (Dickinson, 1940), 227–28

Gasnier, Louis J.: *The Virtuous Sin* (with Cukor, 1930), 46, 65, 66–68, *67*

Gaynor, Janet, 302, 306

Gaynor, Mitzi, 324–25, 326

G-D-C (Cukor production company), 321, 382

General, The (Zilahy), 66

Genet, Jean, 385

Gentlemen Prefer Blondes (Hawks, 1953), 332, 336

George Cukor: Interviews (Long), 40

George Raft Story, The (Newman, 1961), 355

Gerrard, Henry, 116–17

Gershwin, Ira, 309

Gibbons, Cedric, 223

Gibson, William, 372

Gilbert, John, 144

Girls About Town (Cukor, 1931), 65, 66, 68–71, *69*, 80, 89, 150

Glass Menagerie, The (Harvey, 1973), 427

Glass Menagerie, The (Williams), 318

Godard, Jean-Luc, 83, 389

Goddard, Paulette, 172, 191–92, *191*

Goldschmidt-Rothschild, Veronika (Bina) von, 362–63

Goldsmith, Jerry, 388

Gone with the Wind (Fleming, 1939): *Bhowani Junction* (Cukor, 1956) and, 323; Cukor and, 11, 16, 41, 169–81, 186, 192, 303; Havilland in, 11, 171–73, *173*, 175, 179–81; Leigh in, *168*, 171–73, 176, *177*, 178–79, 180–81; McDaniel in, 172–75, *173*; McQueen in, 179; Old South in, 174; *River of Romance* (Wallace, 1929) and, 44; screenplay for, 175–76

Gone with the Wind (Mitchell), 169, 175

Good Wives (Alcott), 118–19

Goodbye, Mr. Chips (Hilton), 146

Goodman, Ezra, 341

Gordon, Michael: *Move Over, Darling* (1963), 339

Gordon, Ruth: *Adam's Rib* (Cukor, 1949) and, 237–38, 242; Cukor and, 9, 13–14, 16; *A Double Life* (Cukor, 1947) and, *13*, 239–40; life and career of, 238–39, 289–90; *The Marrying Kind* (Cukor, 1952) and, 260, 266; *Pat and Mike* (Cukor, 1952) and, 237–38, 249, 254–55; in *Two-Faced Woman* (Cukor, 1941), 239. See also *Actress, The* (Cukor, 1953); *Years Ago* (Gordon)

Gossett, Lou, 407

Goulding, Edmund: *Grand Hotel* (1932), 97, 101

Grace, Henry, 144

Grand Hotel (Goulding, 1932), 97, 101

Granger, Stewart, 290, 321–23

Granger, Tracy, 290

Grant, Cary: in *Bringing Up Baby* (Hawks, 1938), 140, 210; in *Holiday* (Cukor, 1938), 16–17, 51–52, 140, 157, 159, 161–64, *163*, 165–67, 215–16; life and career of, 140–41; *My Fair Lady* (Cukor, 1964) and, 365; in *My Favorite Wife* (Kanin, 1940), 339; in *The Philadelphia Story* (Cukor, 1940), 140, 157, 209, 211–12, 215–16, *215*, 219; *A Star Is Born* (Cukor, 1954) and, 307–8; in *Sylvia Scarlett* (Cukor, 1935), 33, *126*, 128–29, 132–34, *133*, 139–41, 161, 215–16; on Tracy, 294

Grapes of Wrath, The (Ford, 1940), 219

Graves, Robert, 45

Great Expectations (Dickens), 290

Great Expectations (Lean, 1946), 290

Greatest Story Ever Told, The (Stevens, 1965), 386

Great Gatsby, The (Fitzgerald), 57

Greed (Stroheim, 1924), 302, 317

Greeks Had a Word for Them, The (Sherman, 1932), 76

Greene, Graham, 20, 290, 383, 394, 396, 405

Greenspun, Roger, 395–96

Gribble, Henry Wagstaff, 88

Griffith, D. W., 326, 382; *The Birth of a Nation* (1915), 281; *Enoch Arden* (1911), 339–40; *Intolerance* (1916), 281; *Isn't Life Wonderful?* (1924), 45; *Way Down East* (1920), 75

Griffith, Edward H.: *The Animal Kingdom* (1932), 158; *Holiday* (1930), 37, 162–63, 164–65; *No More Ladies* (1935), 188

Griffith, Raymond, 68

Gross, Ilona (Helen), 154, 321

Grumpy (Cukor and Gardner, 1930), 46, 58

Guess Who's Coming to Dinner (Kramer, 1967), 1, 242

Gunga Din (Stevens, 1939), 140

Gwenn, Edmund, *133*

Hadden-Paton, Harry, 364

Hamilton, Patrick, 224, 226

Hamlet (Olivier, 1948), 290

Hardin, Ty, 354–55, 356

Harding, Ann, 37, 158, 164

Harlow, Jean: Cukor and, 16; in *Dinner at Eight* (Cukor, 1933), 100–101, *102*, 105–9, *107*, 263; life and career of, 106–8

Harmetz, Aljean, 170, 171

Harold and Maude (Ashby, 1971), 290

Harpman, Fred, 386, 419

Harrison, Rex: Kendall and, 325; in *My Fair Lady* (Cukor, 1964), 16–17, *31*, 362, 363–75, *370*, 377, 378–79; on *My Fair Lady* (Cukor, 1964), 376

Hart, Moss: *Dinner at Eight* (Cukor, 1933) and, 60; *A Star Is Born* (Cukor, 1954) and, 32, 74, 190, 302, 309, 311–13, 314; *Winged Victory* (Cukor, 1944) and, 247; *The Women* (Boothe) and, 190

Harvey, Anthony: *The Glass Menagerie* (1973), 427

Haskell, Molly: on *Adam's Rib* (Cukor, 1949), 246–47; on female stars, 187; on *Gone with the Wind* (Fleming, 1939), 181; on *Justine* (Cukor, 1969), 381, 386, 389; on *The Philadelphia Story* (Cukor, 1940), 214

Hatch, Tony, 399

Hathaway, Henry: *The Desert Fox* (1951), 307

Haver, Ronald, 303, 308, 310–11, 312

Havilland, Olivia de: on Ayres, 51; Cukor and, 11, 37, 171–72; in *Gone with the Wind* (Fleming, 1939), 11, 171–73, *173*, 175, 179–81; life and career of, 193

Hawks, Howard: auteur theory and, 9–10; on early talkies, 43–44; Monroe and, 331–32; Wayne and, 29

Hawks, Howard—films: *Bringing Up Baby* (1938), 140, 210, 214; *Gentlemen Prefer Blondes* (1953), 332, 336; *His Girl Friday* (1940), 190–91; *Monkey Business* (1952), 332; *Red River* (1948), 276; *Rio Bravo* (1959), 328; *Twentieth Century* (1934), 105

Hays, Will, 34

Hays Code. *See* Motion Picture Production Code (Hays Code)

Hayworth, Rita, 201

Head, Edith, 328

Hecht, Ben, 78, 105, 174, 176

Heerman, Victor, 14, 115–16

Heflin, Van, 210

Hell Bent (Ford, 1918), 327

Heller in Pink Tights (Cukor, 1960), 18, 25, 97, 319, 326–29

Heller with a Gun (L'Amour), 326

Hemingway, Ernest, 45, 319

Henry V (Shakespeare), 302

Hepburn, Audrey: Cukor and, 16, 382; life and career of, 367–68; in *My Fair Lady* (Cukor, 1964), *31*, 77, 358, *359*, 361–62, 366–77, *367, 370*, 378–79

Hepburn, Katharine: in *Adam's Rib* (Cukor, 1949), 21, 221, 237–38, *240*, 241–49, *245, 248*, 253–54; *The Animal Kingdom* (Barry) and, 158; in *A Bill of Divorcement* (Cukor, 1932), 85, 86–88, *86*, 89–93, 95, 161; as "box office poison," 113, 131, 161, 170, 189, 210; in *Bringing Up Baby* (Hawks, 1938), 210, 214; in *Christopher Strong* (Arzner, 1933), 95; C. Collier and, 200; in *The Corn Is Green* (Cukor, 1979), 435; Cukor and, 23, 38, 85–87, 93–95, 185, 382; *Gone with the Wind* (Fleming, 1939) and, 170; in *Guess Who's Coming to Dinner* (Kramer, 1967), 1; in *Holiday* (Barry), 93–94; in *Holiday* (Cukor, 1938), 37, 51–55, 157, *158*, 159, 161–64, *163*, 165–67, *166*, 210, 213; in *Keeper of the Flame* (Cukor, 1942), 239; life and career of, 112–14, 138, 139, 189, 210, 213–14, 216–17; in *Little Women* (Cukor, 1933), 35, 38, 85–86, 111, 112–13, 114–16, *115*, 117–22, *118*, 127, 154, 295; in *Love Among the Ruins* (Cukor, 1975), *39*, 85–86, 101, 213, 394, 395, 427–32, 434–37, *436*; in *The Madwoman of Chaillot* (Forbes, 1969), 394–95; in *Morning Glory* (Sherman, 1933), 76, 95; in *Pat and Mike* (Cukor, 1952), 221, 237–38, 249–55, *252, 254*, 394; in *The Philadelphia Story* (Cukor, 1940), 37,

85–86, 157, 209–14, *211*, *215*, 216–17, *218*, 219–20, 238; in *Philadelphia Story, The* (Barry), 113, 161, 210–11, 214; Red Scare and, 94–95, 241; on *Rich and Famous* (Cukor, 1981), 424; in *Sylvia Scarlett* (Cukor, 1935), 33, 111, *126*, 127–30, 131–41, *133*, 161, 254–55, 403; television and, 427; Tracy and, 220, 237–39, 241–47; *Travels with My Aunt* (Cukor, 1972) and, 394–95, 401, 408; in *Woman of the Year* (Stevens, 1942), 220–21

Hepburn, Tom, 113–14

Her Cardboard Lover (Cukor, 1942), 205, 206

High Stakes (Sherman, 1931), 76, 78–79

Hiller, Wendy, 376

Hilton, James, 146

His Girl Friday (Hawks, 1940), 190–91

His Monkey Wife (Collier), 129

Hitchcock, Alfred: Cukor and, 28, 193, 226, 229; Truffaut and, 24, 28; films: *Family Plot* (1976), 28; *The Lady Vanishes* (1938), 230; *Rear Window* (1954), 275; *Rebecca* (1940), 193; *Suspicion* (1941), 193; *Vertigo* (1958), 219

Hobart, Rose, 201

Hoch, Winton C., 309–10

Hold Back the Dawn (Leisen, 1941), 181, 193

Holden, William, *261*, 263

Holender, Adam, 419

Holiday (Barry), 36, 51–53, 55, 93–94, 157–59, 162–63

Holiday (Cukor, 1938): auteur theory and, 5–7; Ayres in, 36, 51–55, *52*, 158–59, *158*, 164; cinematic style of, 164; drinking in, 36, 37, 80, 158–59; Grant in, 16–17, 51–52, 140, 157, 161–64, *163*, 165–67, 215–16; Hepburn in, 37, 51–55, 85–86, 157, *158*, 159, 161–64, *163*, 165–67, *166*, 210, 213; Nolan in, 158, 165; screenplay

for, 159–60, 162–63, 263; surrogate-director figure in, 32

Holiday (E. Griffith, 1930), 37, 162–63, 164–65

Holliday, Judy: in *Adam's Rib* (Cukor, 1949), 21, 237–38, 247–49, *248*; in *Born Yesterday* (Cukor, 1950), 35, 101, 247, 249, 258, 259, 260, 261–63, *261*, 264–65; Cukor and, 257; in *It Should Happen to You* (Cukor, 1954), 17–18, 249, *258*, 259, *269*, 270–72; life and career of, 257–58, 259–60; in *The Marrying Kind* (Cukor, 1952), 249, 259, 260–61, 266–68, *267*; Red Scare and, 160; in *Winged Victory* (Cukor, 1944), 247

Hollywood Reporter (newspaper), 113

Holt, Tim, 15

homophobia, 176–77, 413–15. *See also* queer sensibility

Hope, Fred, 105–6

Hopkins, Miriam, 76, 418

Hopper, Hedda, 342

Horner, Harry, 263

Horning, William A., 324

Horton, Edward Everett, 162

Houghton, Katharine, 242

House Committee on Un-American Activities (HUAC), 160, 241

Houseman, John, 257–58

Howard, John, 212

Howard, Leslie: in *The Animal Kingdom* (E. Griffith, 1932), 158; in *Gone with the Wind* (Fleming, 1939), 172, 174, 178; in *Romeo and Juliet* (Cukor, 1936), 145

Howard, Leslie—film directed by: *Pygmalion* (with Asquith, 1938), 358, 369, 376, 378

Howard, Sidney, 170, 175–76, 319

Howard, Trevor, 322

Howland, Jobyna, 68

Hoyningen-Huene, George: *The Chapman Report* (Cukor, 1962) and, 347; *Heller in Pink Tights* (Cukor, 1960) and, 328; *Les Girls* (Cukor, 1957) and, 324; *Let's Make Love* (Cukor, 1960) and, 337; Paley and, 136; *A Star Is Born* (Cukor, 1954) and, 20, 303–4, 309, 405

Hudson, Rock, 336

Huldschinsky, Paul, 223

Hussey, Ruth, 201, 202, 215, 219

Huston, John, 14, 51, 331–32

Huston, John—films: *The Misfits* (1961), 275, 332–33; *The Red Badge of Courage* (1951), 287

Huston, Walter, 66–68, *67*

Hutchinson, Ron, 176

Hyde-White, Wilfrid, 337–38, 362, 365, *370*

I Am a Fugitive from a Chain Gang (LeRoy, 1932), 99–100

Il etait une fois (Once Upon a Time) (Croisset), 203

I Lost It at the Movies (Kael), 8

I'm No Angel (Ruggles, 1933), 140

Incomparable Rex, The (Garland), 366

Independent Theatre Owners Association, 113

Informer, The (Ford, 1935), 130

Inside Daisy Clover (Mulligan, 1965), 289–90

Intolerance (D. W. Griffith, 1916), 281

Irving, Washington, 326

Irwin, Hobe, 116–17

Isherwood, Christopher, 387

Isn't Life Wonderful? (D. W. Griffith, 1924), 45

Italian neorealism: characteristics and influence on Hollywood of, 237, 260, 265; Cukor and, 261, 265–66, 276, 385–86

It Happened One Night (Capra, 1934), 210

It's a Wonderful Life (Capra, 1946), 265

It Should Happen to You (Cukor, 1954): Bennett in, 74–75; cinematic style of, 18–19; comedy and drama in, 17–18; Holliday in, 17–18, 249, *258*, *259*, *269*, 270–72; Lemmon in, 15, 27–29, *269*, 270–72; neorealism and, 261; O'Shea in, 278; queer sensibility in, 34–35; satire of modern cult of celebrity in, 260; screenplay for, 269–72; Truffaut on, 10

James, Henry, 147

Jefferson, Joseph, 326, 328–29

Johnny Guitar (Ray, 1954), 280

Johns, Glynis, 344, 345–46, 347, 354–55

Johnson, Nunnally, 340

Jones, Clinton, 286

Journey's End (Whale, 1930), 93

Joyce, James, 385

Julius Caesar (Mankiewicz, 1953), 307

Justine (Cukor, 1969): Aimée in, 387–89; Bogarde in, 384, *384*, 389–90; cinematic style of, 405; critical and commercial reception of, 97, 381, 385, 386; drinking in, 389–90; as *film maudit* (cursed film), 381; Karina in, *384*, 386–87, *388*, 389–90; mise-en-scène in, 25, 419–20; political subplot in, 387–88; queer sensibility in, 34–35; sexuality in, 25–27, 344, 351–52, 384–86, 388–89; Strick and, 381–82, 385, 389; suicide in, 389–90; "wonderful gamey quality" of Cukor in, 38–39; York in, 386–87

Justine (Durrell), 381

Kael, Pauline, 8, 14, 414–15

Kammerer, Felix, 47

Kanin, Garson: *The Actress* (Cukor, 1953) and, 286, 297; *Adam's Rib* (Cukor, 1949) and, 237–38, 242; *Born Yesterday* (Cukor, 1950) and, 259, 262; on Capra, 263; Cukor and, 9, 13–14; *A Double Life* (Cukor, 1947) and, *13*, 239–40; *It Should Happen to You* (Cukor, 1954) and, 269–71; life and career of, 238–39, 289; *The Marrying Kind* (Cukor, 1952) and, 260, 266; *Moviola* miniseries and, 170–71; *My Favorite Wife* (1940) and, 339; *Pat and Mike* (Cukor, 1952) and, 237–38, 249, 251–52, 254–55; on Tracy and Hepburn, 238, 241. See also *Born Yesterday* (Kanin)

Kanin, Michael, 239

Kanter, Hal, 336

Karina, Anna, 16, *384*, 386–87, *388*, 389–90

Kate (Mann), 95, 113–14, 165, 214, 241

Kaufman, George S., 58–60, 190

Kaye, Danny, 270

Kazan, Elia, 14, 313

Keeper of the Flame (Cukor, 1942), 160, 200, 239

Kehr, Dave, 411, 421–22

Kelly, Gene, 24–25, 287, 323–24, 325–26, 337–38

Kelly, Grace, 303

Kendall, Kay, 16, 318–19, 325, *325*

Kennedy, John F., 203, 338

Kennedy, Madge, 260

Kerr, Deborah, 16, 36, 243, 361

Kidder, Margot, 365

King and I, The (Lang, 1956), 361

Kiss, The (Feyder, 1929), 53

Kiss the Boys Good-Bye (Boothe), 192

Kiss the Boys Goodbye (Schertzinger, 1941), 192

Knechtel, Lloyd, 83

Kramer, Stanley: *Guess Who's Coming to Dinner* (1967), 1, 242

Krantz, Judith, 412

Krasna, Norman, 336

Kulp, Nancy, 278, 281–83, *282*

Kuri, Emile, 286

Kurosawa, Akira: *One Wonderful Sunday* (1947), 265

La Bohème (K. Vidor, 1926), 154

La Cava, Gregory: *My Man Godfrey* (1936), 210

La dame aux camélias (*The Lady of the Camellias*) (Dumas *fils*), 144, 145–46, 147–48, 153

Ladies of Leisure (Capra, 1930), 70

Lady Gaga, 306

Lady Vanishes, The (Hitchcock, 1938), 230

Laemmle, Carl, Jr., 46

Lambert, Gavin, on Cukor as partially closeted gay man, 417. Also see *On Cukor* (Lambert)

L'Amour, Louis, 326

Lancaster, Burt, 318

Lang, Walter: *The King and I* (1956), 361

Langley, Noel, 243

Langlois, Henri, 11, 390

Lansbury, Angela: on Cukor, 343; in *Gaslight* (Cukor, 1944), 38–39, 231–35, *232*, *234*, 240; life and career of, 231–32, 235

Lardner, Ring, Jr., 239, 305

La ronde (Ophüls, 1950), 399

La strada (Fellini, 1954), 328

La traviata (Verdi), 144

Lattanzi, Matt, 413–14, *413*, 416–17

Laurents, Arthur, 224

Laverne & Shirley (TV series), 408

Lawford, Peter, 338

Lawrence, Gertrude, 196

Lawrence of Arabia (Lean, 1962), 405

Lawton, Frank, 124

Lean, David, 320, 369; *Doctor Zhivago* (1965), 405; *Great Expectations* (1946), 290; *Lawrence of Arabia* (1962), 405

Leave Her to Heaven (Stahl, 1945), 385

Leavitt, Sam, 303–4

Lehrer, Tom, 278

Leigh, Vivien: Cukor and, 171–72; in *Gone with the Wind* (Fleming, 1939), *168*, 171–73, 176, *177*, 178–79, 180–81

Leisen, Mitchell: *Hold Back the Dawn* (1941), 181, 193; *The Mating Season* (1951), 276

Lelouch, Claude: *Un homme et une femme* (1966), 387

Lemmon, Jack, 15, 27–29, *269*, 270–72

Lennart, Isobel, 10, 280

Leopard, The (Visconti, 1963), 399–400

Lerner, Alan Jay, 358, 364

LeRoy, Mervyn: *I Am a Fugitive from a Chain Gang* (1932), 99–100

Les amants (Malle, 1958), 323

Les Girls (Cukor, 1957), 25, 318–19, 323–26, *325*

Let's Make Love (Cukor, 1960): Berle in, 337–38; camp style in, 337; cinematic style of, 337; critical and commercial reception of, 337; Monroe in, 109, 331, 333–37, *334*; Montand in, 336–38; screenplay for, 336; sexuality in, 334–35; surrogate-director figure in, 337–38

Letter from an Unknown Woman (Ophüls, 1948), 164, 399

Levien, Sonya, 322

Levy, Emanuel, 179, 318

Life of Her Own, A (Cukor, 1950), 10, 18–19, 280

Lipstein, Harold, 328, 347

Liszt, Franz, 319–20

Little Women (Alcott), 14, 38, 111, 118–19

Little Women (Cukor, 1933): auteur theory and, 5–7; cinematic style of, 4, 18, 116–17, 122, 422; critical and commercial reception of, 111–12, 128; Cukor as "woman's director" and, 16; as Cukor's favorite film, 33, 110, 111; Cukor's style in, 12; directing of literary adaptations and, 145, 175; as ensemble piece, 97, 120–21; Hepburn in, 35, 38, 85–86, 111, 112–13, 114–16, *115*, 117–22, *118*, 127, 154, 295; Oliver in, 282; queer sensibility in, 34–35, 111–13, 121; screenplay of, 14, 115–16, 124–25; surrogate-director figure in, 32

Lodge, John Davis, 121

Loewe, Frederick, 358

Lombard, Carole, 165

Lonergan, Arthur, 286

Lonesome Cowboys (Morrissey, 1968), 416

Long, Harry, 131

Long, Louise, 68

Long, Robert Emmet, 40

long takes: Cukor on, 21, 436; in *The Actress* (Cukor, 1953), 293–94; in *Adam's Rib* (Cukor, 1949), 242, 247–49, *248*; in *Born Yesterday* (Cukor, 1950), 264; in *Love Among the Ruins* (Cukor, 1975), 435–36; in *The Marrying Kind* (Cukor, 1952), 268, 271; Monroe and, 337; in *My Fair Lady* (Cukor, 1964), 375; in *Pat and Mike* (Cukor, 1952), 255; in *A Star Is Born* (Cukor, 1954), 309, 311–12, 313; in *Travels with My Aunt* (Cukor, 1972), 401; in *The Women* (Cukor, 1939), 192

Loos, Anita, 16, 183, 185, 195, 198, 199

Loren, Sophia, 18, 318, 319, 326–28

Los Angeles Times (newspaper), 95, 214

lost generation, 45

Lost Horizon (Capra, 1937), 212

Lost Horizon (Hilton), 146

Lost Weekend, The (Wilder, 1945), 37

Love Among the Ruins (Cukor, 1975): auteur theory and, 5–7; comedy and drama in,

429–30; Costigan's screenplay and, 427, 428, 431, 434–35; critical and commercial reception of, 383, 394; Hepburn in, *39*, 85–86, 101, 213, 394, 395, 427–32, 434–37, *436*; long takes in, 435–36; mise-en-scène in, 25, 430; Olivier in, 16–17, 35, 101, 394, 427–34, *432*, 435–37, *436*; sexuality in, 393; surrogate-director figure in, 428, 430

Low, Bill, 364

Lowe, Edmund, 105

Lubitsch, Ernst: Cukor and, 98–99, 371; screenwriters and, 9; *The Women* (Cukor, 1939) and, 169–70, 186

Lubitsch, Ernst—films: *The Man I Killed* (*Broken Lullaby*) (1932), 281; *The Marriage Circle* (1924), 98; *Ninotchka* (1939), 62, 144, 150, 169; *One Hour with You* (1932), 98; *The Smiling Lieutenant* (1931), 58; *So This Is Paris* (1926), 68; *Trouble in Paradise* (1932), 66, 210

Lucas, George: *American Graffiti* (1973), 408

Luce, Clare Boothe, 183, 189–90, 192

Luce, Henry, 183

Lucy, Arnold, *48*

Luft, Sidney, 303

Lukas, Paul, 118, *118*, 122

Lunt, Alfred, 427

Lupino, Ida, 374

Lusk, Norbert, 95

Lust for Life (Minnelli, 1956), 318

MacArthur, Charles, 105

Macgill, Moyna, 231–32

MacKenna, Kenneth, 66

Mackenzie, Compton, 129

MacLaine, Shirley, 338–39, 382

Madame de . . . (Ophüls, 1953), 153, 399

Madwoman of Chaillot, The (Forbes, 1969), 394–95

Maeterlinck, Maurice, 383

Magnani, Anna, 318, 319

Magnificent Ambersons, The (Welles, 1942), 15, 302, 317

Magnolia (Tarkington), 43

Mahin, John Lee, 172, 181, 220–21, 226, 305

Main, Marjorie, 201

Malle, Louis: *Les amants* (1958), 323

Mamoulian, Rouben, 76; *Queen Christina* (1933), 144, 150

Man I Killed, The (*Broken Lullaby*) (Lubitsch, 1932), 281

Mankiewicz, Don M., 346–47

Mankiewicz, Herman J., 60, 97, 99

Mankiewicz, Joseph L.: *Justine* (Cukor, 1969) and, 381; *The Philadelphia Story* (Cukor, 1940) and, 210–11, 221; *Woman of the Year* (Stevens, 1942) and, 221

Mankiewicz, Joseph L.—films: *All About Eve* (1950), 249, 275; *Julius Caesar* (1953), 307

Mann, Daniel: *Hot Spell* (1958), 318

Mann, William J., 95, 113–14, 135, 165, 214, 216, 241

Manners, David, 93

Mannheimer, Albert, 259

Mao Zedong, 99

March, Fredric: Mason and, 307; in *The Royal Family of Broadway* (Cukor, 1930), 58–60, *59*, 61, 306; in *A Star Is Born* (Wellman, 1937), 37–38, 198, 302; in *Susan and God* (Cukor, 1940), 198–201, *199*, 202; in *Years Ago* (Gordon), 286

Marcus, Lawrence B., 381–82

Marilyn (Koster documentary, 1963), 341

Marilyn Monroe: The Final Days (2001 documentary), 339–40

Marion, Frances, 97, 99, 146

Marlow, Brian, 68

Marriage Circle, The (Lubitsch, 1924), 98

Marrying Kind, The (Cukor, 1952): auteur theory and, 5–7; cinematic style of, 18–19; Cukor as "woman's director" and, 16; death and grieving in, 267–69; Holliday in, 249, 259, 260–61, 266–68, *267*; Kulp in, 282–83; marriage in, 276–77; neorealism and, 265–66; queer sensibility in, 34–35; Ray in, 260–61, 266–68, *267*; screenplay for, 260, 266, 271; Shaughnessy in, 271

Marsh, Mae, 281

Marsh, Oliver T., 124

Martin, Dean, 338–39, 340–41

Martin, Mary, 192

Marton, Andrew, 323

Mary Poppins (Stevenson, 1964), 361

Mason, James: life and career of, 74; in *A Star Is Born* (Cukor, 1954), 16–17, 25, 32, 74, 101, 301–2, 306, 307–11, 313–16

Mason, Sarah Y., 14, 115–16

Masters, John, 321

Mating Season, The (Leisen, 1951), 276

Matthews, Francis, 321–23

Maugham, Somerset, 12–13, 203

Mayer, Louis B., 122–23, 184–85, 203, 205, 210–11

Mazeppa (Byron), 327

McBride, Raymond, 294

McCarey, Leo, 340; *The Awful Truth* (1937), 161, 210

McCarthy, Todd: interview with Bisset and, 414, 420–21; interview with Cukor (1981) and, 2, 40, 86, 413, 418

McCowen, Alec, 400–401, *402*, 403–5, 407–8

McCrea, Joel, 70, 74, 100

McDaniel, Hattie, 172–75, *173*

McElhaney, Joe, 310

McGilligan, Patrick: on *The Blue Bird* (Cukor, 1976), 383; on Cukor as partially closeted gay man, 12, 38, 40; on Cukor family, 320–21; on H. Cukor's death, 154; on Cukor's military service, 224; on Cukor's unmade projects, 318; on Cukor's youth, 129; on *A Double Life* (Cukor, 1947), 240; on Gable, 176–77; on Gordon and Kanin, 238–39; on *Heller in Pink Tights* (Cukor, 1960), 18, 326, 329; on *Rich and Famous* (Cukor, 1981), 415; Sarris on, 220; on *Sylvia Scarlett* (Cukor, 1935), 134; on *Travels with My Aunt* (Cukor, 1972), 394–95, 406–7

McGiver, John, 338

McQueen, Butterfly, 179

Me (Hepburn), 119, 213

Meet John Doe (Capra, 1941), 239

Menjou, Adolphe, 88–89

Menken, Adah, 327

mental illness, 36–7, 88, 350

Menzies, William Cameron, 170, 177

Merchant of Venice, The (Shakespeare), 430

Merrill's Marauders (Fuller, 1962), 356

Messenger, Lillie, 93

Metamorphoses (Ovid), 361

MGM (Metro-Goldwyn-Mayer): *The Actress* (Cukor, 1953) and, 286, 296–97; Allyn and, 412; Barrymore and, 306; *Bhowani Junction* (Cukor, 1956) and, 317–18, 322–23; *Camille* (Cukor, 1936) and, 146–47; Cukor and, 15, 169, 225–26, 318–19, 358, 405; *David Copperfield* (Cukor, 1935) and, 122–23; effects of World War II on, 205–6; Fontaine and, 192; Garland and, 301, 304–5; *Gaslight* (Cukor, 1944) and, 224, 232; *Her Cardboard Lover* (Cukor, 1942) and, 206; Holliday and, 259–60; Kelly and, 323–24; *A Life of Her Own* (Cukor, 1950) and, 10, 280; *Pat and Mike* (Cukor, 1952) and, 252, 394; *The Philadelphia Story* (Cukor, 1940) and,

157, 210–11; *Rich and Famous* (Cukor, 1981) and, 413–14; Smith and, 386; *Susan and God* (Cukor, 1940) and, 195–96, 200; *Travels with My Aunt* (Cukor, 1972) and, 394–95; *A Woman's Face* (Cukor, 1941) and, 202–3, 204–5; *The Women* (Cukor, 1939) and, 183, 187

Mildred Pierce (Curtiz, 1945), 189

Milestone, Lewis: *All Quiet on the Western Front* (1930), 43–52, *44*, *48*, 68, 94, 145; *Two Arabian Knights* (1927), 43

Milland, Ray, 10, 37

Miller, Arthur, 332–33, 336

Mills, John, 322

Milwaukee Journal (newspaper), 294

Minnelli, Vincente, 361; *The Band Wagon* (1953), 326; *Bells Are Ringing* (1960), 259–60; *Lust for Life* (1956), 318

Miracle on 34th Street (Seaton, 1947), 275

Miracle Woman, The (Capra, 1931), 93

Miracle Worker, The (Gibson), 372

Miracle Worker, The (Penn, 1962), 372

Misfits, The (Huston, 1961), 275, 332–33

Mitchell, Margaret, 169, 175, 176

Model and the Marriage Broker, The (Cukor, 1951): Brady in, 275, 279–80; character actors in, 97, 275, 278–79, 281–83, *282*; cinematic style of, 18–19; Crain in, 275, 276, 277–78, 279–81; neorealism and, 261; O'Shea in, *274*, 277–78; Ritter in, *274*, 275, 276–81; screenplay for, 276–77; surrogate-director figure in, 32

Modern Screen (magazine), 131

Moffat, Ivan, 322, 381

Mogambo (Ford, 1953), 323

Molander, Gustaf: *A Woman's Face* (1938), 196, 203

Mommie Dearest (C. Crawford), 196

Mommie Dearest (Perry, 1981), 196–97

Monkey Business (Hawks, 1952), 332

Monroe, Marilyn: Cukor and, 331, 333–34; in *Let's Make Love* (Cukor, 1960), 109, 331, 333–37, *334*; relationships with directors and, 331–33; in *Something's Got to Give* (Cukor, 1962), 109, 331, 338–39, *339*, 340–42, 382

Montand, Yves, 336–38

Montgomery, Douglass, 34, 172–73

Moonlight and Magnolias (Hutchinson), 176

Moore, Dennie, *133*, 134, 135, 278, *282*

Moore, Jack D., 144

Moore, Roger, 327

Moreau, Jeanne, 323

Morley, Karen, 105

Morley, Robert, 243

Morning Glory (Sherman, 1933), 76, 95

Morris, Sylvia Jukes, 189

Morrison, Toni, 412

Morrissey, Paul, 179; *Flesh* (1968), 39–40, 416; *Lonesome Cowboys* (1968), 416; *Trash* (1970), 416

Most Dangerous Game, The (Schoedsack, 1932), 116–17

Mostel, Zero, 278, 281–82, 283

Motion Picture Alliance for the Preservation of American Ideals, 241

Motion Picture Production Code (Hays Code): *Bhowani Junction* (Cukor, 1956) and, 323; *The Chapman Report* (Cukor, 1962) and, 343–44, 350–52, 356; Cukor and, 27; *Justine* (Cukor, 1969) and, 385; *Let's Make Love* (Cukor, 1960) and, 337; *The Marrying Kind* (Cukor, 1952) and, 265; *Our Betters* (Cukor, 1933) and, 33–34; *Rich and Famous* (Cukor, 1981) and, 423; screwball comedy and, 210; *Sylvia Scarlett* (Cukor, 1935) and, 135

Mountolive (Durrell), 381

Mr. Deeds Goes to Town (Capra, 1936), 162

Mr. Smith Goes to Washington (Capra, 1939), 30, 162, 219, 263–64
Mulhare, Edward, 377–78
Mulligan, Robert, 419–20; *Inside Daisy Clover* (1965), 289–90
Murfin, Jane, 16, 183
Murnau, F. W.: *Sunrise* (1927), 81
Murphy, Gerald, 197–98
Museum of Modern Art, 132
My Fair Lady (Cukor, 1964): Academy Award and, 1, *3*, 317, 359, 360, 393; Andrews and, 361–62, 376–77; auteur theory and, 5–7; Brett in, 375–76; cinematic style of, 369–71, 376; comedy and drama in, 370–71; Cooper in, 377; critical and commercial reception of, 357, 359–61, 381; Goldschmidt-Rothschild in, 362–63; Harrison in, 16–17, *31*, 362, 363–75, *370*, 377, 378–79; Hepburn in, *31*, 77, 358, *359*, 361–62, 366–77, *367*, *370*, 378–79; Hyde-White in, 337–38, 362, 365, *370*; long takes in, 375; mise-en-scène in, 25; as personal film, 357–58; queer sensibility in, 34, 373–74, 434; screenplay for, 358, 364; setting of, 428; suicidal feelings in, 375; surrogate-director figure in, 32, 227, 365
My Man Godfrey (La Cava, 1936), 210
Myrick, Susan, 176

Naremore, James, 23–24, 132, 307
Nazimova, Alla, 269
Neame, Ronald: *Prime of Miss Jean Brodie, The* (1969), 395
Negulesco, Jean, 339
Newman, Joseph M.: *The George Raft Story* (1961), 355
Newman, Robert, 130–31
New York (magazine), 415
New Yorker (magazine), 414–15

New York Times (newspaper): on French Nouvelle Vague, 130–31; on *Gone with the Wind* (Fleming, 1939), 170; on Holliday, 265; on *Justine* (Cukor, 1969), 381, 385, 386; on *Let's Make Love* (Cukor, 1960), 337; on McGilligan's Cukor biography, 220; on *Sylvia Scarlett* (Cukor, 1935), 131; on *Travels with My Aunt* (Cukor, 1972), 395–96
Nichols, Dudley, 327
Nine Tiger Man, The (Blanch), 382
Ninotchka (Lubitsch, 1939), 62, 144, 150, 169
Niven, David, 98
Nixon, Marni, 361, 377
Nolan, Doris, 158, 165
No More Ladies (E. Griffith, 1935), 188
None but the Lonely Heart (Odets, 1944), 140
Noonan, Tom, 309, *314*, 315
"Notes on 'Camp'" (Sontag), 138–39, 402–3
Nouvelle Vague. See *politique des auteurs* and auteur theory; Truffaut, François
Novak, Kim, 338–39

Oates, Joyce Carol, 412
O'Brien, Edmond, 247
O'Brien, Margaret, 328
O'Brien, Pat, 241
Odd Man Out (Reed, 1947), 307
Odets, Clifford: *None but the Lonely Heart* (1944), 140
Offner, Mortimer, 129
O'Hara, Maureen, 88–89
O'Keeffe, Georgia, 393
Old Acquaintance (Sherman, 1943), 411, 418, 422
Old Acquaintance (Van Druten), 225–26, 411, 418

Old Man and the Sea, The (Hemingway), 319
Oliver, Edna May, 120, 123–24, 282
Olivier, Laurence: *Hamlet* (Olivier, 1948)
    and, 290; in *Love Among the Ruins*
    (Cukor, 1975), 16–17, 35, 101, 394,
    427–34, *432*, 435–37, *436*
O'Malley, Rex, 150
On Acting (Olivier), 427–28
On Cukor (Lambert): on *The Actress*
    (Cukor, 1953), 286; on auteur theory, 7;
    as autobiography, 2; on *Bhowani*
    Junction (Cukor, 1956), 175; on *A Bill of*
    Divorcement (Cukor, 1932), 91; on
    "climate," 25; on Gable, 177; on *Gone*
    with the Wind (Fleming, 1939), 172–73,
    177–78; on *Her Cardboard Lover*
    (Cukor, 1942), 206; on Holliday,
    261–62; language of Cukor in, 40; on
    Little Women (Cukor, 1933), 422; on *The*
    Marrying Kind (Cukor, 1952), 269; on
    My Fair Lady (Cukor, 1964), 359–61,
    376; review of, 8; on the rich, 51–52,
    159; on *The Women* (Cukor, 1939),
    186–87
One Hour with You (Lubitsch and Cukor,
    1932), 98, 371
One Wonderful Sunday (Kurosawa, 1947),
    265
Ophüls, Max, 14; *De Mayerling à Sarajevo*
    (*From Mayerling to Sarajevo*) (1940),
    121; *Letter from an Unknown Woman*
    (1948), 164, 399; *Madame de . . .* (1953),
    153, 399; *La ronde* (1950), 399
Orry-Kelly, 324, 347
O'Shea, Michael, *274*, 277–78
Othello (Shakespeare), 13
Other Side of the Wind, The (Welles,
    1970–1976; 2018), 14–15, 50, 385
O'Toole, Peter: *My Fair Lady* (Cukor,
    1964) and, 365

Our Betters (Cukor, 1933), 12–13, 33–34, 74,
    139
Our Betters (Maugham), 12–13
Overstreet, Richard, 344
Ovid, 361
Owsley, Monroe, 164
Ozu, Yasujiro, 9

Paley, Natalie, 33, 135–36
Pan, Hermes, 372
Paramount Pictures: Cukor and, 224, 319;
    Grant and, 140; *Heller in Pink Tights*
    (Cukor, 1960) and, 319, 327, 328–29;
    Zukor and, 321
Parker, Dorothy, 305, 306–7
Parker, Jean, 120
Pat and Mike (Cukor, 1952): auteur theory
    and, 5–7; cinematic style of, 249–50;
    Gordon-Kanin screenplay for, 237–38,
    249, 254–55; Hepburn in, 85–86, 221,
    237–38, 249–55, *252*, *254*, 264–65, 394;
    queer sensibility in, 34–35; surrogate-
    director figure in, 32; Tracy in, 35, 221,
    237–38, 249–50, 251–55, *252*, *254*
Patrick, John, 324
Patterson, Elizabeth, 88
Paul, Elliot, 204
Pawle, Lennox, 123–24
Pearson, Richard, 434, 435
Peck, Gregory, 326, 336, 382
Penn, Arthur: *Bonnie and Clyde* (1967),
    130–31; *The Miracle Worker* (1962), 372
Penny Serenade (Stevens, 1941), 267
Pereira, Hal, 328
Perry, Frank: *Mommie Dearest* (1981),
    196–97
Peter Pan (Barrie), 382
Peterman, Don, 419
Philadelphia Story, The (Barry), 51–52, 161,
    213, 217

Philadelphia Story, The (Cukor, 1940): auteur theory and, 5–7; critical and commercial reception of, 51–52, 214; Cukor's work with young actresses in, 200; drinking in, 37; Grant in, 140, 157, 159, 209, 211–12, 215–16, *215*, 219; Hepburn in, 37, 85–86, 113, 157, 161, 209–14, *211*, *215*, 216–17, *218*, 219–20, 238; Hussey in, 201, 215, 219; ideological project of, 212; queer sensibility in, 34–35; screenplay for, 214–15, 217–18; sexuality in, 216–17, 348; Stewart in, 30, 211–12, 217–19, *218*; Weidler in, 188–89

Phillips, Margaret, 10

Pickford, Mary, 81

Pickup on South Street (Fuller, 1953), 275–76

Pilgrimage (Ford, 1933), 63, 239

Pink Lady, The (musical comedy), 285, 291

Place in the Sun, A (Stevens, 1951), 265

Planck, Robert, 203

Planer, Franz, 164

Planet of the Apes (1968), 386

Platinum Blonde (Capra, 1931), 106, 162

Playboy (magazine), 341

Plunkett, Walter, 116–17

Poitier, Sidney, 1

Polanski, Roman: *Rosemary's Baby* (1968), 289–90

politique des auteurs, 5, 9–10, 357–58. *See also* auteur theory

Ponti, Carlo, 327

Porter, Cole, 246, 324

Portrait of the Artist as a Young Man, A (Joyce), 385

Powell, Anthony, 401–2

Preminger, Otto, 9–10

Producers, The (Brooks, 1967), 283

Purcell, Gertrude, 60

Pye, Merrill, 124

Pygmalion (Asquith and Howard, 1938), 358, 369, 376, 378

Pygmalion (Cooke, 1983), 365

Pygmalion (Shaw): *Born Yesterday* (Cukor, 1950) and, 262; *My Fair Lady* (Cukor, 1964) and, 227, 358, 363–65, 368, 369, 377–78

Queen Christina (Mamoulian, 1933), 144, 150

queer, use of term, 33, 424

queer sensibility: in *Adam's Rib* (Cukor, 1949), 34–35, 246; in *Born Yesterday* (Cukor, 1950), 34–35; in *Camille* (Cukor, 1936), 34–35; in *The Chapman Report* (Cukor, 1962), 34–35, 354; Cukor and, 32–35, 40, 63, 68–69; in *David Copperfield* (Cukor, 1935), 35; in *It Should Happen to You* (Cukor, 1954), 34–35; in *Justine* (Cukor, 1969), 34–35; in *Little Women* (Cukor, 1933), 34–35; in *Marrying Kind, The* (Cukor, 1952), 34–35; in *My Fair Lady* (Cukor, 1964), 34, 373–74, 434; in *Our Betters* (Cukor, 1933), 33–34; in *Pat and Mike* (Cukor, 1952), 34–35; in *Philadelphia Story, The* (Cukor, 1940), 34–35; in *Rich and Famous* (Cukor, 1981), 68–69, 423–25; in *Susan and God* (Cukor, 1940), 34–35; in *Sylvia Scarlett* (Cukor, 1935), 17, 33, 35, 254–55, 327; Tracy-Hepburn relationship and, 241

Quigley, Juanita, 200

Quigley, Rita, 198–201

Quinn, Anthony, 319, 327–28

Ralph, Jessie, 123–24

Rathbone, Basil, 123–24

Ratoff, Gregory, 78–79

Ray, Aldo: in *The Marrying Kind* (Cukor, 1952), 260–61, 266–68, *267*; in *Pat and Mike* (Cukor, 1952), 251, 252

Ray, Nicholas, 9–10; *Johnny Guitar* (1954), 280

Rear Window (Hitchcock, 1954), 275

Rebecca (Hitchcock, 1940), 193

Red Badge of Courage, The (Huston, 1951), 287

Red Channels (1950 pamphlet), 259

Red Dust (Fleming, 1932), 106–8

Red-Headed Woman (Conway, 1932), 106

Red River (Hawks, 1948), 276

Red Scare: Buchman and, 52, 159–60; Capra and, 263–64; Cukor and, 160; effects of, 196; Hepburn and, 94–95, 241; Holliday and, 160, 259; Mostel and, 278, 283; Offner and, 129; D. Stewart and, 52, 159–60

Reed, Carol: *Odd Man Out* (1947), 307

Reiner, Carl: *Where's Poppa?* (1970), 290

Reinhardt, Gottfried, 224

Reisch, Walter, 225–26, 231, 276–77

Remarque, Erich Maria, 43, 45, 51

Remick, Lee, 338–39

Renoir, Jean, 11–12, 14, 370, 377, 432; on Garbo, 143, 144, 154; *The Rules of the Game* (1939), 11–12

Reynolds, Debbie, 290

Rich and Famous (Cukor, 1981): Bergen in, 2–4, 68–69, 411–13, 418–19, 421, 422–25, *423*; Bisset in, 2–4, 68–69, 411–25, *413*, *423*, 435; camp style in, 418; critical and commercial reception of, 383, 411, 413–15, 421–22; Harpman and, 386; mise-en-scène in, 25, 419–20; Mulligan and, 419–20; queer sensibility in, 68–69, 139, 423–25; screenplay for, 225–26, 411, 413, 415–16; sexuality in, 25–27, 68–70, 351–52, 393, 411–12, 413–18, *413*, 420–22;

Spielberg and, 38; "wonderful gamey quality" of Cukor in, 38–39

Rio Bravo (Hawks, 1959), 328

"Rip Van Winkle" (Irving), 326

Rise and Fall of Legs Diamond, The (Boetticher, 1960), 355

Riskin, Everett, 162

Riskin, Robert, 162, 239

Ritt, Martin: *The Front* (1976), 283

Ritter, Thelma, 16, *274*, 275–81

River of Romance (Wallace, 1929), 43, 44, 62

Rivette, Jacques, 210

RKO Pictures: *A Damsel in Distress* (Stevens, 1937) and, 192; *Little Women* (Cukor, 1933) and, 128; *Our Betters* (Cukor, 1933) and, 34; *Sylvia Scarlett* (Cukor, 1935) and, 128, 135

Robbins, Jerome: *West Side Story* (with Wise, 1961), 361

Roberts, Roy, 349

Rock, Chris, 314

Rockabye (Cukor, 1932), 74

Romanov family, 136

Romeo and Juliet (Cukor, 1936), 60–61, 105, 145, 184, 282

Rommel, Erwin, 307

Rooney, Mickey, 184–85, 206

Roosevelt, Franklin D., 99

Rosemary's Baby (Polanski, 1968), 289–90

Rosher, Charles, 81

Rosson, Harold, 287, 312

Royal Family, The (Kaufman and Ferber), 58–60

Royal Family of Broadway, The (Cukor, 1930), 46, 58–64, *59*, 90, 102, 306

Ruggles, Wesley: *I'm No Angel* (1933), 140

Rules of the Game, The (Renoir, 1939), 11–12

Russell, Rosalind, 16, 184, 190–92, *191*

Ruttenberg, Joseph, 219, 223, 228, 385

Ryan, Meg, 418

"Sailing to Byzantium" (Yeats), 405

Salt of the Earth (Wilson, 1954), 265

Sarris, Andrew: auteur theory and, 5; on Cukor, 8–9, 36; *Justine* (Cukor, 1969) and, 381; on McGilligan's Cukor biography, 220; on *My Fair Lady* (Cukor, 1964), 360; on "obligatory scenes," 272; on *The Philadelphia Story* (Barry), 213; on screwball comedy, 210; on Sherman, 76; on J. Stewart, 218; on *Travels with My Aunt* (Cukor, 1972), 20, 397

Sawdust and Tinsel (Bergman, 1953), 328

Scarlet Empress, The (Sternberg, 1934), 121

Scarlett O'Hara War, The (Erman, 1980), 170–71, 192

Schertzinger, Victor: *Kiss the Boys Goodbye* (1941), 192

Schoedsack, Ernest B.: *The Most Dangerous Game* (1932), 116–17

Schulberg, Budd, 305

Schulman, Arnold, 319

Scorsese, Martin, 370

Scott, Walter M., 386

screwball comedy, 165, 210

Seaton, George: *The Country Girl* (1954), 303; *Miracle on 34th Street* (1947), 275

Selznick, David O.: *All Quiet on the Western Front* (Milestone, 1930) and, 44; *A Bill of Divorcement* (Cukor, 1932) and, 87, 88–89, 93; *David Copperfield* (Cukor, 1935) and, 122–23, 124, 175; *Dinner at Eight* (Cukor, 1933) and, 97–98, 101; Fontaine and, 193; *Gaslight* (Cukor, 1944) and, 229–30; *Gone with the Wind* (Fleming, 1939) and, 16, 169–73, 175–76, 178; *Little Women* (Cukor, 1933) and, 175; *A Star Is Born* (Cukor, 1954) and, 306; *A Star Is Born* (Wellman, 1937) and, 198; *What Price Hollywood?* (Cukor, 1932) and, 73, 76–77, 89, 302

Sennwald, Andre, 131

Senses of Cinema (online magazine), 23–24, 36

Seven Year Itch, The (Wilder, 1955), 336

sexuality: in *Avanti!* (Wilder, 1972), 396–97; in *Bhowani Junction* (Cukor, 1956), 27, 323; in *Camille* (Cukor, 1936), 27, 147; in *The Chapman Report* (Cukor, 1962), 343–56, 416, 417; Cukor as partially closeted gay man and, 12, 16, 40, 139, 176–77, 224, 318, 417, 423–25; "frigidity" and, 216, 219–20; in *Gaslight* (Cukor, 1944), 232–35; in *Heller in Pink Tights* (Cukor, 1960), 327–28; in *Justine* (Cukor, 1969), 25–27, 344, 351–52, 384–86, 388–89; in *Let's Make Love* (Cukor, 1960), 334–35, 336–37; in *Love Among the Ruins* (Cukor, 1975), 393; in *The Philadelphia Story* (Cukor, 1940), 216–17, 348; in *Rich and Famous* (Cukor, 1981), 25–27, 68–70, 351–52, 393, 411–12, 413–18, *413*, 420–22; screwball comedy and, 210; in *Something's Got to Give* (Cukor, 1962), 340–41; in *Travels with My Aunt* (Cukor, 1972), 396–97, 403–5, 407–8

Shakespeare, William, 130, 291, 302, 430, 433

Shamroy, Leon, 385, 386

Shane (Stevens, 1953), 258–59

Shaughnessy, Mickey, 271

Shaw, George Bernard. See *Pygmalion* (Shaw)

Shearer, Norma: Cukor and, 16; *Gone with the Wind* (Fleming, 1939) and, 170; in *Her Cardboard Lover* (Cukor, 1942), 205, 206; life and career of, 184–85, 205; in *Romeo and Juliet* (Cukor, 1936), 145, 184; *Susan and God* (Cukor, 1940) and, 196; in *The Women*

(Cukor, 1939), 183–85, *184*, 186–88, 193–94

She Done Him Wrong (Sherman, 1933), 76, 140

Sheekman, Arthur, 346–47

shell shock, 88

Sher, Bartlett, 364

Sherman, Lowell: Cukor and, 307; in *What Price Hollywood?* (Cukor, 1932), 16–17, 73–83, *75*, *79*, 102, 305

Sherman, Lowell—films as director: *The Greeks Had a Word for Them* (1932), 76; *High Stakes* (1931), 76, 78–79; *Morning Glory* (1933), 76, 95; *She Done Him Wrong* (1933), 76, 140

Sherman, Vincent: *Old Acquaintance* (1943), 411, 418, 422

Shirley, Bill, 375

Shootist, The (Siegel, 1976), 29

Show Boat (Sidney, 1951), 322

Sidney, George: *Show Boat* (1951), 322

Siegel, Don: *The Shootist* (1976), 29

Silvers, Phil, 338

Simmons, Jean: in *The Actress* (Cukor, 1953), 35, 148, *284*, 285–86, 287–94, *288*, 295–96, 310; life and career of, 290

Singin' in the Rain (Kelly and Donen, 1952), 287

Sjöström, Victor: *The Divine Woman* (1928), 129, 147

Slide Area, The (Lambert), 159

Slocombe, Douglas, 398, 405, 429, 435

Smiling Lieutenant, The (Lubitsch, 1931), 58

Smith, Jack Martin, 386

Smith, Ludlow Ogden, 213

Smith, Maggie: in *The Prime of Miss Jean Brodie* (Neame, 1969), 395; in *Travels with My Aunt* (Cukor, 1972), 32, 35, 395–96, 397–407, *397*, *402*, *404*, 418

Smith, Will, 314

Sofaer, Abraham, 322

Some Like It Hot (Wilder, 1959), 332, 333, 335

Something's Got to Give (Cukor, 1962), 109, 331, 338–42, *339*, 382

Some Versions of Cary Grant (Naremore), 23–24, 132

Song Without End (C. Vidor, 1960), 318, 319–20, 384

Sontag, Susan, 138–39, 402–3

Sort of Life, A (Greene), 290

So This Is Paris (Lubitsch, 1926), 68

Spewack, Bella and Samuel, 340

Spielberg, Steven, 38

Sprechstimme (speak-singing), 364

Stagecoach (Ford, 1939), 327

Stahl, John M.: *Leave Her to Heaven* (1945), 385

Stanwyck, Barbara, 70

Star Is Born, A (Cukor, 1954): auteur theory and, 5–7; Carson in, 103; cinematic style of, 4, 19–21, 303–4, 309–10, 405; comedy and drama in, 17–18; critical and commercial reception of, 9, 20, 41, 317; drinking in, 37–38; as *film maudit* (cursed film), 381; Garland in, 74, 301–3, 304–6, *304*, 308, 309–16, *314–15*, 318, 323; Kulp in, 282–83; Mason in, 16–17, 25, 32, 74, 101, 301–2, 306, 307–11, 313–16; mise-en-scène in, 25; Rosson and, 287, 312; screenplay for, 190, 302, 311–13, 314; surrogate-director figure in, 32, 305; *What Price Hollywood?* (Cukor, 1932) and, 73, 77, 82

Star Is Born, A (Haver book), 303

Star Is Born, A (Wellman, 1937), 37–38, 198, 302, 305, 306

Starlight (Unger), 129

Stein, Gertrude, 45

Steiner, Max, 116–17

Stenn, David, 108

Stephens, Robert, *397*, 398–400, 406

Stern, Bert, 334

Sternberg, Josef von, 178, 287; *Blonde Venus* (1932), 140; *The Scarlet Empress* (1934), 121; *Thunderbolt* (1929), 116–17

Stevens, George: *Alice Adams* (1935), 129; *A Damsel in Distress* (1937), 192; *The Greatest Story Ever Told* (1965), 386; *Gunga Din* (1939), 140; *Penny Serenade* (1941), 267; *A Place in the Sun* (1951), 265; *Shane* (1953), 258–59; *Woman of the Year* (1942), 220–21, 239

Stevenson, Robert: *Mary Poppins* (1964), 361

Stewart, Donald Ogden: Cukor and, 13–14, 66; *Dinner at Eight* (Cukor, 1933) and, 101; *Holiday* (Cukor, 1938) and, 36, 52, 159–60, 162; *Keeper of the Flame* (Cukor, 1942) and, 160, 239; *The Philadelphia Story* (Cukor, 1940) and, 214–15; political viewpoint of, 52, 159–60, 239; *Tarnished Lady* (Cukor, 1931), 66; *A Woman's Face* (Cukor, 1941) and, 204; *The Women* (Cukor, 1939) and, 185

Stewart, James: Academy Award and, 30; Capra and, 29–30; life and career of, 206, 219; in *Mr. Smith Goes to Washington* (Capra, 1939), 30; in *The Philadelphia Story* (Cukor, 1940), 30, 211–12, 217–19, *218*

St. Johns, Adela Rogers, 73

"Story of a New York Lady, A" (Stewart), 66

Stothart, Herbert, 148

Stradling, Harry Sr., 358, 362

Strasberg, Lee, 29–30

Streisand, Barbra, 306

Strick, Joseph, 381–82, 385, 389

Stroheim, Erich von: *Greed* (1924), 302, 317

Sturges, John, 319

Sturges, Preston: *Sullivan's Travels* (1941), 100

suicide: in *The Chapman Report* (Cukor, 1962), 350, 353; in *Dinner at Eight* (Cukor, 1933), 17–18, 100, 101, 103, *104*; in *Justine* (Cukor, 1969), 389–90; in *A Life of Her Own* (Cukor, 1950), 10, 280; in *My Fair Lady* (Cukor, 1964), 375; in *A Star Is Born* (Cukor, 1954), 25, 302, 315–16; in *Sylvia Scarlett* (Cukor, 1935), 141; in *What Price Hollywood?* (Cukor, 1932), 81–83, 101–2, 302

Sullivan's Travels (Sturges, 1941), 100

Sunrise (Murnau, 1927), 81

Sunset Blvd. (Wilder, 1950), 249, 354

Surtees, Robert, 324

Susan and God (Cukor, 1940): cinematic style of, 201–2; Crawford in, 189, 196, 197, 198–99, *199*, 207; Hussey in, 201, 202, 219; March in, 198–99, *199*, 202; proposal for remake (1982) of, 195–96; queer sensibility in, 34–35; R. Quigley in, 198–201, *199*; screenplay for, 195, 198, 199; supporting cast of, 201–2

Susann, Jacqueline, 412

Suspicion (Hitchcock, 1941), 193

Swanson, Gloria, 249

Sylvia Scarlett (Cukor, 1935): auteur theory and, 5–7; camp style in, 138–40, 402, 403; cinematic style of, 4, 18, 130; comedy and drama in, 132; critical and commercial reception of, 112, 131, 140; as Cukor's "secret favorite" film, 2, and as favorite film, 33, 111; as *film maudit* (cursed film), 131, 381; Grant in, 33, *126*, 128–29, 132–34, *133*, *137*, 139–41, 161, 215–16; Hepburn in, 33, 85–86, 111, *126*, 127–30, 131–41, *133*, *137*, 161, 254–55, 403; Moore in, 278; queer sensibility in, 17, 33, 35, 111, 127–40, 254–55, 327; screenplay for, 129–30; surrogate-director figure in, 32, 137–38

Tarkington, Booth, 43, 129
Tarnished Lady (Cukor, 1931), 66, 101
Tashman, Lilyan, 65, 68–71, *69*
Taylor, Laurette, 57, 206, 318
Taylor, Robert, 206; in *Camille* (Cukor, 1936), 148–49, *149*, 151–55
television: Collier and, 129; Cukor and, 394. See also *Corn Is Green, The* (Cukor, 1979); *Love Among the Ruins* (Cukor, 1975); Hepburn and, 213; Welles and, 129
Tennyson, Alfred, 339
Thackeray, William Makepeace, 76
Thalberg, Irving, 109, 146–47, 175, 184, 333
They Knew What They Wanted (Howard), 319
Thomas, Bob, 196
3 Bad Men (Ford, 1926), 223
Thunderbolt (Sternberg, 1929), 116–17
Tierney, Lawrence, 279–80
Time (magazine), 51, 341
Tirez sur le pianiste (*Shoot the Piano Player*) (Truffaut, 1960), 130–31
Toback, James, 382–83
Too Much Johnson (Welles, 1938), 258
Towne, Robert, 108–9
Tracy, Lee, 103
Tracy, Spencer: in *The Actress* (Cukor, 1953), 286, 287–89, *288*, 291–97; in *Adam's Rib* (Cukor, 1949), 16–17, 221, 237–38, *240*, 241–47, *245*, 253–54; in *Edward, My Son* (Cukor, 1948), 243; Hepburn and, 220, 237–39, 241–47; in *Keeper of the Flame* (Cukor, 1942), 239; in *Pat and Mike* (Cukor, 1952), 35, 221, 237–38, 249–50, 251–55, *252*, *254*; *The Philadelphia Story* (Cukor, 1940)

and, 211; in *Woman of the Year* (Stevens, 1942), 220–21
Tracy and Hepburn (Kanin), 238, 241, 251–52
Trash (Morrissey, 1970), 416
Travels with My Aunt (Cukor, 1972): camp style in, 393, 395, 402–3, 418; cinematic style of, 405; comedy and drama in, 401; critical and commercial reception of, 20, 383, 395–96, 397, 408; Gossett, Lou in, 407; long takes in, 401; McCowen in, 400–401, *402*, 403–5, 407–8; mise-en-scène in, 25, 397, 419–20; screenplay for, 394–95, 396, 405; sexuality in, 396–97, 403–5, 407–8; Slocombe and, 398, 405, 435; Smith in, 32, 35, 395–96, 397–407, *397*, *402*, *404*, 418; Stephens in, *397*, 398–400, 406; surrogate-director figure in, 32; Williams in, 407–8; "wonderful gamey quality" of Cukor in, 38–39
Travels with My Aunt (Greene), 20, 383, 394, 396, 405
Travers, Bill, 321–23
Tree, Dolly, 124
Trouble in Paradise (Lubitsch, 1932), 66, 210
Truffaut, François: on American audiences, 130; auteur theory and, 5, 9–10; Cukor and, 5, 10; Hitchcock and, 24, 28; *Mommie Dearest* (Perry, 1981) and, 197; *politique des auteurs* and, 5, 9–10, 357–58; on "privileged moments," 87; on Strick, 385
Truffaut, François—films: *Day for Night* (1973), 414; *Tirez sur le pianiste* (*Shoot the Piano Player*) (1960), 130–31
Truman, Harry S., 241
Turner, Lana, 10, 280
Twain, Mark, 264
Twelfth Night (Shakespeare), 291
Twentieth Century (Hawks, 1934), 105

Twentieth Century-Fox: *The Chapman Report* (Cukor, 1962) and, 343–44, 382; *Justine* (Cukor, 1969) and, 381–82, 387; *Let's Make Love* (Cukor, 1960) and, 336; *Marilyn* (Koster documentary) and, 341; *The Model and the Marriage Broker* (Cukor, 1951) and, 276; Monroe and, 338, 341; Mostel and, 283; *Something's Got to Give* (Cukor, 1962) and, 338, 339, 340; *Winged Victory* (Cukor, 1944) and, 247

Two Arabian Knights (Milestone, 1927), 43

Two-Faced Woman (Cukor, 1941), 74–75, 205–6, 224, 239, 289

Tynan, Kenneth, 154, 325, 333, 334, 335, 383

Ulmer, Edgar G.: *The Black Cat* (1934), 93

Ulric, Lenore, 151

Unger, Gladys, 129

Un homme et une femme (Lelouch, 1966), 387

Universal Pictures, 43, 336, 412

Van Druten, John, 225–26, 231–32, 411, 418

Van Heusen, James, 335–36

Vanity Fair (Thackeray), 76

Variety (newspaper), 70, 140

Vaughan, Frankie, 335–36

Veidt, Conrad, 204

Verdi, Giuseppe, 144

Vertigo (Hitchcock, 1958), 219

Vidor, Charles: *Song Without End* (1960), 318, 319–20, 384

Vidor, King, 12–13; *The Big Parade* (1925), 45; *La Bohème* (1926), 154; *The Crowd* (1928), 267

Village Voice (newspaper), 20, 360, 381, 397, 414

Virtuous Sin, The (Cukor and Gasnier, 1930), 46, 65, 66–68, 67

Visconti, Luchino: *The Leopard* (1963), 399–400

Vogue (magazine), 334

Vorkapich, Slavko, 83

Wagon Master (Ford, 1950), 276

Walbrook, Anton, 228

Walker, Alexander, 368

Walker, Alice, 412

Walker, Joseph, 265

Wallace, Henry, 241

Wallace, Irving, 343

Wallace, Richard: *River of Romance* (1929), 43, 44, 62

Wall Street Journal (newspaper), 216

Walpole, Hugh, 124

Walsh, Raoul, 9–10; *What Price Glory* (1926), 45

Wand, Betty, 325

War and Peace (Tolstoy), 44

Warhol, Andy, 270

Warner, Jack L.: *The Chapman Report* (Cukor, 1962) and, 344, 354, 356; *My Fair Lady* (Cukor, 1964) and, 360, 361, 365, 378; *A Star Is Born* (Cukor, 1954) and, 313

Warner Bros.: *The Chapman Report* (Cukor, 1962) and, 343–44; Crawford and, 205; Cukor and, 319; *My Fair Lady* (Cukor, 1964) and, 358, 365; *A Star Is Born* (Cukor, 1954) and, 301, 303

Warren, Robert Penn, 262–63

Waters, John, 204–5

Waxman, Franz, 217–18

Way Down East (D. W. Griffith, 1920), 75

Wayne, David, 34, 246

Wayne, John, 29

Weidler, Virginia, 188–89, 200

Weill, Kurt, 326

Weingarten, Lawrence, 296–97

Weinstein, Henry, 331

Welles, Orson: on actors, 15; auteur theory and, 9; directing the author,

14–15, 50; on directors, 22; Mercury Theatre and, 257–58; on J. Stewart, 30; television and, 129

Welles, Orson—films: *The Fountain of Youth* (1956), 129; *The Magnificent Ambersons* (1942), 15, 302, 317; *The Other Side of the Wind* (1970–1976; 2018), 14–15, 50, 385; *Too Much Johnson* (1938), 258

Wellman, William: *Beggars of Life* (1928), 116–17; *A Star Is Born* (1937), 37–38, 73, 302, 305, 306; *Wild Boys of the Road* (1933), 99–100

West, Mae, 76, 140; as "box office poison," 113

West Side Story (Wise and Robbins, 1961), 361

Whale, James: *Bride of Frankenstein* (1935), 346; *Journey's End* (1930), 93

What Price Glory (Walsh, 1926), 45

What Price Hollywood? (Cukor, 1932): Barrymore and, 37–38; cinematic style of, 98; drinking in, 78–80; Selznick and, 73, 76–77, 89, 302; Sherman in, 16–17, 73–83, *75, 79*, 102, 305; suicide in, 81–83, 101–2, 302; surrogate-director figure in, 32, 305

Wheeler, Hugh, 394–95, 396

Where's Poppa? (Reiner, 1970), 290

Whitty, May, 230

Wiene, Robert: *The Cabinet of Dr. Caligari* (1920), 204

Wild Boys of the Road (Wellman, 1933), 99–100

Wild Is the Wind (Cukor, 1957), 318, 319

Wilde, Oscar, 47, 138

Wilder, Billy, 9, 181, 276, 331–32; *Avanti!* (1972), 396–97; *A Foreign Affair* (1948), 258–59; *The Lost Weekend* (1945), 37; *The Seven Year Itch* (1955), 336; *Some Like It Hot* (1959), 332, 333, 335; *Sunset Blvd.* (1950), 249, 354

Williams, Cindy, 407–8

Williams, Emlyn, 383

Williams, Hope, 93, 161

Williams, Hugh, 124

Williams, Kay, 285

Williams, Tennessee, 318

Willis, Edwin B., 124, 203–4, 223, 286

Wilson, Michael: *Salt of the Earth* (1954), 265

Wingate, James, 34

Winged Victory (Cukor, 1944), 18, 247

Winters, Shelley: in *The Chapman Report* (Cukor, 1962), 346, 347, 355; in *A Double Life* (Cukor, 1947), 239–40

Wise, Robert: *West Side Story* (with Robbins, 1961), 361

Wizard of Oz, The (Fleming, 1939), 169, 287, 301

Wolheim, Louis, 49

Woman of the Year (Stevens, 1942), 220–21, 239

Woman's Face, A (Cukor, 1941): cinematic style of, 203–4; Crawford in, 189, 196, 197, 202–5, *202*; screenplay for, 204; special effects in, 204–5; surrogate-director figure in, 32

Woman's Face, A (Molander, 1938), 196, 203

Women, The (Cukor, 1939): camp style in, 185; comedy and drama in, 186, 419; Crawford in, 106, *184*, 185, 186–89, 197; critical and commercial reception of, 97; Cukor as "woman's director" and, 15; Fontaine in, 192–93, *192–93*; Lubitsch and, 169–70, 186; mise-en-scène in, 185; modeling in, 280–81; Moore in, 278; Russell in, *184*, 190–92, *191*; screenplay for, 183–84, 185–86, 189–90; Shearer in, 183–85, *184*, 186–88, 193–94; Weidler in, 188–89, 200

Women, The (Luce), 183, 189–90

women's pictures (a.k.a. chick flicks), 15–16, 111–12, 419
Wood, Audrey, 427, 428
Wood, Natalie, 361
Wood, Sam, 174, 177
Woodhull, Victoria, 40, 382–83
World War I, 45. See also *All Quiet on the Western Front* (Milestone, 1930)
World War II, 50–51, 205–6
Wright, Teresa, 286, 295
Writers Guild of America, 395
Writers Guild of America, West, 5
Wyler, William: *The Best Years of Our Lives* (1946), 265
Wylie, I. A. R. (Ida Alexa Ross), 160, 239
Wynyard, Diana, 228

Years Ago (Gordon), 35, 272, 286. See also *Actress, The* (Cukor, 1953)
Yeats, William Butler, 405

York, Michael, 386–87
You Can't Take It with You (Capra, 1938), 60
You Can't Take It with You (Kaufman and Hart), 60
Young, Clara Kimball, 146
Young, Freddie, 323
Young, Roland, 123–24

Zaharias, Babe Didrikson, 250
Zanuck, Darryl, 343–44, 356
Zanuck, Richard D., 343–44, 350–51, 354, 356, 381–82
Zaza (Cukor, 1938), 169
Ziegler, William, *19*, 369
Zilahy, Lajos, 66
Zimbalist, Efrem, Jr., 344–45, 347–48, 355–56
Zinnemann, Fred, 319
Zukor, Adolph, 321